Trading in the
Global Currency Markets

Trading in the
Global Currency Markets

Cornelius Luca

Prentice Hall
Englewood Cliffs, New Jersey 07632

Library of Congress Cataloging-in-Publication Data

Luca, Cornelius.
    Trading in the global currency markets / Cornelius Luca.
      p.   cm.
    ISBN 0-13-293424-8
    1. Foreign exchange market.   2. Investment analysis.   I. Title.
  HG3851.L83   1995   94-33520
    332.4'5—dc20   CIP

Printed in the United States of America

10 9 8 7 6 5 4 3

This publication is designed to provide accurate and authoritative information in regard to the subject matter covered. It is sold with the understanding that the publisher is not engaged in rendering legal, accounting, or other professional service. If legal advice or other expert assistance is required, the services of a competent professional person should be sought.
—*From the Declaration of Principles jointly adopted by a Committee of the American Bar Association and a Committee of Publishers and Associations*

Text and illustrations in Chapter 28, copyright © 1978, 1994
Robert R. Prechter, Jr. and A.J. Frost. Reprinted with permission.

ISBN 0-13-293424-8

ATTENTION: CORPORATIONS AND SCHOOLS

Prentice Hall books are available at quantity discounts with bulk purchase for educational, business, or sales promotional use. For information, please write to: Prentice Hall Career & Personal Development Special Sales, 240 Frisch Court, Paramus, New Jersey 07652. Please supply: title of book, ISBN number, quantity, how the book will be used, date needed.

 PRENTICE HALL
Career & Personal Development
Paramus, NJ 07652
A Simon & Schuster Company

On the World Wide Web at http://www.phdirect.com

Prentice-Hall International (UK) Limited, *London*
Prentice-Hall of Australia Pty. Limited, *Sydney*
Prentice-Hall Canada Inc., *Toronto*
Prentice-Hall Hispanoamericana, S.A., *Mexico*
Prentice-Hall of India Private Limited, *New Delhi*
Prentice-Hall of Japan, Inc., *Tokyo*
Simon & Schuster Asia Pte. Ltd., *Singapore*
Editora Prentice-Hall do Brasil, Ltda., *Rio de Janeiro*

To my wife, Sandra
and my daughter, Gwendolyn

Contents

Part 2
Chapter 2: Historical Development of Foreign Exchange   8

Chapter 3: The European Monetary System   19

Part 3
Chapter 4: Currency Characteristics   36

Chapter 5: Foreign Exchange Risks   53

Chapter 6: Central Banks   78

Chapter 16: Major Option Strategies on Currencies   269

Part 5
Chapter 17: Economic Fundamentals   306

Chapter 18: Financial and Socio-Political Factors   345

Part 6
Chapter 19: Technical Analysis   355

Chapter 20: Trend Reversal Patterns   388

Chapter 21: Continuation Patterns   404

Chapter 22: Formations Unique to Bar Charts for Futures   419

Chapter 23: Point and Figure Charting   427

Chapter 24: Candlestick Charting   440

Chapter 25: Quantitative Trading Methods   466

Chapter 26: Oscillators   474

Chapter 27: W.D. Gann Analysis   488

Chapter 28: The Elliott Wave   492

Preface

Foreign exchange took off in earnest as recently as 1973, when currencies were finally allowed to float freely. Ostensibly a new industry, its origins can actually be traced to ancient times, when foreign coins started to be exchanged. Since stocks and bonds took several more millennia to come into existence, foreign exchange is, in fact, the oldest financial market.

Few financial instruments generate as much excitement and profitability. Traders from around the world enter positions for weeks, days, hours or only split seconds. The market can have explosive moves or steady flows. Money changes hands quickly, for a staggering daily average of $1 trillion. The foreign exchange profitability is legendary. George Soros' Quantum fund realized a profit in excess of U.S. $1 billion for a couple of days' work in September 1992. And Hans U. Hufschmid of Salomon Brothers, Inc. netted an income package of $28 million for 1993. Even by Wall Street standards, these numbers are heart stoppers.

It is impossible to envision a world without foreign exchange. Even the smallest transaction across borders triggers a currency exchange at one point or another. Whether importing or exporting raw materials, labor, manufactured goods or services, foreign exchange is an integral part of the transaction.

In addition to the corporate demand, currency trading provides a leading source of income for most financial institutions. In terms of profitability, commercial banks have steadily switched their focus from lending to foreign exchange. Along with investment banks, they set up sophisticated individual dealing rooms, somewhat resembling the NASA mission control rooms.

The latest newcomer to the markets, the hedge funds, rose to prominence in the early 1990s. Extremely aggressive, the hedge fund is able to concentrate billions of dollars into a single position, betting not only on the capacity of "reading" the market correctly, but also on its capability of "making" the market due to its sheer trade size.

Despite its high trading volume and its fundamental role, the foreign exchange market is rarely in the limelight. Since only a tiny fraction of the transactions are conducted on regulated exchanges, the currency markets are generally less visible and receive less media coverage.

There are no geographic, temporal or man-made boundaries to foreign exchange. This is a vibrant 24-hour market open to all eligible players. There are no official openings or closings, with the exception of the currency futures and the options on currency futures. Should the trading session not provide enough satisfaction, traders can deal after normal hours. And if there is a national holiday, players are generally able to find other markets open.

This book introduces you to all the significant aspects of foreign exchange in a practical manner, to best answer your typical questions, such as:

- Why do we trade currencies?
- Who are the players?
- What currencies do we trade?
- What makes them move?
- What instruments can we trade?
- How can we use them?
- How can we forecast currency behavior?
- How do we access the pertinent information?

The book is divided into six parts:

Part 1: Presents the basis of foreign exchange and the factors that contributed to the growth of the industry, from market developments to technological breakthroughs.

Part 2: Presents the historical developments in the market and how these elements have shaped the contemporary environment.

Part 3: Focuses on the mechanics of the market, the major players and markets, the risks pertinent to foreign exchange, corporate trading, methods of trading execution and dealing settlements.

Part 4: Analyzes foreign exchange instruments and provides comprehensive coverage of the major option strategies.

Part 5: Focuses on fundamental analysis, the economic indicators vital to the financial markets that may be disregarded in the currency markets, and the mind of the trader, for a point of view different at times from the typical theoretical expectation.

Part 6: Provides an exhaustive view on technical analysis, including an indepth chart analysis comparing the major chart types, chart formations and oscillators, and a comprehensive discussion of candlestick and point and figure charts as they apply to foreign currencies only.

Leading experts in these fields have courteously contributed their significant knowledge and experience to this book. In addition to taking advantage of their level of sophistication, you will have the opportunity to learn and compare their financial services for your own use.

There are no miracle answers, of course—at least not in this book. In fact, I generally shy away from rules of thumb. The only solid answer I favor is, "It depends." What you will learn is what makes the market move and the traders tick.

You are presented with a comprehensive arsenal of trading weapons, many of them on the cutting edge of technology. You will answer yourself "on what it all depends." Based on these elements, you will be able to make your own choices, test them and ultimately use them for your own benefit.

Cornelius Luca

Acknowledgments

Many thanks to William Rini, SVP Director of International Seminars at the New York Institute of Finance, for making this book possible. I also want to extend my thanks to everyone at the New York Institute of Finance, especially to Robert Gulick, Director of the Institute; Paul McQuarry, Director of Residence Programs; Dana Orenstein, Director of Seminars; and Abe Mastbaum, CPA Program Coordinator for all their gracious and professional cooperation over the years. The help and support of Drew Dreeland, Caroline Carney, Barry Richardson, Judy Weiss-Brown and Judy Sjo-Gaber from Simon & Schuster and Fred Dahl, director of Inkwell Publishing Services were vital for the completion of the book.

The revision of several chapters and many of the illustrations have been made possible through the kind efforts of the following:

Gerald Becker, Publisher, Commodity Perspective, Knight-Ridder

Krishna Biltoo, Marketing Director, Reuters International

Philip Brittan, President, Astrogamma, Inc.

Suzanne Brown, Marketing Manager, Quotron Foreign Exchange

Julian Childs, Executive Vice President, Dow Jones Telerate, Inc.

John Christopherson, Senior Vice President, Banco Portugues do Atlantico; Vice-Chairman of the Committee for Professionalism of ACI

Rich Curtin, Director, Surveys of Consumers, The University of Michigan

Elizabeth DeMorse, Director of Marketing, Bloomberg Financial

John Gray, Editor, Chartcraft, Inc.

Harry Guardiola, Vice President/Manager, Harris Trust & Savings

Robert Hafer, Director of Research, Commodity Research Bureau, Knight-Ridder

Ira Kawaller, Vice President-Director, Chicago Mercantile Exchange

Kurt Klein, Chief Editor, FutureSource

Joe Laurenzano, Senior Market Manager Foreign Exchange/Money, Knight-Ridder

Zoran Lazarevic, Marketing Manager, MMS International

Richard McKeever, Manager, Harlow Meyer Savage Inc.

Gary Meshell, Vice President, Dow Jones Telerate, Inc.

Stephen Onstad, National Marketing Representative & New York Regional Manager, CQG

Jim Pilgrim, Manager, Dow Jones Telerate, Inc.

Richard Pisani, Vice President, Transactions Product, Reuters America, Inc.

Robert Prechter, President, Elliott Wave International

Peter Rotondo, Executive Vice President of Foreign Exchange Division, Noonan, Astley & Pierce

Tim Slater, Past President CompuTrac Managing Director Telerate Seminars, Dow Jones Telerate, Inc.

Melanie Stevens, Marketing/Advertising Assistant, CQG

Nick VanNice, Chief Editor, Commodity Trend Service

Peggy Willie, Director of Marketing, Technical Data, a Thomson Financial Services Division

Chapter 1

What Is Foreign Exchange?

Foreign exchange is simultaneously a simple and complex notion, depending on the end-user. Despite the wide ranging points of view, they all have a common element. *Foreign exchange* is simply the mechanism which values foreign currencies in terms of another currency. An *exchange rate* is therefore the price of one currency in terms of another.

Why Foreign Exchange Occurs

Tourists around the world generate substantial foreign exchange flow. Whether the American tourists abroad in 1985 or the foreign tourists in the United States in the early 1990s, they all must convert their currencies to the local currencies to pay for traveling expenses. These small individual transactions generate important cash flow when compounded.

Investors around the world, large and small, are continuously hunting for investment opportunities. Whether in the equity markets, or real estate, or bank deposits, any international investment must, at one point or another, go through foreign exchange.

An American shopper may buy an American-made silk tie in an American boutique. Chances are that the silk was produced abroad. Even if an American buys an American car from an American dealer, if the car was assembled in Canada or Mexico, foreign exchange was executed.

The presence of foreign exchange in one or more stages of production is deeply ingrained, albeit not always obvious.

Global markets have become so competitive that corporations must continuously search the world for new markets and cheaper sources of raw materials and labor.

The degree of international integration generates interest rates adjustments, which in turn affect the foreign exchange rates.

Political changes are also major factors in foreign exchange. For instance, the fall of the Soviet Empire, despite its historic proportions, did not itself directly affect the foreign exchange market. However, a consequence of the fall, the German unification, generated a long term rally in the Deutsche mark, based on expectations of future economic might and short term high interest rates geared against inflation.

In terms of political or economic uncertainty, local currencies are quickly discarded in favor of safe-haven currencies, such as US dollars or Swiss francs. For instance, in the war-torn former Yugoslavia, where inflation rampages at incredulous rates of tens of million percent per year, the currencies of choice are US dollars and Deutsche marks.

In future chapters we will discuss in detail the major factors affecting the foreign exchange markets. For the time being, we must remember several of their general characteristics. The foreign exchange markets are:

1. sensitive to a large and continuously changing number of factors,
2. open to all players in the major currencies,
3. large and liquid in the major currencies,
4. concentrated on several currencies, and
5. extremely efficient relative to other financial markets.

Factors That Have Contributed to Foreign Exchange Volume Growth

The volume in foreign exchange has experienced a spectacular growth ever since currencies were allowed to float freely against each other. While the daily turnover in 1977 was US $5 billion, it increased to US $600 billion in 1987, to reach the US $1 trillion mark in September 1992 (see Figure 1.1).

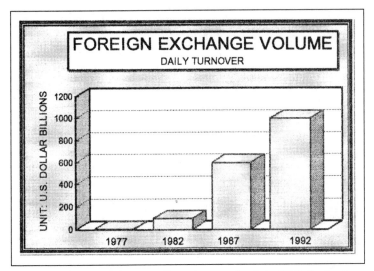

Figure 1.1.   Since the currencies were allowed to float freely in 1973, the foreign exchange daily turnover was estimated to have reached the US $1 trillion mark by September 1992.

Volume in foreign exchange cannot be measured directly the way it is done in the stock market. Foreign exchange is generally conducted in a decentralized manner, with the notable exceptions of the currency futures and the options on currency futures. What is behind this spectacular growth?

Exchange Rates Volatility

During the last days of the fixed exchange rates system, few envisioned the volatility potential of the currency markets. People generally assumed that economic forces just needed occasional self adjutment in an otherwise quiet activity. Were they wrong. The unchecked increase of the US dollar in the 1980s had a destructive effect on the American exporters' international trade competitiveness. The US dollar's record highs were capped in September 1985 and the currency was sent into a two year nosedive, which trimmed 50 percent of its value (see Figure 1.2). The impact of the exchange rate activity on the international economy and trade is difficult to gauge.

For foreign exchange, currency volatility is a prime factor in the growth of volume. In fact, volatility is a *sine qua non* condition for trading. The only instrument which may be profitable under conditions of low volatility is currency options.

Figure 1.2. The US dollar reached record highs against the Deutsche mark, along with other European currencies, in 1985. The negative impact on American exports triggered the G-5 dollar devaluation process, which lowered the US dollar value by 60 percent by 1995. (*Courtesy of Bloomberg Financial Markets*)

Interest Rates Volatility

Economic internationalization generated a significant impact on the interest rates as well. Willingly or not, economies became much more interrelated, a factor which exacerbated the need to change interest rates faster. Interest rates are generally changed in order to adjust the growth in the economy and interest rate differentials (see Figure 1.3) have a substantial impact on exchange rates. However, the correlation between the two is not mechanical. This will be discussed in Part 5, which deals with fundamental analysis.

Business Internationalization

In the past decades we have witnessed an unprecedented internationalization in the business world. The competition has intensified, triggering a worldwide hunt for more markets and cheaper raw materials and labor. The pace of economic internationalization picked up even more since 1989, due to the fall of Communism in Europe and the economic and financial growth in both Southeast Asia and South America. These changes have been positive toward foreign exchange since more transactional layers were added.

The New York, or London or Tokyo markets' clear boundaries are being blurred by the 24-hour trading and brokerage desks.

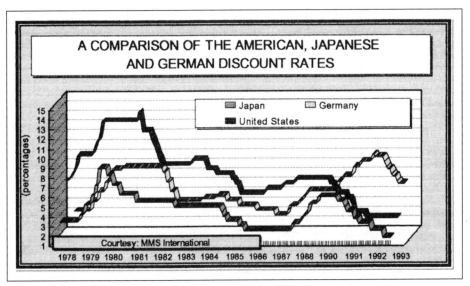

Figure 1.3. The interest rates in the G-7 countries have been more volatile in the past decades, as a result of economic internationalization. Above you can see the history of the discount rates in the most significant economies, the United States, Germany and Japan, between 1978 and 1993. Courtesy of MMS International.

Increased Corporate Interest

Foreign exchange has been perceived by many corporations as a transaction cost, albeit a rather volatile one. This passive approach proved costly for many corporations, large and small. A successful performance of a product or service overseas may be pulled down from the profit point of view by adverse foreign exchange conditions. However, the opposite is true as well.

The overall international performance of a product or service may be enhanced by an accurate handling of the foreign exchange. Experience has proven over and over again that it is worth focusing not on what you pay for foreign exchange, but on what foreign exchange can pay to you. Proper handling of foreign exchange generally adds substantially to the rate of return. Therefore, the interest in foreign exchange has increased dramatically in the past decade, although the full potential has not yet been reached. Many corporations are using currencies not only for hedging, but also for capitalizing on opportunities solely in the currency markets.

Increased Players' Sophistication

Advances in computers, computer software, telecommunications and the increased experience have sharpened the players' sophistication. This enhanced the traders's confidence in their ability to both generate profits and properly handle the exchange risks. Therefore, trading sophistication lead toward volume increase.

Developments in Telecommunications

In the 1970s and early 1980s, foreign exchange was mostly conducted via telephone, and to a much lesser extent on the telex machine. Both mediums are slow and error-prone. The introduction of automated dealing systems in the second half of the 1980s completely altered the way foreign exchange was conducted. The dealing systems are on-line computer systems which link market players on one-on-one basis. They are reliable and much faster, allowing traders to conduct four simultaneous trades, rather than one, or a maximum of two on the phone. They are also safer, as players are able to see the deals which they execute. Finally, the dealing systems have many other features which facilitate trading which will be presented in detail in Chapter 3. The dealing systems had a major role in expanding the foreign exchange business due to their reliability, speed and safety. Although it may be difficult to recall the days before the fax machines were introduced, it is only fair to mention their share into helping foreign exchange. In an industry where the speed of transfer of accurate information is paramount, faxes are currently commonplace.

Computer (Hardware and Software) Development

Computers have a significant role at many stages of conducting foreign exchange. In addition to the dealing systems, matching systems simultaneously connect all players around the world, electronically duplicating the brokers market.

The new front end-back office systems provide full accounting coverage, ticket writing, back office processing and risk management implementation at a fraction of the cost.

Unlike the limited technical analysis of the early 1980s, advanced software now makes it possible to generate all types of charts, augment them with sophisticated technical studies and put them at the traders' fingertips on a continuous basis at a rather limited cost.

Also, currency options can hardly be traded professionally without the aid of computers, because complex strategies require the help of advanced software for pricing.

New FX Instruments

Among the first new foreign exchange instruments were the currency futures, which were developed on the Chicago International Monetary Market about two decades ago. Foreign exchange is continuously enriched by new products in the currency options area. The gamut of options strategies has expanded significantly, as a result of the more sophisticated approach of corporations to foreign exchange trading. Options generally allow for customized strategies for hedging and speculation.

Profitability

One of the biggest fears among the equity players is the bear market. There is no such thing in the foreign exchange markets. Whether the US dollar reaches record highs or record lows, the market is active and liquid. The foreign exchange market is concentrated in four major currencies—Deutsche mark, Japanese yen, British pound and Swiss franc—which are quoted against the US dollar, ensuring a high degree of efficiency. Other financial markets tend to be fragmented among different issues and instruments, with much less liquidity available.

The major foreign exchange instrument is spot, which generally matures in two business days. The profit may be realized that fast. Even the long dated forward contracts mature a lot faster and safer than most of the loans, the former bread and butter instrument for banks. That is why commercial banks have allocated significant resources to trade currencies. Even profits from the credit card business pale in comparison with the size of foreign exchange profits.

Chapter 2

Historical Development of Foreign Exchange

Foreign exchange is a relatively new industry, having started only in 1973. However, it occured in ancient times, as coins started to be exchanged among traders. This chapter deals with the more recent developments which shaped foreign exchange into the vibrant and complex market of today.

A Historical Perspective

Foreign exchange as we know it, began in earnest in 1973. Money, though, goes back a long time, over 4500 years, when the Egyptians coined the first metal money, and the Babylonians wrote the first bills and receipts. The incipient foreign exchange markets can be traced back to the ancient Middle East, where money changers initiated the exchange of coins. Later, during the Middle Ages, as the number of travelers increased, people realized that metal coins may be impractical. Due to highway robberies and the sheer weight of the coins, foreign exchange started to take shape. International merchant bankers devised bills of exchange, which were transferable third party payments which allowed flexibility and growth in foreign exchange dealings.

Closer to the present, the twentieth century has thus far comprised periods of high volatility and of relative stability. Foreign exchange meant, mostly, commercial transactions. The idea of currency speculation has not always been regarded favorably. Money speculators were considered immoral and, at various times in history, they could even face imprisonment. In fact, as recently as the summer of 1993, following the Exchange Rate Mechanism's *de facto* demise, voices in Europe, especially France, only half jokingly reminded us of the efficiency of the guillotine in combating currency speculators.

World War I was immediately followed by extreme volatility and high speculation in foreign exchange; therefore, hedging with forward contracts became commonplace. The Great Depression, combined with the suspension of the gold standard in 1931, created a serious diminution in foreign exchange dealings. Nowadays, currencies around the world are generally quoted against the US dollar. Things haven't always been this way. By the mid-1930s London had gained prominence as the leading center for foreign exchange. At the apex of the British empire, the pound was *the* currency to trade and to keep as a reserve currency. Beside quid, the pound has generally been known as cable, from the fact that in the old times foreign exchange was traded on the telex machines, or cable. In 1930, the Bank for International Settlements was established in Basle, Switzerland. Its goals were to oversee the financial efforts of the newly independent countries, along with providing monetary relief to countries experiencing temporary balance of payments difficulties. The implementation was not perfect. Governments were generally weak, yet reluctant to take advice. Financially, money was scarce, and the ghost of the Depression was ever present. Germany was experiencing a disastrous hyperinflation. It all seemed to create a perfect doomsday scenario. The political and economic disequilibria were overwhelming, and new geographic boundaries had to be drawn in the sand . . .

World War II had a crashing effect on the pound. The British economy was, for all the practical reasons, destroyed, the empire was crumbling, and international confidence in the currency had sunk as a result of Germany's counterfeiting the pound in its all out war effort against England.

In the period following the United States' entrance in the second world war, the US dollar became the prominent currency of the entire globe. Previously, the dollar had been perceived as more of a has been, due to the Stock Market Crash of 1929 and the subsequent Great Depression. In fact, the United States had been reluctant to enter the war, so soon after the painful rebalancing of the Depression scarred economy. In the meantime, the ravages of war were turning Europe and Japan to ashes. The only country unscarred by war was the United States. It was only natural that the future had to be shaped by this country.

The Bretton Woods Accord

Toward the end of the war, in July 1944, the allies, the United States, Great Britain and France met at the United Nations' Monetary and Financial Conference at Bretton Woods, New Hampshire, to discuss and design the financial future of the new economic order. A North American location was selected because the United States was spearheading the Allies' war efforts and had the only major economy unscathed by the ravages of war.

In contrast with the volatility in foreign exchange markets which prevailed in the inter-bellic era, the post-World War II period was designed to be stable, in part due to the tight governmental controls on currency values. The objective was to bring about economic growth and prosperity internationally, through stable currencies. In order to implement it, the Bretton Woods Accord focused on two major building blocks: *the pegging of currencies and the International Monetary Fund (IMF)*.

Currency Pegging

The major trading currencies were pegged to the US dollar in the sense that they were allowed to fluctuate only one percent on either side of that rate. When a currency exceeded this range, marked by intervention points, the central bank in charge had to buy it or sell it, and thus bring it back to the range. In turn, the US dollar was pegged to gold at $35 per ounce. Thus, the US dollar became the world's reserve currency.

The near-fixed monetary system served several purposes. First, it attempted to avoid the stop-and-go situation of the inter-bellic era, when governments tended to resort frequently to floating exchange rates in the wake of economic pressures. Secondly, and at the time, most importantly, the world needed a nurturing environment within which it could rebuild itself. With the majority of the world's industrial base gone up in smoke, major social disruptions and the prewar political balance severely distorted, the last thing needed was currency speculation. Moreover, immediately after the war, there really weren't many currencies left, except the dollar. The world economy needed a warm and smooth cocoon, and the Bretton Woods Accord achieved that by keeping the currencies fixed against the US dollar. The key requirement was the cooperation of the central banks to implement the intervention points. In addition to the technical aspect, this continuous and common effort was meant to assist into bringing together and eventually cementing long-lasting relationships among parties with divergent interests.

The International Monetary Fund (IMF)

The International Monetary Fund (IMF), which has its headquarters in Washington, D.C., has the following general objectives, as presented in The International Monetary Fund, Its Evolution, Organization and Activities— Pamphlet # 37—IMF:

- Promote international cooperation by providing the means for members to consult and collaborate on international monetary issues
- Facilitate the growth of international trade and thus contribute to high levels of employment and real income among member nations
- Promote stability of exchange rates and orderly exchange agreements, and to discourage competitive currency depreciation
- Foster a multilateral system of international payments, and to seek the elimination of exchange restrictions that hinder the growth of world trade
- Make financial resources available to members, on a temporary basis and with adequate safeguards, to permit them to correct payments imbalances without resorting to measures destructive to national and international prosperity."

Structure of the IMF. The fund is governed by the Board of Governors and the Executive Board. The Board of Governors, which manages the Fund, consists of a governor and an alternate governor from each of the member countries. The Executive Board, which is in charge of implementing the daily activities, is comprised of 22 executive directors, representing one or more countries. The Executive Board is led by a Managing Director.

Membership. The International Monetary Fund is open to all countries with a responsible foreign policy. Each of the over 147 members is assigned a specific quota derived from the relative economic performance of each member. Members must pay 25 percent of this quota in standard reserve assets, such as US dollars or SDRs, and the balance in their own currencies. The size of the quota limits both the voting rights and the amounts available to borrow (see Figure 2.1).

Borrowing Facilities. The funds thus raised are available to its members. These resources may be increased through borrowing. Members may borrow funds under the following five facilities:

1. *Reserve tranche* is the most common source of funds. This facility allows a member to draw on its own reserve asset quota at the time of payment. Although proof of need is required, the IMF may not challenge it.

QUOTA = $(0.02Y + 0.05R + 0.10M + 0.10V) \times (1 + X/Y)$

where

Y = national income as of 1940
R = gold and dollar balances
M = average imports during 1934 - 1938
V = maximum variation in exports during 1934 - 1938
X = average exports during 1934 - 1938

Figure 2.1.   The formula used to determine the quota for the original members. The formula was eventually changed in order to provide larger weights to smaller nations (*Source: The International Letter, Federal Reserve Bank of Chicago, October 5, 1984*)

2. *Credit tranche drawings and stand-by arrangements* are the standard form of IMF loans. Once approved by the Executive Board, the loans are available in four equal tranches of 25 percent of the individual quota. Each consecutive tranche is lent under increasingly stringent conditions linked to the implementation of sound economic policies. Loans are received either directly or over the period of the stand-by arrangement.

3. *The compensatory financing facility* extends financial help to countries with temporary problems generated by reductions in export revenues. The financial support consists of up to 83 percent of a specific quota.

4. *The buffer stock financing facility* is geared toward assisting the stocking up on primary commodities in order to ensure price stability in a specific commodity. To this end, up to 45 percent of the quota may be borrowed.

5. *The extended facility* is designed to assist members with financial problems in amounts or for periods exceeding the scope of the previous facilities.

The Special Drawing Rights (SDRs). *The special drawings rights* (SDRs) are international reserve assets created and allocated by the International Monetary Fund to supplement the existing reserve assets. The idea for the SDRs was born out of the necessity for a stable and consistent source of lending, independent of the traditional reserve assets, such as US dollars. At the recommendation of the "Group of Ten", the United States, Great Britain, West Germany, Belgium, the Netherlands, France, Italy, Japan, Canada and Sweden, the SDRs were created at the IMF meeting in Rio de Janeiro in September 1967.

All the IMF members are eligible for allocations. The SDRs are used for payments and for obtaining currencies of other members.

The value of the SDR is calculated by the International Monetary Fund on a daily basis as the sum total of the weighted US dollar values of the five currencies in the basket: the US dollar, the Deutsche mark, the British pound, the Japanese yen and the French franc (see Figure 2.2).

Why the Bretton Woods Accord Failed

Certainly, the Bretton Woods System was not a marriage made in heaven for many of the participants. Some countries found the 1 percent allowed divergence from the value of the US dollar to be constrictive. In addition, under the gold standard, the price of gold was fixed by the United States at US $35 per ounce. This was dragging down on the American gold reserves and consequently on the international confidence in the US dollar. Despite these problems, the Bretton Woods Accord lasted between 1944 and 1971, successful for most of its life. Under its auspices, a broken Europe and Japan were able to reinvent themselves. From its inception, this system had been mostly a one nation show. Once recovered, though, both Europe and Japan started to provide competition within the US dollar block. The expenses were rather high, and after 1965, the United States was perceived as

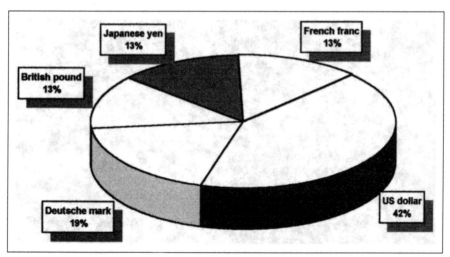

Figure 2.2.   The special drawing right is calculated as the sum of the daily weighted US dollar value of the five currencies in the basket: the US dollar (42 percent), the Deutsche mark (19 percent), the British pound (13 percent), the Japanese yen (13 percent) and the French franc (13 percent). These are the original weights.

exporting inflation. By the late 1960s, the differences in the rates of growth and the rates of inflation among the new major economies were widening. To answer the international pressures, the intervention points were underlined. But they could not provide the answer in 1971, when the Bretton Woods System faltered, and they could not provide the answer 27 years later either, when the European Monetary System failed. The artificially designed ranges could not reign the natural economic forces. In fact, they have just outlived their usefulness. Parallel to the demise of the Bretton Woods Accord, the United States abandoned the pegging the price of gold, in effect annulling the gold standard.

After Bretton Woods

Switching away from the fixed currency system after 27 years out of necessity, not by choice, was a difficult task. *The Smithsonian Agreement,* reached in Washington in December 1971, had a transitional role to the free floating markets. This agreement failed to address the real causes behind the international economic and financial pressures, focusing instead on increasing the ranges of currency fluctuations. From 1 percent, the fluctuation band for currencies relative to the US dollar was expanded to 4.5 percent. Against each other, then, foreign currencies could fluctuate 9 percent.

Parallel to the Washington efforts, the European Economic Community, established in 1957, tried to move away from the US dollar block toward the Deutsche mark block, by designing its own European monetary system. In April 1972, West Germany, France, Italy, the Netherlands, Belgium and Luxembourg developed the *European Joint Float.* Under this system, the member currencies were allowed to fluctuate within a 2.25 percent band, known as *the snake,* against each other, and collectively within 4.5 percent band, known as *the tunnel,* against the US dollar.

Unfortunately, both the Smithsonian Institution Agreement and the European Joint Float did not address the independent domestic problems of the member countries from the bottom up, attempting instead to focus solely on the large international picture and maintain it by artificially enforcing the intervention points. By 1973, both systems collapsed under heavy market pressures.

The idea of regional currency stability with the goal of financial independence from the US dollar block persisted. By July 1978, the plans for the European Monetary System were approved by the members of the European Community: West Germany, France, Italy, the Netherlands,

Belgium, Great Britain, Denmark, Ireland and Luxembourg. The system was launched in March 1979, as a revamped European Joint Float, or a mini Bretton Woods Accord. Additional features, such as the threshold of divergence, were designed to protect this monetary system from the fate of the previous ones. Judging from its expanded life span, until 1993 at least, the European Monetary System was obviously better. However, the continued focus on the macroeconomic picture at the expense of the historically significant changes in Europe at country level, and the stubborn attempts to fix natural economic divergences by means of maintaining the artificial intervention points triggered the collapse of the EMS. The heralded, but widely unexpected fall of the Communist system set off a series of economic imbalances difficult enough even to fully comprehend, let alone fix, by means of intervention points. Seriously rocked by the British pound's exit under heavy foreign exchange selling in September 1992, the European Monetary System folded for all practical purposes at the end of July 1993. The traditional intervention bands were abandoned for politically correct and insignificantly wide intervention bands. (For more details, refer to Chapter 3 on the European Monetary System.)

The Free Floating Foreign Exchange Markets

The 1973 double demise of the Smithsonian Institution Agreement and the European Joint Float signified the official switch of the foreign exchange markets to free floating. The switch occurred pretty much by default, since it was the only available option. However, it is important to keep in mind that currency free-floating was not, by any means, imposed. In other words, countries are free to peg, semipeg or free-float their currencies. In fact, only in 1978 was free-floating officially mandated by the International Monetary Fund.

Free-Floating

The major currencies, such as the US dollar, move independently of the other currencies. The currency may be traded by anybody so inclined. Its value is a function of the current supply and demand forces in the market, and there are no specific intervention points that have to be observed. Of course, the Federal Reserve Bank irregularly intervenes to change the value of the US dollar, but no specific levels are ever imposed (see Figure 2.3). Naturally, free-floating currencies are in the heaviest trading demand. Free-floating is not the sine qua non condition for trading. Liquidity is also an indispensable condition.

Figure 2.3. The US dollar against the Deutsche mark. The value of the USD/DEM is solely a function of the current supply and demand. (Courtesy of Bloomberg)

Currency Blocks

The major currencies tend to have a polarizing effect over currencies from smaller economies. Sometimes, this phenomenon occurs as a result of the former colonial ties. For instance, the former British Empire was metamorphisized into the Commonwealth. Consequently, the currencies of the Commonwealth members, such as the Indian rupee, are closer to the British pound. The same is true for the French franc. Some African nations, such as Cameroon or Cote d'Ivoire, have pegged their currencies to the French franc. At times, the polarizing effect is generated by the fact that the majority of a smaller economy's business is done with a single larger economy or with a group of economies. For instance, within the European Monetary System, the members generally focused their economic ties among themselves, gravitating as a whole around the German economy. Therefore, currency blocks naturally occurred around the US dollar, the Deutsche mark, the British pound, the French franc and the Japanese yen.

Semipegged Currencies

The semipegged currencies seem to be going the way of the dinosaurs. The standard example of semipegging used to be the member currencies of the European Monetary System. They were allowed to fluctuate within 2¼ percent (see Figure 2.4) or, exceptionally, within 6 percent intervention bands

Figure 2.4. The Deutsche mark/French franc. Note the smoothness of the French franc price relative to the Deutsche mark, typical of the EMS crosses, but highly unusual for a free-floating currency. (Courtesy of Bloomberg)

till July 31, 1993. Following the foreign exchange crisis of the summer of 1993, the new EMS intervention rates are 15 percent.

Semi-pegging generally had a slowing down effect on speculative currency trading. However, trading was enhanced when currencies reached the extreme values of the allowed range.

Pegged Currencies

Moving away from the Bretton Woods Accord, some smaller economies naturally gyrated around larger economies with which they had the majority of their economic liaisons. For instance, many of the Caribbean nations, such as Jamaica, have pegged their currencies to the US dollar. In addition, some countries have quasipegged their currencies to the US dollar, by allowing minor divergences. For instance, the Saudi Riyal spot exchange rate (see Figure 2.5) has been closely kept against the US dollar at around 3.7500, although small divergences occurred.

Dirty Floating

Dirty floating, although not widely spread, creates a phenomenon of inefficiency in an industry known to be very efficient. Although officially free-

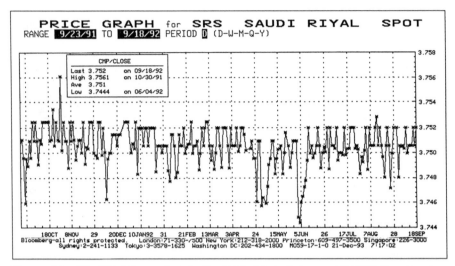

Figure 2.5. The US dollar against the Saudi Riyal is traded around 3.7500. Despite minor divergences, the USD/SAR spot exchange rate shows limited fluctuations. (Courtesy of Bloomberg)

floating, some minor currencies are covertly and irregularly maneuvered by local governments and central banks to better suit domestic or even personal interests. For instance, one of the small countries which officially has a free-floating currency, regularly revalues its currency against the US dollar prior to and during receiving oil shipments. The oil price is quoted in US dollars, and the payment in this case is executed at the dock. Therefore, the temporary revaluation of the domestic currency reduces the total oil bill. Although this type of inefficiency is potentially profitable in foreign exchange, the market size and the limited liquidity of small currencies greatly reduces the profit opportunities.

Currency Reserves

In times of economic or political uncertainty, people and corporations worldwide try to protect their investments and wealth by purchasing currencies or commodities perceived as safe haven instruments. In addition, certain international transactions are executed in currencies other than the domestic ones. This type of currencies are known as *currency reserves*. Prior to the Second World War, the reserve currency used to be the British pound. In the post World War II era, the reserve currency around the world has been the US dollar. Currently, other reserve currencies are the Deutsche mark and, to a lesser extent, the Japanese yen. The portfolio of reserve currencies may change depending on the specific international conditions, to include the Swiss franc or the French franc.

Chapter 3

The European Monetary System

Out of the ravages of World War II, and, at first, within the financial environment of the American-led Bretton Woods Accord, the premier European economic powers began to design different venues for their economic future. Their competitive efforts against American and Japanese economic might over the years culminated in the establishment of the European Monetary System in 1979. This chapter presents the historic path to the system, its characteristics and its future in the international context of the 1990s.

Historical Background

The creation of the European Monetary System was the result of a long and continuous series of post–World War II efforts aimed at creating closer economic cooperation among the capitalist European countries. The European Community (EC) commission's officially stated goals were to improve the inter-European economic cooperation, create a regional area of monetary stability and act as "a pole of stability in world currency markets."

Foreign exchange went through several ups and downs during the destabilized period between the wars but, by and large, foreign exchange speculation was not the name of the game, even when it was allowed. Such speculation still had a negative connotation, and it eventually became a punishable offense.

The end of World War II painted a ravaged picture of the former industrial and financial Europe. Foreign exchange was completely out of the picture, as currencies had lost their value. But even under better circumstances, trading would have been impossible, as currency fluctuations were tied in very narrow ranges against the US dollar, under the Bretton Woods Accord of 1944. The accord had created a much needed nurturing environment for the European economies. Currency stability was vital to the enormous task of rebuilding Europe.

The first steps in this rebuilding were taken in 1950 when the *European Payment Union* was instituted to facilitate the inter-European settlements of international trade transactions. In 1951, the Treaty of Paris established the *European Coal and Steel Community,* formed by West Germany, France, Italy, the Netherlands, Belgium and Luxembourg. Great Britain declined to join. The purpose of the community was to promote the inter-European trade in general, and to eliminate restrictions on the trade of coal and raw steel in particular. Plans for a joint European Defense Community were derailed by the French National Assembly in 1954.

In 1957, the Treaty of Rome established the *European Economic Community*, with the same signatories as the European Coal and Steel Community. The stated goal of the European Economic Community was to eliminate customs duties and any barriers against the transit of capital, services and people among the member nations. The EC also started to raise common tariff barriers against outsiders.

The European Community consists of four executive and legislative bodies:

1. *The European Commission.* The executive body in charge of making and observing the enforcement of the policies. Since it lacks an enforcement arm, the commission must rely on individual government to enforce the policies. There are 23 departments, such as foreign affairs, competition policy and agriculture. Each country selects its own representatives for four year terms. The commission is based in Brussels and consists of 17 members.

2. *The Council of Ministers.* Makes the major policy decisions. It is composed of ministers from the 12 member nations. The presidency is held for 6 months by each of the members, in alphabetical order. The meet-

ings take place in Brussels or in the capital of the nation holding the presidency.

3. *The European Parliament.* Reviews and amends legislative proposals and has the power to adopt or reject budget proposals. It consists of 518 elected members. It is based in Luxembourg, but the sessions take place in Strasbourg or Brussels.

4. *The European Court of Justice.* Settles disputes between the EC and the member nations. It consists of 13 members and it is based in Luxembourg.

In 1963, the *French-West German Treaty of Cooperation* was signed. This pact was designed not only to end centuries of bellicose rivalry, but to settle the postwar reconciliation between two major foes. The treaty, signed by President Charles de Gaulle and Chancellor Konrad Adenauer, stipulated that West Germany will lead economically through the cold war, and France, the former diplomatic powerhouse, will provide the political leadership. The premise of this treaty was obviously correct, in an environment defined by a foreseeable long term continuing cold war and a divided Germany. Later in this chapter, we will discuss the implications of this pact for the present.

In 1964, a common agricultural market was instituted and uniform prices were introduced.

A conference of national leaders in 1969 set the objective of establishing a monetary union within the European Community. This goal was supposed to be implemented by 1980, when a common currency was planned to be used in Europe. The reasons behind the common currency unit were to stimulate inter-European trade and weld together the individual member economies into an all-European superpower. Only this type of economy was perceived to be able to fully compete with the economies of the United States and Japan.

The monetary union strategy of semipegging the nation members' currencies allowed a 2 percent fluctuation against each other. Of course, by the end of 1971, the Bretton Woods Accord collapsed and was replaced for two years by a transitional system, the Smithsonian Accord. This accord raised the stakes in the currency band of fluctuation, by allowing the currencies to move within 4.5 percent against the dollar or a hefty 9 percent against each other.

Faced with the prospect of a rapidly deteriorating international monetary system, the EC members established the *European Joint Float Agreement* in 1972. By 1973, Great Britain, Ireland and Denmark were also members.

The agreement allowed the member currencies to move within a 2.25 percent fluctuation band. Due to its curvaceous movement, this band was nicknamed *the snake*. As a joint group, the agreement allowed these currencies to gyrate within a 4.5 percent band. This larger band was nicknamed *the tunnel*. All in all, the entire agreement became known as *the snake in the tunnel*.

The economic fundamentals did not provide much support to the monetary agreement. The members pursued independent economic policies. Consequently, one by one, the British pound, the Danish krone and the Italian lira were forced out of the snake by early 1973. By and large, the Joint Agreement was gone, despite efforts to prolong its life. A little later in the same fateful year, the Smithsonian Accord collapsed as well, due to immense pressure on the US dollar.

However, the ideals of economic unification, planned to be achieved in large measure through foreign exchange stability, stayed all the contrarian forces and persevered through the engulfing tide of the free-floating markets.

The European Monetary System

In 1978, a new plan for stability—the European Monetary System—was ratified by the nine members of the European Community. After several inadvertent delays, the new system was established in 1979. Out of the nine members, only seven were full members: West Germany, France, the Netherlands, Belgium, Luxembourg, Denmark and Ireland. Great Britain did not participate in all of the arrangements and Italy joined under special conditions. Greece joined in 1981, Spain and Portugal in 1986. Great Britain joined the Exchange Rate Mechanism in 1990. Also in 1990, West Germany became Germany as a result of its political unification with East Germany.

Features of the EMS

The European Currency Unit (ECU). This currency was created by the European Monetary System with the eventual goal of replacing the individual European member currencies. The European currency unit is a basket of the member currencies. As a composite unit, the ECU consists of all the European Community currencies, which are individually weighted. The weights are a direct function of:

1. relative GDP and

2. share of inter-EMS trading.

These weights are examined every five years or upon request.
Figure 3.1 presents the ECU currency weights as of August 3, 1992.
(See also Figure 3.2.)

To obtain the individual currency in the ECU composition, the following calculations are made:

Composition = ECU value × Weight ×
    Currency exchange rate against the US dollar

In the case of the Deutsche mark, its contribution in the ECU is:

$$1.1425 \times .3038 \times 1.7978 = .6240$$

(I used the average rates for both the ECU and the USD/DEM.)

The ECU has not been developed as a physical entity. The currency is not printed, so that, unfortunately, shopping bills still must be paid in other currencies.

The ECU has two functions:

1. Monetary

2. Accounting

ECU Composition		Brussels Fixing Against the US Dollar	Weight (%)
.6242	DEM	1.7975–1.7981	30.38
.0878	GBP	1.6313–1.6318	12.56
1.332	FRF	6.1088–6.1094	19.09
151.8	LIT	1.335–1.341	9.96
.2198	NGL	2.0248–2.0254	9.51
3.431	BFR	36.9950–37.0350	7.81
.1976	DKK	6.9301–6.9307	2.50
.008552	IEP	1.4879–1.4885	1.12
.130	LFR	36.9950–37.0350	.31
1.440	GRD	197.10–197.40	.64
6.885	ESP	112.92–112.98	5.34
1.393	PES	156.93–156.99	.78
		1 ECU = 1.1422 − 1.1428	100

Figure 3.1. The individual components of the European currency unit, and their respective weights. (*Source: Telerate®; Reprinted by Permission. © 1993 Dow Jones Telerate, Inc.*)

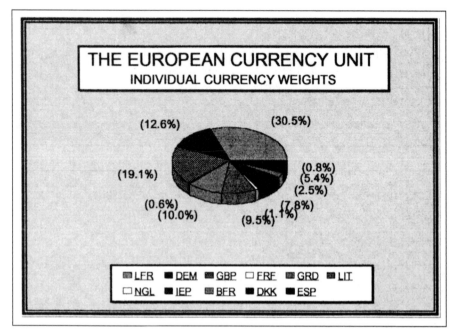

Figure 3.2. The individual components of the European currency unit and their respective weights.

Under the *monetary function*, ECU is considered to be a reserve currency. EMS central banks use it for loans and issue ECUs for debts settlement. Also, the ECU is an actively traded currency in the cash market around the world. In this trading capacity, the ECU is quoted in American terms, just like the British pound. In the futures market, mid-1980s efforts on the Chicago Mercantile Exchange (CME) to trade the ECU failed.

This currency is expected by its creators to eventually become an internationally held asset in the mold of the special drawing rights (SDR), which are issued by the International Monetary Fund.

Under the *accounting function*, the ECU price is used as a benchmark against which the member currencies are valued. The individual currency valuation is made at the fixing time in Europe and is based on the middle rate (the average between the bid and the offer).

The Bilateral Grid. The *bilateral grid* links all of the central rates of the EMS currencies in terms of the ECU. A central rate is the average rate between the bid and the offer at the fixing time. It is used on a daily basis to indicate whether the member currencies are observing the bands' fluctuation limits. These bands had been 2.25 percent for most the members, and 6 percent for Italy until 1990 and later for Spain until July 1993.

	BEF	NLG	DKK	DEM	FRF	IEP	ESB	PTE
BEF 100	**40.212**	5.5870	18.9143	4.9590	16.631	2.0566	407.30	509.23
		5.4626	18.4938	4.8484	16.261	2.0109	383.50	479.59
		5.3415	18.0931	4.7400	15.899	1.9662	631.30	451.67
NLG 100	1872.2	**2.1967**	346.240	90.770	304.44	37.648	7455.8	9321.4
	1830.5		338.537	88.753	297.66	36.810	7021.8	8779.2
	1789.6		331.020	86.780	291.04	35.993	6613.2	8267.9
DKK 100	553.00	30.210	**7.43679**	26.810	89.925	11.121	2202.3	2753.5
	540.72	25.539		26.216	87.926	10.873	2075.2	2593.2
	528.70	28.883		25.630	85.970	10.632	1953.4	2443.3
DEM 100	2109.5	115.24	390.160	**1.94964**	343.05	42.427	8403.0	10504
	2062.6	112.67	381.443		335.39	41.476	7911.7	9891.8
	2016.6	110.17	373.000		327.92	40.552	7451.5	9319.7
FRF 100	628.97	34.360	116.320	30.4950	**6.5388**	12.648	2504.8	3131.6
	614.98	33.595	113.732	29.8164		12.367	2358.9	2949.4
	601.23	32.848	111.200	29.1500		12.092	2221.7	2777.7
IEP 100	5086.0	277.84	940.60	246.600	827.03	**0.8086**	20254	25323
	4972.3	271.66	919.68	241.105	808.63		19076	23850
	4862.3	265.62	899.22	235.700	790.64		17965	22462
ESB 100	27.681	1.5121	5.11927	1.34201	4.5011	0.5563	**154.25**	132.75
	26.070	1.4241	4.81880	1.26395	4.2393	0.5242		125.04
	24.552	1.3412	3.99233	1.19005	3.9923	0.4937		117.74
PTE 100	22.140	1.2095	4.09450	1.07299	3.6001	0.4452	84.926	**192.854**
	26.070	1.1391	3.85617	1.01094	3.3906	0.4193	79.893	
	19.638	1.0728	3.63174	0.95200	3.1933	0.3949	75.330	

Figure 3.3. The Bilateral Central Rate grid reflecting the old intervention bands (May 14, 1993).

The extraordinary foreign exchange volatility of 1993 forced the EMS to expand the fluctuation band to 15 percent up or down against the central rate for all the members. Each central bank is responsible for its currency. If it exceeds the boundaries, the specific central bank is responsible for intervening in the foreign exchange markets and repositioning its currency back into the band. Figure 3.3 presents the bilateral grid of central rates as of May 14, 1993. Figure 3.4 presents the new bilateral grid in effect after the catastrophical foreign exchange events on the EMS.

The Threshold of Divergence. The threshold of divergence is a very important safety feature for the EMS. It creates an emergency exit for currencies which become the singular focus of various adverse forces. The threshold of divergence indicates when the specific country with the pressured currency should take additional steps other than simple central bank intervention in the foreign exchange markets. These steps will be changes in the economic policies or devaluation or revaluation of the currency.

This feature limits the responsibility of the rest of the EMS members toward the currency in trouble. Whereas the other countries will provide support for the distressed currency in the short run, they will stop once the threshold of divergence is reached. Therefore, isolated problems become the sole responsibility of the specific country and the financial and economic exposures of its peers are minimized.

The threshold of divergence was set at 1.69 percent (with the exceptions for countries in the wider 6 percent band, for which it is at 4.5 percent) from its ECU value. This EMS safety feature is an improvement over its predecessor, the snake.

It performed well in September 1992, when the unusual selling pressure on the British pound set up all the defensive measures on the EMS. First, Bank of England attempted to support its battered currency by direct purchases in the interbank market. When this step failed, the other EMS members stepped in and also purchased the pound. This failed as well.

Due to the divergence of the British pound's price from the allowed percentage on the band, the threshold of divergence was activated. The other central banks halted their costly but unsuccessful support of the pound. Bank of England raised its base rate by a hefty 5 percent in the same day, trying to shore up the massive selling pressure. Yet the market was not impressed by the magnitude of the interest rate increase, as it understood that the rate change was triggered only by the crisis, rather than economic policies. Therefore the selling of the pound continued unabated.

With no alternative left, Bank of England was forced to pull its currency out of the Exchange Rate Mechanism (ERM) two years after joining it. Despite the high cost of trying to keep the pound within the permissible

	BEF	NLG	DKK	DEM	FRF	IEP	ESB	PTE
BEF **100**	**40.212**	6.3434 / 5.4626 / 4.7545	21.4747 / 18.4938 / 15.9266	5.6300 / 4.8484 / 4.1750	18.880 / 16.261 / 14.005	2.3350 / 2.0109 / 1.7318	445.42 / 383.50 / 330.34	556.89 / 479.59 / 413.02
NLG **100**	2125.6 / 1830.5 / 1576.5	**2.1967**	393.105 / 338.537 / 291.544	90.770 / 88.753 / 86.780	345.65 / 297.66 / 256.35	42.744 / 36.810 / 31.701	8153.7 / 7021.8 / 6047.1	10194 / 8779.2 / 7560.5
DKK **100**	627.88 / 540.72 / 465.67	34.300 / 25.539 / 25.439	**7.43679**	30.445 / 26.216 / 22.575	102.10 / 87.926 / 75.720	12.626 / 10.873 / 9.364	2408.5 / 2075.2 / 1786.2	3011.2 / 2593.2 / 2233.3
DEM **100**	2395.0 / 2062.6 / 1776.2	115.24 / 112.67 / 110.17	442.968 / 381.443 / 328.461	**1.94964**	389.48 / 335.39 / 288.81	48.170 / 41.476 / 35.714	9191.2 / 7911.7 / 6812.8	11481 / 9891.8 / 8517.9
FRF **100**	714.03 / 614.98 / 529.66	39.009 / 33.595 / 28.938	132.066 / 113.732 / 97.943	34.6250 / 29.8164 / 25.6750	**6.5388**	14.360 / 12.367 / 10.650	2739.3 / 2358.9 / 2031.5	3424.8 / 2949.4 / 2540.0
IEP **100**	5774.4 / 4972.3 / 4282.6	315.45 / 271.66 / 233.95	1067.9 / 919.68 / 792.01	280.000 / 241.105 / 207.600	938.95 / 808.63 / 696.40	**0.8086**	22150 / 19076 / 16428	27694 / 23850 / 20539
ESB **100**	30.272 / 26.070 / 22.451	1.6537 / 1.4241 / 1.2264	5.59850 / 4.81880 / 4.15190	1.46800 / 1.26395 / 1.08800	4.9225 / 4.2393 / 3.6505	0.6087 / 0.5242 / 0.4515	**154.25**	145.18 / 125.04 / 107.67
PTE **100**	24.212 / 26.070 / 17.957	1.3227 / 1.1391 / 0.9809	4.47770 / 3.85617 / 3.32090	1.17400 / 1.01094 / 0.87100	3.9370 / 3.3906 / 2.9199	0.4869 / 0.4193 / 0.3611	92.876 / 79.893 / 68.880	**192.854**

Figure 3.4. The Bilateral Central Rate grid reflecting the new +/− 15 percent intervention bands, established since August 2, 1993.

band (estimated to be anywhere between US$6 to 20 billion), the threshold of divergence performed its emergency exit function, minimizing the losses for the rest of the EMS members.

Supporting Credit Facilities. The supporting credit facilities offer the EMS's central banks an alternative to using their currency reserves for parity maintenance intervention. These facilities consist of three different maturity loans:

a. *Short term* (45-90 days) *loans* for virtually unlimited amounts

b. *Medium term* (90-270 days) *loans* from a limited ECU pool, based on each member's quota

c. *Long term loans* from a limited ECU pool, which are conditioned by the borrower's promise of following domestic economic policies to minimize future need of using this type of loan

The European Monetary Cooperation Fund. The European Monetary Cooperation Fund was established to manage the EMS credit arrangements. In order to increase the acceptance of the ECU, countries which hold more ECU deposits or accept as loan repayment more than their share of ECU, receive interest on the excess ECU deposits, and vice versa. This interest rate is the weighted average of all the EMS members' discount rates.

Performance of the European Monetary System
There was a short maiden voyage for the EMS before problems reminiscent of the time of the snake occurred. Divergences in the rate of growth and the rate of inflation among the members continued to generate unwanted changes in the interest rates and economic policies. And yet, despite many obstacles and several realignments EMS had successfully sailed through the 1980s (see Figure 3.5).

The 1990s were much stormier years for the European Monetary System. Despite a long opposition to full economic union in Europe, starting in 1987, Great Britain successfully (but at a high domestic inflation cost) maneuvered the British pound to stay within the limits of the EMS. Great Britain had been a special member of the EMS since its inception, but not a member of the Exchange Rate Mechanism (ERM).

As one of the major European powerhouses, Great Britain had to be close to the core of the discussions on the future of the European Monetary Union. Yet the British economy has been marked by high inflation and the British government opposed any type of economic or financial unification which would hinder the national sovereignty. The perceived future political benefits outweighed the short term economic concerns. In September 1990,

	DEM	FRF	NLG	BFR	ITL	IEP	DKK	ESP	PTE	GBP
09/1979	+2.0						−3.0			
11/1979							−5.0			
03/1981					−6.0					
10/1981	+5.5	−3.0	+5.5		−3.0					
02/1982				−8.5			−3.0			
06/1982	−4.3	−5.8	+4.3		−2.8					
03/1993	+5.5	−2.5	+3.5	+1.5	−2.5	−3.5	+2.5			
07/1985	+2.0	+2.0	+2.0	+2.0	−6.0	+2.0				
04/1986	+3.0	−3.0	+3.0	+1.0			+1.0			
08/1986							−8.0			
01/1987	+3.0		+3.0	+2.0						
01/1990					−3.7					
09/1992					−7.0				−5.0	OUT
11/1992								−6.0	−6.0	

Figure 3.5.   The EMS realignments between September1979 and November 1992.

Great Britain joined the Exchange Rate Mechanism at the cross rate of GBP/DEM 2.9500.

The move was widely perceived as beneficial for the British economy. Previously, the GBP/DEM cross had become a sure bet to sell just under the 3.0000 level. Both the Bank of England and the Bundesbank would intervene to protect that level. Upon the announcement, the foreign exchange market reacted aggressively by buying (or attempting to buy) large amounts of pounds, despite a simultaneous 1 percent cut in the base rate. The 3.0000 barrier was shattered in a matter of minutes.

The day was an embarrassing one for the cable traders, as it was virtually impossible to trade the currency. There aren't many instances in the careers of spot traders when they are totally unable to make a price.

From the very beginning, objections had been raised regarding the high cross rate, GBP/DEM 2.9500, at which Great Britain joined the ERM. The British position remained consistent, that the move was part of the long term strategy of combating inflation.

Even after entering the ERM, the British government maintained its long standing objections toward advanced economic policy coordination and control, and a single currency. Eventually, its position softened with regard to the currency unification, but not toward European federalism.

By the end of 1991, with the shocks of the surprisingly fast demise of the Communist block and the equally unexpected unification of Germany still in the process of psychological digestion, the skies over the EMS looked very calm and encouraging.

In February 1992, the 12 EMS members signed the *European Union Treaty*, in the Dutch city of Maastricht, an ambitious agreement with the stated goal of a "closer union among the peoples of Europe." It consists of a series of amendments to the 1957 Treaty of Rome. It was planned to become law only upon ratification by all the EMS members and was supposed to be implemented by January 1993, parallel to the establishing of the single European market. According to the Maastricht Treaty, the European Community leaders would have a central bank by 1994, a single currency by January of 1997 or January 1999 and a joint economic and foreign policy by 1999.

The convergence tests for the ERM members were based on *inflation, interest rates, exchange rates, budget deficit* and *debt stock*. In terms of inflation, the individual country rate could not exceed the rate of 1.5 percent above the lowest three members in the previous year. Interest rates had to be kept within 2 percent above the lowest three members in the previous year. With regard to exchange rates, a country had to be an ERM bands member for two years, without realignment. The budget deficit could not exceed 3 percent of the GDP. And finally, the outstanding stock of public sector debt could not be higher than 60 percent of GDP.

As of the beginning of 1993, only France was able to clear all of these stringent rules. It was followed by Germany and Denmark, which were able to clear four out of five rules. At the other end of the spectrum, Greece and Portugal failed all the convergence tests.

Although the discrepancies in the rates of growth and inflation were still there, the decision balance was shifting away from economic convergence first, toward a political convergence first then deal with the problems later. Perhaps the recent unification of Germany was influencing some of the general enthusiasm.

As the costs of political change in Europe started to become apparent, the enthusiasm among the EMS members also started to wear thin. By June 1992, the Danish referendum rejected the treaty by a minuscule margin. And by September 1992, the British pound and the Italian lira had to be (temporarily, it was officially announced) withdrawn from the ERM. Red flags were raised.

The Danes were the only nation to reject the treaty, although they passed it on the second referendum.

The foreign exchange shock of having the pound suspended from the ERM had a longer term impact. How could it happen?

A lot of fingers in the market pointed towards the Bundesbank's tight monetary policy. The traditional German distaste for inflation continued to be fueled by the specific inflationary characteristics of their nation's unification. With an overheated consumer demand from the former East Germany, the Bundesbank had little choice but to pursue a high interest rate policy. The policy paid off domestically, but raised huge problems abroad. As the

September 1992 events were quickly unfolding, Germany only produced a .25 percent interest rate cut, far less than its neighbors' expectations.

Within a worldwide economic slowdown and an East European political turmoil, each nation was looking to stay economically afloat. Faced with either the expensive choice of propping up their currencies to the agreed levels or the economically suffocating choice of raising the interest rates, most of the EMS members felt cornered. The monetary system, after all, was designed to reduce the currencies' gyrations, as the member economies converge. The feeling was that stronger currencies like the Deutsche mark, the Dutch guilder and the Belgian franc had to be revalued, while the other currencies had to be devalued.

Therefore, when the run on the EMS currencies finally occurred in September 1992, it looked more like a *fait accomplit*, rather than a totally unexpected surprise. What was surprising, though, was the velocity of the forces in play in the foreign exchange markets. It was no wonder that the average daily trading volume reached the US$1 trillion level toward the end of 1992.

Sterling pound and the Italian lire were not, by any means, the only currencies negatively affected. The Spanish peseta, the Portuguese escudo and the Irish punt were devalued, the Norway krone and the Finnish markka were allowed to fluctuate, the Swedish central bank raised a key interest rate by 500 percent (this is no typo!), before it gave up and let the Swedish krona fluctuate freely and the Danish krone and the French franc came under increasing pressure. Allowing the currencies to gyrate according to the law of supply and demand is a *de facto* devaluation.

The Swedish krona and the Finnish markka are not, of course, members of the EMS but, since they had been planning to join the EMS, the Swedish and Finnish central banks maintained their respective currencies within the accepted bounds in order to show the necessary financial discipline and commitment.

What about the French franc? Relatively speaking, the French franc came under less pressure in the initial stages of the all-out sell-off of the EMS currencies. But sooner rather than later, the French franc became the selling target of traders around the world. The fundamentals had seemed to be supportive of the French franc. The French economy was in better shape than that of the other members. The increased independence of the Bank of France was perceived as a strong force behind the franc.

But after targeting all of the weaker EMS currencies, triggering hefty devaluations across the board, the foreign exchange market finally focused on the core currency vis-à-vis the Deutsche mark: the French franc. The French government policy of maintaining the franc in the ERM without devaluation, a policy known as the *franc fort*, was being tested.

As the French franc sell-off fury was unleashed, the French efforts had been matched by Germany's. To the chagrin of smaller members, the Bundesbank seemed much more inclined to help the French franc, relative to their own currencies.

Surprise? Not entirely. Behind it all there was the *French-West German Treaty of Cooperation.* France and Germany had entered a very deep reaching pact covering their exact economic and political roles relative to each other. And 29 years later, the pact was being put to the test on the foreign exchange markets.

The Bundesbank not only helped with vigorous foreign exchange market interventions, it also cut the interest rates. Cutting the interest rates under pressure across the board, but specifically to support the French franc, was a first for the Bundesbank. And yet, despite the all-out joint efforts, the franc fort could not be saved.

The decision taken by the ERM on the last weekend of July 1993 was to expand the previous fluctuation bands of 2.25 percent and 6 to 15 percent. Whereas it was stated to be a temporary decision, the future of the European Monetary System as envisioned at the Maastricht Treaty is in jeopardy. The system's resolve is under scrutiny, as its goals must be repositioned to better meet the challenges of the current *fin de siecle.*

Conclusion

There is no doubt in anybody's mind that the unification of 354 million people, along with the joint GDP of US$6.01 trillion, or 20 percent more than the United States' and 50 percent more than Japan's (in 1990), present the European Monetary System with a very attractive goal. The European block would not only be better suited to compete with the United States and Japan, it would be the world economic leader.

Achieving such a mighty goal cannot, in the long run, avoid economic and political realities. Despite the efforts toward economic convergence, the facts show that old-fashioned divergences, in terms of economic growth and inflation, are recurring problems.

Economic Divergence

The divergent economic trends and the consequent need for divergent policies cannot help but emphasize the social differences, generally disregarded by most of the studies. The political unification of Germany, which capitalized on the opportunity presented by the weakening of the Communist grip in Europe, acted as a reality test. Despite having a common language, culture and heritage, the unification proved to be an economically burdening undertaking.

When a similar experiment is envisioned but on a 12-nation scale (with all those nations very different), the logistics appear in a very special perspective.

Convergence has been the buzz word for decades, but natural convergence. When the reality of the economic fundamentals is denied, it is only a matter of time before the forces of the free markets make the necessary adjustments. Simply, an artificial mechanism has a limited life.

Financial Cost of Maintaining the Currency Parity

The cost of maintaining divergent currencies in check is staggering. Some of the central banks' foreign exchange intervention bills were US$6–20 billion for the Bank of England's September 1992 intervention, Deutsche mark 24 billion for the Deutsche Bundesbank's one week support of the Italian lira in 1993, US$50.6 billion for the Banque de France's support of its franc in the summer of 1993 and US$7.4 billion for Danish National Bank's July 1993 effort to back the value of its currency. These numbers, as high as they may be, are but a fraction of the total lost by the central banks to avoid the reality of economic fundamentals. One cannot help but wonder whether these costs are worth it.

Currency Responsibility

Not many lessons had been learned from the foreign exchange crisis of September 1992. The European Community officials found it unwise to make any changes on currencies. The same traditional strategies had been reiterated: follow noninflationary policies and use short term interest rates to discourage speculation and devaluation.

In addition, a set of secret economic indicators was supposed to alert the authorities to currencies' imbalance, so that the adjustment via minor devaluations could be made before it becomes obvious. This approach was envisioned to minimize speculation on the foreign exchange market.

The Two-Tiered Mechanism

Both the economic divergence and the financial costs attached to maintaining the currency parity suggested a two-tiered system. The top tier consists of the core currencies: Deutsche mark, Dutch guilder, Belgium franc, the Luxembourg franc and the French franc, but by August 1993, the French franc could not be considered a core currency anymore. The other EMS member currencies formed the second tier. Although a difficult political sell, this approach is consistent with the Darwinian convergence criteria of the Maastricht Treaty. These criteria refer to the need of harmonizing specific economic indicators.

The Form of Leadership

Whereas the EMS members are all political demoncracies, the EMS is not a democracy, but rather a technocracy. This divergence, reminiscent of that between a currency and an oscillator built off it, generates a contrarian signal. Although it is difficult thinking of a viable alternative, it is equally difficult to understand how soundly this approach may perform in the long run.

The European Central Bank

The de facto decision maker on the European Monetary System has been the Bundesbank. The Bundesbank, built in the mold of the United States Federal Reserve in the wake of the Second World War, is widely known and respected for its independent decision making process. The same type of central bank is necessary for the EMS, if the EMS is expected to ever come close to true economic convergence. Currently, the new European Central Bank, known as the *European Monetary Institute (EMI)*, does not have any power over inter-EMS monetary policy. National central banks continue to maintain their full control. Assuming that Europe will be able to overcome its integration problems, how would a newly established super central bank as independent as the Bundesbank deal with some of the larger central banks, say the Bundesbank? As of the writing of this book, this remains an open question.

New European Environment

European geopolitical realities have changed faster than anybody could ever imagine. The self-destruction of the Communist nightmare brought changes not easy to envision. Germany, the de facto leader of the EMS, was presented with an option it could not refuse, its political unification.

The German costs went well beyond the economic bailout of the former East Germany. The costs also reflected withdrawal payments to the former Soviet troops, transportation costs for these troops and investment in housing and infrastructure in the former Soviet Union for the troops.

The costs linked to the fall of the Communist block are not limited solely to the former Soviet Union, nor are they only financial. Artificial borders between Germany, Poland and the former Soviet Union will eventually become an issue. A much shorter term issue is the velocity with which the former Communist block is trying to shake off not only the failed economic legacies, but also the artificial political entities imposed upon them. The bloody nationalistic overtones in some of the cases cannot but weigh down the goals of the EMS.

Impact on the Foreign Exchange Market

Foreign exchange traders around the world had a glorious performance since the fall of 1992, mostly at the expense of the European central banks. George Soros, the famed fund manager, has become a folk hero among the traders for his acute sense of the market and successful determination in his ´ trading. The central banks didn't take lightly his or the rest of the market's dealing. In France, some voices even maliciously recalled the rosy guillotine times of the French Revolution.

In all fairness, however, the FX professionals helped the fundamentals puzzle fall back into place. The foreign exchange market is very efficient and under much less constraint than the old currency fluctuations bands on the EMS. If the fundamentals had been truly sound, the attacks would have never occurred or, if they did, their impact would have been short lived.

For the Europeans, there are definite advantages in having economic unity. That was obvious from the positive final results of the referendums held in all the member nations. However, the fundamental approach to this unity may need further tinkering. As it has been proved over and over again, the forces of the free market find their way through all the monetary mechanisms yet devised by the human brain. Since they have already proven their staying power, it may be advisable to join them, rather than fight them. Only full economic convergence will be able to implement the formidable goals of the European Monetary System.

Chapter 4

Currency Characteristics

The ISO Codes

The foreign exchange operations and most financial information services do not refer to currencies by their full name. Rather, they use standardized codes, developed by the International Organization for Standardization (ISO) and known as the *ISO codes*. The US dollar is called USD and the Deutsche mark is called DEM (see Figure 4.1), for example. Codification is a practical necessity in the complex global environment of the foreign exchange markets. Throughout this book, we will refer to currencies alternatively by their full names and codes. Figure 4.2 displays the ISO codes for the most traded foreign currencies.

Traders, customer traders and support assistants use the ISO codes extensively for inputting the data. The codes are used on individual basis or more commonly in currency pairs. For instance, US dollar/Swiss franc is entered as USD/CHF.

The ISO abbreviations are not used, however, in normal conversations. Traders use nicknames for the currencies. The US dollar is known as the *buck* or *greenback*. The British pound is generally called *cable* or, less commonly, *quid*. The Swiss franc is commonly referred to as *swissy* and the

```
0732 CCY  PAGE  DLNG    SPOT RATE     LOC  PREV      US   HI & LO WRLD
0732 DEM  BMMA  BMMA*D  1.7422/29     TOR  20/30     1.7422      1.7400
0732 JPY  MIDI  MIDI*J  109.10/20     LON  15/25     109.12      109.00
0732 CHF  CHFX  CHML*C  1.4641/46     LON  39/46     1.4644      1.4635
0731 GBP  RBSX  RBSL*G  1.4981/86     LON  82/92     1.4981      1.4981
0732 CAD  BMMA  BMMA*R  1.3229/34     TOR  30/35     1.3230      1.3218
0719 AUD  NABX  NABL*T  0.7088/93     LON  90/95     0.7105      0.7080
0731 FRF  CHFX  CHML*F  5.9155/75     LON

0727 XAU  UBZB          378.35/378.85  30YR  TB 100.13-15 +19 YTM  6.22
0713 XAG  UBZB          5.04/ 5.06  *  OIL  WTI  15.34/39  USDX 96.00
1640 FED  FRED          3.00- 3.06  *  ED3  3.00- 3.25 ED6  3.12- 3.37
```

Figure 4.1. Page WRLD displayed on Reuters uses ISO currency codes. (Courtesy of Reuters)

CURRENCY	ISO CODE
Australian dollar (A$)	AUD
Austrian shilling	ATS
Belgian franc	BEF
British pound (£)	GBP
Canadian dollar (C $)	CAD
Danish kroner	DKK
Deutsche mark	DEM
Dutch guilder	NLG
French franc	FRF
Hong Kong dollar (HK$)	HKD
Irish punt (I £)	IEP
Italian lira	ITL
Japanese yen (¥)	JPY
New Zealand dollar (NZ$)	NZD
Norway krone	NOK
Portuguese escudo	PTE
Saudi Riyal	SAR
Singapore dollar (S$)	SGD
Spanish peseta	ESP
Swedish krona	SEK
Swiss franc	CHF
US dollar (US$)	USD

Figure 4.2. The ISO codes for the most commonly traded currencies.

French franc, *Paris*. The Australian dollar is called *aussie* and the New Zealand dollars *kiwi*.

The US Dollar

The United States dollar is the main currency in the world (see Figure 4.3). All currencies are generally quoted in US dollar terms. In foreign exchange,

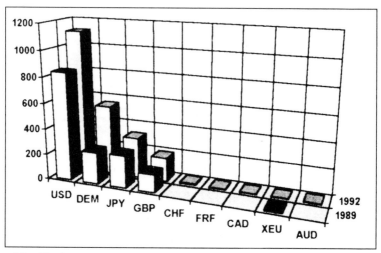

Figure 4.3.   Total gross reported foreign exchange turnover involving selected currencies on one side of transactions; daily averages. The blank spaces on the chart are due to the lack of data. (*Source*: Bank for International Settlements, "*Central Bank Survey of Foreign Exchange Market   Activity in April 1992*")

the US dollar figured on one side in over 80 percent of the transactions in 1992. In the currency swap market, the role of the US dollar is even more powerful, as it occurred in 95 percent of all transactions in 1992, according to Bank for International Settlements. In addition, commodities and international debt are also quoted in terms of US dollar.

In terms of international economic and political unrest, the US dollar is the main haven currency. The US dollar is not backed by gold any longer, but by the sheer size of the United States' economy. Although challenged by Japanese and German competition, the United States remains the preeminent economy in the world and the dollar the world's financial standard.

The US dollar became the leading currency toward the end of the Second World War and the center of the Bretton Woods Accord, as the other currencies were virtually pegged against it. The breakdown of the Bretton Woods system in 1971 and the semipegging of selected European currencies to the Deutsche mark reduced the US dollar's importance only marginally.

The currency was devalued by approximately 50 percent between September 1985 and December 1987 in a relief effort for American exporters and in an attempt to rebalance the trade deficit. The US dollar reached record lows against the European and the Japanese currencies in 1995 (see Figures 4.4 and 4.5).

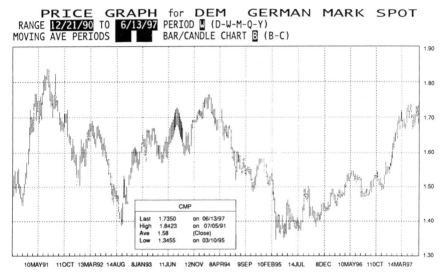

Figure 4.4. The record low of the US dollar against the Deutsche mark in 1995. (*Courtesy of Bloomberg Financial Markets*)

There are no restrictions on foreign exchange, and the Federal Reserve has a minimum of interference, although it intervenes if market conditions require.

The US dollar's significance differs among currencies. Whereas it features in 98 percent of deals against the Canadian dollar and 87 percent against Japanese yen deals, it is only involved in 64 percent of Deutsche mark deals.

The major currencies traded against the US dollar are Deutsche mark, Japanese yen, British pound and Swiss franc (see Figure 4.6).

The Deutsche Mark

The Deutsche mark is second only to the US dollar, representing approximately 25 percent of the international reserves. The USD/DEM is the most liquid and most traded pair of currencies (see Figure 4.6).

Like the US dollar, the Deutsche mark has a strong international presence (see Figure 4.7), although mainly focused on its fellow members of the

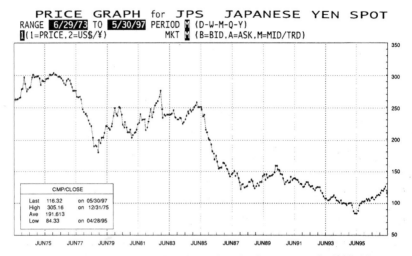

Figure 4.5.   The record low of the US dollar against the Japanese yen in 1995. (*Courtesy of Bloomberg Financial Markets*)

European Monetary System (see Figure 4.8). The seemingly smooth road toward economic integration of the system was derailed by the high costs of the German unification. The unification gave the Deutsche mark an unprecedented boost, as the world perceived Germany to be on its way to becoming an economic superpower.

However, the unexpected breakup of the Soviet empire also triggered a series of negative developments. The costs associated with the unification,

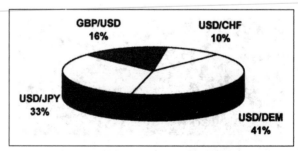

Figure 4.6.   Total net foreign exchange turnover of the major currencies against the US dollar in April 1992. (*Source: Bank for International Settlements, "Central Bank Survey of Foreign Exchange Market Activity in April 1992"*)

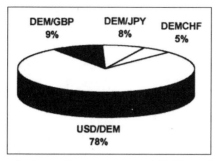

Figure 4.7. Total net foreign exchange turnover of the Deutsche mark against the major currencies in April 1992. (*Source: Bank for International Settlements, "Central Bank Survey of Foreign Exchange Market Activity in April 1992"*)

including the repatriation of the former Soviet troops, were unexpectedly high. German domestic responsibilities necessitated high interest rates, which negatively affected the other EMS members. This artificially created recession in Europe culminated with the double EMS crisis, which signaled practically the end of the European Monetary System in 1993.

The Deutsche mark will remain sensitive to any political shocks in the Russian political arena, due to its geographical proximity to Russia and its financial and economic commitment to different factions of the former Soviet Union.

The Bundesbank has a special position toward inflation, since it is the only major central bank which has special provisions in this regard.

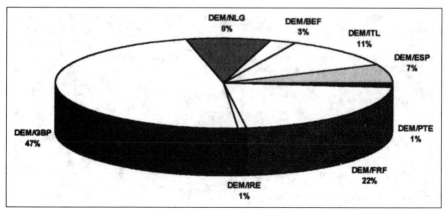

Figure 4.8. Total net foreign exchange turnover of the Deutsche mark against its fellow EMS currencies in April 1992. (*Source: Bank for International Settlements, "Central Bank Survey of Foreign Exchange Market Activity in April 1992"*)

Germany, as a whole, has an unusual sensitivity toward inflation, as a result of the post–World War I hyperinflation which made possible the rise of fascism. Its tough stance on inflation via stubbornly high interest rates gained Germany few friends after the unification. The relatively high interest rates are naturally supportive to the Deutsche mark.

The Japanese Yen

The Japanese yen is the third most traded currency in the world. The currency has a much smaller international presence outside the US dollar and the Deutsche mark. This is reflected in a reduced liquidity on the crosses (see Figure 4.9).

As some foreign companies found the Japanese market tough to crack, the natural demand to trade the yen concentrated mostly among the Japanese *keiretsu*, the economic giants. The yen is theoretically sensitive to changes in the price or structure of the raw material markets. However, after absorbing the *oil shoku* of 1973, the Japanese economy successfully learned how to weather this type of crisis. Therefore, the Kuwait takeover

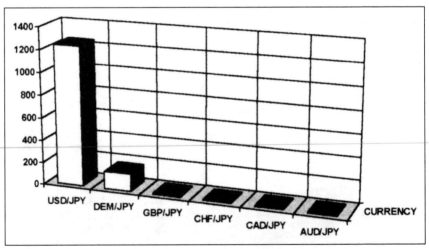

Figure 4.9. The breakdown of the foreign currencies against the Japanese yen in April 1992. Outside the markets for US dollars and Deutsche marks, the turnover is very light. (*Source*: *Bank for International Settlements, "Central Bank Survey of Foreign Exchange Market Activity in April 1992"*)

in 1990 failed to affect the oil price, the Japanese economy and consequently, the Japanese yen.

The currency is much more sensitive to the fortunes of the Nikkei Dow, the Japanese stock market, and the real estate market. The 1989 attempt of the Bank of Japan to deflate the double bubble in these two markets had a negative effect on the Japanese yen. Japan had more than its share of political scandals, from old-fashioned geisha affairs to bribery at the highest government levels. The political scandals had a much smaller impact on the currency, as traders became confused about the significance of those events vis-à-vis the traditional Japanese political arena. The lack of significant resolve generated a lack of interest in the foreign exchange market.

The Japanese yen reached record lows after September 1993 (see Figure 4.5), after the comments made by newly elected President Bill Clinton and Secretary of the Treasury Lloyd Bentsen, regarding the level of the US trade deficit with Japan. The yen had previously been revalued following the G-5's Plaza Accord of September 1985 precisely for the same purpose. However, the yen high of around 120, reached by December 1987, failed to stick or make a serious dent in the Japanese trade surplus with the United States (see Figure 4.10).

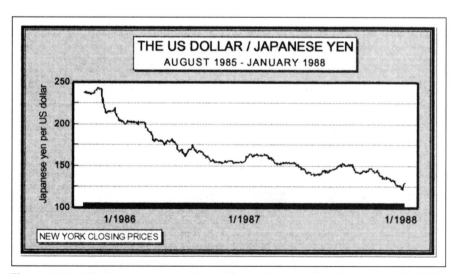

Figure 4.10. The Japanese yen reached a high against the US dollar of around 120 by December 1987. The yen rally was not sustained, and the Japanese trade surplus with the United States was not reduced.

The currency is very liquid around the world, practically around the clock.

Why is the yen quoted at a rate different in format from the other major currencies? According to Professor Paul Aron, the former Vice Chairman at Daiwa Securities in New York, that has to do with a very complex exercise in high finance. In post–World War II Japan, American occupation forces had to decide on a new exchange rate for the yen. Since the day starts in Asia and the Japanese flag displays the sun, this idea was extrapolated to foreign exchange. The sun is represented as a circle, circles have 360 degrees, so the USD/JPY spot exchange rate became 360. *Et voila!*

The British Pound

Fifty percent of the British pound transactions are dealt in the largest foreign exchange market: London. Sterling pound, nicknamed *cable,* has only 14 percent of the world market currently. Until the end of the World War II, though, it was the central currency. Its nickname, cable, is derived from the telex machine, which was used to trade it in its heyday. The currency is heavily traded against the US dollar and the Deutsche marks but has a minimal presence against other currencies (see Figure 4.11).

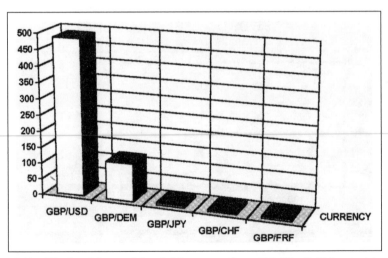

Figure 4.11.   The breakdown of the foreign currencies against the British pound in April 1992. Outside the markets for US dollars and Deutsche marks, the turnover is very light. (*Source: Bank for International Settlements, "Central Bank Survey of Foreign Exchange Market Activity in April 1992"*)

In the recent past, the pound has behaved like a roller coaster, due to British inflation and labor problems. Whereas excellent in London, the currency's liquidity in the other markets is less deep. Therefore, in the New York market, many banks have to stop quoting cable at noon.

The temporary bout with the Exchange Rate Mechanism had a soothing effect on the British pound, as it had to generally follow the Deutsche mark's fluctuations, but the crisis conditions under which the pound had to be withdrawn from the ERM has had a psychological effect on the currency (see Figure 4.12), as the traders are more cautious.

Although less obvious, the British pound is a petrocurrency. Therefore, cable is sensitive to oil price gyrations.

The Swiss Franc

The Swiss franc is the only currency that belongs to neither the European Monetary System nor the G-7 countries. This position is, however, typical of Switzerland, a country known for its neutrality (see Figure 4.13).

Although the Swiss economy is relatively small, the Swiss franc is part of the major four currencies. Why? The Swiss franc closely resembles the strength and quality of the Swiss economy and finance. Switzerland has

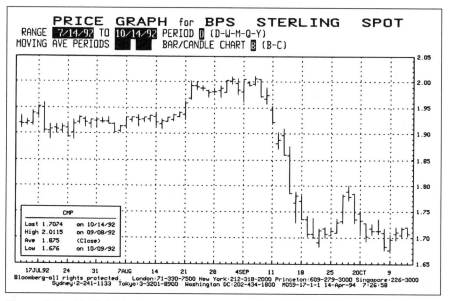

Figure 4.12. The British pound was sharply sold against the US dollar in September 1992, due to the European Monetary System pressures. (Courtesy of Bloomberg)

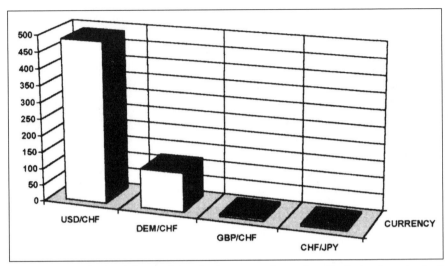

Figure 4.13. The breakdown of the foreign currencies against the Swiss franc in April 1992. Outside the markets for US dollars and Deutsche marks, the Swiss franc turnover is light. (*Source: Bank for International Settlements, "Central Bank Survey of Foreign Exchange Market Activity in April 1992"*)

no political and economic exposure to the former Soviet Union, but a very close economic relationship with Germany. Therefore, in terms of political uncertainty in the East, generally the Deutsche mark is sold in favor of the Swiss franc (see Figure 4.14).

Moreover, a Swiss referendum rejected the possibility of joining the EMS, to the chagrin of Switzerland's neighbors. Only months later, the EMS came under unprecedented pressure which practically dismantled the system. Swissy was one of the few European currencies which did not come under pressure during the 1993 currency attack.

The Swiss banking system has had an unusually high reputation for service. Although the famous secrecy laws have been very helpful, the banking service goes well beyond that, maintaining a widespread network of customers around the world.

Typically, it is believed that the Swiss franc is a stable currency. From a foreign exchange point of view, this is simply not true. The Swiss franc closely resembles the patterns of the Deutsche mark, but lacks its liquidity. Therefore, swissy is more volatile than the Deutsche mark.

The Major Foreign Exchange Markets

The foreign exchange markets function nonstop 24 hours a day. The cash markets are fully decentralized, unlike the currency futures and options on currency futures, which trade on special exchanges. There are no official

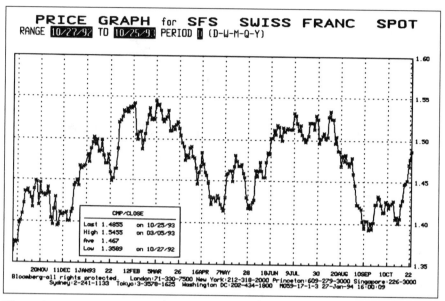

PRICE GRAPH for **SFS SWISS FRANC SPOT**
RANGE `10/27/92` TO `10/25/93` PERIOD ▯ (D-W-M-Q-Y)

Figure 4.14. The Swiss franc may look like the Deutsche mark, but it does not have the responsibilities of its neighboring currency. Therefore, in terms of political uncertainty in Russia, the Swiss franc is the prime currency to buy against the Deutsche mark. (Courtesy of Bloomberg)

opening and closing hours for foreign exchange trading. However, in the New York market, for instance, the unofficial standard trading hours are 8:30 AM to 3:00 PM EDT. Outside these hours banks do not have the obligation to make prices, although most of them will quote.

Although the market never closes, traders find it rather hard to get a currency quote in the New York market after 4:30 PM EDT, because Auckland starts trading around 3:00 PM EDT. California attempted to fill this time niche in the late 1980s, but was unable to do so because of the limited liquidity at that time.

The advance in telecommunications greatly blurred the differences among the markets. From the trader's point of view, the main significance of the market relates to the presence of liquidity since more players generate more trades. Otherwise, there is little practical difference, as traders only have to use a different code when calling out directly.

However, the presence of local customers and money markets still keeps the regional foreign exchange markets separated. The major ones are London, with 32 percent of the market, New York, with 20 percent and Tokyo, with 13 percent. Zurich, Frankfurt, Hong Kong and Singapore follow with about 7 percent share each, and Paris and Sydney have 4 percent and 3 percent, respectively (see Figure 4.15).

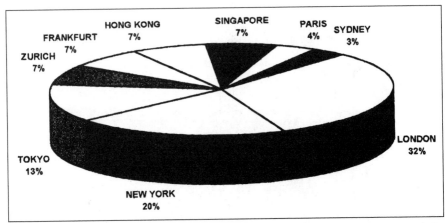

Figure 4.15. The major foreign exchange markets as of April 1992. (*Source: Bank for International Settlements, "Central Bank Survey of Foreign Exchange Market Activity in April 1992"*)

The London market had the most significant growth in foreign exchange between 1989 and 1992, approximately 50 percent (see Figure 4.16). More US dollars (26%) and Deutsche mark (27%) are traded in

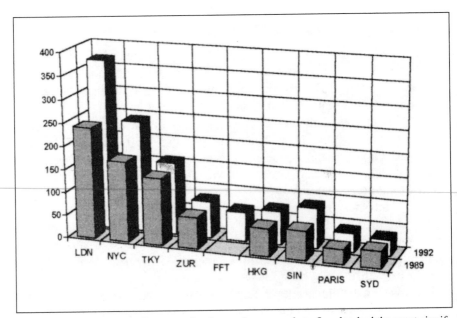

Figure 4.16. Among the European foreign exchange markets, London had the most significant growth in foreign exchange trading between 1989 and 1992. The 1989 data for the Frankfurt market was not available. (*Source: Bank for International Settlements, "Central Bank Survey of Foreign Exchange Market Activity in April 1992"*)

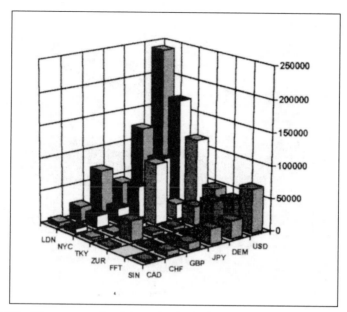

Figure 4.17. The currency breakdown in the major foreign exchange markets in 1992 (daily averages, in million of US dollars). The data for the Canadian dollar turnover in the Frankfurt market was not available. (*Source: Bank for International Settlements, "Central Bank Survey of Foreign Exchange Market Activity in April 1992"*)

London than either New York (18%) or Frankfurt (10%), respectively (see Figure 4.17). With the exception of Singapore, the Asian markets registered the lowest increases in foreign exchange trading in the same period.

The Major Players

The major players in the foreign exchange arena are commercial banks, investment banks, central banks, trading institutions, hedge funds, corporations, high net worth individuals and individual investors (see Figure 4.18).

Commercial and Investment Banks

Commercial and investment banks are the natural players in foreign exchange. Currency trading started as an additional service to the core of commercial banking business, deposits and loans. As currencies were allowed to float freely, and as writing off loans became more of a practice than an exception, banks had to look for other sources of profit.

Foreign exchange has the perfect characteristics for banks. It is profitable, the spot market provides limited credit exposure, the forward market

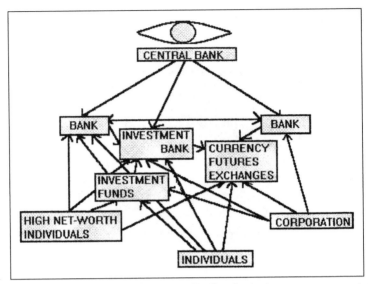

Figure 4.18. The foreign exchange players. Trading institutions are not presented in the diagram, since they have the general characteristics of investment banks.

provides significantly less credit exposure than loans and, since the worldwide interest is concentrated on a handful of currencies, the liquidity is excellent.

The commercial and investment banks are in the market on behalf of both their customers and themselves.

Central Banks

Central banks are a different type of player. Although the largest on individual basis in most instances, central banks are not in the market for the money. They are actually nonprofit organizations. The major central banks do not speculate. Their main purpose regarding foreign exchange is to provide adequate trading conditions. They may also intervene in the market in the attempt to adjust economic or financial imbalances, and also for commercial reasons.

But, though profit is not their target, central banks tend to be profitable, since they generally trade on a long term basis. For instance, all the major central banks sold US dollars against the European and Japanese currencies after the Plaza Accord in September 1985, when the exchange rates were around USD/JPY 245, and they bought back the US dollar at around USD/JPY 121 in January 1988.

The currency crises of September 1992 and July 1993 had an exceptionally negative impact on the profitability of the European central banks.

Hedge Funds

Hedge funds are relative newcomers to foreign exchange. They consist of partnerships of high net worth investors who invest at least $1 million. Using this money as collateral, the funds borrow a multiple of the seed money. The funds research potential investments in markets world wide and focus the capital on one or few instruments. Hedge funds' managers are compensated based on performance, not as a fixed percentage of assets under management. However, they brought to the market significant amounts of currency and flexibility. More funds are entering the currency markets, as the international investment opportunities increase. The impact on the markets of the large funds, such as George Soros' $10 billion Quantum group of Funds, is a matter of study for the regulatory bodies. This fund grossed over $1 billion in profits in September 1992 against the British pound, and lost $600 million on a long USD/JPY position in February 1994. On both occasions, the fund's dealing generated highly volatile conditions in the market.

Corporations

Corporations used to have a love-hate relationship with foreign exchange which was difficult to manage and looked chaotic. The internationalization of business and the increased competitiveness forced them to take a closer look at foreign exchange. Corporations are becoming increasingly sophisticated at risk management. The days when the hedging decisions were made on an all-or-nothing basis seem to be gone. More and more, corporations go beyond their commercial needs and take speculative positions, as opportunities occur.

High Net Worth Individuals

High net worth individuals access foreign exchange either through investment banks or private banking departments. Private banking is generally geared toward European, Asian and South American investors. The North American individual interest in foreign exchange is still under par.

Individuals

Individuals have a limited impact on a one-on-one basis. Most of the transactions are not speculative and are generally related to travel expenses or purchasing of foreign made products. However, when compounded, the individual trading interest may be substantial. For instance, until 1985, summer vacations triggered sell-offs of the US dollars against the European currencies by the American tourists. The strong dollar encouraged traveling abroad and, consequently, purchases of foreign currencies. The opposite has been true in the 1990s. The weak dollar encouraged foreign tourists to visit America and, therefore, dollar purchases.

Conclusion

Foreign exchange can be a profitable game. And the larger the amounts in play, the better opportunity to be profitable. But it can also be an expensive game. In addition to the capital requirement, trading implementation is generally expensive. The support systems come with high price tags, from the phone turrets, resembling hotel phone switching stations, to computers and software, and the list can continue. Commercial and investment banks have deep pockets, so that they can withstand temporary unrealized losses, and even real setbacks.

Generally, individuals are not yet easily attracted by the currency markets. Foreign exchange is still misunderstood at the personal investment level and is more often than not superficially dismissed as "really nuts" or gambling. Forays in the right direction have already been made, as investment and commercial banks, along with some trading companies, offer individual investors and speculators the opportunity to participate in currency trading.

The potential for this market segment has not yet been reached. As foreign exchange financial information becomes more available at mass level via personal computers, individual investors are likely to be attracted, given the faster opportunities for profit.

The futures exchanges provide the best setup for individual traders, or locals, as they are known. Locals buy or lease a seat on the organized exchanges, such as Chicago Mercantile Exchange, and can trade directly the currency futures contracts.

Chapter 5

Foreign Exchange Risks

Foreign exchange is not only a very profitable industry; it is also a risky business. The multitude of players, trading increasingly sophisticated instruments in staggering amounts, naturally exacerbates the trading risks. It is therefore vital to understand where the risks lie in order to develop the correct policies to manage these risks.

The following chapter owes greatly to the research done by the Group of Thirty in *Derivatives: Practices and Principles,* published in July 1993.

The main categories of foreign exchange risk are :

1. exchange rate risk,
2. interest rate risk,
3. credit risk, and
4. country (sovereign) risk.

Although these risks apply to the foreign exchange market as a whole, they apply selectively to the different instruments.

Exchange Rate Risk

Exchange rate risk is the effect of the continuous shift in the world wide market supply and demand balance on an outstanding foreign exchange position. This risk is pertinent to spot, forward outrights, futures and options. The previous instruments have one element in common: the spot price. Forward outrights, futures and options are all derivative instruments. Spot deals mature in two business days. Forward outrights and futures mature past two business days. Options are drawn on both forward outrights and futures.

A trader opens a position by either buying or selling a foreign currency. For the period it is outstanding, the position will be subject to all the price changes. The position will be *closed* or *covered* when the trader executes the opposite deal (sell if first bought, and vice versa) for the same amount of currency.

Exchange risk does not apply to swaps directly. In a swap deal, a party buys and sells the same amount of the same currency with the same counterparty, at different exchange rates and different value dates. Since the same amount of currency is simultaneously bought and sold, there is no exchange risk per se. However, the exchange risk may find its way to the swaps as well, via the back door.

The formula (discussed in Chapter 12) for calculating the forward points, which are applied to the spot rates in order to determine the forward rates, also includes the spot price. Should the spot rate change dramatically, the forward points will also be affected. Volatility is by no means the enemy of the trader; it is in fact the vital element that creates the market. Without continuous price fluctuations, trading would not be possible. However, price volatility is only good when it is used properly.

Compounding the Risk

From the managerial point of view, the *gross dealing exposure* should be measured by adding together the absolute values of all the outstanding exposures. At any given time, a dealing room may be short in some currencies and long in others (or even in the same ones). Since the positions are kept in the same currency, say US dollars, the positions will partly or completely offset each other.

However, from the volatility point of view, this offsetting process is not sound. Currencies move in different degrees of correlation relative to each other. Incidental tendencies for moving in tandem do not reduce the overall exchange risk. Therefore, the gross dealing exposure must always be kept in absolute values, and its total size must be carefully managed.

Exchange Risk Management at Micro Level

Exchange risks start with the traders. A good trader knows to cut losses short and ride the profitable positions. In order to ensure that losses are kept within manageable limits, certain systems are in place. The most popular measures are the *position limit* and the *loss limit.*

There are two types of position limits : daylight and overnight.

1. The *daylight position limit* refers to the maximum amount of a certain currency a trader is allowed to carry at any single time, between the regular trading hours. There is no rule or average regarding the magnitude of the position. But each bank and each treasurer may have a different policy. Each trader should have a trading limit, regardless of his or her level of profitability or seniority. The limit should reflect both the trader's level of trading skills and the amount at which a trader peaks. It is less important whether the daylight limit is $5 million or $50 million than whether the trader can provide a peak performance with the respective position.

2. The *overnight position limit* refers to any outstanding position kept overnight by traders. As a rule of thumb, overnight limits should be smaller than daylight limits. Again, the limits are a function of the policy of the banks and their treasurers, along with the skills of the traders and their specific areas of expertise. The majority of foreign exchange traders do not hold overnight positions.

Most of the trading occurs in the spot market, both in terms of total volume and number of deals and the spot positions generally have a life span of seconds to hours.

The limits, daylight or overnight, may be increased (or decreased) temporarily by a senior officer from the treasury to better encompass special market conditions. For instance, the kidnapping of Michail Gorbachev, the last Soviet President, triggered a sharp rally in the US dollars against the Deutsche mark (see Figure 5.1). The political crisis was difficult to gauge because of the lack of precedent.

Despite the magnitude of the rally, foreign exchange trading was curtailed by many players because they feared the lack of liquidity. Normal position limits were temporarily reduced in order to avoid unacceptable levels of exchange risks. Of course, this action further reduced the liquidity. However, the point is that this type of market behavior is a reality and, therefore, it must be addressed properly.

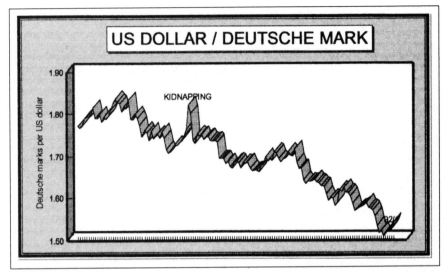

Figure 5.1. The kidnapping of Michail Gorbachev in the summer of 1991 generated a significant rally in the US dollar/Deutsche mark.

The *loss limit* is a measure designed to avoid unsustainable losses made by traders and it is enforced by the senior officers in the dealing room. The loss limits are selected on a daily and monthly basis by the top management. Psychologically, this measure is of great help, as it removes the added pressure on the trader of deciding on the size of the loss in an already hectic environment.

Exchange Risk Management at Macro Level

Management is responsible for designing a clear set of rules encompassing the policies of risk management in a trading entity. These rules refer to the dealing room's objective, the ways of implementation and the general approaches to extraordinary trading circumstances. The risk management policies must be revised regularly, or in reaction to unusual market developments. Flexibility and speed of adjustment are vital requirements in the fast changing financial markets.

In the case of derivatives, and especially in the case of options, market participants should enter master agreements with each other. These agreements document all the outstanding and future transactions and provide for close-out and settlement netting.

The following *International Foreign Exchange Master Agreement* (as of November 1993) was designed by The Foreign Exchange Committee and The British Bankers' Association.

INTERNATIONAL FOREIGN EXCHANGE
MASTER AGREEMENT

MASTER AGREEMENT dated as of _____ , 19____ , by
and between _____ , a _____ ,
and _____ , a _____ .

Section 1. Definitions

Unless otherwise required by the context, the following terms shall have the following meanings in the Agreement:

"Agreement" has the meaning given to it in Section 2.2.

"Base Currency" means as to a Party the Currency agreed as such in relation to it in Part VIII of the Schedule hereto.

"Base Currency Rate" means as to a Party and any amount the cost (expressed as a percentage rate per annum) at which that Party would be able to fund that amount from such sources and for such periods as it may in its reasonable discretion from time to time decide, as determined in good faith by it.

"Business Day" means (i) a day which is a Local Banking Day for the applicable Designated Office of both Parties, or (ii) solely in relation to delivery of a Currency, a day which is a Local Banking Day in relation to that Currency.

"Close-Out Amount" has the meaning given to it in Section 5.1.

"Close-Out Date" means a day on which, pursuant to the provisions of Section 5.1, the Non-Defaulting Party closes out and liquidates Currency Obligations or such a close-out and liquidation occurs automatically.

"Closing Gain" means, as to the Non-Defaulting Party, the difference described as such in relation to a particular Value Date under the provisions of Section 5.1.

"Closing Loss" means, as to the Non-Defaulting Party, the difference described as such in relation to a particular Value Date under the provisions of Section 5.1.

"Confirmation" means a writing (including telex, facsimile or other electronic means from which it is possible to produce a hard copy) evidencing an FX Transaction governed by the Agreement which shall specify (i) the Parties thereto and their Designated Offices through which they are respectively acting, (ii) the amounts of the Currencies being bought or sold and by which Party, (iii) the Value Date, and (iv) any other term generally included in such a writing in accordance with the practice of the relevant foreign exchange market.

"Credit Support Document" means, as to a Party (the "first Party"), a guaranty, hypothecation agreement, margin or security agreement or document, or any other document containing an obligation of a third party ("Credit Support Provider") or of the first Party in favor of the other Party supporting any obligations of the first Party hereunder.

"Credit Support Provider" has the meaning given to it in the definition of Credit Support Document.

"Currency" means money denominated in the lawful currency of any country or the Ecu.

"Currency Obligation" means any obligation of a Party to deliver a Currency pursuant to an FX Transaction governed by the Agreement, or pursuant to the application of Sections 3.3(a) or 3.3(b).

"Custodian" has the meaning given to it in the definition of Event of Default.

"Defaulting Party" has the meaning given to it in the definition of Event of Default.

"Designated Office(s)" means, as to a Party, the office(s) specified in Part II of the Schedule hereto, as such Schedule may be modified from time to time by agreement of the Parties.

"Effective Date" means the date of this Master Agreement.

"Event of Default" means the occurrence of any of the following with respect to a Party (the "Defaulting Party", the other Party being the "Non-Defaulting Party"):

(i) the Defaulting Party shall default in any payment under the Agreement to the Non-Defaulting Party with respect to any sum when due under any Currency Obligation or pursuant to the Agreement and such failure shall continue for two (2) Business Days after written notice of non-payment given by the Non-Defaulting Party to the Defaulting Party;

(ii) the Defaulting Party shall commence a voluntary case or other proceeding seeking liquidation, reorganization or other similar relief with respect to itself or to its debts under any bankruptcy, insolvency or similar law, or seeking the appointment of a trustee, receiver, liquidator, conservator, administrator, custodian or other similar official (each, a "Custodian") of it or any substantial part of its assets; or shall take any corporate action to authorize any of the foregoing;

(iii) an involuntary case or other proceeding shall be commenced against the Defaulting Party seeking liquidation, reorganization or other similar relief with respect to it or its debts under any bankruptcy, insolvency or similar law or seeking the appointment of a Custodian of it or any substantial part of its assets, and such involuntary case or other proceeding is not dismissed within five (5) days of its institution or presentation;

(iv) the Defaulting Party is bankrupt or insolvent, as defined under any bankruptcy or insolvency law applicable to such Party;

(v) the Defaulting Party shall otherwise be unable to pay its debts as they become due;

(vi) the Defaulting Party or any Custodian acting on behalf of the Defaulting Party shall disaffirm, disclaim or repudiate any Currency Obligation;

(vii) (a) any representation or warranty made or deemed made by the Defaulting Party pursuant to the Agreement or pursuant to any Credit Support Document shall prove to have been false or misleading in any material respect as at the time it was made or given and one (1) Business Day has elapsed after the Non-Defaulting Party has given the Defaulting Party written notice thereof, or (b) the Defaulting Party fails to perform or comply with any obligation assumed by it under the Agreement (other than an obligation to make payment of the kind referred to in Clause (i) of this definition of Event of Default), and such failure is continuing thirty (30) days after the Non-Defaulting Party has given the Defaulting Party written notice thereof;

(viii) the Defaulting Party consolidates or amalgamates with or merges into or transfers all or substantially all its assets to another entity and (a) the creditworthiness of the resulting, surviving or transferee entity is materially weaker than that of the Defaulting Party prior to such action, or (b) at the time of such consolidation, amalgamation, merger or transfer the resulting, surviving or transferee entity fails to assume all the obligations of the Defaulting Party under the Agreement by operation of law or pursuant to an agreement satisfactory to the Non-Defaulting Party;

(ix) by reason of any default, or event of default or other similar condition or event, any Specified Indebtedness (being Specified Indebtedness of an amount which, when expressed in the Currency of the Threshold Amount, is in aggregate equal to or in excess of the Threshold Amount) of the Defaulting Party or any Credit Support Provider in relation to it: (a) is not paid on the due date therefor and remains unpaid after any applicable grace period has elapsed, or (b) becomes, or becomes capable at any time of being declared, due and payable under agreements or instruments evidencing such Specified Indebtedness before it would otherwise have been due and payable.

(x) the Defaulting Party is in breach of or default under any Specified Transaction and any applicable grace period has elapsed, and there occurs any liquidation or early termination of, or acceleration of obligations under that Specified Transaction or the Defaulting Party (or any Custodian on its behalf) disaffirms, disclaims or repudiates the whole or any part of a Specified Transaction; or

(xi) (a) any Credit Support Provider in relation to the Defaulting Party or the Defaulting Party itself fails to comply with or perform any agreement or obligation to be complied with or performed by it in accordance with the applicable Credit Support Document and such failure is continuing after any applicable grace period has elapsed; (b) any Credit Support Document relating to the Defaulting Party expires or ceases to be in full force and effect prior to the satisfaction of all obligations of the Defaulting Party under the Agreement, unless otherwise agreed in writing by the Non-Defaulting Party; (c) the Defaulting Party or its Credit Support Provider (or, in either case, any Custodian acting on its behalf) disaffirms, disclaims or repudiates, in whole or in part, or challenges the validity of, the Credit Support Document; (d) any representation or warranty made or deemed made by any Credit Support Provider pursuant to any Credit Support Document shall prove to have been false or misleading in any material respect as at the time it was made or given or deemed made or given and one (1) Business Day has elapsed after the Non-Defaulting Party has given the Defaulting Party written notice thereof; or (e) any event set out in (ii) to (vi) or (viii) to (x) above occurs in respect of the Credit Support Provider.

"FX Transaction" means any transaction between the Parties for the purchase by one Party of an agreed amount in one Currency against the sale by it to the other of an agreed amount in another Currency both such amounts being deliverable on the same Value Date, and in respect of which transaction the Parties have agreed (whether orally, electronically or in writing): the Currencies involved, the amounts of such Currencies to be purchased and sold, which Party will purchase which Currency and the Value Date.

"Local Banking Day" means (i) for any Currency, a day on which commercial banks effect deliveries of that Currency in accordance with the market practice of the relevant foreign exchange market, and (ii) for any Party, a day in the location of the applicable Designated Office of such Party on which commercial banks in that location are not authorized or required by law to close.

"Master Agreement" means the terms and conditions set forth in this master agreement.

"Matched Pair Novation Netting Office(s)" means in respect of a Party the Designated Office(s) specified in Part V of the Schedule, as such Schedule may be modified from time to time by agreement of the Parties.

"Non-Defaulting Party" has the mean ing given to it in the definition of Event of Default.

"Novation Netting Office(s)" means in respect of a Party the Designated Office(s) specified in Part IV of the Schedule, as such Schedule may be modified from time to time by agreement of the Parties.

"*Parties*" means the parties to the Agreement and shall include their successors and permitted assigns (but without prejudice to the application of Clause (viii) of the definition of Event of Default); and the term "Party" shall mean whichever of the Parties is appropriate in the context in which such expression may be used.

"*Proceedings*" means any suit, action or other proceedings relating to the Agreement.

"*Settlement Neeting Office(s)*" means, in respect of a Party, the Designated Office(s) specified in Part III of the Schedule, as such Schedule may be modified from time to time by agreement of the Parties.

"*Specified Indebtedness*" means any obligation (whether present or future, contingent or otherwise, as principal or surety or otherwise) in respect of borrowed money, other than in respect of deposits received.

"*Specified Transaction*" means any transaction (including an agreement with respect thereto) between one Party to the Agreement (or any Credit Support Provider of such Party) and the other Party to the Agreement (or any Credit Support Provider of such Party) which is a rate swap transaction, basis swap, forward rate transaction, commodity swap, commodity option, equity or equity linked swap, equity or equity index option, bond option, interest rate option, foreign exchange transaction, cap transaction, floor transaction, collar transaction, currency swap transaction, cross-currency rate swap transaction, currency option or any other similar transaction (including any option with respect to any of these transactions) or any combination of any of the foregoing transactions.

"*Split Settlement*" has the meaning given to it in the definition of Value Date.

"*Threshold Amount*" means the amount specified as such for each Party in Part IX of the Schedule.

"*Value Date*" means, with respect to any FX Transaction, the Business Day (or where market practice in the relevant foreign exchange market in relation to the two Currencies involved provides for delivery of one Currency on one date which is a Local Banking Day in relation to that Currency but not to the other Currency and for delivery of the other Currency on the next Local Banking Day in relation to that other Currency ("Split Settlement") the two Local Banking Days in accordance with that market practice) agreed by the Parties for delivery of the Currencies to be purchased and sold pursuant to such FX Transaction, and, with respect to any Currency Obligation, the Business Day (or, in the case of Split Settlement, Local Banking Day) upon which the obligation to deliver Currency pursuant to such Currency Obligation is to be performed.

Section 2. FX Transactions

2.1. *Scope of the Agreement.* (a) Unless otherwise agreed in writing by the Parties, each FX Transaction entered into between two Designated Offices of the Parties on or after the Effective Date shall be governed by the Agreement. (b) All FX Transactions between any two Designated Offices of the Parties outstanding on the Effective Date which are identified in Part I of the Schedule shall be FX Transactions governed by the Agreement and every obligation of the Parties thereunder to deliver a Currency shall be a Currency Obligation under the Agreement.

2.2 *Single Agreement.* This Master Agreement, the particular terms agreed between the Parties in relation to each and every FX Transaction governed by this

Master Agreement (and, insofar as such terms are recorded in a Confirmation, each such Confirmation), the Schedule to this Master Agreement and all amendments to any of such items shall together form the agreement between the Parties (the "Agreement") and shall together constitute a single agreement between the Parties. The Parties acknowledge that all FX Transactions governed by the Agreement are entered into in reliance upon the fact that all items constitute a single agreement between the Parties.

2.3. *Confirmations.* FX Transactions governed by the Agreement shall be promptly confirmed by the Parties by Confirmations exchanged by mail, telex, facsimile or other electronic means. The failure by a Party to issue a Confirmation shall not prejudice or invalidate the terms of any FX Transaction governed by the Agreement.

Section 3. Settlement and Netting

3.1 *Settlement.* Subject to Section 3.2, each Party shall deliver to the other Party the amount of the Currency to be delivered by it under each Currency Obligation on the Value Date for such Currency Obligation.

3.2 *Net Settlement/Payment Netting.* If on any Value Date more than one delivery of a particular Currency is to be made between a pair of Settlement Netting Offices, then each Party shall aggregate the amounts of such Currency deliverable by it and only the difference between these aggregate amounts shall be delivered by the Party owing the larger aggregate amount to the other Party, and, if the aggregate amounts are equal, no delivery of the Currency shall be made.

3.3 *Novation Netting.*

(a) *By Currency.* If the Parties enter into an FX Transaction governed by the Agreement through a pair of Novation Netting Offices giving rise to a Currency Obligation for the same Value Date and in the same Currency as a then existing Currency Obligation between the same pair of Novation Netting Offices, then immediately upon entering into such FX Transaction, each such Currency Obligation shall automatically and without further action be individually cancelled and simultaneously replaced by a new Currency Obligation for such Value Date determined as follows: the amounts of such Currency that would otherwise have been deliverable by each Party on such Value Date shall be aggregated and the Party with the larger aggregate amount shall have a new Currency Obligation to deliver to the other Party the amount of such Currency by which its aggregate amount exceeds the other Party's aggregate amount, provided that if the aggregate amounts are equal, no new Currency Obligation shall arise. This Clause (a) shall not affect any other Currency Obligation of a Party to deliver any different Currency on the same Value Date.

(b) *By Matched Pair.* If the Parties enter into an FX Transaction governed by the Agreement between a pair of Matched Pair Novation Netting Offices then the provisions of Section 3.3(a) shall apply only in respect of Currency Obligations arising by virtue of FX Transactions governed by the Agreement entered into between such pair of Matched Pair Novation Netting Offices and involving the same pair of Currencies and the same Value Date.

3.4 *General*

(a) *Inapplicability of Sections 3.2 and 3.3.* The provisions of Sections 3.2 and 3.3 shall not apply if a Close-Out Date has occurred or an involuntary case or other proceeding of the kind described in Clause (iii) of the definition of Event of Default has occurred without being dismissed in relation to either Party.

(b) *Failure to Record.* The provisions of Section 3.3 shall apply notwithstanding that either Party may fail to record the new Currency Obligations in its books.

(c) *Cutoff Date and Time.* The provisions of Section 3.3 are subject to any cut-off date and cut-off time agreed between the applicable Novation Netting Offices and Matched Pair Novation Netting Offices of the Parties.

Section 4. Representations, Warranties and Covenants

4.1 *Representations and Warranties.* Each Party represents and warrants to the other Party as of the date of the Agreement and as of the date of each FX Transaction governed by the Agreement that: (i) it has authority to enter into the Agreement and such FX Transaction; (ii) the persons executing the Agreement and entering into such FX Transaction have been duly authorized to do so; (iii) the Agreement and the Currency Obligations created under the Agreement are binding upon it and enforceable against it in accordance with their terms (subject to applicable principles of equity) and do not and will not violate the terms of any agreements to which such Party is bound; (iv) no Event of Default has occurred and is continuing with respect to it; and (v) it acts as principal in entering into each and every FX Transaction governed by the Agreement.

4.2 *Covenants.* Each Party covenants to the other Party that: (i) it will at all times obtain and comply with the terms of and do all that is necessary to maintain in full force and effect all authorizations, approvals, licenses and consents required to enable it to lawfully perform its obligations under the Agreement; and (ii) it will promptly notify the other Party of the occurrence of any Event of Default with respect to itself or any Credit Support Provider in relation to it.

Section 5. Close-Out and Liquidation

5.1. *Circumstances of Close-Out and Liquidation.* If an Event of Default has occurred and is continuing, then the Non-Defaulting Party shall have the right to close-out and liquidate in the manner described below all, but not less than all, outstanding Currency Obligations (except to the extent that in the good faith opinion of the Non-Defaulting Party certain of such Currency Obligations may not be closed-out and liquidated under applicable law), by notice to the Defaulting Party. If "Automatic Termination" is specified as applying to a Party in Part VI of the Schedule, then, in the case of an Event of Default specified in Clauses (ii) or (iii) of the definition thereof with respect to such Party, such close-out and liquidation shall be automatic as to all outstanding Currency Obligations. Where such close-out and liquidation is to be effected, it shall be effected by:

(i) closing out each outstanding Currency Obligation (including any Currency Obligation which has not been performed and in respect of which the Value Date is on or precedes the Close-Out Date) so that each such Currency Obligation is cancelled and the Non-Defaulting Party shall calculate in good faith with respect to each such cancelled Currency Obligation, the Closing Gain or, as appropriate, the Closing Loss, as follows:

(x) for each Currency Obligation in a Currency other than the Non-Defaulting Party's Base Currency calculate a "Close-Out Amount" by converting:

(A) in the case of a Currency Obligation whose Value Date is the same as or is later than the Close-Out Date, the amount of such Currency Obligation; or

(B) in the case of a Currency Obligation whose Value Date precedes the Close-Out Date, the amount of such Currency Obligation increased, to the extent permitted by applicable law, by adding interest thereto from the Value Date to the Close-Out Date at the rate representing the cost (expressed as a percentage rate per annum) at which the Non-Defaulting Party would have been able, on such Value Date, to fund the amount of such Currency Obligation for the period from the Value Date to the Close-Out Date.

into such Base Currency at the rate of exchange at which the Non-Defaulting Party can buy or sell, as appropriate, such Base Currency with or against the Currency of such Currency Obligation for delivery on the Value Date of that Currency Obligation, or if such Value Date precedes the Close-Out Date, for delivery on the Close-Out Date; and

(y) determine in relation to each Value Date: (A) the sum of all Close-Out Amounts relating to Currency Obligations under which, and of all Currency Obligations in the Non-Defaulting Party's Base Currency under which, the Non-Defaulting Party would otherwise have been obliged to deliver the relevant amount to the Defaulting Party on that Value Date, adding (to the extent permitted by applicable law), in the case of a Currency Obligation in the Non-Defaulting Party's Base Currency whose Value Date precedes the Close-Out Date, interest for the period from the Value Date to the Close-Out Date at the Non-Defaulting Party's Base Currency Rate as at such Value Date for such period; and (B) the sum of all Close-Out Amounts relating to Currency Obligations under which, and of all Currency Obligations in the Non-Defaulting Party's Base Currency under which, the Non-Defaulting Party would otherwise have been entitled to receive the relevant amount on that Value Date, adding (to the extent permitted by applicable law), in the case of a Currency Obligation in the Non-Defaulting Party's Base Currency whose Value Date precedes the Close-Out Date, interest for the period from the Value Date to the Close-Out Date at the Non-Defaulting Party's Base Currency Rate as at such Value Date for such period;

(z) if the sum determined under (y) (A) is greater than the sum determined under (y) (B), the difference shall be the Closing Loss for such Value Date; if the sum determined under (y) (A) is less than the sum determined under (y) (B), the difference shall be the Closing Gain for such Value Date;

(ii) to the extent permitted by applicable law, adjusting the Closing Gain or Closing Loss for each Value Date falling after the Close-Out Date to present value by discounting the Closing Gain or Closing Loss from the Value Date to the Close-Out Date, at the Non-Defaulting Party's Base Currency Rate, or at such other rate as may be prescribed by applicable law;

(iii) aggregating the following amounts so that all such amounts are netted into a single liquidated amount payable by or to the Non-Defaulting Party: (x) the sum of the Closing Gains for all Value Dates (discounted to present value, where appropriate, in accordance with the provisions of Clause (ii) of this Section 5.1) (which for the purposes of this aggregation shall be a positive figure) and (y) the sum of the Closing Losses for all Value Dates (discounted to present value, where appropriate, in accordance with the provisions of Clause (ii) of this Section 5.1) (which for the purposes of the aggregation shall be a negative figure); and

(iv) if the resulting net amount is positive, it shall be payable by the Defaulting Party to the Non-Defaulting Party, and if it is negative, then the absolute value of such amount shall be payable by the Non-Defaulting Party to the Defaulting Party.

5.2 *Calculation of Interest.* Any addition of interest or discounting required under Clause (i) or (ii) of Section 5.1 shall be calculated on the basis of the actual number of days elapsed and of a year of such number of days as is customary for transactions involving the relevant Currency in the relevant foreign exchange market.

5.3 *Other FX Transactions.* Where close-out and liquidation occurs in accordance with Section 5.1, the Non-Defaulting Party shall also be entitled to close-out and liquidate, to the extent permitted by applicable law, any other FX Transactions entered into between the Parties which are then outstanding in accordance with the provisions of Section 5.1, as if each obligation of a Party to deliver a Currency thereunder were a Currency Obligation.

5.4. *Payment and Late Interest.* The amount payable by one Party to the other Party pursuant to the provisions of Sections 5.1 and 5.3 shall be paid by the close of business on the Business Day following such close-out and liquidation (converted as required by applicable law into any other Currency, any costs of such conversion to be borne by, and deducted from any payment to, the Defaulting Party). To the extent permitted by applicable law, any amounts required to be paid under Sections 5.1 or 5.3 and not paid on the due date therefor, shall bear interest at the Non-Defaulting Party's Base Currency Rate plus 1% per annum (or, if conversion is required by applicable law into some other Currency, either (x) the average rate at which overnight deposits in such other Currency are offered by major banks in the London interbank market as of 11:00 a.m. (London time) plus 1% per annum or (y) such other rate as may be prescribed by such applicable law) for each day for which such amount remains unpaid.

5.5. *Suspension of Obligations.* Without prejudice to the foregoing, so long as a Party shall be in default in payment or performance to the Non-Defaulting Party under the Agreement and so long as the Non-Defaulting Party has not exercised its rights under Section 5.1, the Non-Defaulting Party may, at its election and without penalty, suspend its obligation to perform under the Agreement.

5.6. *Expenses.* The Defaulting Party shall reimburse the Non-Defaulting Party in respect of all out-of-pocket expenses incurred by the Non-Defaulting Party (including fees and disbursements of counsel, including attorneys who may be employees of the Non-Defaulting Party) in connection with any reasonable collection or other enforcement proceedings related to the payments required under this Section 5.

5.7. *Reasonable Pre-Estimate.* The Parties agree that the amounts recoverable under this Section 5 are a reasonable pre-estimate of loss and not a penalty. Such amounts are payable for the loss of bargain and the loss of protection against future risks and, except as otherwise provided in the Agreement, neither Party will be entitled to recover any additional damages as a consequence of such losses.

5.8. *No Limitation of Other Rights; Set-Off.* The Non-Defaulting Party's rights under this Section 5 shall be in addition to, and not in limitation or exclusion of, any other rights which the Non-Defaulting Party may have (whether by agreement, operation of law or otherwise). To the extent not prohibited by applicable law, the Non-Defaulting Party shall have a general right of set-off with respect to all amounts owed by each Party to the other Party, whether due and payable or not due and payable (provided that any amount not due and payable at the time of such set-off shall, if appropriate, be discounted to present value in a commercially reasonable manner by the Non-Defaulting Party). The Non-Defaulting Party's rights under this Section 5.8 are subject to Section 5.7.

Section 6. Illegality, Impossibility and Force Majeure

If either Party is prevented from or hindered or delayed by reason of force majeure or act of State in the delivery or receipt of any Currency in respect of a Currency Obligation or if it becomes or, in the good faith judgment of one of the Parties, may become unlawful or impossible for either Party to deliver or receive any Currency which is the subject of a Currency Obligation, then either Party may, by notice to the other Party, require the close-out and liquidation of each affected Currency Obligation in accordance with the provisions of Sections 5.1, 5.2 and 5.4 and, for the purposes of enabling the calculations prescribed by Sections 5.1, 5.2 and 5.4 to be effected, the Party unaffected by such force majeure, act of State, illegality or impossibility (or if both Parties are so affected, whichever Party gave the relevant notice) shall effect the relevant calculations as if it were the Non-Defaulting Party. Nothing in this Section 6 shall be taken as indicating that the Party treated as the Defaulting Party for the purposes of calculations required hereby has committed any breach or default.

Section 7. Parties to Rely on Their Own Expertise

Each Party shall enter into each FX Transaction governed by the Agreement in reliance only upon its own judgment. Neither Party holds itself out as advising, or any of its employees or agents as having the authority to advise, the other Party as to whether or not it should enter into any such FX Transaction or as to any subsequent actions relating thereto or on any other commercial matters concerned with any FX Transaction governed by the Agreement, and neither Party shall have any responsibility or liability whatsoever in respect of any advise of this nature given, or views expressed, by it or any of such persons to the other Party, whether or not such advise is given or such views are expressed at the request of the other Party.

Section 8. Miscellaneous

8.1 *Currency Indemnity.* The receipt or recovery by either Party (the "first Party") of any amount in respect of an obligation of the other Party (the "second Party") in a Currency other than that in which such amount was due, whether pursuant to a judgment of any court or pursuant to Section 5 or 6, shall discharge such obligation only to the extent that on the first day on which the first Party is open for business immediately following such receipt, the first Party shall be able, in accordance with normal banking practice, to purchase the Currency in which such amount was due with the Currency received. If the amount so purchaseable shall be less than the original amount of the Currency in which such amount was due, the second Party shall, as a separate obligation and notwithstanding any judgment of any court, indemnify the first Party against any loss sustained by it. The second Party shall in any event indemnify the first Party against any costs incurred by it in making any such purchase of Currency.

8.2 *Assignments.* Neither Party may assign, transfer or charge, or purport to assign, transfer or charge, its rights or its obligations under the Agreement or any interest therein without the prior written consent of the other Party, and any purported assignment, transfer or charge in violation of this Section 8.2 shall be void.

8.3. *Telephonic Recording.* The Parties agree that each may electronically record all telephonic conversations between them and that any such tape recordings may be submitted in evidence in any Proceedings relating to the Agreement. In the event of any dispute between the Parties as to the terms of an FX Transaction governed by the Agreement or the Currency Obligations thereby created, the Parties may use electronic recordings between the persons who entered into such FX Transaction as the preferred evidence of the terms of such FX Transaction, notwithstanding the existence of any writing to the contrary.

8.4. *No Obligation.* Neither Party to this Agreement shall be required to enter into any FX Transaction with the other.

8.5. *Notices.* Unless otherwise agreed, all notices, instructions and other communications to be given to a Party under the Agreement shall be given to the address, telex (if confirmed by the appropriate answerback), facsimile (confirmed if requested) or telephone number and to the individual or department specified by such Party in Part VII of the Schedule attached hereto. Unless otherwise specified, any notice, instruction or other communication given in accordance with this Section 8.5 shall be effective upon receipt.

8.6. *Termination.* Each of the Parties hereto may terminate this Agreement at any time by seven days' prior written notice to the other Party delivered as prescribed above, and termination shall be effective at the end of such seventh day; provided, however, that any such termination shall not affect any outstanding Currency Obligations, and the provisions of the Agreement shall continue to apply until all the obligations of each Party to the other under the Agreement have been fully performed.

8.7. *Severability.* In the event any one or more of the provisions contained in the Agreement should be held invalid, illegal or unenforceable in any respect under the law of any jurisdiction, the validity, legality and enforceability of the remaining provisions under the law of such jurisdiction, and the validity, legality and enforceability of such and any other provisions under the law of any other jurisdiction, shall not in any way be affected or impaired thereby.

8.8. *Waiver.* No indulgence or concession granted by a Party and no omission or delay on the part of a Party in exercising any right, power or privilege under the Agreement shall operate as a waiver thereof, nor shall any single or partial exercise of any such right, power or privilege preclude any other or further exercise thereof or the exercise of any other right, power or privilege.

8.9. *Master Agreement.* Where one of the Parties to the Agreement is domiciled in the United States, the Parties intend that the Agreement shall be a master agreement, as defined in 11 U.S.C. Section 101(55)(C) and 12 U.S.C. Section 1832(e)(8)(D)(vii).

8.10. *Time of Essence.* Time shall be of the essence in the Agreement.

8.11. *Headings.* Headings in the Agreement are for ease of reference only.

8.12 *Wire Transfers.* Every payment or delivery of Currency to be made by a Party under the Agreement shall be made by wire transfer, or its equivalent, of same day (or immediately available) and freely transferable funds to the bank account designated by the other Party for such purpose.

8.13. *Adequate Assurances.* If the Parties have so agreed in Part X of the Schedule, the failure by a Party ("first Party") to give adequate assurances of its ability to perform any of its obligations under the Agreement within two (2) Business Days of a written request to do so when the other Party ("second Party") has reasonable grounds for insecurity shall be an Event of Default under the Agreement, in which case during the pendency of a reasonable request by the second Party to the first Party for adequate assurances of the first Party's ability to perform its obligations under the Agreement, the second Party may, at its election and without penalty, suspend its obligations under the Agreement.

8.14. *FDICIA Representation.* If the Parties have so agreed in Part XI of the Schedule, each Party represents and warrants to the other Party that it is a financial institution under the provisions of Title IV of the Federal Deposit Insurance Corporation Improvement Act of 1991 ("FDICIA"), and the Parties agree that this Agreement shall be a netting contract, as defined in FDICIA, and each receipt or payment or delivery obligation under the Agreement shall be a covered contractual payment entitlement or covered contractual payment obligation, respectively, as defined in and subject to FDICIA.

8.15. *Confirmation Procedures.* In relation to Confirmations, unless either Party objects to the terms contained in any Confirmation within three (3) Business Days of receipt thereof, or such shorter time as may be appropriate given the Value Date of the FX Transaction, the terms of such Confirmation shall be deemed correct and accepted absent manifest error, unless a corrected Confirmation is sent by a Party within such three Business Days, or shorter period, as appropriate, in which case the Party receiving such corrected Confirmation shall have three (3) Business Days, or shorter period, as appropriate, after receipt thereof to object to the terms contained in such corrected Confirmation. In the event of any conflict between the terms of a Confirmation and this Master Agreement, the terms of this Master Agreement shall prevail, and the Confirmation shall not modify the terms of this Master Agreement.

8.16 *Amendments.* No amendment, modification or waiver of the Agreement will be effective unless in writing executed by each of the Parties.

Section 9. Law and Jurisdiction

9.1 *Governing Law.* The Agreement shall be governed by, and construed in accordance with the laws of [the State of New York] [England and Wales] without giving effect to conflict of laws provisions.

9.2 *Consent to Jurisdiction.* With respect to any Proceedings, each Party irrevocably (i) [submits to the non-exclusive jurisdiction of the courts of the State of New York and the United States District Court located in the Borough of Manhattan in New York City,] [agrees for the benefit of the other Party that the courts of England shall have jurisdiction to determine any Proceedings and irrevocably submits to the jurisdiction of the English courts], and (ii) waives any objection which it may have at any time to the laying of venue of any Proceedings brought in any such court, waives any claim that such Proceedings have been brought in an inconvenient forum and further waives the right to object, with respect to such Proceedings, that such court does not have jurisdiction over such Party. Nothing in the Agreement precludes either Party from bringing Proceedings in any other jurisdiction nor will the bringing of Proceedings in any one or more jurisdictions preclude the bringing of Proceedings in any other jurisdiction.

9.3. *Waiver of Immunities.* Each Party irrevocably waives to the fullest extent permitted by applicable law, with respect to itself and its revenues and assets (irrespective of their use or intended use) all immunity on the grounds of sovereignty or other similar grounds from (i) suite, (ii) jurisdiction of any courts, (iii) relief by way of injunction, order for specific performance or for recovery of property, (iv) attachment of its assets (whether before or after judgment) and (v) execution or enforcement of any judgment to which it or its revenues or assets might otherwise be entitled in any Proceedings in the courts of any jurisdiction, and irrevocably agrees to the extent permitted by applicable law that it will not claim any such immunity in any Proceedings. Each Party consents generally in respect of any Proceedings to the giving of any relief or the issue of any process in connection with such Proceedings, including, without limitation, the making, enforcement or execution against any property whatsoever of any order or judgment which may be made or given in such Proceedings.

9.4. *Waiver of Jury Trial.* Each Party hereby irrevocably waives any and all right to trial by jury in any Proceedings.

IN WITNESS WHEREOF, the Parties have caused the Agreement to be duly executed by their respective authorized officers as of the date first written above.

_____

By _____
    Name:
    Title:

_____

By _____
    Name:
    Title:

Schedule

Part I: *Scope of Agreement.* The Agree   ment shall apply to [all] [the following] FX Transactions outstanding between any two Designated Offices of the Parties on the Effective Date.

Part II: *Designated Offices.* Each of the following shall be a Designated Office:

Part III: *Settlement Netting Offices.* Net settlement provisions of Section 3.2 shall apply to the following Settlement Netting Offices:

Part IV: *Novation Netting Offices.* Netting by novation provisions of Section 3.3(a) shall apply to the following Novation Netting Offices and shall apply to [all FX Transactions] [FX Transactions with a Value Date more than two Business Days after the day on which the Parties enter into an FX Transaction]:

Part V: *Matched Pair Novation Netting Offices.* Matched pair netting by novation provisions of Section 3.3(b) shall apply to the following Matched Pair Novation Netting Offices and shall apply to [all FX Transactions] [FX Transactions with a Value Date more than two Business Days after the day on which the Parties enter into an FX Transaction]:

Part VI: *Automatic Termination.* The "Automatic Termination" provision in Section 5.1 [shall] [shall not] apply to _____ and [shall] [shall not] apply to _____

Part VII: *Notices*
    Address:
    Telephone Numbers:
    Telex Number:
    Facsimile Numbers:

Name of Individual or Department to Whom Notices are to be sent:
Part VIII: *Base Currency*
Part IX: *Threshold Amount*
    The Threshold Amount applicable to _____ shall be:
    The Threshold Amount applicable to _____ shall be:
Part X: *Adequate Assurances.* The provisions of Section 8.13 [shall] [shall no
apply to the Agreement.
Part XI: *FDICIA Representations.* The provisions of Section 8.14 [shall] [shall
not] apply to the Agreement.

Total Currency Exposure vs. Foreign Exchange Trading

Banks and institutions involved in foreign exchange generally have two main sources of transactions: the total currency exposure and the actual foreign exchange trading. The total currency exposure, consisting of all the foreign denominated assets and liabilities, is generally separated from the daily trading activity for management purposes. The total currency exposure may be subject to position limits as well.

Sources of Risk and Revenues

Foreign exchange instruments have different rates of profitability and different degrees of risk. It is management's responsibility to select the most profitable instruments, relative to the present or projected trading capability of the desk, and identify the specific risks associated with each instrument. Only a clear understanding of business conditions enables the management to design the proper risk management policies.

Marking-to-Market

Marking-to-market is the common valuation procedure to calculate the foreign exchange exposure at current market prices.

In the past, positions and profit and loss were calculated on an end-of-day basis. Currently, the larger trading desks use front end/back office computerized systems which are plugged into the on-line financial services and provide a continuous marking-to-market. The failure to execute at least a marking-to-market on a daily basis may have disastrous consequences. Unchecked high volatility in the foreign exchange markets is highly likely to generate insurmountably adverse trading conditions.

In the United States foreign exchange markets, the most common time for selecting the *end-of-day revaluation rates* is 3:00 PM EDT, which coincides with the end of the trading day on the currency futures exchanges. The common practice is to use the middle rate of a specific spot rate or forward spread, which is the arithmetic average of the bid and offer. If and when administrative costs are necessary, adjustments to these revaluations must be allowed.

The exchange rates used for revaluations should be obtained in an objective manner. Generally, the rates should be printed and updated in the computerized systems by an independent source, such as the back office. In the larger dealing rooms, the front end/back office systems linked to the on-line financial services execute this function, as described above. A common source of information on exchange rates in the spot market is page WRLD on Reuters. Other exchange rates are available in a set of pages following WRLD, such as WRLE, WRLF and WRLG (see Figure 5.2). This approach is important in order to avoid unrealistically favorable rates input by a trader, who may want to improve an unrealized P&L, for instance. Certainly, any unrealized P&L figures have only a limited significance, but they may provide substantial warning signals. The lack of "raised red flags" may trigger serious surprises when the P&L is finally realized.

Value at Risk

According to *Derivatives: Practices and Principles, value at risk* refers to "the expected loss from an adverse market movement with a specified probability over a particular period of time." Commonly, the potential adverse change in the value of a portfolio on a daily basis may be calculated with a probability of 97.5 percent, when using two standard deviations.

The determination of the value at risk is significant, especially for more complex foreign currency portfolios, because the results may be compared to the current financial and human resources, thus allowing for decisions on the most adequate set of risk management rules.

Stress Tests

Although players generally understand the unexpected rises in foreign exchange volatility, few could have forecasted the currency developments on the European Monetary System in July 1993. Those developments (see Figure 5.3) have generated big winners, but also big losers. To better respond to this type of situation, it is imperative that the management requests periodic stress tests, designed to check and prepare the traders' handling of their positions vis-à-vis periods of unusually high or low currency volatility. The historical volatility specific for each instrument is readily available on the financial services (see Figure 5.4).

Exchange Risk Management Implementation

The position and loss limits are very basic management and control tools which can now be implemented better and more conveniently with the help of computerized systems. Once all transactions are entered in the system, the treasurer and the chief trader have continuous, instantaneous and comprehensive access to accurate figures for all the positions and the profit and loss. In addition, this information may be relayed from all the international branches into the headquarters terminals.

Interest Rate Risk

Interest rate risk refers to amount mismatches and maturity gaps among transactions in the foreign exchange book. This risk is pertinent to currency swaps, forward outrights, futures and options.

An *amount mismatch* between a spot deal and a forward outright deal may occur during a deal between the spot trader and a customer. If the customer asks for an odd amount dated forward, the spot trader will most likely cover in the spot market in the closest standard amount possible. The difference between the spot and the forward amounts is a mismatch.

For instance, if a customer buys USD/DEM 910,000 in forward outright, a trader will most likely cover USD/DEM 1,000,000 in the spot market because it is easier to trade an even amount, and he will adjust the forward pips later. However, there is an amount mismatched of USD/DEM 90,000.

A typical *maturity gap* occurs when a customer deals in an odd maturity (say 32 days) and the trader covers in one month (assume 31 days). Another typical example occurs when a forward outright deal is covered

```
1043 CCY  PAGE DLNG   SPOT RATE  LOC  PREV      US  HI & LO WRLD
1043 DEM  LOYA LOYL*D 1.5875/85  LON  77/87     1.6028     1.5870
1043 JPY  BMMA BMMA*J 105.66/73  TOR  70/75     105.90     105.53
1043 CHF  BAFX BOAL*C 1.3845/50  LON  45/55     1.3974     1.3815
1043 GBP  BAFX BOAL*G 1.5527/32  LON  27/34     1.5558     1.5412
1043 CAD  CIBC CIBC*R 1.3108/13  TOR  07/12     1.3200     1.3079
1041 AUD  NABN NABN*T 0.6505/10  NYC  10/15     0.6518     0.6464
1043 FRF  CINY CITN*F 5.5370/00  NYC  90/20     5.5768     5.5325

1043 XAU  RNBG RNBA  348.00/348.50 30YR TB 102.16-17 -42 YTM  6.07
1042 XAG  RNBG RNBA   4.04/ 4.06 * OIL  WTI  16.79/83  USDX 90.40
1037 FED  PREB        3.18- 3.25 * ED3  2.93- 3.18  ED6  3.18- 3.31


ONLINE                                                    Quote Mode
REUTER MONITOR      1800
WRLD
```

Figure 5. 2. Page WRLD is a common source of spot exchange rates used for revaluation purposes as well. (Courtesy of Reuters)

with a spot deal. This is done frequently to avoid the exchange risk. Although the exchange risk is annulled, as the same amount of foreign currency was bought and sold, for the duration of time the maturity dates are different, the party which covered only the spot side of the deal is exposed to any changes in either of the applicable interest rates (the interest rate differential).

For small exchange books, maturity mismatches may be easily avoided. For an active forward desk, despite the increasingly sophisticated computer systems, the complete elimination of the maturity gaps is virtually impossible. However, this may not be a serious problem, if the amounts involved in these mismatches are small.

On a daily basis, the traders balance the net payments and receipts for each currency through a special type of swap, called *tomorrow/next* or *rollover*. This type of swap, discussed in detail in Chapter 12, is geared toward the changing, or rolling-over, the old spot date to the new spot date. It is a powerful and convenient tool in handling the flow of maturing trades.

Risk Management Implementation

To minimize the interest rate risk, the management sets limits on the total size of mismatches. The policies differ among banks, but a common ap-

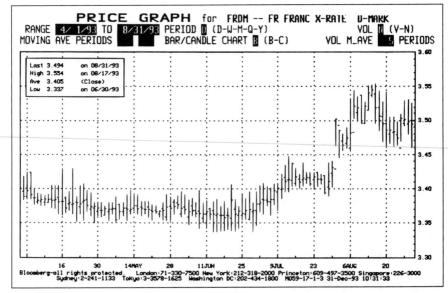

Figure 5. 3. The Deutsche mark/French franc cross rate in the summer of 1993 exemplifies the unexpectedly high volatility in foreign exchange. (Courtesy of Bloomberg)

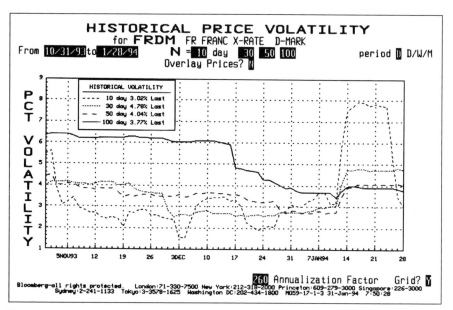

Figure 5. 4. The historical volatility of the Deutsche mark/French franc cross rate. (Courtesy of Bloomberg)

proach is to separate the mismatches, based on their maturity dates, into up to six months and past six months. All the transactions are entered in computerized systems in order to calculate the positions for all the delivery dates and the P&L. The continuous analysis of the interest rate environment is necessary to forecast any changes which may impact on the outstanding gaps. The results of this approach are good, but not perfect.

Credit Risk

Credit risk refers to the possibility that an outstanding currency position may not be repaid as agreed, due to a voluntary or involuntary action by a counterparty. The failure may be triggered by insolvency or prohibition of foreign exchange transactions. An example is the sudden insolvency of Drexel Burnham of New York, the high riding junk bond leader of the 1980s. Although more commonly associated with loan departments, the credit, or settlement risk, also pertains to the foreign exchange markets.

The maturity dates may be closer than for loans, but the same characteristics apply. Credit problems occur not only in the long dated forward contracts, but also in spot contracts, where payments are due in only two business days. Both the credit and the trading departments are responsible for managing credit risk, which is present in all foreign exchange instruments except currency futures and options on currency futures.

In these cases, trading occurs on regulated exchanges, such as the Chicago IMM, where all trades are settled by the Clearing House. On such exchanges, traders of all sizes can deal without any credit concern.

In order to minimize the credit risk for instruments traded off regulated exchanges, the potential and active customers' creditworthiness is essential because commercial and investment banks, trading companies and banks' customers must have credit lines with each other to be able to trade. Even after the credit lines are extended, the counterparties' financial soundness should be continuously monitored.

Traders should use Foreign Exchange Master Agreements to document FX transactions in derivative products. A sample of an International FX Master Agreement as drafted by the British Bankers' Association and the Foreign Exchange Committee is provided at the beginning of this chapter.

Two forms of credit risk are the replacement risk and the settlement risk.

1. *Replacement risk* occurs when counterparties of the failed bank find their books unbalanced to the extent of their exposure to the insolvent party. In order to rebalance their books, these banks must enter new transactions.

2. *Settlement risk* occurs because of the time zones separating nations. Consequently, currencies may be credited at different times during the day. Australian and New Zealand dollars are credited first, then Japanese yen, followed by the European currencies and ending with the US dollars. Therefore, payment may be made to a party which will declare insolvency (or be declared insolvent) immediately after, but prior to executing its own payments.

In this case, we are not facing exchange risk any longer. We are facing a sudden capital disappearance. Foreign exchange traders usually deal in multiples of US$1 million, but these amounts mean little more than tokens. Money is neither seen nor touched. It only exists as an electronic surrealism.

The counterparty's payment failure, however, zooms the concept of money back into reality at a chilling speed. Although rare, and therefore easy to forget, the two major cases, Bankhaus I. D. Herstatt, a small private German bank, and BCCI, sent out clear signals about the seriousness of the situation. After closing down BCCI, Bank of England telexed the news to all the major commercial banks and wished them good luck in recouping the losses through litigation. Some of the losses may be eventually recovered, but the magnitude of the losses incurred by a large, select group of major banks emphasizes the need for better credit risk control.

In addition to selectively opening lines of credit and constantly monitoring the creditworthiness of the counterparties, another measure is available. In assessing the credit risk, end-users must consider not only the market value of their currency portfolios, but also the potential exposure of these portfolios. The potential exposure may be determined through probability analysis over the time to maturity of the outstanding position.

Netting

Netting is a process which enables institutions to settle only their net positions with one another at the end of the day, in a single transaction, not trade by trade. It is a safer procedure, as the cashflow at maturity is clearly reduced. If a bank shows signs of payment difficulty, a group of large banks will provide short term backing from a common reserve pool. In addition, the forward credit lines are not filled, providing room for more business.

Finally, netting is distinctively cheaper. Settlement netting should fall under a single comprehensive master agreement with each counterparty, in order to provide the maximum legal coverage for credit exposure.

Implementation

The computerized systems currently available are very useful in implementing the credit risk policies. The credit lines are easily monitored. In addition, the matching systems introduced in foreign exchange since April 1993 are used by traders for credit policy implementation as well. Traders input the total line of credit for a specific counterparty. During the trading session, the line of credit is automatically adjusted. If the line is fully used, the system will prevent the trader from further dealing with that counterparty. After maturity, the credit line reverts to its original level.

Country Risk

Country (sovereign) risk refers to the government's interference in the foreign exchange markets. Although theoretically present in all foreign exchange instruments, currency futures are, for all practical purposes, excepted from the country risk, because the major currency futures markets are located in the United States.

This type of risk should not be confused with the intervention of the central banks in the foreign exchange markets, which pertains to exchange risk. Country risk happens when governments interfere for such reasons as currency shortage, tightening control over the banking system, freezing foreign funds on deposit or war.

The example of Kuwait's takeover by Iraq, where the foreign exchange transactions (along with all other transactions) were abruptly severed, signifies the difficulty of separating credit from country risk. Of course, this example had a happy ending, at least in the financial markets. The National Bank of Kuwait, which also had a set of books in London, made all the outstanding payments.

Another example is the US freezing of Iranian deposits in US banks following the Iranian government's overthrow and the taking of American hostages.

The impact of restrictions on foreign exchange is generally high if they interfere with the normal payments setup. The failure to receive an expected payment, due to government interference, amounts to the insolvency of an individual bank or institution, a situation described under credit risk. However, the scale is magnified with country risk, as more banks or institutions are affected.

In the past two decades, the trend among the major countries has been one of liberalization. Switzerland and Japan are among the countries which relaxed monetary controls. Sweden relaxed its controls over the krona forward market. But outside the major economies, controls on foreign exchange activities are still present and actively implemented.

From the trader's point of view, it is very important to know or be able to anticipate any restrictive changes concerning the free flow of currencies. If this is possible, though trading in the affected currency will dry up considerably, it is still a manageable situation. The problem occurs at its fullest if there is an element of surprise because the recovery of funds through litigation is a lengthy and frustrating undertaking.

Country risk falls under the joint responsibility of the treasurer and the credit department.

Conclusion

Foreign exchange has skyrocketed in daily turnover from a mere US$5 billion in 1977 to a staggering US$1 trillion in 1992. The industry is thus far subject to limited regulation, save for currency futures. In addition to these factors, the spot market moves at neckbreaking speed. For instance, the US dollar/Deutsche mark exchange rate may change in value 18,000 times daily. Since in this huge and rapidly moving trading environment risks may be substantial, it is imperative to have sophisticated and experienced management able to impose sound policies best suited for the capacity of each particular trading entity.

The introduction of the front end/back office systems has greatly facilitated the implementation of risk management. Instantaneous, accurate and comprehensive information on positions, P&L and credit lines is available to aid in this management.

Chapter 6

Central Banks

The Role of Central Banks

Generally speaking, a central bank's role is to direct the domestic monetary policy of its country. Under the monetary policy, the central bank manages the flow of money and credit that is provided to the economy. Therefore, the role of the central bank vis-à-vis the economy is paramount.

When approaching the subject of the central bank in the context of foreign exchange, there is a tendency to focus on market interventions. Whereas interventions are very important, they are only a fraction of the total role the central banks exercise in affecting the foreign exchange market.

Before we go any further, though, let's take a look at the United States' Federal Reserve.

The Federal Reserve

Historical Background

The Federal Reserve was established in 1913, when Congress passed the *Federal Reserve Act*. The act held that the role of the Federal Reserve was "to furnish an elastic currency, to afford the means of rediscounting commercial paper, to establish a more effective supervision of banking in the United States, and for other purposes."

The act instituted a decentralized system, consisting of the *Federal Reserve Board* in Washington and *12 regional Federal Reserve banks* around the country. These banks around the country had sufficient autonomy to manage financial conditions in their districts. They were also managed by governors.

In 1923, the *Open Market Investment Committee (OMIC)* was established to coordinate the Reserve Bank operations. It was composed of the Governors of the Federal Reserve Banks in New York, Boston, Philadelphia, Chicago and Cleveland. In 1930, the OMIC was replaced by the *Open Market Policy Conference (OMPC)*. It consisted of 12 Federal Reserve banks governors and the members of the Board.

The strains of World War I, the stock market crash of 1929 and the subsequent depression of the 1930s, along with a better understanding of the effects of the monetary tools were all important factors behind changes established by the Roosevelt Administration in 1933. Among those changes were the creation of the *Federal Deposit Insurance Corporation (FDIC)*, the formal recognition of the *Open Market Policy Conference (OMPC)*, already established in 1930, and empowering the Board to change the member bank reserve requirements.

The *Banking Act of 1935* reshaped the structure of the Federal Reserve System into its current form. The Board was renamed the Board of Governors of the Federal Reserve System. The Board of Governors consisted now of seven Governors, one of whom was Chairman of the Board. Also, the Treasury Secretary and the Comptroller of the Currency were disassociated from the Board meetings. The titles of the regional Reserve Bank governors were changed to presidents, and the OPMC's name was switched to its current name, the *Federal Open Market Committee (FOMC)*.

The autonomy of the regional Reserve Banks was curtailed with regard to government debt transaction without FOMC permission. The act also held that the Board must use its powers to generate an appropriate environment for business stability.

The Federal Reserve Bank is independent of Congress and the President. However, all Federal Reserve Governors are selected by the President and must be ratified by Congress.

In contemporary times, Paul Volcker, the Fed Chairman in 1979, linked the economic performance to the growth rates of the *money supply (M1)*. *M1* is composed of currency in circulation (outside the Treasury, the Fed and depositary institutions), travelers checks, demand deposits and other checkable deposits [negotiable order of withdrawal (NOW) accounts, automatic transfer service (ATS) accounts, etc.]. In 1980, the Depositary Institutions Deregulation and Money Control Act (MCA) simplified the structure of the reserve requirements and allowed the elimination of interest rates ceilings on most of the deposits (the exception was the demand deposits). By 1982, however, the M1 as an economic indicator was dropped in favor of the M2. M2 consists of M1 plus repurchase agreements, overnight Eurodollars, money market deposit accounts, savings and time deposits (in amounts under $100,000) and balances in general purposes. Since then, the FOMC has had a love-hate relationship with M2's ability to be a reliable economic indicator.

M3 is composed of M2 plus time deposits over $100,000, term Eurodollar deposits and all balances in institutional money market mutual funds.

The Federal Reserve's Role in Foreign Exchange

Like the other central banks, the Federal Reserve affects the foreign exchange markets in three general ways:

1. The discount rate
2. The money market instruments
3. Foreign exchange operations

Discount Rate. The *discount rate* is the interest rate at which eligible depositary institutions may borrow funds directly from the Federal Reserve Banks. This rate (see Figure 6.1) is controlled by the Federal Reserve and is not subject to trading. It is the single most important interest rate in use.

Prime Rate. The prime rate (see Figure 6.2) is the rate used by commercial banks as a base for retail loan rates. The prime rate is based on the discount rate. The prime rate is always higher than the discount rate. The correlation between the two is not constant. For instance, if the discount rate is increased, it is sure that the prime rate will increase as well. If the discount rate is cut, the prime rate may not follow, giving the banks an extra spread for profit.

The Money Market Instruments

The money market instruments tend to have a generally marginal impact on foreign exchange. Among these instruments, the most significant are:

a. federal funds,

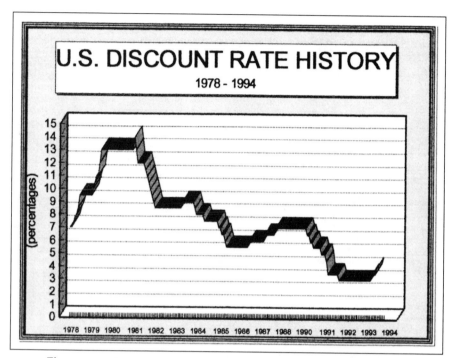

Figure 6.1. The discount rate in the United States between 1978 and 1994.

b. repurchase agreements, and

c. Eurodollars.

Federal Funds. *Federal funds,* largely known as fed funds, are the immediately available reserve balances at the federal reserves. The fed funds (see Figure 6.3) are widely used by commercial banks or large corporations to lend to each other mostly on an overnight basis. Although their level is established by the Fed, the prices fluctuate because they are being traded in the market. The fed funds levels are available on the on-line financial services. Typically, traders find them on Reuters on pages WRLD and PREB, or on Telerate on page 5.

Foreign exchange traders are generally not concerned on a daily basis with the fed funds prices. However, changes in their levels are considered warnings of potential changes in the discount rate. Therefore, at times, the fed funds prices may be a trading signal for the foreign exchange markets.

This scenario came to life in February 1994. The pressure on the Federal Reserve in the United States with regard to openness on their activity, led Alan Greenspan, the Fed's Chairman, to directly announce an increase of the fed funds. This direct approach was unprecedented and generated unusually volatile market conditions in foreign exchange.

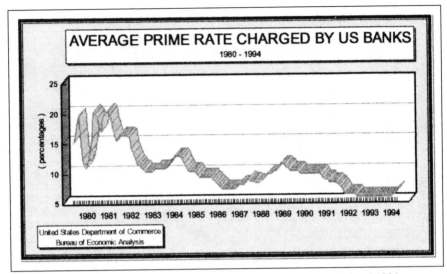

Figure 6.2.   The prime rate in the United States between 1980 and 1994.

Repurchase Agreements. *Repurchase agreements* (*repos*) are almost daily operations executed by the Federal reserve. A repurchase agreement between the Federal reserve and a government securities dealer consists of the Fed's purchasing a security for immediate delivery, with an agreement to sell the same security back at the same price at a predetermined date in the future (usually within 15 days), and receives an interest at a specific rate. This arrangement amounts to a temporary injection of reserves into the banking system. The impact on the foreign exchange market is that the *US dollar should weaken.* The repurchase agreements may be either customer repos or system repos.

Matched Sale-Purchase Agreements. The *matched sale-purchase agreements* are just the opposite of the repurchase agreements. When executing a matched sale-purchase agreement, the Fed sells a security for immediate delivery to a dealer or a foreign central bank, with the agreement to buy back the same security at the same price at a predetermined time in the future (generally within seven days). This arrangement amounts to a temporary drain of reserves. The impact on the foreign exchange market is that the *US dollar should strengthen.* These types of operations occur usually at 11:40 AM EDT (sometime up to 11:55 AM EDT).

The repo activities generally have only a limited impact on the foreign exchange trading. The Fed watchers have become quite adroit and their forecasts are very accurate. Foreign exchange traders generally discounted

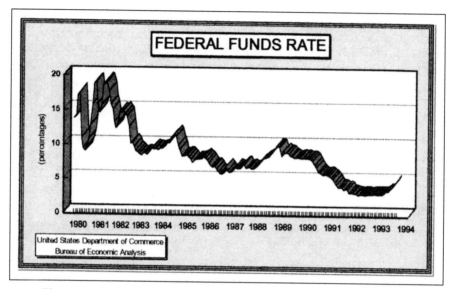

Figure 6.3. The federal funds in the United States between in 1980 and 1994.

these daily operations but, when the Fed refrains from its expected operation, or executes the opposite type of repos, see this as a trading signal.

These open market operations are executed by the New York Federal Reserve Bank as directed by the FOMC.

Eurodollars

Eurodollars are dollar denominated deposits at commercial banks outside the United States. All currency deposits outside the country of origin are called *Eurocurrencies*. These deposits do not have to be placed in Europe. Therefore, Deutsche mark deposits outside Germany are Euromarks, British pounds outside England are known as Eurosterling, etc. Eurodollars have the largest share of the Eurocurrency market.

What's in a Name? The *Eurodollar* name seems to have inadvertently been coined by a French branch of a Soviet bank, La Banque Commerciale pour l'Europe du Nord, S.A., which had as international cable code "Eurobank." Somehow, the name stuck with traders and has been used since.

Origin of the Eurodollars

Currency deposits outside the issuing country are not a novelty, since at all times throughout history, some foreign currencies had more panache for their holders. In the beginning of the twentieth century, the most popular Eurocurrency was the Eurosterling, since the British pound was the currency of reference around the world. The end of World War II brought the end to the pound supremacy and indirectly helped the rise of the Eurodollar market.

In the post-war period money was scarce. The US dollar was the major currency, and the demand for it was widespread. The Communist countries, especially the former Soviet Union, kept dollar deposits in London. Events in 1957—the debilitating British inflation and the Suez crisis—triggered capital controls in the United Kingdom. But the Soviet Union was in no rush to move its dollar deposits from London to New York, because it feared that the United States was going to freeze these deposits in retaliation for the expropriation of American property in the Soviet Union.

United States legislation was also instrumental in the growth of this market. The Federal Reserve had passed Regulation Q, which prohibited payment of interest on demand deposits and prescribed maximum rates banks pay on time deposits. These ceilings had been imposed since 1933 by the United States government. According to *A Guide to Federal Reserve Regulations*, published by the Board of Governors of the Federal Reserve System, "federal law prohibits the payment of interest on demand deposits by member banks. Regulation Q defined 'interest' and restates the prohibitions. In addition, Regulation Q included rules governing the advertising of deposits by member banks." Regulation Q is no longer applicable.

When the European countries returned to free convertibility in 1958, US dollars were still kept in deposits in Europe, to avoid the capped interest rates in the United States. In addition, the investment opportunities were better in Europe, where the economies had been rebuilt.

Finally, the Eurodollar deposits filled the niche for short term money market instruments in Europe.

Creating Eurodollars

Eurodollar deposits can be created by any depositors of US dollars outside the United States, regardless of whether they are American or not. For instance, they could be foreign holders of US dollar deposits at American banks transferring these deposits to foreign banks or American citizens receiving checks drawn on accounts in US banks depositing them in foreign banks.

Foreign Exchange Use of Eurocurrencies

Eurocurrencies rates are used by the forward traders to calculate the forward spread. The formula for the forward spread is:

$$\text{Forward spread} = \text{Spot rate} \times (\text{Eurocurrency} - \text{Eurodollar}) \times \frac{\text{No. of days}}{360}$$

If the result is a positive number, then the forward spread is at premium, and it is added to the spot price. Conversely, if the result is negative, then the spread is at discount, and it is subtracted from the spot rate. The details are covered in Chapter 12.

Eurocurrency rates are posted daily by the major financial information services: Reuters, Telerate, Knight-Ridder and Bloomberg.

Foreign Exchange Operations

The major central banks are involved in the foreign exchange operations in more ways than intervening in the open market. Their operations include payments between central banks or to international agencies. In addition, the Federal Reserve has entered a series of currency swap arrangements with other central banks since 1962. For instance, to help the allied war effort against Iraq's invasion of Kuwait in 1990/1991, payments were executed by the Bundesbank and Bank of Japan to the Federal Reserve. Also, payments to the Worldbank or the United Nations are executed through central banks.

When learning of large currency fluctuations in which the central banks are involved, one cannot help but wonder whether these banks have been motivated by profit. After all, central banks have access to arguably the largest trading capital around. It is very important to dispel this myth.

The major central banks do not engage in speculative trading.

Intervention in the United States foreign exchange markets by the US Treasury and the Federal Reserve is geared toward restoring orderly conditions in the market or influencing the exchange rates. It is not geared toward affecting the reserves.

If, for intervention purposes, the Federal Reserve buys US dollars, then it drains reserves. If it sells, then it adds reserves. The intervention is usually split between the Federal Reserve and the Treasury. If the Treasury pays for its portion in currencies from the Exchange Stabilization Fund, the intervention will not have any impact on the reserves. If the intervention is financed through a sale of special drawing rights (SDRs) from the International Monetary Fund (IMF), then it adds reserves. The change in reserves occurs because the sale of the SDRs, which are financial assets, creates money. Reserves are also increased if the Treasury exchanges foreign currencies for US dollars with the Federal Reserve with the agreement to repurchase them at the same rate. This technique, called warehousing, adds reserves because the Treasury invests the funds.

The actual intervention is executed by the Foreign Exchange Desk at the Federal Reserve Bank of New York.

There are two types of foreign exchange interventions:

1. Naked intervention
2. Sterilized intervention

Naked intervention, or *unsterilized intervention,* refers to the sole foreign exchange activity. All that takes place is the intervention itself, in which the Federal Reserve either buys or sells US dollars against a foreign currency. In addition to the impact in the foreign exchange market, there is also a the monetary effect on the money supply. If the money supply is impacted, then consequent adjustments must be made in interest rates, prices and at all levels of the economy.

Therefore, a naked foreign exchange intervention has a long term effect.

Sterilized intervention neutralizes its impact on the money supply. As there are rather few central banks which want the impact of their intervention in the foreign exchange markets to affect all corners of their economy, sterilized interventions have been the tool of choice. This holds true for the Federal Reserve as well.

The sterilized intervention involves an additional step to the original currency transaction. This step consists of a sale of government securities which offsets the reserve addition which occurs due to the intervention. It may be easier to visualise it, if you think that the central bank will finance the sale of a currency through the sale of a number of government securities.

In addition to selling government instruments to balance the reserve injection, the central banks have two other alternatives: printing money and, well, writing a check to itself. Although central banks are entitled to do so, these are not alternatives to be truly contemplated because of the grave consequences on inflation.

Since a sterilized intervention only generates an impact on the supply and demand of a certain currency, its impact will tend to have a short to medium term effect.

Overview of the Central Banks of the Other G-7 Countries

In the wake of World War II, both Germany and Japan were helped to develop new financial systems. Both countries created central banks fundamentally similar to the Federal Reserve. Along the line, their scope was customized to their domestic needs and they diverged from their mold.

The Deutsche Bundesbank (BUBA)

The German central bank, widely known as the Bundesbank, is a very independent entity, dedicated to a stable currency, low inflation and a controlled money supply. The hyperinflation which developed in Germany after World War I created a perfect economic and political scenario for the rise of an extremist political party and for the start of World War II. The Bundesbank's charter obligates it to avoid any such economic chaos.

In addition to its domestic obligations, the Bundesbank has certain obligations to the European Monetary System, since the Deutsche mark is the backbone of the system. Despite its selective financial commitment to member EMS currencies under stress, it has been obvious that, since 1989, the Bundesbank has had little choice but to concentrate on domestic problems. In fact, those problems were central to the EMS crisis of 1993, because the fall of the Communist system and subsequent German unification generated unforeseen economic strains on Germany that forced the Bundesbank to take domestic actions contrary to the best interests of the EMS. In line with its independent stand, the Bundesbank actually disapproved of German unification, on the grounds that this economically unsound process was inflationary.

When the administration went ahead with unification, the Bundesbank director, Karl Otto Poehl, resigned.

The Bundesbank follows a money supply target, or a corridor, in the M3, generally set in December and revised in June. Bundesbank also sets the discount and the Lombard rate, which are the last resort sources of funds for commercial banks.

The Bank of Japan (BOJ)

The Bank of Japan has deviated from the Federal Reserve mold in terms of independence. Although its Policy Board is still fully in charge of the monetary policy, changes are still subject to the approval of the Ministry of Finance (MOF). The BOJ targets the M2 aggregate. On a quarterly basis, the BOJ releases its Tankan economic survey. Tankan is the Japanese equivalent of the American tan book, which presents the state of the economy. The Tankan's findings are not automatic triggers of monetary policy changes. Generally, the lack of independence of a central bank signals inflation. This is not the case in Japan, and it is yet another example of how different fiscal or economic policies may have opposite effects in separate environments.

Bank of England (BOE)

The Bank of England may be characterized as a less independent central bank, because its decision may be overruled by the government.

The BOE has not had an easy go. Despite the fact that through 1991, British inflation was high, reaching double digit rates, in the late 1980s, the Bank of England did a marvelous job of proving to the world that it was able to maneuver the pound into mirroring the Exchange Rate Mechanism.

After joining the ERM late in 1990, the BOE was instrumental in keeping the pound within its 6 percent allowed range against the Deutsche mark, but the pound had a short stay in the Exchange Rate Mechanism. The divergence between the artificially high interest rates linked to the ERM commitments and the weak domestic economy triggered a massive sell-off of the pound in September 1992 (see Figure 6.4).

Despite significant losses in foreign exchange, rumored to be between US$6 to 20 billion, the Bank of England was able to support the battered British economy by drastically lowering the interest rates.

Banque de France/Bank of France (BOF)

The Bank of France has a joint responsability, with the Ministry of Finance to conduct the domestic monetary policy. Their main goals are noninflation-

Figure 6.4. The British pound activity at the time of its drop from the Exchange Rate Mechanism. (Courtesy of Bloomberg)

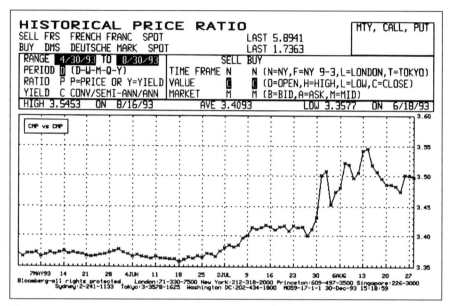

Figure 6.5. The Deutsche mark/French franc cross. Note the smooth chart line prior to August 1993, relative to the following period. The Bank of France held its franc within the old ERM boundaries even after the crisis. (Courtesy of Bloomberg)

ary growth and external account equilibrium. BOF currently targets M3, to which it switched in 1991 from monitoring the M2 aggregate.

Despite its economic strength and political stature, France is not a major player in the foreign exchange markets. In fact, the legal barriers on foreign exchange were only dropped in 1989. The franc fort policy was severely bruised by the ERM crisis of July 1993, when the French franc was yet another victim of the foreign exchange markets.

Ufficio Italiano dei Cambi/Bank of Italy (BOI)

The Bank of Italy is in charge of the monetary policy, financial intermediaries and foreign exchange. Like the other former European Monetary System central banks, BOI's responsibilities shifted domestically following the ERM crisis.

Changes in the discount rates must be approved by the Treasury.

Bank of Canada (BOC)

The Bank of Canada is an independent central bank which has a tight reign on its currency. Due to its complex economic relations with the United States, the Canadian dollar has a limited volatility against the US dollar.

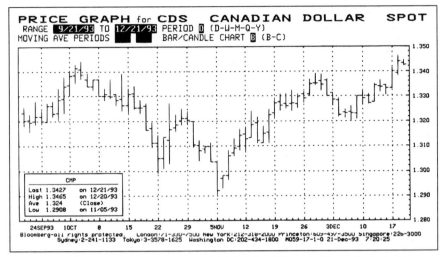

Figure 6.6.   The Canadian dollar versus the US dollar. The volatility is limited. (Courtesy of Bloomberg)

The Bank of Canada intervenes frequently both in the Canadian and United States markets to shore up its Canadian dollar.

Chapter 7

Price Structure and Foreign Exchange Terminology

This chapter presents the typical terminology in foreign exchange, from bids and offers in different instruments to the leave orders left by corporations and in the interbank market. Whereas the definitions of bids and offers are very basic and generally known in the spot market, they may change in the case of other instruments. These differences will be explained.

Spot Market

A *spot deal* takes place between two parties who deliver a certain amount of different currencies to each other, based on an agreed exchange rate, within two business days of the deal date. The exception is the Canadian dollar, in which the spot delivery is executed within one business day.

Let's take an example in the spot market. A bank quotes the USD/CHF at 1.4955/60 on a monitor. In this case, the bank's *bid* is 1.4955 (left side), which means that the bank is interested in buying USD/CHF at this price. The bank's *offer* is 1.4960 (right side), which means that the bank is interested in selling USD/CHF at this price. The difference between the bid and offer is called *spread*. In our example, the spread between

1.4955 and 1.4960 is five pips. A *pip* is the last decimal of the exchange rate. It is the fourth decimal of the exchange rate in the case of currencies such as the Deutsche mark and the British pound, and the second in the case of the Japanese yen or the Italian lira.

Keep in mind that the prices on the monitors are not binding. Although accurate, they are displayed as suggested prices only. If a bank posts the prices during a slow market, it is possible that it will also quote those rates in the interbank dealing. Naturally, banks are generally unable to update prices in a fast market, allowing for gaps between the monitor rates and the quoted prices.

A customer calls this bank for a price in USD/CHF and is quoted 1.4955/60. If the customer wants to buy, he or she will take the offer at 1.4960. Or, if selling, the customer will sell at 1.4955. Conversely, if you set the price of 1.4955/60, then your bid is 1.4955, and your offer is 1.4960.

Forward Market

A forward transaction takes place between two parties who deliver a certain amount of different currencies to each other, based on an agreed exchange rate, past two business days of the deal date. In the forward market, a trader must be a little more careful with the meaning of bids and offers. If you quote a forward price in foreign currency, your bid is on the left side and the offer on the right side, provided that the amount traded is quoted in foreign currency. If the amount is quoted in US dollars, then the right side is your bid and the left side is your offer. In order to cope with this sometime confusing reversal, just remember that buying US dollars is equivalent with selling foreign currency, and vice versa.

Example:

USD/JPY	
Spot	150.00–150.05
Forward	20–25

If you quote 20–25, a counterparty can sell you Japanese yen 250,000,000 at 20 (your bid for foreign currency), or buy Japanese yen 250,000,000 at 25 (your offer for foreign currency), just like in the spot market. However, the counterparty can sell you $2,000,000 at 25 (your bid for US dollars), or buy $2,000,000 at 20 (your offer for US dollars).

We will discuss the forward pricing in appropriate detail in Chapter 12.

Futures Market

Currency futures are a special case of forward outright transactions, or exchange deals which mature past the spot value date. In the spot and forward markets, currencies are quoted in either European terms, i.e., Deutsche mark, or in American terms, i.e., British pound, depending on the generally accepted norm.

In the futures market, prices are only quoted in American terms. The bids and offers are quoted similarly to the spot prices, the bid is on the left side, and the offer is on the right side. For example, if you quote Deutsche mark futures at .6000–.6010, it means that you want to buy at .6000 and sell at .6010. If you want to trade, and this price is quoted to you by another party, you can sell at .6000 and buy at .6010.

Foreign Exchange Terms

Communicating in the foreign exchange markets is an exact and minimalist matter. It could not have been any other way, given the high volatility and the high number of daily transactions.

Selling

To sell, the following terms are used:

- If you hit a bid, you say:

  "Yours."

  "I give you."

  "I sell"

- If you want to sell in the brokers market, without hitting the bid, then you say:

  "Offer join for X amount of currency."

  "I sell X amount of currency at (a lower offer than the current one)."

  Joining or improving the offer does not guarantee the execution.

Buying

To buy, the following terms are used:

- If you take an offer, you say:

"Mine."

"I take."

"I buy"

- If you want to buy in the brokers market, without taking the offer, you say:

"Join the bid for x amount of currency."

"I buy x amount of currency at (a higher bid than the current one)."

Of course, joining the bid or improving the bid in the brokers market does not guarantee any execution.

Price Changing

If you want to change the price, several options are available to you.

1. On the dealing machine, you hit the "INTERRUPT" key. Once this appears on the screen, the price is no longer valid.
2. On the dealing machine or on the phone, you can say "change" or "off" to withdraw your price.

If the counterparty still wants a quote, he or she will ask you either "How now?" or "How are you left?" or "Where are you now?" Of course, you cannot answer, "I'm left heartbroken" or "Downtown" to some trader's chagrin.

Leave Orders

Corporations, high net worth individuals and banks leave currency trading orders with other banks, trading companies and brokers because they cannot trade directly in the interbank market. Of course, they also have the option to request a two-way price and trade on that quote.

Even banks leave orders with other banks either because it is not efficient for them to trade certain currencies, or because they want to maximize the chance of execution by working them 24 hours a day. For instance, a bank specializing in the EMS currencies, which receives an unusual request for a Japanese yen item, is better off leaving the order with another bank which has an active Japanese yen desk, rather than allocating untrained manpower to follow that yen item.

Working currency orders around the clock is a common practice among large banks. If the orders are not executed in a certain market, the orders are transferred to a branch, subsidiary or another bank in the next time zone. Provided that those orders are still not executed, then the transfer will continue to the next time zone, until the time circle is complete: New York, then Auckland or Sydney or Tokyo or Singapore or Hong Kong, then London or Frankfurt or Zurich.

Order execution is obviously very important. To be properly done, it is important for the parties involved to agree on the assignment of risk before the order transfer. Both parties must be clear on what they want and what they can expect from each other.

There are two types of leave orders: *profit taking* and *stop-loss*.

Profit Taking Orders. Profit taking orders may mean two different things. First, as the name states, a trader who is long USD/JPY 5 million at 104.00, leaves an order to sell USD/JPY 5 million at 105.00, as the trader wants to sell at a price currently unavailable. In this case, the trader had a position prior to leaving this order.

Secondly, a trader may leave an order to buy or sell a currency at a price currently unavailable, without a prior position. For instance, a trader may believe that if the GBP/USD reaches 2.0000, it is a good selling opportunity, and leaves a selling order overnight to sell GBP/USD 3 million at that level.

How does one check on the execution of the leave orders? For a bank, the best approach is to ask several brokers what the overnight trading ranges were. For a corporation, the best approach is to ask several banks what the overnight trading ranges were. If the order is well within the trading range, there is no problem.

Potential problems occur when the leave order falls on the extremes of the overnight ranges. For instance, a bank's leave order is to buy USD/DEM 5 million at 2.5000, and the overnight range in one broker is 2.5000–2.5150, and 2.5001–2.5147 in another. The bank with which the order was left says that at 2.5000 only USD/DEM 2 million were sold for someone else. The leave order was regrettably not executed.

Was your order executed or not?

The bank with which the order was left must have access to at least one of the brokers where the low was 2.5000. Also, the two banks should have agreed on the execution rules in advance. If the agreed-upon format gives the counterparty execution latitude, then the bank leaving the order has most of the risk.

Some banks prefer to consider the order executed, based solely on price range, not on liquidity. Therefore, if 2.5000 was given in the brokers market, then the order was filled, despite the fact that only one broker reported that level as the low. In this case, the bank executing the order takes the full risk.

Why would a bank take this approach? Perhaps the bank would like to improve the trading relationship with the counterparty, or it might have a large book of customers, which enables it to protect itself. If there are several orders to buy around 2.5000, USD/DEM 20 million at 2.5020, USD/DEM 20 million at 2.5010 and USD/DEM 20 million at 2.5005, for instance, the chances that 2.5000 will be given are rather small.

Both approaches are valid, as long as the parties agree before hand on the assignment of risk.

Stop-Loss Orders. Stop-loss orders generally mean positioning exiting orders under adverse market conditions. Following up on the previous example, you bought USD/DEM 5 million at 2.5000. The USD/DEM was very steady throughout the day. You left two overnight orders: a profit taking order, to sell USD/DEM 5 million at 2.5200, and a stop-loss order, to sell USD/DEM at 2.4930. If your forecast that the USD/DEM will rally is wrong, then you will limit your loss on the downside by leaving a stop-loss order.

Stop-loss orders can also be used as position entry orders. If you don't have a current outstanding position, and if you expect the market to have a significant move once a certain level breaks, you can leave a so called stop-loss order close to that specific level to enter a position.

For instance, let's assume that your previous order to buy USD/DEM 5 million at 2.5000 was not executed overnight. During your trading day, however, the USD/DEM fell to 2.4940 and remained there for the balance of your trading day. You still expect the USD/DEM to rally, but you are afraid that 2.5000 level turned from a support level into a resistance level once it was broken. Therefore, you may leave an overnight stop-loss order to buy USD/DEM 5 million at 2.5010.

Please notice that the order is placed at a higher level than the initial 2.5000. This is done to avoid the potential resistance at 2.5000.

It is more difficult to execute stop-loss orders than profit taking orders. Chances are that stops are placed at significant levels, which are used by many other traders. Once those levels are reached, large stop-loss orders are going to be triggered, making it close to impossible to execute your order precisely at the requested level. Therefore, it is extremely important to have clear agreements on the type of execution.

There are four types of stop-loss order execution:

At the Price. The stop-loss order must be executed at the precise requested level, regardless of market conditions. The full risk is in the executor's court. This type of stop-loss order can only be executed by banks or trading firms. For example, if the stop-loss order is to sell GBP/USD 3 million at 1.5000, even if the market dropped to 1.4700 under very hectic conditions, and 1.5000 bid was never posted, the order is considered to be filled.

But, whereas traders may take a position to try to execute the order even if the specific price is not available in the market, brokers cannot do that. If the price is not available, they simply cannot execute the order. The price is said to have gapped out.

Next Best Price. The stop-loss order kicks in *after* the requested level was reached.

The trader executing the order must trade on the next available price. Under this format, the risk is fully borne by the customer, who has no guarantee on whether the order will be filled 3 or 30 pips away from the targeted price. This approach may leave room for argument, as the trader may return the customer a worse execution than the actual market deal.

This type of stop-loss order can be executed by banks, trading firms and brokers.

For example, if the stop-loss order is to sell GBP/USD 3 million at 1.5000, a fill will have to be acceptable at 1.4990, but not at 1.5000. The customer wants to be sure that the 1.5000 support level was really broken before exiting the position.

Discretion for Range to Trader. This approach is an imperfect hybrid of the first two types of stop-loss orders. The trader—either a bank or trading firm, but not a broker—has a number of discretionary pips within which the order has to be filled. The customer usually decides on the number of discretionary pips, and whether the currency price must be traded before execution.

For example, if the stop-loss order is to sell GBP/USD 3 million at 1.5000, the customer may:

Either instruct the trader to wait until 1.5000 is given, wait until 1.5000 is offered and then fill the order within 5 pips from the level. In other words, the stop-loss order is shifted from 1.5000 to 1.4995.

Or instruct the trader to fill the order at any price between 1.5000 and 1.4995.

The downside is that, realistically, it is close to impossible to fill a stop-loss order only a handful of pips away from a significant price level, especially if that level must be first traded and then offered, as in our example. Therefore, the trader's discretionary buffer pips are canceled, and most of the risk is borne by the trader.

At Best. Both profit taking and stop-loss orders can be executed at best. This means that the trader wants to trade regardless of the price. This type of order is placed in a fast market, where specific price levels cannot be traded.

Currency Fixings

Currency fixings are a solely European currency market phenomenon (see Figure 7.1). They are executed on a daily basis via an open auction where all players, regardless of size, are welcome to participate with any amount. Unlike the regular trading, there is no anonymity, as all the bids and offers are openly displayed. The highest bid *(geld)* and lowest offer (brief) are averaged to calculate the daily currency fixings *(mitte)* (see Figure 7.2).

The fixings are used by a variety of players. Companies that have a limited foreign exchange exposure and try to avoid both going through a bank and setting up their own desk find the daily operations to be convenient. Large banks may use the fixings to square off either small exposures incurred during the day from customer business, or small positions resulting from netting.

The fixings provide reference levels that are important in Europe. The foreign exchange fixings executed in Frankfurt are used as reference points for the daily end-of-day revaluations. In addition, they are used as legal agreements and as basis for foreign exchange agreements between banks and customers.

These agreements are executed by the banks at three different levels:

• *At the fixing* is the best price and it is used in the interbank trades.

```
0821 FRANKFURTER EXCHANGE FIXING                                    FXGF
      GELD    MITTE   BRIEF  VORTAG         GELD    MITTE   BRIEF  VORTAG

USD 1.6998   1.7038  1.7078 +.0049  NOK 22.995  23.055  23.115 -0.005
GBP  2.551    2.558   2.565 +0.012  SEK 20.465  20.545  20.625 -0.140
IEP  2.428    2.435   2.442 +0.003  ITL  1.0080  1.0130  1.0180 -.0100
CAD 1.2763   1.2803  1.2843 +.0025  ATS 14.203  14.223  14.243 +0.001
NLG 89.110   89.220  89.330 -0.060  ESP  1.211   1.216   1.221 -0.003
CHF 17.775  117.875  17.975 -0.335  PTE  0.972   0.982   0.992 +0.004
BEF  4.795    4.805   4.815 -0.010  JPY 1.5285  1.5300  1.5315 -.0050
FRF 29.265   29.345  29.425 -0.010  FIM 29.730  29.830  29.930 -0.130
DKK 25.545   25.605  25.665 +0.015

                        *27.12.93*
```

Figure 7.1.   The Frankfurt Foreign Exchange Fixings as of December 27, 1993. The information is available on page FXGF on Reuters.

```
        11:08 EST   THE DOW JONES INTERNATIONAL NEWS SERVICE        PAGE  1011
        08:06[FRANKFURT FOREIGN EXCHANGE FIXINGS.......................]

  USA                1.7094      ( 1.7134)
  BRITAIN            2.5430      ( 2.5460)
  IRELAND            2.4320      ( 2.4260)
  CANADA             1.2725      ( 1.2775)
  NETHERLANDS       89.320      ( 89.290)
  SWITZERLAND      117.980      (117.400)
  BELGIUM            4.8140      ( 4.8010)
  FRANCE            29.340      ( 29.335)
  DENMARK           25.550      ( 25.535)
  NORWAY            23.065      ( 23.060)
  SWEDEN            20.395      ( 20.360)
  ITALY              1.0210      ( 1.0165)
  AUSTRIA           14.222      ( 14.220)
  SPAIN              1.2220      ( 1.2200)
  PORTUGAL           0.9790      ( 0.9790)

        11:08 EST   THE DOW JONES INTERNATIONAL NEWS SERVICE        PAGE 31547
        08:06[FRANKFURT FOREIGN EXCHANGE FIXINGS.......................]

  JAPAN              1.5430      ( 1.5515)
  FINLAND           29.780      ( 29.570)

  -0-
```

Figure 7.2.   The Frankfurt Foreign Exchange Fixings as of December 21, 1993. The information is available on page 1011 on Telerate. (*Source: Telerate*® *Reprinted by permission. ©1993 Dow Jones Telerate, Inc.*)

- The *20 pips spread* is the improved corporate spread for the most important customers.

- At *40 pips spread* is reserved for the smaller customers.

Customers generally try to negotiate better spreads with their banks. Currency fixings are not executed in England or in the United States. Japan canceled the currency fixings in the late 1980s.

Chapter 8

Corporate Trading

Willingly or not, corporations have become significant players in foreign exchange. Whereas currency hedging still constitutes the majority of their interest, market speculation is becoming an increasingly attractive activity among corporations of different sizes. Foreign exchange is slowly evolving from its old status of cost of business to a legitimate source of profit.

Role of Foreign Exchange for Corporations

Whereas professional traders start from no position and virtually buy the risk, corporations start from a given position and try to minimize the risk. Corporate customers do not trade among themselves the way banks do. They reach the market via commercial or investment banks.

Corporate interest in foreign exchange derives from several sources. First, companies may need to make payments for raw materials, labor, advertising, distribution, or profit repatriation, to name a few of the typical natural needs to exchange currencies. Second, future expected payments may be hedged in order to eliminate or minimize the risk of adverse currency movement. Finally, corporations may like to enhance their performance by entering foreign exchange markets purely to take advantage of expected currency fluctuations. In other words, to speculate. As speculation is quickly losing its shady connotation, corporations are increasingly joining the ranks of commercial and investment banks, the major foreign exchange players.

Unlike banks, corporations do not trade in-and-out all day long. Their outlook tends to be longer term, not spot oriented. The longer term approach is valid for hedging, covering their commercial needs, and speculation.

Types of Corporations

There are many types of companies involved in foreign exchange, small and large, single-foreign currency oriented and multicurrency oriented, national and multinational. There are product makers, such as electronic services and software, consumer service firms, such as travel agencies, and investment companies, such as equity funds. Corporations may have a temporary or long term interest in international business.

Due to the complexity and speed which characterize the contemporary economy, these factors may overlap or quickly change. For instance, many equity and fixed income funds used to have a predominant focus on the local markets. Some of the more internationally oriented funds diversified primarily in the G-7 countries: the United States, Germany, Japan, the United Kingdom, France, Italy and Canada. The economic and political developments since 1989, notably the fall of Communism in Eastern Europe and the economic rebirth in South America and Southeast Asia, created new high growth stock markets and, consequently, new investment opportunities for the equity and fixed income funds.

Types of Exposures

Exposure reflects the potential effect of currency fluctuations on shareholders' equity.

There are three types of exposures:

1. Transaction or exchange

2. Economic

3. Translation

Transaction Exposure

Transaction—or *exchange*—*exposure*, which is equivalent to exchange risk in the interbank market, reflects the potential profit and loss generated by current foreign exchange transactions by both national and international corporations. For instance, let's consider the situation of an American travel agency, catering to British travelers, which sold trips to the United States in August 1992. The travel payments were received by the agency at a time when the British pound fetched about 2.00 US dollars. Only days later, in early September 1992, the GBP/USD rate was 1.70, and by December 1992, only 1.50 (see Figure 8.1). The repatriation of the receipts from British pounds to US dollars registered a loss of approximately 15 percent within days.

Managing Transaction Exposure

To manage the exposure generated by currency transaction, the management must have a clear set of rules in place. Several questions must be thoroughly answered.

- Do we want the risk?
- Can we shift the risk?
- If we can't shift the risk, how much risk do we want to accept?

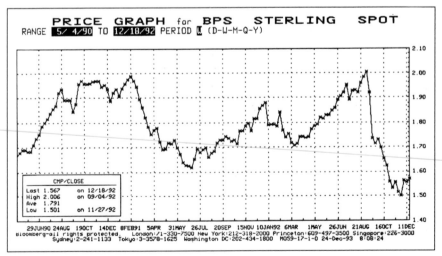

Figure 8.1. The sterling pound fell against the US dollar from around 2.00 in early September 1992 to 1.50 by December 1992, as a result of the crisis on the European Monetary System. (Courtesy of Bloomberg)

- What is our expectation for each of the currencies in which we have an exposure?
- What is the best strategy to handle the currency exposure?
- How can we implement this strategy?

In the case of the travel agency, it seems as if the exposure risk was acceptable, probably for economic reasons, such as competitive prices for the trip. The risk could have been shifted if the prices had been charged in US dollars, rather than British pounds. But realistically speaking, it is not feasible to charge a vacation fee in a foreign currency. Another approach could have been to enter a partnership with a British travel agency and convince that agency to take the currency risk. Provided that neither of these approaches had been made, the agency must decide whether it wants to keep the British pounds in a British bank at a higher rate than in the United States, with full, partial or no hedging, or exchange the money into US dollars at once.

In order to make this decision, the management has to form a view on the behavior of the British pound vis-à-vis the US dollar. A historical chart of the past decade would have indicated that the British pound had been overvalued against the US dollar above the rate of 2.0. Additional fundamental information regarding the state of the British economy vis-à-vis the American and European economies would have shown weak results. A fair conclusion would have been that the British pound was headed down. Therefore, management could have sold the cable in the spot market for US dollars at the earliest possible time, or enter a forward outright deal based on a GBP/USD spot exchange rate of about 2.00.

In addition to the security of hedging, the forward outright transaction would have been advantageous from two points of view. First, the agency had more time to collect the British pounds. Second, the cable could have been deposited in a British bank, provided that the cash was not needed for payments. Certainly, management may customize the above approaches, by executing both spot and forward outright transactions for fractions of the total receipts.

The abrupt fall of cable against both the US dollar and the European currencies was generated by the unexpected EMS crisis. However, the crisis itself was triggered by the same imbalance of the fundamentals which could have been noticed by the management of the travel agency.

Therefore, if management expects the foreign currency to devalue versus the base currency, then the position in the foreign currency must be exchanged quickly at the current rates. Conversely, should the management expect the base currency to ease vis-à-vis the foreign currency, then the position should be translated to the base currency at a later date.

The above approaches assumed that the receipts in foreign currency, in our example the British pounds, have to be repatriated into the base currency, the US dollars. However, if the foreign currency receipts can be invested in the foreign currency, the transaction exposure is eliminated, reduced or postponed, depending on the situation.

Economic Exposure

Economic exposure reflects the impact of foreign exchange fluctuations on the future competitive position of national and international companies.

For instance, let's take the example of IBM personal computers. Developed in the United States, they had the largest segment of the world market in the early 1980s. The high and increasing value of the US dollar in this period had a strong negative effect on IBM's capacity to export the PCs abroad. This was a window of opportunity for the competition, which managed to assemble surprisingly accurate clones at much lower prices. IBM not only reacted slowly to what seemed to be meek competition in the international markets, but ended up seeing its share of the domestic market reduced as well.

By the time the US dollar's rise was capped in September 1985 by the G-5 countries, and eventually devalued by 50 percent in December 1987, IBM had already lost its competitive edge in personal computers. While it is certainly unfair to blame all of IBM's problems in the personal computers market solely on the unfavorable exchange rates, even later, when the dollar reached record lows against the yen, providing American exporters with the opportunity to return the favor, it was precisely the American personal computers makers—including IBM—who were slow to take advantage of the currency edge in the Japanese consumer market.

Managing Economic Exposure

Managing economic exposure is a complex and long term task. The decision depends on the degree of the elasticity of demand for specific goods, the time available for adjustment, and the direction of the base currency relative to the operational foreign currency. The base currency is the currency against which other currencies are quoted. The rule of thumb is, the more inelastic the demand, the longer the time for adjustment.

If the demand for a product is strong in a particular market, a price increase will have a limited negative impact on demand. An example may be the demand for American-made airplanes. Despite the strength of the US dollar in the mid-1980s, the demand for American commercial airplanes was not really affected. Of course, its nearly monopolistic position in the world helped as well.

At the other end of the spectrum, an elastic demand, such as American consumers' demand for cars, had a significantly negative impact on the domestic market share of American car makers, faced with the Japanese competition. Naturally, the shoddy quality of American cars in the 1970s and early 1980s, along with the oil crisis, were also significant factors.

Time for adjustment is crucial. Management may consider importing parts, or even building assembly plants abroad, in order to take advantage of the lower prices generated by the exchange rates. For instance, when faced with steeply declining profits due to the revaluation of the yen against the US dollar, the Japanese producers built assembly plants for consumer electronic products in Southeast Asia, sometimes in countries which have their currencies pegged or semipegged to US dollars, or even directly in the United States, in the case of some auto assembly plants.

Where does foreign exchange fit in this puzzle? Well, consumers tend to care less about the exchange rate of their domestic currency than they do about their domestic prices, even though this rate is a significant determinant of the total price of the product. When faced with the choice between a domestic and an import, consumers generally focus on which product has better features and a better price.

Management must have a good sense of the direction of the base currency relative to the operating currency. Based on an accurate analysis of the price elasticity of demand, expected exchange rate direction and time to adjust, management should be able to set a sound long term strategy. Current economic, financial and political events must be continually monitored in order to better adjust this strategy.

A flexible approach to minimizing economic exposure is paramount, given the potentially severe swings in the currency markets.

Translation Exposure

Multinational companies naturally have a variety of multiple currency exposures generated by their international subsidiaries and branches. For consolidation purposes, all these exposures are translated into a single currency: the base currency. *Translation exposure* reflects the risk of change of the consolidated corporate earnings as a result of past volatility in the base currency. Currency fluctuations may be sizable enough to generate challenging problems for corporate management. Several accounting rules attempted to solve this thorny issue.

FASB 8. Originally, the accounting rules regarding foreign exchange were standardized in 1975 under the Financial Accounting Standards

Board's Statement Number 8 (FASB 8). FASB 8 set the procedures for foreign currency translations into US dollars in the consolidated balance sheets of US multinational corporations.

The immediate effect of this rule was to increase the volatility of the P&L and of the balance sheet statements as a direct result of the exchange rates' volatility. FASB 8 came under heavy criticism because the foreign exchange P&L was directly reported into income, generating volatility in corporate earnings.

FASB 52. In order to answer these concerns, a new, complex set of rules was designed in 1981, under the Financial Accounting Standards Board's Statement Number 52 (FASB 52), and it is currently in use. The FASB's main objective is to move the foreign exchange P&L from the current income into the shareholders' equity.

The P&L resulting from foreign exchange translations is generally contained in an equity account until the investment is liquidated. However, the translation of the foreign exchange P&L may be deferred if the affiliate is a separate entity. This approach is taken for corporations which operate in currencies other than the US dollar. The operating currency, usually the local currency, is called the functional currency. When a corporation has several units, it may use different functional currencies.

If, however, one of the functional currencies happens to be a highly inflationary one, the management should remeasure the results in the reporting currency. In addition, if the functional currency is actually US dollars, then the foreign exchange fluctuations are reflected into current income, in effect using the FASB 8.

Hedging

To hedge or not to hedge, that is the question. The answer depends on a variety of factors, because some corporate investors are comfortable with a full currency hedge while others disregard hedging as useless and costly. Hedging decisions vary, depending on the time frame, the volatility of currency, the market view on the specific currency, management's level of sophistication and the level of risk each company is willing to take.

The expected time frame of the position to maturity is an important factor in deciding whether to hedge. Certain equity fund managers are reluctant to hedge the currency side of investments held for three or more years—the general consensus of long term—but are eager to hedge short term investments

What is best? It depends. In the short term, the British pound lost 15 percent of its value within days in September 1992, and 25 percent in about two months (see Figure 8.1). One and a half years later, the currency was quoted at the same levels. In September 1985, the US dollar was exchanged for 3 Deutsche marks. In the long term, about seven years later, the US dollar could only fetch 1.39 Deutsche marks, or about 54 percent less.

It should be stressed that time, as a hedging factor, should only be considered along with the type of currency and the view on the specific currency. Used alone, the time factor may be unreliable.

Some currencies are more volatile than others. The management of a German company operating in both the Netherlands and the United Kingdom may not feel hard pressed enough hedge the Dutch guilder against the Deutsche mark, but it would surely consider it against the British pound. While the Dutch guilder has a high correlation with the Deutsche mark (see Figure 8.2) due to their EMS links, generating limited fluctuations on the DEM/NGL cross (see Figure 8.3), the correlation between cable and Deutsche mark is much lower after the pound was withdrawn from the EMS in 1992 (see Figure 8.4), which allows for much more fluctuations on the GBP/DEM cross (see Figure 8.5).

If management perceives that the operating currency is expected to perform adversely, and therefore that the outstanding position is at risk, then it must decide on a hedging strategy. To achieve an accurate view on the market, management should use the forecasting techniques explained in Part 5.

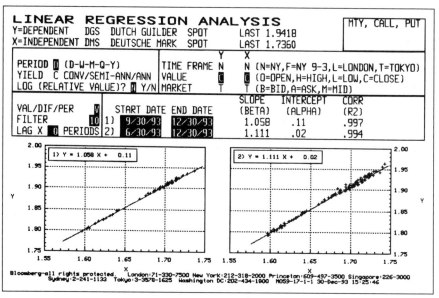

Figure 8.2. The linear regression analysis indicates a high correlation between the Deutsche mark and the Dutch guilder. (Courtesy of Bloomberg)

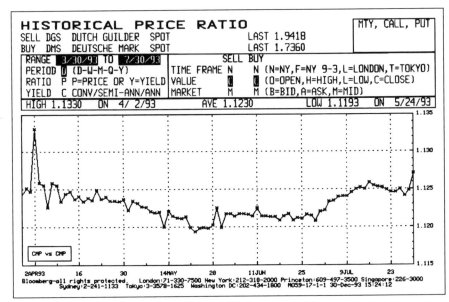

Figure 8.3. The Deutsche mark/Dutch guilder cross chart shows limited fluctuation. (Courtesy of Bloomberg)

Management's level of sophistication, both personnel and equipment is crucial in making hedging decisions. The implementation of the hedging, or the performance of the unhedged outstanding positions must be closely monitored. At the simplest level, the position must be marked to the market at least on a daily basis. The individuals in charge must have the necessary skills, along with full access to the decision support systems such as on-line monitors displaying the running rates and information and adequate software for management and control. Contingency plans for unexpected developments must be in place.

If the outstanding position is not fully or entirely hedged, stop-loss orders must be established and enforced. Conversely, the hedge may be raised if it prevents the outstanding position from generating a profit, and if the elimination of the hedge itself does not neutralize the expected profit.

The level of risk which management is willing to accept differs considerably among companies and it depends on the corporate objective regarding a specific position, the degree of diversification within the compound position and the financial capacity to withstand adverse market behavior.

In terms of corporate objective, the management must determine whether the hedge is passive, that is, purely designed to insulate the out-

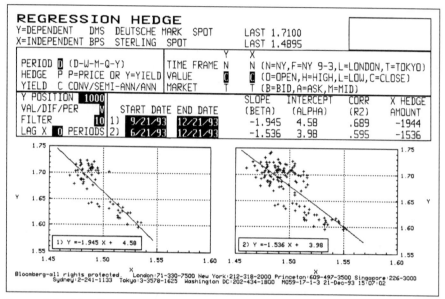

Figure 8.4. The linear regression analysis indicates a lower correlation between the Deutsche mark and the British pound. (Courtesy of Bloomberg)

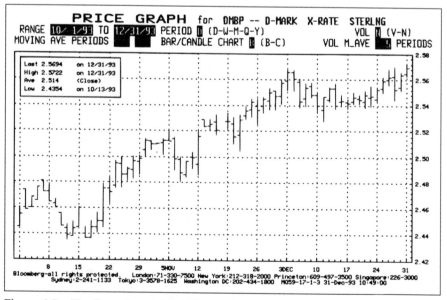

Figure 8.5. The Deutsche mark/British pound cross chart shows much more fluctuation than the Deutsche mark/Dutch guilder cross chart. (Courtesy of Bloomberg)

standing position from the foreign exchange fluctuation, or active, meaning that it is designed to enhance the profit of the original position.

The objective of a passive hedge is to realize a profit and loss as close to zero as possible. This type of hedge may be achieved through forward outright, futures, swaps or options contracts.

An active hedge may only come into existence under adverse currency conditions. This type of hedge may be implemented through stop-loss orders in both the spot and forward markets, along with currency options.

How Foreign Exchange Is Executed

Corporations do not generally trade among themselves. Although exceptions occur, inter corporate foreign exchange is very limited. They reach the currency markets through commercial and investment banks (see Figure 8.6). Corporate customers trade in two ways: ask for a price and trade directly, or leave an order with the bank.

Corporations do not usually contact the traders directly. The two parties are generally linked by the banks' sales force. The sales force, or the corporate traders, have a multitude of tasks. They make cold calls to prospective customers, advise, take orders from customers and pass them

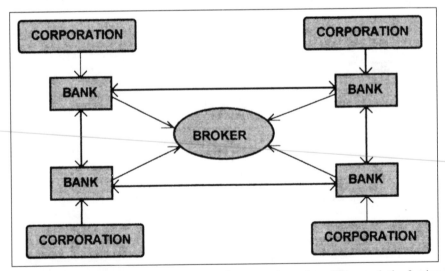

Figure 8.6. Corporate customers do not trade among themselves. They reach the foreign exchange markets through commercial and investment banks. In turn, banks trade with each other directly and through brokers.

to traders, and confirm the orders' execution with the customers (see Figure 8.7).

Corporate customers are very important to banks. Foreign exchange traders welcome the orders as a means of gauging the cash flow and for enhancing their own profits. When the size of orders is large, a trader will get a good "feeling" about the cash flow.

Patterns of profit repatriation, for instance, are often quite important, at least in the short term. An example is the profit repatriation by Japanese companies, a commercial need. The Japanese fiscal semesters end in March and September. In order to repatriate their profits, Japanese companies must purchase yen, generally against US dollars, prior to these dates. Once the new fiscal semesters start in April and October, the Japanese yen is sold again for hedging purposes.

This type of pattern is generally important to foreign exchange traders not only in terms of temporal repetition, but also in terms of transaction size. Since the total of Japanese exports to the United States is so large, it follows that the amounts of US dollars which must be sold for Japanese yen are quite significant.

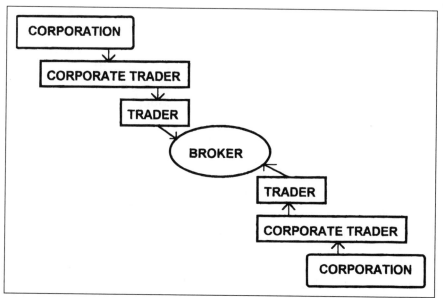

Figure 8.7. Corporate customers do not generally contact the traders directly. The two parties are linked by the banks' corporate traders. Corporate traders make cold calls for prospective customers, take orders from customers and pass them to the trading desk, confirm the orders which were executed and advise their corporate customers.

Corporate orders are also used by traders as part of their daily strategy. If the orders are placed at crucial support or resistance levels, traders may also trade at these levels, once the customer orders are filled. Therefore, both players, the corporation and the trader, will benefit from the execution of the customer's orders.

The quality of the price that banks quote their customers is a function of several factors. First, it is the importance that the bank's management attaches to specific customers. Customers gain in stature when they trade regularly, avoiding calls only to pick the tops and bottoms, and share significant information. The sales force generally reciprocates not only by getting better prices from traders ("Special price for this customer, mate!"), but also by quickly informing the customer of unusual market changes before the rest of the market is informed. The opposite is true when corporations have a habit of pulling orders off just before execution or throwing their weight around with the sales force.

Second, the quote for the customer reflects the position of the bank, along with the individual position. Therefore, the quote may reflect marginal (about 1 to 5 pips) skews from the running market prices. Finally, the quote to the corporate customer must reflect the long term importance of the business relationship.

Some banks will quote their customers the market running prices, similar to quoting in the interbank. The spread between the bid and offer is tight, around 5 pips. This approach generally occurs in the case of larger orders. In this case, there is no commission for the bank. If the orders are large indeed, for instance over $50 million, then the trader may not gain 1 or 2 pips, but will benefit from the flow information instead.

Other banks will have an understanding with their customers to quote the running market prices. Once the deals are executed, the banks will charge a fixed commission of 1 or 2 pips. This approach, which ensures some income for the bank, encourages the trader to quote the price without any personal distortion. This approach seems to be the fairest to all parties involved. The company receives the "real" price, the trader does not have to disrupt his or her trading trying to "read" the customer, and the corporate salesperson does not have to skew the price, as the commission is built in.

Yet another quoting approach is to widen the spread between the bid and offer. This approach limits the risk of the trader, since it offers the buffer of several pips against any adverse currency fluctuations.

The general consensus regarding the prices quoted by banks to corporate customers is that the larger the amounts, the tighter the spread of the quotes. In the interbank market, it is more difficult to trade $500,000 than

$10 million. To partly compensate for small size, some traders w.
spreads of 10 pips or more for small amounts.

In the past, corporations would call the banks and tell them not only
the currency and amount they were looking to trade, but also whether they
were looking to buy or sell. Currently, few large companies will mention
which side they need, if they want to trade directly and some of them behave similarly to the large banks. They call several banks at the same time
and pick the most advantageous price. This approach is not warmly received by traders because they have no margin of profit if the deal is executed, and no information if the deal goes to a different bank.

When a customer has a relatively small order to execute, perhaps less
than $1 million, it is more advantageous to mention the side of interest. This
way, traders tend to quote a better price than the customary ones reserved
for small amounts.

A professional, courteous and quick response by the sales force usually goes a long way in cementing long term, stable business relationships.

Different Points of View

In the regular foreign exchange market, the major market participants are
traders, corporate traders, corporations and brokers. Let's see how their
points of view differ.

Traders. Traders attempt to translate the impact of different fundamental and technical factors on the currencies and to seize the opportunities
in these markets. They need the volatility. The direction of the market and
the price levels are very important.

Corporate Traders. The economic and technical data and market behavior are important to corporate traders only for advisory purposes. They
need some volatility to generate more corporate sales, but they prefer mod-
erate volatility in a two-way market, which attracts more customer orders.

Corporations. Generally, corporations do not like volatility. They already have a natural trading demand stemming from their business. Since
currencies, nevertheless, fluctuate, corporations must be actively involved
in foreign exchange to hedge their positions. Therefore, the direction and
price levels are important.

Brokers. Brokers need market volatility. Volatility gets the market busy and busy traders execute more deals through brokers. However, excessive volatility has a negative impact on the business. Few trades go through when the market is trading under extreme conditions. The direction of the market and the price levels are irrelevant.

The best daily market is a moderately volatile two-way activity.

Chapter 9
Foreign Exchange Settlement

An average $1 trillion changes hands evey day in the foreign exchange markets, often under volatile conditions. The execution of these payments among hundreds of banks around the world is a staggering task. Conversely, the failure to generate timely and accurate payments is sanctioned by steep fines. This chapter focuses on the operational aspect of foreign exchange, a vital part of the trading process.

The Role of the "Back Office"

Foreign exchange transactions do not end when the trader agrees to buy and sell a certain currency with another party. The details of the trade have to be processed, and the amounts agreed to be exchanged must be debited and credited. Responsible for all these activities is the Foreign Exchange Trading Operations Department, or the "back office."

The department is physically separated from the dealing room for internal control. In fact, as communications developments have made it possible, some back offices have been moved to different locations altogether in an effort to save on real estate costs.

Let's take a look at the information which begins the responsibilities of the Operations Department: the *trade ticket*. Every single foreign exchange trade is entered in a ticket. The ticket has a printed serial number if the deal is executed in a commercial bank. There is no sequential number on tickets in investment banks.

The information entered on the ticket can be separated into two categories:

- Information for the trader
- Information for foreign exchange accounting and operations

The most significant information to the trader is: *name and amount of the base currency, exchange rate and the side of the deal* (buying or selling).

Note: Assume that the trader knows both what currency was quoted against the fixed currency (for instance JPY against the USD) and the maturity date (spot, one month, etc.).

Base, or fixed, currency is the primary currency which is traded against another. Generally, the fixed currency is the USD, but it may also be one of the Commonwealth currencies, such as the British pound, or the DEM on a cross deal. If you trade USD/DEM 1,000,000, then the fixed currency is the USD. If the trade is done in GBP/USD 5,000,000, then the base currency is GBP. If you trade DEM/CHF, then the base currency is DEM.

The information necessary for foreign exchange accounting and operations consists of the following:

1. The name and the city location of the counterparty
2. The transaction (deal) date
3 The maturity date (or dates in the case of swaps)
4. Name and amount of the base currency
5. All relevant exchange rates (there are several exchange rates in the case of cross, forward outright and swap transactions)
6. Buying or selling the fixed (base) currency
7. The other foreign currency name and amount
8. Name of the trader
9. Method of execution: *brokers market* or *direct dealing*

   If the deal was executed in the brokers market, the trader must enter the name of the *brokerage house* or *matching system*. This information allows the back office to make the correct commission payments. In the case of a direct deal, the form of telecommunication must be specified: dealing system, phone or telex. If the deal is done on the dealing system, the name of the dealing system must be entered.

10. Payment and receiving instructions (P&R) must be entered for overseas counterparties only. The details of FX transactions with parties on the same continent are confirmed by phone.

Until the mid-1980s, tickets used to be written by hand (Figure 9.1). Needless to say, the process was error prone and it slowed down the trading operation considerably.

Starting in the late 1980s, the dealing rooms have begun to turn "paperless," as tickets are electronically produced and kept in the computer's memory (Figure 9.2). The work load of the back office has been greatly reduced, as most of the relevant information is input in the front office, and sent electronically to the operations department. The processing is executed quickly and accurately by the computerized system.

Let's move over to the operations department and see how they process this information.

After the time of the trade, but *the same day*, the department will go through several steps. They check all the details on the ticket as sent or electronically generated by traders, they calculate any missing amounts (the currencies opposite the base currencies), and exchange rates. Once the tick-

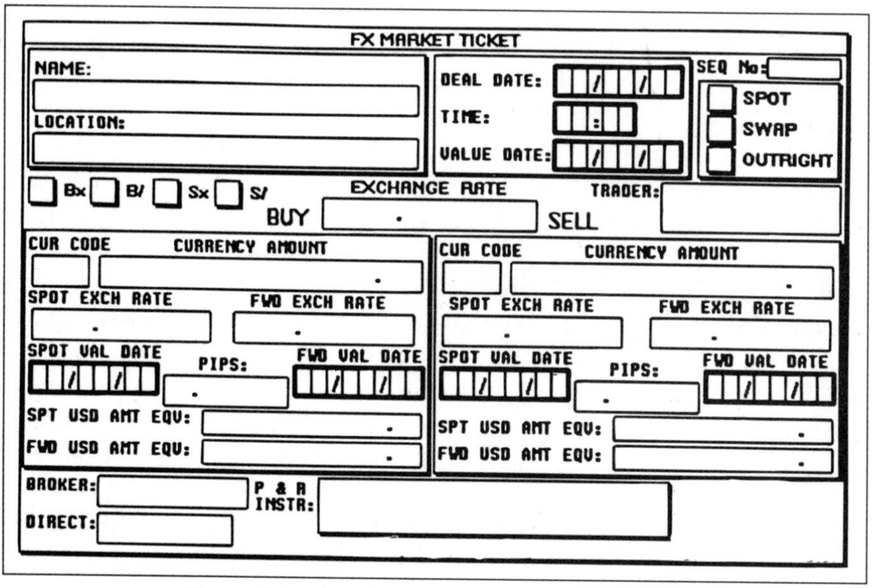

FX MARKET TICKET
NAME:
LOCATION:
DEAL DATE: / /
TIME: :
VALUE DATE: / /
SEQ No:
SPOT
SWAP
OUTRIGHT
Bx B/ Sx S/
EXCHANGE RATE
TRADER:
BUY
SELL
CUR CODE CURRENCY AMOUNT
SPOT EXCH RATE FWD EXCH RATE
SPOT VAL DATE PIPS: FWD VAL DATE
SPT USD AMT EQU:
FWD USD AMT EQU:
CUR CODE CURRENCY AMOUNT
SPOT EXCH RATE FWD EXCH RATE
SPOT VAL DATE PIPS: FWD VAL DATE
SPT USD AMT EQU:
FWD USD AMT EQU:
BROKER:
DIRECT:
P & R INSTR:

Figure 9.1. A typical foreign exchange paper ticket.

Electronically produced Foreign Exchange Screen/Ticket

```
                         OMARK L&D/FX/FXA    MODULE
10:50 AM                                                          10/08/93
                      FX LEVEL-2 INPUT / MAINTENANCE
Branch: PARIS         Trade:      886              Type: F    □ Action:


Trade: 10/08/93                   Value: 11/11/93
  Sell: USD          88,833.12    Spot: 5.0          M
  Buy : FRF         444,165.60    Dealt: 5.0
                                  Status: Input 2 Instr B


   PC:          Salesperson:          Trader: TEST         Deal Method: P
   Port:        Brok:                 A/C Type:            Conf Rcv Method:
   DID:         Ref.:                 Fees:
   Cust: BANK IRL                     Brkrg:
   Pay:
   Narr:

F10 Xmit      PF2 Help      PF3 Print     PF4 Quit      F17 Explode    F18 Query
```

Figure 9.2.   An electronically produced foreign exchange market ticket. (Courtesy of ACT Financial Systems)

ets are filled and checked, the back office confirms every single deal by phone with the counterparties located on the same continent. If the deals are executed over the dealing or matching systems, the trading tickets are checked against the printed confirmations generated by these systems, regardless of the location of the counterparty.

If the deals are executed through brokers, traders bear the responsibility of getting the telex confirmations for all deals with overseas counterparties.

After the time of the trade but *before maturity*, the department sends the payment instructions via automated systems of standardized payment instructions. The system used for foreign currencies is named the Society of Worldwide Interbank Financial Telecommunications (SWIFT). The system used for US dollars is called the Clearing House Interbank Payments System (CHIPS). The dollar payment instructions may also be sent by another system called Fedwire, which links Fed banks to depositary institutions.

In addition, the back office checks to make sure that all the outstanding contracts have been matched and reports any discrepancies. A separate unit specializes in investigating the discrepancies.

After the time of the trade but *on the maturity day,* the department checks to see if the money credited to its own bank is in the *nostro*—or *clearing—account* as instructed and reports if it is not credited.

Nostro Account

A *nostro account*, or *clearing account*, is the account for each foreign currency in the country of origin maintained by the financial institutions for purchase and receiving (P&R) purposes. For instance, all banks have their nostro accounts for Deutsche marks in Germany, either with a German bank or with a German branch of a foreign bank. As an example, let's say that the First Bank of IOU/New York has its CHF nostro account either in its Swiss branch or in a Swiss bank.

Vostro Account

A *vostro account* is identical in scope to a nostro account. The difference is that it belongs to the counterparty. If the First Bank of IOU/New York trades USD/CHF with the Second Bank of UOM/Frankfurt, and First Bank of IOU/New York has a CHF nostro account with the First Bank of IOU/Zurich, this same account will be considered as a vostro account by the Second Bank of UOM/Frankfurt.

SWIFT

Until 1977, all the foreign exchange transactions were settled by following instructions from banks sent via cable messages, known as *cable transfers.* This method was extremely labor intensive, and consequently error prone. The steep increase in the foreign exchange trading volume has generated extreme pressures on the operations departments forced to use the cable transfers, which have been developed in the 1920s. In September 1977, the SWIFT (Society of Worldwide Interbank Financial Telecommunications) automated system was set up in order to send *standardized payment instructions* for *foreign currencies* among European and North American banks. The system proved to be an instant success.

Since the late 1980s, SWIFT has been expanding outside these geographical boundaries, and some 3000 institutions around the world are currently connected to this system.

SWIFT Implementation

There are two types of messages: *financial messages* between SWIFT users and *system messages* between users and the SWIFT system.

SWIFT messages have a common structure:

Header
Text
Trailer

Functions required in the *computer based terminal* (CBT) for message exchange are as follows:

- Message entry/verification /authorization
- Connection with mainframe computer
- Message transmission
- Message reception
- Application management

In the *regional processor* (RGP), messages from a number of users are concentrated, encrypted and sent over to the applicable Operating Center for processing. In the Operating Center, the SWIFT system executes four processes on the messages. They are as follows:

- Checking the syntax on the messages
- Constructing a new header to convert the message to the output form
- Adding trailers to the messages
- Copying and encrypting for storage

Validation of the message to the sender is expressed as:

- ACK = positive acknowledgment
- NAK = negative acknowledgment

Trailers are added to an output message if additional information is necessary. For instance, if the sender is uncertain that the original SWIFT message was received, a new message will be generated, bearing the trailer PDM (possible duplication message). *Message numbering* is done automatically via an Input Sequence Number (ISN) to every message sent. Therefore, safety, accuracy and ease of processing are insured. *Encryption* ensures privacy for all the messages sent through SWIFT and these messages remain private even to SWIFT.

Advisory Bilateral Foreign Exchange Netting Service

Netting is a service which enables institutions to settle their *net positions* with *one another* at the *end of the day* in a *single transaction* instead of at the time each trade is executed.

This process has definite advantages. It is *cheaper*, as there is only one deal to process versus tens of deals on a daily basis. In addition, it is a valuable safety feature, as banks must make only one payment on the net balance with another bank. If this bank shows any sign of payment difficulty, a group of large banks, known as a *banking cooperative*, will provide short term backing from a common reserve pool.

Foreign exchange netting is implemented through ACCORD (discussed next) from SWIFT.

ACCORD

ACCORD is a *central, computerized system* used by banks and brokers to confirm and match foreign exchange and money market trades.

These operations used to be executed primarily by phone and telex. Currently, the majority of the foreign exchange trades are confirmed through SWIFT's ACCORD service because of the system's advantages. It improves efficiency, gives a rapid and accurate picture of settlement positions, spots errors quickly and greatly reduces the operational costs (fines and labor costs).

ACCORD has 88 users in 23 countries.

To improve safety, speed, management and transaction costs, SWIFT proposed to the European Community a new facility for Mass Payments. The Facility for Mass Payments consists of the following components:

- *Interbank File Transfer (IFT)* as the transport vehicle
- *Bulpay* as the standardized format
- *Modules* to translate the national formats into SWIFT formats

The system is designed for international money transfers, checks, direct debits and credits, standing orders and card debits and credits. The system is to become available worldwide (Figure 9.3).

CHIPS

Foreign exchange *dollar settlements* are executed through a computerized system called CHIPS (Clearing House Interbank Payments System). CHIPS is owned by 11 large New York City banks, and links 122 New York City depository institutions which pay and receive dollar funds from their correspondent banks around the world.

To get a sense of the magnitude of the US dollar transactions volume and of the importance of the system, let's compare the total number of transactions versus the total volume of these transactions in the United States.

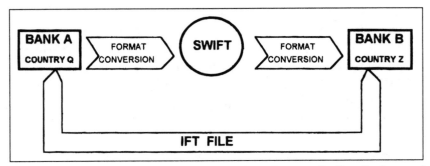

Figure 9.3. Bank-to-bank service of SWIFT's Mass Payment Facility. Banks transfer files internationally through SWIFT, via IFT file transfer mechanism and the bulpay format for bulk instructions in a standardized format.

Number of Payments (in US dollars)

1. 85%—cash
2. 13%—checks
3. 2%—electronic transfers

Volume of Payments (in US dollars):

1. 99%—electronic transfers
2. 1%—cash and checks

CHIPS and the Federal Reserve's network have *80 percent of the total* worldwide dollar transfers business. The size of this market reached in 1991 a staggering *US$1.7 trillion daily.*

Volume rose from 12 times the balances held in accounts at the Federal Reserves in 1980 to 55 times in 1991.

There are several reasons for the growth in CHIPS' volume:

1. The *expansion of the government securities,* a market which was automated in 1980, to finance the federal deficit.

2. *The growth of the world economy* and the increased number of countries.

3. The *low price* (US$.18 per transaction) of execution is very important to make the payment method feasible in a high volume environment.

4. The high *speed* of execution is another feature which is vital to heavy volume markets.

5. *Safety* is a *sine qua non* condition for the execution. In order to ensure the safety of the extraordinarily large amounts of money being trans-

ferred, the system is protected by sophisticated (and generally undisclosed) methods.

6. *Accuracy* is yet another *sine qua non* condition for the execution. Without it, speed and price are inconsequential features.

7. *Reliability* of the system has been proven over and over again. The foreign exchange market is continuously subject to large moves, waves of heavy trading. CHIPS was able to fully process the trades.

CHIPS helps execute some 100,000 to 300,000 transactions a day. To minimize the number of transactions on a bank-to-bank basis, the settlements are *netted.*

Multilateral clearing of accounts through CHIPS depends on each bank's ability of meeting its obligations.

Since 1990, the banks have been *required* by the Federal Reserve *to put up securities as collateral against risk of failure* of any participant bank. The member's failure would thus be absorbed as a group at settlement time and the losses will be settled later through negotiation or litigation.

CHIPS operates between 7:00 AM and 4:30 PM (EDT). Once all the payments and receipts have been executed through CHIPS, the transfers will be final when the CHIPS settle at the Federal Reserves, generally by 6:00 PM (EDT).

Fedwire

US dollar settlements may also be made via *Fedwire.* which consists of a settlement system and a communication network which links the Fed banks to all the depository institutions which want to link up to the Fed.

The main Fedwire features are as follows:

• Securities are transferred free or DVP (delivery versus payment).

• Balances due are paid *transaction by transaction*, not by netting.

• Fedwire money transfers are final, unlike CHIPS transfers, which are not final until CHIPS settles.

Fedwire is used for the following types of trades:

• Large payments and receipts of Fed funds from CHIPS settlement

• Fed funds

• Eurodollar transactions

• Securities delivery

• Funds transfer

Interbank Compensation

Although there is no standard method *per se* currently enforced around the world, the majority of the international banks apply the same set of compensation rules. The *US Council on International Banking, Inc.* provides Interbank Compensation Rules to its 360 members around the world. Their rules are also followed by numerous other banks. The importance of standard (or close to standard, in this case) procedures goes beyond the financial costs; the clarity and fairness of the rules is paramount for maintaining good business relationships in a volatile financial environment. (These compensation rules, courtesy of the *US Council on International Banking, Inc.*, are reproduced at the end of this chapter.)

Conclusion

The operations, or back office, department has a vital role in the continuously moving and changing world of foreign exchange. Simply, the trading activity cannot survive in its absence. Traders focus, fairly enough, on dealing. The foreign exchange transaction is not over until the payment and receiving of foreign currencies around the world are accurately executed. Traders deal millions and billions day in and day out, but the real value of these enormous amounts is not always fully perceived. Nevertheless, it is the back office's responsibility to make sure that all these large amounts are properly debited and credited. Only then is the trading activity complete.

The introduction of the computerized front end-back office systems in the late 1980s has relatively eased the work schedule of the back office. However, the increase in volume and instrument sophistication will keep the back offices around the world quite busy for the foreseeable future.

Appendix: Interbank Compensation Rules (Effective: 1/2/90)*

Part I. General

Rule I.1. Scope. The U.S. Council on International Banking's Interbank Compensation Rules, (the "Rules") govern the settlement of claims for compensation between U.S. Council on International Banking member banks ("banks"), including their head offices and overseas branches, but excluding their subsidiaries, arising from interbank funds payments (other than ACH payments) in United States dollars regardless of:

i. the original source or ultimate beneficiary of any payment, whether foreign or domestic;

ii. the manner of payment (e.g., Fedwire, CHIPS, check, telex);

iii. the type of funds involved (e.g., same day funds, next day funds);

iv. the nature of the underlying transaction (e.g., securities transaction, foreign exchange); or

v. the departments of the banks involved in initiating, processing or receiving the transaction.

*Courtesy of U.S. Council on International Banking, Inc. (One World Trade Center, Suite 1963, New York, NY 10048, (212) 466-3352).

Rule I.2. Nature of the Rules. a. Not every possible situation involving a claim for compensation is explicitly addressed. Not withstanding any provision of these Rules, when a claim for compensation meriting special attention is identified, it is expected that the banks involved will settle such claim so that no bank shall be unjustly enriched or injured by the actions of another member bank.

b. Unless otherwise specified, compensation in connection with a claim meriting special attention shall not exceed the benefit derived by the bank obligated to pay compensation. This limitation may be invoked, for example, in the case of Rule 3, 4 or 5 of Part II, if a beneficiary withdraws the funds from its account so that its bank does not have use of funds.

c. Payment or attempted payment of compensation pursuant to these Rules does not constitute and should not be construed as an admission of negligence or fault on the part of any of the banks involved.

Rule I.3. Manner of Payment. Compensation under the Rules shall be paid in United States dollars. A compensation payment may be made by CHIPS, Fedwire or check. Banks may alter the manner of payment of compensation by prior mutual agreement.

Rule I.4. Ordering Parties/Beneficiaries. The Rules do not confer any right or responsibility on any person, entity or organization not a member of the U.S. Council on International Banking.

Rule I.5. Third Parties. The Rules do not apply to claims for compensation arising from actions of third parties who are non-members of the U.S. Council on International Banking.

Rule I.6. Disputes. Disagreements which arise between member banks, over the application of the rules, may be submitted in writing to the U.S. Council on International Banking Rules Committee for arbitration.

Part II: Interbank Funds Payments

Rule II.1. Definitions. a. "Business day" means a Monday, Tuesday, Wednesday, Thursday or Friday which is not a day on which banking institutions in the United States are authorized or obligated by law or executive order to close.

b. "Fed. Funds Rate" means the average of each day's Federal Funds rate, as published on a daily basis by the Federal Reserve Bank of New York, for the days that a bank must include in the applicable formula(s) in calculating compensation. The daily Fed. Funds Rate for any day on which a published rate is not available shall be deemed to be the same as the immediately preceding published rate.

Rule II.2. Back Valuation. a. A bank which sent a payment may request the bank which received the payment to back values such payment. Generally, such request is accompanied by a payment for the amount of compensation owed pursuant to the formula below. If compensation is paid, the receiving bank is obligated to back value the payment to the date requested, unless i) its customer instructs it not to back value such payment; ii) the account has been closed; iii) the sending bank requests a back valuation to a date more than one year prior to the payment date; or iv) the compensation payment is received more than one year after the payment date.

b. The rules do not require the sending bank to obtain back value. The rules only stipulate the amount required when back valuation is *requested* by the sending bank.

c. If the receiving bank back values the payment pursuant to the request of the sending bank, the sending bank must pay the receiving bank compensation according to the following formula (without regard to whether or not the beneficiary's account was actually in an overdraft position):

$$\text{Compensation} =$$

$$\frac{\text{(Dollar Amount of Payment) x (Fed. Funds Rate) x}}{\text{(No. of Days Back Valued) + \$200*}}{360}$$

Rule II.3. Forward Valuation. a. A bank which sent a payment may request the bank which received the payment to adjust the payment to a future value date. The receiving bank is not obligated to make such an adjustment.

b. If a receiving bank adjusts the payment to a future value date pursuant to the request of the sending bank, the receiving bank must, upon receiving a claim for compensation within 60 days from the date on which the requested adjustment was made, pay the sending bank compensation according to the following formula:

---

*$200 fee is paid to the bank which was requested to make the adjustment to compensate it for its administrative costs in back valuing a payment.

Compensation =

$$\frac{\text{(Dollar Amount of Payment) x (100\%-Reserve Requirement) x (Fed. Funds Rate) x (No. of days Forward Value)}}{360} - \$200^{**}$$

Rule II.4. Return of Payment "Missent Payment." a. There may be circumstances in which a bank that has sent a payment may request the bank that received such payment to return the funds. For example, a bank that has sent i) a payment that should not have been sent; ii) sent a payment to the wrong bank; or iii) sent a duplicated payment or has made an over-payment (each such payment or part thereof constituting an overpayment is hereafter referred to as a "missent payment"), may request the bank which received the payment to return it. To induce the receiving bank to return a missent payment the sending bank may issue an Indemnity conforming to the format of the U.S. Council on International Banking's Compensation Indemnity and Responses (the Indemnity) (Appendix A). The receiving bank is not obligated to return the payment in reliance on the Indemnity.

b. Except as provided under Rule 7 of this Part II (Netting of Compensation), if a receiving bank returns a missent payment, it shall, upon receiving a claim for compensation within 60 days from the date on which it returned the missent payment, pay the sending bank compensation according to the following formula:

Compensation =

$$\frac{\text{(Dollar Amount of Payment) x (100\%-Reserve Requirement) x (Fed. Funds Rate) x (No. of days not to exceed 180)}}{360} - \text{Applicable Deduction}$$

c. A request for compensation received beyond 60 days from the date the missent payment was returned, need not be honored by the receiving bank.

d. A request for compensation included in the body of the Indemnity is a legitimate claim under the new Rules and fulfills the 60 day require-ment.

e. If a missent payment is retained by the receiving bank for more than 180 days, the Fed. Funds Rate means the Fed. Funds Rate in effect during the most recent 180 day time period.

**The $200 deduction is allowed to compensate the receiving bank for its administrative costs in adjusting a payment to a future date. The receiving bank is not entitled to the $200 deduction for for-ward valuation if a request for a change of beneficiary (Rule 5) also accompanies a request for forward valuation. However, the receiving bank is entitled to the $200 fee for amending the beneficiary.

Appendix A: U.S. Council on International Banking Compensation and Indemnity and Responses (the "Indemnity")

1. Purpose. In order to induce a bank receiving a payment (the "Receiving Bank") to return in an expeditious manner, a payment sent to the wrong bank, an overpayment, a duplicated payment or to adjust a credit to the correct account on a payment made to the correct Receiving Bank but for credit to an incorrect or no account, the bank sending such a payment (the "Paying Bank") may issue the Indemnity which appears below to the Receiving Bank. The Receiving Bank may, but is not obligated to act as a result of the Indemnity. The Indemnity may be issued only in connection with payments made in United States dollars.

2. Method of Transmission. A Paying Bank should transmit the Indemnity and a Receiving Bank should transmit any response or release thereof, by telex, S.W.I.F.T., any other mutually agreed upon means of electronic transmission, or by letter. It is recommended that the Indemnity be sent by means of electronic transmission. If transmitted by telex, the telex must be tested. If transmitted by S.W.I.F.T. or any other means of electronic transmission, the transmission must be authenticated. If transmitted by letter, the letter must be executed by an authorized signatory of the sender and must be hand delivered to the receiver by an authorized messenger from the sender. The receiver shall acknowledge in writing receipt of such a letter. Such acknowledgement shall be considered proof that such letter was properly delivered by the sender to the receiver. If transmitted by letter, each Indemnity must be enclosed in a readily identifiable envelope addressed to the Receiving Bank clearly marked with the notation "Indemnity."

3. Format. a. The Indemnity must be in the folowing format:

REF. NO. _____

INDEMNITY

With reference to our payment date_____ by means of (Fedwire # _____),
(CHIPS #_____), (S.W.I.F.T._____), or (check # _____), for
U.S. $_____ in your favor for the account of _____, by order of
._____, we request that you:

    [   ] Adjust the credit from the account of _____ to the account of _____;

    [   ] Refund the amount of U.S. $_____, which was intended for you;

[   ] Refund the amount of U.S. $_____, because the afore-mentioned payment was a duplication of (Fedwire #_____), (CHIPS #_____), (S.W.I.F.T. #_____), or (check #_____);

[   ] Refund the amount of U.S. $_____, which was an over-payment. The correct amount should be U.S. $_____;

[   ] Pay us compensation calculated pursuant to the U.S. Council on International Banking's Interbank Compensation Rules from (payment date) to the date on which you fulfill this request.

In consideration of your complying with the terms of this Indemnity we agree to indemnify you, your officers and employees against any and all claims, liabilities, losses, expenses, (including the reasonable fees and disbursements of your counsel) suits or damages resulting therefrom (each of the foregoing is hereinafter referred to as "loss").

You agree to notify us of any such loss within ten (10) business days of your receipt of notification of any such loss.

We represent and warrant that we are duly authorized by all necessary and appropriate corporate action to execute this Indemnity and that this Indemnity is a valid and legally binding obligation of our bank.

Pursuant to a Recall of Funds notification as provided under the U.S. Council on International Banking's Compensation Indemnity and Responses we will return on demand the amount refunded by you or reimburse you on demand for the amount of the adjustment.

You agree to contact your customer immediately to obtain its debit authorization. Upon receiving such debit authorization, our obligations under this Indemnity will cease and you will notify us of your release hereunder. Please make the appropriate response to this Indemnity.

b. The Indemnity may be sent in an abbreviated format when it bears the statement: "We agree to indemnify you according to the Compensation Indemnity and Responses contained in the U.S. Council on International Banking's Guideline for Issuing and Responding to an Indemnity." Such statement will be deemed to incorporate the entire text of the Indemnity set forth above. The following information must also be provided in the abbreviated format:

1. Date of transfer

2. Amount of transfer

3. Method of transfer

4. Payment system identification

   a) Fedwire number

b) CHIPS number

c) S.W.I.F.T. number

d) Check number

e) Account number or name of party to whom payment was originally sent

f) Account number or name of party to be credited

5. By order party

6. Description of action requested (including claim for compensation).

    c. The Indemnity may be sent by using structured format transaction codes established by procedures in the CHIPS Systems and Operations Manual for CHIPS participants to send and receive such indemnities. Such procedures permit the Paying Bank to cause CHIPS to transmit to the receiving bank a CHIPS Service Message that contains either the statement: "We indemnify you under NYCHA or USCIB Compensation Rules as applicable (Ref. No. _____)" or a structured format transaction code established by such Manual for such indemnities. Such CHIPS Service Message will be deemed to incorporate the entire text of the U.S. Council on International Banking Indemnity set forth in its Compensation Rules between a New York Clearing House Association member bank and a USCIB member bank or between two USCIB members banks. The following information must also be provided in the CHIPS Service Message:

1. Identification of the CHIPS payment message by which the transfer was made as follows:

    a. Paying Bank's payment sequence number ("PSN")

    b. Amount of transfer

    c. Date of transfer

2. Identification of the parties (by name or account number or both where available) as follows:

    a. Party to whom payment was originally sent

    b. By order party

    c. Party to whom corrected payment shall be make (if applicable).

    4. Responses. a. When a Receiving Bank determines it will return principal pursuant to an Indemnity, principal should be returned by CHIPS or Fedwire: and the Receiving Bank should notify the Paying Bank as follows: "Returning your (Fedwire #_____), (CHIPS

#_____) (S.W.I.F.T. # _____), or (check #_____) dated for $_____ pursuant to your Indemnity Ref. No. _____ dated _____. (We are forwarding the appropriate compensation.)"

   b. When in reliance on an Indemnity a Receiving Bank determines to adjust the beneficiary's account and account number, the Receiving Bank should notify the Paying Bank as follows: "On (date), we adjusted your (Fedwire #_____), (CHIPS #_____) (S.W.I.F.T. # _____),or (check # _____) to read (beneficiary and amount) pursuant to your Indemnity Ref. No. _____ dated _____. Please forward compensation of $ _____."

   c. When a Receiving Bank determines to take no action on an Indemnity because it contains insufficient information or is not in the standard format, the Receiving Bank should notify the Paying Bank as follows: "Your Indemnity delivered by (S.W.I.F.T., telex, letter) Ref. No. _____ dated _____ for $ _____ covering instructions via (Fedwire # _____). (CHIPS # _____), (S.W.I.F.T. # _____), or (check # _____) dated _____ by order of _____ cannot be acted upon because it contains (Incorrect Format, Incomplete Information, or Inappropriate Transmittal)."

   d. When Receiving Bank in its sole discretion determines not to take action requested by XXX Indemnity, the Receiving Bank shall notify the Paying Bank as follows: "We have determined to take no action pursuant to your Indemnity delivered by (S.W.I.F.T., telex, letter) Ref. No. _____ dated _____ for $ _____ covering instructions via (Fedwire #_____), (CHIPS #_____), (S.W.I.F.T. # _____), or (check # _____) dated _____ by order of _____. (We are treating the matter as an inquiry and are today, (date), seeking debit authorization from our customer. We shall advise you of its response)."

   5. Confirmation. If the Receiving Bank determines to take the action requested by the Indemnity, it shall attempt to procure confirmation of its action from the party whose account was debited. The Receiving Bank shall notify such party as follows: "On (date), we debited your account #_____ for $_____ in reversal of a credit entry dated _____, our Ref. No._____, cutomer Ref. No. _____ by the order of _____ for the order of _____. The paying bank notified us that it had incorrectly instructed us to credit your account. Please confirm to us that you have no objection to our debiting your account to correct said error."

6. Release. After the Receiving Bank has obtained debit authorization from its customer, the Paying Bank is released from its liabilities and obligations under the Indemnity. The Receiving Bank must notify the Paying Bank as follows promptly upon obtaining said debit authorization: "We hereby notify you that you have been released from all obligations and liabilities arising from and in connection with your Indemnity delivered by (S.W.I.F.T., telex letter) Ref. No._____ dated for $_____ covering instructions via (Fedwire # _____), (CHIPS #) (S.W.I.F.T. #_____), or (check #_____) dated _____ by order of _____."

Once the Receiving Bank has received debit authorization from its customer or notifies the Paying Bank that it releases the Paying Bank of its obligations and liabilities arising from and in connection with such Indemnity, the Paying Bank, shall no longer be liable to the Receiving Bank on the Indemnity in connection with any matter related to, or arising from such Indemnity.

7. Recall of Funds. If the beneficiary whose account has been debited by the Receiving Bank pursuant to a request in the Indemnity from a Paying Bank, requests the return of the amount so debited, the Paying Bank must, as the case may be, return, or reimburse the Receiving Bank for such amount upon receipt of the following notice from the Receiving Bank: "Please (return to us or reimburse us) in the amount of $_____ which we refunded to you via (Fedwire #_____) (CHIPS #_____) or (check #_____) (or credited to the account of _____) pursuant to the Indemnity delivered by (S.W.I.F.T., telex, letter) Ref. No._____, dated _____ covering instructions via (Fedwire #_____), (CHIPS _____) (S.W.I.F.T. #_____), or (check # _____) dated _____ by order of _____because our customer has demanded a return of funds.

Chapter 10

Conducting Foreign Exchange Trading (Brokers' Market vs. Direct Market)

Foreign exchange trading is conducted directly, bank-to-bank, or with the help of an intermediary. Until April 1992, the intermediary had always been the foreign exchange broker. Since then, traders have also had the option of using the matching systems, or electronic brokers.

The technological breakthroughs have changed the manner of trading foreign exchange directly as well. The telephone, the communication tool of choice after the breakup of the Bretton Woods Accord and consequent shift from fixed rates to free-floating rates, has been replaced by dealing systems, which are computer terminals linking the world of finance. These systems have almost entirely replaced phone trading in the larger dealing rooms. Currently, brokered trading and direct dealing are complementary methods.

Market Share

About a third of the foreign exchange deals are executed through the brokers' market. Figure 10.1 displays the share of trades executed through brokers and dealing systems in the major trading centers.

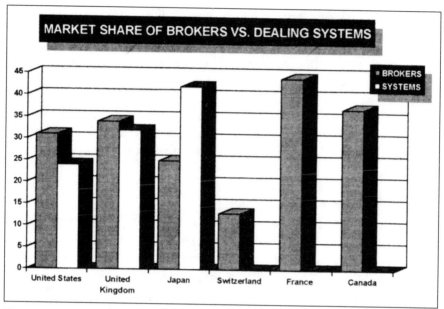

Figure 10.1. Share of the foreign exchange market turnover executed through brokers and dealing systems (in percentages) as of April 1992 in the major foreign exchange markets. Matching systems were introduced in April 1992. (*Source: Bank for International Settlements, "Central Bank Survey of Foreign Exchange Market Activity in April 1992"*)

The Brokers' Market

Role of Currency Brokers

First, I would like to emphasize the difference between an equity brokerage house and a foreign exchange brokerage house. The equity brokerage houses trade for both customers and themselves. They service both individuals and institutions. These institutions may be mutual funds, other investment banks, manufacturing companies, etc.

Foreign exchange brokers *do not take positions* for themselves and only *service banks*. Their roles are:

1. bringing together buyers and sellers in the market,

2. optimizing the price they show to their customers, and

3. quickly, accurately and faithfully executing the traders' orders.

Since they neither assume financial responsibility nor trade for themselves, foreign exchange brokers are not subject to any regulatory requirements per se. Their primary customers are commercial and investment banks and trading firms.

Foreign exchange brokers have an international clientele, as they operate simultaneously in all the major financial centers. Only a fraction of their activity takes place on the dealing systems. The majority of their business is executed via phone. The phone lines between brokers and banks are dedicated, or direct, and are usually installed free of charge by the broker. This is a direct result of the competition from both the other brokers and the dealing systems. A direct phone line means that neither the bank nor the broker has to dial any phone number. They just have to pick up the phone and trade. These dedicated phone lines can only be used by the broker and the individual bank into which they were installed.

Setup

A major foreign exchange brokerage house has direct lines to hundreds of banks around the world. Each of these large houses has a series of departments, each servicing a single major currency or a group of exotic currencies. In addition to foreign exchange, some brokerage houses provide their services for money market instruments as well. Within each department, there are individual brokers, each servicing up to 12 banks. Some brokers may service up to 20 customers, but more than 12 banks is unusual. It is a taxing endeavor, as the brokers not only have to identify which bank called, but also must compete with each other for the prices.

Most of the foreign exchange is executed through an *open box* system, which consists of a microphone in front of the broker which transmits continuously everything he says down the direct phone lines to the speaker boxes in the banks. This way, all banks can hear all the deals being executed. Because of the open box system employed by brokers, a trader is able to hear all prices quoted, whether the bid was hit or the offer taken, and the following price. What the trader will not be able to hear is the amounts on particular bids and offers and the names of the banks showing the prices. *Prices are anonymous.* A very important characteristic of the brokers' market is the anonymity of the banks that are trading in the market. This characteristic ensures the market's efficiency, as all banks have a fair chance to trade.

The open box is a tool used by traders not only to hear the running prices, but also for trading support. Since there are many banks listening to the trading activity in each of the brokerage firms that deal in a specific currency, a trader can create some "trading noise" in the market, by hitting consecutive prices in one broker or by simultaneously dealing with several different brokers.

Characteristics of the Currency Brokers' Price

Let's see how brokers show their customers the prices made by other customers. The broker requests either two-way (bid and offer) prices or one-way (bid or offer) prices from his or her customers. Traders show different prices because they "read" the market differently, have different expectations and different interests. When having more than one price on one or both sides, the broker will automatically optimize the price. In other words, the broker will always show the highest bid and the lowest offer. Therefore, the market will have access to the narrowest spread in the market.

For example, a broker on the spot USD/DEM desk receives the following prices from different banks:

Bank	Bid	Offer
Nonaggresiva	1.7010	1.7020
Bidda	1.7012	1.7022
Offerta	1.7011	1.7017
Taurus	1.7012	1.7019
Notinterestida	1.7010	—
Southoriented	1.7007	1.7017
Uponthefence	—	1.7020

The highest bid is 1.7012, shown by banks Bidda and Taurus, and the lowest offer is 1.7017, shown by banks Offerta and Southoriented. Consequently, the *optimized price* is 1.7012–1.7017.

Once the broker announces the price, all the other prices, the runners-up, are automatically off, and the broker will not use these regardless of the direction of the market—unless the original trader or traders renew their prices.

As you can also notice in the previous example, traders may only show one side of the price. This is characteristic only to the brokers market, as one-sided prices are not generally quoted in the direct market. This dealing approach is less aggressive and from the trader's point of view, this option is attractive, as it involves less risk.

Therefore, one of the advantages of trading in the brokers market is that traders have more trading options than in the direct market.

Let's take a closer look at these options by using the same broker's spot price as above: USD/DEM 1.7012–1.7017. When attempting to buy USD/DEM before it rallies, a trader has three alternatives:

1. *Take the offer at 1.7017.* This is identical to the alternative in the direct market. This option provides *the highest degree of certainty* for executing the deal. Brokers' prices are in competition with the interbank's prices, if they both show an identical price. The broker's advantage is the ready availability, which is vital in a fast market. The downside is that there is no guarantee that the full amount asked by the trader will be executed.

For instance, a trader trying to buy USD/DEM 10,000,000 from the broker may only be able to buy USD/DEM 6,000,000, the only amount that the broker had in the offer at that moment.

Although brokers charge commissions, traders are highly unlikely to miss a deal because of fee considerations. It is much more important to enter a profitable deal or to timely cut a losing position than to miss the opportunity in order to avoid a broker's commission.

Brokers charge a commission for their services, which is equally paid by the buyer and the seller. This helps to ensure the impartiality of the broker. Brokerage is paid per million of US dollars, or British pounds, Australian dollars, etc. These fees are negotiated on an individual basis by the bank and the brokerage firm. They start at $8 per million of foreign currency.

Taking the offer is an aggressive approach and the trader will have to deal on the price shown to him or her. The cost consists of the spread between the bid and the offer, but there is no commission to pay when dealing direct.

2. *Join the Bid at 1.7012.* This alternative provides *the least certainty* of having the deal executed. If you join a bid, you will have to have your deal executed behind previous bids. Brokers use the prices *on first come, first served basis.* In other words, joining the bid is equivalent to joining an invisible queue in the attempt to buy US dollars against Deutsche marks. The trader does not know who is at the front of the queue or how many millions of dollars are posted in the particular bid. Brokers only quote the running price, not the amount. Therefore, it is impossible for a trader to know the size of the bid (or offer, for that matter). It may be an uncertain undertaking, waiting for someone to hit your bid for the exact number of dollars that you want to buy.

Joining the bid is the most defensive approach, but provides a price cost advantage. If your bid is hit, and the USD/DEM does indeed go up as you expected, the profit will be higher by the spread between the bid and the offer, i.e., 5 pips.

3. *Improve the bid, anywhere between 1.7013 and 1.7016, in our example.* This middle-of-the-road alternative has several advantages. By marginally improving (raising) the bid, the trader can ensure that he has the best bid. Anyone joining the bid will not know the size of the bid and will just have to wait to have his order executed in turn.

Although a defensive tool, improving the bid provides *more certainty* than joining the bid. Generally speaking, the more a trader improves the bid, the better the chances of having it dealt on.

The opposite is true if the trader were to sell USD/DEM, on expectations of poor economic data:

1. *Hit the bid* at 1.7012
2. *Join the offer* at 1.7017
3. *Improve the offer* by lowering the offer between 1.7016 and 1.7013

Price anonymity is an important characteristic of the brokers' market. Let's just assume for a second that the market is passing through a stagnant period that is not rich in fundamental or technical signals. Fundamental and technical analyses are used for forecasting the future direction of the currency. A trader might test the market by hitting a bid for a small amount to see if there is any reaction. If he knew there was a large amount in the bid, the trader would have done just the opposite, choosing the path of the least resistance.

Sticking with the spot USD/DEM example, let's add some US dollar amounts to the previous bids and offers.

Bank		Bid	Offer	
Nonaggresiva	1.7010	$5,000,000	1.7020	$20,000,000
Bidda	1.7012	$40,000,000	1.7022	$5,000,000
Offerta	1.7011	$5,000,000	1.7017	$3,000,000
Taurus	1.7012	$150,000,000	1.7019	$3,500,000
Noninterestida	1.7010	$15,000,000	—	0
Southoriented	1.7007	$20,000,000	1.7017	$2,000,000
Uponthefence	—	0	1.7020	$5,000,000
BID	1.7012	$ 190,000,000	OFFER 1.7017	$ 5,000,000

Although prices are almost always anonymous, brokers will state the amounts on a price in some specific instances:

• When the size of the bid or offer is less than the usual marketable amount of USD 5,000,000. The broker will say "on small" or "on tiny" or specify the amount, especially if it an odd amount.

• When a customer expressly asks the broker to look around for a specific amount, most likely late in the afternoon, after 3:00 PM in the New York market.

Among traders, a bank name may have special significance. When the name of the party showing a price belongs to one of the aggressive market makers, this bit of information may be construed as a signal to take their side.

Again, though there are some exceptions, anonymity provides market efficiency by providing each player a fair trading opportunity, and it is an important part of the brokers' approach to the market.

Brokers' Switches

Since prices are anonymous, traders cannot know who is the counterparty. Although a deal is done, names will not be accepted if the banks do not have sufficient credit lines to each other or if there is any kind of dispute between the banks. In this situation, it is the responsibility of the broker to switch, or wash, that name. The broker will look for a third party which can deal with both the organizations and is willing to execute two artificial trades by buying from one and selling to the other at the same price.

Brokers cannot be forced into taking a principal's role if the name switch takes longer than anticipated.

Example:

In the brokers market, Bank Ichisan buys USD/JPY 10,000,000 at 150.00 from Bank Niisan. The two banks cannot accept each other's names. The broker calls on Bank Sansan, which has lines of credit with both Bank Ichisan and Bank Niisan. Bank Sansan will sell USD/JPY 10,000,000 to Bank Ichisan at 150.00 and it will also buy USD/JPY 10,000,000 from Bank Niisan at 150.00. Bank Sansan, in effect, bought and sold the same amount of USD/JPY at the same rate, with no bearing on its P&L. The original deal was a good deal and the only thing that changed was the name of the counterparty.

Switching Pips

Switching pips is a peculiar type of situation which may, theoretically, lead brokers to taking minor positions. At times, due to the turbulence in the market, price liquidity decreases, while demand increases. This imbalance creates additional trading tension.

Brokers scramble to bring fresh prices to the market and, due to the rapid trading activity, a trader who wanted to buy, for instance, USD/DEM at 1.7017, may end up buying at 1.7019. The situation may occur because of the difference between supply and demand. Back tracking to our example of the brokers' price structure, you can see that the amount of USD/DEM in the 1.7017 offer side is minuscule. Once that happens, it is likely that the selling trader will quickly demand that the 1.7019 offer be shown. But if the offer is not properly shown by the broker, or not properly understood by the buying trader, the buyer may ask for compensation— from the broker—for the two pips on each of the US$ millions traded.

Since the broker cannot have a position, but has to maintain the business relation with the specific bank, the broker must either look for a similar mistake on the opposite side or, more realistically, ask a friendly trader for a "pips" loan until that error occurs again. The whole logic in this case is flawed and unbalanced on the trader's side because it is common knowledge that brokers cannot enter trading positions. It is rather difficult to be sure whether the broker is just trying to accommodate the difficult trader or creating some financial position for personal gain.

The Federal Reserve attempted to solve this Catch-22 situation for brokers. On August 1, 1990, the Reserve advised both brokers and traders to cease the "pips" borrowing activity. This should have been an example of "fences making good neighbors" meant to clarify the brokers' professional boundaries and, therefore, to protect them against any undue pressure from the traders.

In reality, exceptions may occur.

Liquidity

Another advantage of the brokers market is that brokers provide a broader selection of banks to their customers. This adds to the price liquidity. For example, the dealing room of an American bank wants to trade in the afternoon. But, because of the time differences, both European and Asian banks are not trading at the same time as the American banks. However, some European and Asian banks have overnight desks which operate at limited capacity. Their primary function, however, is to execute orders and not to make markets. So, their orders are usually placed with brokers, who can deal with the American banks. And this adds to the liquidity of the market.

Lack of Trading Reciprocity

Dealing with brokers has other advantages, especially for smaller banks. One of these is the fact that direct trading is based on the idea of reciprocity. So, if Banque Deuxieme calls Banque Premiere, then Banque Premiere will call back Banque Deuxieme but, Banque Deuxieme may not like to be called back, especially if Banque Deuxieme is a smaller bank with a limited exposure to foreign exchange, and Banque Premiere is a major market maker. A bank will be able to trade with fewer dealers if it trades primarily through the brokers' market.

For smaller banks, using the brokers' market may also translate to savings on personnel, because the cost of training and maintaining a staff qualified to handle a constant flow of calls to and from other banks can be quite high.

Ethics

The structure of the price—the amounts of currency on either side of the price—is very important information. However, the only party having access to this information is the broker. Theoretically, a broker could be the best trader, knowing the short term supply and demand on each of the major currencies. One must remember, however, that foreign exchange brokers always maintain roles of impartial intermediaries and never take positions for themselves.

Brokerage firms carefully enforce this rule in order to maintain their reputation with their clients. A broker engaging in any type of unethical activity runs the risk that traders will simply stop trading with him. Brokers, like the rest of the foreign exchange participants, observe high standards of professionalism and ethics.

Other Services

In order to provide a better service under the pressure of increasing competition, brokers offer additional services, such as posting their rates for the major currencies on different monitors, quoting outside the unofficially "official" trading hours of 8:30 AM EDT to 3:00 PM EDT, quoting exotic currencies and even providing elements of technical analysis. For instance, Noonan, Astley & Pearce, Inc. posts exchange rates on Telerate, on pages 311 and 313 (Figure 10.2).

Potential Disadvantages

Despite all their ordinary and extraordinary efforts, brokers are not always able to provide either a two-way or a one-sided price. In periods of high price volatility, banks may not wish to take on extra risk by showing either a full or even a partial price in the brokers market. Therefore, there are times when brokers will not be able to provide prices.

Broker-Trader Relationship

Brokers and traders work very closely together. A broker will usually service the same bank lines for a long time, learning each trader's idiosyncrasies; therefore, a broker is able to customize his service.

Major Foreign Exchange Brokers

The major foreign exchange brokers are:

Noonan, Astley & Pearce, Inc.

Harlow Meyer Savage Inc.

Lasser-Marshall

Tullet & Tokyo Forex Inc.

Bierbaum Martin

```
          15:08 EST   ITAL.LIRA    D/MARK    CANADIAN  $    YEN      SWISS FRANC
          15:04 EDT   15:04 EDT   15:06 EDT   17:25 EDT   14:46 EDT   14:17 EDT

SPOT    1.4845-55    1700.00-1.0 1.7366-71     0.0-.0    112.57-62   1.4850-60

                     97700 97775
T/N     1.25-1.1       54-55    1.65-1.7      0.0-0.0    0.17-0.16   0.55-0.65
S/N     1.15-1.05      80-81    1.66-1.69     0.0-0.0    0.20-0.18   0.55-0.65
1WK     7.40-7        186-187.8  11-11.2      0.0-0.0    1.50-1.4    3.60-4
1MO     31-30         745-760   45.50-46      0.0-0.0    8.40-8.2   14.25-14.75
2MO     52-50        1380-1400    77-78       0.0-0.0   20.70-20.4  21.50-22.5
3MO     73-71        2075-2100  108.5-109.5   0.0-0.0   35.50-35     25-28
4MO     95-93        2690-2740   135-137      0.0-0.0    52-51       26-29
6MO     127-123      3835-3875   181-183      0.0-0.0    91-90       27-30
9MO     167-159      5225-5325   221-224      0.0-0.0   156-153       8-12
1YR     190-180      6525-6625   231-235      0.0-0.0   230-228     -27--22

TELERATE MATRIX                                                      PAGE 313
        9:55 EDT


                      [ NOONAN, ASTLEY & PEARCE INC - NJ]      08/03 08:05  313
        ! AUSTRALIA !NEW ZEALAND! HONG KONG ! SINGAPORE ! MALAYSIA !   SPOTS    !
        :  8:05 EDT :  8:05 EDT :  8:05 EDT :  8:05 EDT :  8:05 EDT :  8:05 EDT :
        !  DOLLAR   !  DOLLAR   !  DOLLAR   !  DOLLAR   !  RINGGIT  !    INDIA   !
SPOT   ;0.6885 -90  ;0.5517 -24 ;7.7535 -45 ;1.6138 -48 ;2.5600 -10 ; .0318 -319:
T/N    :    4-2     :    4-2    :    -      :    -      :    -      ! ECU-DEM    !
S/N    :    -       :    -      :    -      :    -      :    -      : 1.9100-20  :
1WK    :    -       :    -      :    -      :    -      :    -      !  MEXICO    !
1MO    :  9.9-9.2   :   12-9    :    -      :    -      :    -      :3.1190-10   :
2MO    : 17.7-16.7  :   22-17   :    -      :    -      :    -      ! VENEZUELA  !
3MO    : 25.7-24.2  :   33-27   :    -      :    -      :    -      : 90.26-36   !
6MO    : 44.5-42.5  :   59-52   :    -      :    -      :    -      :            :
1YR    :   76-71    '  115-100  '    -      '    -      '    -      '            '
       !            !           !           :           :           :           :
       :            :           :           :           :           :           :
       ;            ;           ;           ;           ;           ;           ;
       [  SEE PAGES 311, 312, AND 307 FOR OTHER CURRENCIES AND CROSS RATES   ]'
```

Figure 10.2. Exchange rates are posted by Noonan, Astley & Pearce, Inc. on Telerate on pages 311 and 313. In addition to the spot rates, theses pages also offer the forward spreads for the standard periods (*Source: Telerate®. Reprinted by permission.© 1993 Dow Jones Telerate, Inc.*)

Intercontinental Exchange Partners

Prebon Yamane USA, Inc.

Transforex

Direct Dealing

Trading Reciprocity

Direct dealing is an aggressive approach. It is based on trading reciprocity. A market maker—the bank making or quoting a price—expects the bank that is calling to reciprocate with respect to making a price when called upon.

Making a price doesn't mean making just any price. What a trader expects, and is expected to provide in turn, is a fast quote with a tight spread between the bid and the offer. Reciprocity requires banks to develop market relationships. These relationships are very important when the caller needs extra service, such as a quote outside the regular trading time (which in the New York market is 8:30 AM EDT to 3:00 PM EDT), a faster quote in an illiquid market, or a price on an odd amount.

There are some exceptions to full reciprocity, such as the case where banks may reach an understanding to quote each other a handful of different currencies. This situation occurs when smaller banks specialize in one or two currencies, but may call on an irregular basis for prices in other currencies.

Characteristics of the Interbank Currency Price

Unlike the brokers market, quotes in the interbank market are always two-way prices.

When making a market, a bank will quote, or show, only a bid and an offer, known as a spread, to the other bank. Just like the broker, the market maker will not quote the big figure of the exchange rate, which is assumed to be known by all the players. For example, the rate of 1.6510–15 will be quoted as 10–15.

The similarity stops here. The calling bank will only have the option of hitting the bid or taking the offer of the price being quoted. The alternatives available in the brokers market of joining or improving one of the price's sides are no longer available. The price cannot be negotiated. The calling party must decide quickly whether to trade on the price or not. Postponing the answer past 20 seconds or so usually triggers the price annulment.

Since the price quoted by a single bank may not be negotiated, a trader looking to improve the price only has the option of increasing the pool of prices by calling several banks simultaneously or in close sequence and selecting the best price.

If, for instance, a trader from Bank Aggresiva is looking to buy USD/DEM in the direct market, then the trader will call out, mentioning the currency and the amount needed, and get the following prices:

Bank	Bid	Offer
Nonaggresiva	1.7010	1.7020
Bidda	1.7012	1.7022
Offerta	1.7011	1.7017
Taurus	1.7012	1.7019
Supersouth	1.7010	1.7015

The cheapest or lowest offer is quoted by Bank Supersouth at 1.7015 and the trader from Bank Aggresiva will buy USD/DEM at this price.

In a fast market, direct trading may be the only option in getting a price, as the brokers may be bypassed by risk-averse traders. The quoting banks, under these conditions, may be slower than their customary zapping speed, and also show wider spreads than usual. Yet, availability may replace price quality as the traders' top priority.

Discretion

Direct dealing provides more trading discretion, as compared to the brokers market. Sometimes traders take advantage of this characteristic. When a bank needs to trade a large amount of currency quickly, it may simultaneously call an extensive number of banks and hit all or the majority of their prices in rapid succession. Although not endorsed by all the participants, this strategy of lining up banks is an accepted reality of the market.

The downside of direct trading is that it may interfere with the individual trading flows. Let's say that a trader expects the USD/JPY to go up and consequently, that trader buys USD/JPY 10,000,000. Soon, another trader calls directly, asks for a price in USD/JPY and buys USD/JPY 10,000,000 from the first trader. Immediately after, the USD/JPY suddenly rallies, but the first trader does not have the long USD/JPY anymore. Therefore, the trader must develop defensive trading skills.

In order to be able to accurately pick up all the direct calls and call out to trade, a trading desk needs experienced and reliable trading support.

How the Business Is Executed

Direct dealing used to be conducted mostly on the phone. The balance was executed by telex. Phone dealing was error prone and slow. Most traders or their assistants could only make one phone deal at a time, rarely two. When the phone rang, the identity of the caller and the reason for calling would not be known. Moreover, despite the rather limited vocabulary used by traders, communications errors occurred often, due to the noisy and tense trading environment. Dealing errors were difficult to prove and even more difficult to settle. The unofficial working policy was to equally share the resulting cost of the error.

In order to increase the dealing safety, most banks tapped the phone lines on which the trading was conducted. This measure was helpful in recording all the transaction details and enabling the dealers to fairly allocate the responsibility of the error. But tape recorders were unable to prevent the trading errors.

Direct dealing was forever changed in the mid-1980s by the introduction of the dealing systems.

Dealing Systems

Dealing systems are on-line computers which link the contributing banks around the world on a one-on-one basis. This type of service is currently provided by Reuters (see Figure 10.3) and Quotron (see Figure 10.4).

The performance of the dealing systems is characterized by speed, reliability and safety.

Speed

The receiving bank is able to see on its monitor what bank is calling and for what amount. This feature is not only convenient, it also enhances speed, as the call will be picked up by the specific currency trader, rather than randomly.

A trader is able to have up to four simultaneous conversations on Reuters Dealing 2000-2 system, and up to six conversations on Quotron F/X Trader. That's quite a nice departure from struggling to handle two phone dealings in the best case. The deals are clearly posted on the screen. Switching among the calls consists of the simple stroke of a key on the keyboard.

Accessing a bank through a dealing system is much faster than making a phone call, even if using a speed dialer. And the simultaneous accessing

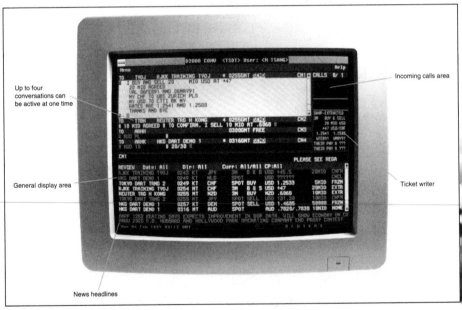

Figure 10.3.   The Reuters Dealing 2000 system perfectly exemplifies the operating complexity available to traders. The screen is divided into five major windows: conversation, monitor, ticket writer, incoming calls area and news headlines. When the matching system is added, more windows are available. Each system operator may contact and trade with four counterparties simultaneously. (*Courtesy of Reuters*)

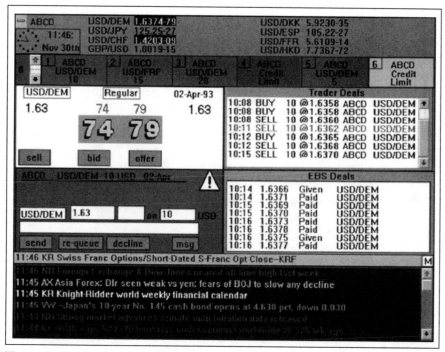

Figure 10.4. The Quotron F/X Trader dealing system. (*Courtesy of Quotron Systems, Inc.*)

of four banks may require only a single key stroke . Immediately following the trade execution, further information regarding value dates, payment and receiving and even greetings may be exchanged (see Figure 10.5).

Instead of typing all this information, useful time is saved by the use of preset keys. Executing four trades totaling USD 40 million or more in about 30 seconds is common among foreign exchange traders. That's fast!

Reliability

Dealing systems are an indispensable trading tool, continuously improved in order to offer maximum support to the dealer's main function: trading. The software is very reliable in picking up the big figure of the exchange rates and the standard value dates. In addition, it is extremely precise and fast in contacting the other parties, switching among conversations and accessing the data base.

Safety

The trader is in continuous visual contact with the information exchanged on the monitor. It is easier to see than hear this information, especially when switching among the conversations.

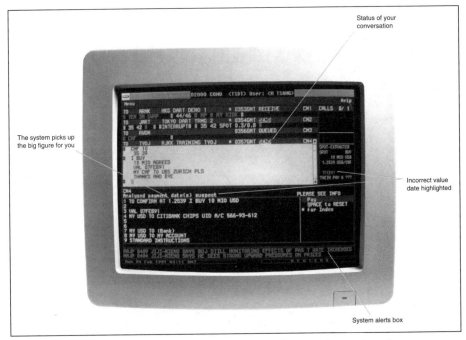

Figure 10.5. The Reuters Dealing 2000 system . Conversation and trading are user-friendly. (*Courtesy of Reuters*)

Traders only use the last two digits of the bid and offer. When confirming, however, all the information must be fully expressed. The software picks up the big figure, not only saving time but also ensuring that typing errors do not occur.

Since all the payment and receiving information is stored in the memory, the trader or assistant is precluded from inadvertently sending the wrong instructions.

At the end of the conversation, all the details will be saved and stored in the data base, ready to be conveniently retrieved any time. If an error still managed to occur, it is significantly faster and easier to retrieve the details from a dealing system than from a tape recorder (see Figure 10.6).

Immediately following the end of communication, the entire trade or conversation will be printed on at least one printer. Dealing tickets may be printed or, as is increasingly the case, electronically generated in paperless systems (see Figure 10.7).

Most banks use a combination of brokers and direct dealing systems. They both reach the same banks, but not the same parties, because corporations, for instance, cannot deal in the brokers market. Traders develop personal relationships with both brokers and traders in the markets, but select their trading medium based on price quality, not personal feelings. The market share between dealing systems and brokers is fluctuating based on the market conditions. Fast market conditions are beneficial to dealing systems, whereas regular market conditions are more beneficial to brokers.

Matching Systems

The biggest competition to brokers is being raised by the introduction of the electronic matching systems, which are, in effect, electronic brokers. Unlike the dealing systems, where the trading is not anonymous and is conducted on a one-on-one basis, the matching systems are anonymous and individual traders deal against the rest of the market, similar to the brokers market.

Unlike the brokers market, there are no individuals to bring the prices to the market and the liquidity may be limited at times. Several incentive programs, which lower the commissions, are geared to increasing the liquidity nearer to that of the dealing systems.

The matching systems are better suited for trading smaller amounts, as brokers generally shy away from amounts under US$3 million.

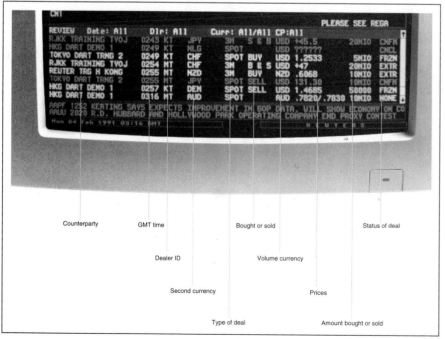

Figure 10.6. The Reuters Dealing 2000-1 system. (*Courtesy of Reuters*)

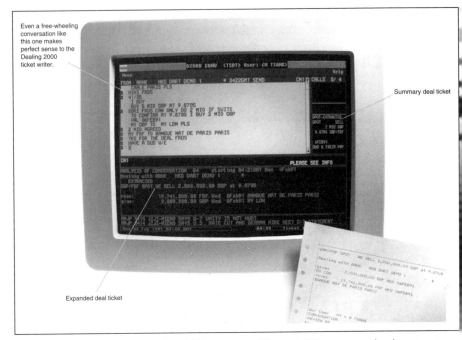

Figure 10.7. The Reuters Dealing 2000-1 system. The end of the conversation is automatically followed by a printout of the entire conversation. (*Courtesy of Reuters*)

The dealing systems' characteristics of speed, reliability and safety are replicated in the matching systems. In addition, credit lines are automatically managed by the systems. Traders input the total credit line for each counterparty. When the credit line has been reached, the system automatically disallows dealing with the particular party by displaying "credit restrictions." As soon as the credit line is restored, the system allows the party to deal again.

The matching systems are user friendly and their acceptance among traders is increasing. The first matching system, *Dealing 2000-2*™, was introduced by Reuters in April 1992 (see Figure 10.8). In 1993, two new matching systems were introduced by MINEX and EBS. *MINEX*™ *Global Electronic Matching System* (see Figure 10.9) was developed by joint venture between the MINEX Corporation and Dow Jones/Telerate in 1992. The MINEX Corporation was formed in 1991 by the Tokyo Forex Company and the Kokusai Denshin Denwa Company (KDD). The *EBS Dealing System* (see Figure 10.4) was developed by the EBS Partners: ABN-AMRO, Bank of America, Barclays Bank, Chemical Bank, Citibank, Credit Suisse, J. P. Morgan, Lehman Brothers, Midland Bank, National Westminster Bank,

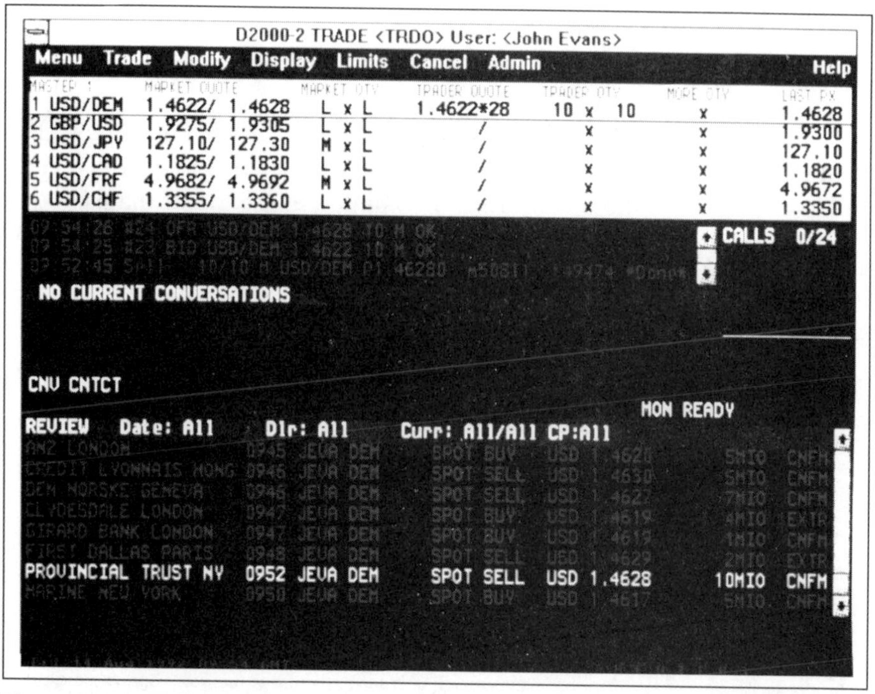

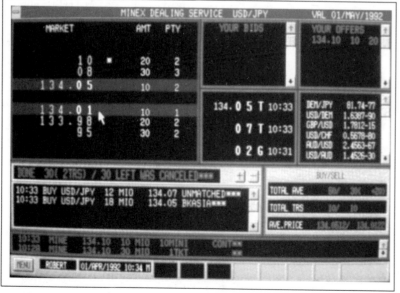

Figure 10.8. The Reuters Dealing 2000-1 and Dealing 2000-2 shared display. (*Courtesy of Reuters*)

Figure 10.9. The MINEX matching system. (*Source: Telerate® Reprinted by permission.© 1993 Dow Jones Telerate, Inc.*)

Quotron Foreign Exchange, Swiss Bank Corporation and Union Bank of Switzerland. Since 1994, the system was acquired by Reuters.

Reuters Dealing 2000-2™. Dealing 2000-2™ is an anonymous, electronic matching system service for spot foreign exchange trading. The system is displayed on the regular Reuters monitor, at the top of the page (see Figure 10.10). This window shows the optimal market price, along with the trader's own one- or two-way price in the major currencies against the dol-

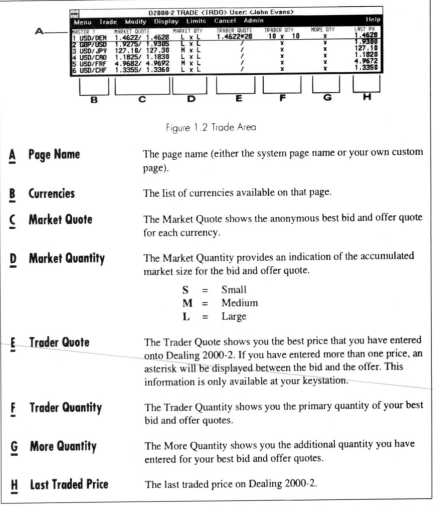

Figure 1.2 Trade Area

A Page Name   The page name (either the system page name or your own custom page).

B Currencies   The list of currencies available on that page.

C Market Quote   The Market Quote shows the anonymous best bid and offer quote for each currency.

D Market Quantity   The Market Quantity provides an indication of the accumulated market size for the bid and offer quote.

                            S = Small
                            M = Medium
                            L = Large

E Trader Quote   The Trader Quote shows you the best price that you have entered onto Dealing 2000-2. If you have entered more than one price, an asterisk will be displayed between the bid and the offer. This information is only available at your keystation.

F Trader Quantity   The Trader Quantity shows you the primary quantity of your best bid and offer quotes.

G More Quantity   The More Quantity shows you the additional quantity you have entered for your best bid and offer quotes.

H Last Traded Price   The last traded price on Dealing 2000-2.

Figure 10.10.   The trade area of the Reuters Dealing 2000-2 matching system. (*Courtesy of Reuters*)

lar and against each other (see Figure 10.10). The additional windows necessary for the matching system do not impede on either the conversation or monitor modes.

MINEX^{TM} Global Electronic Matching System. MINEX is another automated matching system for spot foreign exchange. The service offers prices in the major currencies against the dollar and against each other (see Figure 10.11). In addition to the standard characteristics of speed, reliability and safety, the system provides an audio feature which replicates the voice boxes used by brokers to announce the running prices.

EBS. EBS is another electronic platform for anonymous spot trading. EBS and Quotron F/x Trader are integrated on the same screen in order to offer the trader the maximum of choices in a user-friendly environment (see Figure 10.4).

In the interbank market, traders deal directly on the dealing systems and less frequently on the phone, or through the brokers and the matching

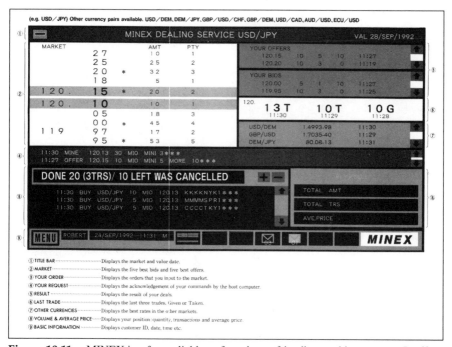

Figure 10.11. MINEX is a fast, reliable, safe and user-friendly matching system . It offers prices in the major currencies pairs, including the major crosses. (*Source: Telerate*® *Reprinted by permission.* © *1993 Dow Jones Telerate, Inc.*)

systems in a complementary fashion. Traders take advantage of the large and sophisticated brokers market, the amount of certainty in direct dealing and the electronic sophistication of the matching systems. Corporations do not use matching systems.

Few players use only one trading venue. The increased competition among these venues brings further efficiency to the foreign exchange markets. Although important, the differences in commissions between brokers and dealing systems are secondary, as traders focus on the best or fastest price available.

Chapter 11

The Spot Market

Currency spot trading is the most popular foreign currency instrument around the world, making up 48 percent of the total activity (see Figure 11.1). The fast-paced spot market is not for the faint hearted, as it features high volatility and quick profits (and losses). This chapter examines how spot trading works and shows how savvy traders stay on top of this exciting market.

The Foreign Currency Spot Marketplace

A spot deal consists of a bilateral contract between a party delivering a specified amount of a given currency against receiving a specified amount of another currency from a second counterparty, based on an agreed exchange rate, within two business days of the deal date. The exception is the Canadian dollar, in which the spot delivery is executed next business day, due to Canada's geographical proximity to the United States.

It is important to notice that the concept of "spot" does not mean that the currency exchange occurs the same business day the deal is executed. Currency trades which require same day delivery are called *cash* transactions. The two-day spot delivery for currencies was developed long before

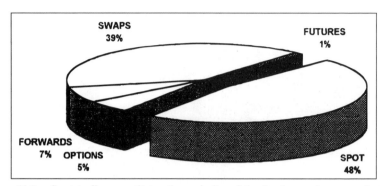

Figure 11.1. Spot trading constitutes the majority of the foreign exchange markets—48 percent. (*Source: Bank for International Settlements, "Central Bank Survey of Foreign Exchange Activity in April 1992"*)

the technological breakthroughs in information processing. This time period was necessary to check out all transactions' details among counterparties. Although technologically feasible, the contemporary markets did not find it necessary to reduce the time to make the payments. Human errors still occur and they need to be fixed before delivery. When currency deliveries are made to the wrong party, fines are applied.

Traders check out all daily transactions executed through brokers at the end of each day, and the back office compares all trading details against printed records when possible. Moreover, the netting agreements developed in the major trading centers such as New York, eliminate the need for executing payments for each individual trade. A single net payment is made at the end of the day to another counterparty. Netting agreements are discussed in detail in Chapter 9. These processes eliminate the possibility of any payments before the end of the day. Occasionally, brokers pass wrong names. The majority of the name errors are generally fixed by the end of the day. However, some counterparty names will only be changed the next business day. Consequently, for all practical purposes, payments could not be executed the same day.

In terms of volume, currencies around the world are traded mostly against the US dollar (40 percent), as the US dollar is the currency of reference. The US dollar's role of currency of reference reflects the United States' economic and political leading position in the international arena. As shown in Figure 11.2, the other major currencies are the Deutsche mark, which is involved in 30 percent of spot foreign exchange volume, followed by the Japanese yen (11 percent), the British pound (8 percent) and the Swiss franc (5 percent). Other currencies with significant spot market shares are the French franc (2 percent), the European Currency Unit (2 percent)

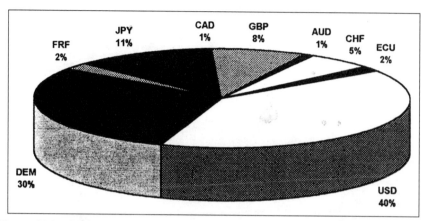

Figure 11.2. Daily market turnover by currency in millions of US dollars. (*Source: Bank for International Settlements, "Central Bank Survey of Foreign Exchange Activity in April 1992"*)

and the Australian dollar (1 percent). These figures refer to trading against all currencies.

In addition, a significant share of trading also takes place in the currencies crosses, a non-dollar instrument, where foreign currencies are quoted against other foreign currencies, such as Deutsche marks against Japanese yen.

There are good reasons for the popularity of the currency spot trading. Profits (or losses) are realized quickly in the spot market, due to the market volatility. In addition, since the spot deals mature in only two business days, the time exposure to credit risk is limited. Turnover in the spot market has been increasing dramatically thanks to the combination of inherent profitability and reduced credit risk. In the United States market, for instance, the daily spot turnover increased from US$81 billion in 1989 to US$95 billion in 1992, according to the Federal Reserve Bank of New York's Central Bank Survey of Foreign Exchange Activity in April 1992 (see Figure 11.3).

The spot market is characterized by high liquidity and high volatility. On an active trading day (24 hours), the US dollar/Deutsche mark exchange rate may change its value 18,000 times (see Figure 11.4). How quickly does the exchange rate move? There is no easy answer, and trying to determine an average time is not too helpful. An exchange rate may "fly" 200 pips in a matter of seconds if the market gets wind of a significant event. For example, when the United Kingdom announced its joining of the Exchange Rate Mechanism in September 1990, there were no spot prices in the British

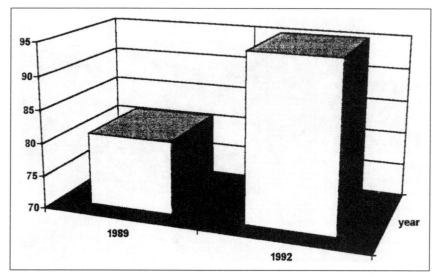

Figure 11.3. Daily market turnover in the United States spot market increased from US $81 billion in 1989 to US$95 billion in 1992. (*Source: Bank for International Settlements, "Central Bank Survey of Foreign Exchange Activity in April 1992"*)

pound for over 30 minutes. But the first quotes had extraordinary wide spreads, between 50 and 100 pips, rather than customary 5 to 10 pips.

On the other hand, the exchange rate may remain quite static for extended periods of time, even in excess of an hour, when one market is almost finished trading and waiting for the next market to take over. This is a common occurrence toward the end of the New York trading day. Since California failed in the late 1980s to provide the link between the New York and Tokyo markets, there is a technical trading gap between around 4:30 PM and 6:00 PM EDT. In the New York market, the majority of transactions occur between 8:00 AM and 12:00 PM, when the New York and the European markets overlap. The activity drops sharply in the afternoon, over 50 percent in fact, when New York loses the international trading support (see Figure 11.5). The overnight trading is limited, as only very few banks have overnight desks. Most of the banks send their overnight orders to branches or other banks which operate in the active time zones.

Typical Spot Trades

In the spot market, any amount may be traded, odd or even, denominated in US dollars, or foreign currency. However, the standard tends to be USD 10,000,000. Unless otherwise specified, a call for spot USD/DEM will be interpreted as for USD/DEM 10,000,000. If the caller tries to execute a dif-

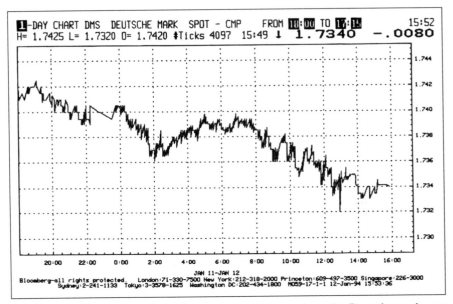

1-DAY CHART DMS DEUTSCHE MARK SPOT - CMP   FROM ▓:▓ TO ▓:▓   15:52
H= 1.7425 L= 1.7320 O= 1.7420 ‡Ticks 4097 15:49 ↓ **1.7340   -.0080**

Figure 11.4. The exchange rate in a major currency, such as the Deutsche mark, may change up to 18,000 times on an active trading day. (*Courtesy of Bloomberg*)

ferent amount, even if it is smaller, the deal may be fully canceled by the market maker. Therefore, the caller must make sure to mention beforehand the amount which he or she wants to trade, if it differs from the standard.

Not all players trade USD 10,000,000. Other typical amounts traded, beside the US$10 million lots are US$5 and US$3 million lots.

The average deal size has increased in the broker market from US$6 million in 1989, to US$7 million in 1992, according to the Federal Reserve Bank of New York's Central Bank Survey of Foreign Exchange Activity in April 1992 (see Figure 11.6).

The Major Players

The major players in the spot market are naturally the commercial banks and the investment banks, followed by hedge funds and corporate customers (see Figure 11.7). In the interbank market, the majority of the deals are international, reflecting the worldwide exchange rate competition and the advanced telecommunication systems. However, corporate customers tend to focus their foreign exchange activity domestically, or to trade through foreign banks operating in the same time zone. Although the hedge funds' and corporate customers' business in foreign exchange has been growing, banks remain the predominant trading force.

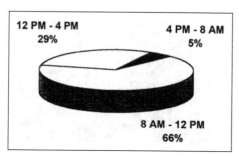

Figure 11.5. In the United States spot market, the majority of the deals are executed be-tween 8 AM and noon, when the European traders are still active. The turnover drops to un-der 50 percent in the afternoon as the liquidity dries up. The overnight activity is limited. (*Source: Bank for International Settlements, "Central Bank Survey of Foreign Exchange Activity in April 1992"*)

Executing the Trade

In executing their deals, spot traders have a language of their own. They use a concise code to get their point across quickly and accurately, leaving no room for interpretation.

Let's take a look at a typical spot trade:

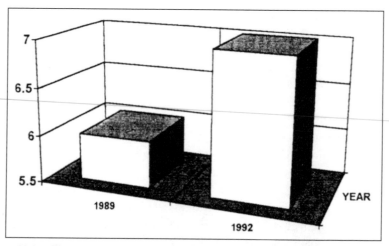

Figure 11.6. The average size deal in the brokers market increased from US$6 million in 1989 to US$7 million in 1992. (*Source: Bank for International Settlements, "Central Bank Survey of Foreign Exchange Activity in April 1992"*)

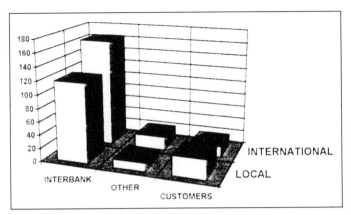

Figure 11.7. Daily market turnover by market segment and counterparty in millions of US dollars. (*Source: Bank for International Settlements, "Central Bank Survey of Foreign Exchange Activity in April 1992"*)

EXAMPLE:
A trader from *Banca Prima*, who just heard from one of her market contacts that a large investment bank is buying USD/DEM, calls *AllesBanken* on Monday, August 1 on a dealing system.
Banca Prima: "DEM 10 PLS." In direct (and polite) translation, this means: "May I have a spot price in USD/DEM 10 million, please?"

AllesBanken's trader replies: "35–40." In a more complete translation, this may stand for "My price for the above amount is 1.7335–40." The big figure (in our case 1.73) is rarely stated, as traders are assumed to know where the market is.

If *Banca Prima*'s trader likes the price and wants to buy USD/DEM at 40, she will press a preset key (B, for instance) and the software will automatically display on the screen in capital letters: "I BUY USD/DEM 10,000,000 AT 1.7340 VALUE AUGUST 3. MY USD TO *Banca Prima*/NEW YORK. THANKS VERY MUCH FOR YOUR NICE PRICE."

Finally, *AllesBanken* confirms the deal by pressing a preset key for confirmation. The software will display the following: "TO CONFIRM I SELL USD 10,000,000 AT 1.7340 VALUE AUGUST 3. MY DEM TO *AllesBanken*/FFT. THKS FOR CALLING. BIFN." BIFN stands for "Bye for now." Done deal.

If the spot trade is done by phone, the same information is exchanged, although the format may be slightly changed.

EXAMPLE:
Banca Prima calls *AllesBanken* on the phone: "Spot dollar mark in 10, please."

AllesBanken replies: "35–40."

Banca Prima: "Mine" (or "I buy" or "I take").

AllesBanken: "All right, I sell you 10 bucks at 40. Big figure is 1.73. All agreed, please?"

Banca Prima: " Yep, all agreed. Thanks, friend. Ciao".

AllesBanken: "Aufwiedersehen."

Profit and Loss

What spot currency trader didn't dream of being "turbo charged" from an abysmal loss to stellar profit by the "divine" intervention of a central bank? The scenario involves three players. In order of their stage entry they are:

1. *A rather aggressive customer,* who is looking to sell a large amount of USD/JPY to a bank, on expectation of worsening trade relationships between the United States and Japan and a consequent appreciation of the Japanese yen.
2. *A weathered currency trader,* who is aware of the US-Japan trade frictions, but believes that the Japanese yen is too strong, and expects the US dollar to strengthen against the yen.
3. *A "divine" central bank,* who fears that the foreign exchange market is getting out of hand in its buying of the Japanese yen.

The customer, Ichiban, calls First International for a price in USD/JPY 100 million. The trader, Don Joe, quotes 101.40–50. Ichiban sells USD 100 million against JPY at 101.40. As Don scrambles for cover, being able to sell only USD 20 million at 101.40, the USD/JPY suddenly drops to 100.60. Understandably tense, Don is just preparing to cut his loss, when all the major central banks intervene at the urge of the "divine" central bank, lifting the USD/JPY to 102.40, 100 pips higher than where he bought. Don Joe sells the balance of the US$80 million, realizing a profit of about $781,250, and he becomes instantaneously a folk hero in the wild world of foreign exchange. Despite its dreamlike quality, this scenario closely described the market behavior of the USD/JPY in April 1994.

The bottom line is important in all financial markets, but in currency spot trading the antes always seem higher as a result of the demand from all around the world.

The profit and loss can be either *realized or unrealized*. The realized P&L is a certain amount of money netted when a position was closed. The unrealized P&L consists of an uncertain amount of money which an outstanding position would roughly generate if it were closed at the current rate. The unrealized P&L will change continuously in tandem with the exchange rate.

Let's take a look at the calculations. For the currencies quoted in European terms, the spot profit and loss (P&L) is calculated as follows:

$$P \& L = \frac{\text{(Selling average rate} - \text{Buying average rate)} \times \text{US dollar amount}}{\text{Closing/revaluation rate}}$$

Example:

Banca Due, which had no previous position in USD/DEM, executed six deals today. The trader first sold USD/DEM 10,000,000 at 1.7025 before the release of economic data , expecting the figure to be worse than expected. The trader was correct, but the dollar fell only 25 pips. The trader took profit by buying USD/DEM 10,000,000 at 1.7000. As the USD started to rebound, two different banks called directly on the dealing system and sold to Banca Due USD/DEM 10,000,000 each at 1.7010 and 1.7005, respectively. However, the USD/DEM rebounded, and the trader at Banca Due took profit by selling USD/DEM 10,000,000 at 1.7030 and USD/DEM 10,000,000 at 1.7035.

Buy	*Sell*
USD/DEM 10,000,000 at 1.7000	USD/DEM 10,000,000 at 1.7025
USD/DEM 10,000,000 at 1.7010	USD/DEM 10,000,000 at 1.7030
USD/DEM 10,000,000 at 1.7005	USD/DEM 10,000,000 at 1.7035

The end-of-day revaluation rate, or closing rate, is 1.7020. This rate is necessary for the P&L calculation for the currencies quoted in European terms.

The average buying rate is 1.7005 for USD/DEM 30,000,000. The calculation of the average is made as follows:

$$(10,000,000 \times 1.7000 + 10,000,000 \times 1.7010 + 10,000,000 \times 1.7005) / 30,000,000 = 1.7005$$

The average selling rate is 1.7030 for USD/DEM 30,000,000. The calculation of the average is made as follows:

$$(10,000,000 \times 1.7025 + 10,000,000 \times 1.7030 + 10,000,000 \times 1.7035) / 30,000,000 = 1.7030$$

$$P\&L = [(1.7030 - 1.7005) \times 30,000,000] / 1.7020 = USD\ 44,065.80$$

For the currencies quoted in American terms, such as the British pound, the spot profit and loss (P&L) is calculated as follows:

$$P \& L = \text{(Selling average rate} - \text{Buying average rate)} \times$$
$$\text{Foreign currency amount}$$

Example:
Banco Tres, which had no previous position in GBP/USD, executed six transactions today. First it bought GBP/USD 10,000,000 at 1.5000 as the currency broke a significant resistance line. Rumors that Bank of England is buying GBP prompted Banco Tres to buy another GBP/USD 10,000,000 at 1.5005 and GBP/USD 10,000,000 at 1.5010. The profit was taken at 1.5025, 1.5030 and 1.5035 for GBP/USD 10,000,000 each, when the rumors were denied.

Buy	*Sell*
GBP/USD 10,000,000 at 1.5000	GBP/USD 10,000,000 at 1.5025
GBP/USD 10,000,000 at 1.5010	GBP/USD 10,000,000 at 1.5030
GBP/USD 10,000,000 at 1.5005	GBP/USD 10,000,000 at 1.5035

The end-of-day revaluation rate is irrelevant for the realized profit and loss in the case of currencies quoted in American terms.

The average buying rate is 1.5005 for GBP/USD 30,000,000. The calculation of the average is made as follows:

$$(10,000,000 \times 1.5000 + 10,000,000 \times 1.5010 + 10,000,000 \times 1.5005)/$$
$$30,000,000 = 1.5005$$

The average selling rate is 1.7030 for GBP/USD 30,000,000. The calculation of the average is made as follows:

$$(10,000,000 \times 1.5025 + 10,000,000 \times 1.5030 + 10,000,000 \times 1.5035) /$$
$$30,000,000 = 1.5030$$

$$P\&L = (1.5030 - 1.5005) \times 30,000,000 = USD \ 75,000.00$$

The *unrealized P&L* is calculated by using these same formulas. The missing rate is replaced by the revaluation rate, and the missing amount will equal the outstanding position.

Example:
La Premiere Banque, has a previous long position of USD/CHF 10,000,000 at 1.4510. The position was correct, and the USD/CHF is higher today. Today, it executes six additional trades in USD/CHF. The market moves in a tight range, but the trader is able to buy USD/CHF 10,000,000 at 1.4600 and sell it back at 1.4625, sell USD/CHF 10,000,000 at 1.4630 and buy back at 1.4610, buy again USD/CHF 10,000,000 at 1.4605 and sell this amount at 1.4635. Expecting the USD/CHF to continue to appreciate, the trader continues to hold a long USD/CHF 10,000,000 position.

Previous position: + USD/CHF 10,000,000 at 1.4510

Buy	*Sell*
USD/CHF 10,000,000 at 1.4600	USD/CHF 10,000,000 at 1.4625
USD/CHF 10,000,000 at 1.4610	USD/CHF 10,000,000 at 1.4630
USD/CHF 10,000,000 at 1.4605	USD/CHF 10,000,000 at 1.4635

The end-of-day revaluation rate is 1.4620. For the unrealized P&L, the end-of-day, or closing rate is important for supplementing the missing exchange rate for currencies quoted in both the European and American terms.

The average buying rate is 1.458125 for USD/CHF 40,000,000. The calculation of the average is made as follows:

$$(10,000,000 \times 1.4510 + 10,000,000 \times 1.4600 + 10,000,000 \times 1.4610 + 10,000,000 \times 1.4605) / 40,000,000 = 1.458125$$

The average selling rate is 1.4630 for USD/CHF 30,000,000. The calculation of the average is made as follows:

$$(10,000,000 \times 1.4625 + 10,000,000 \times 1.4630 + 10,000,000 \times 1.4635) / 30,000,000 = 1.4630$$

$$P\&L \text{ realized} = [(1.4630 - 1.458125) \times 30,000,000] / 1.4620 = USD\ 100,034.20$$

$$P\&L \text{ unrealized} = [(1.4620 - 1.458125) \times 10,000,000] / 1.4620 = USD\ 26,504.79$$

Sources of Information

Foreign exchange traders are information traders. Consequently, traders generally have multiple monitors displaying the most recent rates and events from around the world. The major sources of information are, in alphabetical order, Bloomberg, Knight-Ridder, Reuters and Telerate. Generally, spot currency traders watch pages WRLD on Reuters (see Figure 11.8) and 263 (see Figure 11.9) and 262 (see Figure 11.10) on Telerate. These pages display the most recent spot rates in the major currencies. Some of them, such as WRLD and 262 display additional information. Page WRLD displays the most recent spot exchange rate in each of the major currencies: Deutsche mark Japanese yen, Swiss franc, British pound, Canadian dollar, Australian dollar and New Zealand dollar, along with additional information from other financial markets. Page 263 on Telerate posts the most recent five quotes in each of the major four currencies: Deutsche mark, Japanese yen, Swiss franc and British pound. Page 262 on Telerate posts the most recent quotes in the major currencies, Deutsche mark, Japanese yen, Swiss franc, British pound, Australian dollar, New Zealand dollar, Canadian dollar, and the major currency crosses, Deutsche mark/Japanese yen, Deutsche mark/Swiss franc, British pound/Deutsche

```
                                                         Tue 18 Jan 1994 ####

1352 CCY  PAGE DLNG   SPOT RATE   LOC  PREV        US  HI & LO WRLD
1352 DEM  BBIX BBNY*D 1.7461/66   NYC  60/65       1.7560      1.7438 .
1347 JPY  CINY CITN*J 110.70/80   NYC  70/80       111.05      110.55
1352 CHF  MGTX MGTN*C 1.4605/15   NYC  13/23       1.4760      1.4592
1351 GBP  CIBB CIBV*G 1.4960/70   TOR  60/70       1.4975      1.4933
1352 CAD  HKCT HKBT*R 1.3144/49   TOR  43/48       1.3161      1.3112
1335 AUD  MGTY MGTN*T 0.6972/77   NYC  70/75       0.6980      0.6960
1350 FRF  MGTX MGTN*F 5.9310/45   NYC  15/45       5.9450      5.9240
----------------------------------------------------------------------
1353 XAU  MSGL MSGD 392.80/393.20 30YR TB  99.19-20 +06 YTM   6.28
1343 XAG  MGTY MGTN   5.29/ 5.31 *  OIL  WTI  14.82/85  USDX 96.37
1348 FED  PREB         3.06- 3.12 *  ED3  3.00- 3.25 ED6  3.18- 3.43
```

Figure 11.8. Page WRLD. (*Courtesy of Reuters*)

mark, British pound/Japanese yen, Swiss franc/Japanese yen, Australian dollar/New Zealand dollar and Australian dollar/Japanese yen, along with other financial information.

Reuters offers a series of pages with the most recent spot quotes in other currencies as follows:

• WRLE for New Zealand dollar, French franc, Dutch guilder and Danish kroner (see Figure 11.11).
• WRLF for Italian lire, Belgian franc, ECU and Spanish peseta (see Figure 11.12).

```
TELERATE MATRIX                                              PAGE 263


                  [WORLD SPOT CURRENCY MARKET]          TELERATE PAGE 263
                        [MINEX IS LIVE]
     [IN TKYO, HK, SPORE, NY,CHI AND LDN, TRADING NINE CURRENCY PAIRS, CALL TLR]
  !PAGE BANK           STG        GMT !!PAGE BANK           YEN        GMT !
   3552 D G BANK    FFT 1.5030 -40 14:40   3666 B C I       MIL 104.33 -38  14:40
   6480 NAT WEST    LDN 1.5037 -42 14:39   6592 MIDLAND BK LDN 104.25 -35  14:38
   6418 LLOYDS BK   LDN 1.5040 -50 14:40   7601 BARCLAYS   LDN 104.28 -38  14:38
    815 BNC BRASIL N Y 1.5036 -41 14:38   3552 D G BANK    FFT 104.31 -36  14:39
   3772 ROYAL SCOT LDN 1.5039 -44 14:40    475 IN CAP INV N Y 104.30 -35  14:38
   HI 11:04     1.5075- 1.4947  13:59 LO  '' HI 10:09   104.67- 104.07    1:02 LO  '
  !PAGE BANK           DMK        GMT !!PAGE BANK           SWF        GMT !
   3552 D G BANK    FFT 1.7054 -59 14:40   3552 D G BANK    FFT 1.4978 -83  14:40
    475 IN CAP INV N Y 1.7050 -60 14:40    823 CITIBANK    N Y 1.4970 -80  14:39
   6418 LLOYDS BK   LDN 1.7050 -60 14:40   3666 B C I       MIL 1.4970 -80  14:40
  22220 TRINKAUS    DSD 1.7045 -55 14:40   3435 BASLER KB   BAS 1.4970 -80  14:40
    357 CHEMICAL    N Y 1.7050 -60 14:40   3535 SWISS BANK BAS 1.4968 -78  14:40
  ' HI  9:29     1.7170- 1.7017  11:25 LO  '' HI 13:54    1.5060- 1.4930   1:40 LO  '
                  [DAIWA'S AUTOMATED TREASURY SYS    4500]
```

Figure 11.9. Page 263. (*Source: Telerate® Reprinted by permission.© 1993 Dow Jones Telerate, Inc.*)

```
┌─TELERATE®MATRIX^SM              9:50 EDT                    TERMINAL
                    [WORLD CURRENCY MARKET]                   PAGE 262
    BANK        CTR    SPOT      GMT  PREV1 PREV2   GMT   HIGH - LOW    GMT
DEM B H P       N Y 1.7108 -18  13:50 15-25 20-30 07:51 1.7142-1.7023 11:33
JPY R B C       TOR 104.35 -45  13:50 32-37 30-35 10:10 104.67-104.07 01:02
GBP RABOBANK    UTR 1.4991 -001 13:49 90-95 88-98 11:14 1.5070-1.4950 07:16
CHF NAT WEST    LDN 1.5047 -52  13:50 45-55 50-60 13:49 1.5052-1.4930 01:40
AUD A N Z       FFT 0.6890 -95  13:49 90-95 92-97 07:16 0.6905-0.6886 11:25
NZD A N Z       FFT 0.5520 -27  13:49 18-25 20-24 07:31 0.5523-0.5512 22:02
CAD R B C       TOR 1.2902 -07  13:50 04-09 03-08 11:52 1.2910-1.2890 06:34
FRF MORGAN GTY  N Y 5.9765 -50  13:50 55-05 90-05 07:48 6.0085-5.9555 11:37
    CROSS RATES         HIGH-LOW       EURO      3 MONTH         6 MONTH
DEM/JPY  60.99 -03   61.29- 60.88   USD    3.1875 -3125   3.3750 -5000
DEM/CHF 0.8792 -96  0.8803-0.8737   DEM    6.5625 -6875   6.4375 -5625
GBP/DEM 2.5658 -68  2.5707-2.5565   JPY    3.1250 -2500   3.0937 -1250
GBP/JPY 156.51 -61  157.22-156.04   GBP    5.6250 -8750   5.4375 -6875
CHF/JPY  69.35 -39   70.01- 69.33   TBOND 107.27-29 6.518 GOLD 403.80 -20
AUD/NZD 1.2476 -82  1.2529-1.2472   BRENT  SEP  1664-69   SILU  5.39 -41
AUD/JPY  71.93 -99   72.21- 71.74   SIMEX  DEC  EURO$ S9619 EUROJPY S9708
08/03 09:41 UK SETS 1 BILLION ECU T-BILL SALE -2-: DETAILS.........  4241
08/03 09:44 SECOND IRANIAN SUBMARINE DOCKED AT BANDAR ABBAS......... 3219?
08/03 09:45 *NYMEX CRUDE OIL FUTURES OPEN LOWER; SEPT ON 9C AT $17.88... ----
08/03 09:45 EXISTING HOME SALES UP 1.0% TO 3.96 MLN RATE IN 20........ 4016
08/03 09:46 BEAR STEARNS EARNINGS -3-: YEAR FINANCIAL TABLE........  3220?
08/03 09:49 BEAR STEARNS EARNINGS -4-: 40. YEAR TABLE IN REVENUE.... 3220?

 FX  T-500  HBS  MKTS  7105  500  261  450              MENU  HELP
```

Figure 11.10. Page 262. (*Source: Telerate® Reprinted by permission.© 1993 Dow Jones Telerate, Inc.*)

- WRLG for Hong Kong dollar, Malaysian ringgit, Swedish krona, Norwegian krone, Irish pound, Singapore dollar and Finnish markka (see Figure 11.13).

On Telerate, other spot rates are available on pages 264 (see Figure 11.14), 265 (see Figure 11.15 and 266 (see Figure 11.16). Page 264 displays the

```
                                        Tue 18 Jan 1994 ####

1351            REUTER WORLD SPOT RATES                    WRLE
  NEW ZEALAND DOLLAR (NZD)         FRENCH        FRANC (FRF)
1346 WLG BNZW BNZW   0.5636/43   1350 NYC MGTX MGTN    5.9310/45*
1347 WLG BNZW BNZW   0.5632/39   1346 NYC MGTX MGTN    5.9295/30
1348 WLG NBNZ NBNZ   0.5635/42*  1347 NYC CINY CITN    5.9315/45
HIGH    0.5630   LOW    0.5567   HIGH    5.9495   LOW    5.9250
    DUTCH      GUILDER (NLG)          DANISH      KRONER (DKK)
1343 NYC MGTX MGTN   1.9530/40   1345 NYC MGTY MGTN    6.7690/95
1345 NYC MGTX MGTN   1.9540/50   1348 NYC SEBN SEBN    6.7744/44
1348 NYC CINY CITN   1.9545/55*  1351 NYC MGTY MGTN    6.7710/15*
HIGH    1.9622   LOW    1.9528   HIGH    6.7916   LOW    6.7654
1351 DEM  1.7463/68 JFY  110.70/80 CHF  1.4600/10 GBP  1.4960/70
```

Figure 11.11. Page WRLE . (*Courtesy of Reuters*)

```
                                                      Tue 18 Jan 1994 ####

1351               REUTER WORLD SPOT RATES                           WRLF
  ITALIAN          LIRE (ITL)             BELGIAN        FRANC (BEC)
1348 NYC CINY CITN 1699.00/1.00   1157 BRU CITX CITB   36.310/340L
1350 NYC CPLO CARN 1700.20/1.20L  1153 BRU DEUX DEUB   36.335/345
1346 NYC BDSN BSIN 1700.00/1.00   1153 BRU SGBX GBBS   36.335/345
HIGH    1701.50   LOW    1697.00  HIGH     36.427  LOW      36.334
  EUROPEAN CURRENCY UNIT (ECU)         SPANISH      PESETA (ESP)
1345 NYC MGTX MGTN      1.1115/25  1341 NYC MGTY MGTN    142.30/50
1348 NYC CINY CITN      1.1112/22  1344 NYC MGTY MGTN    142.25/45
1351 NYC MGTX MGTN      1.1115/20L 1351 NYC MGTY MGTN    142.30/50L
HIGH    1.1125   LOW    1.1080    HIGH    142.55  LOW     142.00
1351 DEM   1.7463/68 JPY  110.70/80 CHF   1.4600/10 GBP   1.4960/70
```

Figure 11.12.   Page WRLF. (*Courtesy of Reuters*)

```
                                                      Tue 18 Jan 1994 ####

1352 CCY   PAGE  DLNG     SPOT RATE  LOC  PREV       US  HI + LO WRLG
1359 HKD   CINZ  CICM     7.7252/62  NYC  50/55      7.7255     7.7250
1352 MYR   CINZ  CICM     2.7240/70  NYC  55/80      2.7300     2.7240
1352 SEK   NORV  NBSS     8.0797/97  STO  04/04      8.1111     8.0723
1348 NOK   SEBN  SEBN     7.5050/70  NYC  29/49      7.5291     7.4964
1353 IEP   ICON  IIII     1.4348/58  DUB  18/58      1.4320     1.4320
1339 SGD   MIDN  HSBN     1.6075/85  NYC  75/85      1.6090     1.6075
1101 FIM   KOPX  KIBH     5.6613/13  HEL  36/36      5.6883     5.7150
.................................................................
.................................................................
1351 DEM   1.7463/68 JPY  110.70/80 CHF   1.4600/10 GBP   1.4960/70
```

Figure 11.13.   Page WRLF. (*Courtesy of Reuters*)

	8:26 EST		[WORLD SPOT CURRENCY MARKET]					PAGE 264	
			[FOR ADDITIONAL CURRENCIES SEE 265-266]						
	BANK			GMT		BANK			GMT
HFL	NAT WEST	LDN	1.9604 -09	13:23	DKR	BARCLAYS	LDN	6.7900 -50	13:23
NLG	RABOBANK	UTR	1.9605 -10	13:26	DKK	CHRISTIANI	OSL	6.7865 -915	13:26
	CHRISTIANI	OSL	1.9600 -10	13:25		DEN DANSKE	COP	6.7850 -00	13:25
	BANK			GMT		BANK			GMT
LIR	CHRISTIANI	OSL	1699.5 00	13:26	NKR	CHRISTIANI	OSL	7.5195 -225	13:25
ITL	BARCLAYS	LDN	1699.8 -1.3	13:26	NOK	SE BANKEN	STK	7.5231 -251	13:26
	U B S	GEN	1700.25-1.2	13:26		DEN NORSKE	OSL	7.5215 -45	13:25
	BANK			GMT		BANK			GMT
BEF	BARCLAYS	LDN	36.41 -45	13:23	FFR	B C I	MIL	5.9400 -10	13:26
BEF	U B S	ZUR	36.410- 80	13:22	FRF	U B S	GEN	5.9400 -10	13:26
	SOGENAL	BRU	36.380 -410	13:26		CR SUISSE	ZUR	5.9390 -420	13:26
	BANK			GMT		BANK			GMT
CAN$	R B C	TOR	1.3135 -40	13:12	AUS$	CHEMICAL	LDN	0.6974 -79	13:13
CAD	CITIBANK	N Y	1.3134 -39	13:25	AUD	NAT WEST	LDN	0.6973 -77	13:13
	BK OF MTL	TOR	1.3135 -40	13:23		R B C	TOR	0.6970 -80	13:12

Figure 11.14.   Page 264 on Telerate. (*Source: Telerate® Reprinted by permission © 1993 Dow Jones Telerate, Inc.*)

```
        8:27 EST      [WORLD SPOT CURRENCY MARKET]                        265
      BANK                           GMT        BANK                      GMT
ARS   B E A L      BRU 9981 - -6   13:58  INR   BARCLAYS   LDN 31.34  -44  08:04

ATS   R L B       LIN 12.3100- 50 13:23  IEP   ULSTER     DUB 1.4272 -02  13:26

BHD   SWISS BANK  BAH .37695 -05  10:29  ILS

BRE   B E A L     BRU 273.900-92  13:58  KES   BARCLAYS   LDN 67.15       08:30

FIM   CHRISTIANI  OSL 5.6740 -940 13:26  KRW   STD CHART  SEL 811.10 -30  07:35

GRD   MORGAN GTY  N Y 250.80 -30  13:22  KWD   BURGAN BK  KWT 0.29795-15  08:52

HKD   B E A       LDN 7.7250 -60  09:54  MYR   BARCLAYS   LDN 2.7290 -10  13:10

TRL   MARMARA BK  IST 20000-00    13:23            [CONTINUED NEXT PAGE]
```

Figure 11.15. Page 265 on Telerate. *(Source: Telerate.® Reprinted by permission.© 1993 Dow Jones Telerate, Inc.)*

```
        8:27 EST      [WORLD SPOT CURRENCY MARKET] -                 PAGE 266
      BANK                             GMT        BANK                   GMT
MXP   BANCRESER   MEX 3.1060-1080 14:38  ESP   BARCLAYS    LDN 142.84/94 13:26

NZD   NAT WEST    LDN 0.5627 -32  13:13  QAR   Q N B       DOH 3.6385 -15 06:30

PHP   B O A       MNL 27.73-27.83 07:38  SEK   SVENSKA     STK 8.1070 -170 13:26

PTE   C G D       LIS 175.82 -95  13:15  AED   O I B       MUS 3.6720 -30 05:43

SAR   BARCLAYS    LDN 3.7492 -02  08:10  VEB   CARLSEN CO  FLA 107.50 -60 19:48

SGD   BARCLAYS    LDN 1.6085 -95  11:11  CNY   BANK CHINA  N Y 8.6783 -217 14:01

ZAR   NEDBANK     JHB 3.4135 -50  13:26  OMR   CENTRAL BK  MUS .38496-01  07:26

TWD   TAIPEI FX   TAI 26.4115-423008:00
```

Figure 11.16. Page 266 on Telerate. *(Source: Telerate® Reprinted by permission.© 1993 Dow Jones Telerate, Inc.)*

```
        8:14 EST    [ NOONAN, ASTLEY & PEARCE   INC. -NEW YORK- ]   PAGE 311
            STERLING    ITAL.LIRA   D/MARK      CANADIAN $    YEN    SWISS FRANC
            08:13 EDT   08:04 EDT   08:09 EDT   17:46 EDT  07:50 EDT 07:56 EDT
SPOT   1.4920-25    1611.50-50  1.6282-87      0.0-.0    117.10-15  1.5082-87

                     98950 99050
T/N    0.90-0.8     35-36       2.30-2.35      0.0-0.0   0.12-0.15    1-1.15
S/N    0.95-0.85    0.35-0.365  2-2.2          0.0-0.0   1.50-1.8    0.90-1.1
1WK    7.75-7.25    255-260     16.40-16.7     0.0-0.0   2.25-2.5      6-7
1MO       35-34.25  1125-1135   70-70.5        0.0-0.0   3.45-3.75   26.50-28
2MO    67.50-66     2125-2155   128.5-129.5    0.0-0.0   3.25-4       48-50
3MO    97.50-96     3335-3365   190.5-191.5    0.0-0.0   3-3.75       68-71
4MO    128-126      4375-4450   241-243        0.0-0.0   2.5-3.5      84-89
6MO    183-180      6620-6660   339-341        0.0-0.0   -0.25-0.75  111-116
9MO    257-250      9450-9650   444-446        0.0-0.0   10-8        123-133
1YR    318-310      12400-12500 518-522        0.0-0.0   29-26       125-135
[SEE PG 307 FOR CROSSRATES]  TELERATE SYSTEMS INC [SEE PG 317 FOR SWAP OPTIONS]
```

Figure 11.17. Page 311 provided by Noonan, Astley & Pearce, Inc. on Telerate. *(Source: Telerate ® Reprinted by permission. © 1993 Dow Jones Telerate, Inc.)*

```
TELERATE MATRIX                                                PAGE 312
      9:55 EDT


                      [ NOONAN, ASTLEY & PEARCE INC - NJ]     08/03 08:05  312
      !  BELGIUM  !  SPAIN   !NETHERLANDS!  SWEDEN   !  DENMARK  !  NORWAY  !
      :  8:05 EDT :  8:05 EDT :  8:05 EDT :  8:05 EDT :  8:05 EDT :  8:05 EDT :
      !  FRANC   !  PESETA  !  GUILDER  !  KRONA   !  KRONE   !  KRONE   !
      ; 36.30 -32 ;139.10 -20 ;1.9160 -70 ;7.9990 -190;6.7750 -350;7.3485 -585;
  T/N :    .5-1   :  3.1-3.3  :  1.6-1.9  :   12-13   :   50-100  :    4-6    :
  S/N :     -     :     -     :     -     :   12-13   :   50-150  :    4-6    :
  1WK :    4-5    :     -     :   14-15   :   80-90   :  300-550  :   35-40   :
  1MO :   19-21   :  103-108  :   58-60   :  365-385  :  800-1300 :  172-187  :
  2MO :   28-34   :  180-187  :   99-102  :  620-645  : 1400-1900 :  310-330  :
  3MO :   39-45   :  260-268  :  145-148  :  900-930  : 1600-2100 :  465-485  :
  6MO :   62-72   :  472-482  :  253-258  : 1560-1590 : 2200-2700 :  850-890  :
  1YR :   85-105  :  780-795  :  395-405  : 2500-2550 : 3000-3500 : 1420-1495 :
X/DEM'  21.32-37  :81.70-80   :1.1253 55  '4.6970-20  '3.9700-900 '4.3150-00  :
      ! DM/ATS   !  DM/FRF   ! --SEE PAGE 313 FOR OTHER EXOTICS  !  DM/FIM   !
      :7.0341-46  :3.4960-80  : FORWARD ATS, FRF, & FIM ALSO     :3.4000-100 :
      :          :           : AVAILABLE ON REQUEST             :          :
      ,          ,           ,                                  ,          ,
```

Figure 11.18.   Page 312 provided by Noonan, Astley & Pearce, Inc. on Telerate. (*Source: Telerate* ® *Reprinted by permission.© 1993 Dow Jones Telerate, Inc.*)

most recent three spot rates for Dutch guilder, Italian lire, Belgian franc, Canadian dollar, Danish kroner, Norwegian krone, French franc and Australian dollar. Pages 265 and 266 host a series of more exotic currencies.

Both spot and forward exchange rates are also made available by brokers on the monitors. Noonan, Astley & Pearce, Inc. displays their prices on pages 311, 312 and 313 (see Figure 11.17, Figure 11.18, Figure 11.19). In the morning, traders check the overnight ranges both with the brokers and from the monitors. On Reuters, this information is available on pages TKFE for the Asian market, SPOU for the European market and FXUS for the American market, and on Telerate on page 7779.

The information available on the monitors is supplemented by traders' personal networking. The objective of networking is twofold: find out whether any large customer orders went through, and try to "feel" the mood of the market. This type of information is not available on the regular monitor pages. By the time rumors about large transactions reach the monitors, the market effect is generally diminished. Sometimes, large transactions in some currencies may have an impact on another currency. For instance, a large buying order of Swiss franc against Japanese yen may slow down an otherwise bullish US dollar against Deutsche mark. Swiss franc and Deutsche mark are highly correlated. Therefore, the strength of the Swiss franc will extrapolate to the Deutsche mark as well.

Loss Cutting

Loss cutting is painful for every trader. The ability to cut one's losses in time is the sign of a seasoned trader. Good traders are too busy trying to "read" the market to spend time on blind hope. Lesser traders become trapped hoping for the daily miracle. They dismiss a profitable trading pat-

```
TELERATE MATRIX                                                      PAGE 313
      9:55 EDT


                     [ NOONAN, ASTLEY & PEARCE INC - NJ]      08/03 08:05  313
           ! AUSTRALIA !NEW ZEALAND! HONG KONG ! SINGAPORE ! MALAYSIA  !   SPOTS    !
           :  8:05 EDT :  8:05 EDT :  8:05 EDT :  8:05 EDT :  8:05 EDT :  8:05 EDT  :
           :  DOLLAR   !  DOLLAR   !  DOLLAR   !  DOLLAR   !  RINGGIT  !   INDIA     !
   SPOT ;0.6885 -90 ;0.5517 -24 ;7.7535 -45 ;1.6138 -48 ;2.5600 -10 ; .0318 -319:
   T/N  :   4-2     :   4-2     :    -      :    -      :    -      ! ECU-DEM  !
   S/N  :    -      :    -      :    -      :    -      :    -      ! 1.9100-20 :
   1WK  :    -      :    -      :    -      :    -      :    -      ! MEXICO    !
   1MO  :  9.9-9.2  :  12-9     :    -      :    -      :    -      :3.1190-10  :
   2MO  : 17.7-16.7 :  22-17    :    -      :    -      :    -      ! VENEZUELA !
   3MO  : 25.7-24.2 :  33-27    :    -      :    -      :    -      : 90.26-36  :
   6MO  : 44.5-42.5 :  59-52    :    -      :    -      :    -      !           !
   1YR  :   76-71   '  115-100  '    -      '    -      '    -      '           :
        :           :           !                                              :
        :           :           :                                              :
        ,           ,           ,                                              ,
     [   SEE PAGES 311, 312, AND 307 FOR OTHER CURRENCIES AND CROSS RATES   ]'
```

Figure 11.19. Page 313 provided by Noonan, Astley & Pearce, Inc. on Telerate. (*Source: Telerate* ® *Reprinted by permission.*© *1993 Dow Jones Telerate, Inc.*)

tern as lucky. Even good traders may lose on numerous individual transactions. However, the losing trades are cut quickly, while the profitable trades are allowed to "run."

Characteristics of a Spot Trader

To be successful, spot traders must embody seemingly opposite traits. They must simultaneously be flexible and firm, patient and quick to react.

Why are such contradictory qualities necessary in the current spot market?

Traders have, or at least should have, a view on the market, a scenario, a plan. This view must be backed by some reasons, maybe some fundamental factors, such as the state of the domestic economy relative to other significant economies, maybe some chart signals, maybe a combination of the two. Having such a set plan gives the trader mental toughness and a psychological basis which will provide direction in an otherwise chaotic environment.

With the scenario in place, the trader starts trading, and the market behavior seems to coincide with the plan. But all of a sudden, the exchange rate starts moving abruptly in the "wrong" direction. There is a rumor in the market that a central bank is intervening. The trader feels that his or her view is still fundamentally correct, that in time the market will indeed trade the "right" way. In the short term, however, what is the trader supposed to do?

Imagine yourself hearing on the radio that a train is out of control, quickly running to the railroad tracks, and waiting right in the middle, believing that the train should still be able to stop. If you are correct, that's nice; but if you are wrong, well, you have a problem. A good spot trader soon learns that staying alive is essential to being profitable. A single encounter with the runaway train of the exchange market may prove dangerous to the trader's health. Therefore, while it is important that a trader has a specific market view, and goes about implementing it, it is equally important to be fast and flexible enough to adjust to the changing market conditions.

The spot trader must be able to quickly discern between a major adverse change, or a temporary move. If the trader is long (bought) US$5 million against Deutsche marks at 2.0000 and the exchange rate moves a little lower, to 1.9970, the trader may want to buy US$5 million more at the lower price, while supporting the bids, or simply wait it out, if the move seems to be minor. If buying more, the new average price will be 1.9985, so the rate must move up only by 15 pips to break even. Of course, if the trader is wrong, then the long position will be twice as much as the original one in a falling market.

The reverse is true for a perceived significant adverse exchange rate move. The trader must be able to quickly cut the loss and wait, or reverse the position. If the same long US$5 million against Deutsche marks at 2.0000 position is in place, and the trader decides that 2.0000 was toppish, he may decide at 1.9970 to either cut the position by selling US$5 million against Deutsche marks, or to fully reverse the position, by selling US$10 million against Deutsche marks. The new position is short by US$5 million against Deutsche marks.

Spot traders must be able to readily cut through the abundance of information, and quickly value only the significant factors. This ability is mostly an acquired trait, an art rather than a science. There is only so much quantification to be done. Past that, it is up to the trader to mentally process the information and implement the results.

Types of Traders

Some traders have a strategic approach, some trade "in-and-out" all day long. Both types of traders play a significant role in the market. The strategic players focus more on the "big picture." They tend to trade larger positions and keep them for much longer periods of time. The "in-and-out" traders provide daily liquidity in the market. They rarely have a strong view on the market, focusing instead on the daily market flow. Their profit margin per deal is generally lower than the strategic traders, but they make more deals.

Traders may also be categorized by the level of risk they are able to manage. There is no magic formula for determining the optimum level of risk for each trader. This level can only be determined through trial and error. It is less important to know how much risk a trader is willing to take; it is vital to know at what level the trader's performance peaks. The size of the individual position should reflect therefore not the size of the trader's ego, but his or her capacity of maximizing the trading performance. This decision is made by the chief trader.

The more risk averse traders will take position after the release of the economic data, for instance, rather than going with a position into the number. Most traders do that, since they need reinforcement from the market behavior. Fewer traders will take positions before the release of the economic data. Ultimately, it is the trader's performance that counts, the return on investment, not his or her thirst for risk taking.

Conclusion

Once spot traders decide on a plan, they must stick to their guns, oblivious to any extraneous distractions. Sometimes, a trader would like to get long in a specific currency. Before that happens, however, another counterparty calls and buys from our original trader, who is now short, contrary to the plan. If squaring off now, the trader may incur a small loss, so he or she decides to wait a little longer in order to break even. Once that happens, our trader will go back to the main plan of going long on that currency. But the currency is moving higher, the loss is getting bigger, and the trader remains stuck further with a losing position. No matter how much our trader complains about the unfairness of the market, about the frustration of having the right idea but being pushed in the wrong position, nothing will change. Therefore, a trader must remember to follow his own judgment. Even if small losses result, successful traders should exit positions which do not fit their trading view. If the situation is not clear, it is much better for traders to sit on the fence for a while thinking things over, than to face the runaway train hoping blindly that it will stop.

"Let the profits run, cut the losses short" is a common saying among traders. Its methodical implementation usually extends the trading life of most players. The gambler's approach, going for broke, generally ends in the gambler's own finale, the sad loss. Traders must have a systematic and steady approach to the market. Smaller, consistent profits tend to be preferable to huge P&L fluctuations.

Nobody is bigger than the market. At times, large players, naturally, will be able to have a significant impact on the market. But any artificial move will be very shortlived, regardless of how many billions of dollars have been sacrificed. The living example of this fact was the defeat of the central banks of the European Monetary System in September 1992 and the summer of 1993 in their attempt to prop up manmade ranges in foreign exchange. Since most players are generally small in size and scope, the individual impact will likely be a tad smaller. Therefore, the challenge is not to be the market, but to read the market. Riding the wave is infinitesimally more rewarding than being hit by it.

Chapter 12

The Forward Currency Market: Forward Outright and Swap Transactions

Foreign exchange players have diverse interests in the market, in terms of currencies and delivery dates. Whereas most volume occurs in the spot market, a very large segment of currency trades matures past the spot value date—the standard two business days. Foreign exchange trades which mature beyond the spot dates are known, collectively, as forward trades.

The Forward Foreign Currency Marketplace

The forward currency market consists of two instruments: forward outright deals and swaps. Generally, this market includes only cash transactions. Therefore, currency futures contracts, although a special breed of forward outright transactions, are analyzed separately.

According to figures published by the Bank for International Settlements in the "Central Bank Survey of Foreign Exchange Market Activity in April 1992," the percentage share of the forward market was 46 percent. Seven percent of this occurred in the forward outright market and 39 percent in the swap market. Translated into US dollars, out of an esti-

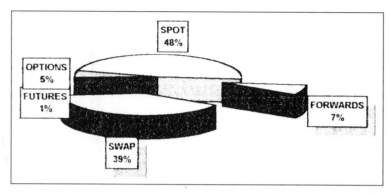

Figure 12.1. The market share of the foreign exchange instruments (*Source: the Bank for International Settlements, "Central Bank Survey of Foreign Exchange Market Activity in April 1992"*)

mated daily gross turnover of US$832 billion (in 1992), the total forward market represents US$383.4 billion: US$58.5 billion in the forward outright market and US$324.9 billion in the swap market. The swap and forward outright markets are heavily concentrated in the US dollar (over 95 percent). In terms of currency pairs, the US dollar/Japanese yen (25 percent) transactions exceed the US dollar/Deutsche mark trades.

General Characteristics of the Forward Market

In the forward market there is no norm with regard to the settlement dates, which range anywhere between three days and three years. Volume in currency swaps over one year tends to be light but, technically, there is no impediment to making these deals. Any date past the spot date, and within the above range, may be a forward settlement, provided that it is a valid business day for both currencies.

The forward markets are decentralized markets, with players around the world entering into a variety of deals either on a one-on-one basis or through brokers. In contrast, the currency futures market is a centralized market, where all the deals are executed on trading floors provided by different exchanges. Whereas in the futures market only a handful of foreign currencies may be traded (futures on the US dollar index can be traded only on the FINEX, in New York) in multiples of standardized amounts, the forward markets are open to any currencies, in any amount.

What is the difference between the forward outright and the swap market?

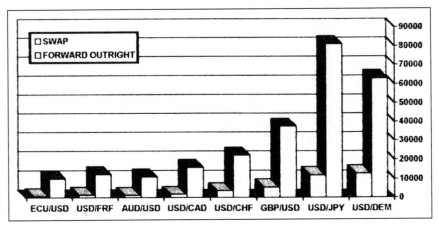

Figure 12.2. The daily average market turnover of the currency swaps versus forward outrights in the major currencies, in millions of US dollars. The forward outright transactions are only a fraction of the volume in the swap market. (*Source: the Bank for International Settlements, "Central Bank Survey of Foreign Exchange Market Activity in April 1992"*)

A *forward outright deal* is an individual trade which matures past the spot delivery date. Since its value date differs from the spot, intuitively, we must expect that the forward rate will also differ from the spot rate.

A *swap deal* is unusual among the rest of the foreign exchange instruments in the fact that it consists of two deals, or legs. All the other individual deals consist of single deals. In its original form, a swap deal is a combination of a spot deal and a forward outright deal.

Before we approach these instruments in more detail, let's take a look at several technical aspects germane to forward pricing.

The Forward Price

The forward price consists of two significant parts: *the spot exchange rate* and the *forward spread*. The forward spread is also known as the *forward points* or the *forward pips*. The forward spread is necessary for adjusting the spot rate for specific settlement dates different from the spot date. It holds, then, that *the maturity date* is another determining factor of the forward price.

The Spot Rate

The spot rate is the main building block. Since the forward price is derived from the spot price, by adjusting the spot price with the forward spread, it follows that both the forward outright and the swap deals are derivative instruments.

Forward Spreads

Figure 12.3 presents major currencies forward outright spreads on page 311 on Telerate provided by Noonan, Astley & Pearce, Inc., a leading international foreign exchange broker. On this page, the spot rates for some of the major currencies are followed by the forward spreads for several standard forward dates: spot/next (S/N), one week, one month, up to one year. Just as in the case of the spot market, the left side of the quote is the bid side, and the right side is the offer side. Note, though, that the bid-offer relationship as just described only applies if the swap is executed in foreign currency amount. If the swap is done in US dollars, the right side of the forward quote becomes the bid and conversely the left side is the offer.

Example:
Your quotes are:

USD/DEM spot = 1.7125 – 30

USD/DEM 3 month forward spread = 147–149

1. A customer sells and buys with you a *DEM 5 million* (foreign currency amount) swap in three months. Therefore you buy and sell DEM 5 million swap at 147. Your prices are:

   1.7130 for spot (because buying DEM is equivalent to selling USD), and

   1.7277 for three months (because the forward spread is added to the spot rate: 1.7130 + 147).

```
TELERATE MATRIX                                              PAGE 311
        9:54 EDT

                         [ NOONAN, ASTLEY & PEARCE  INC. -NEW YORK- ]   PAGE 311
           !  STERLING ! ITAL.LIRA !   D/MARK   !CANADIAN $!    YEN    !SWISS FRANC!
           :  09:54 EDT :  09:30 EDT :  09:53 EDT :  17:01 EDT :  09:51 EDT :  09:54 EDT :
           !           !           !           !          !           !            !
SPOT ;1.4983-88   ;1602.00-00 ;1.7125-30   ;    0.0-.0  ;104.38-41  ;1.5055-60   ;
           :           :           :           :          :           :            :
           :           :93825 93900:           :          :           :            :
T/N : 1.25-1.15 :    30-32   : 1.40-1.45 :  0.0-0.0  :-0.05-0.03 : 0.8-0.9  :
S/N :  1.2-1.1  :    30-32   : 1.4-1.55  :  0.0-0.0  :-0.02-0.0  : 0.80-0.9 :
1WK :    8-7.7  :   205-211  :11.50-12   :  0.0-0.0  : 0.10-0.25 : 5.10-5.6 :
1MO :37.75-37.5 :   890-905  :55.75-56.25:  0.0-0.0  : 0.4-0.6   :   21-23  :
2MO :   68-66   : 1575-1605  :   98-99   :  0.0-0.0  : 0.40-0.7  :   38-39  :
3MO :   97-95   : 2300-2330  :  147-149  :  0.0-0.0  : 1.70-1.5  :   54-56  :
4MO :  119-116  : 2925-3000  :  189-191  :  0.0-0.0  :   6-5.25  :   64-68  :
6MO :  167-164  : 4275-4325  :  263-266  :  0.0-0.0  :21.50-20.5 :   78-82  :
9MO :  210-205  : 5750-5900  :  338-343  :  0.0-0.0  :   45-42   :   87-93  :
1YR '  255-250  ' 7375-7475  '  395-400  '  0.0-0.0  '   74-72   '   92-99  '
[SEE PG 307 FOR CROSSRATES]  TELERATE SYSTEMS INC [SEE PG 317 FOR SWAP OPTIONS]
```

Figure 12.3.   Page 311 provided by Noonan, Astley & Pearce, Inc. (*Source: Telerate*®
Reprinted by permission.© 1993 Dow Jones Telerate, Inc.)

2. A customer sells and buys with you a *USD/DEM 5 million* (US dollar amount) swap in three months. Therefore you buy and sell USD/DEM (equivalent to selling and buying DEM) 5 million swap at 149. Your prices are:

1.7125 for spot , and

1.7274 for 3 months (because the forward spread is added to the spot rate: 1.7125 + 149).

The typical misconception about forward prices is that they represent an expectation on the direction of one currency in terms of another. Drawing on the previous example, since the spot USD/DEM rate is 1.7125 and the three month forward outright USD/DEM rate is 1.7274, that would suggest that the US dollar is bound to be stronger in the future. This is false.

Certainly, any currency price, spot and forward, will always reflect the expectation of future price behavior. But this is not an expectation based on one currency being stronger or weaker than another. The forward spread is simply the result of the interest rate differential between the currencies traded, adjusted for the number of days until the maturity date. This market expectation of future changes in the interest rate differential is, however, essential for forward currency pricing.

Finally, the forward spreads may be influenced for specific periods or as a whole. Let's take an example of a situation where only one of the forward rates for a standard period will be influenced. Let's assume that the real interest rates in a country have been low for a relatively long period of time, and the economy of that country has enjoyed low inflation. If that country's economic indicators which measure inflation, such as the Producer Price Index (PPI) or the Consumer Price Index (CPI), show that inflation has risen in two consecutive months, the market may expect that if these indicators reflect a continuing rise in inflation for a third straight month, then the central bank of that country will increase the discount rate. Higher interest rates constitute, of course, the tool of choice for fighting inflation.

On the market expectation that the central bank will raise interest rates soon, the interest-rate differential has a strong potential to increase for the one month term, but this will have limited or no impact on the other standard settlement dates.

As one of the main factors in the pricing formula of forward spreads, changes in the spot rate will automatically trigger changes in the forward rates. The forward pricing method will be presented in a section on interest rate differential later in this chapter.

Introduction to the Types of Forward Spreads

In the calculation of the three month forward outright USD/DEM rate, the forward spread was added to the spot price. This type of spread is called *premium*. If the forward spread is deducted from the spot price, it is called *discount*. On rare occasions, the forward spread is zero, and naturally the forward price will simply equal the spot price. This type of spread is known as *par*.

Identifying the Types of Forward Spreads

Before learning how to calculate the forward spread, let's see how a player is able to identify a premium spread from a discount spread.

If the bid side (left side) of the forward outright spread is smaller than the offer side (right side), that specific spread is a premium, and it must be added to the spot price to obtain the forward price. For example, the one year forward spread in Deutsche mark, presented in Figure 12.3, is 395–400 and the spot USD/DEM is 1.7125–30. Calculating the offer side, we get 1.7130 + 0.0400 = 1.7530.

Conversely, if the bid side of the forward outright spread is larger than the offer side, then it is a discount spread, and it will be deducted from the spot rate to calculate the forward outright price. For instance, the one year forward spread in Japanese yen, presented in Figure 12.3, is 74–72 and the spot USD/JPY is 104.38–41. Calculating the bid side we get 104.38 – 0.74 = 103.64.

Forward bid < Forward offer ⇒ Premium spread

Forward bid > Forward offer ⇒ Discount spread

To better understand the importance of the spot exchange rate and consequently the significance of the spot value date, we will discuss premium spreads, discount spreads and at par. We will focus on several diagrams and our examples will be for currencies quoted in European terms.

Premium Spread

A *premium spread* is a spread where the interest rates in one foreign currency are higher in all periods than the US interest rates. In such a market, as time progresses, prices go higher, starting from the spot level, rather like climbing a staircase (see Figure 12.4). Alternatively, it may be is easier to visualize the forward dates and the behavior of the forward prices around the spot level on a −∞/+∞ axis, with zero being replaced by the spot level. In a premium market, the prices will increase past the spot price (see Figure 12.5).

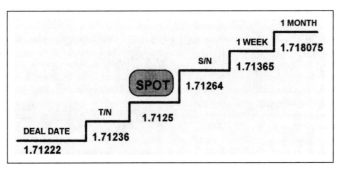

Figure 12.4. In a premium market, the forward prices are higher relative to the spot price, as the time passes. The numerical examples are based on the Deutsche mark rates presented in Figure 12.3.

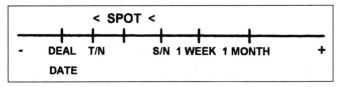

Figure 12.5. In a premium market, the forward prices are higher relative to the spot price, as the time passes.

Discount Spread

The opposite is true for a discount market. The forward prices will decrease relative to the spot exchange rate (see Figure 12.6). Again, it may be is easier to visualize the behavior of the forward prices relative to the forward dates and around the spot level on a $+\infty/-\infty$ axis, with zero being replaced by the spot level. In a discount market, the prices will decrease past the spot price (see Figure 12.7).

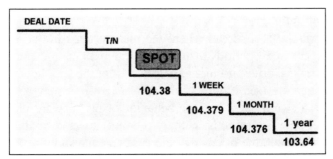

Figure 12.6. In a discount market, the forward prices are lower relative to the spot price, as the time passes. The numerical examples are based on the Japanese yen rates presented in Figure 12.3.

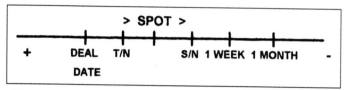

Figure 12.7. In a discount market, the forward prices are lower than the spot price.

At Par

If you refer to Figure 12.3, you will see that in USD/JPY, the spot next (S/N) rate is -0.02–0.0. Calculating the offer side, the forward price will equal:

$$104.41 - 0.0 = 104.41$$

The spot and the forward price are identical, or at par.

Methods of Calculating the Forward Outright Prices

Let's see now why the sum of 1.7125 (the bid of the USD/DEM spot price) and 147 (the bid of the three months USD/DEM forward spread) equals 1.7272 (see Figure 12.3). This is a common source of confusion when first approaching the forward currency markets.

By convention, traders refer to the last decimals as simply points or pips. To be mathematically correct, the three month USD/DEM forward spread should be displayed as 0.0147–0.0149, rather than 147–149. Traders, being pragmatic people, will cut through the less important details and focus on the essential elements only. They disregard, therefore, the full forward spread format. But they don't err on their calculations.

One way to calculate the above forward price is:

$$1.7125 + 0.0147 = 1.7272$$

Let's calculate now the bid side of the one month USD/DEM forward price. The bid remains unchanged at 1.7125. The one month USD/DEM spread is 55.75–56.25. Since the bid is smaller than the offer, you will easily identify a *premium spread* and you will therefore add this spread to the spot rate.

In order to avoid any confusion caused by the decimal points in the forward spread, you may calculate the forward price another way. Drop the decimal point only in the spot price and add it with the forward spread as is:

$$17125 + 55.75 = 17180.75$$

Return the decimal point to its rightful place:

$$17180.75 \Rightarrow 1.718075$$

and you obtain the correct forward price.

Based on the foreign exchange rates you have seen so far, you generally got used to four decimals—or two decimals in the case of the Japanese yen. There is no problem having more decimals and you do not have to round up the forward exchange rates to the perceived "standard" number of decimals.

Of course, both methods of calculation will reach the same result. Yet, if you are just starting, you may find one easier to visualize than the other.

Let's take another example, and calculate the one year forward outright price of the USD/JPY. First, let's identify whether it is a premium or a discount spread, in order to know whether to add or subtract the one year forward spread from the spot price.

The one year forward spread in USD/JPY is 74–72. Since the bid is larger than the offer, this signals a *discount spread*, so you must deduct. If we stick to the same side of the price, the bid side, then the one year forward price in USD/JPY looks like this:

$$104.38 - 0.74 = 103.64$$

Using a different term, three months, the forward price in USD/JPY will be as follows:

$$\text{Forward spread} = 1.70 - 1.50 \Rightarrow \text{discount}$$

$$\text{Spot price} = 104.38 - 41$$

$$\text{Bid side forward price } 10438 - 1.7 = 10436.3 \Rightarrow 104.363$$

Able now to identify all types of forward spreads, let's find out how they are calculated, and what is their relationship with the interest rates.

The Interest Rate Differential

The interest rate differential is a determining factor in forward pricing. Single interest rates are not sufficient in foreign exchange, since any transaction automatically involves two currencies. Therefore, in order to be able to measure the change or the expectations of change in the future value of a currency in terms of another, two interest rates are necessary. Figure 12.8 presents two popular sources of information in foreign exchange: monitor pages 314 and 315 provided by Noonan, Astley & Pearce, Inc. on Telerate. They will be used to help illustrate the interest rate differentials.

```
TELERATE MATRIX                                                    PAGE 314
        9:55 EDT


               NOONAN, ASTLEY & PEARCE  INC. NEW YORK ]    08/03 09:52   314
314!    EURO-DOLLAR    !    FED FUNDS   !     FRA'S       ! INT RATE SWAPS !
   :    09:51 EDT      :    09:52 EDT   :    09:47 EDT :  :  09:52 EDT :   :
   !                   !                !                 !       ACT/360    !
O/N; 3 1/16 - 3 3/16 !    BID      ASK ! 1X4   3.33 -  3.37 ; SXS  3.85 - 3.89;
T/N: 3 1/16 - 3 3/16 : 3 1/16 - 3 1/8  : 2X5   3.54 -  3.58 : DXD  4.15 - 4.19:
S/N: 3 1/16 - 3 3/16 !   LAST    OPEN  ! 3X6   3.66 -  3.70 : MXM  4.43 - 4.47:
1WK: 3 1/16 - 3 3/16 : 3 1/16 - 3 1/16 : 4X7   3.76 -  3.80 : JXJ  4.74 - 4.78:
2WK: 3 1/16 - 3 3/16 !  TERM FED FUNDS ! 5X8   3.70 -  3.74 : 1YR  3.73 - 3.77:
1MO: 3 1/16 - 3 3/16 : 3 1/16 - 3 3/16 : 6X9   3.80 -  3.84 :18MO  4.01 - 4.05:
2MO:  3 1/8 - 3 1/4  :  3 1/8 - 3 1/4  : 9X12  4.07 -  4.11 !   MEDIUM TERM   !
3MO: 3 3/16 - 3 5/16 : 3 3/16 - 3 5/16 : 1X7   3.56 -  3.60 :2 YRS T + 16 - 19:
4MO: 3 3/16 - 3 5/16 : 3 3/16 - 3 5/16 : 2X8   3.64 -  3.68 :3 YRS T + 31 - 34:
5MO:  3 3/8 - 3 1/2  :  3 3/8 - 3 1/2  : 3X9   3.74 -  3.78 :4 YRS T + 30 - 33:
6MO:  3 3/8 - 3 1/2  :  3 3/8 - 3 1/2  : 4X10  3.84 -  3.88 :5 YRS T + 21 - 24:
9MO: 3 9/16 -3 11/16 : 3 9/16 -3 11/16 : 5X11  3.87 -  3.91 :7 YRS T + 24 - 27:
1YR'3 11/16 -3 13/16 '3 11/16 -3 13/16 ' 6X12  3.96 -  4.00 '10YRS T + 32 - 35'
[ TELEPHONE NUMBER: 201 - 200 - 4900/SEE PG 317 FOR CAPITAL MKTS -SWAP OPTIONS ]


TELERATE MATRIX                                                    PAGE 315
        9:55 EDT


              [ NOONAN,ASTLEY,PEARCE (201) 200-5050 ]    08/03 09:53   315
     !  EURO-STERLING !    EURO-YEN    !   EURO-MARKS    !   EURO-SWISS    !
     : 09:52 EDT      : 09:52 EDT      : 09:53 EDT       : 09:52 EDT       :
     !                ;                ;                 ;                 !
O/N  ;                ;                ;                 ;                 !
T/N  :  5 7/8 - 6     :  3 1/8 - 3 1/4 : 6 7/16 - 6 9/16 :  4 7/8 - 5      :
S/N  :  5 7/8 - 6     :  3 1/8 - 3 1/4 : 6 9/16 -6 11/16 :4 13/16 -4 15/16 :
1WK  :  5 7/8 - 6     :  3 1/8 - 3 1/4 : 6 5/8 - 6 3/4   :4 13/16 -4 15/16 :

1MO  :  5 7/8 - 6     :  3 1/8 - 3 1/4 : 6 5/8 - 6 3/4   :  4 5/8 - 4 3/4  :
2MO  :5 13/16 -5 15/16 : 3 3/16 - 3 5/16 : 6 9/16 -6 11/16 :  4 5/8 - 4 3/4  :
3MO  :  5 3/4 - 5 7/8 :  3 1/8 - 3 1/4 : 6 1/2 - 6 5/8   :  4 5/8 - 4 3/4  :
4MO  :5 11/16 -5 13/16 : 3 1/16 - 3 3/16 : 6 1/2 - 6 5/8  : 4 9/16 -4 11/16 :
5MO  :  5 5/8 - 5 3/4 : 3 1/16 - 3 3/16 : 6 7/16 - 6 9/16 :  4 1/2 - 4 5/8  :
6MO  :  5 5/8 - 5 3/4 :         3 - 3 1/8 : 6 3/8 - 6 1/2 : 4 7/16 - 4 9/16 :
9MO  :  5 1/2 - 5 5/8 :         3 - 3 1/8 : 6 3/16 - 6 5/16 :  4 3/8 - 4 1/2 :
1YR  '  5 1/2 - 5 5/8 '         3 - 3 1/8 '       6 - 6 1/8 ' 4 5/16 - 4 7/16 '
             [**NAP NEW DOLLAR, FRA'S AND CD'S LOCATED ON PAGE 314**]
```

Figure 12.8. Pages 314 and 315 provided by Noonan, Astley & Pearce, Inc. (*Source: Telerate.® Reprinted by permission.© 1993 Dow Jones Telerate, Inc.*)

Both pages display the major Eurocurrencies rates: Eurodollars on page 314 and Eurosterling, Euroyen, Euromarks and Euroswiss on page 315. Each of the Eurocurrencies is quoted for different standard forward periods, similar to the periods in the forward currencies quotes.

Eurocurrencies are an excellent tool for traders to calculate the forward spreads. The formula commonly used to determine the forward spread is:

$$\text{Forward spread} = S \times (E_f - E_\$) \times \frac{t}{360 \text{ or } 365} \times 100$$

where S = spot

E_f = Euro foreign currency

$E_\$$ = Eurodollar

t = days to maturity

Notes:

1. If the interest rate differential of two currencies quoted in European terms ($E_f - E_\$$) is positive, then the forward spread is positive, which indicates that the spread is a premium. If the interest rate differential ($E_f - E_\$$) is negative, then the forward spread is negative, which indicates that the spread is a discount. If the interest rate differential ($E_f - E_\$$) is zero, then the spread is at par, and the spot exchange rate equals the forward exchange rate.

2. If the interest rate differential of one currency quoted in American terms and another currency quoted in European terms ($E_f - E_\$$) is positive, then the forward spread is positive, which indicates that the spread is a discount. If the interest rate differential ($E_f - E_\$$) is negative, then the forward spread is negative, which indicates that the spread is a premium. If the interest rate differential ($E_f - E_\$$) is zero, then the spread is at par, and the spot exchange rate equals the forward exchange rate.

3. To annualize the forward spread, the number of days to maturity is divided by 360 days for most of the currencies and by 365 days for the Commonwealth currencies. This is a convention.

4. It is generally irrelevant whether the trader uses the bid, offer or an average of the spot rate to calculate the forward spread, since the object of swap trading is the forward spread itself, not the spot rate.

Example:
The one month spread in USD/CHF is calculated as follows:

S ⠀⠀⠀⠀= 1.5055

Euroswiss $= 4\frac{5}{8} - 4\frac{3}{4}$

Eurodollar $= 3\frac{1}{16} - 3\frac{3}{16}$

t ⠀⠀⠀⠀= 33 days

Forward spread (bid) $= 1.5055 \times (4.625 - 3.1875) \times$
(33/360) $\times$ 100 = 19.84

Forward spread (offer) $= 1.5055 \times (4.75 - 3.0625) \times$
(33/360) $\times$ 100 = 23.29

The forward spread thus calculated is marginally wider than the broker's price : 21–23. The tighter spread is the result of the fact that brokers have access to a larger pool of prices and consequently they are able to optimize the prices.

Another method of obtaining forward spreads involves the individual calculation of the interest rates. The forward spreads are calculated as follows:

$$IR_f = S_f \times E_f \times (t/360 \text{ or } 365)$$
$$IR_\$ = S_\$ \times E_\$ \times (t/360) \qquad ❶$$

where

IR_f = foreign interest rate

$IR_\$$ = US interest rate

S_f = spot exchange rate in terms of the US dollar

$S_\$$ = spot exchange rate in terms of itself

E_f = Euro foreign currency

$E_\$$ = Eurodollar

t = number of days until maturity

$$FR = (S_f + IR_f)/(S_\$ + IR_\$)$$

where

FR = forward rate

$$FS = FR - S_f$$

where

FS = forward spread

Example:
Using one of the previous examples:

E_f = Euroswiss = $4\frac{5}{8} - 4\frac{3}{4}$

$E_\$$ = $3\frac{1}{16} - 3\frac{3}{16}$

t = 33 days (about one month)

S_f = 1.5055

$S_\$$ = 1

The bid is calculated as follows:

$$IR_f = 1.5055 \times 0.04625 \times (33/360) = .0064$$
$$IR_\$ = 1 \times .031875 \times (33/360) = .0029$$

$$FR = (1.5055 + .0064)/(1 + .0029) = 1.5075$$
$$FS = 1.5075 - 1.5055 = .20 \text{ or } 20 \text{ forward pips}$$

The offer is calculated as follows:

$$IR_f = 1.5055 \times 0.0475 \times (33/360) = .0066$$
$$IR_\$ = 1 \times .030625 \times (33/360) = .0028$$
$$FR = (1.5055 + .0066)/(1 + .0028) = 1.5079$$
$$FS = 1.5079 - 1.5055 = .24 \text{ or } 24 \text{ forward pips}$$

This approach compares favorably with the original one.

So far, we have discussed two of the three determining factors in forward pricing: the interest rate differential and, earlier in the chapter, the spot exchange rate. Let's focus now on the last factor: the maturity date.

The Maturity Dates

Just as the spot exchange rate is the most important rate in foreign exchange, the spot value date is also the most significant maturity date. All the other maturity dates are set up based on the spot date. You remember, of course, that the spot date means that the deal matures two business days from the day the deal was made (with the exception of the Canadian dollar). The two business days must be valid in both the countries originating the currencies.

Standard Forward Value Dates

As you can see on Figure 12.3, there are several *standard forward value dates*. Any maturity date falling in one week, one month, one year or a multiple of these periods is known as *standard maturity* or *value date*. Other standard maturity dates are the tomorrow/next (*T/N*), which means that the value date is the next business day or one day prior to the spot date and the spot next (*S/N*), which matures one business day past the spot date or three business days. Finally, there is the *cash date*, when the deal date coincides with the maturity or delivery date.

In addition to the standard forward value dates, there are the *odd maturity dates.* An odd maturity date is any valid day that is not a standard value date. This characteristic emphasizes both the liquidity and the flexibility of the overall forward markets. In contrast, the currency futures markets have only four delivery dates annually.

Let's take a look at Figure 12.9, and discuss several characteristics of the value dates. As already mentioned, the forward dates are based on the spot dates. For instance, when a customer inquires about a one month forward outright price, he means one month *from the spot date*, not from the deal date. In the case of the monthly standard dates, the forward, or long date, is calculated as *date-to-date*. That is, if the current date is July 19, and the spot date falls on July 21, then the one month forward date should fall on August 21. Since August 21 turns out to be a weekend (it is the same situation with a holiday), the delivery date will move ahead, to the next immediate valid business day: August 23.

July

Sunday	Monday	Tuesday	Wednesday	Thursday	Friday	Saturday
				1	2	3
4	5	6	7	8	9	10
11	12	13	14	15	16	17
18	19	20	21	22	23	24
25	26	27	28	29	30	31

August

Sunday	Monday	Tuesday	Wednesday	Thursday	Friday	Saturday
1	2	3	4	5	6	7
8	9	10	11	12	13	14
15	16	17	18	19	20	21
22	23	24	25	26	27	28
29	30	31				

Figure 12.9.

End-of-Month Value Dates

So far, it's all pretty straightforward. Let's change the scenario a little. The new current date is February 24. What is the one month forward date? Tempting as it may be, the value date is not March 26. The reason is that the spot date falls on February 26, the end of the month (in terms of business days). This means that the one month forward value date is March 31, the last business day in March. When the spot date falls on the end of the month, then the one month forward date or any other monthly multiple will fall, by convention, on the end of the month as well. Since this exception is commonly observed in the market, the trader or salesperson must remember it and make sure that the counterparty is aware of it. By mistake or lack of knowledge, the *end-of-month–end-of-month rule* is sometimes not observed by both parties. This failure generally creates animosity among players and, at times, financial penalties.

What happens if, on January 27, a customer asks for a one month forward price? What will be the forward date? Since the spot falls on January 29, the delivery date must fall on the last business day of February, which is February 26.

Two observations are in order. First, unlike the standard monthly delivery dates, when the long date falls on the same day date as the spot, but in a different month, and it will go forward to the next business day if the original long date is not a valid business date, the *end-of-month–end-of-month rule* allows the long date to move either forward or backward. In the previous example, the long date was moved backward. Conversely, if a one month forward price is executed on February 24, the spot falls on February 26 and the long date will fall on March 31. In this case, the long date was moved forward.

Second, how can both January 29–February 26 and February 26–March 31 periods be called one month terms? After all, they do have different numbers of days and different prices, even assuming a similar interest rate differential and a constant spot exchange rate. First, remember the forward pricing formula presented earlier in the chapter:

January

Sunday	Monday	Tuesday	Wednesday	Thursday	Friday	Saturday
					1	2
3	4	5	6	7	8	9
10	11	12	13	14	15	16
17	18	19	20	21	22	23
24	25	26	27	28	29	30
31						

February

Sunday	Monday	Tuesday	Wednesday	Thursday	Friday	Saturday
	1	2	3	4	5	6
7	8	9	10	11	12	13
14	15	16	17	18	19	20
21	22	23	24	25	26	27
28						

March

Sunday	Monday	Tuesday	Wednesday	Thursday	Friday	Saturday
	1	2	3	4	5	6
7	8	9	10	11	12	13
14	15	16	17	18	19	20
21	22	23	24	25	26	27
28	29	30	31			

Figure 12.10.

$$\text{Forward Spread} = S \times (E_f - E_\$) \times (t/360 \text{ or } 365) \times 100$$

where S = spot exchange rate

E_f = Euro foreign currency

$E_\$$ = Eurodollar

$E_f - E_\$$ = Δ Euro

t = days to maturity

Although the traders discussed the forward deal in terms of one month, the calculation is always made in terms of days. None of the players is open to any undue risk or opportunity when asking for a monthly termed price, rather than a price on a number of days, because, solely from this point of view, the number of days in a month is irrelevant.

Forward Pricing for Odd Value Dates (Broken Dates)

Forward pricing for odd value—or broken—dates is executed by using the standard formula. More caution, however, must be exercised, as the trader may not have the same amount of information generally available for the standard dates.

Let's take an example from Figure 12.3. As of August 3, 1993, the spot USD/CHF is 1.5055–60, value August 5, 1993. The six month spread is 78–82, value February 7, 1994. The nine month spread is 87–93 value, May 5, 1994. What is the forward spread for April 8, 1994? The number of days, counted from the spot date, is 216. Checking the rates for Euromarks and Eurodollars in Figure 12.7 for 6 and 9 months, we will have the following information:

Term	Forward spread	Euromarks	Eurodollars
6 months (185 days)	263 –266	6 7/16–6 9/16	3 3/8 –3 1/2
9 months (274 days)	338 –343	6 3/16–6 5/16	3 9/16–3 11/16

The period of 216 days may be broken down into seven months and three days.

One alternative is to receive a broker's or a bank's reliable quote for seven months forward spread. Things would become considerably easier, since the residual period is only three days.

Another alternative is to simply calculate the daily forward points average between the six and nine months forward spreads and adjust the forward price for the number of days in the odd date (216).

$$\frac{(338-263) \times (216 \text{ days}-185 \text{ days})}{274 \text{ days}-185 \text{ days}} = 26 \text{ (bid side)}$$

$$263 + 26 = 289$$

$$\frac{(343-266) \times (216 \text{ days}- 185 \text{ days})}{274 \text{ days} - 185 \text{ days}} = 27 \text{ (offer side)}$$

$$266 + 27 = 293$$

Therefore, a 216 days forward quote may be 289–293.

Convenient as it is, the method is not perfect. This approach assumes that the yield curve will remain linear, a rather risky assumption when the time span is so wide and so far in the future. In our specific example, the Eurodollar rates increase from one month to one year, with an increase of $\frac{3}{16}$ between six and nine months, whereas the Euromark decreases from one month to one year, with a drop of $\frac{4}{16}$ between six and nine months. The trader must look at the preceding periods for further indications and must consider the probability of any upcoming events which may have an impact on the interest rates during the period under consideration.

Currency Forward Outright Deals

As it has become clear by now, a forward outright is a type of trade which matures sometime in the future, past the spot date. Since it is a derivative product (it is derived from the spot price and value date), let's review its components, and what they mean for the trader.

The forward outright price consists, as previously shown, of the spot price and a forward spread, which adjusts—by adding it to or subtracting it from—the spot price. We must remember that while the spot market is very volatile, conceivably every second, the forward prices constitute a much slower market. The trader should take advantage of these features.

In a slow market, a trader looking for a forward outright price should simply inquire for an outright price in its original form. In a fast market, though, the execution should be different. Since the exchange risk is prevalent in the spot market, the spot part of the forward outright should be executed first. Only after the exchange risk is under control, or rather after dealing at the target spot exchange rate, may the forward spread be executed.

Quoting a forward outright price is slower than a spot price, which may mean that the spot rate will move from the current level by the time the trader receives the full quote.

The forward rate adjustment may be executed with the same counter-party with whom the spot deal was done, or it may be done through a swap, with either the same or a different counterparty.

Example:
Let's take the example of a one year forward outright deal in USD/CHF from Figure 12.3.

Spot price = 1.5055

Forward spread = 92 premium

In a steady market, the trader may ask for the straight one year forward outright price of 1.5055 + .0092 = 1.5147

In a fast market, the trader should just ask for and trade on the spot price, 1.5055, and later, either

- ask the same party for a quote in the one year forward spread, .0092, and execute the adjustment, or

- execute a swap for the CHF amount equivalent in size with the spot CHF which matures on the desired long date (one year over spot) with the same or different counterparty.

  Either way, the same result will be achieved: 1.5147 value one year.

Users of the forward outright deals are the common users of foreign exchange: commercial and investment banks, corporations, mutual funds, high net-worth individuals, etc.

Forward outrights are vulnerable to all major risks: market, interest rate, credit and country.

In the previous example, we stripped the spot from the forward in order to avoid the adverse impact of the exchange risk. This risk results mostly from the spot rate, with some additional risk generated by the impact of the spot rate on the forward spread.

The forward spread is linked to the interest rate risk and any change in the interest rate differential triggers a change in the forward spread.

Unlike currency futures, forward outright deals are exposed to the credit risk in the same way that all the other cash products are exposed. Since they mature at a date past the spot value date, the longer time exposures, the greater the default risk of the counterparty.

Finally, the country risk is present in a fashion similar to the other FX instruments. So, longer exposures until maturity increase the potential country risk.

Currency Swaps

A plain vanilla currency swap consists of the simultaneous buying and selling (or the other way around) of the same amount of the same currency with the same counterparty, where the two legs of the transaction mature on different dates (one of the dates being the spot date) and are traded at different exchange rates (one of the exchange rates being the spot rate). (See Figure 12.11.)

Other currency swap versions have different amounts of the base currency being swapped, or the spot leg being replaced by another forward outright leg (forward-forward). An example of a forward-forward currency swap deal is buying and selling CHF 50,000,000 in two months against four months.

The currency swap transactions began in 1971, as a result of the transition from the fixed-rate Bretton Woods Accord to the free-floating currencies. They evolved in the 1970s from the forward foreign exchange contracts (FFECs) and back-to-back/parallel loans (PLs).

Currency swaps have several applications:

1. *Taking advantage of the current and expected changes in the interest rate differentials.* The difference between interest rates generates the forward points which traders deal. The expectations of change and the changes themselves are the focus of the currency forwards market. (see Figure 12.12.)

2. *Hedging.* Hedging is an important application of currency swaps, because their use eliminates exchange rate fluctuations. The counterparties are not exposed to exchange risk, since they buy and sell (or vice versa) the same amount of the same currency.

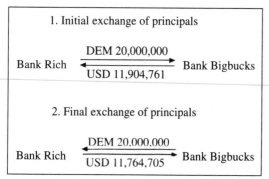

Figure 12.11. The mechanism of a currency swap. This type of foreign exchange deal consists, in its original format, of two exchanges: the initial (generally the at the spot delivery date) and final (at the long delivery date) exchanges of principals. By swapping equal amounts of foreign currency, in this case Deutsche mark, the two counterparties do not have any currency residual amount at the final delivery. The opposite is true if the currency swapped is the US dollar.

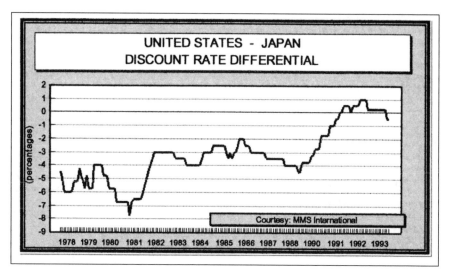

Figure 12.12. The interest rate differential between the Japanese and American discount rates between 1978 and 1993. Based on the chart of this period, we notice that the forward spread was generally at discount, since the interest differential was negative. The spread was at a premium, between January 1991 and January 1993, and then turned negative again.

Trading Currency Swaps

Pricing Currency Swaps—Premium Spread

Example:

$$USD/CHF \text{ spot } = 1.5060-65$$

$$6\text{-month forward spread } = 78-82 \text{ (premium)}$$

On January 5, Bank Prima calls Bank Secunda for a US dollar/Swiss franc 10,000,000 swap in six months. Bank Secunda quotes 78–82. In order to sell and buy—S/B—(or buying and selling Swiss franc) US dollars, Bank Prima takes the offer at 82.

Bank Secunda agrees and confirms the details as follows: "We buy and sell (B/S) US$10,000,000 against Swiss francs at 1.5060 against 1.5142 (because 1.5060 + .0082) value January 7 against July 7." We assume that both the delivery dates are valid trading days.

To make a profit, Bank Secunda must sell and buy (S/B) US$10,000,000 against Swiss francs at a spread lower than 82–in a premium market. Several minutes later, Bank Secunda calls Bank Terza for a US dollar/Swiss franc swap in six months in US$10,000,000. Bank Terza quotes 75–80. Bank Secunda takes the 80 bid. If the same spot rate is used (the spot rate is not important, provided that the market is not too volatile), the rates are 1.5060 and 1.5140, and the dates are identical.

Overall, Bank Secunda bought the forward spread at 80 (in the second transaction) and sold it at 82 (in the first transaction), making a 2 pips profit.

Deal Date	Type of Deal	Amount ($)	Rates	Amount (foreign currency)	Value date
Jan 5	Buy	$10,000,000	1.5060	CHF 15,060,000	Jan 7 (spot)
	Sell	$10,000,000	1.5142	CHF 15,142,000	Jul 7 (forward)
Total		$ 0		CHF 82,000	
Jan 5	Sell	$10,000,000	1.5060	CHF 15,060,000	Jan 7 (spot)
	Buy	$10,000,000	1.5140	CHF 15,140,000	Jul 7 (forward)
Total		$ 0		CHF - 80,000	

P&L (as of July 7) = CHF 15,142,000 - CHF 15,140,000 = CHF 2,000

Bank Secunda made a nominal profit of CHF 2,000. The profit will only be realized six months from now, on July 7, when the final exchange between the two counterparties is executed.

However, when the future profit is discounted to the present value, the current P&L is lower. The present value is calculated as follows:

$$PV = \frac{\text{Amount at future value}}{[\,1 + (IR/100) \times (\text{Tenor}/360 \text{ or } 365)]}$$

where

PV   = present value

IR   = interest rate

Tenor = number of days

Applied to our example:

$$\frac{\text{CHF 2,000}}{1 + (.04625 \times 180/360)} = \text{CHF 1,954.80}$$

Assuming a revaluation rate of 1.5000 for the US dollar/Swiss franc, the P&L in US dollars is CHF 1,954.80/1.5000 = $1,303.20. The longer the period, the less the current profit will be. In addition, taxes will likely reduce the profit further.

Pricing Currency Swaps—Discount Spread

Example:

USD/JPY spot = 104.38–41

6-month forward spread = 21.5–20.5(discount)

On the same date, January 5, Bank Prima calls Bank Secunda for a US dollar/Japanese yen 10,000,000 swap in six months. Bank Secunda quotes 21.5–20.5. To sell and buy (S/B) US dollars [or buy and sell (B/S) Japanese yen], Bank Prima takes the offer at 20.5.

Bank Secunda agrees and confirms the details as follows: "We buy and sell (B/S) US $10,000,000 against Japanese yen at 104.38 against 104.175 (because 104.38–20.5) value January 7 against July 7." We assume that both the delivery dates are valid trading days.

To make a profit, Bank Secunda must sell and buy (S/B) US$10,000,000 at a higher spread. Several minutes later, Bank Secunda calls Bank Terza for a swap in six months in US$10,000,000 against Japanese yen. Bank Terza quotes 23–21. Bank Secunda takes the 21 offer. If the same spot rate is used (the spot rate is not important provided that the market is not too volatile), the rates are 104.38 and 104.17, and the dates are identical.

Deal date	Type of deal	Amount ($)	Rates	Amount (foreign currency)	Vaule date
Jan 5	Buy	$10,000,000	104.38	JPY 1,043,800,000	Jan 7 (spot)
	Sell	$10,000,000	104.175	JPY 1,041,750,000	Jul 7 (forward)
Total		$ 0		JPY −2,050,000	
Jan 5	Sell	$10,000,000	104.38	JPY 1,043,800,000	Jan 7 (spot)
	Buy	$10,000,000	104.17	JPY 1,041,700,000	Jul 7 (forward)
Total		$ 0		JPY 2,100,000	

P&L (as of July 7) = JPY 1,041,750,000 – JPY 1,041,700,000 = JPY 50,000

Bank Secunda made a nominal profit of JPY 50,000. Similar to the previous example, the profit will only be realized six months from now, on July 7, when the final exchange between the two counterparties is executed. Discounted by the net present value, the current P&L is:

$$\frac{JPY\ 50,000}{1 + (.03125 \times 180/360)} = JPY\ 49,230.77$$

At a revaluation rate of 105.00 for the US dollar/Japanese yen, the P&L in US dollars is:

$$\frac{\text{JPY } 49{,}230.77}{105.00} = \$468.86$$

Time and taxation will further reduce the amount of profit.

The Rollover, or Tom/Next Swap

One of the most important concepts in the cash market is *the rollover or to-morrow/next (tom/next, for short) swap*. This swap is peculiar from several point of views. It is the only swap not designed for profit, although it will generally generate a small profit and loss. It is a swap designed for spot traders. Its main role is to change the old spot date to the current spot date.

Let's take an example to understand how using the rollover (or tomor-row/next swap) could have prevented a trader from getting into trouble.

Let's assume that on March 1 (see Figure 12.10), a spot trader buys USD/DEM 10,000,000 at 1.6000 value March 3 (just your standard spot date: two business days). Starting from a zero position in USD/DEM, the trader decides to keep this outstanding position until tomorrow. On March 2, the trader sells USD/DEM 10,000,000 at 1.6200, value March 4. Isn't this great? A nifty profit, and no position to reckon.

However, there is good news and bad news. The good news is that the profit is indeed there. The bad news is a little more complex. Actually, there is still a small position left over from the previous transaction. The position itself is not very risky. But it is confusing and, as a result, the trader is in-formed that he almost gave out an uncovered check for several million Deutsche marks. The gesture is penalized with a hefty compensation claim. Where did we go wrong? And how would using the rollover (tomorrow/next swap) have prevented the error?

Let's take a more detailed look at the previous example.

Deal date	Amount bought	Exchange rate	Amount sold	Spot value date
March 1	USD 10,000,000	1.6000	DEM 16,000,000	March 3
March 2	DEM 16,200,000	1.6200	USD 10,000,000	March 4

The first spot deal executed was valued March 3, whereas the second was valued March 4. The two spot values are not identical. There is a one day gap between the deals that results in a payment and receiving (P&R) problem.

The nostro accounts, which are the accounts kept by each bank or company for each foreign currency in the country of origin, have a positive, but close to zero, balance. On March 3, the trader in our example receives

US$10,000,000 (since the trader bought this amount). This operation poses no problem. Receiving money has never been a problem. However, also on March 3, a reciprocal operation must take place. The trader must pay DEM 16,000,000 to the counterparty's nostro account in a German bank or a German branch of a foreign bank. But our trader's DEM nostro account on March 3 is, for all practical purposes, zero. The DEM payment cannot be executed, although the contract has been made. The payment can only be made a day later, on March 4, after our trader had sold the US dollars, and consequently, bought DEM.

The problem of buying and selling US$10,000,000 at different rates can be easily solved simply by remembering that the nostro accounts are kept in the foreign currency. Therefore, the original position was equivalent to selling DEM 16,000,000. When taking profit on the next day, the trader should have bought DEM 16,000,000, not DEM 16,200,000, or selling US$10,000,000, because:

DEM 16,000,000/1.6200= US$9,876,543.21, not US$10,000,000

Traders around the world solve the payment problems by using the rollover (tomorrow/next swap). Technically, the T/N swap consists of the simultaneous closing of the original position, value the old spot value date, and reopening it in its identical form, save for the spot value date, which will be the current spot value date. Since the dates are different, it follows that the exchange rates are also different. The rates will be identical only in the rare case that the forward spread is at par. The rollover cost is generally very low.

From *a trader's point of view*, the tom/next swap will simply change, or rollover, the old spot value date to the new spot value date. In our example, the original spot value date, March 3, will be rolled over to March 4. This is important, since the spot traders can only trade value spot, not any other values, be it tomorrow or any other date. In order for the trader to really close the position outstanding since the previous day, the value date must coincide with the current spot value date.

The T/N swap will not change in any way the view of the trader, the original position or in any substantial way the profit and loss (P&L) figure. All it will do is enable the trader to currently deal with an outstanding position.

From *the operations department's* point of view, the tom/next swap will enable the company to make the payments stemming from the opening of any foreign exchange transaction.

The trader's expectation of the future behavior of the currency price or the total duration of a position until closing are irrelevant details to the back office. What is relevant is the capacity of the corporation to execute the due payments.

Let's take one last look at the details of the two spot deals, executed on consecutive days, and maturing on different spot value dates.

Deal date	Amount bought	Exchange rate	Amount sold	Spot value date
March 1	USD 10,000,000	1.6000	DEM 16,000,000	March 3
March 2	DEM 16,200,000	1.6200	USD 10,000,000	March 4

To enable both the spot trader to correctly dispose of the overnight position and the back office to execute the P&R instructions, a T/N swap in Deutsche mark must be executed. The following table displays all the deals and their details pertinent to the scenario.

Type of deal	Deal date	Amount bought	Exchange rate	Amount sold	Spot value date	Total position (DEM)
Spot	March 1	USD 10,000,000	1.6000	DEM16,000,000	March 3	(DEM 16,000,000)
Swap	March 2	DEM 16,000,000	1,6000	USD 10,000,000	March 3	0
(B/S)	March 2	USD10,000,625.04	1,5999	DEM 16,000,000	March 4	(DEM 16,000,000)
Spot	March 2	DEM 16,200,000	1.6200	USD 10,000,000	March 4	+DEM 200,00(P&L)

Note: In the second leg of the swap, I assumed that the T/N spread is premium 1. Details on T/N price calculations will follow in the next section of this chapter.

Therefore, as of March 2, the trader is able to trade the original position, short DEM 16,000,000, value the current spot date: March 4. If, on the same day, the trader closes the position by buying DEM 16,000,000 at 1.6200, the total foreign currency position as of March 4 will be zero. But, if the trader sells USD 10,000,000 at 1.6200, then the position will be positive DEM 200,000.

The T/N swap does not need to be made with the same bank with which the spot trade was executed because it is a separate deal.

Why is this type of deal called *tomorrow next*? The swap should theoretically be executed the day after the original spot deal. But the first leg of the swap will mature tomorrow (or the old spot value date) and the second will mature on the current value date (two business days). Therefore, the dates are *tomorrow* and the *next* business day.

In practice, the time of execution of this type of swap should be carefully linked to the ease or availability of trading. If it is difficult or expensive to execute the T/N swap the next business day, simply leave an execution order on the original date of the spot deal. For instance, in the New York market it is easy to trade a T/N swap in Japanese yen during the entire business day following the spot deal. The opposite is generally true for the European currencies in the later part of the day.

In order to avoid any unpleasant consequences, it is advisable to send a leave order on the evening of the original spot trade day to a correspondent bank in the time zone of the country whose currency was traded. In this manner, a trader gains time in the morning, when the market tends to be busier, and the correspondent bank will have the opportunity to execute the T/N swap at a favorable rate.

In the European market, the T/N swaps can be executed during the "normal" trading day, tomorrow, since the time zone overlaps with both the Asian and North American time zones.

Calculating the T/N Price

Let's focus on the calculation of the T/N price. Please keep in mind that this swap is exceptional in terms of value dates. A plain vanilla swap will mature its short leg on the spot value date and the long leg on a specific forward date. The T/N swap will mature its short leg tomorrow and the long leg on the spot date. The exception in value dates extrapolates into an exception regarding the price structure.

Drawing on the previous example, let's use as spot rate just the middle rate, 1.6000, and as the T/N spread 1–1.5. You need both sides of the forward spread in order to identify whether it is a premium or a discount. Let's use the bid side of the T/N spread: 1. You can easily recall the method of identification of the spread:

$$\text{Forward bid} < \text{forward offer} \Rightarrow \text{premium}$$

Applying this rule for the T/N swap, and knowing the price for the long leg, which is equivalent to spot price, 1.6000, what will be the price of the short leg: 1.6001 or 1.5999?

The forward spread is certainly at premium. To better answer this apparently obvious question, please refer to Figures 12.3 and 12.4. As you can see, *the T/N falls before the spot*. T/N is one day away from the deal date, whereas the spot date is two days away. In the case of a premium forward market, that is equivalent to a lower price. Therefore, the correct answer on the T/N exchange rate, which I am sure you have gotten already, is 1.5999.

Conversely, if the T/N spread is at discount, then it will be added to the spot price. For instance, if USD/JPY spot middle rate is 160.00 and the T/N forward spread is 2–1 (discount), the exchange rate for the short leg is 160.01 (if using the offer side of the forward spread).

Covered Interest Rate Arbitrage

Another way of taking advantage of the forward market is the *covered interest rate arbitrage*. Arbitrage is the risk-free type of trading where the same instrument is bought and sold in two different markets in order to cash in on the divergence between the two markets. This approach consists of borrowing currency A, exchanging it for currency B, investing currency B for the duration of the loan, and, after taking off the forward cover on maturity, showing a profit on the entire set of deals.

Theoretically, the covered interest rate arbitrage seems like an attractive option. In reality, this type of trading can be difficult to implement because of possibly serious problems. One problem is that the major currencies operate at a high level of market efficiency. And traders can hardly trade blindly in the more exotic currencies just to arbitrage, because the liquidity in those currencies is generally limited. Another problem is the impact on the balance sheet. From a corporate point of view, the balance sheet will be inflated due to additional assets (the foreign currency denominated loans) and will suffer liabilities (the domestic deposits).

Despite these problems, currency arbitrage is practiced by many corporations and banks.

Example of Currency Arbitrage

The following example is based on the exchange rates and Eurocurrencies rates, as displayed by Noonan, Astley and Pearce, Inc. on pages 311 (see Figure 12.3), 314 and 315 (Figure 12.8) on Telerate.

Example:

Amount	= JPY 1,000,000,000
USD/JPY spot rate	= 104.40
USD/JPY 6 months forward spread	= 21.50 − 20
Time to maturity	= 180 days
Eurodollar 6 months rate	= 3 3/8 − 3 1/2
Euroyen 6 months rate	= 3 − 3 1/8

First step: Cost of deposit

$$\text{Cost 6 months (JPY)} = \text{JPY } 1{,}000{,}000{,}000 \times (3.125/100) \times \left(\frac{180 \text{ days}}{360 \text{ days}}\right) =$$

$$= \text{JPY } 15{,}625{,}000$$

$$\text{Cost 6 months (USD)} = \frac{\text{JPY } 15,625,000}{(104.40 - .2150)} = \text{JPY } 15,625,000/104.1850 =$$

$$= \text{USD } 149,973.60 \text{ (cost of deposit)}$$

Second step: Cost of swap

$$\frac{\text{JPY } 1,000,000,000}{\text{spot rate}} =$$

$$\frac{\text{JPY } 1,000,000,000}{104.40} = \text{USD } 9,578,544.06$$

$$\frac{\text{JPY } 1,000,000,000}{\text{forward outright rate}} =$$

$$\frac{\text{JPY } 1,000,000,000}{104.1850} = \text{USD } 9,598,310.70$$

Cost of swap $= \text{US\$}9,598,310.70 - \text{US\$}9,578,544.06 = \text{US\$}19,766.64$

Total cost of
trade $\quad = \text{US\$}149,973.60 + \text{US\$}19,766.64 \quad = \text{US\$}169,740.24$

Cost of borrowing
USD through JPY $= \left(\dfrac{\text{USD } 169,740.24}{\text{USD } 9,578,544.06}\right) \times (360/180) \times 100$

$$= 3.5442\%$$

3.5442% > 3.50%

CONCLUSION: Borrowing US dollars through Japanese Yen is more expensive than paying the offer side in Euro-dollars.

Chapter 13

Currency Crosses

Despite the international interest in the US dollar, and the consequent pricing of the local currencies in terms of the US dollars, there is also a natural demand of pricing foreign currencies in terms of other currencies. At regional levels, commercial transactions between two neighboring countries may be conducted at the exchange rate between their own currencies, rather than going through the exchange rate against the US dollar. At the international level, the pricing of one currency in terms of another may generate information unavailable in the standard quotes against the US dollar. In the following chapter you will see the advantage of cross currency trading, whether you trade the crosses or not.

The Cross Foreign Currency Marketplace

The US dollar is the currency most actively traded worldwide. Currencies are generally quoted against the US dollar. When currencies are traded against currencies other than the US dollar, these prices are called *cross rates*. Therefore, a cross rate is a nondollar currency.

The most popular currency cross rates are the Deutsche mark/ Japanese yen, the British pound/Deutsche mark and the Deutsche mark/Swiss franc (see Figure 13.1).

Advantages of the Currency Cross Trading

Currency cross trading has been growing significantly since the early 1980s. By 1989, the daily turnover in crosses was estimated to be US $128.9 billion, or 3.6 percent of the interbank business, 2.2 percent of the brokers' market and 4.5 percent of the nonbank transactions, according to the Federal Reserve Bank of New York survey.

In the European market, there is a large commercial need for foreign exchange among the European currencies. If a Swiss exporter to Germany wants to repatriate the profits, he will find it of little use to know the value of the Swiss franc and the Deutsche mark in terms of the US dollar. What the Swiss exporter needs to know is how many Swiss francs he can get in exchange for the Deutsche marks. Figure 13.2 details the daily fluctuations of the Deutsche mark and the Swiss franc cross. The common misconception is that the Swiss franc is a stable currency. Spot US dollar/Swiss franc traders are heavy users of the DEM/CHF. Since the liquidity in spot market for the US dollar/Swiss franc is limited, they tend to cover in the US dollar/Deutsche mark, negotiating these transactions through the cross. Yet, the cross is not "flat" by any means, as the currencies fluctuate against each other. This fluctuation is generally invisible in the exchange rates against the US dollar. In terms of determining on the chart which currency is

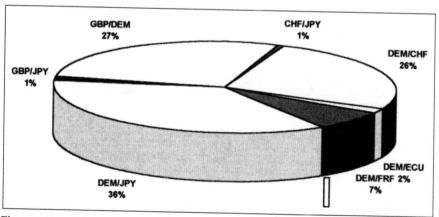

Figure 13.1. The main currency crosses as of April 1992 were the Deutsche mark/Japanese yen, the Deutsche mark/British pound and the Deutsche mark/Swiss franc. (*Source: The Federal Reserve Bank of New York*)

Figure 13.2.   The Deutsche marks/Swiss franc cross rate between 1986 and 1989.

stronger, it is helpful to remember that a high value means the Deutsche mark is stronger relative to the Swiss franc, and vice versa.

Moreover, the German and Swiss economies have a high degree of correlation which is reflected in their currencies as well (see Figure 13.3). This is an important element for the Swiss franc traders. Despite similarities, the Swiss franc market is less liquid than the Deutsche mark market. Therefore, the Swiss franc traders are natural Deutsche mark/Swiss francs users when they cannot trade this currency against the US dollar.

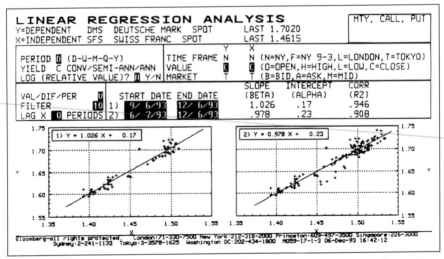

Figure 13.3.   The linear regression analysis of Deutsche marks against Swiss francs shows a high correlation between the two currencies. (*Courtesy of Bloomberg*)

Cross currency trading has been a staple on the European Monetary System since its inception in March 1979. In order to keep them within the prescribed intervention bands, the cross rates of the EMS member currencies against the Deutsche mark were monitored on a daily basis.

Even when the economic relationships between two countries are not very close, the cross rate of their currency may be significant. For instance, the most popular cross rate is the Deutsche mark/Japanese yen rate (see Figure 13.4). Despite their gigantic economies, Germany and Japan do not currently have trade liaisons at par. However, this cross rate is very popular because the Deutsche mark and the Japanese yen rates are the most traded currencies vis-à-vis the US dollar. In fact, the Deutsche mark is involved in 95 percent of all cross trading.

The economic internationalization has been an important factor in the growth of cross currency volume. The opening of Eastern Europe, South America, and South East Asia triggered a significant increase in cross trading. Although the domestic currencies are under limited demand, the hard currencies prevalent in these areas are under increased demand. For instance, there are significant investments denominated in Deutsche marks in the East European countries. Although any hard currency is welcome, investors in these markets tend to exchange their domestic currencies into Deutsche marks.

In addition, US corporations have increased their sophistication in their global management. Cross currencies are used as an effective way of reducing the financial risk especially when a company must concomitantly trade several currencies. Instead, the company may trade a single nondollar currency, before profit repatriation.

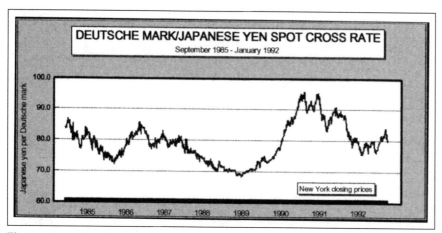

Figure 13.4.   The dominant cross currency is the Deutsche mark/Japanese yen due to the liquidity of the German and Japanese capital markets.

Cross trading can also help traders avoid the wrath of the central banks' intervention. Although theoretically possible, central banks do not generally intervene in the cross markets.

From the technical analysis point of view, crosses are very important sources of information. The same technical rules naturally apply to the crosses. Therefore, the market reacts on signals unavailable outside the cross charts. It is common to have a significant move in Deutsche mark which cannot be forecasted off the US dollar/Deutsche mark chart. However, on the Deutsche mark/Japanese yen or the Deutsche mark/Swiss franc charts, technical points are available.

Price Calculation

Although a currency cross is a nondollar instrument, its calculation is based on currencies' rates in terms of US dollars. For instance, the Deutsche mark/Japanese yen cross is derived from the exchange rates of the US dollar/Deutsche mark and US dollar/Japanese yen, known as *components*.

```
1431 CCY  PAGE DLNG    SPOT RATE    LOC  PREV      US   HI & LO WRLD
1431 DEM  CIBB CIBC*D 1.5180/90    TOR  82/92     1.5265     1.5150
1430 JPY  CMBN CMBN*J 123.92/97    NYC  93/98     124.66     123.77
1429 CHF  DRBN DRBN*C 1.3460/70    NYC  60/70     1.3570     1.3415
1431 GBP  MDNY MIDN*G 1.8770/80    NYC  75/85     1.8805     1.8670
1431 CAD  RBCM RBCR*R 1.1418/23    TOR  20/25     1.1469     1.1418
1430 AUD  CIBB CIBC*T 0.7623/28    TOR  22/27     0.7646     0.7618
1430 FRF  MGTX MGTN*F 5.1820/40    NYC  10/40     5.2095     5.1725

1431 XAU  ARON ARON  349.50/350.00 30YR TB 106.21-23 +15 YTM   7.44
1426 XAG  CSSG CSNY    3.96/ 3.97 * OIL  WTI   19.38/41    USDX 83.27
1421 FED  PREB         3.75- 3.87 * ED3  4.00- 4.12 ED6   4.00- 4.12




1431                      REUTER WORLD CROSS RATES              WXWX
           DEM          GBP         JPY         CHF         FRF
-----------------------------------------------------------------------
DEM     *        0.3503/08   81.56/65    0.8858/71   3.4107/49
-----------------------------------------------------------------------
GBP 2.8510/44        *       232.68/90   2.5271/03   9.7301/410
-----------------------------------------------------------------------
JPY 1.2248/61    0.4294/98       *       1.0857/69   4.1801/42
-----------------------------------------------------------------------
CHF 1.1273/89    0.3952/57   92.00/11        *       3.8474/25
-----------------------------------------------------------------------
FRF 0.2928/32    0.1027/28   23.90/92    0.2596/99       *
```

Figure 13.5. Two popular Reuters pages are WRLD and WXWX. The first one displays primarily the most current bank updates of the spot exchange rates in the major currencies. The latter displays the most popular cross rates, as calculated from the spot exchange rates shown on page WRLD. (*Courtesy of Reuters*)

Cross rates are obtained by either dividing or multiplying two different currencies, or components (see Figure 13.5). To calculate the cross rates between the Japanese yen and the Continental currencies, such as the Deutsche mark, the USD/JPY exchange rate is divided by the USD/DEM exchange rate. The same rule is applied for the all Continental crosses. The currencies considered so far are all quoted in European terms, which means that the exchange rate displays the amount of foreign currency received in exchange for US$1.

If one of the components is a currency quoted in American terms, such as the British pound, then the cross price is calculated by multiplying the components. An exchange rate quoted in American terms shows how many US dollars will be received in exchange for one unit of foreign currency.

Example:

The average (between the bid and offer) rates, of the major four currencies, as shown in Figure 13.5 are:

USD/DEM=1.5185
USD/JPY=123.97
USD/CHF=1.3465
GBP/USD=1.8775

The cross rates are calculated as follows:

$$DEM/JPY = \frac{(USD/JPY)}{(USD/DEM)}$$

$$= \frac{123.97}{1.5185} = 81.64$$

$$CHF/JPY = \frac{(USD/JPY)}{(USD/CHF)}$$

$$= \frac{123.97}{1.3465} = 92.07$$

$$DEM/CHF = \frac{(USD/CHF)}{(USD/DEM)}$$

$$= \frac{1.3465}{1.5185} = 0.8867$$

$$GBP/DEM = (USD/DEM) \times (GBP/USD)$$

$$= 1.8775 \times 1.5185 = 2.8510$$

These calculations are general approximations of the cross prices. To calculate the cross price thoroughly, a two-way (bid–offer) price is necessary.

In order to avoid any errors, it is easier, in the beginning, to start from the end result, and work our way backwards to the components.

Example:

As shown in Figure 13.5, the exchange rate for USD/DEM is 1.5180–1.5190 and the exchange rate for USD/JPY is 123.92–123.97. The task is to calculate the two-way price for the DEM/JPY cross rate.

In other words, our end result is a bid and an offer for the DEM/JPY cross.

A DEM/JPY bid means that you want to buy the DEM and sell the JPY. Buying the DEM is equivalent to selling the USD/DEM, and selling the JPY is the same as buying USD/JPY.

A DEM/JPY offer means that you want to sell the DEM and buy the JPY. Selling the DEM is equivalent to buying the USD/DEM, and buying the JPY is the same as selling USD/JPY.

Therefore, to calculate this type of cross, you must divide either one offer by the other bid or viceversa, but never one bid by the other bid, or one offer by the other offer.

Applying our figures:

$$\text{DEM/JPY BID} = \frac{123.92}{1.5190} = 81.58$$

and

$$\text{DEM/JPY OFFER} = \frac{123.97}{1.5180} = 81.67$$

The DEM/JPY two-way price is therefore 81.58–81.67.

In reality, this approach, although correct, is not good enough. The spread between the bid and offer is, in this case, 9 pips, unacceptable by market standards. The spread should be 3 to 5 pips, such as 81.58–61, or 81.62–67. Therefore, the traders must skew the price depending on the market conditions.

If one of the components of the cross is quoted in American terms, the calculation is different. First, the components are multiplied. Secondly, a bid is multiplied by the other bid, and an offer is multiplied by the other offer.

Example:

GBP/USD = 1.8770–1.8780   USD/DEM = 1.5180–1.5190

The GBP/DEM cross is calculated as follows:

GBP/DEM bid = 1.8770 × 1.5180 = 2.8493
GBP/DEM offer = 1.8780 × 1.5190 = 2.8527

The two-way GBP/DEM cross rate price is therefore 2.8493–2.8527

Relative Strength of a Currency

Looking at Figure 13.4 we see the chart line moving upward, to above 100 yen per mark, signaling an increase in the value of the Deutsche mark/Japanese yen cross. An increase in the cross value reflects the fact that the Deutsche mark is relatively stronger than the Japanese yen, and viceversa. What is the significance of this reading for the components?

DEM/JPY Trades Upward	*DEM/JPY Trades Downward*
Significance for the US dollar:	Significance for the US Dollar:
DEM very strong, JPY strong	DEM strong, JPY very strong
DEM strong, JPY flat	DEM flat, JPY strong
DEM flat, JPY weak	DEM weak, JPY flat
DEM weak, JPY very weak	DEM very weak, JPY weak
DEM strong, JPY weak	DEM weak, JPY strong

Figure 13.6. The relative strength or weakness of one currency in terms of another on the cross has different readings for the components. Understanding these possibilities expands the trading options of a cross trader.

Trading Components

A cross trader is not limited to buying and selling specific currency crosses. By necessity, traders also "leg-in or -out" of a cross. This means that they start or end their trading with a component, rather than always trading crosses. For instance, as mentioned in relation to Figure 13.3, Swiss franc traders frequently get caught with unwanted positions in the interbank market. The optimal solution in the short run to weather a rapid unfavorable market move is to "leg-in" a DEM/CHF cross. When the market stabilizes, the trader can "leg-out."

Another common scenario involves a trader caught in a losing cross position. Generally, a cross position makes a profit on only one of the components. Once it becomes clear which way the market is heading, the trader will leg-out the money losing component, while keeping the profit making component. This type of strategy can minimize a loss or generate a profit.

Position Calculation

Trading in crosses is executed in amounts of foreign currency rather than US dollars, since no US dollars are involved in the first place. The cross amounts are generally quoted in the first currency. This type of quoting is executed both in the case of crosses between American quoted currencies —Deutsche mark (DEM) in the case of Deutsche mark/Japanese yen (DEM/JPY), Deutsche mark/Swiss franc (DEM/CHF) or Deutsche mark/French franc (DEM/FRF). When one or both components are quoted in American terms, then it is the British pound (GBP) in the case of British pound/Deutsche mark (GBP/DEM) or British pound/Australian dollar (GBP/AUD).

Therefore, if someone asks for a price in DEM/JPY 10 million, it is understood by both parties that the quote will be in DEM 10 million, not JPY 10 million. By the way, if the DEM/JPY cross is indeed quoted in DEM 10,000,000, what is the JPY amount? To answer this question, you need to know the cross exchange rate. Using a DEM/JPY cross rate from the Figure 13.5, 81.58 for instance, the Japanese amount is 815,800,000.

$$\text{DEM } 10,000,000 \times 81.58 = \text{JPY } 815,800,000$$

When deciding to leg-out of this DEM/JPY cross position, the trader must know the US dollar value of the components. If USD/DEM spot exchange rate is 1.5180, then the US dollar amount against the Deutsche mark is 6,587,615.28.

$$\text{DEM } \frac{10,000,000}{1.5180} = \text{USD \$ } 6,587,615.28$$

How about the US dollar amount against the Japanese yen? Since we have the cross rate, the USD/DEM rate and the Japanese yen amount, we could easily calculate the US dollar amount.

$$1.5180 \times 81.58 = 123.83844$$

$$\text{JPY } \frac{815,800,000}{123.83844} = \text{US\$ } 6,587,615.28$$

There is not much reason to go through the calculations, though, because the US dollar amounts are always virtually identical on both sides of any cross.

Calculation of the Cross Profit and Loss

In the previous examples we used the DEM/JPY cross rate of 81.58 and the USD/DEM rate of 1.5180. Based on these rates we were able to calculate the USD/JPY rate of 123.8384.

Let's assume that the trader

- buys DEM 10,000,000 at 81.58, and
- sells DEM 10,000,000 at 81.68.

Since the trader bought low and sold high, we know that the trade generated a profit. To calculate the cross P&L, several methods may be employed.

Example:

The first method consists of translating the DEM/JPY rates into USD/JPY rates and then calculating the profit and loss by using the standard formula for the USD/JPY spot exchange rates.

$$81.58 \times 1.5180 = 123.8384$$

$$81.68 \times 1.5180 = 123.9902$$

$$\text{DEM } \frac{10,000,000}{1.5180} = \text{USD } 6,587,615.28$$

Assuming a closing/revaluation price of 124.00, the P&L can be calculated as follows:

$$\text{P\&L} = \frac{(123.9902 - 123.8384)}{124.00} \times \$6,587,615.28 = \$ 8,064.52$$

Please notice that the entire profit was calculated for the Japanese yen. In Deutsche mark there was no P&L since the same DEM amount was bought and sold at the same rate.

The second method is a little faster, since it involves only the cross rates, the cross amount and the closing/revaluation rate for the Japanese yen:

$$\text{P\&L} = (81.68 - 81.58) \times \frac{\text{DEM } 10,000,000}{124.00} = \$ 8,064.52$$

The same methods are applied for a higher number of cross deals.

Example:

A trader executes the following cross deals:

Buy	At	Sell	At
DEM 3,000,000	81.45	DEM 10,000,000	82.00
DEM 5,000,000	81.50	DEM 10,000,000	81.90
DEM 2,000,000	81.40		
DEM 10,000,000	81.70		

The first step in calculating the P&L is averaging the buying and the selling exchange rates.

Buy	At		Sell	At	
DEM 3,000,000 × 81.45 =	244,350,000		DEM 10,000,000 × 82.00 =	820,000,000	
DEM 5,000,000 × 81.50 =	407,500,000		DEM 10,000,000 × 81.90 =	819,000,000	
DEM 2,000,000 × 81.40 =	162,800,000				
DEM 10,000,000 × 81.70 =	817,000,000				
Total					
DEM 20,000,000	1,631,650,000		DEM 20,000,000	1,639,000,000	

Buying exchange rate
1,631,650,000/DEM 20,000,000 = 81.5825

Selling exchange rate
1,639,000,000/DEM 20,000,000 = 81.95

The second step is calculating the P&L. Using the same revaluation rate in USD/JPY as in the previous example, the P&L is calculated as follows:

$$\frac{(81.95 - 81.5825) \times DEM\ 20,000,000}{124.00} = \$59,274.19$$

Conclusion

Currency cross trading has become an increasingly popular instrument in foreign exchange. Volume in the nondollar currencies is still small, and crosses do not represent serious competition to the US dollar.

The importance of crosses is enhanced nowadays by the unprecedented internationalization of business and risk management. As they are increasingly used by a variety of players, the foreign exchange markets will benefit.

Chapter 14

Currency Futures

Currency Futures Marketplace

Currency futures are specific types of forward outright deals. Since they are derived from the spot price, they are a derivative instrument. They are specific with regard to the expiration date and the size of the amount. Whereas, generally, forward outright deals—those that mature past the spot delivery date—will mature on any valid date in the two countries whose currencies are being traded, standardized amounts of foreign currency futures mature only on the third Wednesday of March, June, September and December.

Though currency futures trading is relatively new, commodity futures trading goes back a long time. The Chicago Mercantile Exchange (CME), for instance, was established in 1919, succeeding the Butter and Egg Board, which had been established in 1898 and it is on regulated exchanges—such as the CME—that currency futures are traded.

Currency futures are traded on regulated exchanges similar to the stock markets. The largest currency futures markets are in the United States and the largest of these American markets is the International Monetary Market® (IMM) division of the Chicago Mercantile Exchange.

Foreign currencies futures trading began on May 16, 1972. The Exchange consists of the following three divisions:

1. The International Monetary Market (IMM), for currency and interest rate futures and options, with 1287 members.

2. The Chicago Mercantile Exchange (CME), for agricultural commodities, with 626 members.

3. The Index and Option Market (IOM), established in 1982, for equity related futures and options, with 812 members.

The International Monetary Market®

The trading success of currency futures since 1972 triggered the introduction of options on Deutsche mark futures on the IMM in 1984, on British pound and Swiss franc futures in 1985, and on Japanese yen, Canadian dollar and ECU futures in 1986. By 1992, the IMM had also introduced its first nondollar futures and options: the Deutsche mark/Japanese yen cross contracts.

Other Currency Futures Markets in the United States

In the United States, there are three other currency futures markets: the Philadelphia Stock Exchange (PHLX), FINEX in New York City and MidAmerica Commodity Exchange (MidAm) in Chicago.

The Philadelphia Stock Exchange. Established in 1790, the *Philadelphia Stock Exchange* (*PHLX*) is the oldest US securities exchange. The exchange has 505 members with options privileges. Conceptually similar to the Chicago IMM, the PHLX offers the same size currency futures contracts, differing only in the size of the option contracts. These option contracts on currency futures are half the size of the IMM contracts. The smaller contracts are more affordable for individual investors.

FINEX. *FINEX* is part of the New York Cotton Exchange (NYCE), the oldest futures exchange in New York (founded in 1870). There are 103 FINEX members. The exchange lists futures on the European Currency Unit and the USDX®, a basket of 10 currencies: Deutsche mark, Japanese yen, French franc, British pound, Canadian dollar, Italian lira, Dutch guilder, Belgian franc, Swedish krona, and Swiss franc. The USDX is an unique contract which offers the investor the opportunity to trade the dollar broadly, rather than against a specific currency. The composition and currency weights are described in Figure 14.1.

The size of the USDX contract is $1000 times the US Dollar Index®.

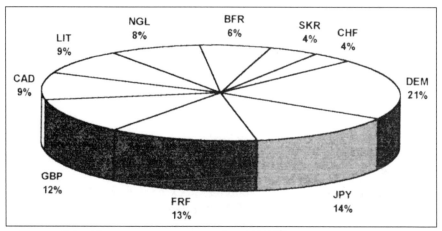

Figure 14.1.   The currency components of the USDX® and their respective weights.

The size of the US Index varies continuously, as the US dollar fluctuates against the basket currencies. It has the same maturity dates as the IMM and PHLX contracts: the third Wednesday in March, June, September and December.

The ticker symbol is DX. The minimum price quotation is .01 of a US. DOLLAR INDEX, which is equivalent to $10.00.

MIDAM. The MidAmerica Commodity Exchange was incorporated in 1880 as Chicago Open Board of Trade, given its current name in 1973, and affiliated with the Chicago Board of Trade in 1987. This exchange has 79 members and 1043 half members. The MidAm exchange offers futures contracts on Deutsche mark (DM 62,500), Japanese yen (JY 6,250,000), British pound (£12,500), Canadian dollar (C$ 50,000), and Swiss franc (SF 62,500).

Currency Futures Markets Around the World
In 1984, the Singapore International Monetary Exchange (SIMEX) opened futures trading in Deutsche mark and Japanese yen. SIMEX contracts are similar to IMM contracts, and they are cleared through a mutual offset system. This agreement enabled traders to deal futures overnight, before the GLOBEX system was established in 1992. GLOBEX is an electronic, after-hours trading system, geared toward global futures trading.

In Asia, currency futures are also traded in:

• *Japan.* US dollar/Japanese yen on the *Tokyo International Financial Futures Exchange (TIFFE),* established in 1989;

- *New Zealand.* US dollar and New Zealand dollar on the *New Zealand Futures & Options Exchange (NZFOE),* established in 1984; and
- *The Philippines.* US dollar/Deutsche mark, US dollar/Japanese yen, US dollar/British pound, US dollar/Swiss franc, US dollar/Philippine peso on the Manila International Futures Exchange (MIFE), established in 1984.

In Latin America, currency futures are traded in:

- Brazil. US dollar on *Bolsa de Mercadorias & Futuros (BM &F),* established in 1991; and
- Chile. US dollar/peso on the *Santiago Stock Exchange (SSE),* established in 1983.

In Europe, currency futures are traded in:

- *Finland.* US dollar/Finnish markka, Deutsche mark/Finnish markka, Swedish krona/Finnish markka, British pound/Finnish markka on the Finnish Options Exchange Ltd., established in 1986;
- *The Netherlands.* US dollar/Dutch guilder on the *Financial Futures Market Amsterdam/Financiele Termijnmarket Amsterdam N.V. (FTA),* established in 1987; and
- *Spain.* Spanish peseta /US dollar, Spanish peseta / Deutsche mark on *Mercado de Opciones Y Futuros Financieros (MEFF Renta Fija),* established in 1990.

Characteristics of Currency Futures

Let's take a look now at two characteristics of currency futures that make them attractive.

1. A futures market provides certain advantages to the trading of futures and options on futures:
   - It is open to all market participants, individuals included. This is different than the spot market, which is virtually closed to individuals— except high net worth individuals—because of the size of the currency amounts traded.
   - It is a central market, just as efficient as the cash market and, whereas the cash market is a very decentralized market, futures trading takes place under one roof. The "open" trading interaction on the floor is very helpful to traders, who interact physically in the trading arena.

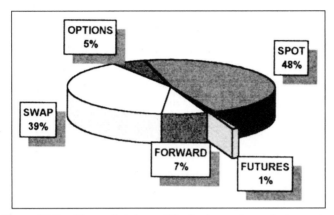

Figure 14.2.   The market share of the foreign exchange instruments.

- It eliminates the credit risk because the Chicago Mercantile Exchange Clearing House acts as the buyer for every seller, and viceversa. In turn, the Clearing House minimizes its own exposure by requiring traders who maintain a nonprofitable position to post a margin equal in size with their loss.

What a futures market does not do is guarantee that the currency will trade at a specific price at any future time. For example, the British pound future price on August 3, 1993 for expiration in September 1993, was 1.4934. On the September expiration date, the British pound was closer to 1.5500. Therefore, one should be aware that the price simply reflects the market expectations at a certain time regarding the future price of a specific currency.

2. Several innate benefits:
   - Hedging tool. Since futures are special types of forward outright contracts, corporations can use them for hedging purposes.
   - Arbitrage opportunities vis-à-vis the spot market. Although the futures and spot markets trade closely together, certain divergences between the two occur, generating arbitraging opportunities.
   - Special technical analysis formations. Gaps, volume and open interest are significant tools solely available in the futures market. Yet their significance extrapolates to the spot market as well.
   - "Price discovery" when the spot market cannot provide a price. In the second part of the trading day in the United States the liquidity may suffer in the Swiss franc or the British pound. The futures prices are used in this instance for approximating the spot prices.

Because of these benefits, the currency futures trading volume has generally been increasing continuously since 1977 (see Figure 14.3). Exceptions include a slight decrease in volume on the Chicago IMM in 1991 as a result of reduced interest from some large corporations. Also, some specific currencies—the Japanese yen, the Swiss franc and the British pound—registered losses in 1992. Only the Deutsche mark registered a volume increase.

At the same time, though, currency futures volume on the Philadelphia Stock Exchange grew.

The Look of Currency Futures

Currency futures look different relative to the cash rates we have seen so far. The only exception may be the British pound because on the IMM, all quotes are in American terms, not European. In the cash market, however, most of the exchange rates are quoted in European terms. The notable exceptions are the Commonwealth currencies—but not the Canadian dollar—and the ECU. The price difference between the futures and the cash quotes occurs because a futures contract is a forward outright, not a spot. The difference in look — no dot between 1 and the rest of the quote—is generated by a technicality: There is not enough space on the screen of the monitor.

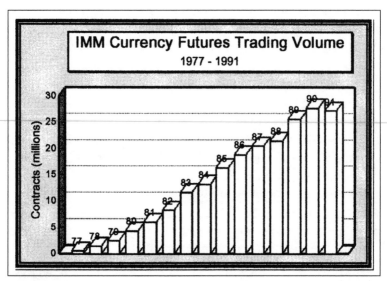

Figure 14.3. IMM currency futures showed a steep increase in volume from 1977 to 1990. A slight reduction occurred in 1991.

To calculate the futures prices for the rest of the currencies, you simply get the inverse of the outright price of the currency quoted in European terms. The outright price, as you recall, is calculated by adding or subtracting the forward pips to or from the spot price.

$$\text{Currency future price} = \frac{1}{\text{Spot price in European terms} +/- \text{Forward pips}}$$

Example:

If the spot USD/DEM average price is 1.7125, and the IMM premium spread is 0.0079, then the IMM dated USD/DEM forward outright will be

$$1.7125 + 0.0079 = 1.7204, \text{ in European terms,}$$

and

$$\frac{1}{1.7204} = 0.5813, \text{ in American terms}$$

Since futures are forward outright contracts, and since the forward prices are generally slow movers, the elimination of the forward spreads will transform the futures contracts into spot contracts. This is important in order to compare the two types of contracts, and it is important to the traders for hedging, arbitrage and price discovery.

Forward Outright Price Calculation

The forward outright pips (or spread) is calculated as follows:

$$FP = S \times (Efc - E\$) \times (t/360^*) \times 100$$

where

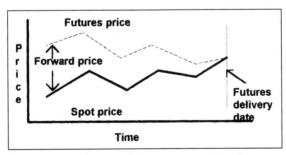

Figure 14.4. The convergence between the futures and the spot prices in a premium market.

*The 360 -day denominator is used for the DM, SF and JY. For the Commonwealth currencies, BP, CD and AD, by convention, a 365 day denominator is used.

$$FP = \text{forward outright pips}$$
$$S = \text{spot price}$$
$$E_\$ = \text{Eurodollar rate}$$
$$E_{fc} = \text{Euro-currency rate}$$
$$t = \text{days to delivery}$$

The forward outright price is calculated as:

$$\text{FWD PRICE} = S + FP$$

Example:

USD/DEM = 1.7130
Eurodollar 2 month = $3\frac{3}{16}\%$
Euromark 2 month = $6\frac{9}{16}\%$
$t = 60$ days
FP = 1.7130 × (0.065625 − 0.031875) × (60/360) = 0.0096356
FWD price = 1.7130 + 0.0096356 = 1.722635625 (in European terms)
The future price, or the forward outright price thus obtained and expressed in American terms, is then:

$$\frac{1}{1.722635625} = 0.5805$$

Futures Market and Cash Market: Comparisons

Let's see how the futures market (FM) compares to the cash interbank market (CM).

Market Environment

- *FM.* Trading takes place in a centralized market, by "open outcry" of prices and amounts, through floor brokers,
  CM. Trading is completely decentralized, being executed, generally, through dealing systems (interbank) and phones (with brokers).
- *FM.* The monitor shows only real prices already traded on the floor.
  CM. The monitor only shows suggested prices.

Market Participants

- *FM.* Players consist of commercial banks, investment banks, corporations, financial institutions and individual speculators.
  CM. By and large, the participants are commercial and investment banks, along with large corporations; individuals or smaller corporations generally have a limited participation.

- *FM*. Conterparty is the exchange.
  CM. The counterparties know their identities, either before the trade (dealing systems) or after the trade (brokers market).

Quoting Style

- *FM*. Players make one-sided prices.
  CM. Players make and request two-way prices.
- *FM*. Trading is executed in foreign currency amounts only.
  CM. Generally, foreign currencies are quoted against the US dollar, except for crosses and small foreign currency fixed amounts.
- *FM*. Futures are traded in multiples of fixed amounts of foreign currencies, known as contracts.
  CM. Generally, the trading unit is US$1,000,000, and the unofficial standard is US $ 10,000,000; crosses are also quoted in million units of foreign currencies; any odd amounts in any currency may be traded.
- *FM*. Prices are quoted in American terms.
  CM. Prices are quoted in European terms, save for most of the Commonwealth currencies and the ECU.

Settlement Dates

- *FM*. The maturity dates are standardized in order to maximize the liquidity: March, June, September and December.
  CM. The settlement dates for spot and forward are spread widely, depending on the agreement between buyers and sellers.
- *FM*. Less than 1 percent of the trades result in physical delivery.
  CM. All trades result in physical delivery.
- *FM*. Settlements are made daily through the Exchange's Clearing House.
  CM. Settlements occur in the spot market two days past the original transaction (except the Canadian dollar, which matures only one day later) or upon an agreed forward date.
- *FM*. Futures may be quoted up to 12 months in advance.
  CM. The long dates are open, as maturities may go well over three years.

Trading Costs

- *FM*. Initial and variation margins are required for all the players.
  CM. Margins are not required.
- *FM*. Commissions are required on single, roundturn basis.
  CM. Commissions are equally paid by the buyer and seller in the brokers market; there are no commissions in the direct market.

Volume

- *FM.* In terms of volume, it is only a fraction of the cash market.
  CM. Out of the $1 trillion traded daily, most of the volume is traded in the spot, forward outright and swap.

Margins

Margin is the amount of money or collateral deposited by a customer with the broker, by a broker with his clearing member or by a clearing member with the Clearing House in order to insure the broker or Clearing House against loss on outstanding futures positions.

There are two types of margins: *initiation* and *variation* or *maintenance.* The initiation margin, which is covered via liquid government instruments, such as T-bills, entitles a trader, or firm, to trade currency futures. The trader's daily loss cannot exceed the size of this margin.

The *variation,* or *maintenance,* margin must fully cover any unrealized loss and must be posted in cash by any trader holding an overnight position with a negative P&L. It must be kept on deposit at all times.

Margins are applied differently to each currency contract and, within each currency, separately to speculative and hedging contracts.

Example:
As of August 24, 1993, some of the initiation margins were as follows:

	BP	CD	DM	SF	JY
Speculative	$ 2295	$ 810	$ 1350	$ 1755	$ 2970
Hedging	$ 1700	$ 600	$ 1000	$ 1300	$ 2200

The margins posted are interest bearing.

Contract Size

The size of a contract in the futures market differs among currencies. The specific amounts for the major currencies contracts are as follows:

Currency	Symbol Chicago	Symbol Philadelphia	Contract Size	
Deutsche mark	DM	ZD	DEM	125,000
Swiss franc	SF	ZS	CHF	125,000
Japanese yen	JY	ZJ	JPY	12,500,000
British pound	BP	ZB	GBP	62,500
Canadian dollar	CD	ZC	CAD	100,000
Australian dollar	AD	ZA	AUD	100,000
French franc	FR	ZF	FRF	500,000
Deutsche mark/Japanese yen	DJ	—	DEM	125,000

Note: Other currency contracts are available as well but, due to the limited trading interest in these contracts, they were omitted.

Price information on foreign currencies futures is available daily in the major newspapers. Figure 14.5 displays the foreign currency futures information from *The Wall Street Journal.*

Floor Trading

There are two types of traders who deal futures on the floor: floor traders, or locals, and floor brokers. *Floor traders* are exchange members who execute their own trades by being physically present in the pit which is the place for

CURRENCY

						Lifetime		Open
	Open	High	Low	Settle	Change	High	Low	Interest
JAPAN YEN (CME) – 12.5 million yen; $ per yen (.00)								
Dec	.9322	.9331	.9232	.9237	– .0086	.9950	.7970	90,112
Mr94	.9322	.9322	.9258	.9263	– .0086	.9930	.8700	4,984
June	.9310	.9310	.9300	.9290	– .0086	.9945	.8540	155
Est vol 26,094; vol Wed 17,582; open int 95,256, + 1,484.								
DEUTSCHEMARK (CME) – 125,000 marks; $ per mark								
Dec	.6067	.6075	.5964	.5970	– .0094	.6650	.5657	105,930
Mr94	.5985	.5995	.5923	.5930	– .0092	.6205	.5646	3,911
June	.5943	.5943	.5905	.5900	– .0090	.6162	.5607	233
Est vol 74,977; vol Wed 62,906; open int 110,075, +5,241.								
CANADIAN DOLLAR (CME) – 100,000 dlrs.; $ per Can $								
Dec	.7574	.7626	.7565	.7622	+ .0048	.8310	.7425	38,953
Mr94	.7558	.7595	.7546	.7598	+ .0049	.7860	.7394	1,217
June	.7535	.7580	.7525	.7574	+ .0050	.7805	.7363	801
Sept	.7505	.7522	.7505	.7548	+ .0051	.7740	.7345	282
Dec	.7485	.7495	.7485	.7526	+ .0052	.7495	.7290	176
Est vol 12,465; vol Wed 15,094; open int 41,429, –3,643.								
BRITISH POUND (CME) – 62,500 pds.; $ per pound								
Dec	1.4880	1.4920	1.4766	1.4790	– .0086	1.5670	1.3930	31,350
Mr94	1.4780	1.4790	1.4688	1.4726	– .0084	1.5550	1.3950	671
Est vol 14,777; vol Wed 9,930; open int 32,090, + 201.								
SWISS FRANC (CME) – 125,000 francs; $ per franc								
Dec	.6875	.6875	.6773	.6789	– .0086	.7212	.6400	42,967
Mr94	.6835	.6835	.6760	.6776	– .0086	.7195	.6470	677
Est vol 32,502; vol Wed 32,389; open int 43,670, –6,530.								
AUSTRALIAN DOLLAR (CME) – 100,000 dlrs.; $ per A.$								
Dec	.6689	.6707	.6682	.6697	+ .0025	.7117	.6392	4,221
Est vol 474; vol Wed 850; open int 4,243, + 62.								
U.S. DOLLAR INDEX (FINEX) – 1,000 times USDX								
Dec	93.83	94.94	93.84	94.81	+ .93	97.30	91.34	6,806
Mr94	94.62	95.65	94.95	95.61	+ .92	98.00	91.78	2,474
Est vol 2,750; vol Wed 2,288; open int 9,321, – 1,290.								
The index: High 94.27; Low 93.25; Close 94.14 + .80								

Figure 14.5. Foreign currency futures information as displayed on a daily basis by The Wall Street Journal. (*Reprinted by permission of The Wall Street Journal, © 1993 Dow Jones & Company, Inc. All rights reserved worldwide.*)

futures trading. *Floor brokers* are any individuals on the exchange floor engaged in executing orders for another person. They may also trade for their own account, but their primary responsibility is executing the customers' orders first. Brokers are licensed by the federal government. CME is enforcing strict rules and the trading activity is monitored by a computerized surveillance system.

To identify the traders on the floor, the members don trading jackets in the colors of the firm they represent. They wear colorful identification badges: green for IMM, blue for IOM and gold for CME. For further ease of identification, each badge also sports a unique set of initials (handle), not necessarily corresponding with the trader's name.

On the CME, up to 4300 members may trade at any given time. The exact number varies.

This total number of people on the floor consists of brokers, traders, runners, supervisors, pit observers and others.

The trading floor itself is divided into four major quadrants: currencies, interest rates, equity and agricultural (in clockwise order). Within each quadrant there are trading pits for the major financial instruments (see Figure 14.6) and each of the four major currency futures is traded in indi-

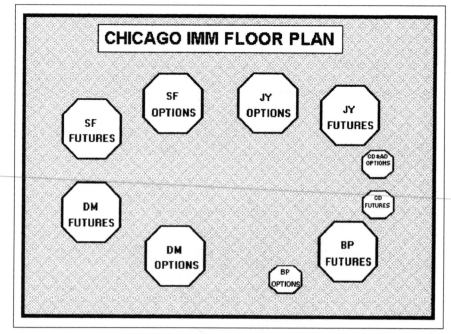

Figure 14.6. The floor plan of the Chicago IMM depicting the general position of the trading pits.

vidual pits. The others share the trading pits. The quadrants are divided by work stations. Large electronic displays continuously show the price activity of the futures traded on the exchanges.

The players on the floor attempt to communicate with each other via lively primal screams, better known as *open outcry*. This method is mercifully supplemented by hand signals, when hearing is temporarily overpowered. Executing the graceful hand signals may be testing even for professional mimes.

Trading Hours

Whereas the cash market trades virtually around the clock, the futures markets trade within certain times. For instance, Chicago IMM trades between 7:20 AM and 2:00 PM CST, except for the days prior to CME holidays and bank holidays when the Exchange is open. On these days trading ends at 12:00 noon CST.

The trading hours in the futures market have an important bearing on the cash market trading hours. The "unofficially official" trading hours in the New York cash market are 8:30 AM to 3:00 PM EDT.

Banks do not have an obligation to quote exchange rates outside these hours. The IMM starts trading at 8:20 AM EDT because the most important economic data is released in the United States at 8:30 AM EDT. Therefore, futures traders have 10 minutes to make last minute adjustments in their positions.

Price Limits

Following the New York stock market crash of 1987, trading safety became a major issue. Price limits were set up in many financial markets, in order to slow down exceptional volatility. The foreign exchange cash—or nonfutures—markets were spared, given their decentralized nature, and henceforth, the impossibility of imposing such limits. In the futures markets, limits are feasible to implement, due to the centralized nature of trading. However, traders who are able to trade in both markets can easily avoid the price limits.

The limits for currency futures may be imposed daily, between 7:20 and 7:35 AM CST, based on the previous day's settlement prices. At other times, the individual currency limits on the IMM are:

- Deutsche mark (DM)—150 pips
- Swiss franc (SF)—150 pips
- Japanese yen (JY)—150 pips
- British pound (BP)—400 pips
- Canadian dollar (CD)—100 pips
- Australian dollar (AD)—150 pips
- Deutsche mark/Japanese yen (DJ)—150 pips

Minimum Price Change
Currency futures prices change in increments of 1 pip, with the exception of the British pound and the French franc prices, which move in increments of 2 pips.

Value of 1 Pip. Every time a currency futures contract moves up or down, it generates a change in profit and loss (P&L), equal to the value of 1 pip.
The values of 1 pip differ among currencies:

- For DM, SF and JY, a pip is worth $12.50.
- For BP, a pip is valued at $6.25 but, since BP moves in increments of 2 pips, the P&L change also equals $12.50.
- For CD and AD, one pip is priced at $10.00.
- For FR, 2 pips are priced at $10.00.
- The DJ pip is the only one not valued in US dollars, but in Japanese yen, since it is a cross contract: JY 1250.

For traders outside the exchange, the prices are available from on-line monitors. The most popular pages are found on Telerate and Reuters. Telerate presents the currency futures on composite pages, while Reuters displays each currency future on an individual page. The information is otherwise similar.
Let's take a look at page 914 from Telerate—in Figure 14.7—and sort out the information. This page displays the futures of the major four currencies, in the following order: the British pound, the Deutsche mark, the Swiss franc and the Japanese yen.
The columns indicate:

- The first column shows the closest expiration dates to the current date. September 1993 contract is the nearest one to be traded.

```
┌─────────────────────────────────────────────────────────────────────────┐
│ ⌐TELERATE®MATRIX SM              9:54 EOT                      TERMINAL │
│          [ TELERATE FUTURES SERVICE ]                         PAGE 914  │
│ STERLING - IMM                                                          │
│        TIME   NET    LAST    PREU1   PREU2   LOW    HIGH   UOL  OPEN   CLOSE│
│ SEP 93 0854 - 66    14934   A14936  14940  14912  15018   389 14980  15000│
│ DEC 93 0852 - 68   A14850   14874   14850  14850  14920   105 14918  14918│
│ MAR 94 0848        A14800  A14810  A14820                            14866│
│ DEUTSCHE MARK - IMM                                                     │
│ SEP 93 0854 - 21    5813    5814    5815   5807   5852   990  5830   5834│
│ DEC 93 0854 - 14   A5768   A5769   A5770   5765   5805   140  5765   5787│
│ MAR 94 0844 - 8     5748    5745   B5600   5745   5748     3  5745   5756│
│ SWISS FRANC - IMM                                                       │
│ SEP 93 0854 - 57    6628    6629    6630   6628   6690   581  6675   6685│
│ DEC 93 0853 - 37   A6615   A6618   A6620   6625   6650     9  42-48  6668│
│ MAR 94 0851        A6610   A6620   A6630                             6661│
│ JAPANESE YEN - IMM                                                      │
│ SEP 93 0854 - 9     9575    9576   A9577   9555   9607   586  9575   9584│
│ DEC 93 0841 - 2     9590    9588   A9589   9575   9594    13  80-85  9592│
│ MAR 94 0006                                                         9614│
└─────────────────────────────────────────────────────────────────────────┘
```

Figure 14.7. The futures market for the major currencies: Deutsche mark, Japanese yen, British pound and Swiss franc on page 314 as shown by Telerate. *(Source: Telerate®. Reprinted by permission. © 1993 Dow Jones Telerate, Inc.)*

- The second column shows the Chicago (Central) time.

- The third column, labeled NET, reflects the price change between the previous day's settlement and the latest available price.

- The fourth column, LAST, shows the latest price actually traded in the market. This is different from the monitor prices in the cash market, which are only suggested prices. When the price is preceded by the letter *S*, that is the current day's *settlement price*. Letter *A* stands for *asked price,* or the offered price, and *B* for *bid price*. When *A* or *B* is posted, it indicates that only a one-sided price had been available (offer or bid), prior to being traded. Letter *R* stands for *revised price* and is used to indicate a change the exchange may make to adjust a price posting error.

- The fifth and sixth columns show the previous two prices traded, in order to indicate the very short term price behavior. The exchange posts seven previous prices on the floor.

- The seventh and eighth columns display the high and the low prices of the day. The trading range is common to the entire futures market. This is different from the cash market situation, where traders generally have close but dissimilar daily ranges.

- The ninth column shows the currency futures trading volume.

- The tenth column shows the opening price. This price is derived from the cash forward outright price as of 7:20 Central Standard Time (CST), the same way we calculated the DEM future example before.

- The last—eleventh—column is labeled CLOSE and it may create confusion in the beginning. The closing price posted in this column always reflects the settlement price of the previous business day. The current day's settlement is always posted in the LAST column—the fourth column—with an S in front of it. But we know this already. The settlement price is common to all the parties involved, unlike the cash market situation. Its importance is based on the margin which has to be posted by the traders holding overnight positions which have a negative P&L. The NET column is therefore a convenient feature for monitoring one's position and profitability.

Mark-to-Market

Mark-to-market is a daily cash flow system used by the United States futures exchanges to maintain a minimum level of margin equity for a specific currency future or option, by calculating the profit and loss at the end of each trading day, in each contract position resulting from the price fluctuation.

The calculation of the profit and loss (P&L) for currency futures is executed as follows:

$$P\&L \text{ futures} = (SP - BP) \times K \times \$12.50^*$$

where

SP = average selling price

BP = average buying price

K = number of contracts traded

Example:

You sold 100 Sep 93 SF contracts at 6685 and 100 Sep 93 SF contracts at 6684. You closed your position by buying back 200 Sep 93 SF contracts at 6628. Let's calculate your P&L.
P&L = (6684.5 − 6628) × 200 × $12.50 = $141,250
Nice profit.

Arbitrage

Arbitrage is the risk-free type of trading where the same instrument is bought and sold simultaneously in two different markets in order to cash in on the divergence between these markets. Let's take a look at the arbitrage opportunities in the futures market.

---

* This is the point value for DM, SF and JY. The point value for BP is $ 6.25, for CD and AD $ 10.00 and for DJ is JPY 1,250.

The futures market activity closely resembles the spot
There is, of course, a good reason for this. Futures are forw
ter all. The forward market moves rather slowly and the f
spread, can be easily stripped. What you are left with is t
derived from the futures price. Therefore, the prices should move in tandem. Well, they do that for most of the time. But there are exceptions, and
the arbitrageurs scramble to bank on these opportunities.

Arbitrage—A Trader's Point of View

How and when do these situations occur? In terms of volume, the futures
market is only a fraction, relative to the spot market. Consequently, it is easier to "move the market." Just imagine extending two rubber bands: a thin
one, and a thick one — about 46 times thicker. Which one can you extend
easier? (Bodybuilders need not apply.)

Timing, as usual, is very important. Arbitrage opportunities occur
when the market is volatile. It is close to impossible to spot a price divergence between the cash and futures in a normally busy market. Since currency futures are less liquid, daily ranges—the number of pips between the
low and the high of the day—tend to overshoot during a fast market (or
overextend the thinner rubber band). It's arbitrage time.

It sounds pretty easy, doing the arbitrage. Doesn't everybody like getting involved in a riskless operation which is so profitable? Well, there is
more exchange risk than meets the eye, especially for a type of deal that is
supposed to be riskless.

Whereas the range is wider for foreign currencies than the spot currencies, the liquidity is more limited. Traders may find it difficult matching the
futures amounts with the spot amounts. It is much easier to execute an order
on the spot side. In addition, translating the cash amounts, generally quoted
against the US dollar, to numbers of standardized foreign currency contracts, may add to the difficulty of the task.

Exchange for Physical (EFP)

Currency futures are, as we remember from the definition, forward outright
deals, with several special characteristics. This is a very basic, but useful issue to recall. Also, as we know by now, futures are traded on centralized
markets, which operate about eight hours per day. What happens if traders
want to trade outside these hours, but lack the access to GLOBEX or
SIMEX? An increasingly popular solution is the *exchange for physical
(EFP)*.

EFPs consist of deals executed in the cash market, outside the exchanges, for amounts equivalent to the currency futures amount, on forward outright prices valued for the futures' expiration. EFPs are generally quoted by commercial and investment banks, even during the regular trading hours.

They differ from the regular forward outright deals not only from the point of view of the standardized amounts and expiration dates, but also from the point of view of the paying and receiving instructions (P&R). The trader asking for, and trading, the EFPs must instruct the market maker to make the payments to the appropriate currency futures broker on the exchange, not to the regular nostro accounts. Unlike a cash forward outright deal, an EFP has the same credit risk coverage as a currency future contract. Therefore, EFPs are the instrument of choice for the credit conscious players.

Moreover, if there is a time difference between the futures and EFP positions, the futures positions will be subject to the margin requirements, even if the position is overall square. Since EFPs may be traded parallel to currency futures, arbitrage opportunities are theoretically possible. In reality, the costs of transactions and the tight market correlation minimize these opportunities.

Regulation in the United States

The *Commodity Futures Trading Commission* (CFTC) was created by Congress in 1974 as an independent agency with a mandate to regulate commodity futures and options markets in the United States. The mandate was renewed in 1978, 1982 and 1986.

The CFTC's responsibilities are to:

• ensure the economic utility of futures markets, via competitiveness and efficiency,
• ensure the integrity of these markets, and
• protect the participants against manipulation, fraud and abusive practices.

The Commission, based in Washington, DC, regulates the activities of 285 commodity brokerage firms, 48,211 salespeople, 8017 floor brokers, 1325 commodity pool operators (CPOs), 2733 commodity trading advisers (CTAs) and 1486 introducing brokers (IBs).

The CFTC reviews the terms and conditions of proposed futures contracts and registers them through the National Futures Association (NFA). NFA is a self regulatory organization, which consists of futures commission merchants (FCMs), commodity pool operators (CPOs), commodity trading advisers (CTAs), introducing brokers (IBs), leverage transaction merchants (LTMs), commodity exchanges, commercial firms and banks. It is responsible for certain aspects of the regulation of futures commission merchants (FCMs), commodity pool operators (CPOs), commodity trading advisers (CTAs), introducing brokers (IBs), leverage transaction merchants (LTMs), focusing primarily on the qualifications and proficiency, financial conditions, retail sales practices and business conduct of these futures professionals.

New Directions in the Futures Markets

Globex

The new direction of the currency futures markets will be influenced by the performance of GLOBEX. GLOBEX is an electronic trading system created through the joint venture of the Chicago Mercantile Exchange (CME), the Chicago Board of Trade (CBT) and Reuters PLC. The system was conceived in 1987 as an after-hours trading system, and geared toward global futures trading. The system, with terminals in Chicago and New York, was launched on June 25, 1992.

GLOBEX is designed to be used between 6:00 PM to 6:00 AM CST, Sunday through Thursday. The system is also designed to allow Far Eastern and European traders to trade futures contracts after the normal business hours in the United States.

The initial reception was less enthusiastic than expected. Despite the trading advantages and state-of-the-art technology, the system has been primarily used by domestic players immediately after hours for "clean-up" purposes. Traders who were left with unwanted positions from the regular trading hours tended to square off their positions through GLOBEX. Despite intense worldwide negotiations, international support was uncertain as of the beginning of 1994.

As the transition between the open outcry trading style to quiet computer trading settles, traders are likely to increase their use of GLOBEX.

Changes in the Trading Habits

Some decline in the currency futures trading volume was registered in 1991 and 1992. The lack of interest can be traced to a number of large corporations which consider the hedging process too cumbersome and to losses inflicted on smaller investors as a result of the unusually volatile conditions in September 1992.

To counterbalance this trend, several proposals are under consideration. They include increasing the size of the contract and a rule for big order execution geared to trading large amounts only among institutions.

New Products

In addition to the cross futures contracts, the Board of Governors of the Chicago Mercantile Exchange approved the trading of a new instrument called *rolling spot contract*. This new currency product is different, as it is focused on the interbank spot currency market, generally used by commercial and investment banks only.

In the spot market, the overnight positions must be "rolled over" in terms of the value date, which is two business days (except for the Canadian dollar). As this operation may be cumbersome, as far as the execution and the accounting are concerned, the Merc is offering an alternative which will automatically roll-over the position to the next business day. The product minimizes the accounting and does not generate delivery of currency. Since the trades are guaranteed by the exchange, the credit risk is minimized.

The first rolling spot contract was offered in the British pound, in the size of BP 250,000, four times the size of the BP future. The larger size is necessary, because the amount being rolled over in the cash market tends to be larger. Rolling spot contracts will be offered for all the currency futures contracts traded on the IMM. Traders should be aware of the fixed amount of the currency futures contract vis-à-vis the amount needed to rollover.

Conclusion

The establishment of the International Monetary Market by the Chicago Mercantile Exchange in 1972 was an innovative step in the long history of the commodity futures markets. Foreign currency futures have offered an alternative to the cash market and a mechanism for hedging. The IMM also opened the market to smaller investors. The IMM was beneficial to the CME as a whole, as it contributed to the overall growth of the futures industry.

The Exchange has been positioning itself for technological steps in the markets. GLOBEX provides a splendid computerized trading environment. Although its use has been hampered by the human need to adjust to changes the trading system is strategically placed to answer the trading requirements of the twenty-first century.

Chapter 15

Currency Options

A *currency option* is a contract between a buyer and a seller, also known as *writer,* which gives the buyer the right, but not the obligation, of trading a specific amount of currency at a predetermined price and within a predetermined period of time, regardless of the market price of the currency, and gives the seller, or writer, the obligation of delivering the currency under the predetermined terms, if and when the buyer wants to exercise the option.

Currency options constitute a unique trading instrument, equally fit for speculation and hedging. Options allow for a comprehensive customization of each individual strategy, a quality of vital importance for the sophisticated investor. More factors affect the option price relative to the prices of the other foreign currency instruments. Unlike spot or forwards, both high and low volatility may generate a profit in the options market. For some, options are a cheaper vehicle for currency trading. For others, options mean added security and exact stop-loss order execution.

The following presentation of the fundamentals of options will enable you to select the most advantageous characteristics for your own trading strategy.

Currency Options Marketplace

Currency options constitute the fastest growing segment of the foreign exchange market. As of April 1992, options represented 5 percent of the foreign exchange market (see Figure 15.1). The average daily volume came to $37.3 billion (according to the Bank for International Settlements, "Central Bank Survey of Foreign Exchange Activity in April 1992").

The biggest options trading center is the United States, followed by the United Kingdom and Japan, with approximately equal volumes.

The four major currency pairs, as reported in the 1992 survey, in options contracts were the US dollar/Deutsche mark (34%) US dollar/Japanese yen (28%), Deutsche mark/Japanese yen (6.0%) and Deutsche mark/British pound (5.8%).

Options prices are based on, or derived off, the cash instruments. Therefore, an option is a derivative instrument. Options are usually mentioned vis-à-vis insurance and hedging strategies. Often, however, traders still have misconceptions regarding both the difficulty and simplicity of using options. There are also misconceptions regarding the capabilities of options. This chapter presents a balanced look at what options are and how they can be of help to you.

Why Options Are Traded

There must be some important advantages in options; otherwise it is impossible to justify the rush to trade them all around the world. Once you see what they are, you can then decide whether options make sense to you and, if so, how you can profitably take advantage of them.

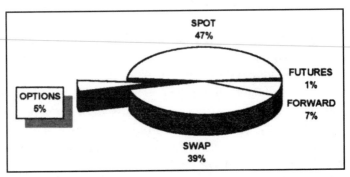

Figure 15.1. Options represented a 5% share of the currency market as of April 1992. (*Source: The Bank for International Settlements, "Central Bank Survey of Foreign Exchange Activity in April 1992"*)

Trade, Do Not Gamble

Let's assume for a moment that you, along with the rest of the market, expect some important news, perhaps the release of economic data or the approach to a significant chart point. It is just one of those "make it or break it" situations. Let's continue to assume, rather safely, that you would rather make it than break it.

The currency is likely to become very volatile after the fact. But if you wait until the information is becoming available, you may find it difficult to join the consequent fast market. In the cash market, you will likely face the choice of either waiting longer than you want to, or gambling and taking a 50-50 chance, plunging in either way and hoping for the best. Of course, hope hasn't so far proven itself to be one of the leading money management theories. And gambling is conducted in institutions better equipped for this type of activity.

The answer for this kind of trading dilemma is options. Unlike the cash market, you can buy both a call and a put, in an option strategy called straddle, and you can realize a profit regardless of the direction of the market.

Flat Market

There are few worse scenarios for currencies traders than a relatively flat market. A quiet market is difficult to bear, especially when traders are flexible enough to consider as a "good" factor both a positive and a negative piece of information for the economy. That is because good refers to the capacity of a factor to create volatility in the market. Reality is that slow trading periods do occur. Again, the solution to the problem is options trading.

In a flat market, a trader may sell, or write, options. Since the writer of the option will receive a premium, or the price of the option, from the buyer of the option, this becomes good old-fashioned trading income.

Traders who expect the currency to rise buy call options from sellers, or writers. Those who expect the currency to ease buy puts from sellers, or writers. Writers have either an opposite expectation than buyers or expect a relatively stable market.

Liquid Market

Once, when a group of students was asked why would they trade currency options instead of cash instruments, one of the answers stood out: "Because they are there." It is absolutely true, at least in terms of liquidity. The market is out there, both on cash and currency futures. The options markets are deep and there are many counterparties ready and willing to intellectually duel with you on the direction or volatility of the market. Liquidity is a con-

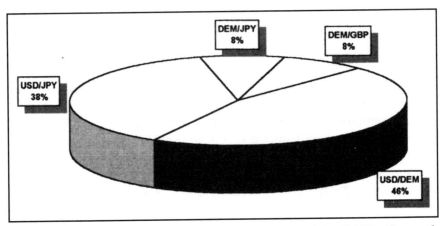

Figure 15.2. The major currency options contracts as of April 1992. (*Source: the Bank for International Settlements, "Central Bank Survey of Foreign Exchange Activity in April 1992"*)

dition *sine qua non* for a successful market, and currency options markets are generally deep.

Insurance

It is important to understand that trading options will not necessarily provide you with any financial insurance. Traders who buy options should realize that they are not securing insurance per se, but insurance as in simply knowing how much they can lose if the market performs differently from their forecast.

If, however, trading options means selling, or writing, options, the insurance aspect will completely and fully disappear, other things being equal. If the market makes an adverse move, the writer has no protection from the option.

Of course, things are not so terrible for the writer. He will be paid the premium and this offers a limited buffer against the adverse move. In addition, the option writer can always hedge or cover the short position.

Hedging

At one time, the usual hedging methods for corporations revolved around swaps, forward outright contracts and futures. However, for some time, currency hedging has become an important tool for corporations. And currency options are increasingly turning into vital tools in this process.

One advantage is that buyers know the maximum loss that they might suffer. This feature is important, as management is able to consider real costs, not expectations, when hedging is considered. Also, with the continuous overall growth of foreign exchange markets, the increased currencies volatility, and the more general internationalization of trade, corporate treasurers have been presented with higher obstacles to clear. Currency options have the advantage of offering more comprehensive hedging possibilities, due to their capacity for customization.

Ranging the Exchange Risk

Not all corporations are willing to hedge the entire currency position. Some players fix either the upside and/or the downside risk, and these single side risks may be fixed through basic options. Limiting the risk—and profitability—on both sides may be achieved through an option known as a *fence*. The ability to fix, or *range*, one or both sides of the exchange risk constitutes a major advantage of trading options. (Options strategies are discussed in Chapter 16.)

Where the Currency Options Are Being Traded

In the currency markets, options are available on either cash or futures. It follows, then, that they are traded either *over-the-counter (OTC) or on the centralized futures markets*.

The Over-the-Counter Market

The majority of currency options, 81 percent in 1992, are traded over-the-counter (see Figure 15.3). The over-the-counter market is a similar to the spot or swap market. Corporations may call banks and banks will trade with

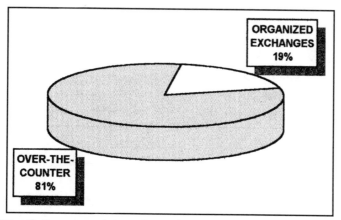

Figure 15.3. Options are traded mostly on the over-the-counter (OTC) market. (*Source: The Bank for International Settlements, "Central Bank Survey of Foreign Exchange Activity in April 1992"*)

each other either directly or in the brokers' market. This type of dealing allows for maximum flexibility: any amount, any currency, any odd expiration date, any time. The currency amounts may be even or odd. The amounts may be quoted in either US dollars or foreign currencies.

Any currency may be traded as an option, not only the ones available as futures contracts. Therefore, traders may quote on any exotic currency, as required, including any cross currencies. The expiration date may be quoted anywhere between hours and years, although the bulk of dates are concentrated around the even dates—one week, one month, two months, etc. Since the cash market never closes, options may be traded literally around the clock.

Customization doesn't come free. The credit and country risks are important factors that add to the decision making process.

Options on Currency Futures

In the United States, three exchanges offer option contracts of currency futures: the Chicago Mercantile Exchange (CME), the Philadelphia Stock Exchange (PHLX) and the New York FINEX.

Options on Deutsche mark futures have been introduced on the Chicago IMM in 1984 by the Chicago Mercantile Exchange's Index and Option Market (IOM). In 1985, options on British pounds and Swiss franc futures were added. Since 1987, options on Japanese yen, Canadian dollar, French franc and Australian dollar have been introduced, as well.

Trading options on futures on either the Chicago (see Figure 15.4) or Philadelphia (see Figure 15.5) centralized markets minimizes the credit and country risks, as the clearinghouse takes the opposite side on every single deal. Therefore, a trader will buy or sell to the exchange, not to another trader. This way, traders can focus on dealing, rather than on securing credit lines with the other participants. However, traders must be aware of the limitations generated by the reduced number of currencies available to trade and by the standardization of currency contract sizes and expiration dates.

Trading an option on currency futures will entitle the buyer to the right, but not the obligation, to take physical possession of the currency future. Unlike the currency futures, buying currency options does not require an initiation margin. The option premium, or price, paid by the buyer to the seller, or writer, reflects the buyer's total risk.

However, upon taking physical possession of the currency future by exercising the option, a trader will have to deposit a margin.

FUTURES OPTIONS PRICES

CURRENCY

JAPANESE YEN (CME)
12,500,000 yen; cents per 100 yen

Strike Price	Calls – Settle			Puts – Settle		
	Nov	Dec	Jan	Nov	Dec	Jan
9150	1.34	....	....	....	0.47	1.05
9200	1.03	1.63	....	0.66	1.26	1.60
9250	0.76	1.37	....	0.89	1.50	....
9300	0.54	1.14	1.73	1.17	1.77	2.10
9350	0.38	0.94	1.52	1.51	2.07	2.38
9400	0.27	0.77	....	1.90	2.39	....

Est vol 27,194   Wed 13,195 calls 13,-
740 puts
Op int Wed   54,467 calls 82,994 puts

DEUTSCHEMARK (CME)
125,000 marks; cents per mark

Strike Price	Calls – Settle			Puts – Settle		
	Nov	Dec	Jan	Nov	Dec	Jan
5850	1.39	1.69	....	0.19	0.50	....
5900	1.01	1.38	....	0.31	0.68	1.19
5950	0.70	1.09	....	0.50	0.89	....
6000	0.46	0.86	....	0.76	1.16	1.72
6050	0.29	0.67	0.84	1.09	1.46	2.03
6100	0.18	0.50	0.68	1.48	1.79	2.37

Est vol 58,787   Wed 9,123 calls 13,-
528 puts
Op int Wed   142,377 calls 111,383 puts

CANADIAN DOLLAR (CME)
100,000 Can.$, cents per Can.$

Strike Price	Calls – Settle			Puts – Settle		
	Nov	Dec	Jan	Nov	Dec	Jan
7500	1.38	1.52	1.52	0.16	0.31	0.55
7550	1.00	1.18	....	0.28	0.46	....
7600	0.68	0.88	....	0.46	0.66	....
7650	0.44	0.64	....	0.72	0.92	....
7700	0.26	0.45	....	....	1.23	....
7750	0.15	0.30	....	....	1.57	....

Est vol 1,362   Wed 1,035 calls 603 puts
Op int Wed   7,847 calls 6,057 puts

BRITISH POUND (CME)
62,500 pounds; cents per pound

Strike Price	Calls – Settle			Puts – Settle		
	Nov	Dec	Jan	Nov	Dec	Jan
1425	....	6.08	....	0.16	0.70	1.54
1450	....	4.18	....	0.52	1.30	2.40
1475	1.72	2.70	....	1.32	2.30	3.56
1500	0.74	1.60	....	2.84	3.68	5.00
1525	0.26	0.90	1.50	4.86	5.48	....
1550	0.12	0.48	0.98	7.20	7.54	....

Est vol 1,402   Wed 337 calls 639 puts
Op int Wed   16,264 calls 12,515 puts

SWISS FRANC (CME)
125,000 francs; cents per franc

Strike Price	Calls – Settle			Puts – Settle		
	Nov	Dec	Jan	Nov	Dec	Jan
6700	....	1.65	....	0.32	0.76	1.23
6750	....	1.36	....	0.50	0.97	....
6800	0.62	1.10	....	0.73	1.21	....
6850	0.42	0.88	....	1.03	1.49	....
6900	0.27	0.70	1.06	1.38	1.80	....
6950	0.17	0.54	....	1.78	2.14	....

Est vol 3,882   Wed 1,041 calls 801 puts
Op int Wed   12,376 calls 8,858 puts

U.S. DOLLAR INDEX (FINEX)
1,000 times index

Strike Price	Calls – Settle			Puts – Settle		
	Nov	Dec	Jan	Nov	Dec	Jan
93	1.99	2.37	....	0.18	0.57	....
94	1.24	1.72	....	0.43	0.91	....
95	0.73	1.19	....	0.87	1.38	....
96	0.33	0.78	1.54	1.51	1.97	....
97	0.13	0.49	....	2.32	2.66	....
98	....	0.29	....	....	....	....

Est vol 277   Wed 184 calls 151 puts
On int Wed   1,374 calls 1,552 puts

Figure 15.4. Options on currency futures traded on the Chicago Mercantile Exchange. (*Reprinted by permission of The Wall Street Journal, © 1993 Dow Jones & Company, Inc. All rights reserved worldwide.*)

The last day of trading in options on currency futures is two Fridays prior to the third Wednesday of the contract month.

For more information regarding the characteristics of currency futures traded on the International Monetary Market, refer to Chapter 14. In addition, you may contact the Chicago Mercantile Exchange at (312) 930-1000.

Expiration months for regular options: March, June, September, December + 2 near-term months.

Last day of trading for regular options: Friday before the third Wednesday of expiring month.

For more information regarding the characteristics of currency futures traded on the Philadelphia Stock Exchange, call 1-800-THE-PHLX or (215) 496-5321.

The U.S. Dollar Index

FINEX, a division of the New York Cotton Exchange, offers a centralized market for trading options on the US Dollar Index. This index—which consists of the weighted average of the prices of ten foreign currencies against

OPTIONS
PHILADELPHIA EXCHANGE

	Calls Vol.	Calls Last	Puts Vol.	Puts Last
FFranc				171.20
250,000 French Franc EOM-European style.				
17½ Oct	...	...	300	4.34
DMark				60.00
62,500 German Mark EOM-European style.				
60 Oct	...	...	450	0.32
61 Oct	35	0.31	...	...
68 Nov	50	0.01	...	...
62,500 German Marks EOM-European style.				
56½ Nov	...	...	50	0.05
59½ Oct	...	...	450	0.16
61½ Nov	150	0.38	...	...
64½ Nov	100	0.06	...	...
SFranc				68.06
62,500 Swiss Francs-European style.				
69 Oct	...	...	10	0.92
Australian Dollar				67.08
50,000 Australian Dollar EOM-cents per unit.				
66 Oct	...	...	5	0.09
67 Oct	5	0.30	25	0.39
68 Oct	5	0.06	...	...
50,000 Australian Dollars-European Style.				
67 Nov	10	0.59	...	...
50,000 Australian Dollars-cents per unit.				
65 Dec	13	2.02	...	...
66 Nov	4	1.09	5	0.28
67 Nov	10	0.52	25	0.70
68 Nov	5	0.20	...	...
68 Mar	4	1.03	...	...
British Pound				148.36
31,250 British Pound EOM-cents per unit.				
147½ Oct	...	...	100	0.54
150 Oct	100	0.48	128	1.82
152½ Nov	2	0.80	...	...
31,250 British Pounds-cents per unit.				
145 Dec	...	...	360	1.60
147½ Nov	...	...	14	1.48
147½ Dec	...	...	776	2.66
147½ Mar	...	...	370	4.70
150 Nov	37	1.20	...	...
152½ Nov	30	0.70	...	...
155 Dec	4	0.88	...	...
157½ Mar	370	1.40	...	...
British Pound-GMark				247.40
31,250 British Pound-German Mark cross.				
244 Nov	...	...	320	0.90
244 Dec	24	4.92	...	...
248 Nov	66	0.88	...	...
250 Nov	10	0.44	...	...
31,250 British Pound-German mark EOM.				
244 Oct	...	...	320	0.58
246 Oct	384	0.76	10	1.02
Canadian Dollar				75.96
50,000 Canadian Dollars EOM-cents per unit.				
75½ Oct	...	...	6	0.29
50,000 Canadian Dollars-European Style.				
74½ Nov	...	...	5	0.16
50,000 Canadian Dollars-cents per unit.				
73 Mar	...	...	20	0.39
74 Dec	...	...	3	0.27
74½ Nov	...	...	150	0.15
75 Nov	...	...	50	0.22
75 Dec	...	...	8	0.48
75½ Nov	...	...	150	0.36
76 Nov	10	0.54	...	...
76 Mar	10	1.06	...	...
76½ Nov	...	...	20	1.06
77 Nov	...	...	14	1.35
77 Dec	...	...	2	1.62
78 Dec	...	...	10	2.38
78 Mar	77	0.45	...	...
78½ Mar	...	...	5	3.24
ECU				114.67
62,500 European Currency Units EOM-cents per unit.				
116 Oct	8	0.37	...	...
62,500 European Currency Units-cents per unit.				
114 Dec	...	...	16	1.72
French Franc				171.20
250,000 French Francs EOM-10ths of a unit per unit.				
17½ Oct	...	...	25	3.92
250,000 French Francs-10ths of a cent per unit.				
16½ Dec	...	...	60	0.98
16¾ Dec	...	...	210	1.62
17 Mar	...	...	86	5.48
17½ Nov	20	0.60	20	4.40
17½ Dec	...	...	2	4.90
17¾ Mar	55	2.04	...	...
18 Mar	110	1.52	...	...
18¼ Dec	210	0.28	...	...
250,000 French Francs-European Style.				
17 Nov	...	...	300	1.62
17¾ Dec	50	0.64	...	...
GMark-JYen				64.97
62,500 German Mark-Japanese Yen cross.				
65 Nov	...	...	65	0.76
66 Nov	65	0.42	...	...
67 Nov	65	0.17	...	...
German Mark				60.00
62,500 German Marks EOM-cents per unit.				
57½ Nov	...	...	500	0.16
58 Nov	...	...	130	0.13
59 Oct	...	...	200	0.11
59 Dec	...	...	150	0.53
59½ Oct	25	0.69	1005	0.20
60 Oct	7	0.55	242	0.33
60 Nov	6	0.84	130	0.87
60 Dec	...	...	150	0.90
60½ Oct	482	0.21	875	0.67
61 Oct	270	0.16	...	...
61½ Oct	200	0.09	...	...
62 Nov	4	0.45	...	...
62½ Oct	100	0.03	...	...
63 Nov	65	0.22	...	...
62,500 German Marks-European Style.				
56 Mar	...	...	52	0.56
57 Nov	...	...	100	0.03
57 Mar	...	...	20	0.80
57½ Nov	...	...	50	0.05
58 Nov	...	...	50	0.09
58½ Dec	...	...	1015	0.55
59 Dec	10	1.81	...	...
59½ Dec	...	...	53	0.92
60 Nov	...	...	15	0.50
60 Dec	200	1.01	505	1.08
60½ Dec	...	...	20	1.37
61 Nov	8	0.37	...	...
61 Dec	515	0.62	15	1.51
61½ Nov	150	0.23	26	1.61
62 Mar	...	...	50	3.26
62½ Nov	800	0.10	...	...
63 Nov	200	0.06	...	...
63 Dec	...	...	5	3.22
63 Mar	20	0.75	...	...
63½ Nov	100	0.07	...	...
64 Nov	100	0.04	...	...
64½ Nov	200	0.03	...	...
62,500 German Marks-cents per unit.				
55 Dec	...	...	15	0.05
55 Mar	1	5.08	...	...
56 Mar	...	...	38	0.61
57 Dec	...	...	350	0.22
57 Mar	...	...	96	0.85
58 Nov	12	2.18	10	0.11
58 Dec	16	2.19	1018	0.40
58 Mar	...	...	244	1.21
58½ Nov	...	...	90	0.20
58½ Dec	...	...	500	0.39
59 Nov	...	...	214	0.37
59 Dec	8	1.59	245	0.78
59 Mar	...	...	39	1.61
59½ Nov	...	...	1219	0.54
59½ Dec	...	...	11	0.99
60 Nov	70	0.72	424	0.78
60 Dec	509	0.97	931	1.20
60 Mar	131	1.75	695	2.20
60½ Nov	217	0.45	41	0.90
60½ Dec	...	...	465	1.50
61 Nov	946	0.30	215	1.21
61 Dec	733	0.60	67	1.74
61 Mar	10	1.22	146	2.60
61½ Nov	1228	0.19	343	1.81
61½ Dec	...	...	6	2.12
62 Nov	302	0.15	10	2.24
62 Dec	406	0.31	124	2.50
62 Mar	1	1.15	6	3.45
62½ Nov	8	0.09	5	1.78
62½ Dec	892	0.30	...	...
63 Nov	130	0.07	7	3.21
63 Dec	90	0.21	2	3.40
63 Mar	48	0.63	...	...
63½ Nov	7	0.06	...	...
64 Nov	5	0.03	...	...
64 Dec	6715	0.12	...	...
64 Mar	10	0.47	...	...
65 Mar	...	...	3	5.78
66 Mar	30	0.25	...	...
Japanese Yen				92.41
6,250,000 Japanese Yen EOM-100ths of a cent per unit.				
91 Oct	...	...	40	0.15
92 Oct	...	...	15	0.45
93 Oct	2	0.35	...	...
6,250,000 Japanese Yen EOM.				
91½ Oct	...	...	345	0.20
92½ Oct	...	...	80	0.58
93½ Oct	30	0.24	...	...
6,250,000 Japanese Yen-100ths of a cent per unit.				
81 Mar	...	...	31	0.06
85 Dec	...	...	9	0.05
87 Mar	...	...	1	0.56
88 Mar	...	...	32	0.86
89 Dec	...	...	260	0.39
90 Nov	...	...	485	0.25
90 Dec	...	...	16	0.58
90½ Nov	...	...	5	0.32
91 Nov	...	...	270	0.45
91 Dec	40	2.46	6	0.90
91½ Nov	...	...	20	0.51
91½ Dec	...	...	2	0.93
92 Nov	...	...	151	0.82
92 Dec	...	...	19	1.26
92 Mar	...	...	302	2.23
92½ Nov	...	...	9	0.91
92½ Dec	75	1.47	110	1.58
93 Nov	12	0.74	127	1.22
93 Dec	...	...	342	1.82
93 Mar	500	2.43	525	2.72
94 Nov	5	0.43	27	1.86
94 Dec	200	0.93	24	2.35
94½ Nov	...	...	1	2.29
95 Nov	20	0.22	...	...
95 Dec	420	0.60	4	3.16
96 Nov	40	0.12	...	...
96 Dec	142	0.40	...	...
97 Dec	30	0.26	...	...
97 Mar	10	1.05	...	...
98 Nov	50	0.05	...	...
98 Dec	7	0.17	...	...
98 Mar	322	0.80	2	6.00
101 Mar	10	0.40	...	...
6,250,000 Japanese Yen-European Style.				
90½ Dec	...	...	250	0.76
92½ Dec	...	...	250	1.56
95½ Dec	250	0.46	...	...
98 Nov	10	0.05	...	...
Swiss Franc				68.06
62,500 Swiss Franc EOM-cents per unit.				
68 Oct	36	0.52	10	0.20
62,500 Swiss Francs EOM.				
68½ Oct	15	0.44	5	0.35
62,500 Swiss Francs-European Style.				
65 Dec	...	...	40	0.19
65½ Dec	...	...	25	0.25
66 Dec	...	...	10	0.34
66½ Dec	...	...	12	0.43
67 Dec	...	...	30	0.82
67½ Dec	...	...	25	0.70
68 Dec	50	1.66	10	0.92
68½ Dec	78	1.40	12	1.11
69 Dec	40	0.84	25	1.36
70½ Dec	12	0.60	...	...
77 Dec	25	0.03	...	...
62,500 Swiss Francs-cents per unit.				
62 Mar	...	...	124	0.38
64 Mar	...	...	10	0.67
65 Dec	...	...	300	0.79
66 Nov	...	...	10	0.14
66 Dec	...	...	230	0.46
67 Dec	20	1.86	10	0.83
67½ Nov	...	...	17	0.67
67½ Dec	...	...	4	0.98
68 Dec	...	...	28	1.24
68 Mar	...	...	31	2.23
69 Nov	9	0.53	3	1.25
69 Dec	...	...	362	1.88
69 Mar	331	1.68	197	2.90
69½ Nov	4	0.41	...	...
69½ Dec	230	0.72	8	2.05
70 Nov	10	0.27	...	...
70 Dec	10	0.57	11	2.56
70 Mar	...	...	9	3.36
71 Dec	10	0.38	...	...
71½ Dec	250	0.27	...	...
72 Dec	20	0.27	...	...
74 Dec	25	0.08	...	...
75 Dec	25	0.04	...	...
Call Vol 25,587		Open Int ... 562,712		
Put Vol 25,307		Open Int ... 542,256		

Figure 15.5. Options on currency futures traded on the Philadelphia Stock Exchange. *(Reprinted by permission of The Wall Street Journal, © 1993 Dow Jones & Company, Inc. All rights reserved worldwide.)*

the US dollar—provides the same general indication of the international value of the US dollar as the Dow Jones Industrial Average provides of the value of the US stock market.

These ten countries have advanced foreign exchange markets and close economic relations with the United States. The currencies, the formula and the weights used to calculate the USDX are identical to those used by the Federal Reserve Board to calculate their own trade-weighted dollar index.

Contract Specifications of Options on Currency Futures on the Chicago Mercantile Exchange (CME)

	Deutsche Mark	Japanese Yen	British Pound	Swiss Franc	Canadian Dollar	Australian Dollar	DEM/JPY
Ticker Symbol	Calls: CM Puts: PM	Calls: CJ Puts: PJ	Calls: CP Puts: PP	Calls: CF Puts: PF	Calls: CV Puts: PV	Calls: KA Puts: JA	Calls: DJ Puts: DJ
Option Coverage	1 DM futures contract (DM 125,000) (DM125,000)	1 JY futures contract (JY12,500,000)	1 BP futures contract (BP 62,500)	1 SF futures contract (SF 125,000)	1 CD futures contract (CD 100,000)	1 AD futures contract (AD 1000,000)	1 DM/JY futures contract
Strike Price Intervals	US 1¢	US .01¢	US 2.5¢	US 1¢	US .5¢	US 1¢	1.00 JY per DM
Quotations	US $ per mark	US $per yen	US $ per pound	US $ per franc	US $ per C $	US $ per A $	JY per DM
Minimum Price Change	.0001	.000001	.0002	.0001	.0001	.0001	.01
Value of 1 Point	$ 12.50	$ 12.50	$ 6.25	$ 12.50	$ 10.00	$ 10.00	¥ 1,250
Months Traded	Jan. / Feb. / Mar.	Apr. / May / Jun.		Jul. / Aug. / Sep.		Oct. / Nov. / Dec.	
Underlying Futures	Mar.	Jun.		Sep.		Dec.	

Figure 15.6.   Contract specifications of the options on currency futures traded on the Chicago Mercantile Exchange (CME).

Contract Specifications of Options on Currency Futures on
The Philadelphia Stock Exchange (PHLX)

	Deutsche Mark	Japanese Yen	British Pound	Swiss Franc	Canadian Dollar	Australian Dollar
Ticker Symbol	Am: XDM Eu: CDM	Am: XJY Eu: CJY	Am: XBP Eu: CBP	Am: XSF Eu: CSF	Am: XCD Eu: CCD	Am: XAD Eu: CAD
Option size	DM 62,500	JY 6,250,000	BP 31,250	SF 62,500	CD 50,000	AD 50,000
Minimum Price Change	.0001	.000001	.0001	.0001	.0001	.0001

	French Franc	European Currency Unit (ECU)	Deutsche Mark/ Japanese Yen	British Pound/ Deutsche Mark	British Pound/ Japanese Yen
Ticker Symbol	Am: XFF Eu: CFF	Am: n.a. Eu: n.a.	MYX	PMX	PYX
Option size	FF 250 ,000	ECU 62,500	DM 62,500	BP 31,250	BP 31,250
Minimum Price Change	.00002	.0001	625 JY	6.25 DM	625 JY

Figure 15.7. Contract specifications of the options on currency futures traded on the Philadelphia Stock Exchange (PHLX).

Following are the details for the spot USDX.

Currency	Base Rate	Weight (%)
Deutsche mark	35.548	20.8
Japanese yen	0.3819	13.6
French franc	22.191	13.1
British pound	247.24	11.9
Canadian dollar	100.33	9.1
Italian line	0.176	9.0
Dutch guilder	34.834	8.3
Belgian franc	2.5377	6.4
Swedish krona	22.582	4.2
Swiss franc	31.084	3.6

The spot USDX is calculated as the geometric trade-weighted average of the changes of the ten major currencies relative to the base period of March 1973, rounded to two decimal points.

$$\text{Multiplier} = (\text{Base rate/Spot rate})^{\text{Currency weight}}$$

where

Base rate = exchange rate in the base period (March 1973) in American terms

Spot rate = current spot rate in American terms

Currency weight = weight assigned to each currency, based on the
respective country's relative share of world trade.

The futures contract (symbol is DX) size is $1000 times the US Dollar Index. FINEX offers options (symbol DO) on USDX futures.
For additional information, call FINEX at (212) 938-2638.

Terminology

Currency Option

A *currency option* is a contract between a buyer and a seller, also known as writer, which gives:

- the *buyer* the right, but not the obligation, of trading a specific quantity of a currency at a predetermined price and within a predetermined period of time, regardless of the market price of the currency, and

- the *seller, or writer,* the obligation of delivering or taking delivery of the currency under the predetermined terms, if and when the buyer wants to exercise the option.

There are two classes of options: calls and puts. Traders who expect the currency to rise, buy calls from option sellers, or writers. Those expecting a currency to ease, buy puts from writers. Writers either have the opposite expectation than the buyers, or expect a relatively stable market.

Premium

Premium is the price of the option paid by the buyer to the seller. It is usually paid at the time of the trade, but it may also be paid at the expiration date. Premium may be quoted in points or in percentages and may be expressed in four different ways:

1. *Percentage in US dollars.* If both the unit of account and the premium are quoted in the same currency, then the price will be quoted in the OTC market as a percentage of the US dollar amount through the strike or exercise price—the price at which the underlying currency will be delivered upon exercise.

Example:
Buy a June 5 Swiss franc call struck at CHF 1.50 for 4 percent.
If the amount is CHF 3,000,000, then the premium will be:

$$\frac{\text{CHF } 3,000,000}{\text{CHF } 1.50} = \text{USD } 2,000,000$$

USD 2,000,000 × 4 percent = USD 80,000

2. *In US dollars where the option quotes are made in foreign currency per US dollar (European terms) in the OTC market.*

Example:
Buy a June 5 Swiss franc call struck at CHF 1.50 for USD .027. If the amount is CHF 3,000,000, then the premium will be:

CHF 3,000,000 × USD .027 = USD 81,000

3. *In US dollars where the option quotes are made in US dollar per foreign currency unit (American terms) on the futures market.*

Example:
A quotation of .88 would represent $.0088 per DM. The option premium would be $550 (62,500 DM × $.0088) on the Philadelphia Stock Exchange.

4. *In foreign currency.*

Example:
A quotation of .60 in a DM/JY contract would be .6 yen per mark on the Philadelphia Stock Exchange. The premium would be 37,500 JY (.6 JY × 62,500 DM)

Theoretical Models: Factors Determining Option Price

Seven major factors have an impact on the option price:

1. Price of the currency
2. Strike (exercise) price
3. Volatility of the currency
4. Expiry date
5. Interest rate differential
6. Call or put
7. American or European option style

In the following seven sections, we will examine these factors in detail and provide numerous figures and examples to illustrate their impact on option prices.

Price of Currency

The currency price is the central building block, as all the other factors are compared and analyzed against it. It is the currency price behavior that both generates the need for options and impacts on the profitability of options.

The impact of the currency price on the option premium is measured by delta, the first of the "Greek letters" that are used to describe aspects of the theoretical pricing models that follow in this discussion of factors determining the option price.

Delta. Delta, or commonly Δ, is the first derivative of the option pricing model. Delta may be viewed from three angles.

1. Generally, it is understood to be the *change* of the currency option price relative to a change in the currency price. For instance, an option with a delta of .5 is expected to move at one half the rate of change of the currency price. Therefore, if the price of a currency goes up 10 percent, then the price of an option on that particular currency is expected to rise by 5 percent.

2. Delta may also be perceived by futures traders to be the *hedge ratio* between the option contracts and the currency futures contracts necessary to establish a neutral hedge. Therefore, an option with the delta = .5 will need two option contracts for each of the currency futures contracts.

3. Finally, delta may be called the *theoretical* or *equivalent share position*. In this case, delta is the number of currency futures contracts by which a call buyer is long or a put buyer is short. If we use the same example of the delta of .5, then the buyer of the put option is short half a currency futures contract.

The value of delta ranges between 0 and 1. Figure 15.8 presents the pricing report and the graph of delta for Deutsche marks calls.

Dynamic Hedging. The relationship between the price of the currency and the premium of the option on that specific currency is intrinsically dynamic. To keep this relationship constant, the position must be *delta hedged*. Since the hedge must be adjusted continuously, this process is known as *dynamic hedging*. The failure to implement dynamic hedging generates additional market risk to the position.

Applying this method in practice may be a taxing undertaking. When volatility significantly exceeds a trader's forecast, the cost of the dynamic hedging may be very high. In addition, the hedge does not provide comprehensive protection in high volatility—crisis—situations where the currency prices are gapped. *Price gapping* means that prices jumped from one level to another, rather than moving continuously to the sequential price. For instance, if the price is 1.6000, then the next price on the upside in a regular market should be 1.6001 and then 1.6002. In a gapping market, the

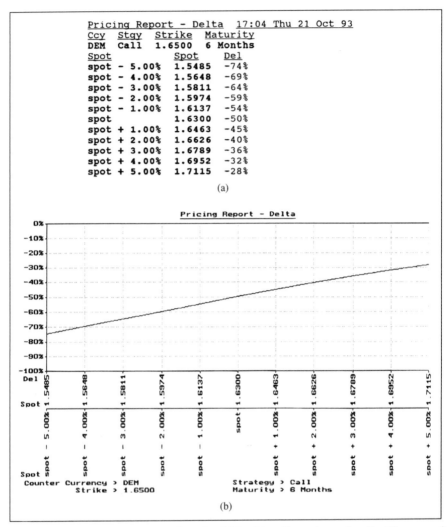

```
Pricing Report - Delta   17:04 Thu 21 Oct 93
Ccy  Stgy  Strike  Maturity
DEM  Call  1.6500  6 Months
Spot            Spot     Del
spot - 5.00%    1.5485   -74%
spot - 4.00%    1.5648   -69%
spot - 3.00%    1.5811   -64%
spot - 2.00%    1.5974   -59%
spot - 1.00%    1.6137   -54%
spot            1.6300   -50%
spot + 1.00%    1.6463   -45%
spot + 2.00%    1.6626   -40%
spot + 3.00%    1.6789   -36%
spot + 4.00%    1.6952   -32%
spot + 5.00%    1.7115   -28%
```

(a)

(b)

Figure 15.8. Pricing report (a) and graph of delta (b) — Deutsche mark calls. (*Courtesy of Astrogamma ©1993 by Astrogamma, Inc.*)

next price after 1.6000 may be 1.6050, allowing the trader no room of adjusting his position.

Traders may be unable to secure prices in the spot, forward outright or futures market, temporarily leaving the position delta unhedged. In order to avoid the high cost of hedging and the risk of unusually high volatility, traders may hedge their original options positions with other options. This method of risk neutralization is called *gamma,* or *vega hedging.*

Gamma. *Gamma* (Γ) is also known as the *curvature of the option*. It is the second derivative of the option pricing model and is the rate of change of an option's delta, or the sensitivity of the delta. For instance, an option with delta = .5 and gamma = .05 is expected to have a delta = .55 if the currency rises by 1 point, or a delta = .45 if the currency decreases by 1 point. Gamma ranges between 0 percent for deep out-of-money options to 100 percent for deep in-the-money options. It may therefore be useful to think of the gamma as the acceleration of the option relative to the movement of the currency.

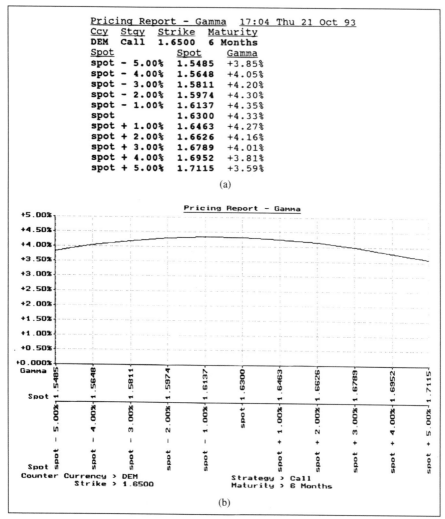

Figure 15.9. Pricing report (a) and graph of gamma (b) for Deutsche mark calls. (*Courtesy of Astrogamma* ©*1993 by Astrogamma, Inc.*)

A Trader's Point of View

- A decrease in volatility or time to expiration may increase sharply the gamma of an option at-the-money.

Strike or Exercise Price

What does it mean to say that the buyer has the right to "exercise" his or her option at a predetermined price? *Exercising* refers to the process in which a buyer converts the option into a currency position. In the case of the call, exercising will create a long currency position, whereas in the case of the put, the buyer will have a short currency position.

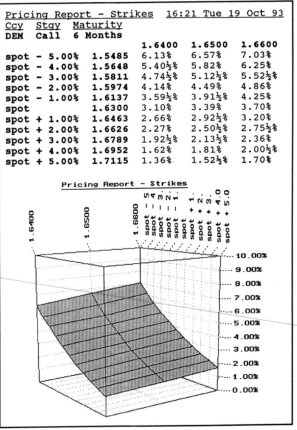

Figure 15.10. Pricing report (a) and graph of strike prices (b) for Deutsche mark calls. (*Courtesy of Astrogamma ©1993 by Astrogamma, Inc.*)

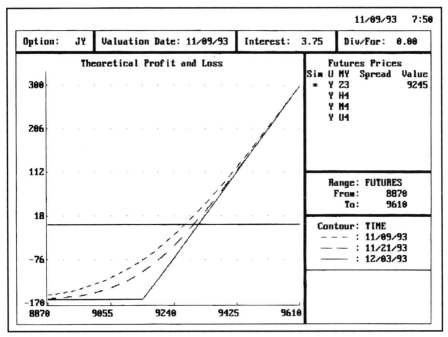

Figure 15.11. Diagram of a call in-the-money (ITM) on Japanese yen futures. (*Courtesy of FutureSource*)

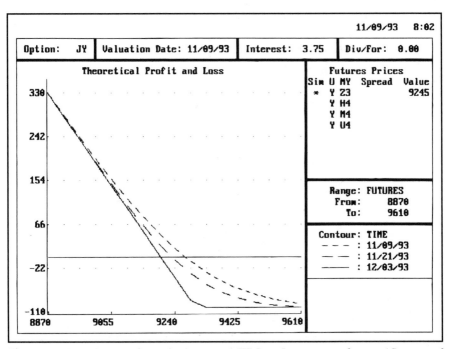

Figure 15.12. Diagram of a put in-the-money (ITM) on Japanese yen futures. (*Courtesy of FutureSource*)

The *exercise*, or *strike, price*, then, is simply the price at which the underlying currency will be delivered upon exercise. How does it relate to the currency price?

In-the-Money. A *call* which has *the present currency price higher than the strike price* is called *in-the-money (ITM)*. A *put* which has *the present currency price lower than the strike price* is called *in-the-money (ITM)*.

In-the-money currency options are *the most expensive*, since the strike price is better than the current price of the underlying currency, and the currency must move only moderately in order to generate a profit.

Example:

Option	Underlying Price	In-the-money	By
DEM Mar 70 call	74.00	Yes	400

Underlying price > Strike price, by 74.00 − 70.00 = 4.00, or 400 pips in-the-money

DEM Mar 75 put	70.00	Yes	500

Underlying price < Strike price, by 75.00 − 70.00 = 5.00, or 500 pips in-the-money

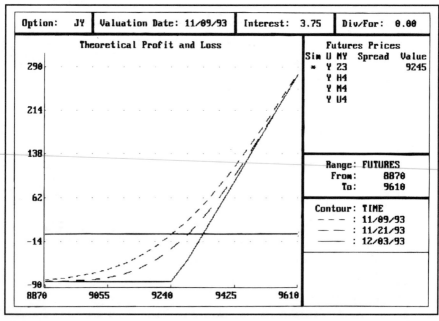

Figure 15.13. Diagram of a call at-the-money (ATM) on Japanese yen futures. (*Courtesy of FutureSource*)

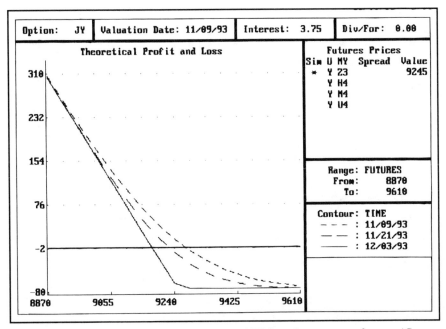

Figure 15.14. Diagram of an at-the-money put (ATM) on Japanese yen futures. (*Courtesy of FutureSource*)

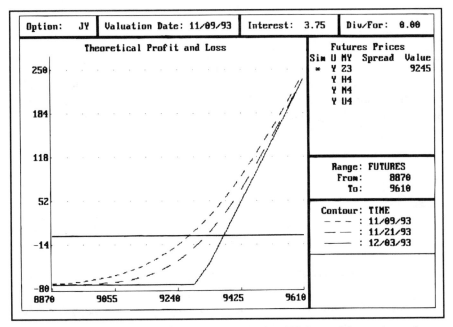

Figure 15.15. Diagram of an out-the-money call (OTM) on Japanese yen futures. (*Courtesy of FutureSource*)

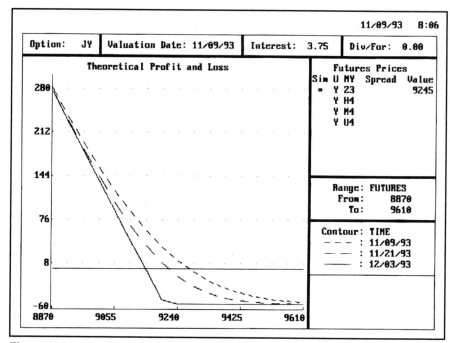

Figure 15.16.   Diagram of a put out-the-money (OTM) on Japanese yen futures. (*Courtesy of FutureSource*)

At-the-Money.   If the present currency price is approximately equal to the strike price, the option is *at-the-money (ATM)*. These currency options have *less expensive premiums,* as the strike price is close or identical to the current price of the underlying currency.

Example:

Option	Underlying Price	At-the-money	By
CHF Sep 69 call	69.00	Yes	0
CHF Sep 69 put	69.00	Yes	0

Underlying price = Strike price

Out-of-the-Money.   A *call* which has the *present currency price lower than the strike price* is called *out-of-the-money (OTM).* A *put* which has the *present currency price higher than the strike price* is called *out-of-the-money (OTM).*

Example:

Option	Underlying Price	Out-the-money	By
GBP Dec 150 call	147.50	Yes	250

Underlying price $<$ Strike price, by 147.50 $-$ 150 $=$ 2.50, or 250 pips

GBP Dec 145 put	147.50	Yes	250

Underlying price $>$ Strike price, by 147.50 $-$ 145 $=$ 2.50, or 250 pips

The premiums for the OTM options are *the cheapest,* since the strike price is worse than the current price of the underlying currency. Therefore, the currency must make a substantial move in order to generate a good profit.

Intrinsic Value. Intrinsic value is the amount by which an option is in-the-money. In the case of a call, the intrinsic value equals the difference between the underlying currency price and the strike price.

Example:

$$IV_{call} = PCP - SP$$

where IV_{call} = intrinsic value of a call
PCP = present currency price
SP = strike price

In the case of a put, the intrinsic value equals the difference between the strike price and the present currency price, when beneficial.

Example:

$$IV_{put} = SP - PCP$$

where IV_{put} = intrinsic value of a put
SP = strike price
PCP = present currency price

It follows, then, that out-of-money options do not have any intrinsic value.

Extrinsic Value or Time Value. The extrinsic or time value (also known as the time premium) consists of the difference between the option premium and its intrinsic value. Since out-of-money options do not have any intrinsic value, these options' premium equals just the time value.

Example:

$TV = P - IV$

where TV = time value

    P = premium

    IV = intrinsic value

In the following example, you can identify each option's *premium, intrinsic value* and *time (extrinsic) value,* based on the currency option, currency price and option price:

Example:

Currency Option	Present Currency Price	Option Premium	Intrinsic Value	Time Value
GBP Jun 150 call	144.00	.25	0	.25
DEM Sep 60 put	59.86	1.59	.14	1.45
CHF Mar 69 call	72.29	3.48	3.29	.19
JPY Dec 89 put	89.00	1.50	0	1.50

Volatility

Volatility is the degree to which the price of currency tends to fluctuate within a certain period of time. Free-floating currencies, such as the Deutsche mark (see Figure 15.17) or the Japanese yen (see Figure 15.18), for example, tend to be volatile against the US dollar. A semi-pegged currency tends to be less volatile. An example is the Netherlands guilder against the Deutsche mark (see Figure 15.19).

The volatility of a pegged currency is 0 versus the currency against which it is pegged.

Sometimes a currency not officially pegged will be quasipegged and, as a result, its volatility is low. The Saudi Ryial, for instance, is quasi-pegged to the US dollar at the rate of 3.75 (see Figure 15.20) and its historical volatility vis-à-vis the US dollar is very low.

Volatility is a key factor in option pricing. Unfortunately, measuring the volatility is a rather strenuous effort.

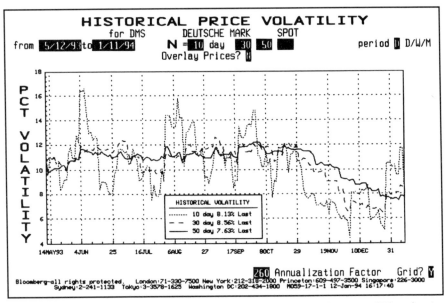

Figure 15.17.   Historical price volatility of the Deutsche mark. (*Courtesy of Bloomberg*)

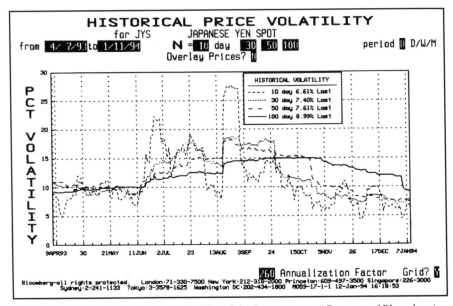

Figure 15.18.   Historical price volatility of the Japanese yen. (*Courtesy of Bloomberg*)

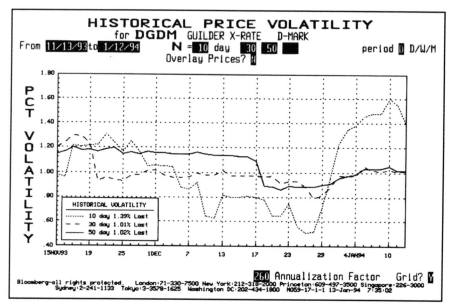

Figure 15.19. Historical price volatility of the Netherlands guilder. (*Courtesy of Bloomberg*)

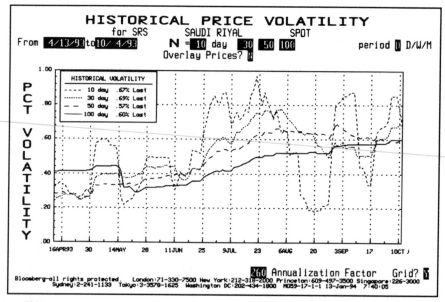

Figure 15.20. Historical price volatility of the Saudi Ryial. (*Courtesy of Bloomberg*)

Example:

$$V^2 = \frac{n \sum\limits_{i-1} (P_i - P)}{n-1}$$

where

V = volatility

n = number of observations

P_i = daily price

P = average price of all P_i

In the probability theory, the bell-shaped curve, known as the normal distribution curve, can be measured in terms of its mean, or the height of the curve, and its standard deviation (σ), or the speed the curve spreads out. The standard deviation helps us measure the probability of a random event to occur. Therefore, traders will use the standard deviation to measure the exact likelihood of a currency level's occurring within a certain range.

- $+/- 1\ \sigma$ takes in 68.3 percent of all the possible outcomes (or 2/3).
- $+/- 2\ \sigma$ takes in 95.4 percent of all the possible outcomes (or 19/20).
- $+/- 3\ \sigma$ takes in 99.7 percent of all the possible outcomes (or 369/370).

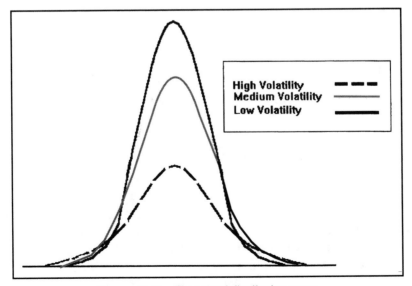

Figure 15.21. The normal distribution curve.

How does this apply to a foreign exchange rate? If USD/DEM is trading today at 1.6200 and has a volatility of 12 percent, then a one standard deviation price change over a year's time would be:

$$1.6200 \times 12 \text{ percent} = 0.1944$$

So, one year from now, we expect the USD/DEM to trade between:

1.4256 and 1.8144 (1.6200 +/− 0.1944) for 2/3 of the time.

1.2312 and 2.0088 (1.6200 +/− 2 × 0.1944) for 19/20 of the time.

1.0368 and 2.2032 (1.6200 +/− 3 × 0.1944) for 369/370 of the time.

Only very rarely will traders concern themselves with the price movement in a year's time, so it may help to calculate the standard deviation in shorter periods of time.

To change a volatility number from a yearly standard deviation to a weekly standard deviation:

$$\sqrt{52} = 7.2$$

To change a volatility number from a yearly standard deviation to a daily standard deviation

$$\sqrt{256} = 16$$

Example:

A JPY Sep futures contract trades at 89.90 and has an annual volatility of 14 percent will have a weekly standard deviation of

$$\frac{14 \text{ percent} \times 89.90}{7.2} = 1.75$$

and a *daily* standard deviation of:

$$\frac{14 \text{ percent} \times 89.90}{16} = 0.79$$

There are basically two ways of considering the volatility. The first is to calculate the standard deviation in a series of rates of changes of spot currency prices which occurred in the past. This is the *historical volatility*. A trader can, therefore, measure the volatility over any time frame. This can be the last 10 days, 30 days, 90 days or any other period in which he is interested. The second method of measuring the volatility is by considering the premiums currently trading in the market, such as OTC, or on the Chicago IMM, and calculating the figure, based on the level of the option premium. This approach is called the *implied volatility*.

Comparing the two types of volatility will show you that, despite a certain degree of correlation, significant differences do exist. These differences emphasize again the difficulty of gauging the volatility.

Vega. The volatility impact on the option premium is gauged by "vega." *Vega* (ς) is the sensitivity of the theoretical value of an option to a change in volatility. For instance, a vega = .2 will generate a .2 percent increase in the premium for each percentage increase in the volatility estimate, and a .2 percent decrease in the premium for each percentage decrease in the volatility estimate.

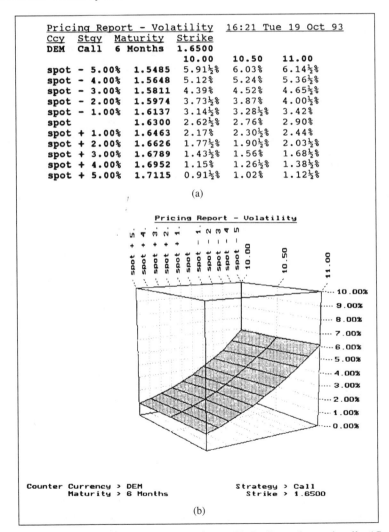

```
Pricing Report - Volatility   16:21 Tue 19 Oct 93
Ccy  Stgy  Maturity  Strike
DEM  Call  6 Months  1.6500
                             10.00     10.50     11.00
spot - 5.00%  1.5485    5.91½%    6.03%     6.14½%
spot - 4.00%  1.5648    5.12%     5.24%     5.36½%
spot - 3.00%  1.5811    4.39%     4.52%     4.65½%
spot - 2.00%  1.5974    3.73½%    3.87%     4.00½%
spot - 1.00%  1.6137    3.14½%    3.28½%    3.42%
spot          1.6300    2.62½%    2.76%     2.90%
spot + 1.00%  1.6463    2.17%     2.30½%    2.44%
spot + 2.00%  1.6626    1.77½%    1.90½%    2.03½%
spot + 3.00%  1.6789    1.43½%    1.56%     1.68½%
spot + 4.00%  1.6952    1.15%     1.26½%    1.38½%
spot + 5.00%  1.7115    0.91½%    1.02%     1.12½%
```

(a)

(b)

Figure 15.22. Pricing report (a) and graph of vega (b) for Deutsche mark calls. (*Courtesy of Astrogamma ©1993 by Astrogamma, Inc.*)

A Trader's Point of View

- Changes in volatility have a maximum dollar impact on at-the-money options and a maximum percentage impact on out-of-money options.
- An increase in volatility generates the delta to converge toward .5, whereas a volatility decrease generates the delta to diverge from .5.
- The impact of a change in volatility will be more significant on a long term option than on a short term option.

Expiry Date

The option is traded for a predetermined period of time and when this time expires, there is a delivery date known as the *expiry date.* If the buyer intends to exercise the option, he must inform the writer on or before expiry. The buyer's failure to inform the writer about exercising the option frees the writer of any legal obligation. However, some exercise is automatic if in-the-money at expiry. An option cannot be exercised past the expiration date.

The writer must be available to be contacted when the option is due to expire.

A Trader's Point of View

- Time is an important factor in an option's pricing and the decrease in the time to expiration has a similar impact on the delta, gamma, theta (discussed below), vega and theoretical value as a decrease in volatility.

Theta.   Theta (T), also known as time decay, occurs as the very slow or nonexistent movement of the currency triggers losses in the option's theoretical value.

For instance, a theta = .02 will generate a loss of 0.02 in the premium for each day that the currency price is flat. Intrinsic value is not affected by time, but extrinsic value is. Time decay accelerates as the option approaches expiry, since the number of possible outcomes is continuously reduced as the time passes.

Time has its maximum impact on at-the-money options and its minimum effect on in-the-money options. Time's effect on out-of-money options occurs somewhere within the above range.

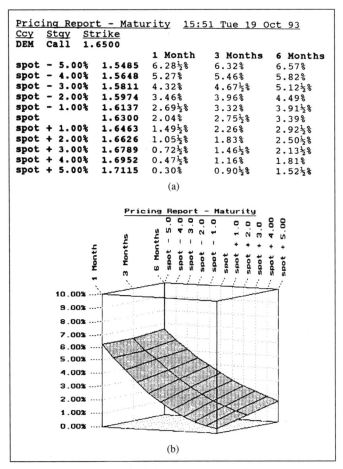

```
Pricing Report - Maturity    15:51 Tue 19 Oct 93
Ccy  Stqy  Strike
DEM  Call  1.6500
                       1 Month    3 Months   6 Months
spot - 5.00%  1.5485   6.28½%     6.32%      6.57%
spot - 4.00%  1.5648   5.27%      5.46%      5.82%
spot - 3.00%  1.5811   4.32%      4.67½%     5.12½%
spot - 2.00%  1.5974   3.46%      3.96%      4.49%
spot - 1.00%  1.6137   2.69½%     3.32%      3.91½%
spot         1.6300   2.04%      2.75½%     3.39%
spot + 1.00%  1.6463   1.49½%     2.26%      2.92½%
spot + 2.00%  1.6626   1.05½%     1.83%      2.50½%
spot + 3.00%  1.6789   0.72½%     1.46½%     2.13½%
spot + 4.00%  1.6952   0.47½%     1.16%      1.81%
spot + 5.00%  1.7115   0.30%      0.90½%     1.52½%
```

(a)

(b)

Figure 15.23. Pricing report (a) and graph of gamma (b) for Deutsche mark calls. (Courtesy of Astrogamma ©1993 by Astrogamma, Inc.)

A Trader's Point of View on Theta

• Theta is always more significant for a short term at-the-money option than a long term at-the-money option.

   The following example shows the relations among the foreign currency, type of option and the delta (hedge ratio), gamma (curvature), theta (time decay), and vega (volatility) positions.

Position	Delta (Δ)	Gamma (Γ)	Theta (Θ)	Vega (ς)
Long currency	+	0	0	0
Short currency	−	0	0	0
Long calls	+	+	−	+
Short calls	−	−	+	−
Long puts	−	+	−	+
Short puts	+	−	+	−

The Interest Rates Differential

Unlike other financial markets, in foreign exchange a single interest rate is insufficient for the decision makers. Every exchange rate means the simultaneous buying of one currency in terms of another.

In options trading, the premium of a call on a foreign currency will increase when the US interest rate increases relative to the foreign interest rate, all else being equal. This will occur either when US interest rates rise and the foreign interest rates are stable, or when US interest rates are stable, but foreign interest rates fall.

The opposite is true in the case of a foreign currency put buying. The option premium will increase when US interest rates decrease relative to the foreign interest rates, or the foreign interest rates increase vis-à-vis the American ones.

Generally, the interest rate used is the risk-free rate (ρ) of government instruments, such as T-bills.

The interest rates are important for options pricing for two reasons. First, the pricing formula includes the forward price, which is calculated on the differential between domestic and foreign interest rates. Second, the premium of an option must be discounted back to the present value by a risk-free interest rate.

Premium is the expected value of the option at expiration. Since the premium is paid up front, its value is discounted through the present value formula:

$$\text{Premium} = \frac{\text{Expected value}}{1 + IR \times \dfrac{\text{number of days}}{365}}$$

The interest rate parity is known among traders as the *cost of carry*, where the forward price is determined by the cost of borrowing money in order to hold the position. For example, the one year forward price of USD/DEM will be determined by the spot USD/DEM 2.0000 and the one year interest rate differential of 3 percent: 2.0600. If the quoted prices differ, the arbitrageurs will cash in on the opportunity.

A Trader's Point of View

• The impact of interest rates on the theoretical value of options is more significant on deep in-the-money options.

Call or Put

Currency Call. A *call*, then, is a contract between the buyer and the seller which holds that:

• the *buyer* has the right, but not the obligation, to buy a specific quantity of a currency at a predetermined price and within a predetermined period of time, regardless of the market price of the currency; and
• the *writer* assumes the obligation of delivering the specific quantity of a currency at a predetermined price and within a predetermined period of time, regardless of the market price of the currency, if the buyer wants to exercise the call option.

A call option is traded because the buyer believes that the underlying currency will rise above a certain price, whereas the seller expects the currency is either going to be stable or move lower.

Currency Put. Conversely, a *put* is a contract between the buyer and the seller which holds that:

• the *buyer* has the right, but not the obligation, to sell a specific quantity of a currency at a predetermined price and within a predetermined period of time, regardless of the market price of the currency; and
• the *writer* assumes the obligation to take delivery of the specific quantity of a currency at a predetermined price and within a predetermined period of time, regardless of the market price of the currency, if the buyer wants to exercise the call option.

In the case of the put, the buyer expects the underlying currency to weaken to, or under, a specific level, while the seller believes the currency will rise, or just trade the range.

Perhaps it is a good time to emphasize that the seller of a call is not the same as the buyer of the put. As we go along, it will become more apparent why.

American or European Option Style

The exercise of an option may occur on or prior to the expiry. Depending on when exercising may occur, there are two types of options: *American* and *European style*.

- The *American style option* may be exercised at any valid business date throughout the life of the option.
- The *European style currency option* may only be exercised on the expiry date.

Early Exercise of American-Style Options

Generally speaking, American options are not exercised prior to expiry but there are exceptions. These occur when either an option is deep in the money, when the option is approaching the expiration date and has no extrinsic value and with call options on high interest currencies or put options on low interest currencies.

The logic behind this exercise of an American style option is that a high interest currency is likely to depreciate against the US dollar, and vice versa.

The additional opportunities offered by American style options will translate into a higher cost, or premium. However, one should keep in mind that early exercise is usually not beneficial.

Advantageous Early Exercising Scenarios

- Bid-offer spreads in the market may make it too expensive to sell the option and trade forward outrights.
- If the option shifts deeply into money, the interest rate differential gained by early exercise may exceed the value of the option
- If the option amount is small and/or the expiration is close and the option value only consists of the intrinsic value, it may be better to use the early exercise.

Option Pricing

Due to the complexity of its determining factors, option pricing is difficult. In the absence of option pricing models, option trading is nothing but inefficient gambling. The flurry of options on equities in the 1920s had an accelerating impact on the stock market crash of 1929.

The Black-Scholes Formula

The pioneering efforts of several researchers have been vital for option pricing. In 1972, professors Myron Scholes and Fischer Black published in the *Journal of Political Economy* a method of calculating the fair price, or premium for an European-style call option on stocks. The method became known around the world as the *Black-Scholes model.* The Black-Scholes fair value model holds that a stock and the call option on the particular stock are comparable investments and, thus, a riskless portfolio may be created by buying the stock and selling the option on the stock, as a hedge. The movement of the price of the stock will be reflected by the movement of the price of the option, but not necessarily by the same amplitude. Therefore, it is necessary to hold only the amount of the stock to duplicate the movement of the price of the option.

$$(C(E) = SN(d_1) - \frac{E}{e^{pt}} N(d_2)$$

and

$$d_1 = \frac{\ln\left(\frac{S}{E}\right) + (p + .5\sigma^2)t}{\sigma\sqrt{t}}$$

$$d_2 = d_1 - \sigma\sqrt{t}$$

where

S   = spot exchange rate

E   = exercise or strike price

e = 2.71828

t = time till expiration

σ = standard deviation of the continuously compounded annual rate of change of the   exchange rate

p = risk-free rate (T-bills)

ln   = the natural logarithm

$N(d)$ = probability that a deviation less than d will occur in a normal distribution with a mean of zero and a standard deviation of 1

The Black-Scholes option pricing model holds, in its original form, several theoretical assumptions which may diverge from the realities of the financial world. Among those assumptions are:

• constant interest rates,

- constant and known volatility,
- no transaction/taxation costs,
- no dividends,
- no early exercise, and
- continuous trading.

One serious problem which, in its original form, the model is unable to answer is the expectation of "normal" or continuous trading behavior of the foreign exchange market. Despite its efficient structure, the foreign exchange market has been affected by a long series of unexpected factors that disrupted the daily continuity of trading. These factors ranged from political crisis, such as the kidnapping of Mr. Mikhail Gorbachev, the former Soviet President in 1991, to the currency crisis on the European Monetary System in 1993.

The log-normal distribution (see Figure 15.21) is unable to include these types of aberrations.

The assumption of market continuity was relaxed in 1973 by Robert Merton, who also adapted several other assumptions made by the Black-Scholes model, such as no dividends and constant interest rates.

Another weakness is the relationship between spot and forward prices.

Despite attempts to make the forward price something more than a "guesstimate," extraneous forces may affect the forward price. Using the EMS example again, semi-pegging the European currencies against the Deutsche mark will generate unexpected changes in the interest differentials used to calculate the forward points. Therefore, the option pricing model tends to underprice out-of-money currency options.

The original Black-Scholes formula can only be applied to European call options. However, there is a relationship between a call option and a put option established through the forward market. This is called the *put-call-forward exchange parity (PCFP) theory.*

$$C - P = \frac{F - E}{(1 + r)^t}$$

where: C = call

P = put

F = forward price

E = exercise price

r = interest rate

The idea is that the option of buying the domestic currency with a foreign currency at a certain price x is equivalent to the option of selling the foreign currency with the domestic currency at the same price x. Therefore, the call option in the domestic currency becomes the put option in the other, and vice versa.

Another pricing model, introduced by Cox, Ross and Rubinstein in 1979, was meant to apply to the early exercise provision of American style options. As it assumes that early exercise will only occur if the advantage of holding the currency exceeds the time value of the option, their binomial method evaluated the call premium by estimating the probability of early exercise for each successive day. The theoretical premium is compared to the holding cost of the cash hedge position until the option's time value is worth less than the forward points of the currency hedge when the option should be exercised.

The practical applications of the Cox-Ross-Rubinstein model are tedious and the binomial pricing models must compromise on the number of trials.

In 1983, Mark Garman and Steven Kohlhagen expanded the Black-Scholes model to foreign exchange, by using the interest rate differential (the difference between two interest rates) rather than a single interest rate and consequently allowing for the currency forward to be traded either at premium or discount.

Also in 1983, Orlin Grabbe provided a different adaptation of the Black-Scholes model to foreign exchange. Yet another foreign exchange option pricing was proposed by Bodurtha and Courtadon in 1987.

The Black-Scholes formula was adjusted for foreign exchange as follows:

$$C = e^{-r_f^t} SN(d) - Ee^{-r_d^t} N(d - \sigma \sqrt{t})$$

and

$$d = \frac{\ln\left(\frac{S}{E}\right) + (r_d - r_f + \frac{\sigma^2}{2})t}{\sigma \sqrt{t}}$$

where S = spot exchange rate

E = exercise or strike price

e = 2.71828

t = time till expiration

σ = standard deviation of the continuously compounded annual rate of change of the exchange rate

r_d = domestic interest rate

r_f = foreign interest rate

ln = the natural logarithm

$N(d)$ = probability that a deviation less than d will occur in a normal distribution with a mean of zero and a standard deviation of 1

Chapter 16

Major Option Strategies on Currencies

Some basic considerations prior to deciding on the best option trading strategy for you are:

- Do you expect the currency to get stronger, weaker, or stay relatively stable?
- Do you expect high or low volatility?
- Why are you choosing to trade an option over a spot, a forward outright, or a futures contract?

This chapter will describe—in detail and with numerous examples and illustrations—the comprehensive gamut of choices available in option trading. This gamut starts with the simple and moves to options with the complexity and flexibility that have characterized option trading and turned it into a fast growing market.

We will start with the simple strategies, including a review of buying and selling call and put options.

Basic Strategies

Buying a Call Option

The *buyer of a DEM call option* acquires the right, but not the obligation, to buy a certain amount of DEM at a certain price, on or before a specified value date. The buyer expects the DEM to rise (whereas the seller expects the currency to remain stable or ease). The maximum risk the buyer may incur is the premium paid to the seller, or writer, of the option. The maximum benefit is theoretically unlimited but it is not known, as it is impossible to know how the DEM will perform. A simple rise in the price of DEM will not guarantee a profit for the buyer because the rise must be enough to cover the premium before any profit is earned (see Figure 16.1).

The premium is the highest for the deep ITM calls and the lowest for deep OTM calls. With an OTM call option, the buyer encounters the smallest financial risk, while having the best leverage. *Leverage* refers to the expected return on investment, the potential profit generated by the buyer's investment.

Of course, OTM options in general, and OTM calls specifically, stand the least chance of performing profitably because, for them to be profitable, the currency needs to make a substantial price move.

Buying a Synthetic Call Option

Synthetic options rarely generate arbitrage opportunities, but help one better understand the intricacies of the market. A trader can easily shift from a long call position to a long put position, or a from a short call position to a short put position. However, the trader cannot turn a long call position into a short put position or a short call position into a long put position.

A *synthetic call option* consists of *a combination of long currency and a long currency put* (see Figure 16.2).

The same characteristics of the long call apply.

Selling A Call Option

Selling a call option is equivalent to writing a naked call on an amount of currency which the writer does not own. In return for the premium, the writer will be ready to sell the predetermined amount of DEM at the predetermined exercise, or strike, price if and when the buyer chooses to do so, on or before the expiry (see Figure 16.3).

The maximum benefit for the seller is the premium received from the buyer. The maximum risk for the seller is unlimited, but unknown. The only financial buffer against loss is the premium. But, even if the currency rises, the seller will not lose as long as the currency advancement does not exceed the amount of the premium.

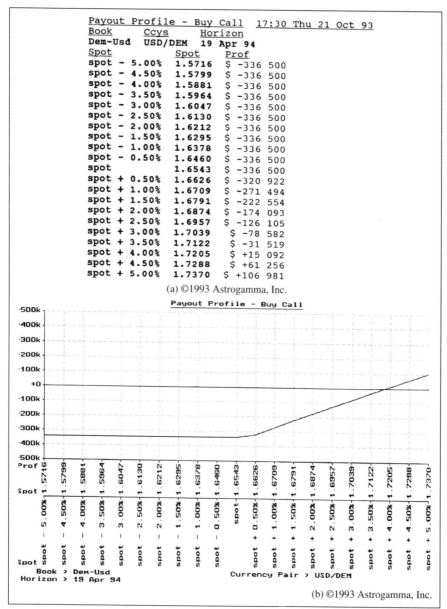

(a) ©1993 Astrogamma, Inc.

(b) ©1993 Astrogamma, Inc.

Figure 16.1. Pricing report (a) and graph (b) of a long USD/DEM call. (*Courtesy of Astrogamma © 1993 Astrogamma, Inc.*)

The break-even point is calculated as the sum of the exercise price and the premium.

$$\text{BEP (call selling)} = S + P$$

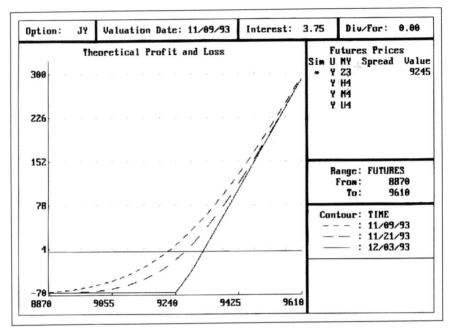

Figure 16.2. Pricing report and graph of a long synthetic call on Japanese yen futures. (*Courtesy of FutureSource*)

where

S = exercise, or strike price

P = premium

A Trader's Point of View on Calls Writing

- Generally, near term call options are more desirable to write, as there is less time available for a wide price swing in currency.
- A sharp rally in the price of the currency immediately following the writing of the option will generate the largest loss, given the fact that there is no time premium amortization.
- In order to avoid or minimize the negative impact of a currency advance, the writer should have a stop-loss order or liquidate the position.

Buying a Put Option

The buyer of a DEM put option acquires the right, but not the obligation to sell a certain amount of DEM at a certain price, on or before a specified value date. The buyer expects the DEM to ease (whereas the seller expects the currency to remain stable or rise).

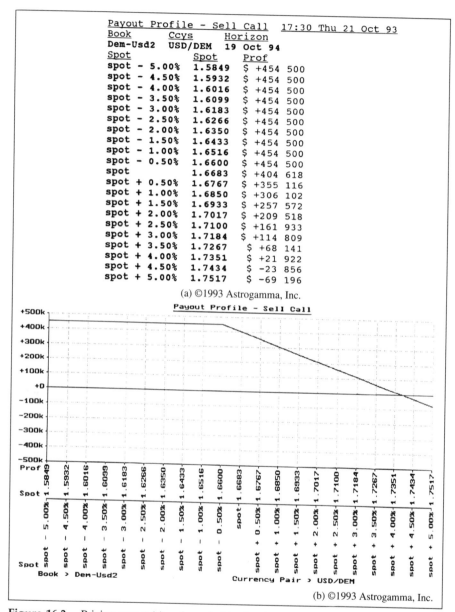

```
Payout Profile - Sell Call    17:30 Thu 21 Oct 93
Book        Ccys        Horizon
Dem-Usd2    USD/DEM    19 Oct 94
Spot                    Spot      Prof
spot - 5.00%            1.5849    $ +454 500
spot - 4.50%            1.5932    $ +454 500
spot - 4.00%            1.6016    $ +454 500
spot - 3.50%            1.6099    $ +454 500
spot - 3.00%            1.6183    $ +454 500
spot - 2.50%            1.6266    $ +454 500
spot - 2.00%            1.6350    $ +454 500
spot - 1.50%            1.6433    $ +454 500
spot - 1.00%            1.6516    $ +454 500
spot - 0.50%            1.6600    $ +454 500
spot                    1.6683    $ +404 618
spot + 0.50%            1.6767    $ +355 116
spot + 1.00%            1.6850    $ +306 102
spot + 1.50%            1.6933    $ +257 572
spot + 2.00%            1.7017    $ +209 518
spot + 2.50%            1.7100    $ +161 933
spot + 3.00%            1.7184    $ +114 809
spot + 3.50%            1.7267    $ +68 141
spot + 4.00%            1.7351    $ +21 922
spot + 4.50%            1.7434    $ -23 856
spot + 5.00%            1.7517    $ -69 196
```

(a) ©1993 Astrogamma, Inc.

Figure 16.3. Pricing report (a) and graph (b) of a short call on USD/DEM. (*Courtesy of Astrogamma © 1993 Astrogamma, Inc.*)

The maximum risk the buyer may incur is the premium paid to the seller of the option. The maximum benefit is theoretically unlimited but it is not known, as it is impossible to know how the DEM will perform. A simple fall in the price of DEM will not guarantee a profit for the buyer because the currency must fall low enough to cover the premium before any profit is earned (see Figure 16.4).

The premium is highest for deep ITM calls and lowest for deep OTM calls. With an OTM call option, the buyer encounters the smallest financial risk, while having the best leverage. Of course, OTM options in general, and OTM calls specifically, stand the least chance of performing profitably, because for them to be profitable, the currency needs to make a substantial price move.

Buying a Synthetic Put Option

A *synthetic put option* consists of *a combination of short currency and a long currency call* (see Figure 16.5).

The same characteristics of the long put apply.

Selling a Put Option

Selling a currency put option for a premium is executed by a trader who expects that specific currency to rise or remain relatively stable for the life of the option. The trader selling the put option is known as the *writer*. In return for the premium, the writer will be ready to buy the predetermined amount

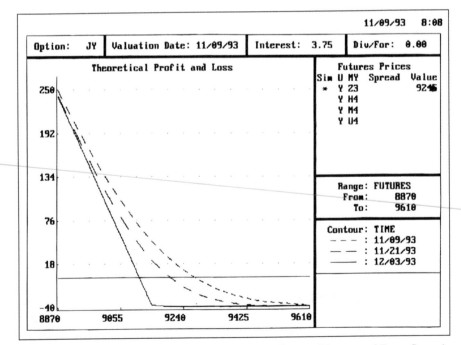

Figure 16.4.   Diagram of a long put on Japanese yen futures. (*Courtesy of FutureSource*)

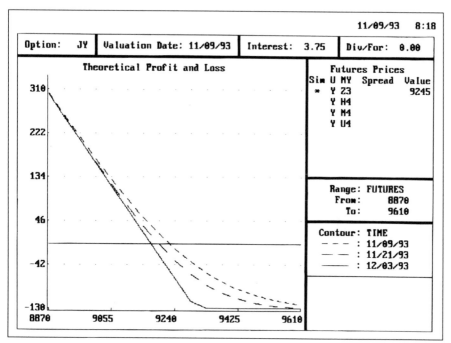

Figure 16.5. Diagram of a synthetic long put on Japanese yen futures. (*Courtesy of FutureSource*)

of DEM at the predetermined exercise, or strike, price, if and when the buyer chooses to do so, on or before the expiry (see Figure 16.6).

The maximum benefit for the seller is the premium received from the buyer. This means that the seller needs the price of the currency to stay at any level above the strike price of the put option. The maximum risk for the seller is unlimited and the only financial buffer against loss is the premium.

The break-even point (BEP) is calculated as the difference between the exercise price and the premium.

$$\text{BEP (put selling)} = S - P$$

where

S = exercise, or strike price

P = premium

A Trader's Point of View on Puts Writing

• In addition to gaining the premium income, traders also write put options in order to acquire a currency below the current market price.

• If the currency price trades below the exercise price, the put will be exer-

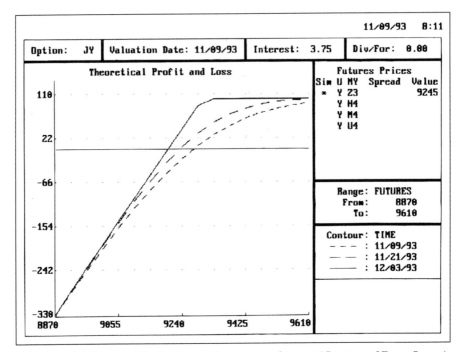

Figure 16.6.   Diagram of a short put on Japanese yen futures. (*Courtesy of FutureSource*)

cised. However, the exercise is likely to occur only if the option is in-the-money and near term.

• In order to avoid or minimize a loss, the put writer can leave a stop-loss order or buy a put identical to the one originally written.

Compound Strategies

Two of the major problems in foreign exchange—at least for the cash traders—are solved by options.

The first problem occurs when the market is very quiet and currency prices are relatively stable. The lack of volatility is generally equaled to lack of profitability. The way out? Options writing.

The second problem appears when traders have certain expectations about a rise in volatility, but lack the confidence to take a view on the direction of the market. Since we have already talked about the opportunities provided by trading individual calls and puts, we can move a step further and combine these classes of options in search of better profits and hedges. These compound strategies are also known as *currency spreads*.

Currency Spreads

A *spread* is *a long currency option and an offsetting short currency option generally in the same currency.* If the spread is executed in two different currencies, then the spread is called an inter market spread.

We will discuss two types of spreads. The first is the nonratio, or regular, spread, which is a compound option strategy in which the number of long options is the same as the number of short options. The second is the ratio spread, in which the number of long options is different from the number of short options.

Nonratio (Regular) Spreads

Under the combinations which pair equal numbers of long and short options, we will present the following spreads:

1. Straddles
2. Strangles
3. Vertical
4. Calendar
5. Box
6. Butterfly
7. Condor
8. Combination

1. Straddles (Buying). Many times, traders are faced with the specter of the release of certain economic data, the expectation of a central bank changing the discount rate or expectations about the breakout of a currency through a special chart level. Traders are confident about a sudden release of energy in the price of a currency and in its volatility, but not quite sure about the direction of the move. Certainly, these traders would like to soar on the news, not be buried.

Long Straddle. A popular choice among option traders in this situation, a quiet market before the big storm, is *buying a straddle.* A *long straddle* consists of a *long call and a long put on the same currency, at the same strike price and with the same expiration dates* (see Figure 16.7). The buyer pays a premium on the call and a premium on the put in order to have the right, but not the obligation, to buy, or to sell, a predetermined amount of foreign currency on or before expiry, at a predetermined price.

The buyer enters a long straddle position in anticipation of a sharp increase in volatility. He buys volatility. In order to make a profit, the cur-

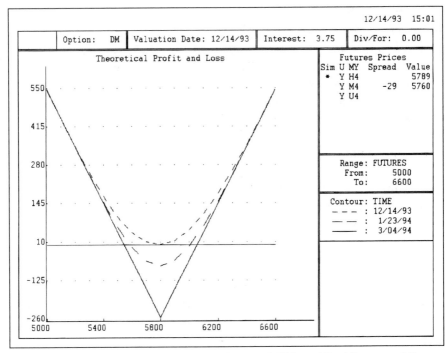

Figure 16.7. Pricing report and diagram of a long DEM straddle. (*Courtesy of Future-Source*)

rency must swing high or low enough to cover investment costs, but once the cost of the premiums is cleared, the profit is theoretically unlimited.

The maximum loss for the buyer is the sum of the premiums. Naturally, the buyer does not have to wait to physically lose the entire investment, as the position can be sold.

Of course, when the price of the currency rises, the value of the call rises, while the value of the put declines. The opposite is true if the value of the currency declines.

The upside break-even point is the sum of the strike price and the premium on the straddle (which is simply the premiums on the individual call and put):

$$BEP \text{ (upside)} = S + P$$

where

S = exercise, or strike, price

P = premium

The downside break-even point is the difference between the strike price and the premium on the straddle (which is simply the compound premium on the individual call and put):

$$\text{BEP (upside)} = S - P$$

. . . *Selling*

Short Straddle. A *short straddle* consists of a *short call and a short put on the same currency, at the same strike price and with the same expiration dates* (see Figure 16.8). The writer expects the currency to be relatively stable. In effect, the writer sells volatility.

The maximum profit consists of the combined premium of the two individual options. The loss occurs once the level of the premium is exceeded by the currency swing and then the loss is unlimited.

2. Strangles. A strangle is nothing but a straddle with a twist. The twist consists of disregarding the condition in the definition of the straddle that both options have the same strike price.

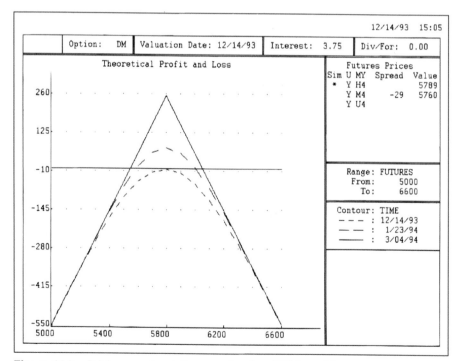

Figure 16.8. Pricing report and diagram of a short DEM straddle. (*Courtesy of Future-Source*)

Buying . . .

Long Strangle. A *long strangle* consists, therefore, of *a long call and a long put on the same currency, at different strike prices, but with the same expiration dates* (see Figure 16.9). In order to minimize the risk, traders generally buy out-of-money options. Exactly as in the case of the straddle, the buyer pays a premium on the call and a premium on the put in order to have the right, but not the obligation, to buy, or to sell, a predetermined amount of foreign currency on or before the expiry, at a predetermined price.

The buyer enters a long strangle strategy in anticipation of a sharp increase in volatility. He buys volatility. In order to make a profit, the currency must swing high or low enough to cover the investment costs but, once the cost of the premiums is cleared, the profit is theoretically unlimited.

The maximum loss for the buyer is the sum of the premiums. Naturally, the buyer does not have to wait to physically lose the entire investment, as the position can be sold.

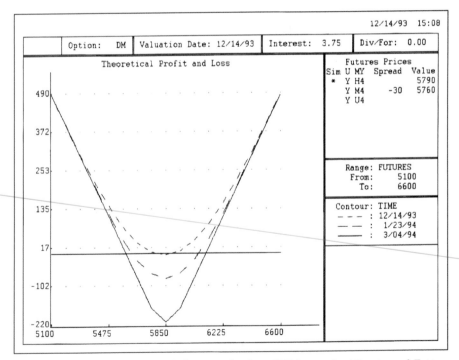

Figure 16.9. Pricing report and diagram of a long DEM strangle. (*Courtesy of Future-Source*)

Of course, when the price of the currency rises, the value of the call rises, while the value of the put declines. The opposite is true if the value of the currency declines.

Short Strangle (Selling). A *short strangle* consists of *a short call and a short put on the same currency, with the same expiration dates, but with different strike prices* (see Figure 16.10). The writer expects the currency to be relatively stable. In effect, the writer sells volatility. The maximum profit consists of the combined premium of the two individual options. The loss occurs once the level of the premium is exceeded by the currency swing, and then the loss is unlimited.

3. Vertical Spreads. A *vertical spread* consists of a strategy with *two similar options (i.e., calls or puts), one being bought and the other sold, on the same currency with the same expiration date, but with different strike prices.*

There are several types of vertical spreads:

- Vertical bull call spreads
- Vertical bull put spreads

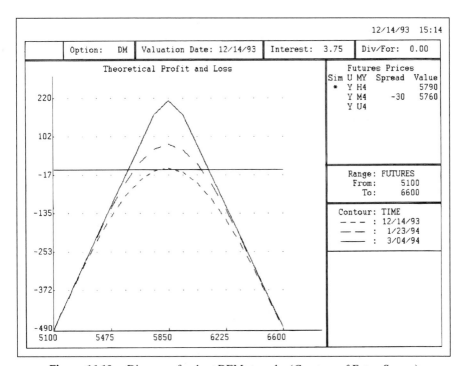

Figure 16.10. Diagram of a short DEM strangle. (*Courtesy of FutureSource*)

- Vertical bear put spreads
- Vertical bear call spreads

Vertical Bull Spreads. A *vertical bull spread* is an option combination whose *theoretical value will rise to a predetermined maximum profit if the price of underlying currency rises and whose maximum loss is also predetermined.*

Vertical Bull Call Spread (Buying). A *vertical bull call spread* is a compound strategy of *two options with a common expiration date, where one option is a long call with a lower strike price and the other is a short call with a higher strike price.*

This strategy offers a less risky alternative to buying a naked call.

The buyer's maximum profit consists of the dollar difference between the two strike prices, minus the total premium paid. The break-even point is calculated as the sum of the lower strike price and the total premium. The maximum loss is limited to the premium paid for the two options.

Vertical Bull Put Spread (Selling). A *vertical bull put spread* is a compound strategy of *two options with a common expiration date, where one option is a long put with a lower strike price and the other is a short put with a higher strike price* (see Figure 16.11).

This strategy is less bullish than a long call.

The buyer's maximum profit consists of the net premium for the two options (one paid, the other received). The break-even point is calculated as the difference between the higher strike price and the net premium received. The maximum loss is limited to the dollar difference between the two strike prices, minus the total premium received.

Vertical Bear Spreads. A *vertical bear spread* is an option combination whose *theoretical value will decline to a predetermined maximum profit if the price of underlying currency declines and whose maximum loss is also predetermined.*

Vertical Bear Put Spread (Long Vertical Put Spread). A *vertical bear put spread* (see Figure 16.12) is a compound strategy of *two options with a common expiration date, where one option is a long put with a higher strike price and the other is a short put with a lower strike price.*

This strategy offers a less risky alternative to buying a naked put.

The buyer's maximum profit consists of the dollar difference between the two strike prices, minus the total premium paid. The break-even point is calculated as the difference between the higher strike price and the total premium. The maximum loss is limited to the premium paid for the two options.

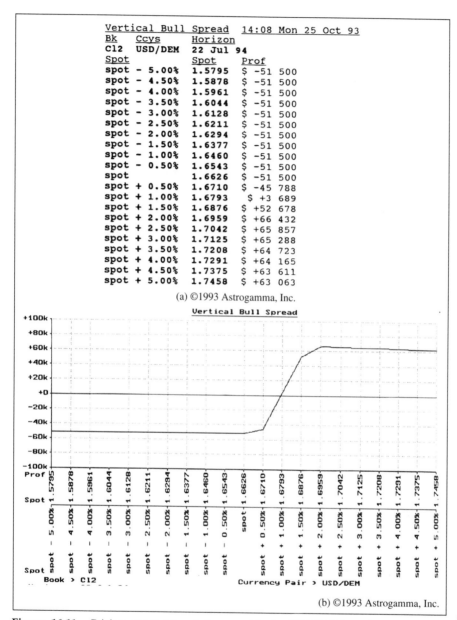

```
Vertical Bull Spread   14:08 Mon 25 Oct 93
Bk   Ccys          Horizon
C12  USD/DEM        22 Jul 94
Spot               Spot      Prof
spot - 5.00%       1.5795    $ -51 500
spot - 4.50%       1.5878    $ -51 500
spot - 4.00%       1.5961    $ -51 500
spot - 3.50%       1.6044    $ -51 500
spot - 3.00%       1.6128    $ -51 500
spot - 2.50%       1.6211    $ -51 500
spot - 2.00%       1.6294    $ -51 500
spot - 1.50%       1.6377    $ -51 500
spot - 1.00%       1.6460    $ -51 500
spot - 0.50%       1.6543    $ -51 500
spot               1.6626    $ -51 500
spot + 0.50%       1.6710    $ -45 788
spot + 1.00%       1.6793    $  +3 689
spot + 1.50%       1.6876    $ +52 678
spot + 2.00%       1.6959    $ +66 432
spot + 2.50%       1.7042    $ +65 857
spot + 3.00%       1.7125    $ +65 288
spot + 3.50%       1.7208    $ +64 723
spot + 4.00%       1.7291    $ +64 165
spot + 4.50%       1.7375    $ +63 611
spot + 5.00%       1.7458    $ +63 063
```

(a) ©1993 Astrogamma, Inc.

(b) ©1993 Astrogamma, Inc.

Figure 16.11. Pricing report (a) and diagram (b) of a USD/DEM vertical bull spread. (*Courtesy of Astrogamma © 1993 Astrogamma, Inc.*)

Vertical Bear Call Spread (Selling, Short Vertical Call Spread). A *vertical bear call spread* is a compound strategy of *two options with a common expiration date, where one option is a short call with a lower strike price and the other is a long call with a higher strike price.*

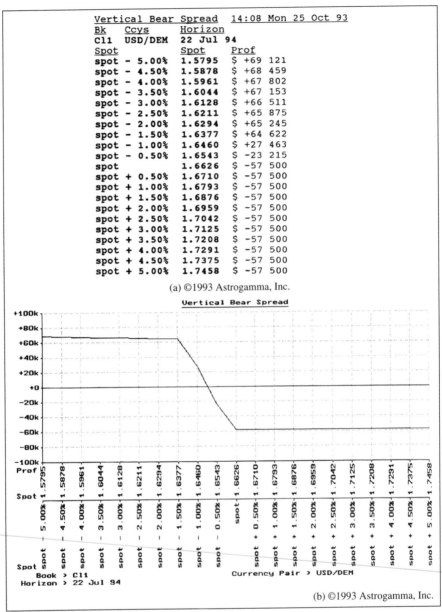

```
Vertical Bear Spread   14:08 Mon 25 Oct 93
Bk   Ccys      Horizon
Cll  USD/DEM   22 Jul 94
Spot           Spot       Prof
spot - 5.00%   1.5795   $ +69 121
spot - 4.50%   1.5878   $ +68 459
spot - 4.00%   1.5961   $ +67 802
spot - 3.50%   1.6044   $ +67 153
spot - 3.00%   1.6128   $ +66 511
spot - 2.50%   1.6211   $ +65 875
spot - 2.00%   1.6294   $ +65 245
spot - 1.50%   1.6377   $ +64 622
spot - 1.00%   1.6460   $ +27 463
spot - 0.50%   1.6543   $ -23 215
spot           1.6626   $ -57 500
spot + 0.50%   1.6710   $ -57 500
spot + 1.00%   1.6793   $ -57 500
spot + 1.50%   1.6876   $ -57 500
spot + 2.00%   1.6959   $ -57 500
spot + 2.50%   1.7042   $ -57 500
spot + 3.00%   1.7125   $ -57 500
spot + 3.50%   1.7208   $ -57 500
spot + 4.00%   1.7291   $ -57 500
spot + 4.50%   1.7375   $ -57 500
spot + 5.00%   1.7458   $ -57 500
```

(a) ©1993 Astrogamma, Inc.

(b) ©1993 Astrogamma, Inc.

Figure 16.12. Pricing report (a) and diagram (b) of a USD/DEM vertical bear spread. (*Courtesy of Astrogamma © 1993 Astrogamma, Inc.*)

This strategy offers a less risky alternative to writing a naked call.

The seller's maximum profit is limited to the premium paid for the two options. The break-even point is calculated as the sum of the lower strike price and the total premium. The maximum loss consists of the dollar difference between the two strike prices, minus the total premium received.

4. Calendar Spreads. There are three types of calendar spreads—also called time and horizontal spreads: calendar spreads, calendar combinations and calendar straddles.

Calendar Spread. A *calendar spread* is a *combination of two similar types of options, either calls or puts, with the same strike price but different expiration dates.* The dissimilarity between the expiration dates allows this type of spread to capitalize on both the impact of the time decay and the interest rate differentials.

Calendar spreads are very complex in terms of both trading and P&L calculation. P&L can only be estimated. The maximum profit will be achieved if the implied volatility of the currency is higher, while the interest rate differential is narrower. The maximum loss is estimated to be the net premium, assuming that both the volatility and the interest rate differential remain stable.

Calendar Combination. An offshoot of the calendar spreads are calendar combinations. A *calendar combination* consists of the *simultaneous call calendar spread and put calendar spread, in which the strike price of the calls is higher than the strike price of the puts.*

Calendar Straddle. Another offshoot is the calendar straddle. The *calendar straddle* consists of *simultaneous buying of a longer term straddle and near term straddle with a common strike price.*

5. The Box Spread. A *box spread* consists of *four options with a common expiration date: a long call and a short put at one strike price and a long put and a short call at a different strike price.*

6. Butterfly Spread. A *butterfly spread* consists of a *combination of a bull spread and a bear spread, using either calls or puts.* Therefore, in the general form, the spread may consist of either:

- *four same-type options with a common expiration date as follows: two long identical options, one short option with an immediately lower strike price and one short option with an immediately higher strike price; or*

- *four same-type options with a common expiration date as follows: two short identical options, one long option with an immediately lower strike price and one long option with an immediately higher strike price.*

Usually it is set up with long term options. The maximum profit for a *long butterfly* (see Figure 16.13) occurs when the price of the currency reaches the level of the middle strike price at expiration. The upside break-even point is the difference between the highest strike price and the net

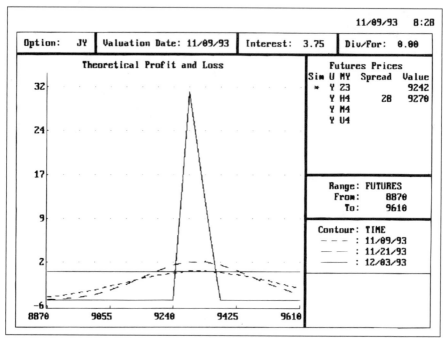

Figure 16.13. Diagram of a long butterfly on Japanese yen futures. (*Courtesy of Future-Source*)

debit. The downside break-even point is the sum of the lowest strike price and the net debit. The maximum loss equals the premium paid.

The maximum profit for a *short butterfly* (see Figure 16.14) equals the premium paid, and occurs when the currency price trades outside the extreme strike prices at expiration. The upside break-even point is the difference between the highest strike price and the net credit. The downside break-even point is the sum of the lowest strike price and the net credit. The maximum loss occurs when the price of the currency reaches the level of the middle strike price at expiration.

7. **Condor Spread.** A *condor spread* consists of either:

* *four same-type options with a common expiration date as follows: two long options with consecutive strike prices, one short option with an immediately lower strike price and one short option with an immediately higher strike price;* or

* *four same-type options with a common expiration date as follows: two short options with consecutive strike prices, one long option with an immediately lower strike price and one long option with an immediately higher strike price.*

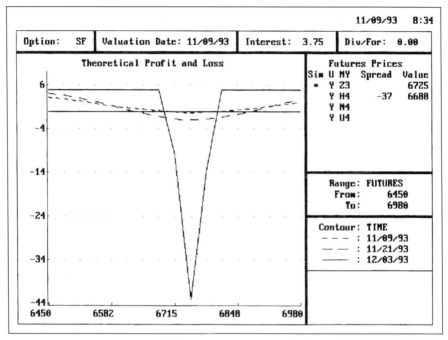

Figure 16.14. Diagram of a short butterfly on Swiss franc futures. (*Courtesy of FutureSource*)

8. Combination Spread or Synthetic Future. A *combination spread (synthetic future) consists of a long call and a short put, or a long put and a short call, with a common expiration date.*

Ratio Spreads

A *ratio spread* is a spread in which *the number of long options is different from the number of short options.* Therefore, there is a certain ratio between the long and short options.

The compound strategies previously discussed in the nonratio spread section—the straddles and the strangles—have a one-on-one ratio in their original form. But, by convention, the one-on-one ratio is not considered a ratio. In terms of these compound strategies, they may be truly "ratioed" by changing the number of one of the option classes.

The following ratio spreads are the most popular:

1. Ratio calls
2. Ratio puts
3. Call ratio backspreads

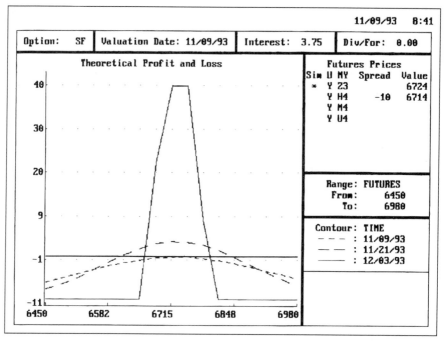

Figure 16.15. Diagram of a long condor on Swiss franc futures. (*Courtesy of Future-Source*)

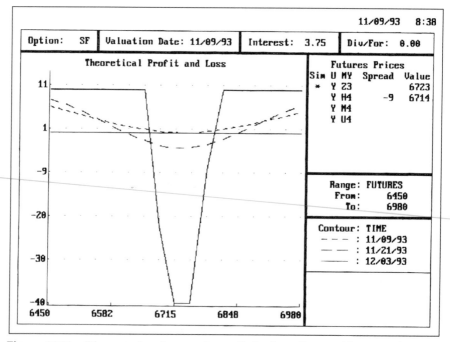

Figure 16.16. Diagram of a short condor on Swiss franc futures. (*Courtesy of Future-Source*)

4. Put ratio backspreads

5. Diagonal ratios

6. Christmas trees

Before presenting these ratio spreads, I would like to introduce the concept of neutral spread, useful in understanding other types of spreads. A *neutral spread,* or a *delta neutral spread,* consists of *a long option position and a short option position which have their respective total delta positions relatively equal.*

Thus being established, we can move along.

Ratio Call Spread

A *ratio call spread* consists of *a number of long calls with lower strike prices and a larger number of short calls with a higher strike price* (see Figure 16.17).

This type of combination is generally delta neutral.

The maximum profit is realized when the currency price is at the higher strike price.

This combination has two break-even points. The downside break-even point consists of the sum of the lower strike price and the debit, divided by the number of long calls. The upside break-even point consists of the sum of the higher strike price and the maximum profit potential, divided by the number of naked calls.

The maximum loss downside risk is the net premium and the upside risk is unlimited.

Ratio Put Spread

A *ratio put spread* consists of *a number of long puts with higher strike prices and a larger number of short puts with a lower strike price* (see Figure 16.18).

This ratio spread is generally designed as delta neutral.

The maximum profit is realized when the currency price is at the lower strike price.

This combination has two break-even points. The downside break-even point consists of the difference between the lower strike price and the maximum profit potential, divided by the number of naked puts. The upside break-even point consists of the difference between the higher strike price and the debit, divided by the number of long puts.

The maximum loss downside risk is unlimited and the upside risk is the net premium.

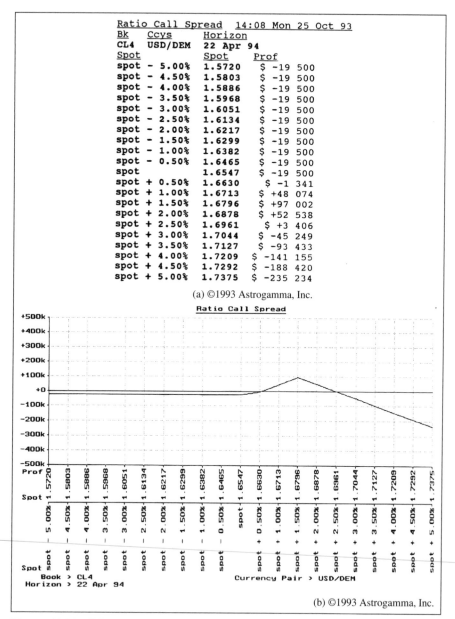

```
Ratio Call Spread   14:08 Mon 25 Oct 93
Bk   Ccys    Horizon
CL4  USD/DEM  22 Apr 94
Spot          Spot      Prof
spot - 5.00%  1.5720    $ -19 500
spot - 4.50%  1.5803    $ -19 500
spot - 4.00%  1.5886    $ -19 500
spot - 3.50%  1.5968    $ -19 500
spot - 3.00%  1.6051    $ -19 500
spot - 2.50%  1.6134    $ -19 500
spot - 2.00%  1.6217    $ -19 500
spot - 1.50%  1.6299    $ -19 500
spot - 1.00%  1.6382    $ -19 500
spot - 0.50%  1.6465    $ -19 500
spot          1.6547    $ -19 500
spot + 0.50%  1.6630    $  -1 341
spot + 1.00%  1.6713    $ +48 074
spot + 1.50%  1.6796    $ +97 002
spot + 2.00%  1.6878    $ +52 538
spot + 2.50%  1.6961    $  +3 406
spot + 3.00%  1.7044    $ -45 249
spot + 3.50%  1.7127    $ -93 433
spot + 4.00%  1.7209    $ -141 155
spot + 4.50%  1.7292    $ -188 420
spot + 5.00%  1.7375    $ -235 234
```

(a) ©1993 Astrogamma, Inc.

(b) ©1993 Astrogamma, Inc.

Figure 16.17. Price report (a) and diagram (b) of a ratio call spread on USD/DEM. (*Courtesy of Astrogamma © 1993 Astrogamma, Inc.*)

Call Ratio Backspread

A *call ratio backspread* consists of *short calls with a lower strike price and more long calls with a higher strike price.*

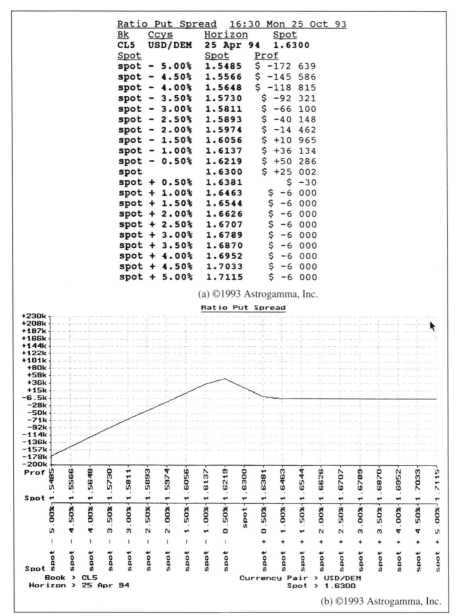

Figure 16.18 (a)

```
Ratio Put Spread   16:30 Mon 25 Oct 93
Bk   Ccys       Horizon      Spot
CL5  USD/DEM    25 Apr 94    1.6300
Spot            Spot         Prof
spot - 5.00%    1.5485       $ -172 639
spot - 4.50%    1.5566       $ -145 586
spot - 4.00%    1.5648       $ -118 815
spot - 3.50%    1.5730       $  -92 321
spot - 3.00%    1.5811       $  -66 100
spot - 2.50%    1.5893       $  -40 148
spot - 2.00%    1.5974       $  -14 462
spot - 1.50%    1.6056       $  +10 965
spot - 1.00%    1.6137       $  +36 134
spot - 0.50%    1.6219       $  +50 286
spot            1.6300       $  +25 002
spot + 0.50%    1.6381           $ -30
spot + 1.00%    1.6463       $   -6 000
spot + 1.50%    1.6544       $   -6 000
spot + 2.00%    1.6626       $   -6 000
spot + 2.50%    1.6707       $   -6 000
spot + 3.00%    1.6789       $   -6 000
spot + 3.50%    1.6870       $   -6 000
spot + 4.00%    1.6952       $   -6 000
spot + 4.50%    1.7033       $   -6 000
spot + 5.00%    1.7115       $   -6 000
```

(a) ©1993 Astrogamma, Inc.

(b) ©1993 Astrogamma, Inc.

Figure 16.18. Price report and diagram of a ratio put spread on USD/DEM. (*Courtesy of Astrogamma © 1993 Astrogamma, Inc.*)

This spread is usually established as a delta neutral ratio spread. It benefits from a price movement in either direction, but it is essentially a bullish position.

The maximum upside profit potential is unlimited and the downside profit potential consists of the total premium received. The maximum loss potential occurs when the currency price reaches the higher strike price at expiration.

Put Ratio Backspread

A *put ratio backspread* consists of *short puts with a higher strike price and more long puts with a lower strike price* (see Figure 16.19).

This spread is usually established as a delta neutral ratio spread. It benefits from a price movement in either direction, but it is essentially a bearish position.

The maximum upside profit potential consists of the total premium received and the downside profit potential is unlimited.

The maximum loss potential occurs when the currency price reaches the lower strike price at expiration.

Christmas Tree Spread

A *Christmas tree spread* is a type of *ratio vertical spread where you sell options at two or more strike prices.*

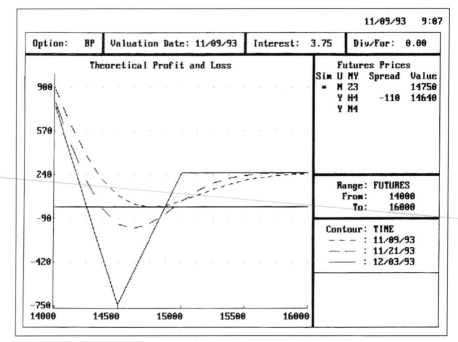

Figure 16.19. Price report and diagram of a put ratio backspread on GBP futures. (*Courtesy of FutureSource*)

Diagonal Spread

A *diagonal spread* consists of *several same type options, in which the long side and the short side have different strike prices and different expirations.*

Spreads with Both Options and Currency

The currency spreads and combinations we have presented so far have been composed of currency options only. In addition to options, the following spreads also consist of the underlying currency, whether cash or futures:

1. Covered long
2. Covered short
3. Fence

Covered Long

A *covered long* means *selling a call against a long currency position.* This strategy was designed to enhance the profitability of currency trading in a quiet market, via the option's premium (see Figure 16.20). A covered long is synonymous to a short put.

Covered Short

A *covered short* means *shorting a put against a short currency position* (see Figure 16.21). This strategy was designed to enhance the profitability of currency trading in a quiet market, via the option's premium. A covered short is synonymous to a short call.

Fence

Fences have become a strategy of choice among corporations due to their insurance features, acquired at minimum or no cost. The idea behind this strategy is that the security against a loss is purchased with the price of limiting the unlimited profitability offered by an individual option (see Figure 16.22). The price in dollars and cents may be low. But is it worth giving up the unlimited profit potential of a currency swing?

The trade-off is not too bad, since the profit potential can be unlimited only in theory. In the real trading world, most currencies tend to have limited price activity. Therefore, a well planned fence will not only provide much needed insurance against unfavorable currency activity at a low price, but will also allow the buyer to take advantage of the trading range.

```
Covered Long   14:08 Mon 25 Oct 93
Bk    Ccys     Horizon
CL6   USD/DEM  26 Apr 94
Z     Spot          Spot       Prof
FX    spot - 5.00%  1.5722   $ -527 398
      spot - 4.50%  1.5805   $ -472 271
      spot - 4.00%  1.5888   $ -417 718
      spot - 3.50%  1.5970   $ -363 730
      spot - 3.00%  1.6053   $ -310 297
      spot - 2.50%  1.6136   $ -257 414
      spot - 2.00%  1.6218   $ -205 070
      spot - 1.50%  1.6301   $ -153 258
      spot - 1.00%  1.6384   $ -101 969
      spot - 0.50%  1.6467    $ -51 195
      spot         1.6549        $ -930
      spot + 0.50%  1.6632    $ +48 835
      spot + 1.00%  1.6715    $ +98 108
      spot + 1.50%  1.6798   $ +146 896
      spot + 2.00%  1.6880   $ +195 206
      spot + 2.50%  1.6963   $ +243 043
      spot + 3.00%  1.7046   $ +290 416
      spot + 3.50%  1.7129   $ +337 332
      spot + 4.00%  1.7211   $ +383 797
      spot + 4.50%  1.7294   $ +429 817
      spot + 5.00%  1.7377   $ +475 398
Put   spot - 5.00%  1.5722   $ +173 398
      spot - 4.50%  1.5805   $ +118 271
      spot - 4.00%  1.5888    $ +63 717
      spot - 3.50%  1.5970     $ +9 729
      spot - 3.00%  1.6053    $ -43 703
      spot - 2.50%  1.6136    $ -96 586
      spot - 2.00%  1.6218   $ -148 930
    · spot - 1.50%  1.6301   $ -200 742
      spot - 1.00%  1.6384   $ -252 031
      spot - 0.50%  1.6467   $ -302 805
      spot         1.6549   $ -353 070
      spot + 0.50%  1.6632   $ -354 000
      spot + 1.00%  1.6715   $ -354 000
      spot + 1.50%  1.6798   $ -354 000
      spot + 2.00%  1.6880   $ -354 000
      spot + 2.50%  1.6963   $ -354 000
      spot + 3.00%  1.7046   $ -354 000
      spot + 3.50%  1.7129   $ -354 000
      spot + 4.00%  1.7211   $ -354 000
      spot + 4.50%  1.7294   $ -354 000
      spot + 5.00%  1.7377   $ -354 000
             (a) ©1993 Astrogamma, Inc.
```

Figure 16.20.   Price report of a covered long—USD/DEM. (*Courtesy of Astrogamma © 1993 Astrogamma, Inc.*)

A *fence* consists of either:

• *a long currency position, a long out-of-money put and a short out-of-money call, where the options have the same expiration date* (this strategy is also known as *risk conversion*); or

• *a short currency position, a short out-of-money put and a long out-of-money call, where the options have the same expiration date* (this strategy is also known as *risk reversal*).

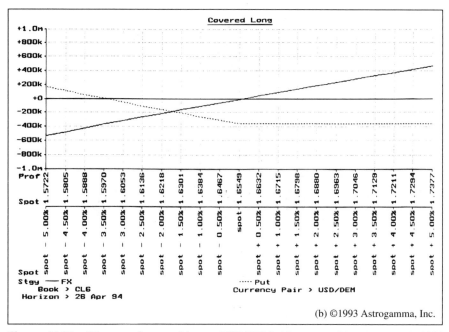

(b) ©1993 Astrogamma, Inc.

Figure 16.20. Diagram of covered long—USD/DEM. (*Courtesy of Astrogamma © 1993 Astrogamma, Inc.*) (Continued)

As an example, a buyer who wants to avoid the risk of a currency upswing at a reduced price will purchase a call and also write a put on the specific currency.

For instance, let's assume that the spot GBP/USD trades at 1.50, and the trader buys a $1.45 6 months GBP call and sells a $1.55 put, where the premium paid (for the call) and the premium received (for the put) are identical. The P&L for the life of the options (6 months, in this example) will be zero if the GBP/USD spot will trade between 1.45 and 1.55 for the period. Since the option cost is zero, the break-even point is the strike price.

The downside of the fence strategy is that the maximum loss is unlimited. Should the trader want to limit the potential loss, an additional option should be bought.

Strategy Box

The strategy box in Figure 16.23 encompasses the basic approaches to the market in terms of volatility.

```
Covered Short   14:08 Mon 25 Oct 93
Book    Ccys      Horizon     Spot
Dem-Usd USD/DEM   19 Apr 94   1.6627
Stay    Spot                Spot      Prof
FX      spot - 5.00%        1.5796    $ +475 033
        spot - 4.50%        1.5879    $ +419 992
        spot - 4.00%        1.5962    $ +365 526
        spot - 3.50%        1.6045    $ +311 624
        spot - 3.00%        1.6128    $ +258 277
        spot - 2.50%        1.6211    $ +205 477
        spot - 2.00%        1.6294    $ +153 216
        spot - 1.50%        1.6378    $ +101 486
        spot - 1.00%        1.6461    $  +50 278
        spot - 0.50%        1.6544       $ -414
        spot                1.6627    $  -50 600
        spot + 0.50%        1.6710    $ -100 286
        spot + 1.00%        1.6793    $ -149 481
        spot + 1.50%        1.6876    $ -198 191
        spot + 2.00%        1.6960    $ -246 424
        spot + 2.50%        1.7043    $ -294 186
        spot + 3.00%        1.7126    $ -341 484
        spot + 3.50%        1.7209    $ -388 325
        spot + 4.00%        1.7292    $ -434 716
        spot + 4.50%        1.7375    $ -480 663
        spot + 5.00%        1.7458    $ -526 172
Call    spot - 5.00%        1.5796    $ -336 500
        spot - 4.50%        1.5879    $ -336 500
        spot - 4.00%        1.5962    $ -336 500
        spot - 3.50%        1.6045    $ -336 500
        spot - 3.00%        1.6128    $ -336 500
        spot - 2.50%        1.6211    $ -336 500
        spot - 2.00%        1.6294    $ -336 500
        spot - 1.50%        1.6378    $ -336 500
        spot - 1.00%        1.6461    $ -336 500
        spot - 0.50%        1.6544    $ -336 500
        spot                1.6627    $ -320 261
        spot + 0.50%        1.6710    $ -270 590
        spot + 1.00%        1.6793    $ -221 412
        spot + 1.50%        1.6876    $ -172 718
        spot + 2.00%        1.6960    $ -124 501
        spot + 2.50%        1.7043    $  -76 755
        spot + 3.00%        1.7126    $  -29 472
        spot + 3.50%        1.7209    $  +17 354
        spot + 4.00%        1.7292    $  +63 730
        spot + 4.50%        1.7375    $ +109 662
        spot + 5.00%        1.7458    $ +155 156
                    (a) ©1993 Astrogamma, Inc.
```

Figure 16.21. Price report of a covered short—USD/DEM. (*Courtesy of Astrogamma* © *1993 Astrogamma, Inc.*)

Exotic Options*

The range of options strategies is continuously expanding to better encompass the diversity of needs in the financial arena. Following is a study of the exotic options developed by Astrogamma.

---

*Excerpted from the "Fenics" FX options trading software Help pages. (© 1993 Astrogamma, Inc. Reproduced with permission.)

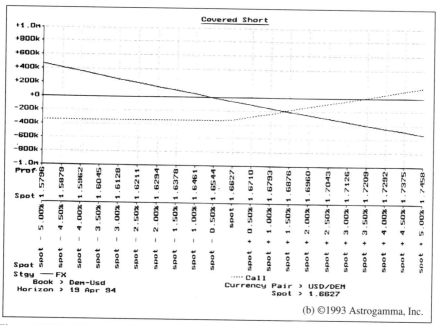

(b) ©1993 Astrogamma, Inc.

Figure 16.21. Diagram of a covered short—USD/DEM. (*Courtesy of Astrogamma © 1993 Astrogamma, Inc.*) (Continued)

Barrier Options

Barrier options are also known as *trigger options, cutoff options, cutout options, stopoptions, down/up-and-outs/ins, knockups,* etc. They are very similar to European-style vanilla options, except that a second strike price—the trigger—is specified which, when reached in the market, automatically

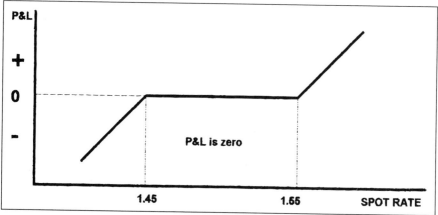

Figure 16.22. Diagram of a fence compound strategy in British pounds.

	BULLISH	BEARISH	UNDECIDED
VOLATILITY RISING	LONG CALL	LONG PUT	LONG STRADDLE
VOLATILITY FALLING	SHORT CALL	SHORT PUT	SHORT STRADDLE
VOLATILITY UNDECIDED	BULL SPREAD	BEAR SPREAD	NO STRATEGY

Figure 16.23. Strategy box.

causes the option to be expired - *knockout options* - or "inspired" (*knockin options*).

With *knockouts*, the trader buys a vanilla option which goes away if the trigger is reached. With *knockins*, the trader is buying a vanilla option which does not exist until the trigger is reached. The determination of when the trigger is hit can be based on the spot currency rate (spot style) or the forward currency underlying the option (forward style).

In standard cases—knockouts and knockins—the bias of the trigger is opposite to that of the underlying vanilla option. In other words, as the likelihood of being triggered increases, the option is losing intrinsic value or becoming more out-of-the-money.

There is also another variant, known as *reverse knockouts* and *reverse knockins*, in which the likelihood of being triggered increases as the option's intrinsic value increases. These are often referred to as "in-the-money" knockouts and knockins, because the trigger must be in-the-money with respect to the strike in order for the option to have any value at all (reverse knockout), or to be any different from a vanilla option (reverse knockin).

Any option that is triggered when it has intrinsic value is virtually impossible to hedge near the trigger, so the reverse varieties are very rare.

Knockouts for Corporate Hedging

From a corporate standpoint, normal knockouts are the most appealing of the barrier types. Assuming that a corporate customer is buying the underlying vanilla option for hedging purposes, it is clear that, when the trigger is reached, FX rates have moved "his or her" way, and the protection of the option may no longer be needed.

For example, consider a corporate customer who is long British pounds against US dollars, value three months from now. Assume that

Cable is now 1.5500, and that the customer's level of pain on the downside is 1.5000. The corporate customer could buy a knockout put (an up-and-out) with a strike price of 1.5000 and a trigger at 1.6000. If Sterling reaches 1.6000 prior to expiry, the customer will sell the pounds there, as the option's protection is not needed any more. Otherwise, the corporate customer either exercises the 1.5000 put or lets it expire out-of-the-money on expiry day.

The advantage of a knockout option in comparison with a pair of orders (a take-profit at 1.6000 and a stop-loss at 1.5000) is that the British pound can drop below 1.5000 without having the customer stopped out, with a possible gain if it recovers. The advantage of a knockout option in comparison with a risk reversal (where the customer would sell a 1.6000 call instead of leaving a sell order there) is that the position is closed as soon as 1.6000 is reached. There is no chance that the customer will have to let the 1.6000 bids go untouched because he needs the long position in Sterling to cover his short option, then watch helplessly as Cable drops below 1.6000 again.

The disadvantage of a knockout option, in comparison with both the pair of orders and the pair of options, is that it costs money, but not as much as the 1.5000 put would cost by itself. How much cheaper the knockout option is than the corresponding normal option depends entirely on how far away the trigger is from the current market. If the trigger is set very close, the knockout option is very cheap, since the likelihood of the trigger being reached before expiry is very great. Conversely, if the trigger is very far away from the current market, the savings are minimal.

The corporate hedging rationale for the remaining types of barrier options is not so clear, particularly for reverses, which get knocked in or out when the option has intrinsic value. Reverse knockins seem appealing, until one realizes that the trigger has to be so far in-the-money to realize meaningful costs savings that the risk of the operation never knocking in is too great to bear.

Hedging a Position in Barrier Options

There is an almost perfect static hedge for a forward knockout option. Let's say that the trader sold a knockout call. To cover himself, the trader buys a vanilla call with the same strike and maturity against it. Then, the trader sells a put with the same maturity struck so that when the forward reaches the trigger, the call bought and the put sold are worth the same.

The idea is that the call covers the vanilla part of the knockout exactly, the put compensates for the difference in premium, and, if the knockout expires early, the trader unwinds the two hedge options at flat.

For forward knockout options, the strike price of this put is a constant over the life of the option. The formula for forward knockouts is:

$$\text{Forward knockout option strike price} = \frac{\text{Trigger}^2}{\text{Strike}}$$

Therefore, the trigger is the geometric average of the strike and the hedge strike, which comes in handy when forward = trigger.

To be a perfect hedge, the hedge option should be executed in a ratio of strike/trigger for calls and trigger/strike for puts. This ratio is usually very close to 1:1.

For spot knockouts the hedge strike unfortunately drifts, so if using this hedging method, the trader will still have the residual risk up to the swap points between spot and the forward. It still is a darn good hedge, though.

The static hedge for a knockin option follows directly from that for the knockout. It is easy to demonstrate that buying both a knockout and knockin with the same specifications is the same as buying a vanilla option: if the trigger is never reached, the trader owns the vanilla option from the knockout , and if the trigger is reached, the trader owns the vanilla option from the knockin. Either way, the trader owns the vanilla option. The following formula holds for reverse knocks, as well:

$$\text{Knockout} + \text{Knockin} = \text{Vanilla}$$

From this discussion, we know that:

1. Knockout call = Vanilla call (at strike) − Vanilla put (at hedge strike)

2. Knockin call = Vanilla call − Knockout call

therefore, substituting from (1):

3. Knockin call = Vanilla call − (Vanilla call − Vanilla put) = Vanilla put

It's a little hard to believe, but the perfect static hedge for a forward knockin call is simply a vanilla put at the same hedge strike and in the same ratio as for the knockout call. Thinking through the logic of this position makes it clear why this is the case.

The trader buys a knockin call and hedges it by selling a vanilla put struck so that when the forward reaches the trigger, the call he bought and the put he sold are worth the same. When the knockin is triggered, the trader is long a call and short a put with the same value (a classic risk reversal), and he unwinds it at flat.

The same conditions apply to hedging spot knockins, but it is a more dynamic hedge since the trader does not know where the forward will be when spot reaches the trigger. It is still a great hedge.

There is no similarly simple hedging strategy for reverses, or for any option that gets triggered when the underlying vanilla has intrinsic value. They become virtually impossible to hedge around the trigger, especially near expiration, because on one side of the trigger they are worthless and on the other side they are worth intrinsic value, which may be substantial if the trigger is deep-in-the-money with respect to strike. This "on-off" feature is much more complicated to hedge than, for example, a vanilla option at expiration.

Barriers II

Risk Management Aspects of Barriers Options

As the preceding discussion makes clear, barrier options have "imbedded" options, in the form of the trigger, that turn traditional notions of risk management on their heads. It's useful to point out a few of the important differences from normal options that the trader should be aware of when dealing barriers.

The most noticeable difference between knockouts and vanilla options is the delta, which is much higher for the knockout than for the vanilla, at least for knockouts with sensible triggers. It's easy to point to the replicating strategy and conclude that, when the trader is long a knockout, the trader is really long a risk reversal with the underlying vanilla as one leg, so the delta of the knockout is obviously higher.

But the real reason is even simpler and more intuitively appealing than that. When the knockout gets triggered, the vanilla underlying it still has time value, but as you move away from the trigger the knockout starts to behave more like the vanilla, until the two are indistinguishable. Obviously, if the knockout loses its value more quickly as you near the trigger, the knockout is more sensitive to movements in spot across the entire range of spot movements, which means its delta must be higher.

High knockout deltas start to seem like an easy concept to grasp when you consider what happens to knockins: knockin calls have *negative* deltas and knockin puts have *positive* deltas. Once again, this isn't hard to understand when you look at the replicating strategy, but it also makes intuitive sense.

Take the example of a USD/DEM knockin USD call (a down-and-in) with a strike of 1.5000 and a trigger of 1.4000. As spot moves toward 1.5000, the underlying vanilla is gaining intrinsic value, but the likelihood that the trader will ever have a vanilla option to exercise (i.e., the chance of the option being knocked in) is diminishing, so the knockin USD call is worth less and less. On the other hand, as spot moves to 1.4000, it is becoming more and more likely that you will own a valuable vanilla option, so the value of the knockin is increasing. As soon as the call is knocked in, its delta becomes positive. Thus, even though it is a call, the knockin loses value when spot rises (away from the trigger) and gains value when spot falls—negative delta.

Because the deltas of standard knockouts and knockins are discontinuous through the trigger, the trader must be prepared to unwind the delta hedge for the knockout, or to flip the direction of the delta hedge for the knockin using an order. Similarly, if the trader has hedged the knock with the replicating strategy, the hedge position will need to be delta-hedged when the offsetting barrier option is triggered.

The most striking feature about the reverse knockouts is their prices, which seem disconcertingly low, unless the trigger is very far in the money. This is because they have the same likelihood of expiring worthless as a vanilla option, but their upside is not only limited but disappears completely if the trigger is reached.

Let's take the example of a USD/DEM reverse knockout USD call (an up-and-out) with a strike of 1.5300 and a trigger of 1.5500. Despite the fact that the option could end up with as much as 200 points of intrinsic value, it is virtually worthless, regardless of where the spot is. The reason is that any time it gets intrinsic value, the likelihood of expiring worthless increases. This is in contrast to a straight vanilla or knockout call, which has unlimited upside, or a 1.5300:1.5500 USD call spread, also with a 200 points of intrinsic value, but which doesn't lose that value when spot goes above 1.5500.

For the same reasons, long positions in the typical reverse knockout have negative vega.

By contrast, the values of reverse knockins are virtually indistinguishable from vanilla options unless the trigger is in-the-money. The deltas of reverse knocks become very unstable near the trigger, especially when approaching expiration.

Optimal Options

Previously known as *lookback options,* the optimal options refer to the most favorable rate of the underlying currency that existed (from the holder's perspective) during the life of the option. This rate becomes the strike in the case of optimal strike options, or it becomes the underlying, determining the intrinsic value when compared to a predetermined fixed strike in the case of optimal rate options. Optimals can be based on the spot rate (spot style) or the forward rate (forward style).

The highest underlying rate achieved during the option's life would become the strike of an optional strike put option and the underlying rate of an optimal rate call option. Conversely, the lowest underlying rate achieved during the option's life would become the strike of an optional strike call and the rate of an optimal rate put option.

Because these options allow the holder to transact at the most favorable rate that existed during the life of the option, they are very expensive—almost twice the premium of the at-the-money options.

Optimals for Corporate Hedging

Despite their high price, optimal options still are good hedging vehicles when the trader expects more volatility than the market does.

Optimals can be hedged quite well with straddles.

Risk Management Aspects of Barriers Options

When looking at the price and volatility sensitivity of optimal strike options, it helps to remember that they can be replicated with straddles. They have virtually no spot sensitivity, but plenty of gamma, vega and time decay.

Average Options

These are options which refer to the average rate of the underlying currency that existed during the life of the option. This rate becomes the strike in the case of the average strike options, or it becomes the underlying, determining the intrinsic value when compared to a predetermined fixed strike in the case of average rate options. Average options can be based on the spot rate (spot style) or the forward underlying the option (forward style). The average can be calculated arithmetically or geometrically, and the rates can be tabulated with a variety of frequencies.

Averages for Corporate Hedging

The appeal of average options for corporate hedging is obvious. In theory, the goal of a corporation in hedging its foreign exchange exposure is to minimize the P&L impact of foreign exchange rates fluctuations. While transacting at the average rate for a given period is not sufficient to achieve this goal, it does help avoid the uncertainties that go along with trying to second-guess the market, and it provides a reasonable measure of downside protection at about half the cost of vanilla options.

Vanilla options are also tremendously valuable in hedging nontransactional (portfolio) exposures, such as interest in a foreign subsidiary or other offshore investments. As static hedges, average rate options may be attractive because they tend to hold their intrinsic value and are not so dependent on where the spot is at expiry.

Hedging a Position in Average Options

Although the most complicated exotic options to price and manage, average options are more like vanilla options than the other exotics when it comes to hedging.

Risk Management Aspects of Average Options

Average options are much less susceptible to market volatility than vanilla options and therefore, somewhat cheaper. Otherwise, the differences between the two classes of average options become more pronounced, and their relationship to vanilla options becomes muddled.

Conclusions

Given a choice, foreign exchange traders will not trade currency options when they are confident about the direction of the market. Dollar per dollar, the profit is lower when trading options vis-à-vis spot, forwards or futures, simply because of the premium involved.

The reverse of the scenario, though, is that at times traders cannot forecast the direction of the market prior to certain events, but expect high volatility. In this case, the best choice is to trade options.

The lack of activity in the currency market signals another opportunity for trading options. Unlike any of the other instruments, options selling, or writing, enables a trader to produce in an otherwise unprofitable environment.

By using options, corporations are able to customize sophisticated strategies for a variety of purposes, such as hedging or insurance. Options trading also allows advanced strategies to be achieved at relatively low cost.

There are certain costs attached to options trading. These costs are pertinent to the adequate capitalization for delta (and/or gamma and vega) hedging and research costs.

Finally, options trading expands and improves the risk management tools. This is a vital feature in a market trading an average daily volume of US$1 trillion.

New Directions in Options Trading

Currently, the options share of the currency market is estimated at 5 percent (1993). The increased complexity of the world economic and political environment will fuel the growth of options trading well into the next century.

More and more corporations around the world are getting involved in options trading for hedging, risk management and speculation purposes.

The developments on the European Monetary System in September 1992 and July 1993 are perfect examples of real life scenarios which may be disastrous for unprotected financial entities. It was estimated that in the time frame encompassing these dates, options trading on the EMS currencies rose by up to 10 percent. It should also be added that, due to the extraordinary circumstances of these events, options trading was concentrated in the top echelon of traders. Premiums skyrocketed up to three times their normal level due to the unprecedented volatility and to the specific needs of various corporations.

The new currency players from emerging economies are increasing their trading efforts around the world. Since 1989, these players have started to become more involved in foreign exchange in general and options trading in particular. From South America to Southeast Asia to Eastern Europe, the demand for derivatives has become substantial.

The options market will also increase due to continuous instrument innovations. In response to the diverse international demand, options strategies are continuously being developed.

In addition, the technological breakthroughs in hardware and software have been pillars for both the increased trading sophistication and affordability.

While players around the world are by and large indifferent to the risks germane to options trading, central banks and even governments are less confident. The specter of mismanaged risks, from market to credit, creates an increasing concern.

The recommendations of the Washington, DC-based Group of Thirty, presented in Chapter 5, have made a significant contribution to the approach to derivatives trading and sound risk management.

The increasing application of these practices and principles will consolidate the soundness and scope of options trading.

Chapter 17

Economic Fundamentals

Forecasting is based on two essential types of analysis: (1) fundamental, discussed in detail in Chapters 17 and 18, (2) and technical, the chart study of past behavior of commodity prices, discussed in Chapters 19 through 28. What are the fundamentals? As the name indicates, they refer to factors which either show the fundamental state of the economy or fundamentally alter the outlook of one economy relative to the world economy. This chapter focuses on the theoretical models of exchange rate determination and on the major economic factors and their likelihood of impacting on the foreign exchange rates.

Economic Fundamentals

Any news which has a direct or indirect bearing on the economy may be considered fundamental. The news may refer to changes in the economy, changes in interest rates, political elections, coup d'état, natural disasters, etc. It's a busy, busy world.

In order to navigate through the large, complex and changing universe of fundamentals, they may be classified into four categories: economic factors, financial factors, political factors and crisis. A rough comparison of these categories provides us with a simple but very important finding. By and large, economic factors differ from the other three factors in terms of

MMS Currency
Global Economic Calendar

Date	GMT	CTRY	Release	For	Forecast	Median	Last
DEC 01	05:00	JPN	Auto sales*	NOV	−7.7% A	N/A	−11.3%
DEC 01	07:00	SWI	Federal CPI, M/M	NOV	−0.1% A	0.2%	0.1%
DEC 01	07:00	SWI	Federal CPI, Y/Y	NOV	2.2% A	2.6%	3.4%
DEC 01	07:30	SWI	GDP, Q/Q	Q3	0.6% A	N/A	0.4%
DEC 01	07:30	GER	Import Prices M/M	OCT	0.1% A	0.1%	−1.1%
DEC 01	07:30	GER	Import Prices Y/Y	OCT	−1.5% A	−1.5%	−1.5%
DEC 01	07:30	JPN	Forex Rsrvs (Mo/Mo)	NOV	0.2% A	N/A	−0.6%
DEC 01	10:30	GER	Indust Prod M/M	OCT	−0.4% A	0.0%	0.0% R
DEC 01	10:30	GER	Manuf Output M/M	OCT	−0.4% A	−0.3%	0.0% R
DEC 01	13:30	US	GDP Preliminary	Q3	2.7% A	2.9%	2.8%
DEC 01	13:30	US	GDP Deflator Pre.	Q3	1.6% A	1.6%	1.6%
DEC 01	15:00	US	NAPM	NOV	55.0%	54.5%	53.8%
DEC 01	15:00	US	Construction Sp.	OCT	1.0%	1.0%	0.8%
01-08	----	GER	Capital account	OCT	N/A	N/A	−18.7B
01-08	----	GER	Long-term cap a/c	OCT	N/A	N/A	20.5B
DEC 02	07:00	JPN	BOJ Corp Serv Price*	OCT	0.4%	N/A	0.6%
DEC 02	07:00	JPN	BOJ Corp Serv Price	OCT	0.2%	N/A	0.1%
DEC 02	09:30	UK	Official Reserves	NOV	100M	50M	$32M
02-06	09:30	GER	Manuf. Orders M/M	OCT	−0.6%	−0.5%	2.1% R
DEC 02	13:30	US	Initial Clms 11/27		332K	331K	339K
DEC 02	13:30	US	Personal Income	OCT	0.6%	0.7%	0.2%
DEC 02	13:30	US	PCE	OCT	0.8%	0.8%	0.3%
DEC 02	15:00	US	New Home Sales	OCT	725K	700K	762K
DEC 02	21:30	US	M2-Wk Ended 11/22		$4.0B	$4.7B	$7.7B
02-05	----	SWI	Unemployment Rate	NOV	4.9%	4.9%	4.8%
02-06	----	DEN	Unemployment, sa	OCT	12.5%	12.5%	12.5%
03-07	06:30	JPN	GDP (SAAR)	Q3	−2.9%	−2.0%	−1.6%
DEC 03	06:30	JPN	Trade Bal(1st 20D)	NOV	N/A	N/A	$5.7B
DEC 03	06:30	JPN	Current A/C (IMF)	OCT	$11.4B	$11.6B	$13.3B
DEC 03	06:30	JPN	Trade Bals (IMF)	OCT	$12.9B	N/A	$14.6B
DEC 03	07:00	JPN	Frgn Bond Invstment	OCT	$7.0B	N/A	−$6.0B
DEC 03	09:00	GER	Unemp. SA West	NOV	45K	45K	56K
DEC 03	09:00	GER	Employment SA West	OCT	−40K	−40K	−34K
DEC 03	13:30	US	Nonfarm Payrolls	NOV	175K	171K	177K
DEC 03	13:30	US	Mfg Payrolls	NOV	10K	10K	12K
DEC 03	13:30	US	Hourly Earnings	NOV	0.1%	0.2%	0.5%
DEC 03	13:30	US	Unemployment Rate	NOV	6.7%	6.7%	6.8%
DEC 03	13:30	US	Leading Indicators	OCT	0.4%	0.6%	0.5%
DEC 03	15:00	US	Factory Orders	OCT	1.3%	1.3%	0.7%

[* = YR/YR, SOME DATES ARE ESTIMATED]

Figure 17.1. The economic data is available on the Global Economic Calendar provided by MMS International on pages 7756, 7757 and 7758 via Telerate. (*Courtesy of MMS International*)

the certainty of their release. The dates and times of economic data release are known well in advance, at least among the industrialized nations (see Figure 17.1).

Political factors vary greatly in terms of the certainty of dates and times. For instance, the time of presidential elections in some countries is known long in advance, such as every four years in the United States. In other countries, like Italy, where governments are less stable, the timing of parliamentary elections cannot be forecast in advance. Moreover, the rapid fall of the Soviet Empire was shockingly unforeseen by anybody, fundamentally oriented or not.

With financial factors, timing remains a mystery. Discount rates are changed by central banks, and this activity is surrounded by secrecy, despite the fact that the markets closely watch the central banks' activities and try to forecast the timing of their moves. For instance, the Bundesbank's cut of the German discount rate in October 1993, shortly after a new director took over, surprised the markets in terms of timing, even though such a move was not unexpected (see Figure 17.2).

A crisis may or may not be an important factor, depending on the predictability of the crisis. That is why the impact on foreign exchange of the Allied Forces military response to the Iraqi aggression against Kuwait in 1991 was minimal, whereas the kidnapping of Michail Gorbachev, the last president of the Soviet Union, had a sharp effect on the foreign exchange markets.

MMS Currency
[Critical Events Calendar]

Date	GMT	Venue	Event/Speech
DEC 14	----	SWIT	Group of ten central bank governors meet
14-16	----	BRUSS	EC Farm Ministers meet, with final approval of the Blair House Accord to be decided.
DEC 14	07:00	FFT	Dec BBK monthly report published
DEC 14	----	SWIT	EC central bank governors monthly meeting
DEC 14	----	BRUSS	ECOFIN council
DEC 15	----	PARIS	French Assembly & Senate to vote on GATT and general policy from the government
DEC 15	----	GER	Second round German metal wage talks in NRW
DEC 15	05:00	WASH	Clintons fast-track authority for the GATT Uruguay round expires.
DEC 15	----	GENEV	GATT Uruguay Round called to final session, to record the results of the negotiations
DEC 15	06:00	TYO	BOJ Gov Mieno has regular press conference

Figure 17.2.   The Critical Events Calendar provided by MMS International on page 7759 on Telerate covers all the potentially market moving factors aside from the economic factors. (*Courtesy of MMS International*)

Theories of Exchange Rate Determination

After spending a long and fruitful life within the Bretton-Woods Accord co-coon, currencies around the world were allowed at last, in 1971, more free-dom to move against each other, to find their own equilibrium level and to take the pressure off governments and central banks in terms of keeping a country's money within the prescribed ranges. Few imagined at the time that, after 27 years of virtual standstill, currencies could have a volatile be-havior under international conditions of relative peace and prosperity. As you can see from Figure 17.3, the US dollar has had quite a "roller coaster" behavior since 1973, the true start toward currency free-floating.

Models of Exchange Rate Determination

Attempting to understand why currencies move so much is a taxing goal. Many attempts have been made to learn the factors determining the volatil-ity of the foreign exchange market. In this section, the three most significant theories on exchange rate determination are discussed.

These three models are traditional theories, modern monetary theories on short term exchange rate volatility and synthesis of traditional and mod-ern monetary views.

Traditional Theories

The traditional theories consist of the Purchasing Power Parity (PPP) and the Views on Elasticities.

Purchasing Power Parity

The oldest and still the most popular of the theories is the purchasing power parity. *Purchasing power parity* was developed in 1556 by Martin de Azpilcueta Navarro. The theory states that the price of a good in one coun-try should equal the price of the same good in another country, exchanged at the current rate—*the law of one price.*

For example, if the foreign currency (such as the USD/JPY in 1985 at about 240) is undervalued, the purchasing power of the domestic currency (USD) is higher abroad. As the flow of USD moves abroad, domestic prices fall and foreign prices rise as the domestic demand rises *or* the foreign cur-rency rises until two currencies reach the parity level.

$$P_d = SPf$$

where

Pd = domestic price of product A

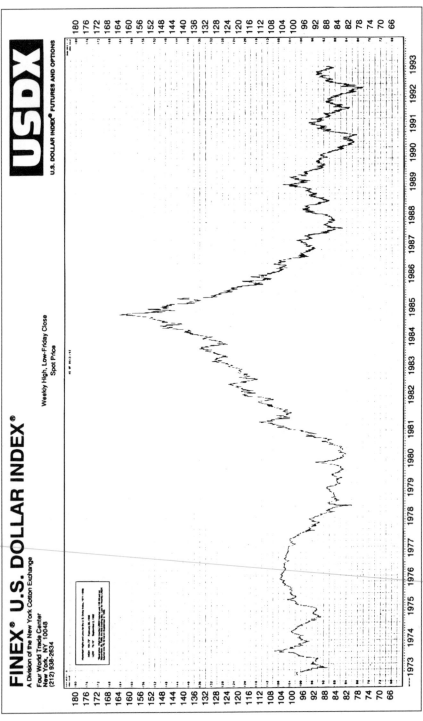

Figure 17.3. The US Dollar Index® between 1973 and 1993. (*Courtesy of FINEX® US*

S = spot exchange rate

Pf = foreign price of product A

There are two versions of the purchasing power parity theory:

• Absolute version
• Relative version

The PPP Absolute Version

Under the *absolute version,* the exchange rate simply equals the ratio of the two countries' general price level, which is the weighted average of all goods produced in a country.

However, this version quickly comes under fire. First, which two countries produce and/or consume the same goods? None. Even if we examine the previous two German states or at the still split Korea, which have the same culture, language and idiosyncrasies despite the political division, we would be hard pressed to find similar production and consumption.

The typical PPP example publicized on a yearly basis is the price of a hamburger around the world. Now, tasty as they may be, hamburgers are much less popular outside the United States. In addition, hamburgers are targeted differently in other countries. Whereas, in the United States, hamburgers are generally considered an inexpensive yet satisfying fast food, in Tokyo or Paris they are more of a *chic* type of meal, and in Moscow they are a rather expensive import. And then there are cultures where beef is not consumed.

Second, the absolute version assumes that transportation costs and trade barriers are insignificant. In reality, transportation costs are significant and dissimilar around the world. In terms of trade barriers, well, that would be an interesting point to raise next time the United States and Japan meet over trade issues. Trade barriers are still alive and well, sometimes obvious and sometimes hidden, and the costs and goods distribution are influenced by them.

Finally, this version disregards the importance of brand names. With many commodities—such as soybeans—price is likely to be the main factor. Cars, however, are chosen not only because of the best price for the same type of engine, but also on the basis of the name. After all, as one might say in California, "you are what you drive." Even with some commodities, brand names are important. Coffee is not just coffee, but Java or espresso or vanilla flavor. And orange juice, as well, comes under different brand names.

These cases show what happens to the absolute version of the purchasing power parity in the real world, where the theory fails.

The PPP Relative Version

In order to eliminate some of these problems, the purchasing power parity theory was designed in a different form—the relative version. Under the *relative version,* the percentage change in the exchange rate from a given base period must equal the difference between the percentage change in the domestic price level and the percentage change in the foreign price level.

For instance, if US prices rose by 6 percent and German prices rose by 2.4 percent between 1985 and 1989, then the US dollar should have fallen by 3.6 percent. However, although the prices in the two countries did increase by approximately those percentages, the US dollar fell about 50 percent.

Obviously, the relative version of the PPP is not free of problems. First, it is difficult or arbitrary to define the base period. Second, trade restrictions remain a real and thorny issue, just as they were in the absolute version. Third, different price index weighting and the inclusion of different products in the indexes make the comparison difficult. And, finally, in the long term, countries' internal price ratios may change, generating the exchange rate to move away from the relative PPP.

In conclusion, the spot exchange rate moves independently of relative domestic and foreign prices. In the short run, the exchange rate is influenced by financial market conditions, not by commodity market conditions.

Despite these problems, the theory behind the Plaza Accord of September 1985, where the G-5 countries decided to devaluate the US dollar relative to the European and Japanese currencies, was purchasing power parity (see Figure 17.4).

How successful was the implementation of the theory in reality? In qualifying the success of the application of this theory, the problems germane to each of the versions must be emphasized.

Trade barriers, which have negatively affected the ability of the devalued US dollar to achieve a more balanced international trade, are still a major problem. And, despite the continuous internationalization of both industries and consumption, countries still do not have common production or consumption. Brand names continue to maintain their importance. Satisfied consumers are loyal consumers, and are difficult to convince otherwise.

Therefore, price by itself generally fails to be the trigger in the consumers' minds. It is value, or the perception of value, and the propensity to spend that will convince the value oriented shopper of the 1990s. These are just some of the reasons the purchasing power parity failed to achieve the original tasks of the Plaza Accord of 1985.

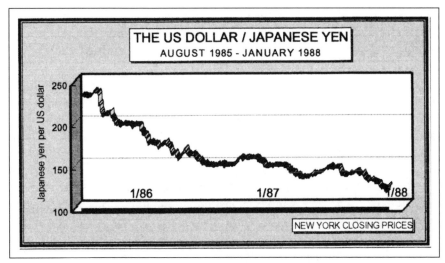

Figure 17.4.   The exchange rate between the US dollar and the Japanese yen fell around 50 percent between September 1985 and January 1988 in an attempt to implement the purchasing power parity.

The J Curve

The application of the purchasing power parity, in reality, creates the J curve effect. The *J curve* theory holds that the devaluation of a currency will trigger exports gains in the long term, rather than short term. The reasons behind this theory are linked to previous contracts, existing inventories and behavior modification.

Theory of Elasticities

The *theory of elasticities* was popular in the post World War II era, when it determined the balance of trade's response to a change in the exchange rate. Later, this theory was modified to examine the exchange rate's response to a disturbance in the trade balance.

The theory of elasticities holds that the exchange rate is simply the price of foreign exchange which maintains the balance of payments in equilibrium. In other words, the degree to which the exchange rate responds to a change in the trade balance depends entirely on the elasticity of demand to a change in price.

Therefore, if the demand is price inelastic, then a decline in imports and a rise in exports is small. Consequently, the exchange rate must rise steeply to eliminate the payment deficit. On the other hand, if the demand is price elastic, then the decline in imports and the rise in exports are large. Therefore, the exchange rates need little adjustment.

For instance, if the imports of country A are strong, then the trade balance is weak. Consequently, the exchange rate rises—due to the growth of country A's exports—and triggers in its turn a rise in its domestic income, along with a decrease in the foreign income.

Whereas a rise in the domestic income (in country A) will trigger an increase in the domestic consumption of both domestic and foreign goods and, therefore, more demand for foreign currencies, a decrease in the foreign income (in country B) will trigger a decrease in the domestic consumption of both country B's domestic and foreign goods, and therefore less demand for its own currency.

The elasticities approach is not problem-free, either. First, in the short term, the exchange rate is more inelastic than the long term. Since the spot market is focusing on the short term, the lack of elasticity will impact the exchange rate. And, second, additional exchange rate variables arise continuously, changing the rules of the game.

Conclusion

The volatility of the spot exchange rate is influenced to a large extent by short term variables not anticipated during the Bretton Woods Accord era. Despite the shortcomings, the traditional views on exchange rate determination still tend to explain the long term behavior of foreign currencies.

The Fisher Effect

The Fisher effect holds that the *nominal interest rate* consists of the *real interest rate* plus the *expected rate of inflation*.

$$I_n = I_r + I_e$$

where

I_n = nominal interest rate

I_r = real interest rate

I_e = expected rate of inflation

Therefore, for the countries with identical real interest rates, their nominal interest rates will differ with respect to their individual expected rates of inflation.

The International Fisher Effect

The international Fisher effect holds that investors will keep assets denominated in depreciating currencies only to the extent that the interest rates are sufficiently high to balance the expected currency losses.

This is a very important point not only for investors but also for the governments of countries with currencies expected to depreciate. In order to attract investments in such countries, it is vital that interest rates exceed expected loses on foreign exchange.

Modern Monetary Theories on Short Term Exchange Rate Volatility

The modern monetary theories on short term exchange rate volatility take into consideration the short term capital markets' role and the long term impact of the commodity markets on foreign exchange. These theories hold that the divergence between the exchange rate and the purchasing power parity is due to the supply and demand for financial assets and the international capability.

One of the modern monetary theories states that exchange rate volatility is triggered by a one-time domestic money supply increase, since this is assumed to raise expectations of higher future monetary growth.

The purchasing power parity is extended to include the capital markets. If, in both countries whose currencies are exchanged, the demand for money is determined by the level of domestic income and domestic interest rates, then a higher income increases demand for transactions balances while a higher interest rate increases the opportunity cost of holding money, reducing the demand for money.

Under absolute PPP, the spot exchange rate equaled the ratio of the domestic price level to the foreign price level. Therefore, the spot exchange rate is determined by the two countries' relative money supply, relative interest rates and relative real incomes.

Under a second approach, the exchange rate adjusts instantaneously to maintain continuous interest rate parity, but only in the long run to maintain PPP.

Volatility occurs because the commodity markets adjust slower than the financial markets. This version is known as the *dynamic monetary approach.*

The Portfolio-Balance Approach

Whereas, in the previous examples, it was assumed that international financial assets were interchangeable, the portfolio-balance approach holds the opposite. Due to the difference between international assets, investors, likely to focus on only a group of financial assets, will have to purchase the specific currency or currencies. Therefore, the portfolio-balance approach holds that the currency demand is triggered by the demand for financial assets, rather than the demand for the currency per se.

Synthesis of Traditional and Modern Monetary Views

In order to better suit the previous theories to the realities of the market, some of the more stringent conditions were adjusted into a synthesis of the traditional and modern monetary theories.

A short term capital outflow induced by a monetary shock creates a payments imbalance that requires an exchange rate change to maintain balance of payments equilibrium. The exchange rate volatility is triggered by speculative forces, commodity markets disturbances and the existence of short term capital mobility. The degree of change in the exchange rate is a function of the consumers' elasticity of demand.

Since the financial markets adjust faster than the commodities markets, the exchange rate tends to be affected in the short term by the capital market changes, and by the commodities changes in the long term.

Economic Indicators

Economic indicators are the bread and butter of the fundamental factors. Unlike other factors, they occur in a steady stream, at certain times, and a little more often than changes in interest rates, governments or underground activity in San Andrea Fault in California.

Knowing the date and time of release is very important to the foreign exchange trader (see Figure 17.5). Based on this information, a trader is able to enter, exit or adjust a foreign exchange position. Eyes glued to the monitor screens, traders around the world act on the economic data.

However, though this information is important, the information alone is not sufficient. It is the skill of the forecaster and trader which will generate a P&L.

```
TELERATE MATRIX                                           PAGE 33051
08/03/93 10:32 EDT


                  THE DOW JONES CAPITAL MARKETS REPORT       PAGE 33051
   >>08/02 17:40[CALENDAR OF INTERNATIONAL ECONOMIC DATA, EVENTS............]

   JAPAN: APRIL-JUNE SERVICE PRICE INDEX, 0730 GMT.
   CANADA: JULY UNEMPLOYMENT RATE, 1100 GMT.
   AUSTRALIA: SECOND-QUARTER GDP, 0130 GMT.
   ===============  ONE DAY IN WEEK  =====================
   WEST GERMANY: JULY UNEMPLOYMENT, JUNE MANUFACTURING
   ORDERS, JULY RESERVES.
   -0-

   -(AP-DJ)--08-02-93 1740EDT
```

Figure 17.5. The economic data from the G-7 countries is available on Telerate on page 33051. (*Source: Telerate® Reprinted by permission. © 1993 Dow Jones Telerate, Inc.*)

```
TELERATE MATRIX                                           PAGE 141
08/03/93 10:33 EDT

                 [TELERATE SYSTEMS INC., ECONOMIC INDICATORS- P5 ] PAGE 141
!RELEASE!          -- U.S. QUARTERLY ECONOMIC DATA -- [ECO SURVEYS: PG 9430-34]
! *DATE  !      QUARTERLY REPORTS     !2 QTR "93!1 QTR "93!4 QTR "92!3 QTR "92!
:*07/29 :REAL GDP  = REVISED MONTHLY  :   5.020 :   5.000 :   4.991 :   4.934 :
:       :   % CHANGE                  :   +1.6  :   +0.7  :   +4.7  :   +3.4   :
:       : IMPLICIT PRICE DEFLATOR     :   +2.6  :   +3.3  :   +2.3  :   +2.0   :
:       : FIXED WEIGHT PRICE INDEX    :   +2.6  :   +4.3  :   +3.4  :   +2.1   :
:       : PERSONAL CONSUMPTN EXPNDTRS :   3.398 :   3.367 :   3.360 :   3.318 :
:       : NET EXPORTS                 :  -0.070 :  -0.070 :  -0.049 :  -0.053 :
:       : CHANGE IN INVENTORIES       :   8.2   :  33.5   :   9.8   :  15.0   :
: 09/01 :CORPORATE PROFITS (AFTER-TAX) :        :$251.1R :$241.0R :$222.2    :
:       :   % CHANGE                  :        :   4.2R  :   5.5R  :  -4.5R   :
:
: 08/30 :US TRADE DEFCT-BAL OF PAYMNTS :       : -29.07 : -25.96 : -26.54   :
: 09/14 :US CURRENT ACCT DEFICIT($BLN) :       : -20.91 : -23.69R : -17.78R :

*[NOTE:] SEE NEW EXPANDED VERSION OF MONTHLY ECONOMIC DATA ON PAGES 137-140
[ALL RELEASE DATES ARE SUBJECT TO CHANGE - SEE PAGE 22 FOR WEEKLY CALENDAR]  .
```

Figure 17.6. The GDP as provided by Telerate on page 141. (*Source: Telerate® Reprinted By Permission. © 1993 Dow Jones Telerate, Inc.*)

Characteristics of the Economic Data Release

Economic data is generally released on monthly basis. The exception is the Gross Domestic Product and the Gross Domestic Product Deflator, which are released quarterly (see Figure 17.6).

There are also several indicators which are released weekly, on preliminary basis (see Figure 17.7). However, the indicators released weekly are not important to the foreign exchange traders, as the data is not complete and, consequently, they are not market shakers.

```
TELERATE MATRIX                                           PAGE 22
08/03/93 10:32 EDT

              [ TELERATE US ECONOMIC CALENDAR* AUG 26 ]      PAGE 22
!AUG 02!NAPM INDEX (JUL) 10:00 ET /CONSTRUCTION SPENDING (JUL) 10 ET  . 137 .
       U.S. TREASURY $24.4 BILLION 3&6 MONTH BILL AUCTION           55-57
       ===============================================================
!AUG 03!LEADING INDICATORS (JUN) 08:30 A.M. EDT                      137
       JOHNSON-REDBOOK RETAIL SALES REPORT                           4
       ===============================================================
!AUG 04!DOMESTIC CAR SALES (JULY)/ HOUSING COMPLETIONS (JUN) 10:00 ET  26336/4
       FED BEIGE BOOK REPORT 12:00 ET                                4
       ===============================================================
!AUG 05!INITIAL JOBLESS CLAIMS FOR WEEK ENDING 7/31 08:30 ET         26340
       FACTORY ORDERS/MFG SHIPMENTS (JUN) 10:00 ET                   137
       FEDERAL RESERVE NYC BANK LOANS & MONEY SUPPLY DATA: 16:30 EDT  101-110
       ===============================================================
!AUG 06!EMPLOYMENT (JUL) 08:30 ET                                    137
       WHOLESALE TRADE (JUN) 10:00 ET                                138
       CONSUMER CREDIT (JUN)                                         137
     '  'FEDERAL RESERVE NATIONAL BANKING STATISTICS: 16:15 ET    '  103  '
```

Figure 17.7. This economic data is either released on a monthly basis, such as the NAPM Index, Leading Indicators or Employment, or on a weekly basis, in the case of the Initial Jobless Claims. This information is available on Telerate on page 22. (*Source: Telerate® Reprinted by permission. © 1993 Dow Jones Telerate, Inc.*)

Every single economic indicator is always released in "pairs." The first number reflects the latest period. The second one is the revised figure of the month prior to the latest period.

For instance, in July, an economic data is released for the month of June, the latest period. In addition, the release also includes the revision of the same economic indicator figure for the month of May. The reason for the revision is that the department in charge of the economic statistics compilation is in a better position to gather more information in a month's time.

This feature is important for traders. If the figure for an economic indicator is better than expected by 0.4 percent for the past month, but the previous month's number is revised lower by 0.4 percent, then traders are likely to ignore the overall release of that specific economic data.

Economic indicators are released at different times. In the United States, economic data is generally released at 8:30, 9:15 and 10:00 AM EDT. It is important to remember that the most significant data for foreign exchange is released at 8:30 AM EDT. In order to allow time for last minute adjustments, the United States currency futures markets open at 8:20 AM EDT.

Sources of Information

Information on upcoming economic indicators is published in all leading newspapers such as *The Wall Street Journal, The Financial Times* and *The New York Times,* and business magazines, such as *Business Week.* More often than not, traders use the monitor sources—Telerate, Reuters, Knight-Ridder or Bloomberg—to gather information both from the above sources and from the sources' own up-to-date information.

The prints on fundamental analysis were made possible courtesy of Dow Jones Telerate Inc., Reuters (see Figure 17.8), Bloomberg, Knight-Ridder, MMS, International, and Technical Data, a Thomson Financial Services Division (see Figure 17.9)

The Gross National Product (GNP)

The *Gross National Product* (see Figure 17.10) is perhaps the most significant economic indicator. According to professor Paul Samuelson, GNP "measures the economic performance of the whole economy." This indicator consists, at macro scale, of the sum of the consumption spending, investment spending, government spending and net trade.

$$GNP = C + I + G + T$$

where

C = consumption spending

I = investment spending

```
                    Data printed 15:03 GMT   Tue 14 Dec 1993 ####


            REFERENCE INFORMATION INDEX                          REFF

.GENERAL ECONOMIC STATISTICS.
TRADE BALANCES                    RTAD    MONETARY RESERVES          RTAY
CURRENT ACCOUNT                           US ECONOMIC STATISTICS     NYNQ-R
BALANCE OF PAYMENT                RTAE    CANADA ECOMOMIC STATS      NYNU
CONSUMER PRICES                   RTAF    JAPAN INDICATORS           JPAX-Z
WHOLESALE PRICES                  RTAG
INDUSTRIAL OUTPUT                 RTAH
UNEMPLOYMENT RATE                 RTAI    OECD ECONOMIC FORECAST     OECD
GNP/GDP DATA                      RTAM    NORDIC TRADE AND
MONEY SUPPLY - M1                 RTAX      PAYMENT BALANCES         SCAP



                    Data printed 15:03 GMT   Tue 14 Dec 1993 ####


REUTERGRAPH - U.S. ECONOMIC STATISTICS                            NYNQ
                        JUN    JUL    AUG     SEP     OCT    NOV
CONS PRICE IND (PCT)    UNCH   +0.1   +0.3    UNCH    +0.4   +0.2
PRODCR PRICES  (PCT)    R-0.3  -0.2   -0.6    +0.2    -0.2   UNCH
MERCH TRD -DEF-(BLN)   -12.06 -10.34 -9.71  -10.89   12/16

                       *4Q-92*  *1Q-93*  *2Q-93*   *3Q-93*
BAL OF PYMNTS (BLN)    R-25.96  R-29.31  -34.39    -36.28

GDP    (PCT)                    +4.7R   +0.8R   +1.9    +2.7R
GDP  DEFLATOR (PCT)             +2.3R   +3.6R   +2.3    +1.6
FED BUDGET DEFICIT (BLN) -120   ------  ------  ------
10-DEC-0834. FEP993 NA10670

REUTERGRAPH - U.S. ECONOMIC STATISTICS                            NYNR
                        JUL    AUG     SEPT    OCT     NOV
LEAD IND   (PCT)        0.1    +0.9R   +0.5    +0.5    12/29
PERSON INC (PCT)       -0.3    +1.3    +0.02   +0.06   12/23
UNEMPLYMNT (PCT)        6.8    6.7     6.7     6.8     6.4
NON-FARM (THSNDS)      +211R   -39     +162R   +147R   +208
HOUS STRTS (MLN)       1277R   1314    1359    1396    12/17
IND PROD   (PCT)       +0.4    +0.2    +0.4    +0.8    *****
CONS CREDIT (BLN)      +5.0R   +3.6    +6.7    +6.1R   +8.1
RETAIL SLS (PCT)       +0.3R   +0.2    +0.1    R+1.8   +0.4
BUS INVEN  (PCT)       -0.5    +0.3R   +0.3    12/15   *****
DUR GOODS  (PCT)       -2.8R   +2.6R   +1.1R   +2.0    12/23
14-DEC-0832. FEP092 NA10670
                                                        ENDS
```

Figure 17.8. The economic data may be selected on Reuters from the Reference Information Index on page REFF. The United States economic statistics, for instance, are available on pages NYNQ and NYNR. (*Courtesy of Reuters*)

G = government spending

T = net trade (exports − imports)

Consumption Spending

Consumption is made possible by personal income and discretionary income. The decision by consumers to spend or save is psychological in nature. Consumer confidence is also measured as an important indicator of the

```
3                TECHNICAL DATA - FOREX WATCH TFS(C)93              PAGE 2303
DATE    [MKT]. RELEASE (PER) [LOCAL TIME]  .EST/[ACT]. PREV .[MEDIAN]. REF PAGE.
[18/10] WG E  PPI             (SEP)13:00      0.0%    -0.1%    0.0%      2346
        WG E  M3 SUPPLY       (SEP)14:00     +6.7%    +7.2%   +6.9%      2347
        UK    PSBR, STG       (SEP)10:30    [+5.9B]   +3.45B  +5.3B      2350
        CD    NEW ORDERS      (AUG)08:30    [+3.7%]   -2.7%   -1.3%      2338
        CD    UNFILLED ORDERS (AUG)08:30    [+0.5%]   -0.3%   -0.3%      2338
        CD    INVENTORIES     (AUG)08:30    [+0.75]   +0.8%   +0.4%      2338
        CD    MANUF SHIPMTS   (SEP)08:30    [+3.75]   -1.5%   -0.4       2338
        CD    ADV DPT ST SL Y (AUG)08:30    [-0.2%]   -6.3%   -2.0       2339
        CD    BUILD PERMITS   (AUG)08:30    [-3.3%]   +9.1%   -2.0       2339
        AUS   HOUSE FINANCE   (JUL)11:30    [-3.0%]   12.8%   N/A        2369
        AUS   EXPORT PI       (JUL)11:30     N/A      +0.4%   N/A        2368
        SWE   UNEMPLMT        (SEP)14:00    [+8.4%]   +9.4%   +9.5%      2372
        JP    MERCH TRADE     (SEP) 5:30PM [$12.7B]   +7.5B +$11.7B      2343
        JP    INDUST OUTPUT R (SEP) 2:30PM  [-2.6%]   -4.4%   N/A        2343
[19/10] JP    MONEY SUPPLY    (SEP) 5:45PM  [+2.0%]   +1.7%   +1.8%      2343



3                TECHNICAL DATA - FOREX WATCH TFS(C)93              PAGE 2304
DATE    [MKT]. RELEASE (PER) [LOCAL TIME]  .EST/[ACT]. PREV .[MEDIAN]. REF PAGE.
[19/10] DEN   TRADE BAL, DK   (JUL) - -      +3.0B    +4.5B   N/A        2371
        DEN   UNEMPLMT        (AUG) - -      12.5%    12.4%   N/A        2372
        SWE   TRADE BAL       (AUG)16:00     N/A      N/A     N/A        2371
        SWE   IND ORDERS      (SEP)14:00     N/A      -2.0%   N/A        2371
        US    --- PERMITS     (SEP) 8:30     1.28     1.25    1.23       2335
        US    HOUSING STARTS  (SEP) 8:30     1.32M    1.32    1.31       2335
[20/10] SWE   RETAIL SLS      (AUG)07:30    +7.1%    +6.7%   +6.8%       2371
        FR    INDUS PROD (JUL/AUG)12:00     -0.4%     N/A    -0.1%       2353
        UK    M4 LENDING, STG (SEP)10:30     3.8B     3.4B    2.3B       2351
        UK    RETAIL SLS      (SEP)10:30    +1.2%    +0.1%   +0.3%       2350
[21/10] AUS   IMPORT PI       (AUG)11:30     N/A     +0.1%    N/A        2368
        AUS   PI MFG MAT"S    (AUG)11:30     N/A      0.0%    N/A        2368
        DEN   CURRT ACCOUNT DK(JUL) - -     +2.75B   +4.3B    N/A        2371
        FR    CPI FINAL       (SEP)11:00     0.0%    +0.1%   +0.4%       2353
        UK    NON-EC TRADE,ST (SEP)10:30    -0.85B   -570M   -650M       2351
        US  ' PHILLY FED SURV (SEP) 8:30  '  N/A  '  0.7 '   N/A  '      2335
```

Figure 17.9.   The calendar of economic data as provided by Technical Data, a Thomson Financial Services Division, on pages 2303 and 2304 via Telerate. (*Courtesy Telerate*)

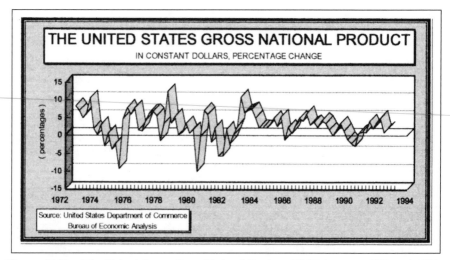

Figure 17.10.   The United States Gross National Product (GNP) between 1972 and 1994 (quarterly).

propensity of consumers, who have discretionary income, to switch from saving to buying.

Investment Spending

Investment—or gross private domestic spending—consists of fixed investment and inventories.

Government Spending

Government spending is very influential both in terms of sheer size and its impact on different other economic indicators, due to special expenditures. For instance, United States military expenditures had a significant role in the total US employment until 1990. The defense cuts that occurred at the time increased unemployment figures in the short run.

Net Trade

Net trade is another major component of the GNP. The continuous worldwide internationalization and the economic and political developments since 1980 have had a sharp impact on United States' ability to compete overseas. The US trade deficit of the past decades has slowed down the overall GNP.

GNP can be approached in two ways: flow of product and flow of cost (see Figure 17.11).

Flow-of-Product Approach	*Flow of Cost Approach*
Personal consumption spending	Wages
Durable goods	
Nondurable goods	Proprietors' income
Services	
	Rental income of persons
Gross private domestic investment	
	Corporate profits
Government spending	
	Net interest
Net trade	
Exports	Business transfer payments
Imports	
	Capital consumption allowances

Figure 17.11. The two approaches summarized above are used by the United States Department of Commerce. This method is known as the National Income and Product Accounts (NIPA). The two sides must balance.

Characteristics

GNP is released on quarterly basis, unlike the rest of the economic indicators. Its release is automatically paired with the release of the implicit GNP deflator, which is an important method used to adjust the GNP for inflation and which is calculated by dividing the current dollar GNP figures by the constant GNP figures.

Due to its quarterly release, the revision of the GNP performance from previous terms is often disregarded by foreign exchange traders because they find it difficult to design future trading strategies based on fundamentals which occurred six months ago.

The Gross Domestic Product (GDP)

Whereas the gross national product refers to the sum of all goods and services produced by United States residents—either in the United States or abroad, the *gross domestic product* (GDP) refers to the sum of all goods and services produced in the United States—either by domestic or foreign companies. The differences between the two are rather nominal in the case of the economy of the United States. GDP figures (see Figure 17.12) are more popular outside the United States. In order to make it easier to compare the performance of different economies, the United States also releases the GDP figures.

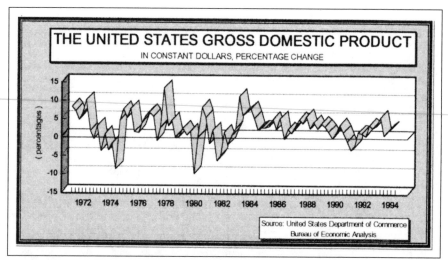

Figure 17.12. The United States gross domestic product (GDP) between 1972 and 1994 (quarterly).

Industrial Sector Indicators

The *industrial sector indicators* consist of *industrial production, capacity utilization, National Association of the Purchasing Managers (NAPM) Index, factory goods orders and durable goods orders.*

Industrial Production

Industrial production (see Figure 17.13) consists of the total output of a nation's plants, utilities and mines. From a fundamental point of view, it is an important economic indicator, which reflects the strength of the economy, and by extrapolation, the strength of a specific currency. Therefore, foreign exchange traders use this economic indicator as a potential trading signal.

The industrial production figures are released on monthly basis.

Capacity Utilization

Capacity utilization (see Figure 17.14) consists of total industrial output divided by total production capability. The term refers to the maximum level of output a plant can generate under normal business conditions.

In general, capacity utilization is not a major economic indicator for the foreign exchange market. However, there are instances where its economic implications are useful for fundamental analysis. A "normal" figure for a steady economy is 81.5 percent. If the figure reads 85 percent or more, the data suggests that the industrial production is overheating, that the econ-

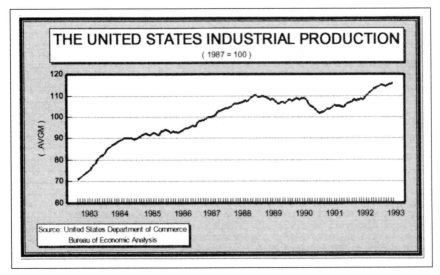

Figure 17.13.   The United States Industrial Production between 1983 and 1993 (monthly).

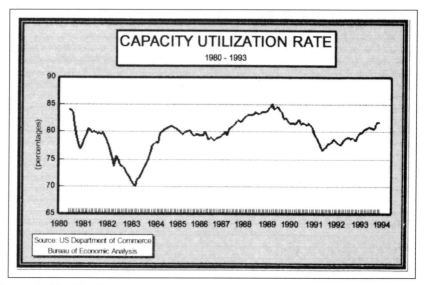

Figure 17.14. The United States capacity utilization rate between 1980 and 1993 (monthly).

omy is close to full capacity. High capacity utilization rates precede inflation, and expectation in the foreign exchange market is that the central bank will raise the interest rates in order to avoid or fight inflation.

The National Association of Purchasing Managers Index

National Association of Purchasing Managers Index (NAPM) is a survey of 250 industrial purchasing managers, conducted to gauge the changes in new orders, production, employment, inventories and vendor delivery speed. A reading under 45–50 percent indicates a worsening economy.

From a trader's point of view, the NAPM index is more of a mixed bag. The survey is based more on psychology than facts, it excludes California and industrial production does not automatically generate consumer demand. Being the first economic indicator, the market may use the NAPM Index as a pretext for a short term move.

Factory Orders

Factory orders refer to the total of durable and nondurable goods orders. Nondurable goods consist of food, clothing, light industrial products and products designed for the maintenance of durable goods. Durable goods orders are discussed separately. This indicator has a limited significance for foreign exchange traders.

Durable Goods Orders

Durable Goods Orders (see Figure 17.15) consist of products with a life span of more than three years.

Examples of durable goods are autos, appliances, furniture, jewelry and toys. They are divided into four major categories: primary metals, machinery, electrical machinery and transportation.

In order to eliminate the volatility pertinent to large military orders, the indicator has a breakdown of the orders between defense and nondefense.

This data is important to foreign exchange markets because it gives a good indication of consumer confidence. Since durable goods cost more, a higher number shows the consumer's propensity to spend. Therefore, a good figure is generally bullish for the domestic currency.

Business Inventories

Business Inventories consist of items produced and held for future sale. The compilation of this information is facile and holds little surprise for the market. Moreover, financial management and computerization help control business inventories in unprecedented ways. Therefore, the importance of this indicator for foreign exchange traders is limited.

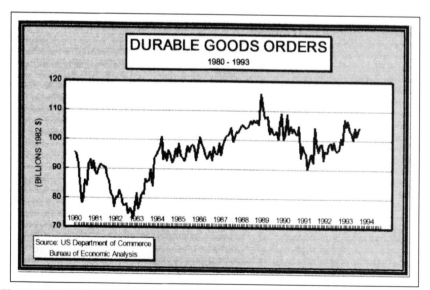

Figure 17.15. The United States durable goods orders between 1980 and 1993 (monthly).

Construction Data

Construction indicators constitute significant economic indicators, which are included in the calculation of the GDP of the United States. Moreover, housing has been, traditionally, the engine which pulled the US economy out of all the recessions after World War II. These indicators are classified into three major categories:

1. Housing starts and permits
2. New and existing one-family home sales (see Figure 17.16)
3. Construction spending

Private housing is monitored closely at all the major stages: *permits, starts, completion* and *sales* (see Figure 17.17). Private housing is classified based on the number of units (one, two, three, four, five and more), region (Northeast, West, Midwest and South) and inside or outside metropolitan statistical areas.

Construction indicators are cyclical and very sensitive to the level of interest rates (and consequently the mortgages) and the level of disposable income. Low interest rates alone may not be able to generate a high demand for housing. As the situation in the early 1990s demonstrated, despite the historically low mortgage rates in the United States, housing increased only marginally, as a result of the lack of job security in a weak economy.

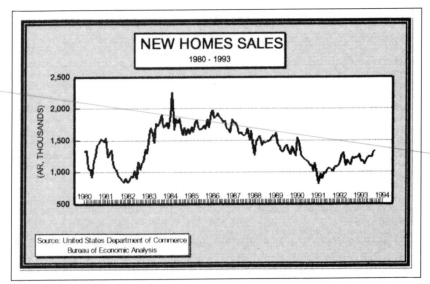

Figure 17.16.   The new homes sales figures in the United States between 1980 and 1993.

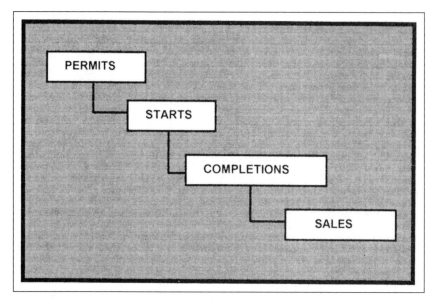

Figure 17.17. Construction of private housing is monitored throughout all the major stages of development.

Housing starts between one and a half and two million units reflect a strong economy, whereas a figure of approximately one million units suggests that the economy is in recession.

Despite their economic significance, construction indicators are not the favorite of the foreign exchange traders. Their unusual volatility is further exacerbated by weather patterns. As a trader, it is difficult to gauge whether sunny summer weather is better for housing shopping or going to the beach. The numbers tend to fluctuate significantly from one month to the other.

Therefore, few traders use the construction figures for their fundamental analysis.

Inflation Indicators

Few other economic problems have the same infamous connotation as does inflation. The rate of inflation is the widespread rise in prices. Therefore, gauging inflation is a vital macro economic task.

Traders are closely watching the development of inflation, since the tool of choice to fight inflation is raising the interest rates, and higher interest rates tend to support the local currency. Moreover, the inflation rate is used to "deflate" nominal interest rates and the GNP or GDP to their real values in order to achieve a more accurate measure of the data.

The values of the real interest rates or real GNP/GDP are of the utmost importance to the money managers and traders of international financial instruments in order to accurately compare the opportunities world wide. Generally, traders use the following economic tools:

- Producer Price Index (PPI)
- Consumer Price Index (CPI)
- GNP Deflator
- GDP Deflator
- Commodity Research Bureau's Index (CRB Index)
- The Journal of Commerce Industrial Price Index (JoC)

The first four, the producer price index, the consumer price index and the deflators are strictly economic indicators. They are released at specific intervals. The others, the Commodity Research Bureau's Index and the Journal of Commerce are commodity indexes. The commodity indexes provide information on inflation quicker and continuously.

Other economic data which measure or suggest inflation are consumer prices and capacity utilization.

Producer Price Index (PPI)

The *producer price index* (see Figure 17.18) has been compiled since the beginning of the twentieth century and was called the wholesale price index until 1978. Currently, the PPI gauges the average changes in prices received by domestic producers for their output at all stages of processing. The PPI data is compiled from most sectors of the economy, such as manufacturing, mining and agriculture. The sample used to calculate the index contains about 3400 commodities. The weights used for the calculation of the index for some of the most important groups are: food—24 percent, fuel—7 percent, autos—7 percent and clothing—6 percent. Unlike the CPI (discussed below), the PPI does not include imported goods, services or taxes. This index is released on a monthly basis.

Consumer Price Index (CPI)

The *consumer price index* (CPI) gauges the average change in retail prices for a fixed market basket of goods and services. The CPI (see Figure 17.19) data is compiled from a sample of prices for food, shelter, clothing, fuel, transportation and medical services which people purchase on daily basis. The weights attached for the calculation of the index to the more important groups are: housing—38 percent, food—19 percent, fuel—8 percent and autos—7 percent. This consumer price index is released monthly.

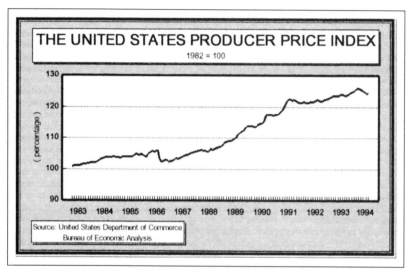

Figure 17.18. The United States Producer Price Index in 1983–1993, on a monthly basis.

The two indexes, PPI and CPI, are instrumental in helping traders measure the inflationary activity, although the Federal Reserve considers them to overstate the strength of inflation.

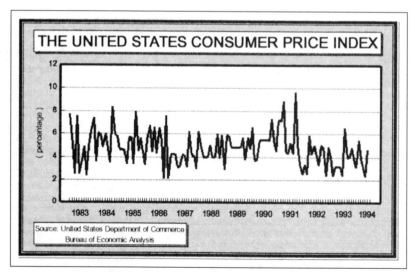

Figure 17.19. The United States Consumer Price Index between 1983 and 1993 (monthly). With the isolated exceptions of several spikes above 8 percent, the CPI levels in the United States had been fairly low and stable.

Gross National Product Implicit Deflator

The nominal GNP figure is not in itself helpful to the trading community. A large number may or may not be good, depending on the inflation in the specific economy. Therefore, the nominal GNP figure must be "deflated" by some price index.

There are several GNP deflators, but the most commonly used is the *implicit deflator* (see Figure 17.20). The implicit deflator is calculated by dividing the current dollar GNP figure by the constant dollar GNP figure.

Gross Domestic Product Implicit Deflator

In the same manner, the *gross domestic product implicit deflator* (see Figure 17.21) is calculated by dividing the current dollar GDP figure by the constant dollar GDP figure.

Both the GNP and GDP implicit deflators are released quarterly, along with the respective GNP and GDP figures.

The implicit deflator is generally regarded as the most significant measure of inflation.

Commodity Research Bureau's Futures Index (CRB Index)

Watching for inflationary trends is made easier by the Commodity Research Bureau's Futures Index. The CRB Index (see Figure 17.22) consists of the equally weighted futures prices of 21 commodities. As of July 7, 1992, the components of the CRB Index were as follows:

- *Precious metals* (14.3 percent): gold, silver, platinum

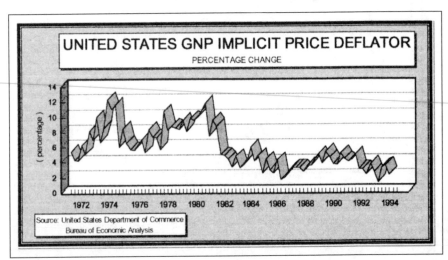

Figure 17.20. The United States gross national product implicit deflator between 1972 and 1993 (quarterly).

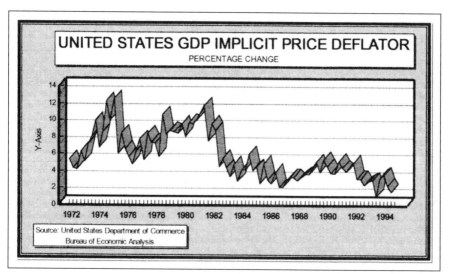

Figure 17.21. The United States gross domestic product implicit deflator between 1972 and 1993 (quarterly).

- *Industrials* (28.6 percent): crude oil, heating oil, unleaded gas, lumber, copper, cotton
- *Grains* (23.8 percent): corn, wheat, soybeans, soy meal, soy oil
- *Livestock and meat* (14.3 percent): cattle, hogs, pork bellies

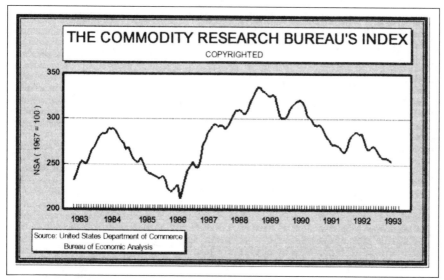

Figure 17.22. The Commodity Research Bureau's Index (1983–1993). Notice the steady decline of the index since April 1989, which coincided with a low inflation period in the United States. The low inflation allowed the Federal Reserve to cut the discount rate and maintain it at a low level in a recessionary economic environment.

- *Imports* (14.3 percent): coffee, cocoa, sugar
- *Miscellaneous* (4.7 percent): orange juice

The preponderance of food commodities (13 out of 21) makes the CRB Index less reliable in terms of general inflation. Nevertheless, the index is a popular tool which proved quite reliable in the late 1980s and early 1990s.

The Journal of Commerce Industrial Price Index (JoC)

The Journal of Commerce Index consists of the prices of 18 industrial materials and supplies processed in the initial stage of manufacturing, building and energy production. It is more sensitive, as it was designed to signal changes in inflation prior to the other price indexes.

A Trader's Point of View on Inflation

Traders have the luxury of a multitude of tools to measure inflation. However, traders cannot expect the central banks to either raise the discount rate every time one of the indicators shows a higher figure, signaling inflation, or to cut it, when the opposite occurs. As illustrated in the preceding Exhibits, the indexes spiked up several times, such as the CPI figure in 1991 due to the shortlived speculation of high oil prices following the Iraqi invasion of Kuwait. One month's economic figures grab attention, but they do not generally trigger the action of a central bank, since one number does not make a trend.

Central banks need confirmation of long term changes in the inflation trend before counteracting with equally long term weapons.

Even a trend does not guarantee the central bank's action in the short term. For instance, the low inflation in the United States in the early 1990s allowed the Federal Reserve to maintain a low discount rate of 3 percent, which was instrumental in the steady process of economic recovery.

By 1993, the discount rate was not perceived by the markets as being sensitive to the low or lower readings of the price indexes. Since the nominal discount rate was already very low, and the real rate approached 0.6 percent, the markets expected the discount rate to be sensitive only on the upside, if inflation was perceived to have picked up. From the point of view of foreign exchange, the inflation indicators in the United States were less important fundamentally in the early 1990s. The downtrend in the discount rate was brought to a hault in May 1994, when the Fed raised this rate along with the Fed funds rate as a pre-emptive strike against inflation. However, the interest rate increase failed to support the US dollar.

Balance-of-Payments

The *balance-of-payments* consists of all the international commercial and financial transactions of the residents of one country. The familiar indicator is the merchandise trade balance. In the long term, the competitiveness of a country is a function of its natural resources, industrial base, skill of the labor force and cost structure. In the short term, international trade is impacted by the changes in the spending patterns generated by the business cycles. Other factors affecting the balance-of-payments are domestic and foreign investments in both goods and services.

The data has a limited following by traders. However, the data is important for foreign exchange on longer term statistical basis.

Merchandise Trade Balance

The *merchandise trade balance* is one of the most important economic indicators. Its value may trigger long lasting changes in the monetary and foreign policies. The trade balance consists of the net difference between the exports and imports of a certain economy. The data includes the following six categories:

1. Food
2. Raw materials and industrial supplies
3. Consumer goods
4. Autos
5. Capital goods
6. Other merchandise

The typical example of the impact of the merchandise trade balance in the financial markets must refer to the coordinated change in foreign exchange, backed by changes in interest rates conceived at the historical Plaza Accord in New York on September 1985 by the G-5 countries. At the time, the US dollar was at post–World War II record highs against the European and Japanese currencies. The United States felt that the American exporters were at a disadvantage, as their high priced products were hardly competitive in the international markets. The devaluation of the US dollar was therefore earmarked to rebalance this economic disequilibrium in the medium term. Trade deficits were not something new in the United States. As a matter of fact, the last time the United States had registered a positive trade balance was in 1975. The economic theory behind this strategy was the *purchase power parity.*

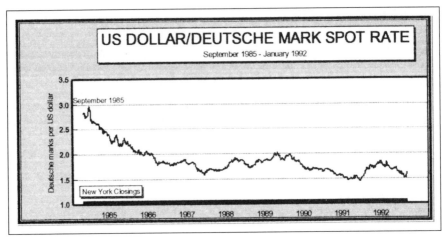

Figure 17.23. The US dollar/ Deutsche mark spot rate based on the spot closing rates in New York between September 1985 and January 1992.

The extent of the success of the US dollar devaluation (see Figure 17.23) strategy in order to reduce and eventually reverse the trade deficit is minuscule. As you can see in the Figure 17.24, the trade numbers improved by 1990, only to fall back to the previous levels soon after.

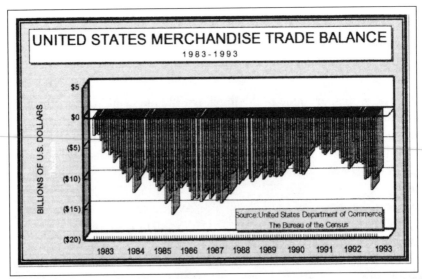

Figure 17.24. The United States Merchandise Trade Balance between 1983 and 1993 (monthly). The devaluation of the US dollar by about 50 percent since 1985 was not able, by itself, to rebalance the United States' trade deficit.

Undoubtedly, the US exporters have been much more successful overseas starting in 1987. However, the American imports kept pace with the exports, maintaining the trade deficit through the early 1990s (see Figure 17.25).

The United States—Japan Merchandise Trade Balance

With a trade surplus of $160 billion in 1993, by far the only G-7 member to post such a performance, it is easy to understand why the Japanese yen had to rise and why the friction over the trade gap between the United States and Japan (see Figure 17.26) is so intense. However, why did the dollar devaluation, which cut the dollar to half of its 1985 value (see Figure 17.27), fail to generate a sound turnaround of the US trade balance in the early 1990s?

Technically, changes in the value of currencies take six to nine months to translate into changes in the trade balance.

A Trader's Point of View on the Trade Deficit

The trade deficit, important as it may be in general, has had a *roller coaster* importance for foreign exchange traders. In the 1980s, both before and after the Plaza Accord, the trade figure was one of the most sought after fundamental data.

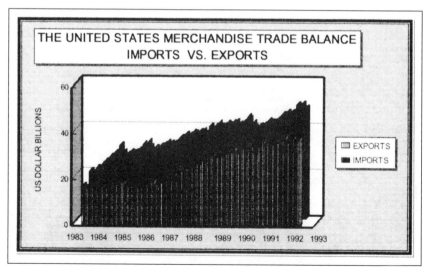

Figure 17.25. The United States merchandise trade balance: imports vs. exports. The exports have grown sharply since 1987, but the imports have grown as well. Despite marginal improvements since 1990, the United States still has a wide gap between imports and exports.

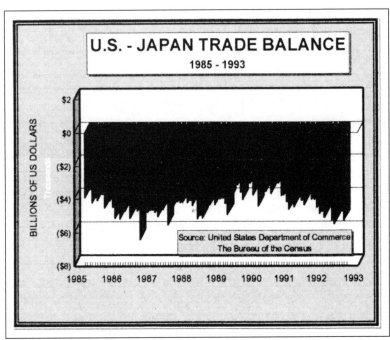

Figure 17.26. The United States merchandise trade balance with Japan has been a sticky political point through the 1980s and 1990s.

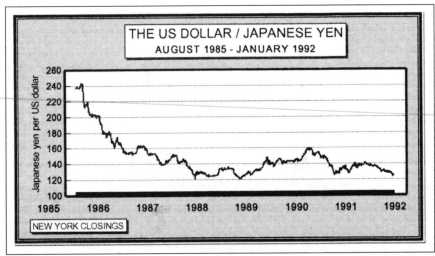

Figure 17.27. The US dollar/Japanese yen spot rate between August 1985 and January 1992.

Before the Accord, the US dollar was an easy, but temporary sell, as the number was worse by the month. The release of the data created a perfect opportunity to take profit on the almighty dollar. After the Accord, the release of the figure generated perfect opportunities to enter new short US dollar positions based on disappointment in the lack of quick translation of the dollar devaluation into trade deficit improvements.

However, the trade figure eventually lost its *panache*. After all, no happy ending was in sight. Traders take positions based on expectations or facts that did not materialize

The trade deficit's importance to the foreign exchange community was suddenly brought back into the limelight by the newly elected Clinton Administration. A series of well timed statements from President Clinton and Treasury Secretary Lloyd Bentsen, regarding the relative weakness of the yen vis-à-vis the dollar and its negative impact on the United States–Japan balance of trade, sent the USD/JPY on a fast downward spiral, from 126.00 to 96.60, a post–World War II record as of September 1994.

Fundamentally, this situation created a tremendous USD/JPY selling opportunity for foreign exchange traders around the world. How long this data will remain a trigger point in foreign exchange only depends on the success of translating the 1993/1994 USD/JPY devaluation into an improvement in the merchandise trade deficit.

Employment Indicators

The employment rate is an economic indicator with multiple significance. The rate of employment, naturally, measures the soundness of an economy. In addition, the indicator is used as a major component in the calculation of other economic indicators, such as the GNP and GDP.

Generally, the most commonly used employment figure is the monthly *unemployment rate,* which is released as a percentage (see Figure 17.28). The figure is calculated as the ratio of the difference of the total labor force and the employed labor force, divided by the total labor force. The data is more complex, though, and it generates more information. The report consists of two separate surveys: business firms and households.

- The Business Firms (Establishments) Survey consists of the payroll, workweek, hourly earnings and total hours of employment in the nonfarm sector. The nonfarm sector refers to jobs in government, federal government, manufacturing, services, construction, mining, retail and others.
- The Households Survey consists of the unemployment rate, the overall labor force and the number of people employed.

In foreign exchange, the standard indicators monitored by traders are the unemployment rate, the manufacturing payrolls, the nonfarm payrolls, the average earnings and the average workweek. Generally, the most significant employment data is the manufacturing and the nonfarm payrolls, followed by the unemployment rate.

This data is released on a monthly basis. Although *initial unemployment claims* are available on a weekly basis, they are not important to the market because they are not complete. The claims underscore the real figures because not all workers are covered by unemployment insurance.

The household data is generally less reliable. This survey tends to show overly optimistic figures due to either individual reluctance to admit being unemployed or to discouraged unemployed women who unwillingly become housewives and stop claiming unemployment.

The unemployment rate is a lagging economic indicator. It is an important feature to remember, especially in times of economic recession. Whereas people focus on the health and recovery of the job sector, employment is the last economic indicator to rebound. Since, in terms of economic contraction jobs are cut, it takes a certain amount of psychological confidence in economic recovery at managerial level before new positions are added. At individual levels, the improvement of the job outlook may be clouded when new positions are added in small companies and thus not fully reflected in the media.

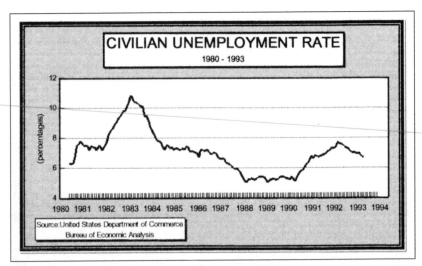

Figure 17.28. The civilian unemployment rate in the United States between 1980 and 1993 (monthly).

The employment reports are very significant to the financial markets in general and to foreign exchange in particular. In foreign exchange, the data is truly affective in periods of economic transition—recovery and contraction. The reason for the indicator's importance in extreme economic situations is the picture it paints with regard to the health of the economy and to the degree of maturity of a business cycle. A decreasing unemployment figure signals a maturing cycle, whereas the opposite is true for an increasing unemployment indicator.

Consumer Spending Indicators

Retail Sales

Retail sales (see Figure 17.29) are a significant consumer spending indicator for foreign exchange traders, as it shows the strength of consumer demand as well as consumer confidence.

As an economic indicator, retail sales are particularly important in the United States. Unlike other countries, such as Japan, the focus of the US economy is the consumer. If the consumer has enough discretionary income, or enough credit for that matter, then more merchandise will be produced or imported. Retail sales create an economic process of "trickling up" to the manufacturing sector.

The seasonal aspect is important for this economic indicator. The retail sales months that are most watched by foreign exchange traders are

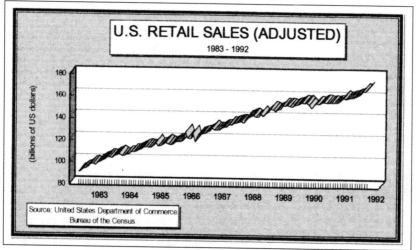

Figure 17.29. The United States monthly retail sales between 1983 and 1992.

December, because of the holiday season, and September, the back-to-school month. Increasingly, November is becoming an important month, as a result of the shift of the former after Christmas sales to the pre-December sales days.

Another interesting phenomenon occurred in the United States. Despite the economic recession in the early 1990s, the volume of retail sales was unusually high. The profit margin was, however, much thinner. The reason is the consumer's shift toward the discount stores.

Retail sales are closely watched by traders for gauging the overall strength of the economy and, consequently, the strength of the currency.

This indicator is released on a monthly basis.

Consumer Sentiment

Consumer sentiment (see Figure 17.30) is a survey of households, designed to gauge the individual propensity for spending. The two studies in this area are conducted by the University of Michigan and the National Family Opinion for the Conference Board. The confidence index measured by the Conference Board is sensitive to the job market, whereas the index generated by the University of Michigan is not.

In the early 1990s, consumer confidence increased sharply twice—after the successful Allied intervention against Iraq and following the 1993 United States presidential election. Both times, however, the increases were short lived, as they occurred against a bleak economic background.

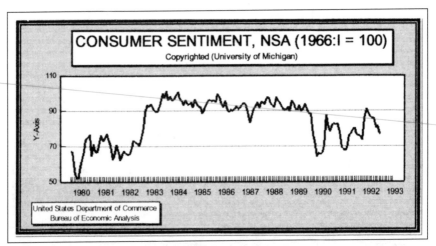

Figure 17.30. The consumer sentiment in the United States between 1980 and 1993 as measured by the University of Michigan (copyrighted) on monthly basis.

Auto Sales

Despite the importance of the auto industry, both in terms of production and sales, auto sales are not an economic indicator widely followed by foreign exchange traders. The American auto makers experienced a long, steady market share loss, only to start rebounding in the early 1990s. But car manufacturing has become increasingly internationalized, with American cars being assembled outside the United States and Japanese and German cars assembled within the United States.

Due to their confusing nature, auto sales figures cannot be easily used in foreign exchange.

Leading Indicators

The *leading indicators* consist of the following economic indicators:

Average workweek of production workers in manufacturing

Average weekly claims for state unemployment

New orders for consumer goods and materials (adjusted for inflation)

Vendor performance (companies receiving slower deliveries from suppliers)

Contracts and orders for plant and equipment (adjusted for inflation)

New building permits issued

Change in manufacturers' unfilled orders, durable goods

Change in sensitive materials prices

Index of stock prices

Money supply, adjusted for inflation

Index of consumer expectations

This index (see Figure 17.31) is designed to offer a six to nine months future outlook of economic performance. Unlike the unemployment rate, which is a lagging economic indicator, the leading indicators are, as the name implies, a leading indicator. In addition to its forecasting value, the data can be used in times of slow economic performance to gauge whether the economy is in recession. Three consecutive negative monthly readings are generally considered to mean recession.

For example, during the Allied intervention in Kuwait, the leading indicators in the United States registered two consecutive months of negative numbers. Foreign exchange traders were apprehensive about the numbers for the third month. When released, the numbers showed an earth-shattering

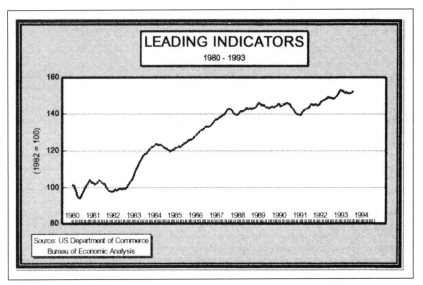

Figure 17.31.   The United States Leading Indicators between 1980 and 1993 (1982 = 100).

change of +.1. Poor number, but positive. The recession, on paper, was avoided.

The next month, however, the revision of the original third month showed a negative figure, because by this time, the paper calculation had finally caught up with the reality in the street.

Personal Income

Personal income (see Figure 17.32) is simply the income received by individuals, nonprofit institutions and private trust funds. Components of this indicator include wages and salaries, rental income, dividends, interest earnings and transfer payments (social security, state unemployment insurance and veteran benefits). The wages and salaries reflect the underlying economic conditions.

This indicator is vital for the sales sector. Without an adequate personal income and a propensity to purchase, sales of durable and nondurable goods are limited.

For FX traders, personal income is not significant.

Economic Fundamentals—Conclusion

Economic fundamentals provide the most significant information to traders. The time of release is well known in advance, a feature specific to the economic indicators. The impact of the economic data tends to be more long

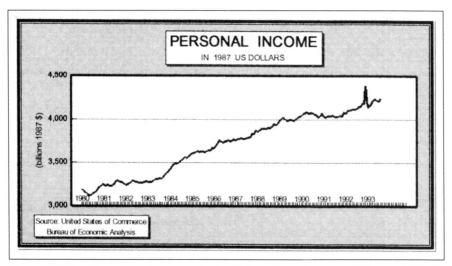

Figure 17.32. The personal income in the United States between 1980 and 1993 (in 1987 $).

term oriented. This effect is not generated only by the need for a deeper understanding of the changes reflected by the data, but also by the flow of the market. The old saying "buy on rumor, sell on fact" may, in the short run, stir in the wrong direction. Traders get long in US dollars on expectation of strong US economic data. They take profit by selling their long position once the good economic data is released. The data is not truly disregarded because it will create a buying opportunity later on.

Not all economic data is significant for the foreign exchange market. Above, we have discussed the most important economic indicators. However, these indicators do not have the same impact on the market every time. Traders react to expectations of change or actual changes. If the economic data fails to show changes in the economy, then the traders will have a mute reaction. If one country's economy over performs or under performs relative to other economies, that specific currency will be bought or sold, respectively. If the correlation between economies is high, then the currency will be less volatile as the overall change is limited.

The relativity of economic performance among countries is particularly important to foreign exchange. Whereas, in other financial markets, domestic data suffices, that is not the case in foreign exchange. Since any FX transaction consists of the simultaneous transaction of two currencies, it is easy to grasp the importance of comparing individual economies in the international arena.

The significance of economic data tends to be cyclical. In the United

States, where the trade balance has had an abysmal showing for years, that indicator has been in and out of the limelight, depending on the market perception of what the government can do and actually does about it.

Also in the United States, inflation numbers have been generally disregarded by the foreign exchange markets in the early 1990s. Being low for so long, these indicators allowed the Federal Reserve to maintain low interest rates. Little change, if any, was expected, so the inflation numbers, excellent otherwise for the economy, were nonevents for the traders. Although there are quite a few economic indicators released in any given month, they do not provide all the information necessary to trade. The information is not always relevant, because either the change is insignificant or it has already been discounted by the market. What these economic indicators do, however, is provide the overall background. The "feeling" of the market is the vital element in trading. If the market focuses on an aspect askew from the theoretical truth, it may be difficult for an individual trader to stop the tidal wave. That is why traders must stay close to the market, trying to gauge any change in other traders' opinions.

This is not an argument to follow the flock, but an attempt to emphasize the importance of understanding and "feeling" the market. In the contemporary environment, the access to information and the processing of information is of unprecedented sophistication and speed and monitors crowding the traders' desks carry continuous flows of information. Currency traders have become information traders.

It is up to the trader to discern which data are important, how to interpret them and what weights to apply. Instantly.

Chapter 18

Financial and Socio-Political Factors

Financial Factors

Currency exchange rates are greatly influenced by financial factors, particularly the interest rates. In fact, some market observers consider interest rates to be the primary determinant of currencies' value. It is a misconception, however, to think that any increase in an interest rate automatically triggers a rally in the domestic currency. This chapter analyzes the importance of interest rates vis-à-vis the exchange rates and explains how traders use interest rate changes in their trading.

The Role of Financial Factors

Financial factors are vital to fundamental analysis. Changes in a government's monetary or fiscal policies are bound to generate changes in the economy, and these will be reflected in the exchange rates. Financial factors should be triggered only by economic factors. Is it always true? Regrettably, no. When governments focus on different aspects of the economy or have additional international responsibilities, financial factors may have priority over economic factors. This was generally true in the case of the European Monetary System. The realities of the market however, revealed the underlying artificiality of this approach. Using the interest rates independently from the real economic environment translated into a very expensive strategy. The European economies came under undue pressure by 1992, and the EMS was in complete disarray by July 1993.

Let's take a look at the financial factors affecting currency exchange rates.

Money Supply

According to Paul Samuelson, the supply of money, M1, incorporates "the sum of coins and currency in circulation outside the banks, plus checkable demand deposits (after various routine adjustments have been made in this magnitude)" (Paul Samuelson, *Economics*, 11th edition, McGraw-Hill Book Company, 1980). The broader M2 also includes time and savings accounts. In addition, the Fed publishes another broader money supply figure, M3, which also includes large denomination time deposits and term repurchase agreements. For further details please refer to Chapter 6.

Money supply is a major factor of the **Quantity Equation of Exchange**.

$$MV = PQ$$

where

M = money supply

V = velocity

P = prices

Q = real transactions

Velocity of money is the rate at which money is turning over on annual basis to facilitate income transactions. Samuelson states that MV "equals GNP."

The money supply data is released in the United States on a weekly basis (Thursdays). This data comes in handy in revealing the cyclical phase of economic recovery. For example, a larger money supply reflects a strengthening economy. Despite their implied importance, the money supply figures have lost some panache since the 1980s. This is due to distortions created by newer types of bank deposits, such as interest bearing checking accounts, money market accounts, etc. By 1993, the Federal Reserve Bank of the United States found the money supply no longer useful for gauging the state of the economy, because of the statistical distortions.

Interest Rates

Interest rates are of paramount importance for foreign exchange. Generally, the first advice on fundamental analysis given to the junior foreign exchange trader is to "watch the interest rates." This is easier said than done, though, as central banks are not particularly eager to change discount rates too often. The realities of the international and domestic economic environment, however, dictate more maneuvering of the discount rates (see Figure 18.1).

The rule of thumb is that higher interest rates generate a stronger currency, and vice versa. However, the investor must focus on the real interest rate rather than on the nominal interest rate. Nominal interest rates, unlike the real ones, take inflation into account (see the Fisher effect). Moreover, in foreign exchange, it takes two to tango, especially when it comes to interest rates. Since foreign exchange, by definition, consists of the simultaneous transaction of two currencies, then it follows that the market must focus on two respective interest rates as well. This is the *interest rate differential*, a basic factor in the markets (see Figures 18.2 and 18.3).

Therefore, traders will react when the interest rate differential changes, not simply when the interest rates themselves are changed. For example, if all the G-5 countries decided to simultaneously lower their respective interest rates by 0.5 percent, then the move would be neutral for foreign

Figure 18.1. The discount rate history in the United States between 1978 and 1994.

Figure 18.2. The discount rate differential between Germany and the United States between 1978 and 1994.

exchange, because the interest rate differentials would also be neutral. Of course, most of the time the discount rates are cut unilaterally, a move which generates changes both in the interest differential and the exchange rate.

Traders approach the interest rates like any other factor, trading on expectations and facts. For example, if rumor says that a discount rate will

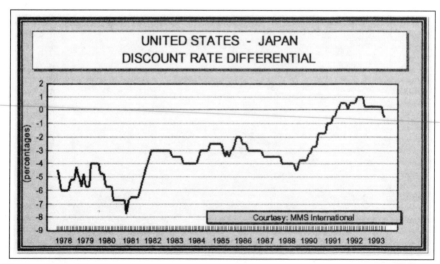

Figure 18.3. The discount rate differential between Japan and the United States between 1978 and 1993.

be cut, the respective currency will be sold before the fact. Once the cut occurs, it is quite possible that the currency will be bought back. Or the other way around. An unexpected change in interest rates is likely to trigger a sharp currency move. "Buy on rumor, sell on fact . . ." Things are not that easy in a market as complex as the foreign exchange market. Other factors affecting the trading decision are the time lag between the rumor and the fact, the reasons behind the interest rate change and the perceived importance of this change.

A discount rate slow in the making is generally already discounted by the market. Since it is a fait accompli, it is neutral to the market. If the discount rate was changed for political rather than economic reasons, a common practice with the European Monetary System, the markets are likely to go against the central banks, sticking to the real fundamentals, not the political ones. This happened in both September 1992 and the summer of 1993, when the European central banks lost unprecedented amounts of money trying to prop up their currencies, despite having high interest rates. The market perceived those interest rates as being artificially high and therefore aggressively sold the respective currencies.

Finally, traders deal on the perceived importance of a change in the interest rate differential. Is this differential divergent from the economic balance of two countries? If so, is it likely that the respective governments, or at least one of them, will do anything about it? Was the change in the discount rate significant enough to help the economy? These are just some of the important questions for which a trader must find answers. In order to be successful on the cutting edge of foreign exchange a trader must rely on a keen analytical ability, sensitivity to the market "feeling" and fast execution.

Political Events

Political events represent an open-ended category of the fundamental factors affecting the global currency market. While certain political events, such as the United States presidential elections, can be anticipated well in advance, most are nearly impossible to forecast. By and large, traders have to "play it by ear," adjusting their reaction relative to each event. As a rule of thumb, the financial instruments which are perceived worldwide as safe havens in times of international uncertainty are the US dollar and the Swiss franc among currencies, and gold, among commodities. Of course, like any other rule of thumb, investors do not follow this course blindly.

Let's take a look at several real life political events and examine what the market reactions have been in the foreign exchange markets.

The Japanese Elections of 1993. When the United States elected a new president, the first Democrat in 12 years, the impact in the foreign exchange market was neutral. After all, the polls had predicted Bill Clinton's victory long before the elections. On the other hand, an unexpected event occurred in Japanese politics. After 38 years of uninterrupted power, the Japanese Liberal Democratic party was replaced by a coalition government, led by Morihiro Hosokawa. The Japanese Liberal Democrat party had been plagued by an astounding number of political scandals since the mid-1980s. Yet, through thick and thin, they managed to hold onto the political reins. How did the foreign exchange market react to this surprising turn of events?

Let's take a look back at the foreign exchange climate prior to the event. Clinton, the new American president, had unleashed a wave of Japanese yen buying, by stating that the United States–Japan trade balance was in deep disequilibrium. The Japanese yen was rising fast from above 120 Japanese yen per US dollar to around 105 Japanese yen per US dollar. Coming in the middle of this yen revaluation, the foreign exchange impact of the Japanese elections was strong. The Japanese yen fell to around 111 per US dollar. Within two months, however, the Japanese yen reached a temporary post–World War II record of 100.35 per US dollar (see Figure 18.4). USD/JPY fell further in 1994 to 96.60.

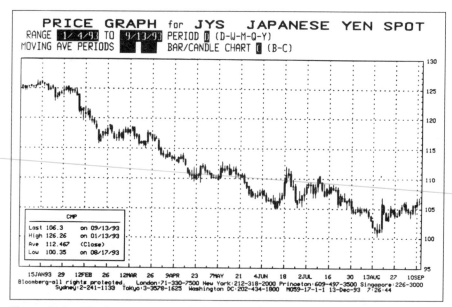

Figure 18.4. The Japanese yen reached a record high against the US dollar in 1993, as a result of the United States' government call for a more equitable trade balance between the United States and Japan. (*Courtesy of Bloomberg*)

Two questions come to mind. Why did the Japanese elections have such a strong impact on the currency? And, since the impact on the currency was so strong, why was it so shortlived?

The Japanese yen fell on the surprising results of the elections due to genuine shock overseas, and immediate international assumptions regarding potential Japanese changes over a variety of issues linked to trade. But the yen quickly rebounded when traders took a closer look at the realities of Japanese politics. On one hand, Morihiro Hosokawa was hardly a new face on the political scene. He had been a top member of the deposed Japanese Liberal Democrat party. On the other, the Japanese government had been perceived over the years as very weak, relative to Japan's economic might. The markets obviously doubted that sweeping changes were around the corner and refocused on the stronger fundamentals, specifically, Mr. Clinton's call for a stronger yen to rebalance the American trade deficit with Japan. In addition, the revaluation of the Japanese yen was not just a call in the wild. The Japanese economy is formidable and the currency should reflect its might.

The Italian Political Scandal of 1993. Few countries have had as many changes of government as Italy. As a result, political crises have been commonplace in the Italian political arena. Yet the icing on the cake occurred toward the end of 1993, when a widespread political scandal engulfed Italian politics. The impact on the Italian lira was swift (see Figures 18.5 and 18.6), despite attempts to support it. The currency was sold aggressively against both the Deutsche mark and the US dollar.

Political Crises

Where as political events generally take place over a period of time, political crises strike suddenly. They are almost always, by definition, unexpected. Currency traders have a knack for responding to crises. Speed is essential, shooting from the hip is the only fighting option. The traders' reflexes take over. Without fast action, traders can be left out in the cold. There is no time for analysis—just a split second, at best—to act. As volume drops dramatically, trading is hindered by a crisis. Prices dry out quickly, and sometimes the spreads between bid and offer jump from 5 pips to 100 pips. Getting back to the market is difficult, as few traders want to get caught on the wrong foot.

The Kidnapping of Michail Gorbachev of 1991. Michail Gorbachev, the last Soviet president, was kidnapped in August 1991. The kidnapping occurred during London trading time, and the US dollar was heavily bought against the Deutsche mark, the currency with the largest exposure to the

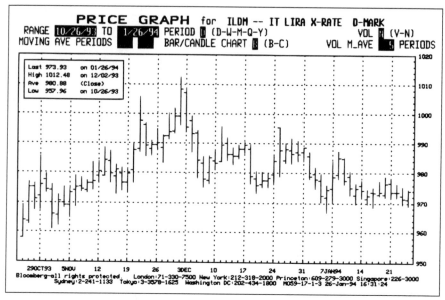

Figure 18.5. The Italian lira fell against the Deutsche mark as a result of the political scandal which engulfed the Italian political arena at the end of 1993. (*Courtesy of Bloomberg*)

Figure 18.6. The Italian lira fell against the US dollar too, as a result of the Italian political scandal of 1993. (*Courtesy of Bloomberg*)

Soviet Union at the time (see Figure 18.7). As far as foreign exchange was concerned, New York was virtually shut out, as few traders ventured to buy US dollars at those stratospheric levels. As it became apparent that Mr. Gorbachev was alive and negotiations were underway, the crisis quickly lost steam, and the US dollar buying against the Deutsche mark turned into selling.

The 1990-1991 Iraqi Invasion of Kuwait. The Iraqi invasion of Kuwait came as a surprise. Fresh out of its long war with neighboring Iran, Iraq seemed to be moving toward more cooperation in the political arena. When the invasion occurred in August 1990, the reaction in the foreign exchange market was quick: buy the US dollar against the Japanese yen. The Japanese economy was perceived as worst suited to a reduction of oil supply. The exchange rate of the US dollar against the Japanese yen reached 160 from 150. By the beginning of 1991, with the Allied troops at the height of the operations against Iraq, the US dollar/Japanese yen was quoted at 125 (see Figure 18.8). How did the Japanese yen manage this comeback?

Japan was not directly involved in the military confrontation in the Persian Gulf. It maintained a neutral stand, and only reluctantly contributed

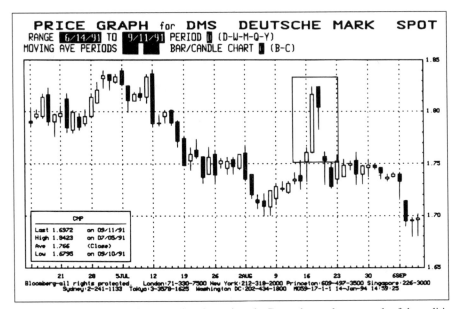

Figure 18.7. The US dollar rose sharply against the Deutsche mark as a result of the political uncertainty in the former Soviet Union in August 1991. (*Courtesy of Bloomberg*)

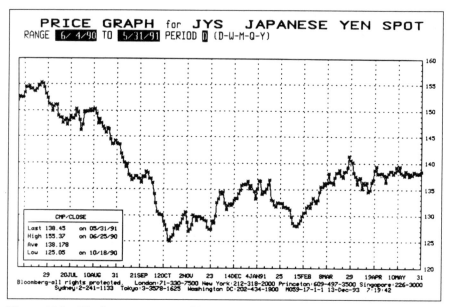

Figure 18.8. The Japanese yen was fairly stable during the Kuwait conflict of 1991. The doomsday scenarios linked to Japan's oil dependency fell short of reality. (*Courtesy of Bloomburg*)

financially to the Allied effort. As a major customer of Gulf oil, Japan was allowed to continue the oil transports throughout the crisis. Moreover, Japan had already stockpiled large quantities of oil. Once they realized that the doom scenarios bore little relation to the reality of the situation, traders turned around, and started buying the Japanese yen.

Conclusion

Fundamental analysis must take into account numerous events which occur in a multitude of areas. Whether they are economic, financial or political, different fundamental factors can have vastly different impacts on foreign exchange. Sometimes the reaction is quick. Other times, the effects are slow to appear, or they occur on the "wrong " side. Astute traders learn to interpret all of these continuously evolving factors, weigh them properly and act on them appropriately. This concerted effort, along with the technical signals, can generate accurate forecasts in an increasingly competitive trading environment.

Chapter 19

Technical Analysis

One of the most significant tools available for the forecasting of financial markets is technical analysis, which is the chart study of past behavior of commodity prices in order to forecast their future performance. Although the use of chart analysis has increased significantly since the mid-1980s, it is nothing new. Such analysis has been an increasingly utilized forecasting tool over the last two centuries. Seiki Shimizu, a famous Japanese commodities trader and the author of a comprehensive study on candlestick charting, speculated that technical analysis could have occurred in Europe in the sixteenth century and in Japan in the seventeenth century. He believes that the beginning of the rice market in 1750 parallels the establishment of charting in Japan.

The Reason of Being

Commodity traders started to analyze the past price behavior, because they felt that commodity prices reflect the action of all available factors. In other words, commodity prices reflect all the changes in the balance between supply and demand as caused by traders' reaction to economic, political or psychological changes. Later, observations on the seasonality of crops evolved into the idea of historical repetition in the market. Finally, the empirical evidence showed that, once the market starts moving one way, the direction and momentum are likely to continue for a while, before new forces are able to change the balance between buyers and sellers, and turn the tide.

These three factors—the *price*, as the ultimate result of all the market forces, the *repetition of the market price behavior* and the *market tendency of moving in trends*—slowly crystalized in the traders' minds to set up the basis of chart analysis. Since then, there has been a vigorous and continuous effort to refine the process of technical analysis in order to profitably forecast future market behavior.

To the untrained eye, technical analysis may seem, at times, confusing. On one hand, it seems that everybody is talking about it, using it and profiting from it. On the other hand, certain academicians compare it with the structure of a house of cards.

Where is the truth?

Pros . . .

The main strengths of technical analysis may be summarized as flexibility, flexibility and flexibility. There is flexibility with regard to the underlying instrument. A trader who deals several currencies, but specializes in one, may easily apply his technical expertise to trading another currency. The trader does this when trading activity in the currency in which he specializes temporarily slows down.

There is also flexibility regarding the markets. A trader who specializes in spot trading can make a smooth transition to dealing currency futures by using chart studies, because the same technical principles apply over and over again, regardless of the market.

And, finally, there is flexibility regarding the time frame. Different players have different trading styles, objectives and time frames. Yet the same technical principles apply, as they easily adapt to many different points of view.

Technical analysis also has a "user-friendly" feature. It is easy to compute and the technical services are becoming increasingly sophisticated and reasonably priced. Currently, the market enjoys a multitude of financial information services that offer printed and electronic charts. The technically inclined traders have only to focus on interpreting them, not on producing them.

. . . And Cons

All good things seem to get their share of criticism, and so does technical analysis. Criticism is healthy, as it keeps the object of its attention "lean and mean." Criticism is good for technical analysis in general and for foreign exchange analysis in particular, as it helps newcomers better understand its characteristics and the ways it can help their performance.

The technical analysis naysayers usually focus on two general aspects:

1. The random walk theory
2. The self-fulfilling prophecy

The Random Walk Theory. Developed by Paul Coorner in 1964, this is based on the efficient market hypothesis, which states that prices move randomly versus their intrinsic value. The random walk theory has three versions: the strong version, the semistrong version and the weak version.

1. The *strong version* holds that it is impossible to forecast anything based on past or current information. Therefore, past chart information is completely meaningless.
2. The *semistrong version* states that forecasting is impossible if it is based on publicly available information. By extrapolation, since most information in foreign exchange—along with the charts reflecting that information—are publicly available, forecasting is generally precluded. Exceptions are allowed in the case of proprietary information. A trading desk receiving an order to buy a very large amount of currency will therefore be able to "forecast" the behavior of the market.
3. The *weak version maintains* that an efficient market with instantaneous access to information, will discount everything, so the past data is useless for forecasting.

Among financial markets, academicians have labeled foreign exchange as the most efficient market. If the hypothesis of market efficiency holds, then all past information has already been reflected in the price and, therefore, there is no niche for an individual trader to speculate at the expense of the rest of the market.

Any "turf advantage" or any other type of "inside information" will be instantly gathered and digested by the markets. Consequently, all market participants are precluded from consistently having any advantage over the rest of the market. The instantaneous access to information around the world should only add to the validity of this theory.

All markets do have a degree of randomness. This is, perhaps, even more so in the foreign exchange market, which has such a large volume that no individual player can have a consistent or long-term impact on the direction of a currency. Until very recently, the academic community has generally been unable to prove the existence of any particular patterns governing price activity. However, new academic studies, such as the tests conducted at the University of Wisconsin, that take advantage of unprecedented computer capability, fully contradict the random walk theory.

Let's take an example to see if charting philosophy clears the reality check.

In the 1985 Plaza Accord the G-7 countries decided that, since the unchecked rise of the US dollar was damaging American exporters' competitiveness abroad and the enormous exchange rate disequilibrium had already triggered a dangerously high trade deficit for the United States, the dollar must be devalued. So a dollar devaluation was achieved over time by massive central bank intervention.

Prior to this historic open market intervention, technical analysis provided ample selling signals. The outcome was proven over the next two years. In addition, the USD/JPY daily chart between 1985 and 1988 (see Figure 19.1) shows an interesting pattern. The dollar/yen spot rate moves in increments of 2,000 pips in the long term. From its high at around 240, the currency dropped to 220, to 200, 180, 160, 140, back up to around 160, 140, and, finally, to 120. Every 2,000 pips, the US dollar/Japanese yen spot rate found a trading plateau. This pattern is not an exception; in fact, it is still continuing. After reaching the 120 level the third time, the dollar/yen spot rate reached and broke the 100 barrier in June 1994.

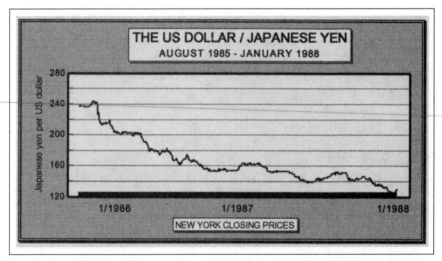

Figure 19.1. The US dollar/Japanese yen spot exchange rate chart shows that the currency follows a price pattern of 2000 pips in the long term (September 1985–January 1988).

The Self-Fulfilling Prophecy. Criticism has been around for a long time and technical analysts wouldn't actually mind this theory—should it hold. Not only would it be the fastest way of getting rich overnight, but think of all the trader-sized egos which would really be touched.

The self-fulfilling prophecy, however, has too many holes to support anything but the most superficial criticism, because chart interpretation is very subjective and personal. It requires an individual, innate talent mixed with personally acquired and refined research and understanding and since different traders have different objectives, time frames and trading styles, it is rather difficult to predict which prophecy will be fulfilled. Moreover, if the time-honored law of supply and demand does not provide the backing, any technical related price overshooting will be shortlived.

Chartists are not trying to create an artificial environment where financial instruments may be maneuvered at will. They are merely trying to identify in the already existing environment any signals in price behavior for future price activity.

This brings us to the matter of whether past information can predict the future. Yes, it can. And one does not have to venture all the way to the foreign exchange world to see this, because the strategy of using past information to build forecasting models is rather the standard in most industries. Since currency trading is not a game of darts, the precedent is very important in helping a chartist forecast a currency's way into the future. It is the lack of historic information, not its availability, that is detrimental. And it may be lack of understanding the lessons of the past, rather than the past itself, that triggered the debate.

Technical analysis has been proved over and over again in the financial markets. The majority of currency traders use it extensively. Very rarely, if ever, was a consistently useful tool such as charting able to make such a powerful impact on the traders' decision process.

Despite all the technological breakthroughs, charting remains closer to art than to science. Yet, the more refined the trader becomes, the better is his forecasting performance.

Arguments may continue to go back and forth. In the meantime, the technicians, in increasing numbers, focus their expertise on forecasting the price activity in the future.

For those still interested in charting, let's move ahead with several important things in mind:

1. The price is a comprehensive reflection of all the market forces.
2. Price movements are historically repetitive.
3. Price movements are trend followers.

Types of Charts: A Comparison

Although the terms *chart* and *graph* are used interchangeably, there is a difference. *Graphs* tend to mechanically record certain information, perhaps the weight and the height of a growing infant or, in less domestic circumstances, the performance of an economic indicator. As long as the numbers come within the expectation, no red flags are raised. *Charts*, however, focus on instruments which are traded, or commodities whose prices are continuously subject to market forces. The information thus condensed in the charts enables the skillful chartist to draw profitable signals for future price activity.

There are four types of charts:

1. *Line chart* (see Figure 19.2).
2. *Bar Chart* (see Figure 19.3).
3. *Candlestick chart* (see Figure 19.4).
4. *Point and figure chart* (see Figure 19.5).

Line Chart

The *line chart* is the original type of chart. In order to plot it, single prices for selected time period are connected by a line. The most popular line chart is the daily chart. Although any point of the day can be plotted, most

Figure 19.2. The Deutsche mark/Swiss franc daily line chart. (*Courtesy of Bloomberg*)

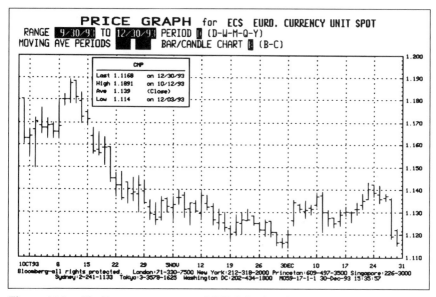

Figure 19.3. The European currency unit/US dollar bar chart. (*Courtesy of Bloomberg*)

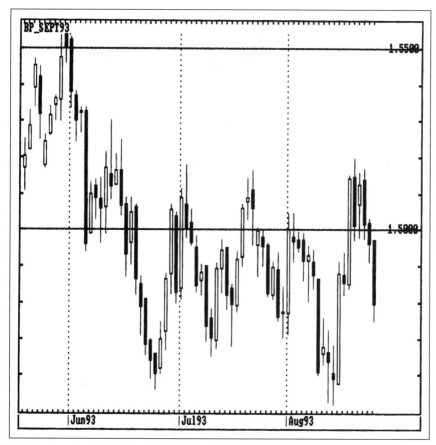

Figure 19.4. The British pound/US dollar candlestick chart. (*Courtesy of TeleTrac. Source: Telerate. Reprinted by permission.* © *1993 Dow Jones Telerate, Inc.*)

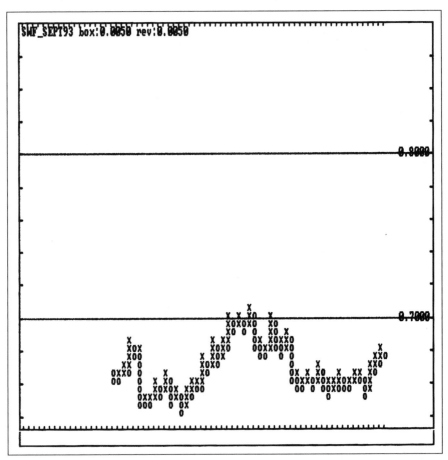

Figure 19.5.   The US dollar/Swiss franc point and figure chart. (*Courtesy of TeleTrac. Source: Telerate. Reprinted by permission. © 1993 Dow Jones Telerate, Inc.*)

traders focus on the closing price, which they perceive as the most important (see Figure 19.6). But an immediate problem with the daily line chart is the fact that it is impossible to see the price activity for the balance of the day.

With so much information missing, should line charts even be considered for technical analysis?

Yes, because due to the sophistication of current charting services, daily price activity does not need to be lost. Simply, change the time span for which you need to see the price fluctuation to a very short period, such as one minute, and virtually all prices will be plotted for you to analyze (see Figure 19.7)

Daily line charts are also useful when looking for the big picture, the major trend because, without line charts, intraday activity would become an unimportant detail. And, when plotted over a long stretch of time, such as

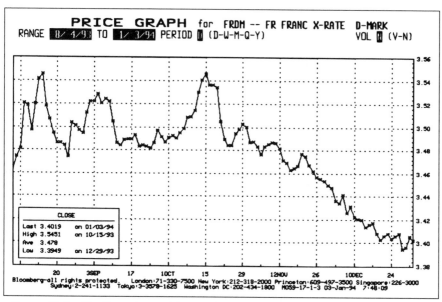

Figure 19.6. The Deutsche mark/French franc daily line chart. (*Courtesy of Bloomberg*)

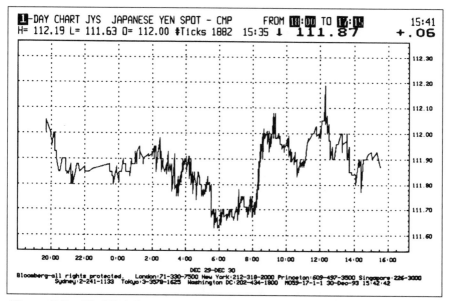

Figure 19.7. The US dollar/Japanese yen one minute line chart. (*Courtesy of Bloomberg*)

several years, a line chart is easier to visualize (see Figure 19.1). Also, technical analysis goes well beyond chart formation; in order to execute certain models and techniques, line charts are better suited than any of the other charts.

However, just like the point and figure chart (discussed below) the line chart is a continuous chart. And this is a disadvantage because price gaps cannot be charted on a continuous chart.

Bar Chart

The *bar chart* is arguably the most popular type of chart currently in use. It consists of four significant points:

- The *high* and the *low* prices, which are united by a vertical bar.
- The *opening* price, which is marked with a little horizontal line to the left of the bar.
- The *closing price*, which is marked with a little horizontal line to the right of the bar (see Figure 19.8).

The opening price is not always important for analysis.

Bar charts have the obvious advantage of displaying the currency range for the period selected. The most popular period is daily, followed by weekly. Other periods may be selected, as well.

An advantage of this chart is that, unlike the line and point and figure charts, the bar chart is able to plot price gaps which are formed in the currency futures market. Although the currency futures market is trading around the clock, the currency futures market is physically open only for about a third of the trading day (Chicago IMM is open for business 7:20 AM to 2:00 PM CDT). Therefore, price gaps may occur between two days' price ranges. Incidentally, the bar chart is the chart of choice among currency futures traders.

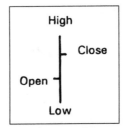

Figure 19.8.   The structure of a bar.

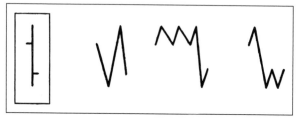

Figure 19.9.   Bar charts cannot show every price fluctuation, even when plotted for very short term time periods.

This chart, however, is unable to plot the whole price fluctuation, even when plotted for short time periods (see Figure 19.9).

Candlestick Chart

The *candlestick chart* was probably developed in Japan around 1750. Despite its venerable age, it was only in the 1980s that it became popular among non-Asian traders. This exposure was by and large possible because of the breakthroughs in electronic charting.

The candlestick chart is closely related to the bar chart. It also consists of four major prices: high, low, open and close (see Figure 19.10). In addition to the common readings, the candlestick chart has a set of particular interpretations. It is also easier to view.

The *body (jittai)* of the candlestick bar is formed by the opening and closing prices. To indicate that the opening was lower than the closing, the body of the bar is left blank (see Figure 19.10–A). In its original form, the

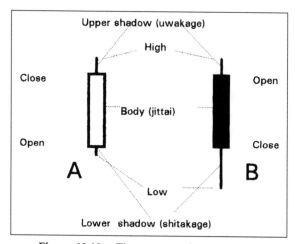

Figure 19.10.   The structure of a candlestick.

body was colored red. However, current standard electronic displays allow you to keep it blank or select a color of your choice. If the currency closes below its opening, the body is filled (see Figure 19.10–B). In its original form, the body was colored black. But the electronic displays allow you to keep it filled or to select a color of your choice.

It is, therefore, very easy to see on a candlestick chart the intraday (or weekly) direction. When the high and the low differ from the opening and closing levels, the rest of the range is marked by two "shadows": the *upper shadow (uwakage)* and the *lower shadow (shitakage)*.

For illustration purposes, we may assume that in Figure 19.10, the following price activity took place:

The USD/DEM opened at 1.7000 and closed at 1.7200. The high was 1.7230 and the low was 1.6980(A).

The USD/DEM opened at 1.7200 and closed at 1.7000. The high was 1.7250 and the low was 1.6900(B).

Just as with a bar chart, the candlestick chart is unable to trace every price movement during a day's activity.

Not all traders use all of the chart types, nor is it a prerequisite of a successful trader. It will be up to you to choose the best chart or set of charts for yourself.

Point and Figure Chart

The *point and figure chart* takes a different approach. All other types of charts have one thing in common: the prices are always plotted against certain periods of time. The point and figure chart completely disregards time, concentrating fully on the price activity. When the currency moves up, the fluctuations are marked with X's. Moves on the downside are plotted with O's. This chart was also designed to minimize the amount of statistical noise. The direction on the chart will only change if the currency is reversed by a certain number of pips.

A very popular point and figure chart is 1 × 3 (see Figure 19.11), which means that as long as the currency continues in the same direction, every single pip will be recorded. The currency must reverse by three pips before they are plotted. This way, minor activities are ignored, allowing the trader to concentrate solely on the price fluctuation.

This chart is very popular among the intraday futures traders because the trading signals are easier to see on the chart and they are more precise and no personal interpretation is necessary. It has become more popular since the late 1980s, due to the electronic charting exposure.

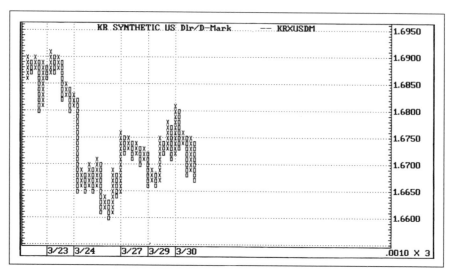

Figure 19.11. US dollar/Deutsche mark point and figure chart. (Courtesy of Knight-Ridder)

Point and figure charting will be discussed in more detail in Chapter 23.

Volume and Open Interest

Volume consists of the total amount of currency traded within a period of time, usually one day. For example, by 1993, the total foreign currency daily trading volume reached $1 trillion. But traders are naturally more interested in the volume of specific instruments for specific trading periods, because large trading volume suggests that there is enough interest and liquidity in a certain market and low volume raises a red flag and warns the trader to veer away from that market.

The risks of a low volume market are usually very difficult to quantify or hedge. In addition, certain chart formations require heavy trading volume for successful development. An example is the head and shoulder formation, which we will present in Chapter 20.

Therefore, despite its obvious importance, volume is not easy to quantify in all foreign exchange markets. Volume figures can be calculated for the futures and for the options on futures markets, because both take place on centralized exchange floors and all the trades go through the clearinghouse. It is a different situation for the spot, forwards and cash options markets, where the trading is completely decentralized and therefore almost impossible to gauge.

In order to minimize this problem, traders have to learn how to estimate volume. One method is to extrapolate the figures from the futures market. Another is "feeling" the size of volume based on the number of calls on the dealing systems or phones, and the "noise" from the brokers' market. It isn't the easiest job in the world, but who ever thought it would be?

Open interest is the total exposure, or outstanding position in a certain instrument. The same problems that affect volume are also present here. As I already mentioned, figures for volume and open interest are available for currency futures. If you have access to printed or electronic charts on futures, you will be able to see these numbers plotted at the bottom of the futures charts. As demonstrated in Figure 19.12, volume is represented by a bar chart, and the open interest is plotted as a line chart.

Volume and open interest figures are available from different sources, although one day late. These figures may be obtained from:

1. *Newspapers: The Wall Street Journal, The Journal of Commerce;*
2. *Weekly printed charts:* Commodity Trend Service, Commodity Perspective;
3. *Monitors:* Telerate, Reuters, Knight-Ridder, Bloomberg;
4. *On-line services;* and
5. *MercLine* at (312) 930-8282.

Trader's Point of View on Open Interest

The open interest figures from the futures market are not fool-proof. The foreign exchange markets are a *zero-sum game*, and this is more evident in the futures markets, where every outstanding contract must be offset by an opposite contract. So, on an individual basis, the figures may be misleading.

For instance, if an investment bank or a fund opens a position in the open futures market by buying a large amount of DEM futures, it is not fully clear whether the real position of that player is long DEM futures. It may also be a hedge for an option position, a cash position, or simply a strategy of throwing the dogs off the scent by showing one hand where everybody sees it, and doubling it up on the opposite side in the cash market.

Trend

The idea of *trend* is paramount to technical analysis. The familiar quote, "the trend is my friend," is deeply rooted in the experience of the markets and it should be respected and attentively observed. A trend simply shows the direction of the market. Therefore, a trend may be:

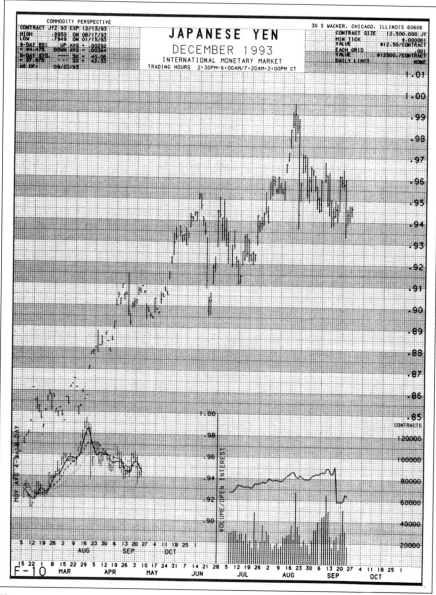

Figure 19.12. The Japanese yen futures bar chart and its trading volume. (*Courtesy of The Commodity Perspective*)

1. *Upward,* such as the trend in British pound against the US dollar between February 1985 and January 1988 (see Figure 19.13);

2. *Downward,* such as the US dollar trend against the Deutsche mark between September 1985 and January 1988 (see Figure 19.14); or

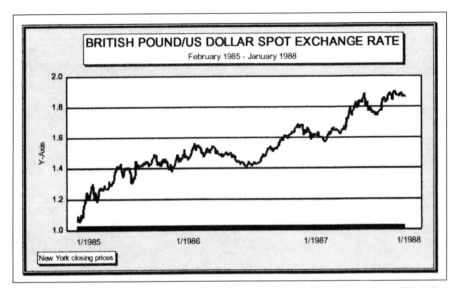

Figure 19.13. The British pound was in a long term upward trend against the US dollar between February 1985 and January 1988.

3. *Sideways,* also known as a "flat market" or "trendless" (see Figure 19.15).

Since the markets do not move in a straight line in any direction, but rather in zigzags, it is the direction of these peaks and troughs that create the market trend.

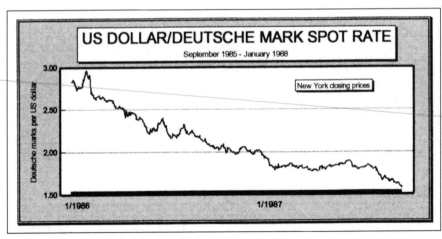

Figure 19.14. The US dollar was in a long term downward trend against the Deutsche mark between September 1985 and January 1988.

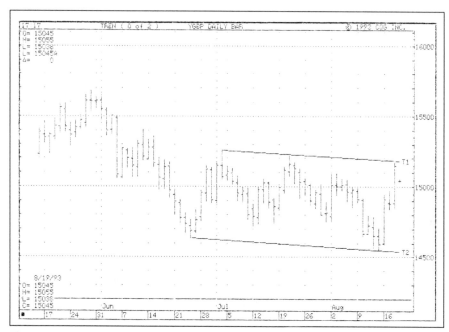

Figure 19.15. The British pound/US dollar was in a sideways market for a period of two months. (*Courtesy of CQG*)

In addition to direction, trends are also classified by time frame: *major or long term trends, secondary or medium term trends and near-term or short term trends.* Any number of secondary and near-term trends may occur within a major trend.

The time frames for each of them vary widely. The Dow Theory, developed at the end of the nineteenth century by Charles Dow, suggests a one year length for a major trend. Currently, for a major trend, the market is expecting a time span between 6 months and 2.5 years (see Figures 19.13 and 19.14). Secondary trends should last for a matter of months, and short term trends for a matter of weeks.

Support and Resistance Levels

The peaks represent the price levels where the selling pressure exceeds the buying pressure and they are known as *resistance levels.* The troughs, on the other hand, represent the levels where the selling pressure succumbs to the buying pressure, and they are called *support levels.* In an uptrend, the consecutive supports and resistance levels must exceed each other respectively. The reverse is true in a downtrend. Although minor exceptions are acceptable, these failures should be considered as warning signals for trend changing.

The significance of trends is a function of time and volume. The longer the prices bounce off the support and resistance levels, the more significant the trend becomes. Trading volume is also very important, especially at the critical support and resistance levels. When the currency bounces off these levels under heavy volume, the significance of the trend increases.

The importance of the support and resistance levels goes beyond their original functions. If these levels are convincingly penetrated, they tend to turn into just the opposite. A firm support level, once it is penetrated on heavy volume, will likely turn into a strong resistance level (see Figure 19.16). Conversely, a strong resistance turns into a firm support after being penetrated (see Figure 19.17).

Trendline

A *trendline* is the natural development in tracking a trend. It simply consists of a straight line connecting the significant highs (peaks) or the significant lows (troughs). Following in the tracks of the trend directions, the trendlines may be classified as:

1. *Up trendlines* (see Figure 19.18),
2. *Down trendlines* (see Figure 19.19), or
3. *Sideways trendlines* (see Figure 19.20).

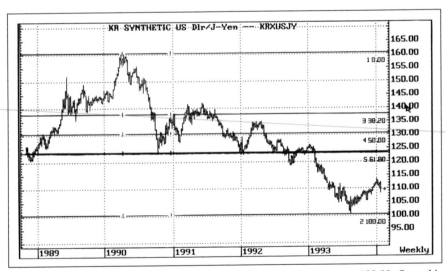

Figure 19.16.   The US dollar/Japanese yen had a very strong support at 120.00. Once this support line was broken, it turned into a strong resistance line. (*Courtesy of Knight-Ridder*)

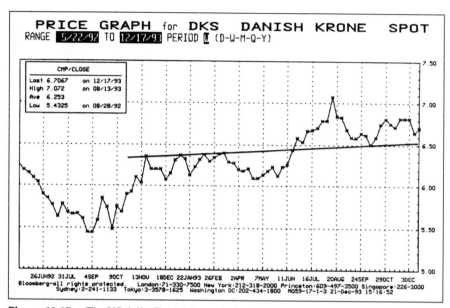

Figure 19.17. The US dollar/Danish krone had a strong resistance at 6.4900. Once broken, the resistance line turned into strong support. (*Courtesy of Bloomberg*)

Figure 19.18. An up trendline can be noticed in the British pound/US dollar in March and April 1993. (*Courtesy of CQG*)

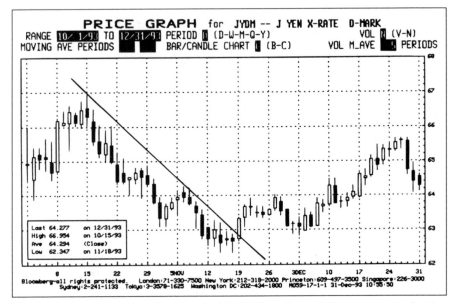

Figure 19.19. A down trendline is noticed in the Deutsche mark/Japanese yen in October and November 1993. (*Courtesy of Bloomberg*)

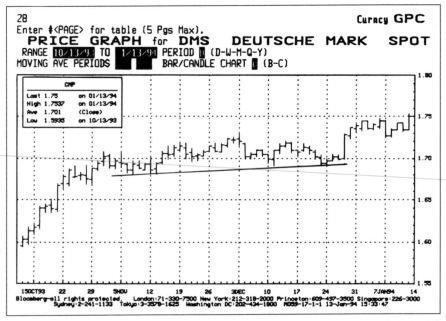

Figure 19.20. A flat market can be observed in November and December 1993 in the US dollar/Deutsche mark. (*Courtesy of Bloomberg*)

Drawing the trendline is rather easy, as only two points are necessary. But this trendline is merely "tentative" as John Murphy, the author of *Technical Analysis of the Futures Markets*, calls it. Most traders expect a *third contact point confirmation*. Once the trend seems to be securely set in its tracks, we must recall an important point made in the beginning of this chapter.

Financial markets are trend followers. Therefore, we can expect now the currency to *maintain the general direction* and *velocity*. The most significant trendlines occur around an angle of 45° (see Figure 19.21). This important technique was established by W. D. Gann, the renowned investor and technical analyst. He noted that a trendline at a sharper angle suggests that the rally is unsustainable. Conversely, a trendline at a low level indi-

Figure 19.21.   The Gann lines marked on British pound futures. (*Courtesy of CompuTrac*)

cates that the trend is close to reverse. He also noted that a longevity of one month or more would provide the trendline with increased weight.

Not only would we like to identify as many significant trendlines as possible, but we also like the trendlines to provide "clean" support and resistance levels. However, since the market has a life of its own, this is not possible. Many times we do have minor trendline penetrations. As a rule of thumb, this type of breakout should be disregarded.

A Trader's Point of View on Trendlines

1. *Anemic breakouts (from a volume point of view) should be disregarded.* Several players were perhaps forced to cut their losses, or attempted to spearhead a new trend but failed to stir sufficient market interest (see Figure 19.22).

2. *A breakout from an up trendline should be confirmed by a close below the original trendline.* Conversely, a breakout from a down trendline should be confirmed by a close above the trendline (see Figure 19.23).

Figure 19.22. Weak violations of trend lines, as the ones on the US dollar/Japanese yen daily bar chart must be disregarded. They show that the market is not looking to break out at that time. (*Courtesy of CQG*)

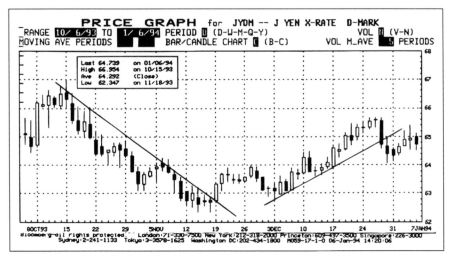

Figure 19.23. Trend breakouts must be confirmed by at least one closing outside the trendline. The trendline breakouts on the Deutsche mark/Japanese yen were confirmed when the following days' markets closed outside the trendlines. (*Courtesy of Bloomberg*)

3. *For more significance of the trend changing signal, a breakout should be followed by two consecutive closes outside the trendline (see Figure 19.24).*

4. *Even after confirmation, the breakout is still likely to be followed by a period of consolidation (see Figure 19.25).* It is relatively rare for a trendline to suddenly reverse its direction.

5. *If a consolidation period does indeed occur, the longer it lasts, the steeper the following rally will be (see Figure 19.26).*

6. *Breakouts from up trendlines will tend to test the strength of the former support line, now turned into a resistance line (Figure 19.27).*

7. *Use a price filter of 1 percent to test the validity of the breakout.*

The Channel Line

A *channel line* is a parallel line that can be traced against the trendline, connecting the significant peaks in an uptrend and the significant troughs in a downtrend (see Figure 19.28). Along with the trendline, the channel line creates a channel which borders the currency trend. In a downtrend, the channel line is at the bottom of the channel (the support line). In an uptrend, the channel line is at the top of the channel (the resistance line).

Figure 19.24. Trendline breakouts are confirmed by two or more closings outside the trendlines. On the US dollar/Swiss franc chart you can see an example of this rule of confirmation. (*Courtesy of CQG*)

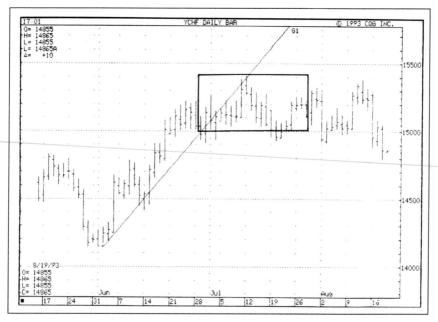

Figure 19.25. The breakout of the US dollar/Swiss franc trend was followed by a period of consolidation near the trendline. (*Courtesy of CQG*)

Figure 19.26. After breaking out of a sharp downtrend, the British pound consolidated for three months. The consolidation period was followed by a sharp breakout. (*Courtesy of TeleTrac. Source: Telerate. Reprinted by permission. © 1993 Dow Jones Telerate, Inc.*)

A Trader's Point of View on Channel Breakouts

1. *A channel is a very attractive chart pattern for traders, as the number of buying signals is approximately doubled by the number of selling signals, and viceversa.* The price will basically gyrate between the trendline and channel line.

2. *The price failure of reaching the trendline should be interpreted as a possible trend acceleration (see Figure 19.29).*

3. *The break of the channel line confirms a trend acceleration (see Figure 19.30).*

4. *The price failure of reaching the channel line should be construed as a case of a weakening trend (see Figure 19.31).*

5. *A channel breakout suggests a target for the currency price equal to the width of the channel.*

Figure 19.27. The US dollar/Deutsche mark daily chart displays the breakout from an uptrend. The currency test the strength of the new resistance line before weakening. (*Courtesy of CQG*)

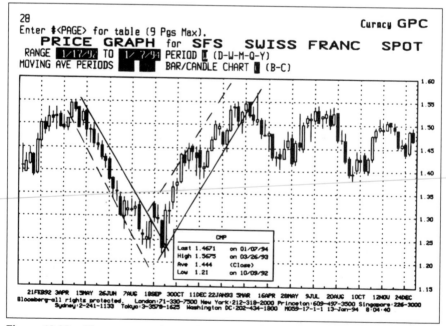

Figure 19.28. There are two channel lines traced against the trendlines. In our example, the US dollar/Swiss franc channel lines are marked with dashed lines. (*Courtesy of Bloomberg*)

Figure 19.29.   The failure of the US dollar/Japanese yen to reach the trendline was a signal that the downtrend is accelerating. (*Courtesy of TeleTrac. Source: Telerate. Reprinted by permission. © 1993 Dow Jones Telerate, Inc.*)

Speedlines

An innovative analysis based on trends was perfected by Edson Gould and quickly embraced by the technicians. It is called *speedlines*. To calculate these speedlines, the total range of a trend is divided into thirds on a vertical line which originates at the top of the range for an up trend and at the bottom of the trend for a down trend. The two speedlines are plotted by using as coordinates the origin and the 1/3 and 2/3 prices respectively. The speedlines are a useful tool in gauging the direction of the trend. A price fluctuation away from the trend which finds support at the first (1/3) speedline indicates that the trend continues smoothly ahead. The penetration of the first (1/3) speedline is a trend weakening warning and the next level to watch is the second speedline (2/3). Should the currency price

Figure 19.30. The breakout of the US dollar/Canadian dollar's channel line confirmed the acceleration of the trend. (*Courtesy of CQG*)

Figure 19.31. The failure of the US dollar/Deutsche mark to reach its channel line was a signal that the trend was weakening. (*Courtesy of CQG*)

bounce back we may be faced with an uncertain (or consolidation) period between the first ($1/3$) and second ($2/3$) speedlines. If this last speedline gives way as well, then the next target is the range origin (see Figure 19.32). The previous rule, that a penetrated support level will turn into a resistance level, and vice versa, remains valid for the speed lines as well.

Speedlines may be applied to all charts. They present the most significance in the short and medium term bar charts and long term line charts.

The Importance of the Long Term Charts

As previously mentioned, the tools of technical analysis are flexible in terms of instruments, markets and time frames. Although in terms of time frame, the most popular charts are the daily charts, the longer period charts are very important, too. By longer period charts I mean *weekly* and *monthly charts.*

In addition, the electronic charting and the weekly printed charts services offer maximum convenience to the traders.

Why are the weekly and monthly charts useful?

1. These charts make it possible to *compress very long term information in a single chart* (Figure 19.33).

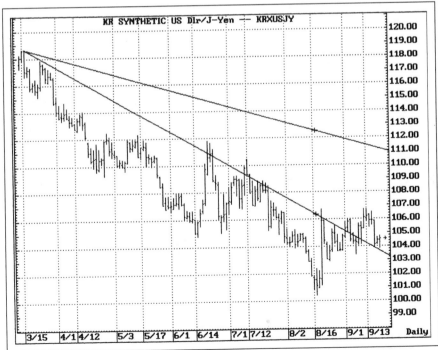

Figure 19.32. An example of speedlines in the US dollar/Japanese yen. (*Courtesy of Knight-Ridder*)

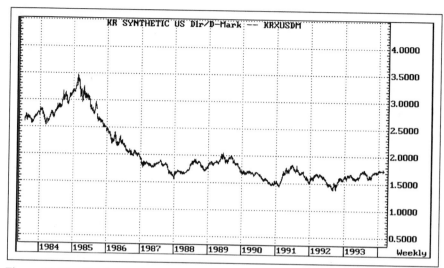

Figure 19.33. The bar weekly chart of US dollar/Deutsche mark between 1984 and 1993. (*Courtesy of Knight-Ridder*)

2. Very long term charts provide very important information regarding the long term trends or cycles. Therefore, the trader can get a correct perspective regarding *the real direction of the market in the long run, the strength or direction of the current trend occurring within that trend, or the possibility of breakout from the long term trend (Figure 19.34).*

Figure 19.34. The weekly bar chart of US dollar/Japanese yen between 1984 and 1993. The downtrend in this currency is obvious between the beginning of 1985 and the end of 1993. (*Courtesy of Knight-Ridder*)

3. Long term charts may also *provide other technical sign*
*lost in the daily charts. For instance, a long term triple t*ᵤₗ
pound was approaching completion in September 1992 (see ~
19.35). The massive sell-off triggered by George Soros helped the
British pound break the support line. This pattern was not evident on
short term charts.

Percentage Retracements

As we are well aware by now, foreign currencies, like all the other financial
instruments, do not move straight up or down, even in the healthiest of the
trends. Traders watch several percentage retracements, in search of price
objectives.

The typical percentage retracements are:

1. The *traditional percentage retracements* were developed by Charles
   Dow at the turn of the last century. They are ⅓, ½ and ⅔, or 33 percent,
   50 percent and 66 percent. A retracement past 66 percent is considered
   to be a trend failure (Figure 19.36).
2. The *Fibonacci ratios* are very popular among the Elliott Wave students.
   These ratios are .382 and .618, or approximately 38 percent and 62 per-

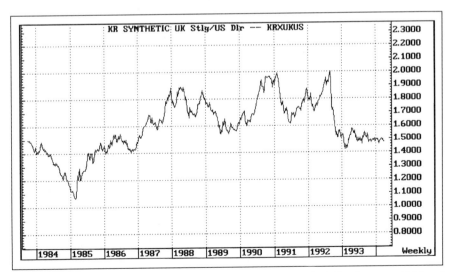

Figure 19.35. The weekly bar chart of the British pound/US dollar between 1984 and
1993. (*Courtesy of Knight-Ridder*)

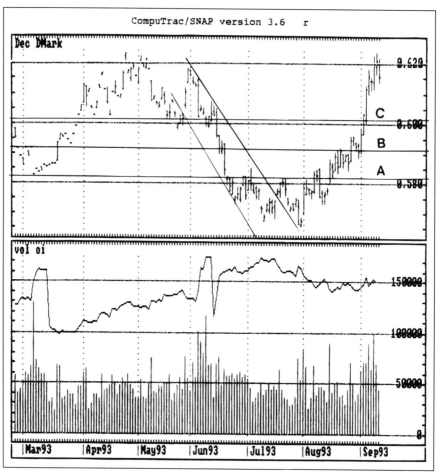

Figure 19.36. A market example of Charles Dow's retracement percentages in Deutsche mark futures: 33%(A), 50%(B), 60%(C). (*Courtesy of CompuTrac*)

cent (Figure 19.37). The Fibonacci ratios are discussed in more detail in Chapter 28.

3. The *Gann percentages* attach importance to the ⅛ breakdowns. The Gann theory focuses mostly on the ⅜, ⅘, and ⅝, or 38 percent, 50 percent and 62 percent retracement figures (Figure 19.38).

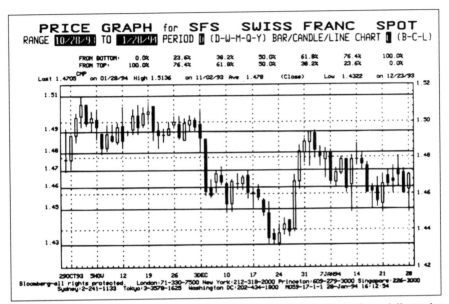

Figure 19.37. A market example of Fibonacci ratios in US dollar/Swiss franc daily market. (*Courtesy of Bloomberg*)

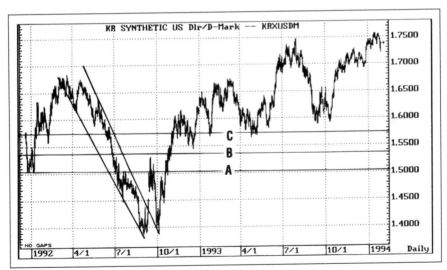

Figure 19.38. An example of Gann percentage retracements: 38%(A), 50%(B), 62%(C). (*Courtesy of Knight-Ridder*)

Chapter 20

Trend Reversal Patterns

Chart formations are generally sorted on the basis on their significance to the current trend of the underlying currency. Formations signaling the end of the trend are known as *reversal patterns.* Conversely, chart formations which confirm that the underlying currency trend is intact are called *continuation patterns.* This chapter presents trend reversal formations.

Introduction

The most significant trend reversal patterns are:

1. head and shoulders (and inverse head and shoulders),
2. double tops (and double bottoms),
3. triple tops (and triple bottoms),
4. rounded tops (and rounded bottoms),
5. V-formations, and
6. diamond.

Head and Shoulders

The *head and shoulders* pattern, one of the most reliable and well-known chart formations, hardly needs an introduction. As you can see in see Figure 20.1, the underlying currency broke the trendline of the *channel xx'-yy'*. In a typical move, the currency rallied back to the previous support line, which turned into a resistance line. As the currency fell, the trend breakout was confirmed.

The head and shoulders pattern consists of three consecutive rallies, where the first and third rallies—the *shoulders*—have about the same height, and the middle one—the *head*—is the highest. All three rallies are based on the same support line (or on the resistance line in the case of the reversed head and shoulders formation), known as the *neckline*.

Prior to point A, the neckline was a resistance line (see Figure 20.1). Once the resistance line was broken, it turned into a significant support line. The price bounced off it twice, at points B and C. The neckline was eventually broken in point D, under heavy volume and the trend reversal was confirmed. As the significant support line was broken, a retracement could be expected to retest the neckline (E), now a resistance line again. If the resistance line held, the price was expected to eventually decline to around level F, which was the price target of the head and shoulders formation. The target was approximately equal in amplitude with the distance between the top of the head and the neckline. The price target was measured from point D, where the neckline was broken (see the dotted lines). A market example of a head and shoulders reversal formation is presented in Figure 20.2.

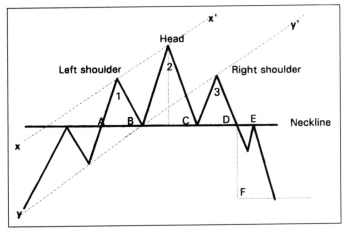

Figure 20.1. Example of a typical head and shoulders pattern.

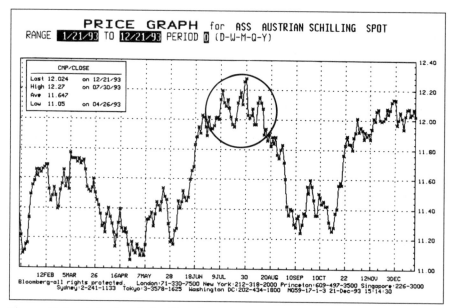

Figure 20.2. A head and shoulders formation was formed on the US dollar/Austrian shilling spot in July–August 1993. (*Courtesy of Bloomberg*)

Signals Generated by the Head and Shoulders Pattern

The head and shoulders formation provides excellent information on:

1. The *support line* is based on points B and C.

2. The *resistance line*. After giving in at point D, the market may retest the neckline at point E.

3. The *price direction*. If the neckline holds the buying pressure at point E, then the formation provides information regarding the *price direction*: diametrically opposed to the direction of the head and shoulders (*bearish*).

4. The *price target*. This is provided by the confirmation of the formation (by breaking through the neckline under heavy trading volume).

One of the main requirements of the successful development of this formation is that the breakout through the neckline occurs under heavy market volume. As you remember, though, gauging volume is only possible in the currency futures market. The trader will have to estimate the size of the cash market volume by extrapolating the currency futures' volume and on the trading "noise." A breakout on light volume is a strong warning that it is a false breakout and will trigger a sharp backlash in the currency price.

The time frame for this chart formation's evolution is anywhere from several weeks to several months. The intraday chart formations are not reliable. The longer the formation time is, the more significance should be attached to this pattern.

The target is unlikely to be reached in a very short time frame. Whereas there is no immediate suggestion regarding the length of target reaching time, common sense would link it to the duration of development of the chart pattern.

I want to emphasize the importance of *measuring the target from the point where the neckline was broken.* There is a tendency among the new technicians to measure the target price not only from under the neckline but also from the middle of the formation. This may happen as they measure the height of the head.

Most head and shoulders formations, of course, look different than that in the Figure 20.1. Prices fluctuate enough to forego any possibility of a clean-looking chart line. Also, the neckline is seldom a perfectly horizontal line.

Potential Problems

1. The height of the shoulders should be about equal. More importantly though, the shoulders must not be taller than the head.

2. It is very important that the significant points A, B, C and D are all tangential to the neckline. The failure of this requirement nullifies the characteristics of the formation.

3. The head and shoulders formation is confirmed only when the completion of the three rallies and their reversals is followed by a breach of the neckline. The failure of the price to *break through the neckline on closing prices basis* puts on hold or negates the validity of the formation.

A Trader's Point of View on the Head and Shoulders Pattern

1. Traders use many types of charts based on different time periods. It is important to remember that the breakout confirmation is a closing *price outside the neckline.* It is recommended that either a daily bar chart or a daily line chart be used.

2. Most traders will wait for the formation to penetrate the neckline before attempting to jump on the bandwagon. Price quotes are likely to be very wide and any hesitation may make it difficult to get in the market, as it is possible that the market will retest the neckline.

3. A minority of the market, the high-risk traders, will take positions prior to the breakout. If the market penetrates the neckline, they will have the highest profitability. If the market fails, very tight stop-loss orders must

be set, although the high speed and low liquidity of the situation may make it almost impossible to execute them.

4. Due to the market expectation for imminent completion, it is likely that there are large positions outstanding in the direction of the future target. Therefore, the chart failure is likely to trigger steep position reversals.

5. The target should be considered as simply a suggested objective. The price will only accidentally stop exactly at the target price. Generally, it may fall somewhat short or overshoot. The trader must consider any additional information to fine tune the profit-taking level.

6. Cash traders must remember both the importance of volume and the lack of volume information. The correct estimation of volume in the cash market is a matter of personal skill.

The Inverse Head and Shoulders

The *inverse head and shoulders formation* (see Figure 20.3) is a mirror image of the previous pattern. Therefore, you can apply the same characteristics, potential problems, signals and the trader's point of view from the preceding presentation.

The underlying currency broke out of the downtrend ranged by the *xx' -yy' channel*. The currency retested (the rally number 3) the previous resistance line, now turned into a support line. Among the 3 consecutive rallies, the shoulders (1 and 3) have approximately the same height, and the head is the lowest. Prior to point A, the neckline was a support line. Once this line was broken, it turned into a significant resistance line. The price bounced off the neckline twice, at points B and C. The neckline was eventually broken at point D, under heavy volume. As the significant resistance

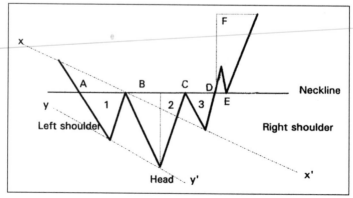

Figure 20.3. Example of a typical inverse head and shoulders pattern.

line was broken, a retracement could be expected to retest the neckline (E), now a support line again. If it held, the price was expected to eventually rise to around level F, which is the price target of the head and shoulders formation.

The price objective is approximately equal in amplitude to the distance between the top of the head and the neckline, and is measured from the breakout point, D.

Figure 20.4 presents an example of an inverse head and shoulders pattern at work in the foreign exchange markets.

Double Top

Another very reliable and common trend reversal chart formation is the *double top*. As the name clearly and succinctly describes, this pattern consists of two tops (peaks) of approximately equal heights (see Figure 20.5). A parallel line is drawn against a resistance line which connects the two tops. We should think of this line as identical to the head and shoulders' neckline.

As a resistance line, it is broken at point A. It turns into a strong support for price level C, but eventually fails at point E. The support line turns into a strong resistance line, which holds the market backlash at point F. The price objective is at level G, which is the average height of the double top formation, measured from point E (see the dotted lines).

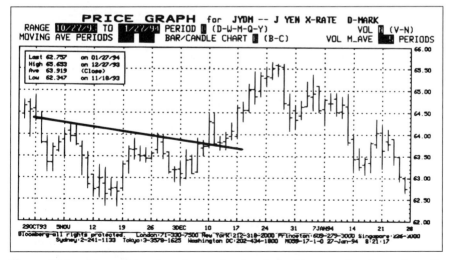

Figure 20.4. An example of an inverse head and shoulders can be observed on the Deutsche mark/Japanese yen daily chart. (*Courtesy of Bloomberg*)

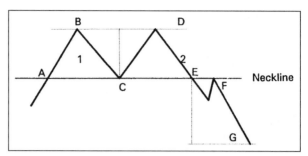

Figure 20.5.   Example of typical double top formation.

Signals Provided by the Double Top Formation
The double top formation provides information on:

1. the *support line*, set between points A and E;
2. the *resistance line*, set between points B and D;
3. the *price direction* [if the neckline holds the buying pressure at point F, then the formation provides information regarding the *price direction*: diametrically opposed to the direction of the peaks (*bearish*)]; and
4. the *price target*, provided by the confirmation of the formation (by breaking through the neckline under heavy trading volume).

Exactly as in the case of the head and shoulders pattern, a vital requirement for the successful completion of the double top formation is that the breakout through the neckline occurs under heavy market volume. And again, please remember that gauging volume in traditional ways is only possible in the currency futures market. Therefore, the trader must estimate the size of the cash market volume by extrapolating the currency futures' volume and based on the trading "noise." A breakout on light volume is a strong case for a false breakout, which would trigger a sharp backlash in the currency price.

The time frame for this chart formation's evolution is anywhere from several weeks to several months. The intraday chart formations are less reliable. There is a strong correlation between the length of time to develop the pattern and the significance of the formation.

The target is unlikely to be reached in a very short time frame. There is no direct suggestion regarding the length of target reaching time. But, foreign exchange common sense links it to the duration of development.

It is important to *measure the target from the point where the neckline was broken.* Avoid the trap of measuring the target price from the middle of the formation under the neckline. This may happen as you measure the average height of the formation.

Most double top formations look different than that in Figure 20.5. As shown in Figure 20.6, prices fluctuate enough to create a rather "weathered" looking line and the neckline is seldom a perfectly horizontal line.

Potential Problems

1. The height of the peaks should be about equal.

2. It is very important that the significant points A, C and E are all tangential to the neckline. The failure of this requirement nullifies the characteristics of the formation.

3. The double top formation is confirmed only when the full completion of the two rallies and their respective reversals is followed by a breach of the neckline (the closing price is outside the neckline). The failure of the price to break through the neckline puts on hold or negates the validity of the formation.

A Trader's Point of View on the Double Tops Formation

1. It is important to remember that the breakout confirmation consists of a *closing price outside the neckline.* It is recommended that a daily chart be used, rather than 5 or 15 minute charts.

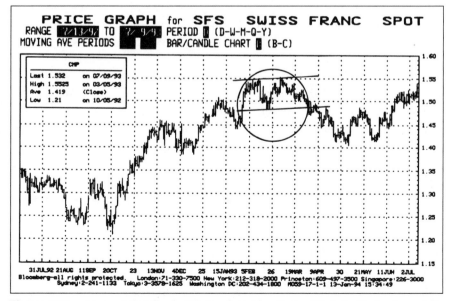

Figure 20.6. An example of a double top formation in the US dollar/Swiss franc daily chart. (*Courtesy of Bloomberg*)

2. The majority of the market will wait for the confirmation of the neck-line's breaching before attempting to jump on the bandwagon. As the price quotes will likely be very wide and highly volatile, this makes it difficult to join in, especially since it is possible that the market will retest the neckline.

3. The high risk takers will take positions prior to the breakout. If the market penetrates the neckline, they will have the highest profitability. Very tight stop-loss orders must be set, if the market fails. Yet, it may be nearly impossible to execute them, due to the high speed and low liquidity.

4. Due to the market expectation for imminent completion, it is likely that there are large positions outstanding in the direction of the future target. Therefore, the chart failure is likely to trigger steep position reversals.

5. The target should be considered as simply a suggested objective. The price will only accidentally stop exactly at the target price. Generally it may either fall somewhat short or overshoot. The trader must consider any additional information in order to fine tune the profit-taking level.

6. The cash traders must remember both the importance of volume and the lack of volume information. Correctly estimating volume in the cash market is a matter of personal skill.

Double Bottom

The *double bottom formation* (Figure 20.7) is a mirror image of the previous pattern. Therefore, you may apply the same characteristics, potential problems, signals and the trader's point of view from the preceding presentation.

The bottoms have about the same amplitude. A parallel line (the neckline) is drawn against the line connecting the two bottoms (B and D). As a support line, it is broken at point A. It turns into a strong resistance for price level C, but eventually fails at point E. The resistance line turns into a strong support line, which holds the market backlash at point F. The price objective is at level G, which is the average height of the bottoms, measured from point E (see the dotted lines).

Figure 20.8 presents an example of a double bottoms pattern at work in the foreign exchange markets.

Triple Top and Bottom

The *triple top* (see Figure 20.9) is a hybrid of the head and shoulders and double top trend reversal formations. Conversely, the *triple bottom* (see Figure 20.10) is a hybrid of the inverse head and shoulders and double bot-

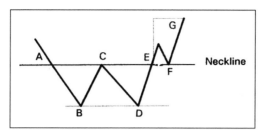

Figure 20.7. Example of typical double bottom formation.

toms formations. Consequently, they have the same characteristics, potential problems, signals and the trader's point of view as the double top, or double bottom, respectively.

As shown in Figure 20.9, in a typical triple top formation, the tops have about the same height. A parallel line (the neckline) is drawn against the line connecting the three tops (B, D and F). As a resistance line, the neckline is broken at point A. It turns into a strong support for price levels C and E, but eventually fails at point G. The support line turns into a strong

Figure 20.8. An example of a double bottoms formation in the US dollar/Swiss franc daily bar chart. Please notice that the price objective was not fully reached. (*Courtesy of CQG*)

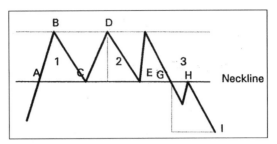

Figure 20.9. Typical triple top formation.

resistance line, which holds the market backlash at point H. The price objective is at level I, which is the average height of the three tops formation, as measured from point D (see the dotted lines).

As a double top, the formation fails at point E. The price moves up steeply towards point F. The resistance line is holding once more and the price drops sharply again towards point G. At this level, the market pressure is able to penetrate the support line. After a possible retest of the neckline, the prices drop further, to eventually reach the price objective.

The opposite is true for the triple bottom.

As shown in Figure 20.10, in a triple bottom formation, the bottoms have about the same amplitude. A parallel line (the neckline) is drawn against the line connecting the three bottoms (B, D and F). As a support line, the neckline is broken at point A. It turns into a strong resistance for price levels C and E, but eventually fails at point G. The resistance line turns into a strong support line, which holds the market backlash at point H. The price objective is at level I, which is the average length of the triple bottoms formation, as measured from point D (see the dotted lines).

Market examples of a triple top and triple bottom are presented in Figures 20.11 and 20.12.

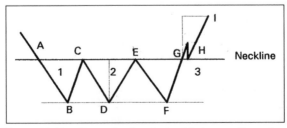

Figure 20.10. Example of typical triple bottom formation.

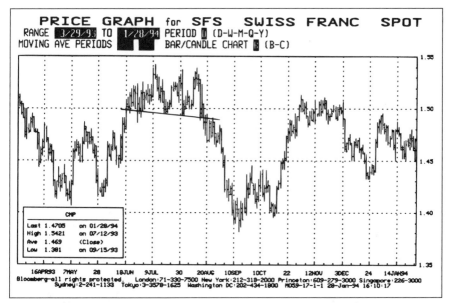

Figure 20.11. This is an example of a triple top formation in the US dollar/Swiss franc. (*Courtesy of Bloomberg*)

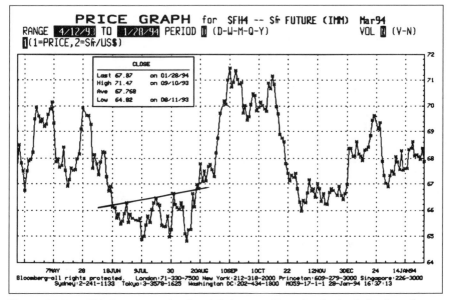

Figure 20.12. This is an example of a triple bottoms formation in the Swiss franc futures. (*Courtesy of Bloomberg*)

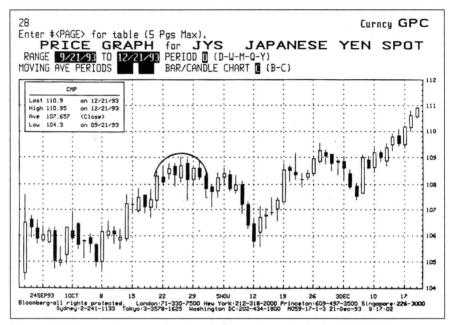

Figure 20.13. A market example of a rounded top formation in the US dollar/Japanese yen daily chart. (*Courtesy of Bloomberg*)

Figure 20.14. A market example of a rounded bottom formation in the Deutsche mark/Japanese yen daily chart. (*Courtesy of Bloomberg*)

Rounded Top and Bottom Formations

The *rounded top and bottom* (see Figures 20.13 and 20.14), also known as *saucers*, are infrequent trend reversal chart patterns. They consist of a very slow and gradual change in the direction of the market. These patterns reflect the indecision of the market at the end of a trend. The trading activity is slow. It is impossible to know when the formation is indeed completed. Like any other consolidation pattern, the longer it takes to complete, the higher the likelihood of a sharp price move in the new direction.

V-Formations (Spikes)

The *V-formations*—V-top and V-bottom (see Figures 20.15 and 20.16)—are the opposite of the rounded top and bottom. In their case, the trend changes suddenly, and they are accompanied by a heavy trading volume. Unlike the previous patterns, this reversal formation provides no warning or consolidation period.

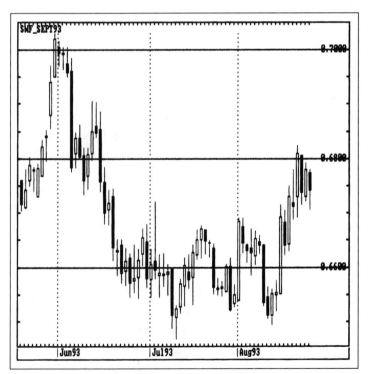

Figure 20.15. A market example of a V-top formation in the Swiss franc futures daily chart. (*Courtesy of TeleTrac. Source: Telerate. Reprinted by permission. 1993 Dow Jones Telerate, Inc.*)

Figure 20.16.   A market example of a V-bottom formation in the British pound monthly chart. (*Courtesy of CQG*)

The Diamond Formation

The *diamond formation* is a minor reversal pattern which tends to occur at the top of the trend. The price activity may be outlined by a shape resembling a diamond (Figure 20.17). The combination of divergent and convergent support and resistance lines is closely mimicked by the increase and decrease in trading volume. Upon breakout, volume picks up substantially. The price target is the height of the diamond, measured from the breakout

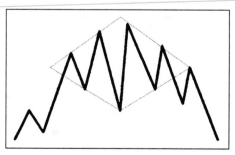

Figure 20.17.   Example of a typical diamond formation.

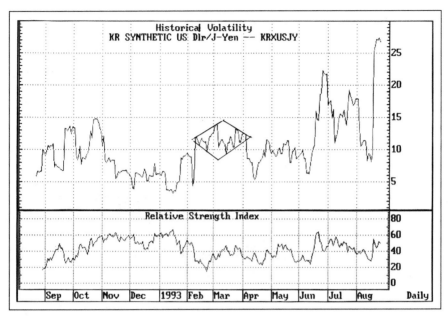

Figure 20.18 An example of a diamond formation in the Japanese yen daily volatility. (*Courtesy of Knight-Ridder*)

point. An example of a diamond reversal formation is provided in the Figure 20.18, in the Japanese yen market.

Among the previous reversal chart formations, the head and shoulders and the double tops and bottoms are by far the most common, followed by the V-formations and the triple top and bottom. Due to their significance in trend reversals, they are generally known as *major reversal patterns*.

Chapter 21

Continuation Patterns

We have previously explored the major reversal patterns. Technical analysis also provides signals which reinforce the current trends. These chart formations are known as *continuation patterns*. Unlike the reversal patterns, they consist of fairly short consolidation periods. The breakouts occur in the same direction as the original trend. The most important continuation patterns are:

1. flags,
2. pennants,
3. triangles,
4. wedges, and
5. rectangles.

The Flag Formation

The *flag formation* is yet another reliable chart pattern which provides two vital signals: direction and price objective. This formation consists of a brief consolidation period within a solid and steep upward trend or downward trend. The consolidation itself tends to be sloped in the opposite direction from the slope of the original trend, or simply flat. The consolidation is bordered by a support line and a resistance line, which are parallel to each other or very mildly converging, making it look like a flag (parallelogram). The previous sharp trend is known as a *flagpole.*

Once the currency resumes its original trend by breaking out of the consolidation, the price objective is the total length of the flagpole, measured from the breakout price level. If the original trend is up, the formation is called a *bullish flag.* As Figure 21.1 shows, the original trend is sharply up. The flagpole is measured between points A and B. The consolidation period occurs between the support line D to E and the resistance line B to C. When the market penetrates the resistance line at point C, the trend resumes its rally, with the price objective F, measured from C. The price target is measured as the flagpole's length (A to B), calculated from the breakout point through the resistance line (B to C).

In the numerical example, the height of the flag pole is measured as the difference between 1.7000 and 1.6000—1000 pips. Once the resistance line is broken at 1.6800, the price target is 1.7800, as 1000 pips from 1.6800.

Conversely, if the original trend is going down, the formation will be called a *bearish flag* (see Figure 21.2). As Figure 21.2 displays, the original trend is sharply down. The flagpole is measured between points A and B. The consolidation period occurs between the support line B to E and the resistance line C to D. When the market penetrates the support line at point E, the trend resumes its fall, with the price objective F, measured from E. The price target is of about equal amplitude with the flagpole's length (A to B), measured from the breakout point through the support line (B to E).

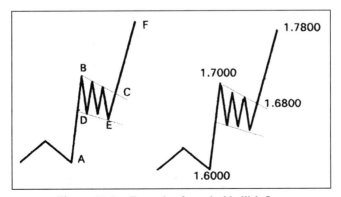

Figure 21.1. Example of a typical bullish flag.

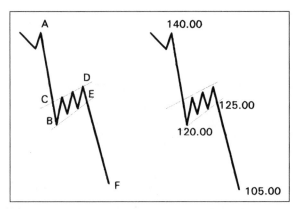

Figure 21.2.   Example of a typical bearish flag formation.

In the numerical example, the height of the flag pole is measured as the difference between 140.00 and 120.00—2000 pips. Once the support line is broken at 125.00, the price target is 105.00, as 2000 pips from 125.00.

As you can see from the Figures 21.3 and 21.4, the flag formations are very reliable. They tend to develop in a period of days to months. However, the support and resistance lines may have to be adjusted several times, due to false breakouts.

The Pennant Formation

The *pennants* are closely related to flags. The same principles apply. The sole difference is that the consolidation area better resembles a pennant, as the support and resistance lines converge. If the original trend is bullish, then the chart pattern will be a *bullish pennant.* In Figure 21.5, the pennant pole is A to B. The pennant-shaped consolidation is framed by C, B and D. When the market brakes through the resistance line B to D, the price objective is E. The amplitude of the target price is D to E, and it is equal to the pennant pole A to B. The price target measurement starts from the breakout point.

In the numerical example, the height of the pennant pole is measured as the difference between 1.5500 and 1.4500—1000 pips. Once the resistance line is broken at 1.5200, the price target is 1.6200, as 1000 pips from 1.5200.

If the original trend is going down, then the formation will be a *bearish pennant.* In Figure 21.6, the pennant pole is A to B. The pennant-shaped consolidation is framed by C, B and D. When the market brakes through the support line B to D, the objective price is E. The amplitude of the target

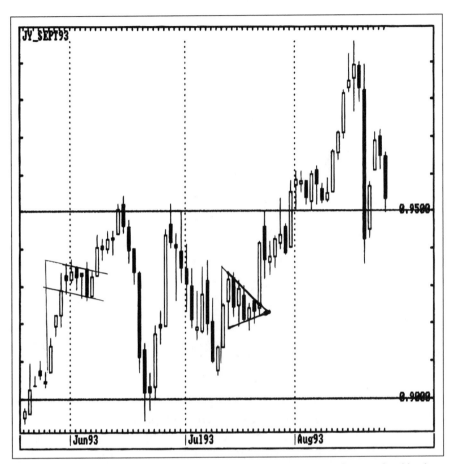

Figure 21.3. An example of a flag formation (a) in Japanese yen futures. On this chart, you can also see an example of a bullish pennant (b). (*Courtesy of Teletrac. Source: Telerate. Reprinted by permission. 1993 Dow Jones Telerate, Inc.*)

price is D to E, and it is equal to the pennant pole A to B. The price target measurement starts from the breakout point.

In the numerical example, the height of the flagpole is measured as the difference between 139.00 and 119.00—2000 pips. Once the support line is broken at 120.00, the price target is 100.00, as 2000 pips from 120.00.

As you can see, the pennant formations are reliable. They may develop in different time frames, from days to months. However, the support and resistance lines may have to be adjusted, due to false breakouts.

The Triangle Formation

Triangles can be visualized as pennants with no poles. There are four types of triangles: symmetrical, ascending, descending and expanding (broadening).

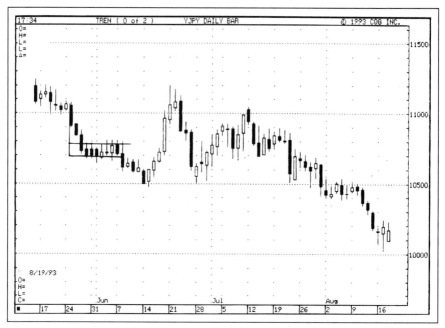

Figure 21.4. An example of an inverse flag formation in the US dollar/Japanese yen. On this chart, you can also see an example of a pennant. (*Courtesy of CQG*)

A *symmetrical triangle* consists of two symmetrically converging trendlines, defined by at least four significant points (see Figure 21.8). The two symmetrically converging trendlines suggest that there is a balance between the supply and demand in the foreign exchange market. Consequently, a break may occur on either side. In the case of a bullish symmetrical triangle, the breakout will occur in the same direction, qualifying the formation as a continuation pattern.

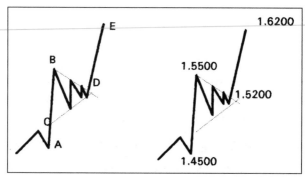

Figure 21.5. Example of a typical bullish pennant.

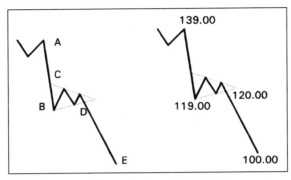

Figure 21.6.   Example of a typical bearish pennant.

As Figure 21.8 shows, the converging trendlines are symmetrical. The up trendline is defined by points B, D and F. The down trendline is defined by points A, C, E and G. The price target is either (1) equal to the width of the base of the triangle BB′, measured from the breakout point H (HH′), or (2) at the intersection of line BI (which is a parallel line to the up trendline AG) with the price line.

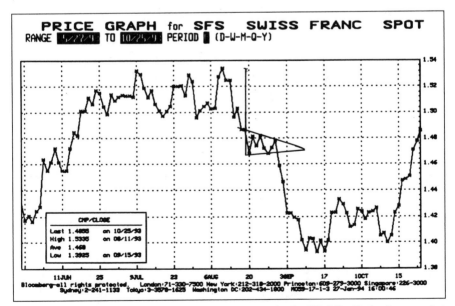

Figure 21.7.   A market example of a bearish pennant in the US dollar/Swiss franc market. (*Courtesy of Bloomberg*)

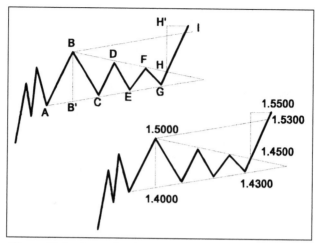

Figure 21.8. Example of typical bullish symmetrical triangle.

Trading volume will visibly decrease towards the end of the triangle, suggesting the ambivalence of the market. The breakout is accompanied by a rise in volume.

In the numerical example, the price objective is either 1.5500, as the difference between 1.5000 and 1.4000, measured from 1.4500, or 1.5300, as the difference between 1.5000 and 1.4000, measured from 1.4300. A currency market example is presented in Figure 21.9.

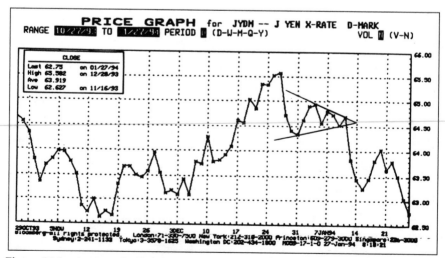

Figure 21.9 An example of a symmetrical triangle in the Deutsche mark/Japanese yen spot market. (*Courtesy of Bloomberg*)

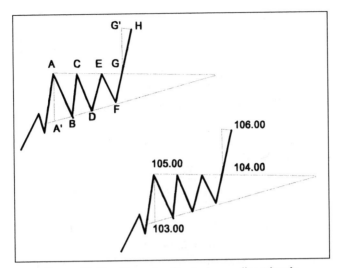

Figure 21.10. Example of typical ascending triangle.

The *ascending triangle* consists of flat upper trendline and an upward sloping bottom trendline (Figure 21.10). The formation suggests that the demand is stronger than the supply. The breakout should occur on the upside, and it consists of the width of the base of the triangle as measured

Figure 21.11. An example of an ascending triangle in the US dollar/Deutsche mark daily chart. (*Courtesy of CQG*)

from the breakout point. As you can see in Figure 21.10, the upper trendline, defined by points A, C and E, is flat. The converging bottom line, defined by points B, D and F is sloped upward. The price objective is the width of the base of the triangle (AA′) measured above the upper trendline from the breakout point G (GG′). In the numerical example, the price objective is 106.00, as the 200-pip difference between 105.00 and 103.00, measured from 104.00.

Trading volume is decreasing steadily towards the tip of the triangle, but increases rapidly on the breakout.

Figure 21.11 presents a market example of an ascending triangle.

The *descending triangle* is simply the mirror image of the ascending triangle, which we just discussed. It consists of a flat lower trendline and a downward sloping upper trendline (see Figure 21.12). This pattern suggests that the supply is larger than the demand. The currency is expected to break on the downside. The descending triangle also provides a price objective. This objective is also calculated by measuring the width of the triangle base and then transposing it to the breakpoint. As shown in Figure 21.12, the bottom trendline, defined by points A, C, E and G is flat. The converging top line, defined by points B, D, F and H is sloped downward. The price objective is the width of the base of the triangle (AA′), measured above the lower trendline from the breakout point I (II′).

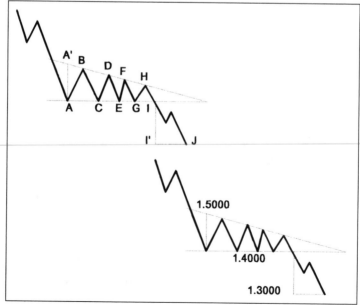

Figure 21.12.   Example of typical descending triangle.

Figure 21.13. An example of a descending triangle in the US dollar/Japanese yen weekly chart. (*Courtesy of CQG*)

In the numerical example, the price objective is 1.3000, as the 1000 pip difference between 1.5000 and 1.4000, measured from 1.4000.

Trading volume is decreasing steadily towards the tip of the triangle, but increases rapidly on the breakout. Figure 21.13 displays an example of a descending triangle.

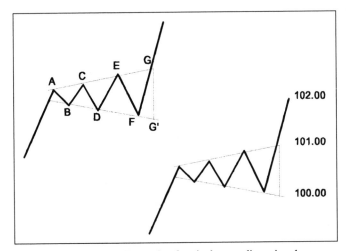

Figure 21.14. Example of typical expanding triangle.

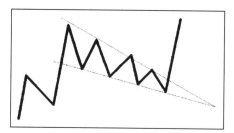

Figure 21.15. Example of typical falling wedge.

The *expanding (broadening) triangle* is a fairly unusual pattern. It consists of a horizontal mirror image of a triangle, where the tip of the triangle is next to the original trend, rather than its base (see Figure 21.14). Volume also follows the horizontal mirror image switch and increases steadily as the chart formation develops. As shown in Figure 21.14, the bottom trendline, defined by points B, D and F and the top line, defined by points A, C and E, are divergent. The price objective should be the width—GG′—of the base of the triangle, measured from the breakout point G.

In the numerical example, the price objective is 102.00, as the 100-pip difference between 101.00 and 100.00, measured from 101.00.

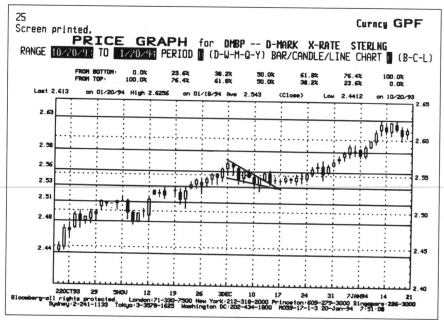

Figure 21.16. A falling wedge in the British pound/Deutsche mark daily chart. (*Courtesy of Bloomberg*)

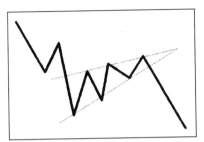

Figure 21.17.   Example of typical rising wedge.

The Wedge Formation

The *wedge formation* is a close relative of the triangle and of the pennant formations. It resembles both the shape and the development time of the triangles. But it really looks and behaves like a pennant without a pole. The wedge is markedly sloped, and the breakout occurs in the direction opposite to its slope (see Figures 21.15 and 21.17), but similar to the direction of the original trend. The signal we receive from the wedge formation is the direction only. There is no reliable price objective. Depending on the trend direction, there are two types of wedges: *falling* (see Figures 21.15 and 21.16) and *rising* (see Figures 21.17 and 21.18).

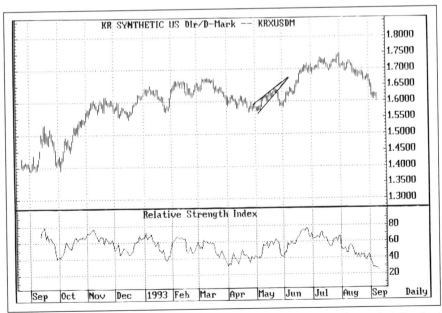

Figure 21.18.   An example of the rising wedge in US dollar/Deutsche mark daily chart. (*Courtesy of Knight-Ridder*)

The Rectangle Formation

Also known as a *trading range* (*or congestion*), the *rectangle formation* reflects a consolidation period. Upon breakout, it is likely to continue the original trend. Its failure will change it from a continuation to a reversal pattern. This pattern is easy to spot, as it can be considered a minor sideways trend.

If it occurs within an up trend and the breakout occurs on the up side, it is called a *bullish rectangle* (see Figure 21.19). The price objective is the height of the rectangle. As Figure 21.19 presents, the currency moves between well defined, flat support and resistance levels. A valid breakout may occur on either side from this consolidation period. Please note the failed double top (A, B, C, D, E). The price target (GH) is equal to the height of the rectangle (G′H), measured from the breakout point H. In the numerical example, the price objective is 1.6200, as the 100 pip difference between 1.6100 and 1.6000, measured from 1.6100.

If the consolidation occurs within a down trend and the breakout continues the original trend, then it is called a *bearish rectangle* (see Figure 21.20). As shown in Figure 21.20, the currency moves between well defined, flat support and resistance levels. A valid breakout may occur on either side of this consolidation period. Please note the failed double bottom (A, B, C, D, E). The price objective (HG′) is equal in size with the height of the rectangle (GH), measured from the breakou point H. In the numerical

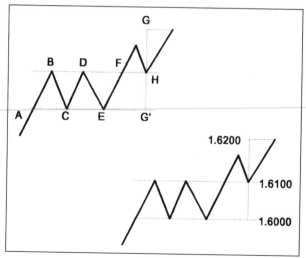

Figure 21.19.   Example of typical bullish rectangle.

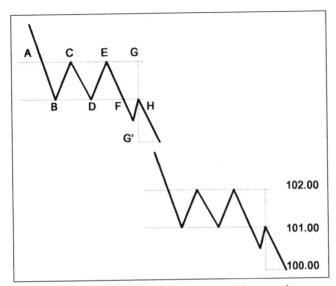

Figure 21.20 Example of typical bearish rectangle.

example, the price objective is 100.00, as the 100 pip difference between 102.00 and 101.00, measured from 101.00.

A market example of a rectangle is presented in Figure 21.21.

Volume should give further indication at, or close to the points tangential to the support and resistance levels. As usual, a heavier volume predicts, or substantially increases the chance of a breakout.

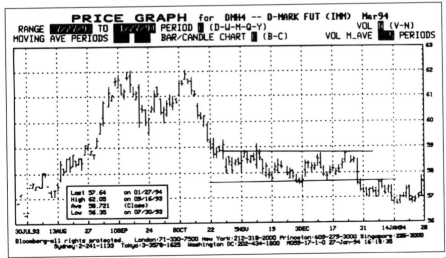

Figure 21.21. A market example of a rectangle in Deutsche mark futures. (*Courtesy of Bloomberg*)

A Trader's Point of View on Continuation Patterns

1. Both the reversal and the continuation patterns are primarily used on line and bar charts. Somewhat similar readings may occur in the other types of charts. We will approach both the point and figure and the candlestick charts separately.

2. In the case of the continuation patterns, false breakouts tend to occur more often. Therefore, filters should be used.

3. Also in the case of the continuation patterns, especially in the case of triangles, more adjustments may be necessary.

4. Traders should consider the term "continuation pattern" with restraint. A valid breakout on the "wrong" side will turn the formation into a reversal pattern.

5. Throughout the presentation, I kept mentioning the significance of the volume. I have no choice but remind you of the difficulty of volume gauging in foreign exchange markets other than the futures.

Chapter 22

Formations Unique to Bar Charts for Futures

Unlike line and point and figure charts, which are continuous charts, bar and candlestick charts for futures are not. Currency futures trading sessions are shorter than cash trading sessions and price gaps may occur on a daily basis, if the overnight activity occurs outside of the previous day's range. Although the following patterns are applicable to both bar and candlestick charts, we will analize each type of chart separately.

The chart formations unique to bar charts are gaps, island reversals and key reversals.

Gaps

Gaps refer to the price gaps between consecutive trading ranges. Price gaps occur when a range's low is higher than the previous range's high or the high of a range is lower than the preceding range's low.

In order to capture these price gaps, only certain bar charts may be used. Charts plotted for weekly, daily, hourly or shorter periods generally fail to display the gaps, as they will show some inherent overlapping, due to continuity. Only currency futures markets provide the opportunity to chart these gaps. Since the currency futures are traded on centralized markets, which open and close at fixed times—trading roughly only a third of the day—they can naturally provide these price gaps between consecutive trading days.

The Chicago IMM trades between 7:20 AM and 2:00 PM Central time. If, for instance, the trading range for the previous day was 0.6000–0.6100 for Deutsche marks, and today's opening price is 0.6150, as the market bought the marks overnight, then there is a 50 pip gap relative to yesterday's range.

There are four types of gaps: common, breakaway, runaway and exhaustion.

The Common Gap

Common gaps have the least technical significance. They do not give any indication of the market's direction or of price objective (Figure 22.1). Common gaps tend to occur in relatively quiet periods or in illiquid markets. When they occur in illiquid markets, such as distant currency futures expiration dates, the common gaps must be completely ignored. When occurring within regular trading ranges, the word in the street has been that *gaps must be filled.*

Common gaps are short term. When currency futures open higher than yesterday's high, they will be quickly sold, targeting the level of the previous day's high. Should the sell-off fail, the market will turn on a dime, reversing the short term position. For instance, if the previous day's range was 0.7030–0.7100 and today's opening price is 0.7130, traders tend to sell the futures contracts from 0.7130 to 0.7100 to fill the price gap. If they cannot reach 0.7100, then the market will quickly turn to buying the futures contracts. The reverse is true if the market opens lower than yesterday's low, as the traders will buy the futures contracts to fill the price gap between the current lower price and yesterday's low. For instance, if the previous day's range was 0.7030–0.7100 and today's opening price is 0.7000, traders tend to buy the futures contracts from 0.7000 to 0.7030 to fill the price gap. If they cannot reach 0.7030, then the market will quickly turn to selling the futures contracts.

Once again, *the common gap lacks technical significance*, a fact that is generally accepted among professional traders. However, at times, it is not clear whether a common gap is just a common gap or another type of gap. So the "gap filling" temptation is likely to continue.

The Breakaway Gap

Breakaway gaps occur in the beginning of a new trend, many times at the end of a long consolidation period. They may also appear after the completion of some chart formations. They signify a brisk change in trading senti-

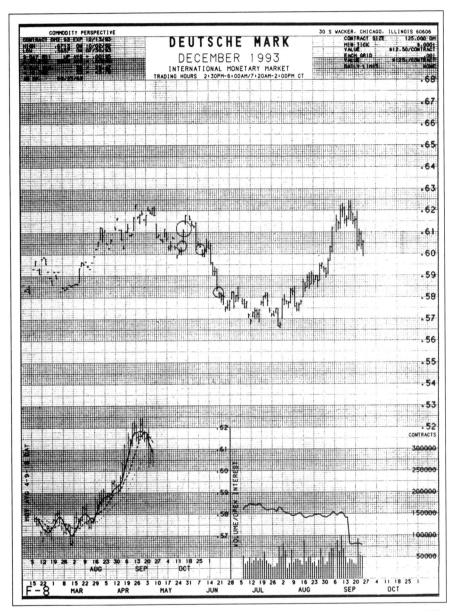

Figure 22.1. Examples of common gaps in Deutsche mark futures. (*Courtesy of The Commodity Perspective, Knight-Ridder Financial Publishing*)

ment and they occur on very heavy trading. The price takes a secondary place to participation (Figure 22.2). For instance, if the Japanese yen futures traded sideways in a 200 pip range—0.9520 to 0.9720—for two months and a price gap occurred between 0.9720 and 0.9750, the market is likely to buy the yen futures further.

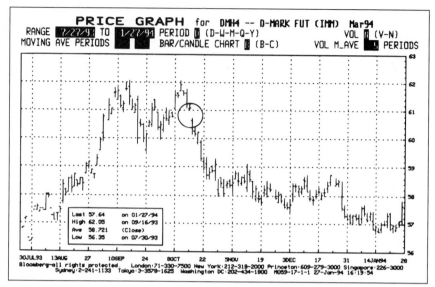

Figure 22.2. Example of a breakaway gap in Deutsche mark futures. (*Courtesy of Bloomberg*)

A Trader's Point of View on Breakaway Gaps

1. A breakaway gap provides us the direction of the market.
2. Although there is no price objective per se, the steep demand for a currency will ensure a solid rally in the foreseeable future.

The Runaway or Measurement Gap

Runaway or *measurement gaps* are special gaps which occur within solid trends. They are known as measurement gaps because they tend to occur about midway through the life of a trend (Figure 22.3). For example, if a 30 pip runaway gap occurs at the top of an up trend measuring 200 pips—between 0.6250 and 0.6050—then the price objective for the trend is 0.6480, as the previous 200 pip range is added to 0.6280.

A Trader's Point of View on Runaway Gaps

1. The runaway or measurement gap provides the direction of the market. This gap confirms the health and the velocity of the trend.
2. It is the only type of gap which also provides a price objective. This price objective is the previous length of the trend, measured from the runaway gap, in the same direction as the original trend.

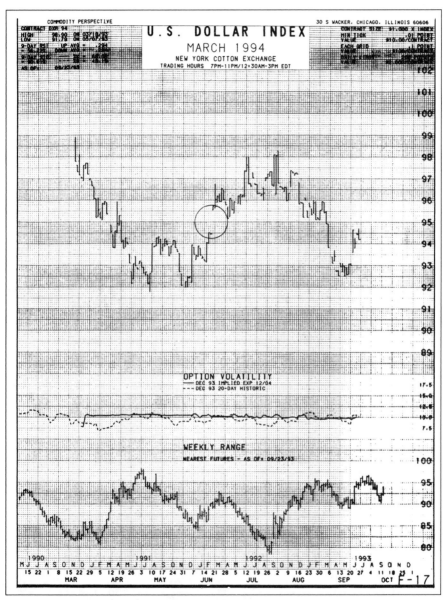

Figure 22.3. Example of runaway or measurement gap in the US Dollar Index futures. (*Courtesy of The Commodity Perspective, Knight-Ridder Financial Publishing*)

The Exhaustion Gap

Exhaustion gaps occur at the top or at the bottom of a V reversal formation. Trends change direction in a rather uncharacteristically quick manner. There is no consolidation next to the broken trendline. The trend reversal is very sharp (see Figure 22.4).

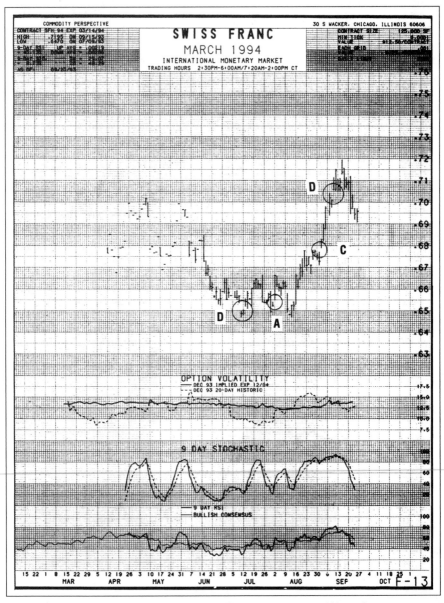

Figure 22.4. Examples of exhaustion gaps (D), a common gap (A), and a measurement gap (C) in Swiss franc futures. (*Courtesy of The Commodity Perspective, Knight-Ridder Financial Publishing*)

A Trader's Point of View on Exhaustion Gaps

1. The exhaustion gap provides the direction of the market.

2. In addition, this type of gap provides information on the high demand for a specific currency, which will ensure price velocity in the medium term.

Island Reversals

One or more ⅓ day ranges will be separated from the ante and post ranges. These isolated ranges are known as *island reversals* and they are a direct result of exhaustion gaps. Occurring at the tip of a V-formation, an island reversal consists of a one or more days' ranges, separated in an insular fashion from both the original trend and the new one (see Figure 22.4). The reversal signal is very strong. In the market example, in the Swiss franc futures, the island reversal, which is separated by the exhaustion gap (D) from the rest of the range, consists of two days' ranges. The same principles from the exhaustion gap apply.

Key Reversal Days

A *reversal day* consists of a trading range which reaches a new high—in a bullish market—but closes lower than the previous day. A *key reversal day* occurs when the daily price range on the bar chart of the reversal day fully

Figure 22.5. A market example of a key reversal day in the British pound daily chart. (*Courtesy of CQG*)

engulfs the previous day's range, and the close is also outside the previous day's range.

Upgrading a reversal day to a key reversal day is not a fast process. Due to a fairly high rate of failure, a trader must wait several days for confirmation, which consists of a solid and sustained reversal of the previous trend.

A key reversal day example is illustrated in Figure 22.5. The British pound daily range on June 6, 1993 was 1.5380 to 1.5500. On June 7, 1993, the market reversed from 1.5500 to 1.5070 and closed 1.5090, much lower than the previous day's low of 1.5380.

Despite the difficulty in categorizing reversal days, the formation provides at least an excellent opportunity to spot a major trend reversal. In order to better and faster capitalize on this opportunity, a trader must use the signal only when supplemented with other information.

Chapter 23

Point and Figure Charting

The point and figure chart originated towards the end of the nineteenth century when it was known as the book method. Interest in this type of chart has been continuously growing, due to its accuracy in providing trading signals. But it was the electronic charting of the 1980s that brought this charting system into prominence.

The point and figure chart is the only one which plots only the price activity, whereas all the other charts plot the price in terms of time periods. Time is irrelevant for the purposes of the chart. If a chartist wants to make any personal notation regarding the time period, that is fine, of course. But time will be a non-factor in the analysis. This means that, at times, there may be few or no entries for the standard periods of time used in other types of charts, if the market is flat. This is a different concept, as we got used to a flatter line or a short bar, but not to the prospect of no chart entry. That is why the point and figure chart is a purer approach to charting. In addition, just like the other continuous chart, the line chart, it reveals price fluctuations missed by the bar chart.

The point and figure chart was designed to better plot price activity and one of the important things this chart does is to *avoid plotting the lack*

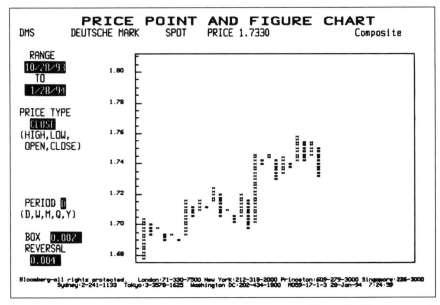

Figure 23.1. An example of a point and figure chart in US dollar/Deutsche mark. (*Courtesy of Bloomberg*)

of activity. All irrelevant market activity, the so-called market noise, is filtered out. To understand how it works, let's remember how the chart is plotted. The rising prices are marked with X's and the falling prices are entered as O's. Therefore, a point and figure chart looks like a series of alternating X's and O's columns (Figure 23.1).

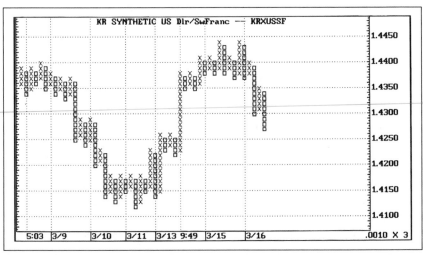

Figure 23.2. An example of a point and figure chart in US dollar/Swiss franc. (*Courtesy of Knight-Ridder*)

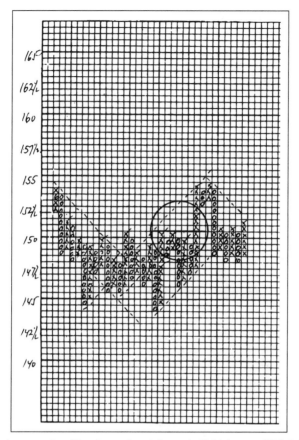

Figure 23.3. An example of breakout of a triple top in British pound/US dollar. (*Courtesy of Chartcraft Inc.*)

Let's take the very popular example of a 1 × 3 point and figure chart (also known as the *3-box reversal*). Every single pip that continues the original direction is entered. When the market changes direction, no entry will be posted before the price reverses by 3 pips. At that point, all 3 pips will be recorded, plus all the additional pips which maintain the direction, on an individual basis. This way, all the insignificant moves are tuned out, allowing the trader to focus on the real price behavior (see Figure 23.2).

Incidentally, it is quite possible to use a 1 × 1 reversal box. However, it may not be the best possible choice, as the trading signals will lose some of their sensitivity, due to statistical noise. As a rule of thumb, which should be adjusted for personal preference, the higher the number of reversal boxes, the sharper the sensitivity to the more significant price fluctuations.

Volume is not recorded or available in the forex cash market the same way as in the currency futures market, yet it is an integral part of the chart. Since volume creates trading activity, the heavier the volume, the more activity will be charted. Therefore, volume is alive and well, albeit in this indirect manner.

Before we take a look at the popular point and figure chart formations and see how clear the trading signals are, let me just point out the *significance of number 3* in technical analysis in general and for point and figure charting in particular. Previously, empirical evidence pointed out the importance of this number—the head and shoulders, triple top and triple bottom formations, along with categorizing the trends in terms of importance and direction. Number 3 will become very obvious in the following point and figure chart formations. There is no known scientific reasoning behind it, but it is a reality which we have to observe.

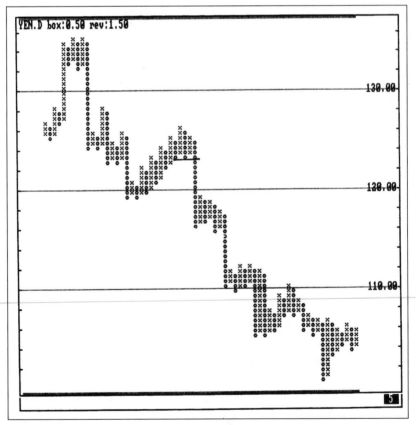

Figure 23.4. An example of breakout of a triple bottom in US dollar/Japanese yen. (*Courtesy of TeleTrac. Source: Telerate. Reprinted by permission. © 1993 Dow Jones Telerate, Inc.*)

It should be noted that the 45° trendline is very important. Please notice the frequency of this trendline in the following point and figure chart formations.

Breakout of a Triple Top

This formation is similar in aspect and behavior to a very short term double bottom formation, where the third upside attack will result in the penetration of the resistance line. The breakout of the neckline will be followed by a currency rally equal in size to the height of the bottoms (Figure 23.3).

Breakout of a Triple Bottom

This formation is similar in shape and performance to a very short term double top formation, where the third attack on the downside will result in the penetration of the support line. The breakout of the neckline will be fol-

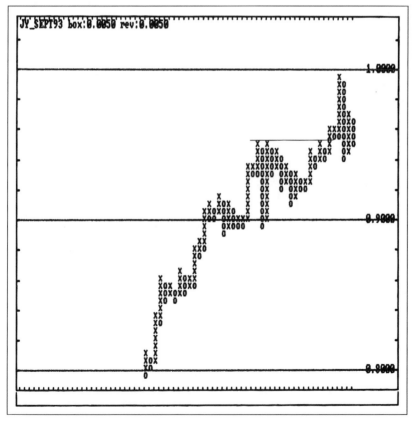

Figure 23.5. An example of breakout of a spread triple top in Japanese yen futures. (*Courtesy of TeleTrac. Source: Telerate. Reprinted by permission. © 1993 Dow Jones Telerate, Inc.*)

lowed by a currency drop equal in size to the height of the tops (Figure 23.4).

Breakout of a Spread Triple Top

The *breakout of a spread triple top* pattern is a spin-off of the breakout of a triple top. The difference consists of a failure of the third X's column to reach the resistance line (Figure 23.5). However, the next attack (still the third), will break through the resistance level. The breakout of the neckline will be followed by a currency rally equal in size to the height of the bottoms.

Breakout of a Spread Triple Bottom

This formation is the mirror image of the breakout of a spread triple top (Figure 23.6). The breakout of the neckline will be followed by a currency drop equal in size to the height of the tops.

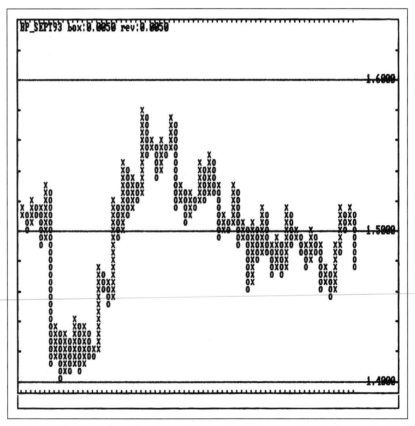

Figure 23.6. An example of breakout of a spread triple bottom in British pound/US dollar. (*Courtesy of TeleTrac. Source: Telerate. Reprinted by permission. © 1993 Dow Jones Telerate, Inc.*)

The Ascending Triple Tops Formation

The *ascending triple tops* formation is another spin-off of the breakout of a triple tops formation. Each new top is higher than the previous one. The third top is generally a buying signal (Figure 23.7). The break of the resistance line confirms a buying signal.

Upward Breakout of a Bullish Resistance Line

The *upward breakout of a bullish resistance line pattern* confirms the ascending triple top formation by adding 1 or more X's to the chart. Although the same general rules apply, remember that the importance of this resistance line is enhanced by the larger number of significant tangential highs (see Figure 23.7).

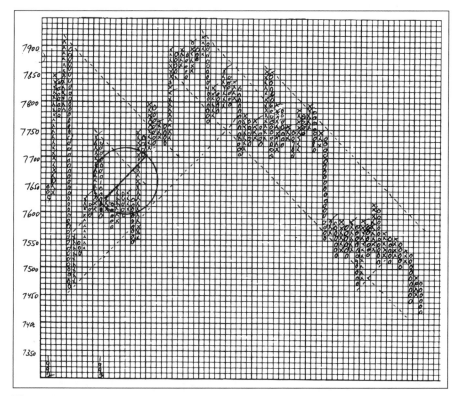

Figure 23.7. An example of a breakout of an ascending triple top in US dollar/Canadian dollar. (*Courtesy of Chartcraft, Inc.*)

The Descending Triple Bottoms Formation

The *descending triple bottoms* formation is a spin-off of the breakout of the triple bottoms formation. However, each consecutive bottom is lower than the preceding one (Figure 23.8). The breakout of the support line generates a selling signal.

Downward Breakout of a Bearish Support Line

The *downward breakout of a bearish support line* is a confirmation of the previous formation, the descending triple bottom formation (see Figure 23.8). Once the bearish support line is broken, one or several O's are entered.

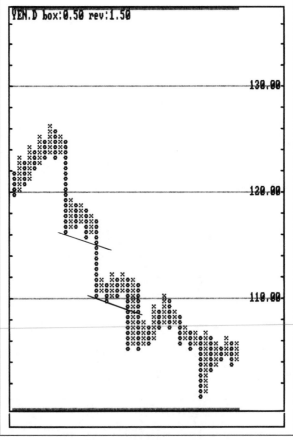

Figure 23.8. Examples of a descending triple bottom formations in US dollar/Japanese yen. (*Courtesy of TeleTrac. Source: Telerate. Reprinted by permission.* © *1993 Dow Jones Telerate, Inc.*)

Downward Breakout of a Bullish Support Line

The *downward breakout of a bullish support line* pattern generates a selling signal (see Figure 23.9). In this pattern, the currency seems to be under a bullish bias as it moves within a bullish channel. However, if the currency has a valid breakout through the support line, the trader receives a bearish signal.

Upward Breakout of a Bearish Resistance Line

The *upward breakout of a bearish resistance line* pattern occurs when the currency breaks out on the upside from the bearish channel. When the breakout is valid, this formation generates a buy signal (Figure 23.10).

Figure 23.9. Examples of a downward breakout of a bullish support line in US dollar/Japanese yen. (*Courtesy of TeleTrac. Source: Telerate. Reprinted by permission.* © *1993 Dow Jones Telerate, Inc.*)

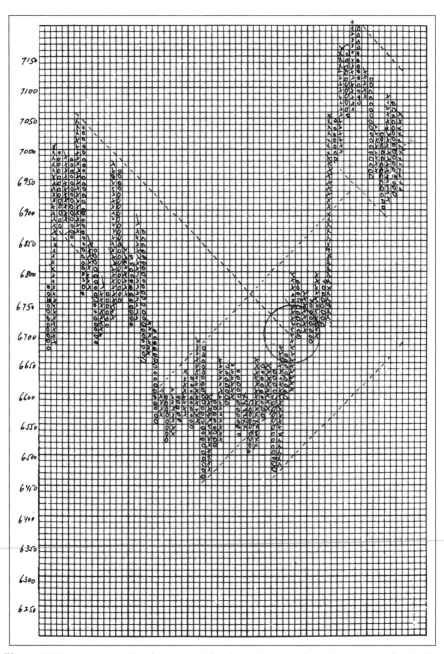

Figure 23.10. An example of an upward breakout through a bearish resistance line in the US dollar/Swiss franc market. (*Courtesy of Chartcraft, Inc.*)

Upward Breakout from a Consolidation Formation

The *upward breakout from a consolidation formation* (Figure 23.11) may be visualized as a bullish flag or pennant formation. A valid upside breakout will have a price objective equal in size to the total length of the flagpole, or pennant pole. If the pole is not obvious, the formation will resemble a symmetrical triangle, or a rectangle. This is important to notice, since the currency may break out either way.

Downward Breakout from a Consolidation Formation

The *downward breakout from a consolidation formation* resembles a bearish flag, or a bearish pennant formation applied to point and figure charting. The breakout of the support line generates a selling signal (see Figure 23.12).

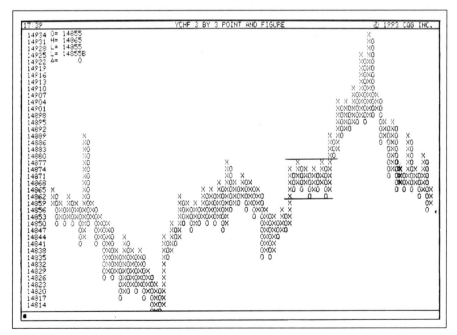

Figure 23.11. An example of an upward breakout from a consolidation formation in the US dollar/Swiss franc market. (*Courtesy of CQG*)

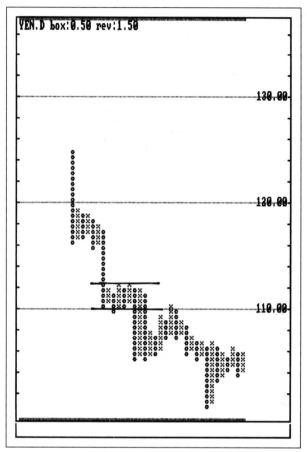

Figure 23.12. An example of an downward breakout from a consolidation formation in the US dollar/Japanese yen market. (*Courtesy of TeleTrac. Source: Telerate. Reprinted by permission.* © *1993 Dow Jones Telerate, Inc.*)

In addition to the above formations, all the reversal and continuation chart formations previously presented apply as well.

The intraday one-box reversal charts offer yet another type of signal, specific only to point and figure: the *horizontal count*. The idea behind this approach is that a period of consolidation is generally followed by a sharp move. And, as you remember, the longer the consolidation period, the

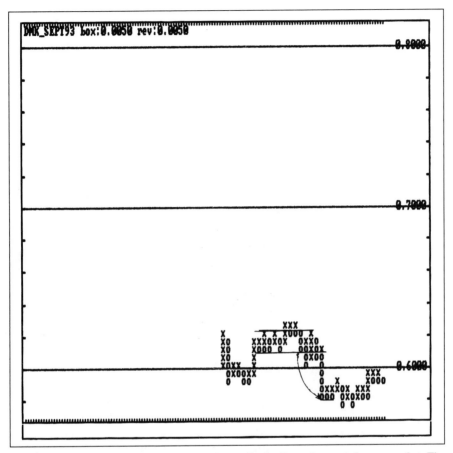

Figure 23.13. An example of a horizontal count in the Deutsche mark futures market. The horizontal count of the number of columns where the currency was stable was extrapolated in the vertical price target. (*Courtesy of TeleTrac. Source: Telerate. Reprinted by permission.* © *1993 Dow Jones Telerate, Inc.*)

sharper the subsequent price activity. This method counts the number of columns that form the consolidation area (the horizontal count) and extrapolates this number vertically to the breakout price level (Figure 23.13). The level thus obtained is the new price objective.

Chapter 24

Candlestick Charting

One of the most fascinating types of chart is the candlestick chart. Used in Japan for over two hundred years, candlestick charting is becoming very popular around the world. In terms of structure, they are similar to the bar charts and consist of opening, high, low and closing prices.

The body (*jittai*) consists of the range between the opening and closing price. A filled (black) body indicates that the currency closed lower than it opened. The reverse is true for a blank body.

The Japanese consider the real body paramount in their technical interpretation. The candlestick's body provides the most significance regarding the direction of the market.

The high and low prices create the upper and lower shadows, respectively—when different from the open or close. The upper shadow (*uwakage*) occurs if the daily high is higher than either the closing price of a blank body or the opening price of a black body. The *lower shadow* (*shitakage*) occurs if the daily low is lower than either the closing price of a black body or the opening price of a blank body.

For example, let's assume that the USD/JPY opened at 100.00 and closed at 99.00, the high was 100.30 and the low was 98.50. The candlestick's body is black because the closing price (99.00) is lower than the opening price (100.00). The candlestick has an upper shadow between 100.00 and 100.30 and a lower shadow between 99.00 and 98.50.

As already mentioned, in their original form, the blank bodies were colored red. Since some electronic services post them as blank (they may be colored as well, depending on the system and printer used), we will do likewise in this book.

In addition to the chart patterns presented in Chapters 20, 21 and 22, candlestick charting provides other significant trading signals.

Let's get familiar with the basic types of candlesticks, their characteristics and their Japanese nicknames, when available.

The Daily Blank Candlesticks

We will focus first on the *blank bars*, which show that *the currency closed higher than it opened* (Figure 24.1). They are as follows:

Name	Nickname	Interpretation
1. Long blank bar		Very bullish
2. Short blank bar		Stable to bullish
3. Blank upper shadow		Bearish
4. Blank lower shadow		Bullish
5. Long blank bar (no shadows)	Blank marubozu	Very bullish
6. Long blank bar (upper shadow)	Blank opening bozu	Bullish
7. Long blank bar (lower shadow)	Blank closing bozu	Bullish

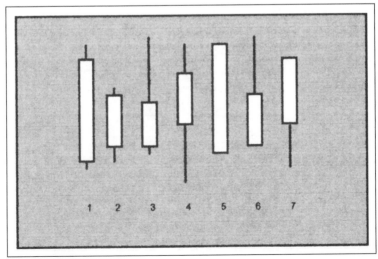

Figure 24.1. Examples of typical blank candlesticks. A blank candlestick indicates that the currency's closing price is higher than its opening price.

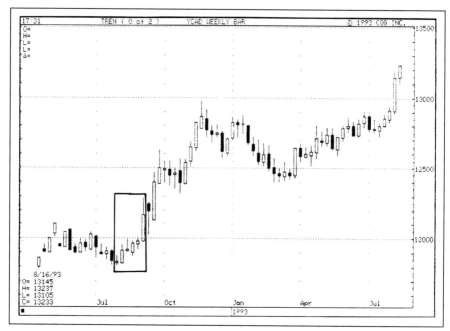

Figure 24.2. Market examples of blank candlesticks in the US dollar/Canadian dollar weekly chart. (*Courtesy of CQG*)

Figure 24.2 displays several market examples of blank candlesticks in a box in the US dollar/Canadian dollar weekly chart.

The Daily Black Candlesticks

Let's take a look now at the *black (filled) bars* where *the closing is lower than the opening* (Figure 24.3). They are as follows:

Name	Nickname	Interpretation
8. Long black bar		Very bearish
9. Short black bar		Stable to bearish
10. Black upper shadow		Bearish
11. Black lower shadow		Bullish
12. Long black bar (no shadow)	Black *marubozu*	Very bearish
13. Long black bar (upper shadow)	Black closing *bozu*	Bearish
14. Long black bar (lower shadow)	Black opening *bozu*	Bearish

Several black, or filled, candlestick market examples are shown in a box in Figure 24.4, in the US dollar/Japanese yen weekly chart.

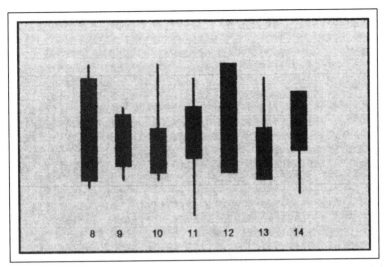

Figure 24.3. Examples of typical black, or filled, candlesticks. A black candlestick indicates that the currency's closing price is lower than its opening price.

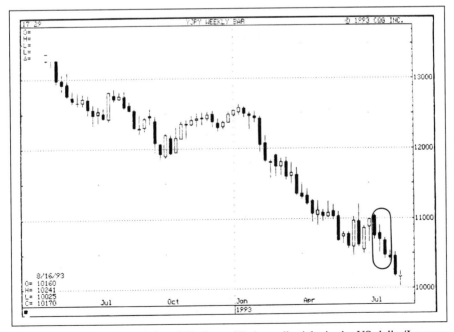

Figure 24.4. Market examples of black, or filled, candlesticks in the US dollar/Japanese yen weekly chart. (*Courtesy of CQG*)

Perhaps a couple of words about the nicknames would be in order. The Japanese are quite fond of nicknames and this characteristic was also applied in candlestick charting. Here are some of them: A *marubozu (shaven head)* is a candlestick bar with a full body, but no shadow. This means that in the case of a *blank marubozu*, the opening price is similar to the low, and the closing price is the high. In the case of a *black marubozu*, the opening price is similar to the high (*yoritsuki takane*), and closing price is the low (*yasunebike*).

Daily Reversal Patterns

So far we saw the basic bullish and bearish patterns. Let's take a look at the *daily reversal patterns* (Figure 24.5). They are as follows:

Name	Nickname	Interpretation
15. Opening and closing *doji* bar	Long legged shadows' *doji*	Reversal
16. Short black bar	*Koma*	Either way
17. Short blank bar	*Koma*	Either way
18. Opening and closing *doji* bar	*Tonbo* (dragonfly)	Reversal
19. Opening and closing *doji* bar	*Tonbo*	Reversal
20. Opening and closing *doji* bar	*Tohbu*	Reversal/stable
21. Opening and closing *doji* bar	4 price *doji* line	Special reversal

The nicknames, again, are very interesting. *Komas* (16 and 17) are *spinning tops*, not quite sure which way to go. *Tonbo* (18 and 19) is a drag-

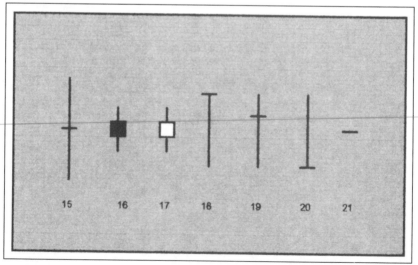

Figure 24.5.   Examples of typical daily reversal pattern in candlestick charting.

onfly, it signals a reversal, yet it may move either way. *Tohba* or tohbu (20) is the gravestone doji.

The *long legged shadows' doji bar* (15) is one of the most recognized candlestick reversal patterns outside Japan and also a very reliable reversal formation. A doji bar resembles a bar. The candlestick does not have a real body, as the opening and closing price are identical (see Figure 24.6). This shows that the market reached the end of the trend and temporarily balanced before reversing itself. The market tends to reverse immediately after the signal. At times, exceptional pressure on the opposite side was able to post-pone the reversal by one day.

The *4 price doji bar* (21) is an exceptional reversal formation. Due to the complete lack of activity, the trader should wait for further information.

Two other reversal candlesticks (Figure 24.7) are known as:

Name	Nickname	Interpretation
22. Black lower shadow	*Karakasa* (hangman at the top,	Sell at the top
23. Blank lower shadow	Hammer at the bottom)	Buy at the bottom

Initially known as *karakasa* (paper umbrella), it is better known now as the *hangman,* when it occurs at the top of the trend, because the traders who may fall in the trap and buy that currency will be caught long at the top

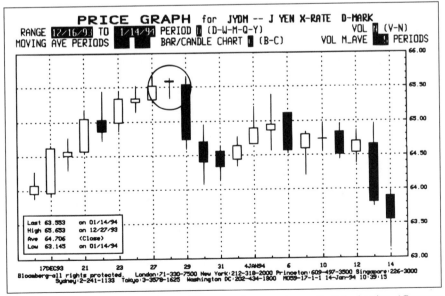

Figure 24.6.   Example of a doji bar daily reversal pattern in candlestick charting. (*Courtesy of Bloomberg*)

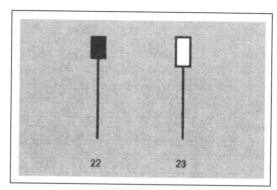

Figure 24.7. Examples of additional reversal candlesticks.

of the range. The opposite is true when this formation occurs at the bottom of the trend. The only difference is the name: the *hammer*. A market example of a *hangman* can be observed in the Deutsche mark/Japanese yen market (see Figure 24.8).

Although these candlesticks may seem to give either bullish signals at the top or bearish signals at the bottom, a closer look and a little caution should help. It is important to remember that the body is small—only one-half or one-third of the length of the shadow. Obviously, the signals are to sell at the top and buy at the bottom. (Don't we always want to do just that, anyway?)

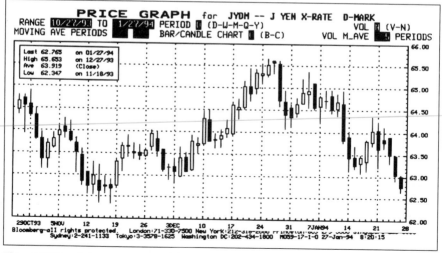

Figure 24.8. A hangman reversal formation can be seen in the Deutsche mark/Japanese yen daily chart. (*Courtesy of Bloomberg*)

The single candlesticks introduced so far are the fundamental tools, either by themselves or in combination. Since we know now their individual interpretation, let's move on and mix them up, in search of further signals.

Two-Day Candlesticks Combinations

When two consecutive candlesticks show the same direction, based on the trendiness quality of the market, we tend to look for continuation. But can we get any signal when the *consecutive candlesticks point out different directions?* Let's find out.

The Bullish Signals

Name
24. Kirikomi
25. Bullish tasuki
26. Upside gap tasuki
27. Bullish tsutsumi (the engulfing bar)

The *kirikomi bar* (24) is a blank marubozu bar which opens the second day lower (than the previous low of a long black bar) and closes above the 50 percent level of the previous day's range (Figure 24.9). The formation generates a *bullish* signal.

The *bullish tasuki bar* (25) is a long black bar which has a high above the 50 percent of the previous day's long blank body, and closes marginally below the previous day's low (Figure 24.10). The signal is *bullish*.

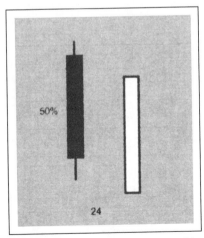

Figure 24.9.   Example of the kirikomi bar.

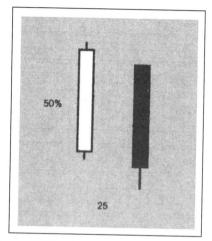

Figure 24.10. Example of a bullish tasuki bar.

The *upside gap tasuki bar* (26) occurs in an uptrend. It is a second day black bar which closes an overnight gap opened on the previous day by a blank bar (Figure 24.11). This is similar to a common gap in the currency futures bar chart which was indeed closed, but had little meaning otherwise, as it occurred against the direction of the trend. The signal of the upside gap tasuki bar is bullish.

The *bullish tsutsumi bar (the engulfing pattern)* (27) is a second day long blank candlestick whose body "engulfs" the previous day's small black

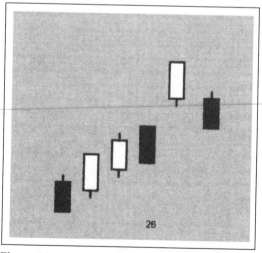

Figure 24.11. Example of the upside gap tasuki bar.

body (Figure 24.12). This is the equivalent of a bullish key reversal in the bar charts. Examples of bullish tsutsumi bars can be observed on the daily Japanese yen chart in Figure 24.13.

The Bearish Signals

Name
28. *Kabuse* (dark cloud cover)
29. *Atekubi*
30. *Irikubi*
31. *Sashikomi*
32. Bearish *tsutsumi*
33. Bearish *tasuki*
34. Downside *tasuki* gap

The *kabuse bar (a dark cloud cover)* (28) is a second day black bar which set a higher price, but closed midway through the previous day's blank long closing bozu body. The kabuse bars give a *bearish reversal signal.*

Based on the price behavior on the second day, there are three *types of kabuse bars* (Figure 24.14):

28a. Long black closing *bozu,* which settles under the 50 percent level of the original blank bar
28b. Black *marubozu*
28c. Long black opening *bozu,* which settles under the 50 percent level of the original blank bar

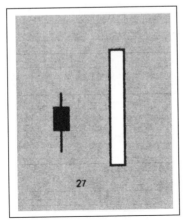

Figure 24.12.   Example of the bullish tsutsumi bar, or engulfing pattern.

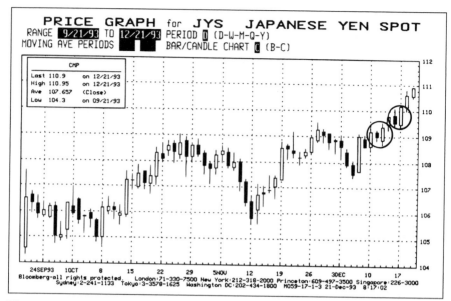

Figure 24.13. Examples of the bullish tsutsumi bars as they appear on the daily Japanese yen chart. (*Courtesy of Bloomberg*)

A market example of a kabuse bar can be observed in Figure 24.15, in the US dollar/Deutsche mark daily chart.

The *atekubi bar* (29) is a blank bar that closes at the daily high (Figure 24.16). The current closing price equals the previous day's low. The origi-

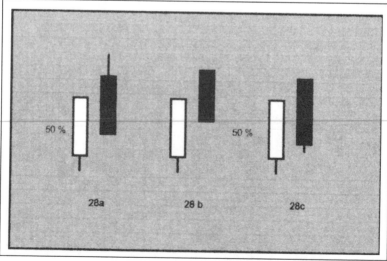

Figure 24.14. Examples of kabuse bars (dark cloud cover).

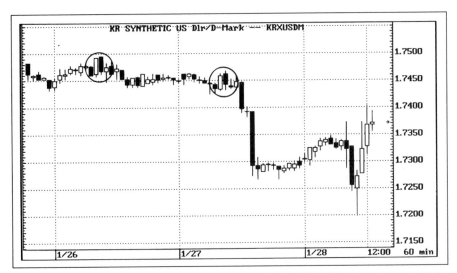

Figure 24.15. A market example of a kabuse bar in the US dollar/Deutsche mark daily chart. (*Courtesy of Knight-Ridder*)

nal day's range is a long black bar. This is a typical case of the market closing an overnight gap in the currency futures market, with no impact on the previous trend. The atekubi bar signals *selling*.

The *irikubi bar* (30) is a modified atekubi bar. All the characteristics are the same, except that the second day's closing high is marginally higher than the original day's low (Figure 24.17). The signal remains *bearish*.

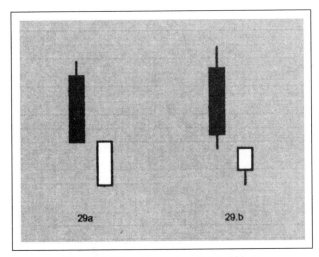

Figure 24.16. Examples of atekubi bars.

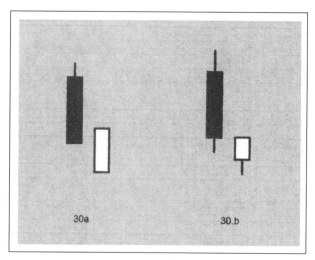

Figure 24.17.   Example of irikubi bars.

The *sashikomi bar* (31) is, in turn, a modified irikubi bar (Figure 24.18). Therefore, all the characteristics are the same, and the signal remains *bearish*. The difference is that the opening of the second day's blank bar is much lower than that of the irikubi bars. Despite the wider gap thus formed, the blank candlestick only closes just above the previous day's low.

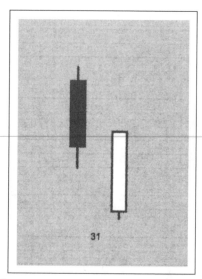

Figure 24.18.   Example of a sashikomi bar.

The *bearish tsutsumi bar (the engulfing pattern)* (32) is a second day long black candlestick whose body "engulfs" the previous day's small blank body (Figure 24.19). This is the equivalent of a bearish key reversal in the bar charts.

A market example of the bearish tsutsumi bar may be observed in the Deutsche mark futures daily chart from Figure 24.20.

The *bearish tasuki bar* (33) is a long blank bar which has a low above the 50 percent of the previous day's long black body and closes marginally above the previous day's high (Figure 24.21). The second day's rally is temporary, as it is caused only by profit taking. The sell-off is likely to continue the next day. The tasuki bar's signal is *bearish*.

The *downside gap tasuki bar* (34) occurs in a downtrend. It is a second day blank bar which closes an overnight gap opened on the previous day by a black bar (Figure 24.22). This is similar to a common gap in the currency futures bar chart which was indeed closed, but had little meaning otherwise, since it occurred against the direction of the trend.

The "Wait and See" Signals

---

35. Harami bar
36. Hoshi (star)
37. Kenuki (tweezers)

The *harami bar* (35) is just the opposite of the tsutsumi bar, as the engulfing range occurs first. The second day's range results within the previ-

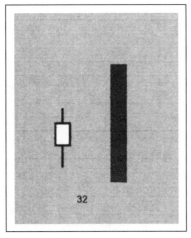

Figure 24.19.   Example of the bearish tsutsumi bar.

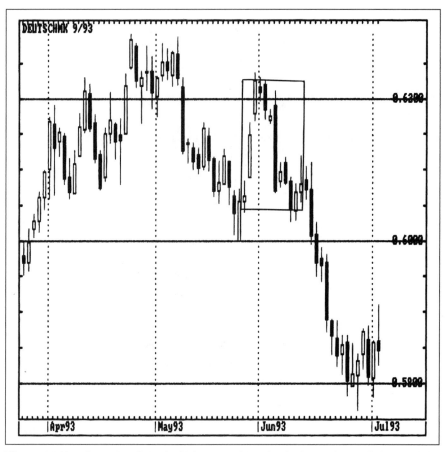

Figure 24.20. Example of the bearish tsutsumi bar in the Deutsche mark futures daily chart. (*Courtesy of TeleTrac. Source: Telerate. Reprinted by permission. © 1993 Dow Jones Telerate, Inc.*)

ous day's body. The two consecutive ranges have opposite directions, but it does not matter which one is first (Figure 24.23). The market's focus remains on the activity of the first day, so the trading volume will slow down until further information becomes available. However, when the second day's range is a doji bar (Chart 35 c and d), then the harami bar becomes a reversal signal. A market example is available in the US dollar/Japanese yen daily chart in Figure 24.24.

The *hoshi (star) bar* (36) is essentially identical in nature with the harami bar. It consists of a tiny body which appears the following day out-

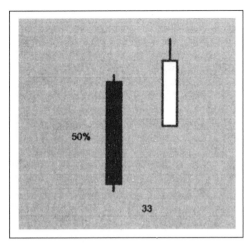

Figure 24.21.   An example of the bearish tasuki bar.

side the original body (see Figure 24.25). It is not important whether the star reaches the previous day's shadows. The direction of the two consecutive ranges is also irrelevant. The reading is also "wait and see." Market examples of *hoshi bars* are provided in Figures 24.26 and 24.27, on the US dollar/Deutsche mark daily chart, and the British pound/US dollar daily chart, respectively.

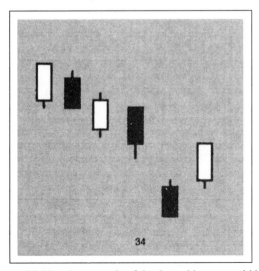

Figure 24.22.   An example of the downside gap tasuki bar.

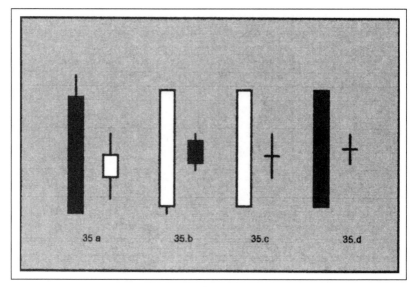

Figure 24.23.   Examples of the harami bars.

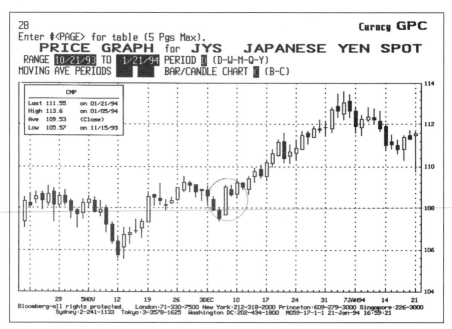

Figure 24.24.   A market example of the harami bar in the US dollar/Japanese yen daily chart. (*Courtesy of Bloomberg*)

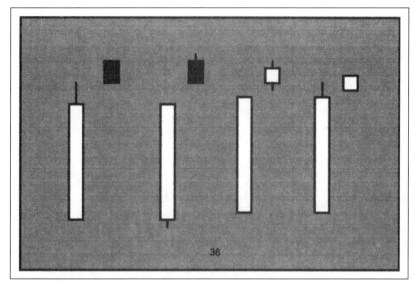

Figure 24.25.   Examples of the hoshi (star) bars. The signal is "wait and see."

Figure 24.26.   A market example of the hoshi bar on the US dollar/Deutsche mark daily chart. (*Courtesy of Bloomberg*)

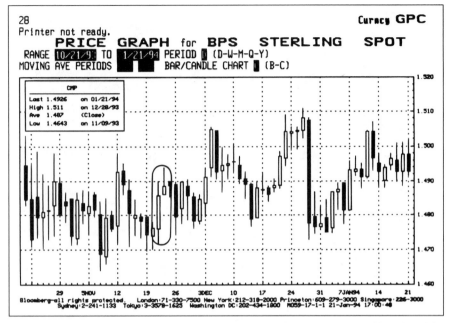

Figure 24.27. A market example of the hoshi bar on the British pound/US dollar daily chart. (*Courtesy of Bloomberg*)

The *kenuki (tweezers) bars* (37) refer to consecutive bars which have matching highs or lows (Figure 24.28). In a rising market, a tweezers top occurs when the highs match. The opposite is true for a tweezers bottom. The "wait and see" interpretation changes to reversal when the formation occurs after an extended move. A market example can be observed in Figure 24.29, on the Australian dollar/US dollar weekly chart.

The Reversal Signals
We already came across several reliable reversal signals, such as the doji bar and the engulfing patterns. We observed that some of the uncertain signals may turn into reversal signals under certain conditions, for example the tweezers bars. Now we will focus on other reversal patterns, described by "Sakata's 5 methods." These strategies date back about 200 years. They are:

1. *Sanzan* (three mountains)
2. *Sansen* (three rivers)
3. *Sangu* (three gaps)

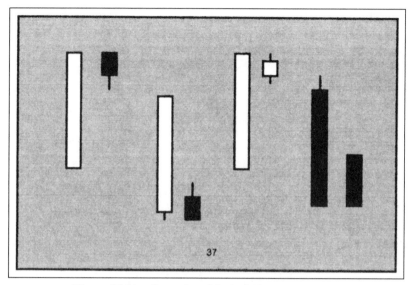

Figure 24.28. Examples of the kenuki (tweezers) bars.

Figure 24.29. Example of the kenuki bar on the Australian dollar/US dollar weekly chart. (*Courtesy of CQG*)

4. *Sanpei* (three parallel bars)

5. *Sanpo* (three methods)

Please note the omnipresence of number 3. It seems somehow that number 3 has a lot of attraction among technicians, regardless of the geographical or time frames.

The following reversal patterns generally have more daily entries than we were accustomed to so far.

1. When considering *sanzan (three mountains)*, think of the triple top formation (Figure 24.30). This strategy holds that prices move up in three waves and then descend in three waves. If the middle mountain is higher than the other two, the formation is called the *three Buddha top* formation. This candlestick formation closely resembles the head and shoulders chart formation.

2. The *sansen (three rivers)* method is also known as the *three river evening star*. It consists of three daily entries. The first day is a long blank bar (a bullish move), followed by a bullish but short ranged one day island and it ends with a bearish long black line (Figure 24.32). It is

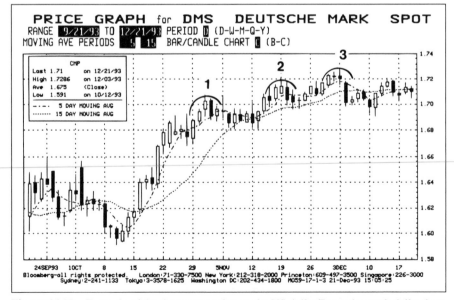

Figure 24.30. Example of the three mountains on the US dollar/Deutsche mark daily chart. (*Courtesy of Bloomberg*)

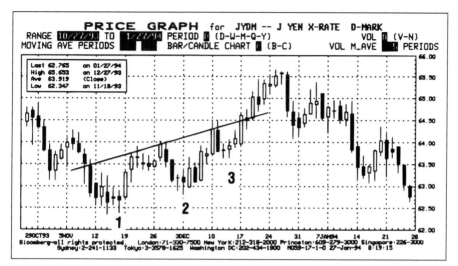

Figure 24.31. Example of the inverse three Buddha on the Deutsche mark/Japanese yen chart. (*Courtesy of Bloomberg*)

easy to visualize if you remember the exhaustion gap from the currency futures bar charts.

A spin-off of the three rivers evening star is a rather poetically named formation called (40) the *upside gap's two crows* (Figure 24.33). It differs in the second and third bars, since they are both bearish, yet unable to close the exhaustion gap in the very short term. It may be remem-

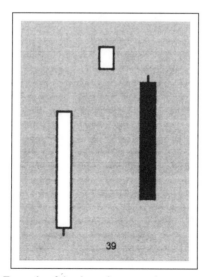

Figure 24.32. Example of the three rivers evening star reversal formation.

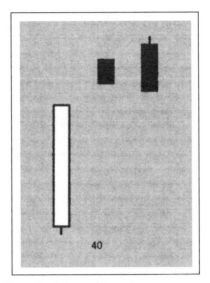

Figure 24.33. Example of the upside gap's two crows reversal formation.

bered from the exhaustion gaps, again, this time as the two or three day island.

There are several other versions of the three rivers, such as the *evening Southern cross* and the *two crows,* but they have the same reversal function.

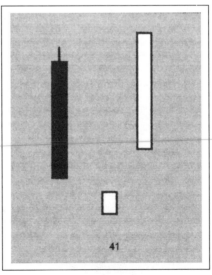

Figure 24.34. Example of the three rivers morning star reversal formation.

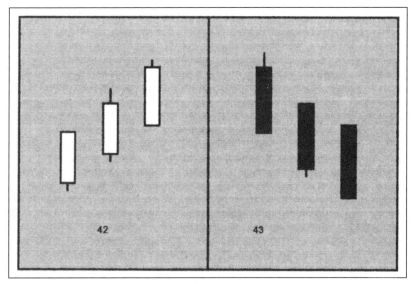

Figure 24.35. Example of the three soldiers (42) and the three crows (43) reversal formations.

Figure 24.36. A market example of the three soldiers is provided on the US dollar/ Deutsche mark daily chart. (*Courtesy of Bloomberg*)

The opposite of the three rivers evening star is the three rivers morning star (Figure 24.34). The same rules apply.

3. The *sangu (three gaps)* is a method applicable in either a steeply rising or falling market, where the daily limits will break the trading. The theory holds that after the third gap, the market will reverse at least to the second gap. There is not much reason to focus on this method as it is hardly applicable in the currency markets. Daily limits do not exist in the full sense in the currency futures markets. Therefore, it is highly unlikely for this formation to appear on the charts.

4. *Sanpei (three parallel bars)* refers to the similarity of direction and velocity of three consecutive bars, as otherwise, all the entries are parallel (Figure 24.35). They generate a reversal formation after an extended rally. When bullish, the formation is known as the *three soldiers* (42); when bearish, the name switches to *three crows* (43) because calling it the inverted three soldiers may have caused confusion over the years. A market example is available for the *three soldiers* in Figure 24.36.

5. *Sanpo (three methods)* advises a trader to occasionally pause when following a trend. In direct translation, no market will go straight up or down. Retracements are in order before the market will make new highs, and, respectively, new lows (Figure 24.37). Although they may be con-

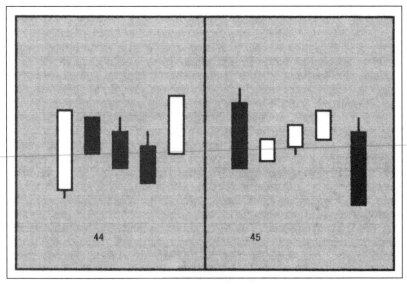

Figure 24.37. Example of the rising three methods (44) and the falling three methods (45) formations.

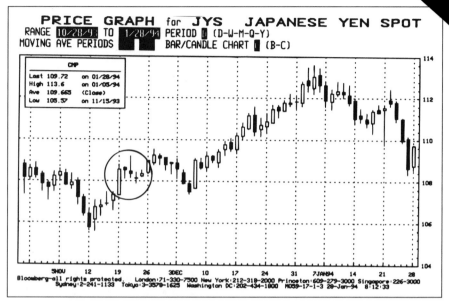

Figure 24.38. An example of the three rising method is provided on the US dollar/Japanese yen daily chart. (*Courtesy of Bloomberg*)

strued as very short term reversals (within the pattern), these formations are basically continuation patterns. I kept them along with the previous reversal patterns since they all are generally quoted together. These formations may be both bullish (44) and bearish (45). A market example of the three rising method is provided on the US dollar/Japanese yen daily chart in Figure 24.38.

Chapter 25

Quantitative Trading Methods

Now that we have been introduced to all the chart types and major chart formations, we can move from chart interpretation to the *quantitative,* or *mathematical,* trading methods which provide *a more objective view of price activity.* In addition, the quantitative methods tend to provide signals prior to their occurrence on the currency charts.

The tools of the quantitative methods are the *moving averages,* discussed in this chapter, and the *oscillators,* which are discussed in Chapter 26.

Moving Averages

The *moving average* is an average of a predetermined number of prices over a number of days, divided by the number of entries. The higher the number of days of the average, the smoother the line is. The moving average makes it easier to visualize the currency activity without the daily statistical noise. It is a common tool in technical analysis and is used either by itself or as an oscillator.

As you can see from Figure 25.1, a moving average is a smoother line than the underlying currency. The daily closing price is commonly included in the moving averages. The average may also be based on the midrange level or on a daily average of the high, low and closing prices.

It is important to observe that the moving average is a follower, rather than a leader. Its signals occur after the new movement started, not before.

There are three types of moving averages:

1. The simple moving average or arithmetic mean
2. The linearly weighted moving average
3. The exponentially smoothed moving average

1. As described above, the *simple moving average or arithmetic mean* is the average of a predetermined number of prices over a number of days, divided by the number of entries. So if you want to have a three-day average, you simply add the closing prices of the last three days and divide their

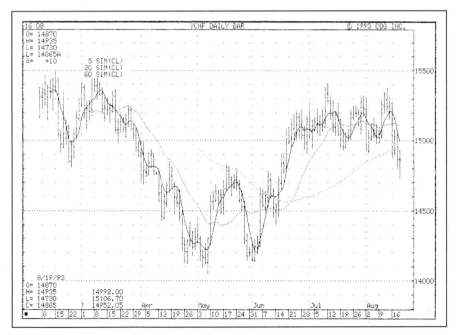

Figure 25.1. An example of three simple moving averages, 5, 20 and 60-day, traced along the US dollar/Swiss franc daily bar chart. (*Courtesy of CQG*)

sum by three. In order to have the average "move," each day you add the new closing price to the previous sum and deduct the oldest price.

$$\frac{P4 + P3 + P2 + P1 - P4}{3} = \text{Simple moving average}$$

You now have a simple moving average (Figure 25.2).

2. Traders who dislike allocating equal weights to each of the daily prices considered always have the option of using a *linearly weighted moving average*. This type of average assigns more weight to the more recent closings. This is achieved by multiplying the last day's price by one, and each closer day by an increasing consecutive number. In our previous ex-

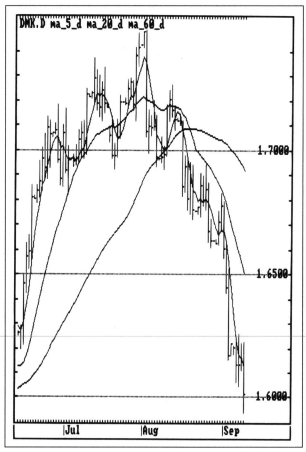

Figure 25.2. An example of three simple moving averages, 5, 20 and 60 day, traced along the US dollar/Deutsche mark daily bar chart. (*Courtesy of TeleTrac. Source: Telerate. Reprinted by permission. © 1993 Dow Jones Telerate, Inc.*)

ample, the fourth day's price is multiplied by 1, the third by 2, the second by 3 and the last one by 4 and the fourth day's price is deducted. The new sum is divided by 9, which is just the sum of its multipliers.

$$\frac{(P4 \times 1) + (P3 \times 2) + (P2 \times 3) + (P1 \times 4) - P4}{9} = \text{Linearly weighted moving average}$$

3. The most sophisticated moving average available is the *exponentially smoothed moving average* (Figure 25.3). In addition to assigning different weights to the previous prices, the exponentially smoothed moving average also takes into account the previous price information of the underlying currency.

The traders choose a number of averages to use with a currency. A suggested number is 3, as more signals may be available. But, be wary of using 3 very close moving averages, in order to avoid confusing signs. It may be helpful to use intervals which better encompass short-term, medium-term and long-term periods, for a more complex set of signals.

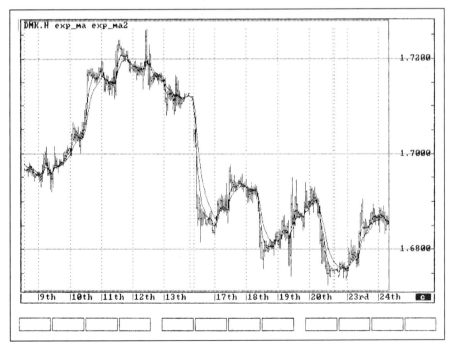

Figure 25.3. An example of an exponentially smoothed moving average on US dollar/Deutsche mark hourly chart. (*Courtesy of TeleTrac. Source: Telerate. Reprinted by permission. © 1993 Dow Jones Telerate, Inc.*)

Some of the more popular periods are 4-9-18 days, 5-20-60 and 7-21-90 days. Unless you focus on a specific combination of moving averages (for instance, 4-9-18 days), the exact number of days for each of the averages is less important, as long as they are spaced far enough apart from each other to avoid insignificant signals.

Trading Signals

A *buying signal* on a two moving average combination occurs when the shorter term of two consecutive averages intersects the longer one upwards. A *selling signal* occurs when the reverse happens, and the longer of two consecutive averages intersects the shorter one downwards (Figure 25.4)

A *signal* involving three moving averages is generated by a moving averages combination of 4–9–18 days. The *buying warning* occurs when the four day moving average crosses upwards both the nine and 18 day averages, and the *buying signal* is confirmed when the nine day moving average also crosses upwards the 18 day average (Figure 25.5).

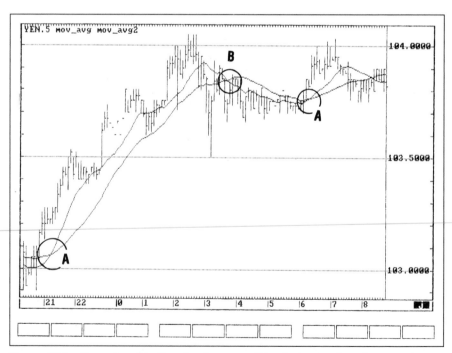

Figure 25.4. Examples of trading signals generated by the intersection of two moving averages in US dollar/Japanese yen: (A) buying signals, and (B) selling signal. (*Courtesy of TeleTrac. Source: Telerate. Reprinted by permission.* © *1993 Dow Jones Telerate, Inc.*)

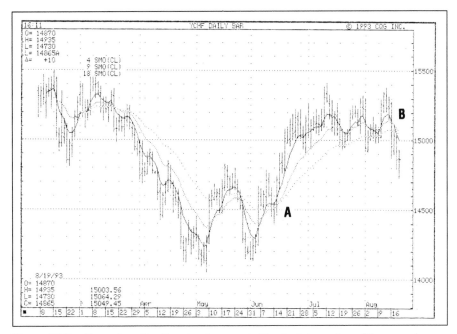

Figure 25.5. Examples of trading signals generated by the intersection of three moving averages in US dollar/Swiss franc: (A) buying signal, and (B) selling signal. (*Courtesy of CQG*)

The reverse is true for the selling signal. The *selling warning* appears when the four day average intersects downwards the nine and 18 day moving averages. This warning becomes a *selling signal* when the nine day moving average falls below the 18 day average as well (Figure 25.5).

A type of signal based on a two moving average combination, and more popular in Japan, is known as the *cross*. There are two kinds of crosses. When two consecutive moving averages intersect each other as they move in opposite directions, this is called a *dead cross*, and the intersection should be disregarded. If, however, the two consecutive moving averages intersect as they move in the same general direction, this is called a *golden cross,* and it is a signal that the currency will move in the same direction (Figure 25.6).

Single moving averages are frequently used as *price and time filters*, mirroring the filters first described under the trendline breakout confirmation rules.

- As a *price filter*, a short-term moving average has to be cleared by the currency closing price, the entire daily range or a certain percentage (chosen at the discretion of the trader)

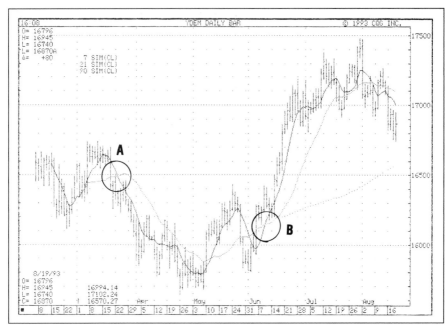

Figure 25.6. An example of moving averages intersections: (A) dead cross and (B) golden cross. A dead cross consists of the intersection of two moving averages moving in different directions. A golden cross consists of two moving averages moving in the same direction. (*Courtesy of CQG*)

- As a *time filter*, a short number of days may be used to avoid any false signals.

Two very popular versions of the price filters are the *envelope model* and the *high-low band*.

The *envelope model* consists of a short term (perhaps five day) closing price based moving average to which you add and subtract a small percentage (2 percent suggested for foreign currencies). The two winding parallel lines above and below the moving average will create a band bordering most price fluctuations. When the upper band is penetrated, a *selling signal* occurs. When the lower band is penetrated, a *buying signal* occurs. Since the signals generated by the envelope model are very short term and they occur many times against the ongoing direction of the market, speed of execution is paramount.

The *high-low band* is set up the same way, with the difference that the moving average is based on the high and the low prices. The resulting two moving averages define the edges of the band. A close above the upper band suggests a *buying signal* and one below the lower band gives a *selling signal.*

Due to the comprehensive number of foreign exchange topics covered in this book, it is impossible to present all the formulas. In order to balance this shortcoming, I will provide the appropriate sources of information, should you require a more detailed analysis. Note that, whereas it is very important to understand the concept behind the mathematical formulas, the calculations are provided by the charting services—Teletrac, Knight-Ridder, CQG and Bloomberg.

Chapter 26

Oscillators

The idea behind the oscillators is that as the market gyrates, prices tend to overshoot, to overextend. The oscillators, therefore, have been designed to provide signals regarding the overbought and oversold conditions. They come in particularly handy during trading ranges, when traders have no available trends on which to focus.

As we present the oscillators in more detail, three rules will become apparent:

1. The signals are mostly useful at the extremes of their scales.
2. Warnings and/or signals are triggered when a divergence occurs between the price of the underlying currency and the oscillator.
3. Crossing the zero line usually generates direction signals.

The major types of oscillators are as follows:

1. Moving averages (as oscillators)
2. Momentum

3. Relative strength index (RSI)

4. Stochastics

Moving Averages Oscillators

As oscillators, the values of two consecutive moving averages are subtracted from each other (the larger number of days from the previous one) and the new values are plotted (Figure 26.1).

1. When the line that results intersects the zero line upwards, a *buying signal* occurs, and vice versa.

2. When a divergence occurs between the moving averages oscillator and the currency, a *warning signal* is triggered.

3. In addition, minor trends may be spotted within the major trends.

Another oscillator, built not on simple moving averages but rather on exponentially smoothed moving averages is known as the *moving average*

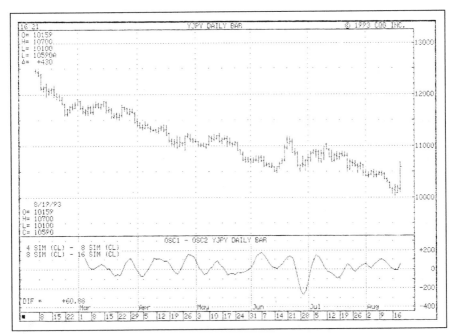

Figure 26.1. An example of the moving average oscillator based on the US dollar/ Japanese yen daily bar chart. (*Courtesy of CQG*)

convergence/divergence (*MACD*) method. This method is attributed to Gerald Appel. The MACD consists of two exponential moving averages which are plotted against the zero line. The zero line represents the times the values of the two moving averages are identical.

In addition to the signals generated by the averages intersection with the zero line and by divergence, additional signals occur as the shorter average line intersects the longer average line. The *buying signal* is generated when this intersection is upwards, whereas the *selling signal* occurs when the intersection takes place on the downside (Figure 26.2).

The *Bollinger bands,* named after John Bollinger, combine a moving average with the instrument's volatility. The bands were designed to gauge whether the prices are high or low on relative basis. He chose standard deviation to measure the volatility, because of its sensitivity to extreme deviations. They are plotted two standard deviations above and below a simple moving average.

The bands look a lot like an expanding and contracting envelope model. When the band contracts drastically, the signal is that volatility will expand sharply in the near future. An additional signal is a succession of two top formations, one outside the band, followed by one inside. If it occurs above the band, it is a selling signal. When it occurs below the band, it is a buying signal (Figure 26.3).

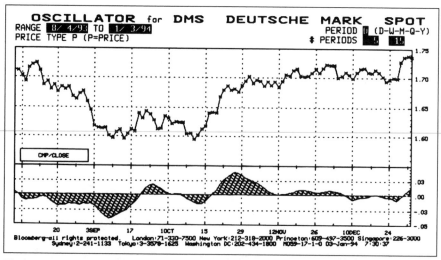

Figure 26.2. An example of moving average convergence/divergence(MACD) based on the US dollar/Deutsche mark daily chart. (*Courtesy of Bloomberg*)

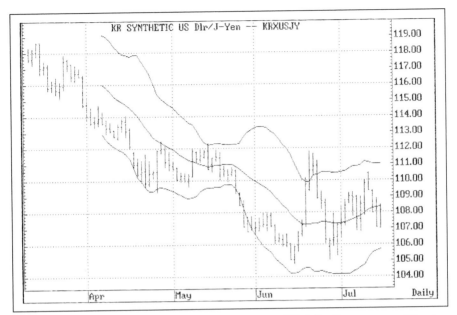

Figure 26.3. An example of Bollinger Bands based on US dollar/Japanese yen. (*Courtesy of Knight-Ridder*)

Momentum

Momentum is an oscillator designed to measure the rate of price change, not the actual price level. This oscillator consists of the net difference between the current closing price and the oldest closing price from a predetermined period.

The formula for calculating the momentum (*M*) is:

$$M = CCP - OCP$$

where

CCP = current closing price

OCP = old closing price for the predetermined period.

The new values thus obtained will be either positive or negative numbers, and they will be plotted around the zero line. At extreme positive values, momentum will suggest an overbought condition, whereas at extreme negative values, the indication is for an oversold condition (Figure 26.4). The momentum is measured on an open scale around the zero line.

This may create potential problems when a trader must figure out what exactly an extreme overbought or oversold condition means. On the simplest level, the relativity of the situation may be addressed by analyzing the previous historical data and determining the approximate levels which de-limitate the extremes.

In terms of time frame, needless to say, the shorter the number of days included in the calculations, the more responsive the momentum will be to short term fluctuations, and vice versa.

The signals triggered by the crossing of the zero line remain in effect. However, they should be followed only when they are consistent with the ongoing trend.

Other Momentum Oscillators

Swing Index (SI). The *swing index (SI)* is an oscillator developed by Welles Wilder. This momentum is plotted on a scale of −100 to +100. The spikes reaching the extremes suggest reversal.

Accumulation Swing Index (ASI). The *accumulation swing index (ASI)* is based on the *swing index* (SI). A *buying signal* is generated when the daily high exceeds the previous SI significant high, and a *selling signal* occurs when the daily low dips under the significant SI low.

Figure 26.4. An example of the momentum oscillator based on the British pound/US dollar daily chart. (*Courtesy of CQG*)

Commodity Channel Index (CCI). The commodity channel index (CCI) was developed by Donald Lambert. It is consists of the difference between the mean price of the currency and the average of the mean price over a predetermined period of time. A *buying signal* is generated when the price exceeds the upper (+100) line, and a *selling signal* occurs when the price dips under the lower (−100) line (Figure 26.5).

Rate of Change (ROC). The *rate of change* (see Figure 26.6) is another version of the momentum oscillator (Figure 26.4). The difference consists in the fact that, while the momentum's formula is based on subtracting the oldest closing price from the most recent, the ROC's formula is based on *dividing* the oldest closing price into the most recent one.

The formula for calculating the ROC is:

$$ROC = \left(\frac{CCP}{OCP}\right)100$$

where

CCP = current closing price

OCP = old closing price for the predetermined period

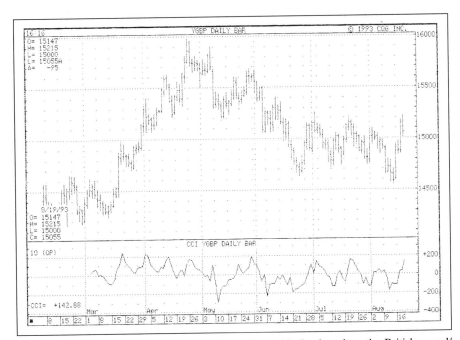

Figure 26.5. An example of the Commodity Channel Index based on the British pound/ US dollar daily chart. (*Courtesy CQG*)

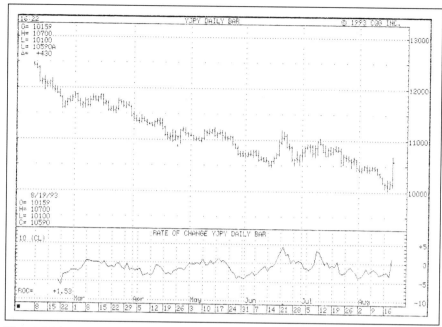

Figure 26.6.   An example of the rate of change based on the US dollar/Japanese yen daily chart. (*Courtesy of CQG*)

In the case of the ROC, the former zero line becomes the 100 line. The standard momentum rules of interpretation apply.

Trix Index. The **Trix index** was devised by Jack Hutson. As analyzed by Martin Pring, it consists of one day ROC calculation of a triple exponentially smoothed moving average of the closing price. This momentum oscillator may be plotted in several ways. Since we do not have the pages to analyze it here, I will just mention that it is useful to either indicate that a minor downward move following the completion of a chart formation means a reversal of the uptrend, or that its own top reversal is a warning that a head and shoulder formation will have an extended lower target.

The Relative Strength Index (RSI)

The *relative strength index* (see Figure 26.7) is yet another popular oscillator devised by Welles Wilder. The RSI measures the relative changes between the higher and lower closing prices.

The formula for calculating the RSI is:

$$RSI = 100 - \left[\frac{100}{(1 + RS)} \right]$$

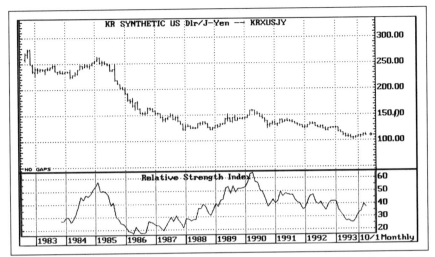

Figure 26.7. An example of the relative strength index (RSI) based on the US dollar/ Japanese yen daily chart. (*Courtesy of Knight-Ridder*)

where

RS = (average of X days up closes/average of X days down closes)

X = predetermined number of days

The original number of days, as used by its author, was 14 days. Currently, a nine day period is more popular.

The RSI is plotted on a 0 to 100 scale. In addition to the electronic charting services, the RSI figures are conveniently displayed by the major financial services on Telerate and Reuters.

The 70 and 30 values are being used as warning signals, whereas values above 85 indicate an overbought condition (*selling signal*) and under 15, an oversold condition (*buying signal*). Wilder identified the RSI's forte as its divergence versus the underlying price. Some traders use only the numerical values.

Stochastics

Unlike moving averages, which constitute a lagging indicator, stochastics generate trading signals before they appear in the price itself. Unfortunately, though, it is rather hard to know how long in advance.

The stochastics concept is based on George Lane's observations that, as the market gets toppish, the closing prices tend to approach the daily highs, whereas in a bottoming market, the closing prices tend to draw near the daily lows.

The oscillator consists of two lines called %K and %D. Visualize %K as the plotted instrument, and %D as its moving average.

The formulas for calculating the stochastics are:

$$\%K = \left[\frac{(CCL - L9)}{(H9 - L9)}\right]100$$

where

CCL = current closing price

$L9$ = the lowest low of the past 9 days

$H9$ = the highest high of the past 9 days

and

$$\%D = \left(\frac{H3}{L3}\right)100$$

where

$H3$ = the three day sum of $(CCL - L9)$

$L3$ = the three day sum of $(H9 - L9)$

The resulting lines are plotted on a 1 to 100 scale. Just as in the RSI, the 70 percent and 30 percent values are used as warning signals. The *buying (bullish reversal) signals* occur under 10 percent, and conversely the *selling (bearish reversal) signals* come into play above 90 percent (see Figure 26.8).

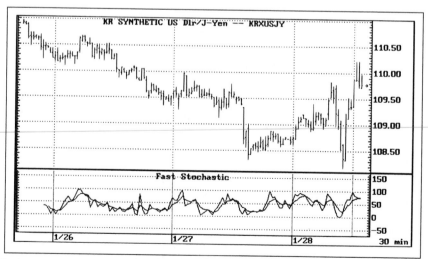

Figure 26.8. An example of the fast stochastic study based on the 30 minute US dollar/ Japanese yen chart. (*Courtesy of Knight-Ridder*)

In addition to these signals, the oscillator/currency price divergence generates significant signals.

The intersection of the %D and %K lines generate further trading signals. There are two types of intersections between the %D and %K lines:

1. The *left crossing,* when the %K line crosses prior to the peak of the %D line.
2. The *right crossing,* when the %K line occurs after the peak of the %D line.

Lane suggests using only the right intersection trading signals.

The Slow Stochastics

The slower version of the stochastics is popular among many traders, as they believe that the signals are more accurate. The new slow %K line consists of the original %D line. The new slow %D line formula is calculated off the new %K line (see Figure 26.9).

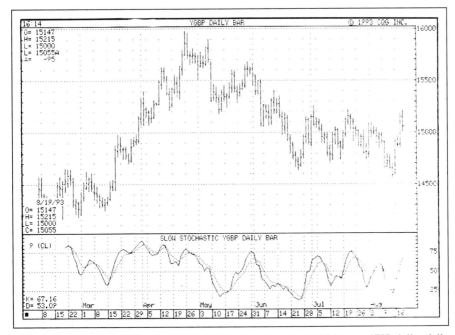

Figure 26.9.   An example of slow stochastics based on the British pound/US dollar daily chart. (*Courtesy of CQG*)

Larry Williams %R

The *Larry Williams %R* is a version of the stochastics oscillator. It consists of the difference between the high price of a predetermined number of days and the current closing price, which difference in turn is divided by the total range. This oscillator is plotted on a reversed 0 to 100 scale. Therefore the bullish reversal signals will occur under 80 percent, and conversely the bearish signals will appear above 20 percent. The interpretations are similar to those discussed under stochastics (see Figure 26.10).

A Trader's Point of View

It is important to remember that the scale of the stochastics ranges from 0 to 100. As the %K line reaches the extremes of the scale, it should not be interpreted to mean that the currency will necessarily reverse in the immediate period. The currency will indeed reverse, but it may do so anytime between the next day and the next several days (in the case of a daily chart). This is important to remember, since most traders have loss limit constraints which may inadvertently be triggered in the very short run. The correct price reaction, even a day later may offer little comfort and sympathy.

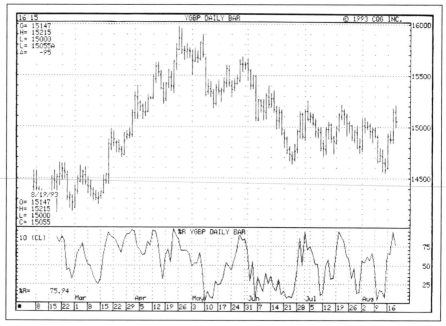

Figure 26.10. An example of the Larry Williams %R oscillator based on the British pound/US dollar daily chart. (*Courtesy of CQG*)

Conclusion

Oscillators are a favorite tool among traders. Some use them as the "main dish," and take the majority of their trading signals off the oscillators. However, most of the traders use them as a "side dish," and try to avoid acting prematurely on a reversal signal. Regardless of the importance each individual trader attaches to them, oscillators are vital in the continuous search for more accurate technical forecasting.

The Parabolic System (SAR)

This is yet another technical tool designed by Welles Wilder. The *parabolic system* is a stop-loss system, based on price and time. The system was devised to supplement the inadvertent gaps of the other trend following sys-

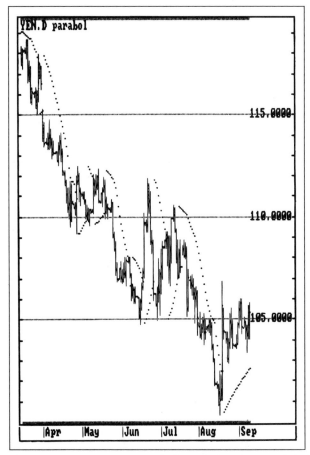

Figure 26.11. An example of the SAR parabolic study based on the US dollar/Japanese yen daily chart. (*Courtesy of TeleTrac. Source: Telerate. Reprinted by permission. © 1993 Dow Jones Telerate, Inc.*)

tems. Although not technically an oscillator, the parabolic system can be used with the oscillators.

"SAR" stands for *stop and reverse.* The stop moves daily in the direction of the new trend. The built-in acceleration factor pushes the SAR to catch up with the currency price. If the new trend fails, the SAR signal will be generated.

The name of the system is derived from its parabolic shape, which follows the price gyrations. It is represented by a dotted line. When the parabola is placed under the price it suggests a long position. Conversely, an above the price parabola indicates a short position (see Figure 26.11).

SAR performs well in trending markets, but it is not quite reliable in trading ranges. John Murphy suggests as a possible solution another device from Welles Wilder: the directional movement index.

The Directional Movement Index (DMI)

The *directional movement index* provides a signal of trend presence in the market. The line simply rates the price directional movement on a scale of 0 to 100. The higher the number, the better the trend potential of a movement, and vice versa (see Figure 26.12). This system can be used by itself or as a filter to the SAR system. DMI is beyond the scope of our discussion here, but is described in full detail by Welles Wilder in *New Concepts in*

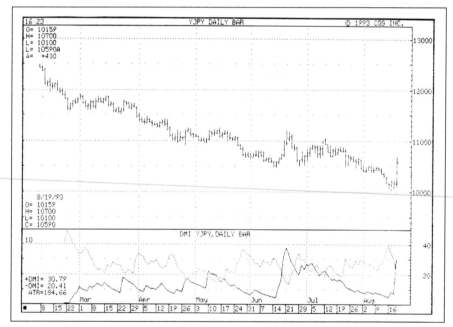

Figure 26.12. An example of the directional movement index (DMI) based on the US dollar/Japanese yen daily chart. (*Courtesy of CQG*)

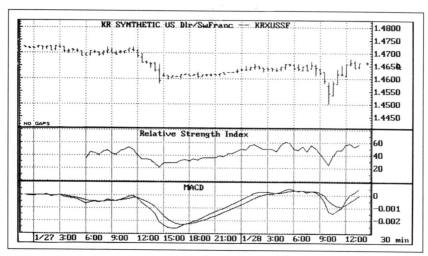

Figure 26.13. Example of oscillator combinations used for daily trading. (*Courtesy of Knight-Ridder*)

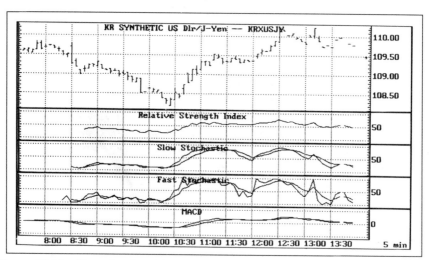

Figure 26.14. Example of oscillator combinations used for daily trading. (*Courtesy of Knight-Ridder*)

Technical Analysis, by John Murphy in *Technical Analysis of the Futures Markets* and by Martin Pring in *Market Momentum.*

Traders use different combinations of technical tools in their daily trading and analysis. Some of the more popular oscillators are the relative strength index and the MACD, as shown in Figure 26.13, and the relative strength index, the fast and slow stochastics and the MACD, as shown in Figure 26.14.

Chapter 27

W. D. Gann Analysis

One of the most influential approaches to technical analysis was developed by William D. Gann (1878–1955), the eminent stock and commodity trader. The Gann analysis is a complex approach based on traditional chart formations. His mathematical approach to technical analysis generates unique trading signals.

The most important features of his analysis are as follows:

1. The cardinal square
2. The squaring of price and time
3. Geometric angles

The Cardinal Square

The *cardinal square* is a technique of forecasting future significant chart points by counting from the all-time low price of the currency. It consists of a square divided by a cross into four quadrants. The all-time low price is housed in the center of the cross. Each of the following higher prices are entered in clockwise order. The numbers positioned in the cardinal cross are the most significant chart points. Figure 27.1 shows an application for the US dollar/Deutsche mark. The lowest price (1.3430) was entered in the center of the cross. The rates displayed on the cross are the most significant levels. If broken, these levels trigger sharp movements.

1.5740	1.5745	1.5750	1.5755	1.5760	1.5765	1.5770	1.5775	1.5780	1.5785	1.5790	1.5795	1.5800	1.5805	1.5810	1.5815	1.5820	1.5825	1.5830	1.5835	1.5840	1.5845	1.5850
1.5735	1.5330	1.5335	1.5340	1.5345	1.5350	1.5355	1.5360	1.5365	1.5370	1.5375	1.5380	1.5385	1.5390	1.5395	1.5400	1.5405	1.5410	1.5415	1.5420	1.5425	1.5430	1.5855
1.5730	1.5325	1.4960	1.4965	1.4970	1.4975	1.4980	1.4985	1.4990	1.4995	1.500	1.5005	1.5010	1.5015	1.5020	1.5025	1.5030	1.5035	1.5040	1.5045	1.5050	1.5435	1.5860
1.5725	1.5320	1.4955	1.4630	1.4635	1.4640	1.4645	1.4650	1.4655	1.4660	1.4665	1.4670	1.4675	1.4680	1.4685	1.4690	1.4695	1.4700	1.4705	1.4710	1.5055	1.5440	1.5865
1.5720	1.5315	1.4950	1.4625	1.4340	1.4345	1.4350	1.4355	1.4360	1.4365	1.4370	1.4375	1.4380	1.4385	1.4390	1.4395	1.4400	1.4405	1.4410	1.4715	1.5060	1.5445	1.5870
1.5715	1.5310	1.4945	1.4620	1.4335	1.4090	1.4095	1.4100	1.4105	1.4110	1.4115	1.4120	1.4125	1.4130	1.4135	1.4140	1.4145	1.4150	1.4415	1.4720	1.5065	1.5450	1.5875
1.5710	1.5305	1.4940	1.4615	1.4330	1.4085	1.3880	1.3885	1.3890	1.3895	1.3900	1.3905	1.3910	1.3915	1.3920	1.3925	1.3930	1.4155	1.4420	1.4725	1.5070	1.5455	1.5880
1.5705	1.5300	1.4935	1.4610	1.4325	1.4080	1.3875	1.3710	1.3715	1.3720	1.3725	1.3730	1.3735	1.3740	1.3745	1.3750	1.3935	1.4160	1.4425	1.4730	1.5075	1.5460	1.5885
1.5700	1.5295	1.4930	1.4605	1.4320	1.4075	1.3870	1.3705	1.3580	1.3585	1.3590	1.3595	1.3600	1.3605	1.3610	1.3755	1.3940	1.4165	1.4430	1.4735	1.5080	1.5465	1.5890
1.5695	1.5290	1.4925	1.4600	1.4315	1.4070	1.3865	1.3700	1.3575	1.3490	1.3495	1.3500	1.3505	1.3510	1.3615	13760	13945	1.4170	1.4435	1.4740	1.5085	1.5470	1.5895
1.5790	1.5285	1.4920	1.4595	1.4310	1.4065	1.3860	1.3695	1.3570	1.3485	1.3440	1.3445	1.3790	1.6005	1.3620	1.3765	1.3950	1.4175	1.4420	1.4745	1.5090	1.5475	1.5900
1.5685	1.5280	1.4915	1.4590	1.4305	1.4060	1.3855	1.3690	1.3565	1.3480	1.3435	1.3430	1.3455	1.3520	1.3625	1.3770	1.3955	1.4180	1.4445	1.4750	1.5095	1.5480	1.5805
1.5680	1.5275	1.4910	1.4585	1.4300	1.4055	1.3850	1.3685	1.3560	1.3475	1.3470	1.3465	1.3640	1.3525	1.3630	1.3775	1.3960	1.4185	1.4450	1.4755	1.5100	1.5485	1.5910
1.5675	1.5270	1.4905	1.4580	1.4295	1.4050	1.3845	1.3680	1.3555	1.3550	1.3545	1.3540	1.3535	1.3530	1.3635	1.3780	1.3965	1.4190	1.4455	1.4760	1.5105	1.5490	1.5915
1.5670	1.5265	1.4900	1.4575	1.4290	1.4045	1.3840	1.3675	1.3670	1.3665	1.3660	1.3655	1.3650	1.3645	1.3640	1.3785	1.3970	1.4195	1.4460	1.4765	1.5110	1.5495	1.5920
1.5665	1.5260	1.4895	1.4570	1.4285	1.4040	1.3835	1.3830	1.3825	1.3820	1.3815	1.3810	1.3805	1.3800	1.3795	1.3790	1.3975	1.4200	1.4465	1.4770	1.5115	1.5500	1.5925
1.5660	1.5255	1.4890	1.4565	1.4280	1.4035	1.4030	1.4025	1.4020	1.4015	1.4010	1.4005	1.4000	1.3995	1.3990	1.3985	1.3980	1.4205	1.4470	1.4775	1.5120	1.5505	1.5930
1.5655	1.5250	1.4885	1.4560	1.4275	1.4270	1.4265	1.4260	1.4255	1.4250	1.4245	1.4240	1.4235	1.4230	1.4225	1.4220	1.4215	1.4210	1.4475	1.4780	1.5125	1.5510	1.5935
1.5650	1.5245	1.4880	1.4555	1.4550	1.4545	1.4540	1.4535	1.4530	1.4525	1.4520	1.4514	1.4510	1.4505	1.4500	1.4495	1.4490	1.4485	1.4480	1.4785	1.5130	1.5515	1.5940
1.5645	1.5245	1.4875	1.4870	1.4865	1.4860	1.4855	1.4850	1.4845	1.4840	1.4835	1.4830	1.4825	1.4820	1.4815	1.4810	1.4805	1.4800	1.4795	1.4790	1.5135	1.5520	1.5945
1.5640	1.5240	1.5230	1.5225	1.5220	1.5215	1.5210	1.5205	1.5200	1.5195	1.5190	1.5185	1.5180	1.5175	1.5170	1.5165	1.5160	1.5155	1.5150	1.5145	1.5140	1.5525	1.5950
1.5635	1.5630	1.5625	1.5620	1.5615	1.5610	1.5605	1.5600	1.5595	1.5590	1.5585	1.5580	1.5575	1.5570	1.5565	1.5560	1.5555	1.5550	1.5545	1.5540	1.5535	1.5530	1.5955
1.6070	1.6065	1.6060	1.6055	1.6050	1.6045	1.6040	1.6035	1.6030	1.6025	1.6020	1.6015	1.6010	1.6005	1.6000	1.5995	1.5990	1.5985	1.5980	1.5975	1.5970	1.5965	1.5960

Figure 27.1. Example of the Gann cardinal square for the US dollar/Deutsche mark.

The Squaring of Price and Time

In his analysis, Gann used basic forms of geometry, such as the square, the circle and the triangle. The 360 degrees are a staple in his time analysis. In order to reach his time targets, he counted forward from the significant chart points by 30, 90, 120, 180 and 360. These forward days are potential reversal days.

In addition, Gann also considered 7 as a significant number.

The squaring of the price and time refers to his technique of converting a significant commodity dollar price into time units (from days to years) and adding these time periods to the day the significant price was reached. When the time targets were reached, time and price were squared, and the market was likely to reverse.

Geometric Angles

Gann divided the price movements into both thirds and eighths, the same percentages he used to calculate the price retracements. The resulting percentages will be, therefore, as follows:

$\frac{1}{8}$	=	12.5%
$\frac{2}{8}$	=	25%
$\frac{1}{3}$	=	33%
$\frac{3}{8}$	=	37.5%
$\frac{4}{8}$	=	50%
$\frac{5}{8}$	=	62.5%
$\frac{2}{3}$	=	67%
$\frac{6}{8}$	=	75%
$\frac{7}{8}$	=	87.5%
$\frac{8}{8}$	=	100%

The most important number is 50 and the rest of the numbers' importance decreases symmetrically on the upper and lower side. The most significant percentages, used as retracement levels, are in bold fonts. The 33 percent, 50 percent and 66 percent levels coincide with the retracement percentages from the Dow Theory, and the 37.5 percent and 62.5 percent levels to the Fibonacci retracement ratios.

The geometric angles are trendlines drawn from significant highs and lows at specific angles (see Figures 27.2 and 27.3). As mentioned under trendlines, the most important one is the 45° angle. The penetration of the 45° line signals a trend reversal.

This angle is a result of a combination of price and time ratio of 1 × 1. Steeper trendlines are determined by a ratio of 1 × 2, 1 × 3, 1 × 4 and

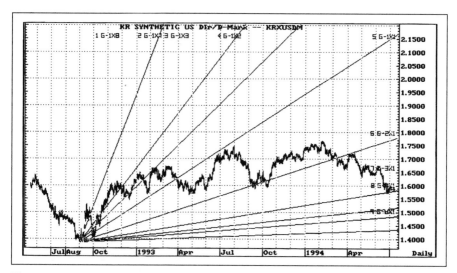

Figure 27.2. Gann geometric angles on a US dollar/Deutsche mark daily bar chart. (*Courtesy of Knight-Ridder*)

1 × 8. Flatter trendlines are determined by price and time ratios of 2 × 1, 3 × 1, 4 × 1 and 8 × 1. These lines work in the same manner as the speed-lines. The penetration of one line suggests that the price will move to the next line. They tend to work better on weekly or monthly charts.

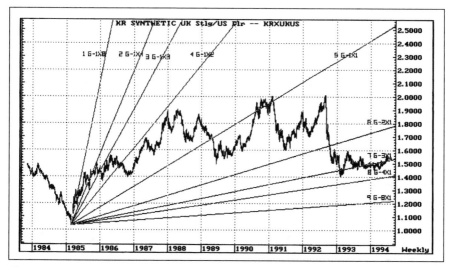

Figure 27.3. Gann geometric angles on a British pound/US dollar weekly bar chart. (*Courtesy of Knight-Ridder*)

Chapter 28

The Elliott Wave

Ralph Nelson Elliott (1871–1948) developed his approach to technical analysis in the latter part of a life he spent as an accountant. Elliott discovered—through an exhaustive study of the DJIA—that the ever-changing stock market reflects a basic harmony found in nature. From this discovery, he developed a rational system of stock market analysis. He postulated that price movements in financial markets are repetitive in form but not necessarily in time or amplitude, and he claimed predictive value for what is now called the *Elliott Wave Principle.*

In essence, the Elliott Wave Principle is a system of empirically derived rules for interpreting action in the markets. It is a tool of unique value, whose most striking characteristics are generality and accuracy. Its generality gives market perspective most of the time, and its accuracy in identifying changes in direction is at times remarkable. For the trader, it is important to know that the rules of wave analysis have stood the test of time and that market action can be understood usefully within the context of Elliott's principles.

Authored by Robert R. Prechter, Jr. and A. J. Frost.

Basics of Wave Analysis

In general, the basic objective of wave analysis is to follow and interpret correctly the development of patterns in the markets. The Wave Principle's rules and guidelines provide both an objective basis for making these interpretations and for trading signals.

In a series of articles published in 1939 by *Financial World* magazine, Elliott pointed out that the stock market unfolds according to a basic rhythm or pattern of five waves in the direction of the trend at one larger scale and three waves against that trend. In a rising market, this five-wave/three-wave pattern forms one complete bull market/bear market cycle of eight waves. The five-wave upward movement as a whole is referred to as an *impulse* wave, while the three-wave countertrend movement is described as a *corrective* wave. This basic structure is illustrated in Figure 28.1.

Within the five-wave bull move, waves 1, 3 and 5 are themselves impulse waves, subdividing into five waves of smaller scale, while waves 2 and 4 are corrective waves, subdividing into three smaller waves each. As shown in Figure 28.1, subwaves of impulse sequences are labeled with numbers, while subwaves of corrections are labeled with letters.

Following the cycle shown in the illustration, a second five-wave upside movement begins, followed by another three-wave correction, fol-

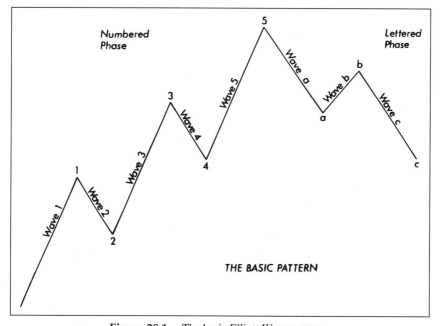

Figure 28.1.   The basic Elliott Wave pattern.

lowed by one more five-wave upmove. This sequence of movements constitutes a five-wave impulse pattern at one larger degree of trend, and a three-wave corrective movement at the same scale must follow. Figure 28.2 shows this larger-scale pattern in detail. As the illustration shows, waves of any degree in any series can be subdivided and resubdivided into waves of smaller degree or expanded into waves of larger degree. This structure is an example of "fractal" geometry, incorporating self-similarity and scaling symmetry, and is consistent with numerous scientific insights into the nature of growth and evolution.

Three essential rules govern the interpretation of these patterns:

1. A second wave may never retrace more than 100 percent of a first wave; for example, in a bull market, the low of the second wave may not go below the beginning of the first wave.

2. The third wave is never the shortest wave in an impulse sequence; often, it is the longest (see "Extensions" below).

3. A fourth wave can never enter the price range of a first wave, except in one specific type of wave pattern (see "Diagonal Triangles" below).

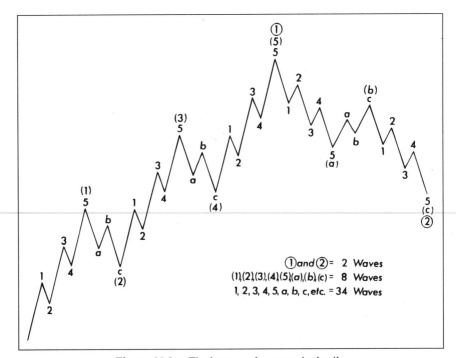

Figure 28.2. The larger scale pattern in detail.

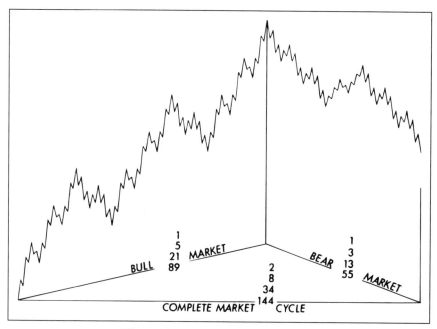

Figure 28.3. A complete market cycle.

Overall, the form of market movements is essentially the same, irrespective of the size or duration of the movements. Furthermore, smaller scale movements link up to create larger scale movements possessing the same basic form. Conversely, large scale movements consist of smaller scale subdivisions with which they share a geometric similarity. Because these movements link up in increments of five waves and three waves, they generate sequences of numbers that the analyst can use (along with the rules of wave formation) to help identify the current state of pattern development, as shown in Figure 28.3.

Impulse Waves—Variations

Extensions

In any given five-wave sequence, a tendency exists for one of the three impulse subwaves (i.e., wave 1, wave 3 or wave 5) to be an *extension*—an elongated movement, usually with internal subdivisions. At times, these subdivisions are of nearly the same amplitude and duration as the larger degree waves of the main impulse sequence, giving a total count of nine waves of similar size rather than the normal count of five for the main sequence. In a nine-wave sequence, it is sometimes difficult to identify which wave is extended. However, this is usually irrelevant, since a count of nine and a count of five have the same technical significance. Figure 28.4 shows why this is so, as examples of extensions in various wave positions make it clear that the overall significance is the same in each case.

Extensions can provide a useful guide to the lengths of future waves. Most impulse sequences contain extensions in only one of their three impulsive subwaves. Thus, if the first and third waves are of about the same magnitude, the fifth wave probably will be extended, especially if volume during the fifth wave is greater than during the third. On the other hand, if wave three already has extended, wave five should be simply constructed and should resemble wave one.

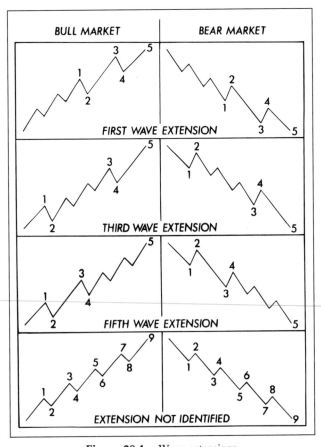

Figure 28.4. Wave extensions.

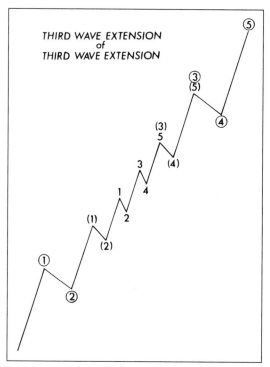

Figure 28.5. Wave extensions.

Extensions may also occur within extensions. Although extended fifth waves are not uncommon, extensions of extensions occur most often within third waves, as shown in Figure 28.5.

Diagonal Triangles

Two types of diagonal triangle have been identified. Both types are found relatively rarely, and each has highly specific implications for future market movements. (These formations should not be confused with the more common corrective triangles found in fourth wave positions within impulse waves and B wave positions within corrections (see "Corrective Waves" below).

The diagonal triangle type 1 occurs only in fifth waves and in C waves, and it signals that the preceding move has "gone too far too fast," as Elliott put it. Essentially a rising wedge formation defined by two converging trendlines, type 1 diagonal triangles indicate exhaustion of the larger movement. Unlike other impulse waves, all of the patterns' subwaves, including waves 1, 3 and 5, consist of three-wave movements, and their

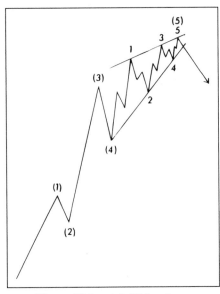

Figure 28.6. A bullish pattern.

fourth waves often enter the price range of their first waves, as shown in Figures 28.6 and 28.7.

A rising diagonal triangle type 1 is bearish, since it is usually followed by a sharp decline, at least to the level where the formation began. In contrast, a falling diagonal type 1 is bullish, since an upward thrust usually follows.

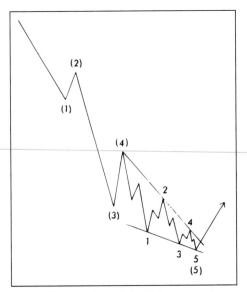

Figure 28.7. A bearish pattern.

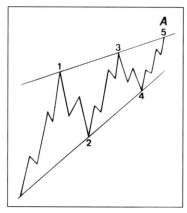

Figure 28.8

The diagonal triangle type 2 occurs even more rarely than type 1. This pattern, found in first wave or A wave positions in very rare cases, resembles a diagonal type 1 in that it is defined by converging trendlines and its first wave and fourth wave overlap, as shown in Figure 28.8. However, it differs significantly from type 1 in that its impulsive subwaves (waves 1, 3 and 5) are normal, five-wave impulse waves, in contrast to the three-wave subwaves of type 1. This is consistent with the message of type 2 diagonal triangle, which signals continuation of the underlying trend, in contrast to the type 1's message of termination of the larger trend.

Failures (Truncated Fifths)

Elliott used the word *failure* to describe an impulse pattern in which the extreme of the fifth wave fails to exceed the extreme of the third wave. Figures 28.9 and 28.10 show examples of failures in bull and bear markets. As the illustration shows, the truncated fifth wave contains the necessary impulsive (i.e., five-wave) substructure to complete the larger movement. However, its failure to surpass the previous impulse wave's extreme signals weakness in the underlying trend, and a sharp reversal usually follows.

Corrective Waves

Stock market swings of any degree tend to move more easily *with* the trend of one larger degree than *against* it. As a result, corrective waves can be highly complex and "choppy" and often are difficult to interpret precisely until they are finished. Thus, the terminations of corrective waves are less predictable than those of impulse waves, and the wave analyst must exer-

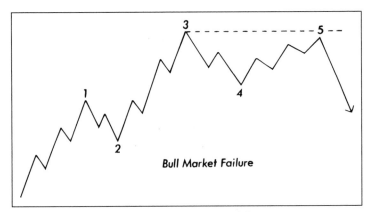

Figure 28.9.   Bull market failure.

cise greater caution when the market is in a meandering, corrective mood than when prices are in a clearly impulsive trend. Moreover, while only three main types of impulse wave exist, there are a total of ten basic corrective wave patterns, and all can link up to form extended corrections of great complexity.

The single most important thing to remember about corrections is that they can never be "fives." Only impulse waves can be fives. Thus, an initial five-wave movement against the larger trend is never a complete correction, but only part of it.

Corrective patterns fall into four main categories:

1. Zigzags (5-3-5)
2. Flats (3-3-5)
3. Triangles (3-3-3-3-3)
4. Combined structures

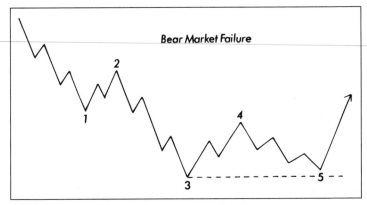

Figure 28.10.   Bear market failure.

Zigzags

A *zigzag* is a simple three-wave pattern, subdivided into a 5-3-5 structure, in which the extreme of wave B remains a significant distance from the beginning of wave A. Figures 28.11-28.14 show examples in bull and bear markets. (A zigzag rally within a bear market is sometimes referred to as an *inverted* zigzag.)

Occasionally, in larger formations, two zigzags can occur in succession, separated by intervening three-wave structures of any type. This produces a *double zigzag,* illustrated in Figure 28.15. Although double zigzags are uncommon, they occur often enough that the analyst should be aware of their existence.

Flats

Flat corrections subdivide as 3-3-5 structures, as shown in Figures 28.16-28.19. The initial movement, wave A, seems to lack sufficient force to develop into a full five waves, as in a zigzag. Wave B appears to share

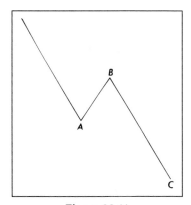

Figure 28.11

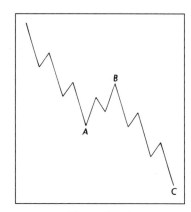

Figure 28.12

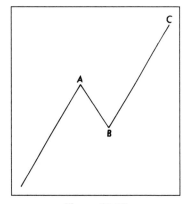

Figure 28.13

Figure 28.14

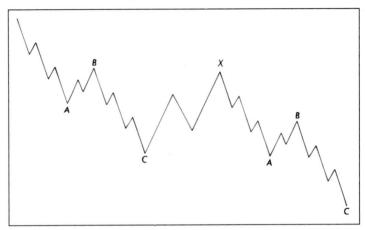

Figure 28.15. Double zigzag.

this lack of countertrend pressure and often ends at or beyond the start of wave A, and wave C usually terminates near the extreme of wave A, rather than significantly beyond it, as in a zigzag.

Flat corrections, overall, do less damage than zigzags to the larger trend. They appear to indicate strength underlying the larger trend and thus often precede or follow extensions. As a rule, the longer the flat, the more dynamic is the next impulse wave.

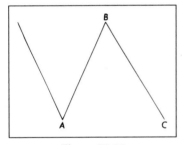

Figure 28.16

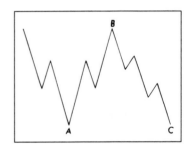

Figure 28.17

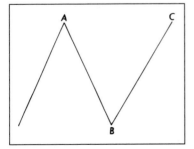

Figure 28.18

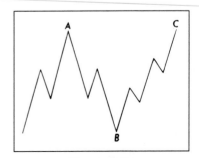

Figure 28.19

Four types of flats have been identified:

1. *Regular,* in which wave B ends at or very slightly beyond the level of the *start* of wave A and wave C ends at or slightly beyond the level of the extreme of wave A.

2. *Expanded,* in which wave B significantly exceeds the level of the start of wave A and wave C significantly exceeds the level of the extreme of wave A (Figures 28.20-28.23).

3. *Irregular,* in which wave B ends near the start of wave A, as in a regular flat, but wave C fails to move all the way to the extreme of wave A (Figures 28.24-28.27).

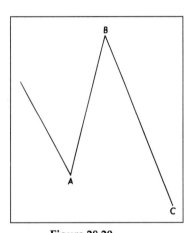

Figure 28.20

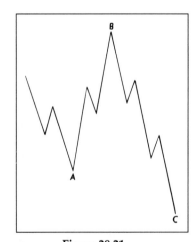

Figure 28.21

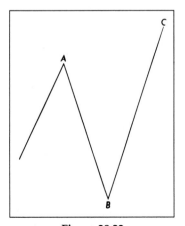

Figure 28.22

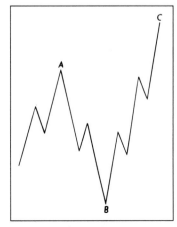

Figure 28.23

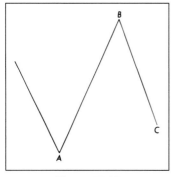

Figure 28.24

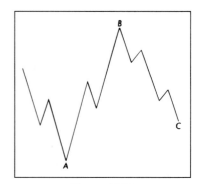

Figure 28.25

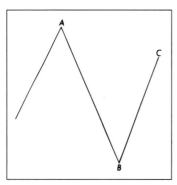

Figure 28.26

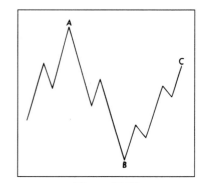

Figure 28.27

4. *Running,* a rare formation in which wave B carries well beyond the level of the start of wave A and wave C fails to carry back past that level. In other words, the end of wave C in a downward correction ends above the beginning of wave A, and in an upward correction below the level of the beginning of wave A (Figure 28.28).

   This formation signals strength in the larger trend and occurs when the market moves so quickly that corrective patterns have no time to develop normally. It is essential that the internal subdivisions of a running correction adhere to the Wave Principle's rules. For example, the B wave must contain only three subwaves and not five, which would probably make it, instead, the first wave of an impulse pattern of the next larger degree.

Triangles

Generally, triangles occur only in positions just prior to the final movement in the direction of the larger trend. They tend to be protracted and reflect a balance of forces that creates a sideways movement, usually associated

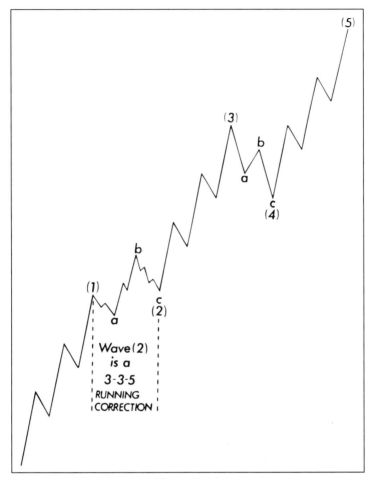

Figure 28.28

with relatively low volume and low volatility. All triangles consist of five waves, labeled A-B-C-D-E, subdivided into three waves each. Four main types exist, as shown in Figure 28.29. (Corrective triangles must not be confused with the impulsive patterns called diagonal triangles (see "Impulse Waves—Variations" above).

The trendlines that contain a triangle usually are highly accurate; that is, touch points rarely fall short of or exceed these boundaries. The one exception is wave E, which often overshoots the trendline, especially in expanding and contracting triangles.

After completion of a triangle, the final impulse wave of the larger trend is usually swift and travels a distance approximately equal to the widest part of the triangle. This movement is known as a *thrust*.

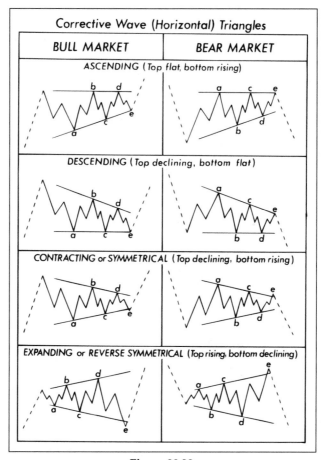

Figure 28.29

Combined Structures

In wave analysis, a zigzag or flat is often referred to as a *three*. Occasionally, these patterns, as well as triangles, may combine into more complex *double three* or *triple three* formations, consisting of two or more "threes" separated by smaller three-wave movements labeled as X waves. Figures 28.30 and 28.31 illustrate the basic structure of these formations. A double three may consist of a flat, a smaller zigzag forming wave X and a second flat, or of a zigzag , a smaller flat in wave X and a second zigzag, or of any similar combination.

The combined structures appear to reflect hesitation in the market, as if stock prices are waiting for economic fundamentals to catch up with investor expectations. Usually, these formations move generally sideways, although Elliott indicated that the entire formation could slant against the

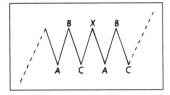

Figure 28.30

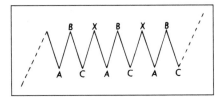

Figure 28.31

larger trend. Action subsequent to a double or triple three often is quite strong.

As far as has been determined, the formations listed here are all that can be identified in the movements of financial markets. As a result of detailed study of a large number of charts at every conceivable time frame, from 15 minute bar charts covering a few days' action to monthly charts covering nearly three centuries of market history, we are convinced that no other formations exist.

Fibonacci Analysis

Perhaps Elliott's most important contribution to the study of patterns in the markets was his discovery that movements of the same degree tend to be related to one another by a specific mathematical ratio, known variously as the *Fibonacci ratio,* the *golden ratio* or *phi.* With this discovery, Elliott was able to place social change, as reflected in the financial markets, into a continuum of evolution reaching from the molecular scale to the cosmological.

The Fibonacci ratio is named after Leonardo Fibonacci of Pisa, an Italian mathematician of the late twelfth and early thirteenth centuries, who introduced Hindu-Arabic numerals to Western Europe in a work titled *Liber Abaci.* In the same book, in a problem concerning the dynamics of population growth in rabbits, he introduced an additive numerical series that has come to be called the Fibonacci sequence in his honor.

To obtain the Fibonacci sequence, begin with 1 and add 1 to it. Take the sum of this operation (2) and add it to the previous term in the sequence (1). Then take the sum of his second operation (3) and add it to the previous term in the sequence (the sum of the first operation, i.e., 2). Continue iterating in this manner, adding the most recent sum to the previous term, which is itself the sum of the two previous terms, etc. This yields the following series of numbers:

$$1, 1, 2, 3, 5, 8, 13, 21, 34, 55, 89, 144, 233, 377,$$
$$610, 987, 1597, 2584, 4181, \text{(etc.)}$$

These numbers exhibit several remarkable relationships, in particular the ratio of any term in the series to the next higher term. This ratio tends asymptotically to 0.618. . . . In addition, the ratio of any term to the next lower term in the sequence tends asymptotically to 1.618, which is the inverse of 0.618. Similarly constant ratios exist between numbers two terms apart, three terms apart and so on. The ratio 0.618, referred to as the Fibonacci ratio, is an irrational number (i.e., it never resolves to a single solution no matter how many decimal places one carries it), calculated as

$$\left(\frac{\sqrt{5} - 1}{2}\right) = 0.6180339$$

Because 3 and 5 are Fibonacci numbers (i.e., numbers in the basic Fibonacci sequence), combinations of 3s and 5s will tend to add up to larger Fibonacci numbers. For example, Elliott's basic 5-3-5-3-5 impulse wave sequence adds up to 21, which is a Fibonacci number. Adding a 5-3-5 corrective wave sequence raises the total to 34, which is also a Fibonacci number. Thus, there are Fibonacci numbers and ratios embedded in the number of waves at various degrees.

The Fibonacci ratio underlies the geometry of the logarithmic spiral, a geometric form found widely in nature. The log spiral's expansion (or contraction) is determined by the cotangent of the angle of the radius vector to the tangent. In the case where that cotangent equals

$$-\left(\frac{\pi}{2}\right) \times \log (0.618)$$

The figure is sometimes referred to as the golden spiral. This figure also possesses the noteworthy property that the ratio of the length of the arc to its diameter is 1.618, the inverse of 0.618.

Golden spirals appear in a variety of natural objects, from seashells to hurricanes to galaxies. Many other natural forms exhibit additional Fibonacci proportions in various ways. In the human body, the bronchial tubes branch fractally in a pattern that exhibits the Fibonacci ratio. The double helix of the DNA molecule possesses precise Fibonacci geometry. Indeed, the Fibonacci ratio occurs at every scale from the molecular to the cosmological and it is most associated with processes of growth.

The financial markets exhibit Fibonacci proportions in a number of ways. As noted earlier, most five-wave sequences contain an extension in one impulse wave. The two nonextended waves tend to be approximately equal in magnitude, and the extended wave tends to be a Fibonacci multiple (most often 1.618 times) of the nonextended waves. Corrective waves tend to retrace a Fibonacci percentage (most often 61.8 percent, 38.2 percent or

23.6 percent) of the preceding impulse wave. Within corrective waves, Fibonacci relationships often exist among the subwaves.

These relationships, combined with Elliott's detailed rules and guidelines, constitute a powerful tool for calculating price targets and placing stops for example, if a corrective wave is expected to retrace 61.8 percent of the preceding impulse wave, an investor might place a stop slightly below that level. This will ensure that if the correction is of a larger degree of trend than expected, the investor will not be exposed to excessive losses. On the other hand, if the correction ends near the target level, this outcome will increase the probability that the investor's preferred wave interpretation is accurate.

Further Study

This discussion has touched on only the most basic concepts of wave analysis. Successful forecasting and trading using the Wave Principle require a thorough knowledge of the method's rules and guidelines. *Elliott Wave Principle: Key to Stock Market Profits,* by A.J. Frost and Robert R. Prechter, Jr. (Elliott Wave International, PO Box 1618, Gainesville, GA 30503, USA, 404-536-0309), is the standard textbook of wave analysis, presenting the highly sophisticated technical analysis method in comprehensive detail.

Conclusion

This concludes our exploration of the main tools currently used by traders. We have covered all types of charts, major chart formations, quantitative methods, theories and studies. Some of these topics may look more familiar to you than others. Few traders are familiar with all the technical tools. Perhaps the mere analysis of all the formations would take too much from the trading time. Luckily, most traders will be able to reach significant signals from a much lighter load of technicals. And, even more, our analysis time has been greatly reduced and our analytical sharpness seriously enhanced by the splendid on-line electronic charting services and weekly printed charts.

What is the best technical combination for you is really only up to you. You have the opportunity to see for yourself what is available in the fascinating world of technical analysis. If you feel familiar and confident with certain techniques, and especially if they prove profitable to you, then you probably got it.

Glossary

Accumulation swing index (ASI)   An oscillator based on the *swing index* (SI). A *buying signal* is generated when the daily high exceeds the previous SI significant high, and a *selling signal* occurs when the daily low dips under the significant SI low.

American-style currency option   An option which may be exercised at any valid business date throughout the life of the option.

Arbitrage   A risk-free type of trading where the same instrument is bought and sold simultaneously in two different markets in order to cash in on the divergence between these markets.

Ascending triangle   A triangle continuation formation with a flat upper trendline and a bottom sloping upward trendline (*see* Triangle).

Ascending triple top   A bullish point and figure chart formation which suggests that the currency is likely to break a resistance line the third time it reaches it. Each new top is higher than the previous one.

At-the-money (ATM) option   An option whose present currency price is approximately equal to the strike price.

Atekubi   A bearish two-day candlestick combination. It consists of a blank bar that closes at the daily high; the current closing price equals the previous day's low. The original day's range is a long black bar.

At par forward spread   Forward price is zero; therefore, the spot price is similar to the forward price. It reflects the fact that the foreign interest rate is similar to the US interest rate for that particular period.

At the price stop-loss order   A stop-loss order which must be executed at the precise requested level, regardless of market conditions.

Average options   Options which refer to the average rate of the underlying currency that existed during the life of the option. This rate becomes the strike in the case of the average strike options, or it becomes the underlying, determining the intrinsic value when compared to a predetermined fixed strike in the case of average rate options. Average options can be based on the spot rate (spot style) or the forward underlying the option (forward style). The average can be calculated arithmetically or geometrically, and the rates can be tabulated with a variety of frequencies.

Balance-of-payments   All the international commercial and financial transactions of the residents of one country.

Bank of Canada (BOC)   The central bank of Canada. It has a tight reign on its currency. The Bank of Canada intervenes frequently both in the Canadian and the United States markets to shore up its Canadian dollar.

Bank of England (BOE)   The central bank of the United Kingdom. It is a less independent central bank. Its decision may be overwritten by the government.

Bank of France (BOF)   The central bank of France. It has a joint responsability with the Ministry of Finance to conduct the domestic monetary policy. Their main goals are noninflationary growth and external account equilibrium.

Bank of Italy (Ufficio Italiano dei Cambi)   The central bank of Italy. It is in charge of the monetary policy, financial intermediaries and foreign exchange. Changes in the discount rates must be approved by the Treasury.

Bank of Japan (BOJ)   The Japanese central bank. Although its Policy Board is still fully in charge of the monetary policy, changes are still subject to the approval of the Ministry of Finance (MOF). The BOJ targets the M2 aggregate.

Bar chart   A type of chart which consists of four significant points: *the high* and *the low* prices, which form the vertical bar, *the opening* price, which is marked with a little horizontal line to the left of the bar, and the closing price, which is marked with a little horizontal line to the right of the bar.

Barrier options (trigger options, cutoff options, cutout options, stop options, down/up-and-outs/ins, knockups)   Options very similar to European-style Vanilla options, except that a second strike price (the *trigger*) is specified which, when reached in the market, automatically causes the option to be expired (*knockout options*) or "inspired" (*knockin options*).

Bearish tasuki   A bearish two-day candlestick combination. It consists of a long blank bar which has a low above the 50 percent of the previous day's long black body, and closes marginally above the previous day's high. The second day's rally is temporary, as it is caused only by profit taking. The sell-off is likely to continue the next day.

Bearish tsutsumi (the engulfing pattern)   A bearish two day candlestick combination. It consists of a second day long black candlestick whose body "engulfs" the previous day's small blank body.

Bilateral grid   An exchange rate system which links all of the central rates of the EMS currencies in terms of the ECU.

Black closing bozu   A bearish candlestick formation which consists of a long black bar (upper shadow).

Black marubozu (shaven head)   A bearish candlestick formation which consists of a long black bar (no shadow).

Black opening bozu   A bearish candlestick formation which consists of a long blank bar (lower shadow).

Black-Scholes fair value model   The original option pricing model which holds that a stock and the call option on the particular stock are comparable investments and thus a riskless portfolio may be created by buying the stock and selling the option on the stock, as a hedge. The movement of the price of the stock will be reflected by the movement of the price of the option, but not necessarily by the same amplitude. Therefore, it is necessary to hold only the amount of the stock to duplicate the movement of the price of the option.

Blank opening bozu   A bullish candlestick formation which consists of a long blank bar (upper shadow).

Blank closing bozu   A bullish candlestick formation which consists of a long blank bar (lower shadow).

Bollinger bands   A quantitative method which combines a moving average with the instrument's volatility. The bands were designed to gauge whether the prices are high or low on relative basis. They are plotted two standard deviations above and below a simple moving average. The bands look like an expanding and contracting envelope model. When the band contracts drastically, the signal is that volatility will expand sharply in the near future. An additional signal is a succession of two top formations, one outside the band followed by one inside. If it occurs above the band, it is a selling signal. When it occurs below the band, it is a buying signal.

Book method   Point and figure chart's original name.

Blank marubozu (shaven head)   A bullish candlestick formation which consists of a long blank bar (no shadows).

Breakaway gap   A price gap which occurs in the beginning of a new trend, many times at the end of a long consolidation period. It may also appear after the completion of major chart formations.

Breakout of a triple top   A bullish point and figure chart formation which suggests that the currency is likely to break a resistance line the third time it reaches it.

Breakout of a triple bottom   A bearish point and figure chart formation which suggests that the currency is likely to break a support line the third time it reaches it.

Breakout of a spread triple top   A bullish point and figure chart formation which suggests that the currency is likely to break a resistance line the third time it reaches it. The currency failed to reach the resistance line once.

Breakout of a spread triple bottom   A bearish point and figure chart formation which suggests that the currency is likely to break a support line the third time it reaches it. The currency failed to reach the support line once.

Bullish tasuki   A bullish two-day candlestick combination. It consists of a long black bar which has a high above the 50 percent of the previous day's long blank body, and closes marginally below the previous day's low.

Box spread   A compound option strategy which consists of four options with a common expiration date: a long call and a short put at one strike price and a long put and a short call at a different strike price.

Bullish tsutsumi (the engulfing bar)   A bullish two-day candlestick combination. It consists of a second day long blank candlestick whose body "engulfs" the previous day's small black body.

Bundesbank   The German central bank, also known as Buba, has the obligation in their charter to preserve the strength of the Deutsche mark and to avoid the possibility of economic chaos. In addition to its domestic obligations, the Bundesbank has had international obligations since 1979 as the front player of the European Monetary System. The Bundesbank is a very independent central bank.

Business firms (establishment) survey   Survey of the payroll, workweek, hourly earnings and the total hours of employment in the nonfarm sector.

Business Inventories   An economic indicator which consists of the items produced and held for future sale.

Butterfly spread   A compound option strategy which consists of a combination of a bull spread and a bear spread, using either calls or puts.

Calendar spread   A combination option of two similar types of options, either calls or puts, with the same strike price but different expiration dates. The dissimilarity between the expiration dates allows this type of spread to capitalize on both the impact of the time decay and the interest rate differentials.

Calendar combination   A compound option strategy which consists of the simultaneous call calendar spread and put calendar spread, in which the strike price of the calls is higher than the strike price of the puts.

Calendar straddle   A compound option strategy which consists of simultaneous buying of a longer term straddle and near term straddle with a common strike price.

Call ratio backspread   A compound option strategy which consists of short calls with a lower strike price and more long calls with a higher strike price. The profit is twofold. The maximum upside profit potential is unlimited. The downside profit potential consists of the total premium received. The maximum loss potential occurs when the currency price reaches the higher strike price at expiration.

Candlestick chart   A type of chart which consists of four major prices: high, low, open and close. The *body (jittai)* of the candlestick bar is formed by the opening and closing prices. To indicate that the opening was lower than the closing, the body of the bar is left blank. If the currency closes below its opening, the body is filled. The rest of the range is marked by two "shadows": the *upper shadow (uwakage)* and the *lower shadow (shitakage)*.

Capacity utilization   An economic indicator which consists of total industrial output divided by total production capability. The term refers to maximum level of output a plant can generate under normal business conditions.

Cardinal square   A Gann technique of forecasting future significant chart points by counting from the all-time low price of the currency. It consists of a square divided by a cross into four quadrants. The all-time low price is housed in the center of the cross. Each of the following higher priced are entered in clockwise order. The numbers positioned in the cardinal cross are the most significant chart points.

Channel line   A parallel line that can be traced against the trendline, connecting the significant peaks in an uptrend, and the significant troughs in a downtrend.

Chaos theory   A theory which holds that statistically noisy behavior may occur randomly, even in simple environments. This seemingly random behavior may be predicted with decreasing accuracy if the source is known.

CHIPS (Clearing House Interbank Payments System)   A computerized system used for foreign exchange dollar settlements.

Christmas tree spread   A compound option strategy which consists of several short options at two or more strike prices.

Classes of options   The types of options: calls and puts.

Commodity Channel Index (CCI)   An oscillator which consists of the difference between the mean price of the currency and the average of the mean price over a predetermined period of time. A *buying signal* is generated when the price exceeds the upper (+100) line, and a *selling signal* occurs when the price dips under the lower (−100) line.

Common gap   A price gap which occurs in relatively quiet periods or in illiquid markets. It has a limited technical significance.

Commodity Futures Trading Commission (CFTC)   An independent agency created by Congress in 1974 with a mandate to regulate commodity futures and options markets in the United States. The CFTC's responsibilities are to ensure the economic utility of futures markets, via competitiveness and efficiency; ensure the integrity of these markets and protect the participants against manipulation, fraud and abusive practices. The Commission, based in Washington, DC., regulates the activities of 285 commodity brokerage firms, 48,211 salespeople, 8017 floor brokers, 1325 commodity pool operators (CPOs), 2733 commodity trading advisers (CTAs) and 1486 introducing brokers (IBs).

Commodity Research Bureau's (CRB) Futures Index   Index formed from the equally weighted futures prices of 21 commodities. The preponderance of food commodities (13 out of 21) makes the CRB Index less reliable in terms of general inflation.

Consumer Price Index (CPI)   An economic indicator which gauges the average change in retail prices for a fixed market basket of goods and services.

Consumer sentiment   A survey of households designed to gauge the individual propensity for spending. There are two studies conducted in this area, one survey by the University of Michigan, and the other by the National Family Opinion for the Conference Board. The confidence index measured by the Conference Board is sensitive to the job market, whereas the index generated by the University of Michigan is not.

Continuation patterns   Technical signals which reinforce the current trends.

Country (sovereign) risk   A trading risk emerging from a government's interference in the foreign exchange markets.

The Council of Ministers   The legislative body of the European Economic Community in charge of making the major policy decisions. It is composed of ministers from all the 12 member nations. The presidency rotates every six months by all the 12 members, in alphabetical order. The meetings take place in Brussels or in the capital of the nation holding the presidency.

Covered interest rate arbitrage   An arbitrage approach which consists of borrowing currency A, exchanging it for currency B, investing currency B for the duration of the loan, and, after taking off the forward cover on maturity, showing a profit on the entire set of deals.

Credit risk   The possibility that an outstanding currency position may not be repaid as agreed, due to a voluntary or involuntary action by a counterparty.

Cross rates   Currencies traded against currencies other than the US dollar. A cross rate is a nondollar currency.

Combination spread (synthetic future)   A compound option strategy which consists of a long call and a short put, or a long put and a short call, with a common expiration date.

Condor spread   A compound option strategy which consists of either four same-type options with a common expiration date—two long options with consecutive strike prices, one short option with an immediately lower strike price and one short option with an immediately higher strike price, or four same type options with a common expiration date—two short options with consecutive strike prices, one long option with an immediately lower strike price and one long option with an immediately higher strike price.

Cost of carry   The interest rate parity, where the forward price is determined by the cost of borrowing money in order to hold the position.

Covered long   A compound option strategy which consists of selling a call against a long currency position. A covered long is synonymous with a short put.

Covered short   A compound option strategy which consists of shorting a put against a short currency position. A covered short is synonymous to a short call.

Cox, Ross and Rubinstein pricing model   An option pricing model which takes into consideration the early exercise provision of the American style options. As it assumes that early exercise will only occur if the advantage of holding the currency exceeds the time value of the option, their binomial method evaluated the call premium by estimating the probability of early exercise for each successive day. The theoretical premium is compared to the holding cost of the cash hedge position, until the option's time value is worth less than the forward points of the currency hedge and the option should be exercised.

Currency call   A contract between the buyer and seller which holds that the buyer has the right, but not the obligation, to buy a specific quantity of a currency at a predetermined price and within a predetermined period of time, regardless of the market price of the currency. The writer assumes the obligation of delivering the specific quantity of a currency at a predetermined price and within a predetermined period of time, regardless of the market price of the currency, if the buyer wants to exercise the call option.

Currency option   A contract between a buyer and a seller, also known as writer, which gives the buyer the right, but not the obligation, of trading a specific quantity of a currency at a predetermined price and within a predetermined period of time, regardless of the market price of the currency, and the seller the obligation of delivering or buying the currency under the predetermined terms, if and when the buyer wants to exercise the option.

Currency put   A contract between the buyer and the seller which holds that the buyer has the right, but not the obligation, to sell a specific quantity of a currency at a predetermined price and within a predetermined period of time, regardless of the market price of the currency. The *writer* assumes the obligation of buying the specific quantity of a currency at a predetermined price and within a predetermined period of time, regardless of the market price of the currency, if the buyer wants to exercise the call option.

Currency fixings   An open auction executed in Europe on a daily basis where all players, regardless of size, are welcome to participate with any amount.

Currency futures   A specific type of forward outright deal with regard to the expiration date and the size of the amount.

Current account balance   The broadest current dollar measure of the United States trade which incorporates services and unilateral transfers into the merchandise trade data.

Daylight position limit   The maximum amount of a certain currency a trader is allowed to carry at any single time, between the regular trading hours.

Dead cross   An intersection of two consecutive moving averages which move in opposite directions and which should technically be disregarded.

Dealing systems   On-line computers which link the contributing banks around the world on a one-on-one basis.

Delta (Δ)   (1) The change of the currency option price relative to a change in the currency price; (2) the *hedge ratio* between the option contracts and the currency futures contracts necessary to establish a neutral hedge; (3) the *theoretical or equivalent share position*. In this case, delta is the number of currency futures contracts a call buyer is long or a put buyer is short. Delta ranges between 0 and 1.

Descending triple bottom   Bearish point and figure chart formation which suggests that the currency is likely to break a support line the third time it reaches it. Each new bottom is lower than the previous one.

Descending triangle   A triangle continuation formation with a flat lower trendline and a downward sloping upper trendline (*see* Triangle).

Diagonal spread   A compound option strategy which consists of several same-type options, in which the long side and the short side have different strike prices and different expirations.

Diamond   A minor reversal pattern which resembles a diamond shape.

Directional Movement Index   A signal of trend presence in the market. The line simply rates the price directional movement on a scale of 0 to 100. The higher the number, the better the trend potential of a movement, and vice versa.

Direct dealing   An aggressive approach in which banks contact each other outside the brokers market.

Discount forward spread   A forward price which is deducted from a spot price to calculate a forward price. It reflects the fact that the foreign interest rate is lower than the US interest rate for that particular period.

Discount rate   The interest rate at which eligible depository institutions may borrow funds directly from the Federal Reserve Banks. This rate is controlled by the Federal Reserve and is not subject to trading.

Discretion for range to trader stop-loss order   A stop-loss order which gives the trader a number of discretionary pips within which the order has to be filled.

Double bottoms   A bullish reversal pattern which consists of two bottoms of approximately equal heights. A parallel (resistance) line is drawn against a line which connects the two bottoms. The break of the resistance line generates a move equal in size with the price difference between the average height of the bottoms and the resistance line.

Double tops   A bearish reversal pattern which consists of two tops of approximately equal heights. A parallel (support) line is drawn against a resistance line which connects the two tops. The break of the support line generates a move equal in size with the price difference between the average height of the tops and the support line.

Downside tasuki gap   A bearish two day candlestick combination. It consists of a second day blank bar which closes an overnight gap opened on the previous day by a black bar.

Downward breakout of a bearish support line   A bearish point and figure chart formation which confirms the currency's breakout of a support line the third time it reaches it.

Downward breakout of a bullish support line   A bearish point and figure chart formation which confirms the currency's breakout of a support line the third time it reaches it. The support line is sloped upward.

Downward breakout from a consolidation formation   A bearish point and figure chart formation which resembles the inverse flag formation. A valid downside breakout form the consolidation formation has a price target equal in size with the length of the previous downtrend.

Durable Goods Orders   An economic indicator which measures the changes in sales of products with a life span in excess of three years.

Economic exposure   Reflects the impact of foreign exchange changes on the future competitive position of a company.

Elliott Wave Principle   A system of empirically derived rules for interpreting action in the markets. It refers to a five-wave/three-wave pattern which forms one complete bull market/bear market cycle of eight waves.

Envelope model   A band created by two winding parallel lines above and below a short term moving average will create a band bordering most price fluctuations. When the upper band is penetrated, a *selling signal* occurs, and when the lower band is penetrated, a *buying signal* is generated. Since the signals generated by the envelope model are very short term geared and they occur many times against the ongoing direction of the market, speed of execution is paramount.

Eurocurrency   Currency deposit outside the country of origin.

Eurodollars   US dollar deposits placed in commercial banks outside the United States.

European Coal and Steel Community   European entity established in 1951 by the Treaty of Paris, with the purpose of promoting the inter-European trade in general, and to eliminate restrictions on the trade of coal and raw steel in particular. This community was formed by West Germany, France, Italy, the Netherlands, Belgium, Luxembourg and Great Britain.

European Commission   The executive body of the European Economic Community in charge of making and observing the enforcement of policy. It consists of 23 departments, such as foreign affairs, competition policy and agriculture. Each country selects its own representatives for four year terms, but the commissioners may only act for the benefit of the community. The commission is based in Brussels and consists of 17 members.

European Court of Justice   The European Economic Community body in charge of settling disputes between the EC and member nations. It consists of 13 members and it is based in Luxembourg.

European currency unit   A basket of the member currencies. As a composite unit, the ECU consists of all the European Community currencies, which are individually weighted. It was created by the European Monetary System with the eventual goal of replacing the individual European member currencies.

European Economic Community   A community established by the Treaty of Rome in 1957, with the goals eliminating customs duties and any barriers against the transit of capital, services and people among the member nations. The signatories were West Germany, France, Italy, the Netherlands, Belgium and Luxembourg.

European Joint Float Agreement   European monetary system established in April 1972 by the EC members: West Germany, France, Italy, the Netherlands, Belgium and Luxembourg. Great Britain, Ireland and Denmark were admitted by January, 1973. The agreement allowed the member currencies to move within a 2.25 percent fluctuation band (nicknamed the *snake*). As a joint group, the agreement allowed these currencies to gyrate within a 4.5 percent band (nicknamed the *tunnel*). The entire agreement was known as *the snake in the tunnel.*

European Monetary System   European monetary system established in March, 1979 by seven full members: West Germany, France, the Netherlands, Belgium, Luxembourg, Denmark and Ireland. Great Britain did not participate in all of the arrangements and Italy joined under special conditions. New members: Greece in 1981 and Spain and Portugal in 1986. Great Britain joined the Exchange Rate Mechanism in 1990. Also in 1990, West Germany became Germany as a result of its political unification with East Germany.

European Monetary Cooperation Fund   EMS fund established to manage the EMS credit arrangements.

European Monetary Institute (EMI)   The new European Central Bank created to govern the EMS. As of March, 1994 it did not have any power over inter-EMS monetary policy.

European Parliament   The European Economic Community body in charge of reviewing and amending legislative proposals. It has the power to reject the budget proposals. It consists of 518 members who are elected. It is based in Luxembourg, but the sessions take place in Strasbourg or Brussels.

European Payment Union   European entity instituted in 1950 to facilitate the inter-European settlements of international trade transactions.

European-style currency option   An option which may only be exercised on the expiry date.

European Union Treaty Treaty signed by the 12 EMS members on February 1992 in the Dutch city of Maastricht, with the stated goal of a "closer union among the peoples of Europe."

Exchange for physical (EFP) Consists of deals executed in the cash market, outside the exchanges, for amounts equivalent to the currency futures amount, on forward outright prices valued for the futures' expiration. EFPs are generally quoted by commercial and investment banks, even during regular trading hours.

Exchange rate risk Foreign exchange risk which is the effect of the continuous shift in the world wide market supply and demand balance on an outstanding foreign exchange position.

Exchange rate risk Trading risk pertinent to the market fluctuation.

Exhaustion gap Price gap which occurs at the top or at the bottom of a V reversal formation. The trend changes direction in a rather uncharacteristically quick manner.

Expanding (broadening) triangle A triangle continuation formation which looks like a horizontal mirror image of a triangle, where the tip of the triangle is next to the original trend, rather than its base (*see* Triangle).

Exercise (strike price) The price at which the underlying currency will be delivered upon exercise.

Expiry date The delivery date.

Exponentially smoothed moving average A moving average which also takes into account the previous price information of the underlying currency.

Factory orders An economic indicator which refers to the total orders of durable and nondurable goods. The nondurable goods orders consist of food, clothing, light industrial products and products designed for the maintenance of the durable goods.

FASB # 8 (Financial Accounting Standards Board's Statement Number 8) The original accounting rules regarding foreign exchange were standardized in 1975, which set the procedures for foreign currency translations into US dollars in the consolidated balance sheets of US multinational corporations.

FASB # 52 (Financial Accounting Standards Board's Statement Number 52) A complex set of rules, designed in 1981, whose main objective is to move the foreign exchange P&L from the current income into the shareholders' equity.

Federal funds (fed funds) Immediately available reserve balances at the federal reserves. The fed funds are widely used by commercial banks or large corporations to lend to each other on an overnight basis. Although their level is established by the Fed, the prices fluctuate because they are being traded in the market.

Federal Reserve The central bank of the United States. It was established in 1913, when Congress passed the *Federal Reserve Act*. The Act held that role of the

Federal Reserve was "to furnish an elastic currency, to afford the means of rediscounting commercial paper, to establish a more effective supervision of banking in the United States, and for other purposes."

Federal Open Market Committee (FOMC)   A committee established in 1935, through the Banking Act, to replace the *Open Market Policy Conference (OMPC)*. Currently active.

Federal Reserve Board   The board consists of a Governor and four other regular members. The Secretary of the Treasury and the Comptroller of the Currency are closely consulted. The 12 regional Federal Reserve Banks around the country have sufficient autonomy to manage financial conditions in their districts. They are also managed by governors.

Fedwire   An automated communications and settlement system linking the Federal Reserve banks with other banks and with depository institutions.

Fence   A compound option strategy which consists of either a long currency position, a long out-of-money put and a short out-of-money call, where the options have the same expiration date (*risk conversion*), or a short currency position, a short out-of-money put and a long out-of-money call, where the options have the same expiration date (*risk reversal*).

Fibonacci percentage retracements   Price retracements of .382 and .618, or approximately 38 percent and 62 percent.

Fibonacci ratio   0.618 and 0.312.

Fibonacci sequence   Takes a sequence of numbers which begins with 1 and adds 1 to it, takes the sum of this operation (2) and adds it to the previous term in the sequence (1). Then it takes the sum of this second operation (3) and adds it to the previous term in the sequence (the sum of the first operation, i.e., 2). The Fibonacci sequence continues iterating in this manner, adding the most recent sum to the previous term, which is itself the sum of the two previous terms, etc. This yields the following series of numbers: 1 1 2 3 5 8 13 21 34 55 89 144 233 377 610 987 1597 2584 4181 (etc.)

FINEX   A currency market part of the New York Cotton Exchange (NYCE), the oldest futures exchange in New York. The exchange lists futures on the European Currency Unit and the USDX®, a basket of 10 currencies: Deutsche mark, Japanese yen, French franc, British pound, Canadian dollar, Italian lira, Dutch guilder, Belgian franc, Swedish krona, and Swiss franc.

Fisher effect   A theory holding that the nominal interest rate consists of the real interest rate plus the expected rate of inflation.

Flag   A continuation formation which resembles the outline of a flag. It consists of a brief consolidation period within a solid and steep upward trend or downward trend. The consolidation itself tends to be sloped in the opposite direction from the slope of the original trend, or simply flat. The consolidation is bordered by a support line and a resistance line, which are parallel to each other or very mildly converging, making it look like a flag (parallelogram).

The previous sharp trend is known as the *flagpole*. Once the currency resumes its original trend by breaking out of the consolidation, the price objective is the total length of the flagpole, measured from the breakout price level.

Floor traders (locals)   Exchange members who execute their own trades by being physically present in the pit or place for futures trading.

Floor brokers   Any individuals on the exchange floor engaged in executing orders for another person. They may also trade for their own account, with the primary responsibility of executing the customers' orders first. Brokers are licensed by the federal government.

Foreign exchange   The mechanism which values foreign currencies in terms of another currency.

Foreign exchange exposure   The potential effect of currency fluctuations on shareholders' equity.

Foreign exchange brokers   Intermediaries among banks who bring together buyers and sellers to the market, optimize the price they show to their customers and do not take positions for themselves.

Foreign exchange rate   The price of one currency in terms of another.

Forward outright   Foreign exchange deal which matures at a day past the spot delivery date (generally two business days).

Forward spread (forward points or forward pips)   Forward price used to adjust a spot price to calculate a forward price. It is based on the current spot exchange rate, interest rate differential and the number of days to delivery.

Fractal geometry   Geometry theory which refers to the fact that certain irregular objects have a fractal number of dimensions. In other words, an object cannot fill an integer number of dimensions.

French-West German Treaty of Cooperation   A treaty, signed in 1963 by President Charles de Gaulle and Chancellor Konrad Adenauer, which established that West Germany will lead economically through the cold war, and France, the former diplomatic powerhouse, will provide the political leadership.

Fuzzy logic   Method which attempts to weigh the quality of the patterns recognized by neural networks. Since not all patterns have equal financial significance for foreign currency forecasting, this method qualifies the degree of certainty of the results.

Gamma (Γ)   The rate of change of an option's delta, or the sensitivity of the delta.

Gann percentage retracements   The Gann theory focuses mostly on the 3⁄8, 4⁄8 and 5⁄8 or *38 percent, 50 percent and 62 percent* retracement figures.

Gap   The price gap between consecutive trading ranges (i.e., the low of the current range is higher than the high of the previous range).

Genetic algorithms   Method used to optimize a neural network. Trial and error is applied to an evolution like system, which generates natural selection for financial forecasting purposes.

Golden cross   An intersection of two consecutive moving averages which move in the same direction and suggests that the currency will move in the same direction.

GLOBEX   An electronic trading system conceived in 1987 as an after-hours trading system and geared toward global futures trading created through the joint venture of the Chicago Mercantile Exchange (CME), the Chicago Board of Trade (CBT) and Reuters PLC.

Gross national product   The sum of government expenditure, private investment and personal consumption.

Gross national product implicit deflator   Deflator tool designed to adjust the gross national product for inflation. It is calculated by dividing the current dollar GNP figure by the constant dollar GNP figure.

Harami bar   A "wait-and-see" two day candlestick combination. It consists of two consecutive ranges having opposite directions, but it does not matter which one is first. The second day's range results within the previous day's body.

Head and shoulders   A bearish reversal pattern which consists of a series of three consecutive rallies, where the first and third rallies (the shoulders) have about the same height and the middle one (the head) is the highest. The rallies are based on the same support line, known as the neckline. When the neckline is broken, the price target is approximately equal in amplitude with the distance between the top of the head and the neckline.

Hedging   A method used to minimize or eliminate the risk of exchange rate fluctuations.

Hoshi (star)   A "wait-and see" two-day candlestick combination. It consists of a tiny body which appears the following day outside the original body. It is not important whether the star reaches the previous day's shadows. The direction of the two consecutive ranges is also irrelevant.

High-low band   A band created by two winding parallel lines above and below a short term moving average will create a band bordering most price fluctuations. The moving average is based on the high and low prices. The resulting two moving averages define the edges of the band. A close above the upper band suggests a buying signal and one below the lower band gives a selling signal.

Households survey   Consists of the unemployment rate, the overall labor force and the number of people employed.

Implied volatility   Method of measuring the volatility by considering the premiums currently trading in the market and calculating the figure based on the level of the option premium.

Industrial production   An economic indicator which consists of the total output of a nation's plants, utilities and mines.

Initiation margin   A margin paid by the trading party in order to trade currency futures. Trader's daily loss cannot exceed the size of this margin.

Interest rate risk   Amount of mismatches and maturity gaps among transactions in the foreign exchange book.

International Fisher effect   Theory holding that investors will hold assets denominated in depreciating currencies only to the extent that the interest rates are sufficiently high to balance the expected currency losses.

International Monetary Market®   The major currency futures and options on currency futures market in the world. It is a division of the Chicago Mercantile Exchange in Chicago.

In-the-money (ITM) call   A call which has the present currency price higher than the strike price.

In-the-money (ITM) put   A put which has the present currency price lower than the strike price.

Intrinsic value   The amount by which an option is in-the-money. In the case of a call, the intrinsic value equals the difference between the underlying currency price and the strike price. In the case of the put, the intrinsic value equals the difference between the strike price and the present currency price, when beneficial.

Inverse head and shoulders   A bullish reversal pattern which consists of a series of three consecutive sell-offs. Among the three consecutive sell-offs, the shoulders have approximately the same amplitude, and the head is the lowest. The formation is based on a resistance line called neckline. After the neckline is penetrated, the target is approximately equal in amplitude with the distance between the top of the head and the neckline.

Irikubi   A bearish two day candlestick combination. It consists of a modified *atekubi bar*. All the characteristics are the same, except that the second day's closing high is marginally higher than the original day's low.

Island reversal   An isolated range or ranges which occur at the tip of a V-formation.

ISO codes   Standardized currency codes developed by the International Organization for Standardization (ISO).

J curve theory   Devaluation of a currency will trigger exports gains in the long term, rather than short term, because of previous contracts, existing inventories and behavior modification.

Jittai   Body of the candlestick (*see* Candlestick charts).

Journal of Commerce Index   Index which consists of the prices of 18 industrial materials and supplies processed in the initial stage of manufacturing, building and energy production. It is more sensitive, as it was designed to signal changes in inflation prior to the other price indexes.

Kabuse (dark cloud cover)   A bearish two day candlestick combination. It consists of a second day long black bar which opens above the high of the previous day's blank bar and closes within the previous day's range (in an uptrend).

Karakasa (hangman at the top, hammer at the bottom)   A bearish candlestick at the top of the trend, bullish at the bottom of the trend. The candlestick can be either blank or black. The body of the candlestick is very small and only half of the length of the shadow.

Kenuki (tweezers)   A "wait-and-see" two day candlestick combination. It consists of consecutive bars which have matching highs or lows. In a rising market, a tweezers top occurs when the highs match. The opposite is true for a tweezers bottom.

Key reversal day   The daily price range on the bar chart of the reversal day fully engulfs the previous day's range, and also the close is outside the preceding day's range.

Kirikomi   A bullish two day candlestick combination. It consists of a blank marubozu bar which opens the second day lower (than the previous low of a long black line) and closes above the 50 percent level of the previous day's range.

Knockouts   A plain vanilla option which goes away if the trigger is reached.

Knockins   A plain vanilla option which does not exist until the trigger is reached.

Koma (spinning tops)   A reversal candlestick formation which consists of a short bar, either blank or black. This candlestick may also suggest lack of direction.

Larry Williams %R   A version of the stochastics oscillator. It consists of the difference between the high price of a predetermined number of days and the current closing price, which difference in turn is divided by the total range. This oscillator is plotted on a reversed 0 to 100 scale. Therefore the bullish reversal signals will occur under 80 percent and the bearish signals will appear above 20 percent. The interpretations are similar to those discussed under stochastics.

Leading indicators index   An economic indicator designed to offer a six to nine months future outlook of economic performance. It consists of the following economic indicators: average workweek of production workers in manufacturing; average weekly claims for state unemployment; new orders for consumer goods and materials (adjusted for inflation); vendor performance (companies receiving slower deliveries from suppliers); contracts and orders for plant and equipment (adjusted for inflation); new building permits issued; change in manufacturers' unfilled orders, durable goods; change in sensitive materials prices; index of stock prices; money supply, adjusted for inflation and the index of consumer expectations.

Line chart   The line connecting single prices for each of the time periods selected.

Linearly weighted moving average   A moving average which assigns more weight to the more recent closings.

Long legged shadows' doji   A reversal candlestick formation which consists of a bar in which the opening and closing prices are equal.

Long straddle   A compound option which consists of a long call and a long put on the same currency, at the same strike price and with the same expiration dates. The maximum loss for the buyer is the sum of the premiums. The upside break-even point is the sum of the strike price and the premium on the straddle. The downside break-even point is the difference between the strike price and the premium on the straddle. The profit is unlimited.

Long strangle   A compound option which consists of a long call and a long put on the same currency, at the different strike prices, but with the same expiration dates. The profit is unlimited.

M1   Money supply measure which is composed of currency in circulation (outside the Treasury, the Fed and depository institutions), travelers checks, demand deposits and other checkable deposits [negotiable order of withdrawal (NOW) accounts, automatic transfer service (ATS) Accounts, etc.].

M2   Money supply measure which consists of M1 plus repurchase agreements, overnight Eurodollars, money market deposit accounts, savings and time deposits (in amounts under $100,000) and balances in general purposes.

M3   Money supply measure which is composed of M2 plus time deposits over $100,000, term Eurodollar deposits and all balances in institutional money market mutual funds.

Margin   The amount of money or collateral deposited by a customer with a broker, by a broker with a clearing member or by a clearing member with the clearinghouse in order to insure the broker or clearinghouse against loss on outstanding futures positions.

Mark-to-market   Daily cash flow system used by the United States futures exchanges to maintain a minimum level of margin equity for a specific currency future or option by calculating the profit and loss at the end of each trading day in each contract position resulting from the price fluctuation.

Matched sale-purchase agreements   Daily operations executed by the Federal Reserve, in which the Fed sells a security for immediate delivery to a dealer or a foreign central bank, with the agreement to buy back the same security at the same price at a predetermined time in the future (generally within seven days). This arrangement amounts to a temporary drain of reserves.

Matching systems   Electronic systems duplicating the traditional brokers market. A price shown by a bank is available to all traders.

Maturity date   The date when the foreign exchange contract expires.

Merchandise trade balance   An economic indicator which consists of the net difference between the exports and imports of a certain economy. The data includes food, raw materials and industrial supplies, consumer goods, autos, capital goods and other merchandise.

Momentum   An oscillator designed to measure the rate of price change, not the actual price level. This oscillator consists of the net difference between the current closing price and the oldest closing price from a predetermined period. The momentum is measured on an open scale around the zero line.

Moving average   An average of a predetermined number of prices over a number of days, divided by the number of entries.

Moving average convergence/divergence (MACD)   An oscillator which consists of two exponential moving averages (other inputs may be chosen by the trader as well) which are plotted against the zero line. The zero line represents the times the values of the two moving averages are identical. The *buying signal* is generated when this intersection is upwards, whereas the *selling signal* occurs when the intersection takes place on the downside.

Moving averages oscillator   An oscillator in which the values of two consecutive moving averages are subtracted from each other (the larger number of days from the previous one) and the new values are plotted.

Naked intervention (unsterilized intervention)   A central bank type of intervention in the foreign exchange market which consists solely of the foreign exchange activity. This type of intervention has a monetary effect on the money supply and a long term effect on foreign exchange.

National Association of Purchasing Managers Index (NAPM)   A survey of 250 industrial purchasing managers, conducted in order to gauge the changes in new orders, production, employment, inventories and vendor delivery speed.

National Futures Association (NFA)   A self-regulatory organization, which consists of futures commission merchants (FCMs), commodity pool operators (CPOs), commodity trading advisers (CTAs), introducing brokers (IBs), leverage transaction merchants (LTMs), commodity exchanges, commercial firms and banks. It is responsible for certain aspects of the regulation of FCMs, CPOs, CTAs, IBs, LTMs, focusing primarily on qualifications and proficiency, financial conditions, retail sales practices and business.

Netting   A process which enables institutions to settle only their net positions with one another at the end of the day, in a single transaction, not trade by trade.

Neural networks   Computer systems which recognize patterns. They may be used to generate trading signals or to be part of trading systems.

Neutral spread (delta neutral spread)   A compound option strategy which consists of a long option position and a short option position which have their respective total delta positions relatively equal.

Next best price stop-loss order   A stop-loss order which must be executed after the requested level was reached.

Nonfarm sector   Jobs in government, federal government, manufacturing, services, construction, mining, retail and others.

Nostro account (clearing account)   The account for each foreign currency in the country of origin maintained by the financial institutions for purchase and receiving (P&R) purposes.

Open interest   The total outstanding position in a currency.

Open Market Investment Committee (OMIC)   Committee established in 1923 in order to coordinate the Reserve Bank operations. It was composed of the Governors of the Federal Reserve Banks in New York, Boston, Philadelphia, Chicago and Cleveland. Not currently active.

Open Market Policy Conference (OMPC)   Committee established in 1930 to replace the OMIC. It consisted of 12 Federal Reserve Banks governors and the members of the Board. Not currently active.

Optimal options   Options which refer to the most favorable rate of the underlying that existed (from the holder's perspective) during the life of the option. This rate becomes the strike in the case of optimal strike options, or it becomes the underlying, determining the intrinsic value when compared to a predetermined fixed strike in the case of optimal rate options. Optimals can be based on the spot rate (spot style) or the forward rate (forward style).

Option currency spread   A long currency option and an offsetting short currency option generally in the same currency.

Option writers   Option sellers.

Out-of-the-money (OTM) call   A call which has the present currency price lower than the strike price.

Out-of-the-money (OTM) put   A put which has the present currency price higher than the strike price.

Overnight position limit   A position kept overnight by traders.

Oscillators   Quantitative methods designed to provide signals regarding the overbought and oversold conditions.

Parabolic system   A stop-loss technical system, based on price and time. The system was devised to supplement the inadvertent gaps of the other trend following systems. Although not technically an oscillator, the parabolic system can be used with the oscillators. *SAR* stands for *stop and reverse*. The stop moves daily in the direction of the new trend. The built-in acceleration factor pushes the SAR to catch up with the currency price. If the new trend fails, the SAR signal will be generated. The name of the system is derived from its parabolic shape, which follows the price gyrations. It is represented by a dotted line. When the parabola is placed under the price, it suggests a long position. Conversely, a price above the parabola indicates a short position.

Pennants   A continuation formation which resembles the outline of a pennant. It consists of a brief consolidation period within a solid and steep upward trend or downward trend. The consolidation itself tends to be sloped in the opposite direction from the slope of the original trend, or simply flat. The consolidation is bordered by a support line and a resistance line, which converge, creating a triangle. The previous sharp trend is known as the pennant pole. Once the currency resumes its original trend by breaking out of the consolidation, the price objective is the total length of the pole, measured from the breakout price level.

Personal income   An economic indicator which consists of the income received by individuals, nonprofit institutions and private trust funds. Some of the components of this indicator are wages and salaries, rental income, dividends, interest earnings and transfer payments (social security, state unemployment insurance and veteran benefits).

Philadelphia Stock Exchange (PHLX)   The oldest US securities exchange which offers currency futures and options on currency futures.

Point and figure chart   A type of chart which plots price activity without regard to time. When the currency moves up, the fluctuations are marked with X's. The moves on the downside are plotted with O's. The direction on the chart will only change if the currency reversed by a certain amount of pips.

Premium   The price of the option paid by the buyer to the seller.

Premium forward spread   Forward price which is added to a spot price to calculate a forward price. It reflects the fact that the foreign interest rate is higher than the US interest rate for that particular period.

Prime rate   The rate that the commercial banks charge customers, which is based on the discount rate.

Producer price index   An economic indicator which gauges the average changes in prices received by domestic producers for their output at all stages of processing.

Purchasing power parity (PPP)   Model of exchange rate determination stating that the price of a good in one country should equal the price of the same good in another country, exchanged at the current rate (*the law of one price*).

Put ratio backspread   A compound option strategy which consists of short puts with a higher strike price and more long puts with a lower strike price. The profit is twofold. The maximum upside profit potential consists of the total premium received. The downside profit potential is unlimited. The maximum loss potential occurs when the currency price reaches the lower strike price at expiration.

Put-call-forward exchange parity (PCFP) theory   A relationship between a call option and a put option established through the forward market. The theory holds that the option of buying the domestic currency with a foreign currency at a certain price X is equivalent to the option of selling the foreign currency with the domestic currency at the same price X. Therefore, the call option in the domestic currency becomes the put option in the other, and vice versa.

Random walk theory   An efficient market hypothesis, stating that prices move randomly versus their intrinsic value. Therefore, no one can forecast market activity based on the available information.

Rate of change   A momentum oscillator in which the oldest closing price is divided into the most recent one.

Ratio call spread   A compound option strategy which consists of a number of long calls with lower strike prices and a larger number of short calls with a higher strike price. The maximum profit is realized when the currency price is at the higher strike price. This combination has two break-even points. The downside break-even point consists of the sum of the lower strike price and the debit, divided by the number of long calls. The upside break-even point consists of the sum of the higher strike price and the maximum profit potential, divided by the number of naked calls. The maximum loss is twofold. The maximum downside risk is the net premium. The upside risk is unlimited.

Ratio put spread   A compound option strategy which consists of a number of long puts with higher strike prices and a larger number of short puts with a lower strike price. The maximum profit is realized when the currency price is at the lower strike price. This combination has two break-even points. The downside break-even point consists of the difference between the lower strike price and the maximum profit potential, divided by the number of naked puts. The upside break-even point consists of the difference between the higher strike price and the debit, divided by the number of long calls. The maximum loss is also twofold. The maximum downside risk is unlimited. The upside risk is the net premium.

Ratio spread   A compound option strategy in which the number of long options is different from the number of short options.

Rectangle   A continuation formation which resembles the outline of a parallelogram. The price objective is the height of the rectangle.

Relative Strength Index   An oscillator which measures the relative changes between the higher and lower closing prices. The RSI is plotted on a 0 to 100 scale. The 70 and 30 values are used as warning signals, whereas values above 85 indicate an overbought condition (*selling signal*), and, under 15, an oversold condition (*buying signal*).

Resistance level   The peaks representing the price level where the supply exceeds the demand.

Reversal patterns   Patterns that occur at the end of the trend, signaling the trend change.

Rounded top (saucer)   A bearish reversal pattern which consists of a very slow and gradual change in the direction of the market.

Rounded bottom   A bullish reversal pattern which consists of a very slow and gradual change in the direction of the market.

Regulation Q   Regulation passed by the Federal Reserve which prohibited payment of interest on demand deposits and prescribed maximum rates banks pay on time deposits. These ceilings had been imposed since 1933 by the United States government. The regulation is not currently in effect.

Replacement risk   A form of credit risk which holds that counterparties of failed banks will find their books unbalanced to the extent of their exposure to the insolvent party. In order to rebalance their books, these banks must enter new transactions.

Repurchase agreements (repos)   Daily operations executed by the Federal Reserve. A repurchase agreement between the Federal Reserve and a government securities dealer consists of the Fed's purchasing a security for immediate delivery, with the agreement to sell the same security back at the same price at a predetermined date in the future (usually within 15 days). This arrangement amounts to a temporary injection of reserves in the banking system.

Rollover (tomorrow/next or tom/next) swap   A swap designed for spot trades' maintenance. It was designed to change the old spot date to the current spot date (on the front office's side) and to enable the bank to make the payments to the counterparty (on the back office's side).

Runaway or measurement gap   A price gap which occurs within solid trends. It is also called a measurement gap because it tends to occur about midway through the life of a trend.

Sangu (three gaps)   A reversal candlestick method applicable in either a steeply rising or falling market, where the daily limits will break the trading. The theory holds that after the third gap, the market will reverse at least to the second gap.

Sanpei (three parallel bars)   A reversal candlestick combination. It refers to the similarity of direction and velocity of three consecutive bars, as otherwise, all the entries are parallel. They generate a reversal formation after an extended rally. When bullish, the formation is known as the *three soldiers*. When bearish, the name is the *three crows.*

Sanpo (three methods)   A candlestick combination which advises that retracements are in order before the market will reach new highs and new lows.

Short straddle   A compound option which consists of a short call and a short put on the same currency, at the same strike price and with the same expiration dates. The maximum profit consists of the combined premium of the two individual options. The loss occurs once the level of the premium is overpassed by the currency swing and is unlimited.

Short strangle   A compound option which consists of a short call and a short put on the same currency, with the same expiration dates, but with different strike prices. The maximum profit consists of the combined premium of the two individual options. The loss is unlimited.

Simple moving average or arithmetic mean   An average of a predetermined number of prices over a number of days, divided by the number of entries.

Sansen (three rivers) method   A reversal candlestick combination. It consists of three daily entries. The first day is a long blank bar (a bullish move), followed by a bullish but short ranged one day island and it ends with a bearish long black line.

Sanzan (three mountains)   A reversal candlestick combination. It consists of a triple top formation.

Sashikomi   A bearish two day candlestick combination. It consists of a modified irikubi bar. The difference is that the opening of the second day's blank bar is much lower than that of the irikubi bars. Despite the wider gap thus formed, the blank candlestick only closes just above the previous day's low.

Settlement risk   A form of credit risk which may occur due to the time zones separating the nations. Payment may be made to a party which will declare insolvency (or be declared insolvent, whatever the case may be) immediately after, but prior to executing its own payments.

Shitakage   Lower shadow of the candlestick (*see* Candlestick charts).

Slow stochastics   A version of the original stochastic oscillator. The new slow %K line consists of the original %D line. The new slow %D line formula is calculated off the new %K line.

Snake   The nickname of the European Joint Float Agreement's 2.25 percent fluctuation band of the European currencies against each other, due to its curvaceous movement.

Speedlines   Support or resistance lines, which divide the range of the trend in thirds on a vertical line. The two resulting speedlines are plotted by using as coordinates the origin and the $\frac{1}{3}$ and $\frac{2}{3}$ prices respectively.

Spot deal   A foreign exchange deal which consists of a bilateral contract between a party delivering a certain amount of a currency against receiving a certain amount of another currency from a second counterparty, based on an agreed exchange rate, within two business days of the deal date. The exception is the Canadian dollar, in which the spot delivery is executed within one business day.

Spot next (S/N)   A foreign exchange deal which matures one business day past the spot date, or three business days.

Sterilized intervention   A central bank type of intervention in the foreign exchange market which consists of a sale of government securities which offsets the reserve injection which occurs due to the foreign exchange intervention. The money market activity sterilizes the impact of the foreign exchange intervention on the money supply. Sterilized interventions have a short to medium term effect.

Stochastics   An oscillator which consists of two lines called %K and %D. Visualize %K as the plotted instrument and %D as its moving average. The resulting lines are plotted on a 1 to 100 scale. Just like in the case of the RSI, the 70 percent and 30 percent values are used as warning signals. The *buying* (*bullish reversal*) *signals* occur under 10 percent and the *selling* (*bearish reversal*) *signals* come into play above 90 percent.

Strike price   *See* Exercise price.

Support level   The troughs representing the level where the demand exceeds the supply.

Symmetrical triangle   A triangle continuation formation in which the and resistance lines are symmetrical (*see* Triangle).

Swap deal   A foreign exchange deal which consists of a spot deal and a forward outright deal. A party simultaneously buys and sells (or sells and buys) the same amount of a currency with the another counterparty, where the two legs of the transaction mature on different dates (one of the dates being the spot date) and are traded at different exchange rates (one of the exchange rates being the spot rate). Exceptions may be made with regard to the value dates (forward-forward) and amount (different amounts).

SWIFT (Society of Worldwide Interbank Financial Telecommunications)   An automated system set up to send standardized payment instructions for foreign currencies among international banks.

Swing Index (SI)   A momentum oscillator which is plotted on a scale of −100 to +100. The spikes reaching the extremes suggest reversal

Synthetic call option   A combination of a long currency and a long currency put.

Synthetic put option   A combination of a short currency and a long currency call.

Tan book   An economic report prepared by the Federal Reserve for FOMC meetings.

Tankan economic survey   The Japanese equivalent of the American tan book which is released by the Federal Reserve. The survey is released on a quarterly basis.

Technical analysis   The chart study of past behavior of commodity prices for forecasting their future performance.

Theory of elasticities   A model of exchange rate determination stating that the exchange rate is simply the price of foreign exchange which maintains the BOP in equilibrium. The degree to which the exchange rate responds to a change in the trade balance depends entirely on the elasticity of demand to a change in price.

Theta (T) or time decay   Occurs as the very slow or nonexistent movement of the currency triggers losses in the option's theoretical value.

Three Buddha top formation   A reversal candlestick combination. It consists of a head and shoulders formation, or three consecutive rallies in which the first and the third are of approximately the same height, and the second is the highest.

Threshold of divergence   A safety feature for the EMS which creates an emergency exit for currencies which become the singular focus of various adverse forces. The threshold of divergence indicates when the specific country with the pressured currency should take additional steps other than simple central bank intervention in the foreign exchange markets.

Time decay   *See* theta.

Time value (time premium or extrinsic value)   The difference between the option premium and its intrinsic value.

Tomorrow/next (T/N) deal   A foreign exchange deal which matures the next business day, or one day prior to the spot date.

Tonbo (dragonfly)   A reversal candlestick formation.

Tohbu (gravestone doji)   A reversal candlestick formation.

Traditional (Charles Dow) percentage retracements   ⅓, ½ and ⅔, or *33 percent, 50 percent* and *66 percent.*

Transaction exposure   Potential profit and loss generated by current foreign exchange transactions.

Translation exposure   The risk of change of the consolidated corporate earnings as a result of past volatility in the base currency.

Trend   The general direction of the market, as shown by the significant peaks and troughs of the currency fluctuations.

Trendline   A straight line connecting the significant highs (peaks) in a downtrend, and the significant lows (troughs) in an uptrend.

Triangles   A continuation formation which resembles the outline of a pennant, but without the pole. It consists of a brief consolidation period within a solid and steep upward trend or downward trend. The consolidation itself tends to be sloped in the opposite direction from the slope of the original trend, or simply flat. The consolidation is bordered by converging support and resistance lines, making it look like a triangle. Once the currency resumes its original trend by breaking out of the consolidation, the price objective is the height of the triangle, measured from the breakout price level.

Triple top   A bearish reversal pattern which consists of three tops of approximately equal heights. A parallel—support—line is drawn against a resistance line which connects these tops. The break of the support line generates a move equal in size with the price difference between the average height of the tops and the support line.

Triple bottom   A bullish reversal pattern which consists of three bottoms of approximately equal heights. A parallel—resistance—line is drawn against a line which connects these tops. The break of the resistance line generates a move equal in size with the price difference between the average height of the bottoms and the resistance line.

The tunnel   The nickname of the European Joint Float Agreement's $4\frac{1}{2}$ percent total fluctuation band of the European currencies.

TRIX Index   An oscillator which consists of one day ROC calculation of a triple exponentially smoothed moving average of the closing price.

Unemployment rate   An economic indicator released as a percentage which is calculated as the ratio between the difference of the total labor force and the employed labor force, divided by the total labor force.

Upside gap tasuki   Bullish two-day candlestick combination. It consists of a second day black bar which closes an overnight gap opened on the previous day by a blank bar.

Upward breakout of a bullish resistance line   Bullish point and figure chart formation which confirms the currency's breakout of a resistance line the third time it reaches it.

Upward breakout of a bearish resistance line   Bullish point and figure chart formation which confirms the currency's breakout of a resistance line the third time it reaches it. The resistance line is sloped downward.

Upward breakout from a consolidation formation   Bullish point and figure chart formation which resembles the flag formation. A valid upside breakout from the consolidation formation has a price target equal in size with the length of the previous uptrend.

USDX   Currency index which consists of the weighted average of the prices of ten foreign currencies against the US dollar: Deutsche mark, Japanese yen, French franc, British pound, Canadian dollar, Italian lira, Dutch guilder, Belgian franc, Swedish krona and Swiss franc.

Uwakage   Upper shadow of the candlestick (*see* Candlestick charts).

Value at risk   The expected loss from an adverse market movement, with a specified probability over a particular period of time.

Variation (maintenance) margin   Margin paid by the trading party in order to fully cover any unrealized loss. It must be posted in cash by any trader holding an overnight position with a negative P&L. It must be kept on deposit at all times.

Vega (ς)   The sensitivity of the theoretical value of an option to a change in volatility.

Velocity of money   The rate at which money is turning over on an annual basis to facilitate income transactions.

Vertical bull spread   An option combination whose theoretical value will rise to a predetermined maximum profit if the price of underlying currency rises and whose maximum loss is also predetermined.

Vertical bull call spread   A compound option strategy of two options with a common expiration date, where one option is a long call with a lower strike price and the other is a short call with a higher strike price. The buyer's maximum profit consists of the dollar difference between the two strike prices, minus the total premium paid. The break-even point is calculated as the sum of the lower strike price and the total premium. The maximum loss is limited to the premium paid for the two options.

Vertical bull put spread   A compound option strategy of two options with a common expiration date, where one option is a long put with a lower strike price and the other is a short put with a higher strike price. The buyer's maximum profit consists of the net premium paid for the two options (one paid, the other received). The break-even point is calculated as the difference between the higher strike price and the total premium received. The maximum loss is limited to the dollar difference between the two strike prices, minus the total premium received.

Vertical bear spread An option combination whose theoretical value will decline to a predetermined maximum profit if the price of underlying currency declines and whose maximum loss is also predetermined.

Vertical bear put spread A compound option strategy of two options with a common expiration date, where one option is a long put with a higher strike price and the other is a short put with a lower strike price. The buyer's maximum profit consists of the dollar difference between the two strike prices, minus the total premium paid. The break-even point is calculated as the difference between the higher strike price and the total premium. The maximum loss is limited to the premium paid for the two options.

Vertical bear call spread A compound option strategy of two options with a common expiration date, where one option is a short call with a lower strike price and the other is a long call with a higher strike price. The seller's maximum profit is limited to the premium paid for the two options. The break-even point is calculated as the sum of the lower strike price and the total premium. The maximum loss consists of the dollar difference between the two strike prices, minus the total premium received.

Vertical spread A compound option which consists of two similar options (i.e., calls or puts), one being bought and the other sold, on the same currency with the same expiration date, but with different strike prices.

Volatility The degree to which the price of currency tends to fluctuate within a certain period of time.

V-formations (spikes) Reversal formation which shows sudden trend changes and is accompanied by a heavy trading volume. This pattern may include a key reversal day, or an island reversal and an exhaustion gap.

Volume The total amount of currency traded within a period of time, usually one day.

Vostro account A nostro account from the point of view of the counterparty.

Wedges A continuation formation which resembles the outline of a pennant, but without the pole. It consists of a brief consolidation period within a solid and steep upward trend or downward trend. The consolidation is sharply angled in the opposite direction from the slope of the original trend. The consolidation is bordered by a support line and a resistance line which converge, making it look like a sharply angled triangle. Once the currency resumes its original trend by breaking out of the consolidation, the price objective is the height of the wedge, measured from the breakout price level.

Appendix A

World Currencies and Their Swift Codes

Afghanistan	Afghani	AFA
Albania	Lek	ALL
Algeria	Algerian dinar	DZD
American Samoa	US dollar	USD
Andorra	Andorran peseta	ADP
	Spanish peseta	ESP
Angola	New kwanza	AON
Anguilla	E. Caribbean dollar	XCD
Antigua, Barbuda	E. Caribbean dollar	XCD
Argentina	Argentina peso	ARS
Armenia	Russian ruble	RUR
Aruba	Aruban guilder	AWG
Australia	Australian dollar	AUD
Austria	Austrian schilling	ATS
Bahamas	Bahamian dollar	BSD
Bahrain	Bahraini dollar	BHD
Bangladesh	Taka	BDT
Barbados	Barbados dollar	BBD
Belgium	Belgian franc	BEF
Belize	Belize dollar	BZD
Benin	CFA franc	XOF

Bermuda	Bermudian dollar	BMD
Bhutan	Ngultrum	BTN
	Indian rupee	INR
Bolivia	Boliviano	BOB
Bosnia-Herzegovina	Yugoslavia dinar	YUN
Botswana	Pula	BWP
Brazil	Cruzeiro	BRR
Brunei Darusalam	Brunei dollar	BND
Bulgaria	Lev	BGL
Burkina Faso	CFA franc	XOF
Burundi	Burundi franc	BIF
Cambodia	Riel	KHR
Cameroon	CFA franc	XAF
Canada	Canadian dollar	CAD
Cape Verde	Capeverde escudo	CVE
Cayman Islands	Cayman Island dollar	KYD
Central African Republic	CFA franc	XAF
Chad	CFA franc	XAF
Chile	Chilean peso	CLP
China	Yuan renminbi	CNY
Colombia	Colombian peso	COP
Comoros	Comoro franc	KMF
Congo	CFA franc	XAF
Cook Islands	New Zealand dollar	NZD
Costa Rica	Costa Rica colon	CRC
Cote d'Ivoire	CF franc	XOF
Croatia	Croatian dinar	HRD
Cuba	Cuban peso	CUP
Cyprus	Cyprus pound	CYP
Czech Republic	Koruna	CSK
Denmark	Danish Krone	DKK
Djibouti	Djibouti franc	DJF
Dominica	Caribbean dollar	XCD
Dominican Republic	Dominican peso	DOP
East Timor	Rupiah	IDR
	Timor escudo	TPE
Egypt	Egyptian pound	EGP
El Salvador	El Salvador colon	SVC
Equatorial Guinea	CFA franc	XAF
Estonia	Kroon	EEK
Ethiopia	Ethiopian birr	ETB
Faeore Islands	Danish Krone	DKK
Falkland Islands	Falkland Islands pound	FKP
Fiji	Fiji dollar	FJD
Finland	Markka	FIM
France	French franc	FRF
French Guyana	French franc	FRF
Gabon	CFA franc	XAF

Gambia	Dalasi	GMD
Georgia	Russian ruble	RUR
Germany	Deutsche mark	DEM
Ghana	Cedi	GHC
Gibraltar	Gibraltar pound	GIP
Greece	Drachma	GRD
Greenland	Danish Krone	DKK
Grenada	Caribbean dollar	XCD
Guadeloupe	French franc	FRF
Guam	US dollar	USD
Guatemala	Quetzal	GTQ
Guinea	Guinea franc	GNF
Guinea-Bissau	Guinea-Bissau peso	GWP
Guyana	Guyana dollar	GYD
Haiti	Gourde	HTG
	US dollar	USD
Honduras	Lempira	HNL
Hong Kong	Hong Kong dollar	HKD
Hungary	Forint	HUF
Iceland	Icelandic krona	ISK
India	Indian rupee	INR
Indonesia	Rupiah	IDR
Iran	Iranian rial	IRR
Iraq	Iraqi dinar	IQD
Ireland	Irish pound	IEP
Isle of Man	Pound sterling	GBP
Israel	Shekel	ILS
Italy	Italian lira	ITL
Jamaica	Jamaican dollar	JMD
Japan	Yen	JPY
Jordan	Jordanian dinar	JOD
Kazakhstan	Russian ruble	RUR
Kenya	Kenyan shilling	KES
North Korea	North Korean won	KPW
Republic of Korea	Won	KRW
Kuwait	Kuwaiti dinar	KWD
Kyrygystan	Som	KGS
Lao	Kip	LAK
Latvia	Latvian lats	LVL
Lebanon	Lebanese pound	LBP
Lesotho	Loti	LSL
	Financial rand	ZAL
	Rand	ZAR
Liberia	Liberian dollar	LRD
Libyan Arab Jamahiriya	Libyan dinar	LYD
Liechtenstein	Swiss franc	CHF
Luxembourg	Belgian franc	BEF
	Luxembourg franc	LUF

Lithuania	Lithuani talas	LTT
Macao	Pataca	MOP
Madagascar	Malagasy franc	MGF
Malawi	Kwacha	MWK
Malaysia	Malaysia ringgit	MYR
Maldives	Rufiyaa	MVR
Mali	CFA franc	XOF
Malta	Maltese lira	MTL
Marshall Islands	US dollar	USD
Martinique	French franc	FRF
Mauritania	Ouguiya	MRO
Mauritius	Mauritius rupee	MUR
Mexico	Mexican peso	MXP
Micronesia	US dollar	USD
Moldavia	Moldovan leu	MDL
Monaco	French franc	FRF
Mongolia	Tugrik	MNT
Monserrat	Caribbean dollar	XCD
Marocco	Maroccoan dirham	MAD
Mozambique	Metical	MZM
Myanmar	Kyat	MMK
Namibia	Rand	ZAR
Nauru	Australian dollar	AUD
Nepal	Nepalese rupee	NPR
Netherlands Antilles	Netherlands Antilles guilder	ANG
Netherlands	Netherlands guilder	NLG
New Caledonia	CFP franc	XPF
New Zealand	New Zealand dollar	NZD
Nicaragua	Oro	NIO
Niger	CFA franc	XOF
Nigeria	Naira	NGN
Niue	New Zealand dollar	NZD
Norfolk Island	Australian dollar	AUD
Norway	Norwegian krone	NOK
Oman	Rial omani	OMR
Pakistan	Pakistan rupee	PKR
Palau	US dollar	USD
Panama	Balboa	PAB
	US dollar	USD
Papua New Guinea	Kina	PGK
Paraguay	Guarani	PYG
Peru	Nuevo sol	PEN
Philippines	Philippine peso	PHP
Poland	Zloty	PLZ
Portugal	Portuguese escudo	PTE
Puerto Rico	US dollar	USD
Quatar	Quatari Rial	QAR
Romania	Leu	ROL

Russia	Ruble	RUR
Rwanda	Rwanda franc	RWF
Saints Kitts & Nevis	Caribbean dollar	XCD
Saint Lucia	Caribbean dollar	XCD
Saint Vincent and the Grenadines	Caribbean dollar	XCD
Samoa	Tala	WST
San Marino	Italian lira	ITL
Sao Tome and Principe	Dobra	STD
Saudi Arabia	Saudi riyal	SAR
Senegal	CFA franc	XOF
Seychelles	Seychelles rupee	SCR
Sierra Leone	Leone	SLL
Singapore	Singapore dollar	SGD
Slovenia	Tolar	SIT
Solomon Islands	Solomon Islands dollar	SBD
Somalia	Somali shilling	SOS
South Africa	Rand	ZAR
Spain	Spanish peseta	ESP
Sri Lanka	Sri Lanka rupee	LKR
Sudan	Sudanese dinar	SDD
Suriname	Suriname guilder	SRG
Swaziland	Lilangeni	SZL
Switzerland	Swiss franc	CHF
Syria	Syrian pound	SYP
Taiwan	New Taiwan dollar	TWD
Tajikistan	Russian ruble	RUR
Tanzania	Tanzania shilling	TZS
Thailand	Baht	THB
Togo	CFA franc	XOF
Tonga	Pa'anga	TOP
Trinidad and Tobago	Trinidad and Tobago dollar	TTD
Tunisia	Tunisian dinar	TND
Turkmenistan	Manat	TMM
Turkey	Turkish lira	TLR
Turks and Caicos Islands	US dollar	USD
United Arab Emirates	UAE dirham	AED
Uganda	Uganda shilling	UGX
Ukraine	Karbovnet	UAK
United Kingdom	Pound sterling	GBP
United States of America	US dollar	USD
Uruguay	Uruguayan peso	UYP
Vanuatu	Vatu	VUV
Vatican	Italian lira	ITL
Venezuela	Bolivar	VEB
Vietnam	Dong	VND
Virgin Islands	US dollar	USD
Western Sahara	Moroccan Dirham	MAD
Yemen	Yemeni rial	YER

Yugoslavia	Yugoslavia dinar	YUN
Zaire	Zaire	ZRZ
Zambia	Kwacha	ZMK
Zimbabwe	Zimbabwe dollar	ZWD
*European Monetary System	European Curency Unit	XEU
*International Monetary Fund	Special Drawing Rights	XDR

Designates no country assignment

Source: Telerate. Reprinted by permission. © 1993 Dow Jones Telerate, Inc.

Appendix **B**

Forex USA, Inc.
A Membership Corporation
By-Laws

Table of Contents

By-Laws Forex USA, Inc. A Membership Corporation

Preamble

Forex USA, Inc. is the successor to Forex USA, an unincorporated association which was in turn the successor to the Forex Association of North America, itself the successor to Forex Club of North America. The Forex Club of North America was founded in 1958 for the primary purpose of fomenting good relations among members of the Foreign Exchange community and to provide them an opportunity to meet together and exchange information on the foreign exchange market. As the market has grown, so have the goals of the Corporation, which now lists among its goals and purposes:

Educating members of the profession and of the public at large both with respect to the business of foreign exchange and with respect to general economic and financial topics, striving to improve the market environment, striving to give the profession the highest sense of responsibility and sophistication, and establishing the profession's reputation as one of honesty, responsibility, sophistication and dignity, specifically by, but not limited to,

(a) Conducting seminars, open to non-members as well as members, designed to instruct both novice and experienced foreign exchange and eurocurrency professionals in the basics and in the fine points of the business;

(b) Conducting meetings, and other presentations, open to members, their guests and, at times, the general public, at which guest speakers will deliver remarks on the topics of foreign exchange and eurocurrency dealing, banking, the economy, and other subjects in order not only to increase the members' understanding of the business, but also to further educate the members and the public with respect to the larger importance of foreign exchange and its role in the financial markets.

(c) Participating in the affairs of other organizations devoted to promoting the profession of foreign exchange and eurocurrency dealing worldwide as well as in the United States;

(d) Working in conjunction with, and assisting and cooperating with other individuals, groups, associations, corporations, government officials and agencies to effectuate any and all of the foregoing purposes;

(e) Conducting any and all lawful activities that may be necessary, useful, or desirable for the furtherance of accomplishment of the foregoing purposes.

Article I. Members

Section 1. Memberships. Membership shall be limited to individuals who are in sympathy with the purposes of the Corporation. Membership shall be open to, but not specifically limited to, any individual who is employed by a bank, or financial institution of a banking nature, and is directly involved in the decision making or trading of Foreign Exchange, Eurocurrency deposits or related instruments, or who acts as a broker in those markets. There will be three classifications of membership:

(a) International Membership.

International membership shall be open to individuals who meet the above requirements, who meet all of the requirements for international membership of a national club set forth in the By-Laws of the Association Cambiste Internationale, and who have been National members of the Corporation for at least one year.

(b) National Membership.

National membership shall be open to individuals who meet the membership requirements, and who have had at least one year market experience. National members may participate fully in all Corporate events but shall not be entitled to vote in Corporate elections until after the first anniversary of their admission to membership.

(c) Honorary Membership.

Honorary membership shall be extended automatically to all international and national members who retire from active business and may be extended to others at the discretion of the Board of Directors. Honorary members shall not be entitles to vote in Corporate elections.

(d) Sponsorship.

Applications for new membership, regardless of category, must be sponsored by two (2) voting members in good standing who have been members of the Corporation for at least three years. Both sponsors will attest to the applicant's market experience. Sponsors must certify that they have known the applicant for a minimum of one (1) year.

Section 2. Admission to Membership. Any person who certifies that he or she meets the membership criteria set forth above may be admitted to membership by act of the Board of Directors. Application shall be made to the Membership Committee which shall screen all applications for membership before presenting such applications to the Board of Directors for final approval. Members of Forex USA at the time of incorporation shall automatically become members of the Corporation, but renewal of membership shall be contingent upon meeting the membership criteria set forth herein.

Section 3. Renewal of Membership. Each renewal applicant must certify that he or she continues to meet the membership criteria.

Section 4. Duration and Termination of Membership. Membership shall be on a yearly basis and shall be contingent upon payment of yearly dues set forth herein. Renewal of membership is contingent upon timely payment of dues. Membership will be automatically cancelled if dues are not paid within the first three months of the new fiscal year.

Section 5. Expulsion. Any member who ceases to meet the qualifications required for membership may, at the discretion of the Board of Directors, be deprived of the right to remain a member. Other grounds for expulsion may be adopted at the discretion of the Board.

Section 6. Dues. Dues will be established by the Board of Directors and are nonrefundable.

Section 7. Meetings. There will be a minimum of four meetings of the membership each year, one of which will be the Annual General Meeting which shall be held no later than September 30 of each year, at a date and place to be fixed by the Board of Directors, or, if not so fixed, as may be determined by the Chairman of the Board of Directors. Additional membership meetings may be called at the discretion of the Board of Directors.

Section 8. Notice of Meetings. Written notice of the place, date and hour of any membership meeting shall be given to each member by mailing the notice by first class mail, postage prepaid, or by personal delivery, not less than ten or more than fifty days before the date of the meeting. The Secretary may, at his or her discretion, also employ any other method of providing notice permitted by law.

Section 9. Special Meetings. Special meetings of the members may be called by the Board of Directors or upon written demand of ten percent of the voting members. Such written demand shall specify the location and date of the meeting. The date be more than two but less than three months from the date of the meeting. Upon receiving the written demand the

Secretary of the Corporation shall promptly give notice to the membership within five business days. If the secretary does not provide such notice, any member who signed the demand may do so. The notice shall indicate the purpose for which the meeting is called and identify the persons calling the meeting.

Section 10. Quorum. The number of members necessary to constitute a quorum for the transaction of business at any meeting of the members shall be not less than one-tenth of the total number of members entitled to cast votes, or one hundred members, whichever is less, present in person or by written proxy. The members present at any meeting at which a quorum is lacking shall have the power to adjourn such meeting from time to time, without notice other than an announcement at the meeting of the time when and place where the meeting will be reconvened, until a quorum shall be present, at which time any business may be transacted that could have been transacted at the meeting as originally convened.

Section 11. Voting. At any meeting of the members, each voting Member present in person or by written proxy shall be entitled to vote. Except as otherwise provided by law or by these By-Laws, the vote of a majority of members entitled to vote, if a quorum is present at such time, shall be the act of the members.

Article II. Board of Directors

Section 1. Powers and Numbers. The Corporation shall be managed by a sixteen member Board of Directors, consisting of the President, Vice President, Secretary, Treasurer and twelve other members. There shall be at least one director from each regional chapter. Each Director shall be an active member of the Corporation. A Director attending less than 50% of the meetings of the Board of Directors between Annual General Meetings shall be deemed to have resigned and will be so notified.

Section 2. Election and Term of Office. Directors shall be elected at the annual meeting of the members by a plurality vote as provided in Article I, Section 10. Each director shall hold office for three years, with one-third of the Directors' terms expiring each year by rotation. Directors whose terms have expired shall be eligible for re-election but no one may serve more than three consecutive full terms. Each member of the Executive Committee of Forex USA at the time of incorporation shall automatically become a Director of the Corporation with his or her term expiring at the same time as if the Association had not incorporated.

Section 3. Qualifications. Candidates for the Board of Directors must have had at least seven years of active trading experience as well as three consecutive years of voting membership in the Corporation.

Section 4. Resignations and Vacancies. Any Director may resign from office at any time by delivering his or her resignation in writing to the Chairman of the Board of Directors. In the case of a vacancy on the Board of Directors, a successor shall be appointed by the Board of Directors to serve until the next annual general meeting at which time a successor shall be elected by the membership to serve the unexpired portion of the departing Director's term.

Section 5. Meetings. Meetings of the Board may be held at any place that the Board may from time to time set or as shall be specified in the respective notice thereof. The annual meeting of the Board of Directors in each year shall be held following the annual meeting of the members. Other regular meetings of the Board shall be held at the discretion of the Board. Special meetings of the Board may be held whenever called by the Chairman of the Board at such time and place as he or she shall set.

Section 6. Quorum and Voting. Unless a greater proportion is required by law, eight Directors shall constitute a quorum for the transaction of business or of any specified item of business. The President, or whoever is serving as Chairman of the Board in his or her stand, shall not vote except when necessary to break a tie, but he or she shall be counted toward making up a quorum. Except as otherwise provided by law or by these By-Laws, the vote of a majority of the Directors present at the time of the vote, if a quorum be present at such time, shall be the act of the Board.

Section 7. Action by the Board. Any action required or permitted to be taken by the Board may be taken without a meeting if all members of the Board consent in writing to the adoption of a resolution authorizing the action. The resolution and the written consents thereto by the members of the Board shall be filed with the minutes of the proceedings of the Board. Any one or more members of the Board may participate in a meeting of the Board by means of a conference telephone or similar communications equipment allowing all persons participating in the meeting to hear each other at the same time. Participation by such means shall constitute presence in person at the meeting.

Section 8. Notice of the Meetings. Notice of the time and place of each regular or special meeting of the Board, together with a written agenda stating all matters upon which action is proposed to be taken, and, to the extent possible copies of all documents on which action is proposed to be taken, shall be communicated to each Director in writing, at least seven days before the day on which the meeting is to be held; provided, however, that notice of special meetings to discuss matters requiring prompt action may be communicated to him or her not less than forty-eight hours before the time at which such meeting is to be held.

Article III. Officers, Employees and Agents

Section 1. Number and Qualifications. The offices of the Corporation shall be a President, a Vice President, a Secretary, and a Treasurer, as well as such other officers, if any, as the Board of Directors may from time to time appoint. Any member in good standing who meets the eligibility requirements for any elective position may run for that position. No one person may hold more than one office in the Corporation at one time.

Section 2. Election and Term of Office. The officers of the Corporation shall be chosen at the annual meeting of the membership by a majority vote as provided in Article I, Section 10. Each officer shall hold office for a term of three years. The officers of Forex USA at the time of incorporation shall continue in position as officers of the Corporation with their terms expiring at the same time as if the Association had not been incorporated.

Section 3. Employees and Other Agencies. The Board of Directors may appoint from time to time such employees and other agents as it shall deem necessary, each of whom shall hold office at the pleasure of the Board, and shall have such authority and perform such duties and may receive such reasonable compensation, as the Board of Directors may from time to time determine.

Section 4. Vacancies. In a case of vacancy in the office of President, the Vice President shall succeed the President and serve until the next Annual General Meeting at which time a successor shall be elected by the membership to serve the unexpired portion of the President's term. In the case of vacancy in any other office, a successor shall be appointed by the Board of Directors to serve until the next Annual General Meeting at which time a successor shall be elected by the membership to serve the unexpired portion of the departing officer's term.

Section 5. President. Powers, Duties and Qualifications: The President shall preside at all meetings of the members of the Board of Directors, shall have general supervision of the affairs of the Corporation and shall keep the Board of Directors duly informed about the activities of the Corporation. The President shall serve as Chairman of the Board of Directors. As such he shall not vote on matters before the Board except when necessary to break a tie vote. The President shall have the power to sign alone in the name of the Corporation all contracts authorized either generally or specifically by the Board unless the Board of Directors shall specifically require an additional signature. A candidate for President must have had at least ten years active trading experience, and must have at least five years consecutive voting membership in the Corporation.

Section 6. Vice President. Powers, Duties and Qualifications: The Vice President shall have such powers and duties as may be assigned to him by the Board. In the absence of the President, the Vice President shall perform the duties of the President. A candidate for Vice President must meet the same qualifications as a candidate for President.

Section 7. Secretary. Powers, Duties and Qualifications: The secretary shall act as secretary of all meetings of the members of the Board of Directors, and shall keep the minutes of all such meetings. The Secretary shall also keep the records of the Corporation as well as handle all correspondence deemed necessary, including the dissemination of appropriate information to the general membership. The Secretary shall be responsible for the giving and serving of all notices of the Corporation and shall perform all the duties customarily incident to the office of Secretary. A candidate for Secretary must have had at least seven years active trading experience and five years consecutive voting membership in the Corporation.

Section 8. Treasurer. Powers, Duties and Qualifications: The Treasurer shall keep or cause to be kept full and accurate accounts of receipts and disbursements of the Corporation and shall account for dues and all moneys disbursed at least once a year at the annual meeting and at any other time deemed appropriate by the Board of Directors. A candidate for Treasurer must have had at least seven years active trading experience and five years consecutive voting membership in the Corporation.

Article IV. Committees

Section 1. Membership Committee. There shall be a Membership Committee consisting of five members. The members shall be elected by the general membership at the annual meeting and will serve terms of three years. The functions of the Membership Committee shall be to screen all applications for membership or change in membership status before presenting such applications to the Board of Directors for final approval. The Membership Committee shall also review all suggestions received from the membership regarding matters affecting the Corporation and its improvement, and make recommendations to the Board for consideration and action. Candidates for the Membership Committee must have had at least three years consecutive voting membership in the Corporation.

      Section 2. Nominating Committee. There shall be a Nominating Committee consisting of five members, two of whom will be appointed by the Board of Directors and three elected by the general membership at an annual meeting. Members of the Nominating Committee will serve terms of three years. The Committee will receive nominations from the general membership for elective positions to be filled, adjudge eligibility and availability of candidates nominated, and submit to the Board of Directors the names of no more than three candidates for each elective position to be filled at the ensuing annual meeting. Only nominations made as provided by this by-law shall be voted upon. Candidates for membership on the Nominating Committee shall have had at least three years continuous voting membership in the Corporation.

      Section 3. Other Committees. The Board may, at its discretion, appoint or create such other committees as it deems necessary or appropriate.

      Section 4. Vacancies. In the case of an elective position on any committee becoming vacant, a successor to the departing member shall be appointed by the Board of Directors and shall serve until the next Annual General Meeting at which time a successor shall be elected by the membership to serve the unexpired portion of the departing member's term.

Article V. Election Procedures

      Section 1. Notice; Ballots. The Secretary, thirty days prior to the date of the annual meeting, shall mail every member of the Association a ballot listing persons nominated in accord with Article IV, Section 3. Ballots will be returned by mail or by personal delivery and must be received by the Chairman of the Nominating Committee no later than noon (Eastern Time) of the day of the Annual General Meeting in order to be considered valid. Each member with voting rights shall be entitled to one vote for each office and to as many votes for membership on the Board of Directors and Committees as there are vacancies to be filled. No member may cast more than one vote for any single candidate.

Section 2. Tabulation; Results. The votes shall be tabulated at a meeting of the Board of Directors immediately preceding the Annual General Meeting. Election shall be plurality. Results of the election will be announced at the Annual General Meeting by the Chairman of the Nominating Committee. Ties will be resolved by hand vote of those members with voting rights present at the meeting.

Section 3. The Board of Directors may promulgate regulations not inconsistent with this by-law.

Article VI. Chapters

Regional chapters of the Corporation may be formed if approved by the Board of Directors and ratified by the general membership. Chapters of Forex USA in existence before incorporation shall be deemed approved and ratified as of the date of incorporation. Each chapter shall be governed by these By-Laws and shall submit any proposed by-laws of their own to the Board of Directors for approval. Each chapter shall report all income derived from any sources to the Board of Directors at such times and in such manner as the Board may designate.

Article VII. Activities

Section 1. Seminars. At the discretion of the Board the Corporation may conduct junior, and senior, or other, seminars annually. With the approval of the Board of Directors, the chapters may also conduct seminars.

Section 2. Meetings. At least three of the four general meetings shall be devoted to a presentation on a topic of relevance to the business of foreign exchange and eurocurrency dealing. Additional meetings may be held at the discretion of the Board.

Article VIII. Contracts, Checks, Bank Accounts and Investments

Section 1. Checks, Notes and Contracts. The Board of Directors is authorized to select such depositories as it shall deem proper for the funds of the Corporations and shall determine who shall be authorized on the Corporation's behalf to sign bills, notes, receipts, acceptances, endorsements, checks, releases, contracts and documents.

Section 2. Investments. The funds of this Corporation may be retained in whole or in part in cash or be invested and reinvested from time to time in such property, real, personal, or otherwise or stocks, bonds or other securities as the Board of Directors in its discretion may deem desirable.

Article IX. Office and Books

Section 1. Office. The office of the Corporation shall be located at such place as the Board of Directors may from time to time determine.

Section 2. Books. There shall be kept at the office of the Corporation correct books of account of the activities and transactions of the Corporation including a Minute Book which shall contain a copy of the Certificate of Incorporation, a copy of these By-Laws, and all minutes of meetings of the members and of the Board of Directors. There shall also be kept at that office copies of the following from each regional chapter: (1) by-laws; (2) minutes of membership meetings; (3) minutes of executive committee meetings.

Section 3. Audit. Each year the Board of Directors shall appoint an independent public or certified accountant or a firm of such accountants to conduct a complete financial audit of the books of the Corporation in the first month of the new fiscal year. Such an audit shall also be conducted immediately preceding the accession to office of a newly appointed or elected Treasurer.

Section 4. Fiscal Year. The fiscal year of the Corporation shall be determined by the Board of Directors, but must end within the first six months preceding the annual meeting.

Article X. Indemnification

The Corporation may, to the fullest extent now or hereafter permitted by law, indemnify any person made, or threatened to be made, a party to any action or preceding by reason of the fact that he, his testator or intestate, was a director, officer, employee or agent of the Corporation, against judgments, fines, amounts paid in settlement and reasonable expenses, including attorneys' fees.

Article XI. Amendments

These By-Laws may be amended at any meeting of the Board of Directors by the vote of a two-thirds majority of the Directors in office. These By-Laws may also be amended by the members of the Corporation at a special meeting duly called for that purpose. Notice of the adoption of any amendment shall be mailed to each member.

Bibliography

Bank for International Settlements. *Central Bank Survey of Foreign Exchange Market Activity in April 1992.* Basle, March 1993.

Bergstrand, Jeffrey H. *Selected Views of Exchange Determination after a Decade of "Floating" New England Economic Review,* Federal Reserve Bank of Boston, May/June 1983.

Frost, A.J. and Prechter Jr., Robert R. *Elliott Wave Principle,* 5th ed. New Classics Library, 1985.

Global Derivatives Study Group. *Derivatives: Practices and Principles.* The Group of Thirty, Washington, D.C., 1993.

Levich, Richard. *Empirical Studies of Exchange Rates: Price Behavior, Rate Determination and Market Efficiency—Handbook of International Economics.* Elsevier Science Publishers B.V., 1985.

Meulendyke, Ann-Marie. *U.S. Monetary Policy and Financial Markets.* Federal Reserve Bank of New York, 1989.

Murphy, John J. *Technical Analysis of the Futures Markets.* New York Institute of Finance, New York, 1986.

Plocek, Joseph E. *Economic Indicators.* New York Institute of Finance, New York, 1991.

Pring, Martin J. *Martin Pring on Market Momentum.* International Institute for Economic Research, Inc., 1993.

Samuelson, Paul A. *Economics,* 11th ed. McGraw-Hill Book Company, 1980.

Shimizu, Seiki. *The Japanese Chart of Charts.* Tokyo Futures Trading Publishing Co., Tokyo, 1986

Stigum, Marcia. *After the Trade: Dealer and Clearing Bank Operations in Money Market and Government Securities.* Dow Jones-Irwin, Chicago, 1988.

Sutton, W.H. *Trading in Currency Options.* New York Institute of Finance, New York, 1987

Chart Services

Astrogamma, 3 Hanover Square, New York, NY 10004
Bloomberg Financial, 499 Park Avenue, New York, NY 10022
Chartcraft, Inc., 30 Church Street, New Rochelle, NY 10801
Commodity Perspective, 30 S. Wacker Dr., Chicago, IL 60606
Commodity Trend Service, 1224 U.S. Highway 1, N. Palm Beach, FL 33408
CompuTrac/Dow Jones Telerate, 1017 Pleasant Street, New Orleans, LA 70115
CQG, Inc., PO Box 758, Glenwood Springs, Colorado 81602-0758
FutureSource, 955 Parkview Boulevard, Lombard, IL 60148
Knight-Ridder, 75 Wall Street, New York, NY 10005
Teletrac/Dow Jones Telerate, Harborside Financial Center, 600 Plaza Two, Jersey City, NJ
    07311

Index